The Principles of Learning & Behavior

2nd Edition

Michael Domjan
University of Texas at Austin

Barbara Burkhard
State University of New York at Stony Brook

Brooks/Cole Publishing Company
Pacific Grove, California

Brooks/Cole Publishing Company
A Division of Wadsworth, Inc.

Printed in the United States of America
10   9   8   7   6   5   4

Library of Congress Cataloging in Publication Data

Domjan, Michael, [date]
    The principles of learning and behavior.

    Bibliography: p.
    Includes index.
        1. Learning in animals.   2. Cognition in animals.
    3. Learning, Psychology of.   I. Burkhard, Barbara,
    [date]   II. Title.
    QL785.D63   1985   150.19′43   85-5276
    ISBN 0-534-05208-8

Sponsoring Editor: *C. Deborah Laughton*
Editorial Assistant: *Mary Tudor*
Production Editor: *Fiorella Ljunggren*
Manuscript Editor: *Rephah Berg*
Permissions Editor: *Mary Kay Hancharick*
Interior and Cover Design: *Victoria A. Van Deventer*
Art Coordinator: *Judith Macdonald*
Interior Illustrations: *Barbara Hack*
Typesetting: *Allservice Phototypesetting Company of Arizona, Phoenix*
Printing and Binding: *R. R. Donnelley & Sons Company, Crawfordsville, Indiana*

(Credits continue on p. 365)

The Principles of Learning & Behavior

2nd Edition

*To Katherine and Paul
and to Hannah, Jacob, Zachary, and Abigail*

Preface

From the early 20th century to the mid-1960s, the study of learning constituted the foundation of the study of psychology in North America. Prominent investigators of learning, such as Hull, Spence, Mowrer, Tolman, Miller, and Skinner, were prominent in the field of psychology as a whole rather than just major figures in a subspecialty. The thrust of the effort during this period was devoted to developing a general theory of behavior based on extensive laboratory study of a few specialized experimental situations. Findings derived from this research were used to build theories of learning and behavior that were assumed to apply to a variety of species and circumstances. The concepts and findings were also used to construct models of abnormal behavior, personality, and the acquisition of special skills, such as language. Students training in psychology were all taught the principles of learning and behavior even if they ended by specializing in some other area.

The field of psychology has changed dramatically during the past 20–25 years with the growth of such subfields as cognitive psychology, psycholinguistics, physiological psychology, behavior genetics, and developmental psychology. The study of learning and behavior no longer has the dominant position in psychology it once enjoyed. Nevertheless, it remains a vital area of study addressed to certain basic aspects of how behavior is governed by environmental events. The contemporary study of learning and behavior is enriched by numerous new findings and new ways of thinking. Our basic ideas of classical and instrumental conditioning have undergone profound changes in the past 15 years, and this vigorous progress continues. In addition, the study of conditioning and learning is becoming better integrated with related investigations of the biological bases of behavior and studies of cognitive processes.

Conditioning and learning investigations are also providing techniques for analyzing behavior that are becoming invaluable in many newly emerging fields such as behavioral neuroscience, developmental psychobiology, psychopharmacology, behavioral medicine, behavioral toxicology, and teratology. Dramatic advances in neurophysiology are providing renewed hope that the neural substrates of learning will soon be discovered, and this renewed interest in the neurophysiology of learning is, in turn, creating a resurgence of interest in the basic behavioral mechanisms of learning. Thus, whereas the study of conditioning and learning began as mainly a concern of psychologists, it is now an integral part of a broad network of interdisciplinary approaches to the study of behavior.

The purpose of our book is to introduce students to contemporary investigations of learning and behavior. We endeavor to emphasize the development of ideas rather than familiarize the student with all the complications that often accompany particular investigations. The historical antecedents of ideas are presented only insofar as they are important to the understanding of current issues. Given the rapid and major changes taking place in the field, some contemporary ideas about learning and behavior cannot be fully integrated with previous findings yet. Nevertheless, we try to provide an integrated approach wherever possible. For example, recent information about biological constraints on learning is interwoven into the fabric of the presentation rather than discussed in a separate chapter divorced from the basic phenomena of conditioning.

To assist the student, we give numerous examples

of the major points in the text. Most of the research examples are drawn from animal experiments. However, we frequently point out the potential relevance of the findings and concepts to the analysis of human behavior. In addition, we have felt free to rehearse certain ideas by pointing out analogous human situations. These extensions to human behavior should be treated as food for thought rather than as the outcome of definitive scientific reasoning. Technical terms are presented in boldface the first time they appear, so that readers can easily identify them.

The book is organized hierarchically, early chapters providing the foundation for information presented later. However, concepts are repeated as they come up in later chapters so that all the preceding chapters do not necessarily have to be read. The book begins with a statement of the basic elements of the behavioral approach to the study of psychology, a definition of learning, and some comments about the historical antecedents of the study of learning and behavior. Chapter 2 describes elicited behavior and two of the most elementary processes of behavior change, habituation and sensitization. Various conditioning and learning procedures and phenomena are then described in order of increasing complexity. Chapters 3 and 4 present some old and many contemporary issues in classical conditioning. The basic concepts and theoretical foundations of the study of instrumental conditioning are presented in Chapter 5. Chapter 6 is devoted to a description of schedules of reinforcement and choice behavior, and theoretical issues concerning the mechanisms of reinforcement are discussed in Chapter 7. Chapters 8, 9, and 10 present procedures and phenomena that have been analyzed in terms of the interaction of classical and instrumental conditioning processes. Chapter 8 discusses the stimulus control of learned behavior. Avoidance and punishment are discussed in Chapter 9, and Chapter 10 treats in a more general fashion theoretical issues concerned with the interaction of classical and instrumental conditioning processes. The last two chapters of the book present some of the extensive recent research on animal cognition. Chapter 11 covers memory mechanisms, and Chapter 12 describes a variety of information-processing mechanisms, including timing, counting,

serial pattern learning, concept formation, reasoning, and language in nonhuman animals.

The present edition of the book, though similar to the first edition in its goals and basic approach, differs from the first edition in many details. For example, material from Chapters 2 and 3 of the first edition has been incorporated into a single chapter here, and coverage of research on animal cognition has been expanded from one chapter to two. In making the various changes, we sought to improve the clarity of the presentation and to incorporate many research findings and ideas that have become prominent since publication of the first edition. Throughout, we worked to end up with a book that is, we hope, a reasonably accurate reflection of the field. One of us (M.D.) was primarily responsible for rewriting the basic text, and the other (B.B.) was primarily responsible for providing new examples of the applications of conditioning and learning principles to human behavior problems.

We are indebted to many individuals, including J. J. B. Ayres, P. Balsam, M. Bouton, M. Cantor, M. Fanselow, C. Flaherty, A. W. Logue, M. Rashotte, D. Thomas, W. Timberlake, and G. Whitney, who made thoughtful suggestions for revisions of the first edition of the book and/or directed our attention to important new areas of research. We are also grateful for the comments we received on earlier drafts of the second edition from numerous individuals, including James Allison of the University of Indiana, Michael R. Best of Southern Methodist University, Douglas Gillan of Lockheed Corporation, Bill Gordon of the University of New Mexico, Peter Killeen of the University of Texas at Austin, Richard Miller of the University of Western Kentucky, David Riccio of Kent State University, Mark Rilling of Michigan State University, Robert A. Rosellini of the State University of New York at Albany, Michael Scavio of California State University, Fullerton, W. Scott Terry of the University of North Carolina at Charlotte, Ronald Ulm of Salisbury State College, Gary Walters of the University of Toronto, Edward Wasserman of the University of Iowa, and Ben Williams of the University of California at San Diego. We would also like to thank the staff of Brooks/Cole for its continuing support of the book: C. Deborah Laughton for prodding us to undertake the revision, Fiorella Ljunggren for guiding the book through production, and Rephah Berg for her expert manuscript editing. Finally, we wish to thank Nancy Marlin for writing *Directed Readings for Domjan and Burkhard's Principles of Learning* *and Behavior, 2nd Edition* (Brooks/Cole, 1986), to accompany the present text, and Stuart Hall for helping with the test bank for our book.

Michael Domjan
Barbara Burkhard

Brief Contents

Contents

CHAPTER 4

Classical Conditioning: Mechanisms 73

CHAPTER 5

Instrumental Conditioning: Foundations 100

CHAPTER 6

Schedules of Reinforcement and Choice Behavior 128

CHAPTER 7

Reinforcement: Theories and Experimental Analysis 153

CHAPTER 8

Stimulus Control of Instrumental and Classical Conditioning 181

CHAPTER 9

Aversive Control: Avoidance and Punishment 216

CHAPTER 10

Interactions of Classical and Instrumental Conditioning 248

CHAPTER 11

Animal Cognition: Memory Mechanisms 272

CHAPTER 12

Animal Cognition: Diverse Information-Processing Mechanisms 302

The
Principles
of
Learning
&
Behavior

2nd Edition

CHAPTER 1
Introduction

The goal of Chapter 1 is to introduce students to the study of learning and behavior and the method of investigation used in this field. Modern experiments on learning are based on the behavioral approach to the study of psychology. The chapter describes the behavioral approach and its historical antecedents and contrasts the behavioral approach to other strategies used in the study of psychology. Because numerous experiments on learning have been performed with animal subjects, the chapter also discusses the rationale for using animals in research and the generality of animal learning results. The chapter ends with a discussion of the relationship between behavioral investigations and other aspects of psychology.

People have always been interested in understanding their own and others' behavior. This interest is much more than idle curiosity. Because we live in a complex society, many aspects of our lives are governed by the actions of others. How much you get paid in your work depends on what your boss decides to give you. Whether your home life is pleasant or unpleasant depends on how accommodating or hostile your housemates are. Whether you get admitted to college depends on the decision of an admissions officer. Whether you get to school on time depends on traffic and how well your car was repaired the last time you had it in the shop.

Because we depend a great deal on other people in nearly every aspect of our lives, it is important for us to be able to predict how others will behave. Life would be unbearable if you could not predict when your mother was about to scold you or when your classes were to be held or if the grocery checker were as likely to hit you as to ring up your groceries. Much of our interest in behavior is motivated by a desire to better predict the actions of others.

Informal Reflections about Behavior

There are many possible approaches to understanding and predicting behavior, ranging from the reading of tea leaves to scientific observation. Everyone probably adopts certain unique strategies in figuring out why others act as they do. However, informal reflections about behavior often also share certain common features. First, in the absence of specific training in psychology, people who try to figure out what makes someone do certain things are likely to think about how they themselves would act in similar situations. That is, by reflecting on one's own reasons for doing something, one tries to gain insight into the reasons others act as they do. This method of reaching understanding about behavior is called *informal introspection*. For most of human history, introspection was the primary means of gaining information about behavior. However, informal introspection is not used in systematic investigations of behavior. Many areas of psychology have abandoned the use of

introspection altogether. In other areas, introspection is used only under highly restricted and controlled circumstances. For example, a subject may be asked to respond to a carefully worded questionnaire item or to make a judgment about a stimulus presented in a laboratory situation.

In addition to using informal introspection as their primary method for obtaining insights into behavior, people not trained in psychology are likely to attribute actions to forces within the actors. That is, behavior is assumed to be caused by internal factors, such as the person's free will or wishes. If we see someone running toward a bus stop, we are likely to explain this by assuming that the person wants to catch the bus. If one of our friends spends a great deal of time studying, we interpret this by concluding that she wants to get As in school. Internal motivation is also frequently used to explain the behavior of animals. If a dog stands facing the door, we are likely to say that it wants to go out. If a cat jumps on the kitchen counter when dinner is being prepared, we are likely to conclude that it wants to steal pieces of food.

A third common characteristic of informal reflections about behavior is that they are stated in terms of large and complex units of behavior. On the basis of their behavior, we describe people as being energetic, clever, polite, angry, happy, or in love. Each of these descriptions refers to a complex array of activities. For example, being in love may involve making frequent phone calls to the loved one, not paying close attention to other people, eagerly anticipating meetings with the loved one, buying gifts, being much more careful than usual about one's grooming, and other behaviors. Similarly, many responses are involved in being angry. An angry person may shout, threaten people, throw things, drive too fast, or engage in physical aggression.

Disadvantages of Informal Reflections about Behavior

Informal reflections have not contributed much to the understanding of behavior, because of their reliance on unsystematic introspection, their focus on internal causes, and their consideration of large and complex units of behavior. Each of these aspects of the informal approach has certain shortcomings.

Unsystematic introspection is generally not very useful in furthering our understanding of behavior, because people are not very skillful at accurately interpreting their own behavior. Introspective accounts of behavior are often self-serving and grossly inaccurate. An overweight person may report not eating frequent snacks although he often eats between meals. A husband with marital difficulties may regard himself as a model spouse who is being ignored by his wife, when in fact he rarely compliments her or pays attention to her. Parents may think of themselves as very much interested in what their teenagers are doing, even though they may inquire about these activities but once or twice a week. Often the task of a therapist is to get past such self-serving introspective accounts of behavior and teach people to pay closer attention to what they actually do. For example, the overweight person may be asked to make a note in a diary each time he eats something.

The focus on internal sources of motivation in informal reflections about behavior also often gets in the way of meaningful insights into behavior. The major problem here is that independent evidence of the inferred motive is typically not available. Rather, the internal cause of an action is merely inferred from the behavior we are trying to explain, and the "explanation" therefore does not give us any new information about the behavior. Consider, for example, a stranger running toward a bus stop. We are likely to "explain" this behavior in terms of internal motives by saying that the person is trying to catch the bus. However, such use of an internal motive does not help us understand the behavior, because we do not have independent evidence that the person is trying to catch the bus. (Perhaps he is running to a nearby office.) Since our only evidence for the internal motive is the behavior we are trying to explain, postulation of the internal motive provides no new information, no new insight into the behavior.

Internal motives used in informal reflections about behavior are often inferred from the behavior itself. We may say that Mary must be trying to do well on a test because she spends a lot of time in the library, that Joe must be hungry because he hurries to get his food and eats fast, or that Beth must not be interested in a club because she is always late to its meetings. Such internal motives provide a false sense of understanding and may in fact be entirely incorrect. The truth may be that Mary is spending a lot of time at the library in an effort to attract someone else's attention, Joe hurries to get and eat his food because he is eager to go play basketball, and Beth is habitually late to club meetings because she cannot get a baby sitter to come earlier. Internal motives are useful in explaining behavior only if evidence for the motives comes from sources independent of the behavior we are trying to explain. For example, assuming that Mary is trying to do well on a test would be a more meaningful explanation of all the time she is spending at the library if we know that she has been placed on academic probation. We are often not careful to obtain such independent evidence of internal motives in informal reflections about behavior.

The third characteristic of informal analyses of behavior, the focus on large, complex behavioral units, sometimes also hampers understanding of behavioral processes. Human experiences such as love (broadly defined) are very complex and are likely to be determined by a multiplicity of factors. Before one can gain much insight into such complicated psychological processes, one has to define and analyze their components. Simple behavior patterns are presumably governed by less complicated mechanisms, which should be easier to discover. The knowledge gained from the investigation of elementary responses can then be used to guide the study of more complex behavioral systems.

The Behavioral Approach to the Study of Psychology

As we have seen, informal reflections rarely provide meaningful insights into behavior, because they rely on often faulty introspection and unconfirmed internal motives and because they typically deal with large, complex units of behavior. The approach to the study of behavior described in this book differs from informal reflections in several important respects. It does not rely on introspection, does not make careless inferences about internal causes of behavior, and focuses on small rather than large and complex units of behavior. We characterize this approach as *behavioral* to emphasize that the primary object of the study is the behavior of organisms.

The method of investigation that provides the foundation of behavioral studies is the same as that used in natural sciences, such as biology, chemistry, and physics. Basically, behavioral studies are concerned with only those aspects of behavior that can be publicly observed so that the observations can be verified by anyone who wishes to do so. To aid in data collection, experiments are often done with automated recording devices, such as movie or videotape cameras or microswitches that record every time an animal moves some aspect of its environment. One common experimental situation, for example, is shown in Figure 1.1. This apparatus is used to study the pecking behavior of pigeons and other birds. Each time the bird pecks at the response key, it displaces the key slightly, and the displacement is automatically recorded on counters, chart paper, or some other device.

In the interest of studying only those aspects of psychology that can be observed in a publicly verifiable fashion, behavioral investigations have often been limited to observable responses. Many experiments have involved measuring the actions and movements of animals. Other responses that can be objec-

Automatic programming and recording equipment

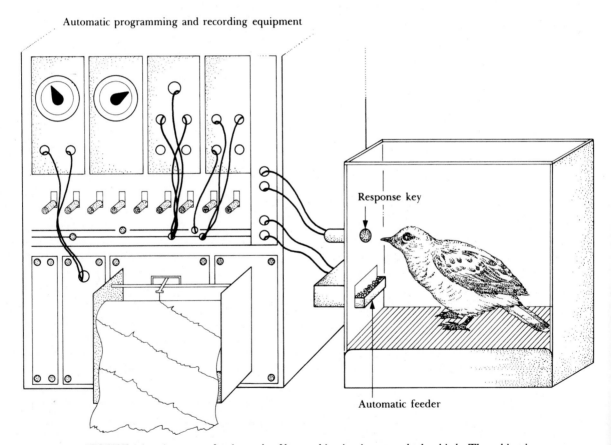

Response key

Automatic feeder

FIGURE 1.1.   Apparatus for the study of key pecking in pigeons and other birds. The subject is placed in a small enclosure with a response key. Each time the bird pecks at the response key, it displaces the key slightly, and the displacement is automatically recorded on counters, chart paper, or some other device.

tively measured are more physiological in nature. Some experiments have involved, for example, measuring salivation, blood sugar level, brain electrical activity, or heart rate. Behavioral experiments are only just beginning to address topics such as thinking, how information is abstracted from pictures, how information is remembered, and how organisms reason and figure out solutions to problems. We will describe some of this research in Chapters 11 and 12. However, much of the book will deal with the causes of motor and emotional responses: how we learn to get around in our environment, how we learn proper table manners, and why we like certain experiences, such as playing baseball. This book will not discuss, for example, what your thought processes are in solving a math problem. However, it will discuss why you study your math assignments, why you attend math classes, and why you may dislike mathematics.

A second important difference between behavioral investigations and informal reflections about behavior is that the behavioral approach does not look for causes of behavior solely inside the organism. Instead, a fundamental assumption is that organisms adjust their behavior to meet the demands of the environment. How they go about doing this often depends on motivation and other internal processes. However, internal processes are viewed as making the individual more (or less) responsive to certain external stimuli, not as being the sole cause of a particular behavior. Thus, for example, animals are more responsive to food-related stimuli when they are hungry and are more sensitive to members of the other sex when their hormonal state makes them sexually receptive.

Some people believe that if you study only actions that are controlled by the external environment, you are limiting yourself to rather uninteresting aspects of behavior. According to this idea, behavior that occurs in response to external stimuli is reflexive, and reflexes are viewed as simple, automatic, and invariant reactions to specific eliciting stimuli. Thus, it is assumed that a behavioral analysis cannot consider the unpredictability, flexibility, and complexity of more interesting aspects of human and animal behavior. This view is unjustified for two reasons. First, studying only responses that are controlled by the external environment does not limit the investigations

to reflexive behavior. We will also be concerned with goal-directed behavior, such as searching for food. Goal-directed behavior is not an invariant, reflexive response to a specific eliciting stimulus. Rather, it is more importantly governed by stimuli signaling the nature and location of the sought-after goal (such as food). Second, reflexive behavior is not necessarily simple, automatic, and invariant. The complex emotional reactions you experience when you listen to a moving piece of music or watch a good movie are elicited responses, but they are very different from simple reflexes such as a startle reaction to a sudden loud noise or constriction of the pupils of the eyes in response to a bright light. Further, many reflexes do not occur every time the appropriate eliciting stimulus is presented, and one can learn to make reflexive responses to new stimuli. One of the goals of this book is to illustrate the richness, complexity, and variability of behavior that occurs in response to external environmental events.

Finally, unlike informal reflections, the behavioral approach is typically concerned with small units of behavior. In fact, many behaviorally oriented investigations of complex psychological processes begin by defining a restricted class of responses that is to be considered indicative of the processes of interest. For example, food gathering in rats may be defined in terms of how often they press a lever for a food reward, aggression may be defined in terms of how often monkeys bite a hose when aversively stimulated, and fear may be defined in terms of how rapidly someone escapes from a dangerous situation. The scientific study of behavior, of course, can be applied to more complex forms of behavior as well. However, the bulk of the research has not been of this sort.

Historical Antecedents of the Behavioral Approach

Cartesian dualism

The behavioral approach to the study of psychology can be traced to the French philosopher René Descartes (1596–1650). Before Descartes, the common belief was that human behavior was entirely

determined by conscious intent and free will. People's actions were not thought to be controlled by external stimuli or mechanistic natural laws. What someone did was presumed to be the result of his or her deliberate intention. Descartes took exception to this view of human nature because he recognized that many things people do are automatic reactions to external stimuli. However, he was not prepared to abandon altogether the idea of free will and conscious control of one's actions. He therefore formulated a dualistic view of human behavior known as Cartesian **dualism.** According to this view, there are two aspects of human behavior. Some actions are involuntary and occur in response to external stimuli. These actions are called **reflexes.** Another aspect of human behavior involves voluntary actions which do not have to be triggered by external stimuli and which occur because of the person's conscious choice to act in a certain way.

The details of Descartes' dualistic view of human behavior are diagramed in Figure 1.2. Let us first consider the mechanisms of involuntary, or reflexive, behavior. Stimuli in the environment are detected by the person's sense organs. The sensory information is then relayed to the brain through nerves. From the brain, the impetus for action is sent through nerves to the muscles that create the involuntary response. Thus, involuntary behavior involves the reflection by the brain of stimulus input into response output.

Several aspects of this system are noteworthy. Stimuli in the external environment are seen as the cause of all involuntary behavior. These stimuli produce involuntary responses by way of a neural circuit that includes the brain. However, only one set of

nerves is involved. Descartes assumed that the same nerves transmitted information from the sense organs to the brain and from the brain down to the muscles. This circuit, he believed, permitted rapid reactions to external stimuli, as when you quickly withdraw your finger from a hot stove.

Descartes assumed that the involuntary mechanism of behavior was the only one available to animals. According to this view, all of animal behavior occurs as reflex responses to external stimuli. Descartes did not believe that animals had free will or were capable of voluntary, conscious actions. Free will and voluntary behavior were considered to be uniquely human attributes. This superiority of humans over animals existed because only human beings were thought to have a mind, or soul. The mind was assumed to be a nonphysical entity. However, if the mind is not physical, how can it generate the physical movements involved in voluntary behavior? Descartes believed that the mind was connected to the physical body by way of the pineal gland, near the brain. Because of its connection to the brain, the mind could be aware of and keep track of involuntary behavior. Through this mechanism the mind could also initiate voluntary actions. Because voluntary behavior was initiated in the mind, it could occur independently of external stimulation.

The mind/body dualism introduced by Descartes was followed by two intellectual traditions. One of these involved discussions about what is in the mind and how the mind works. Because the mind is not considered a physical entity, one cannot discover where the mind is located or any of its characteristics by dissecting the body or conducting some other

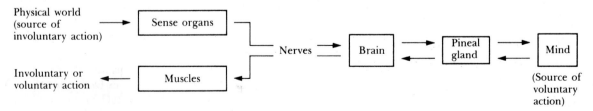

FIGURE 1.2. Diagram of Cartesian dualism. Events in the physical world are detected by sense organs. From here the information is passed along to the brain. The brain is connected to the mind by way of the pineal gland. Involuntary action is produced by a reflex arc that involves messages sent first from the sense organs to the brain and then from the brain to the muscles. Voluntary action is initiated by the mind, with messages sent to the brain and then the muscles.

kind of careful physical investigation. Therefore, the study of the mind was carried out by the method of introspection. The thinkers involved were philosophers rather than experimental scientists. Nevertheless, some of their ideas were important to the foundation of a scientific study of human behavior. The second intellectual tradition has been concerned with the mechanisms of reflexive behavior. Because reflexes are produced entirely by external stimuli acting on body organs, the study of reflexes has been conducted using the methods of direct observation and experimentation.

Historical developments in the study of the mind

As we noted, one set of issues that concerned philosophers involved questions about what is in the mind and how the mind works. Descartes had some things to say about both these questions. Because Descartes thought the mind was connected to the brain by way of the pineal gland, he believed that some of what is in the mind came from sense experiences. However, he also believed that some of the contents of the mind were innate and existed in all human beings independent of worldly experience. He believed that all human beings were born with certain ideas, including the concept of God, the concept of self, and certain fundamental axioms of geometry (such as the fact that the shortest distance between two points is a straight line). The philosophical approach that assumes we are born with innate ideas about certain things is called **nativism.**

Some philosophers after Descartes took issue with the nativist position. The British philosopher John Locke (1632–1704), for example, believed that all the ideas people had were acquired directly or indirectly through experiences after birth. He believed that human beings were born totally innocent of any preconceptions about the world. The mind was considered to start out as a clean slate (*tabula rasa*, in Latin), to be gradually filled with ideas and information as the person had various sense experiences. This philosophical approach to the question of what the mind contains is called **empiricism.** Empiricism was accepted by a group of British philosophers who lived

from the 17th to the 19th century and who came to be known as the British empiricists.

The nativist and empiricist philosophies differed not only on what the mind was assumed to contain but also on how the mind was assumed to operate. Descartes believed that the mind did not function in a predictable and orderly manner according to discoverable rules or laws. One of the first to propose an alternative to this view was the British philosopher Thomas Hobbes (1588–1679). Hobbes accepted the distinction between voluntary and involuntary behavior stated by Descartes and also accepted the notion that voluntary behavior was controlled by the mind. However, unlike Descartes, he believed that the mind operated just as predictably and lawfully as reflex mechanisms. More specifically, he proposed that voluntary behavior was governed by the pursuit of pleasure and the avoidance of pain. Thus, functions of the mind were not determined by reason but by a principle of **hedonism.** Whether or not the pursuit of pleasure and the avoidance of pain were laudable or desirable was not an issue for Hobbes. Hedonism was simply a fact of life. As we shall see, this conception of behavior has remained with us in one form or another to the present day.

According to the British empiricists, another important aspect of how the mind works involved the concept of **association.** Recall that empiricism assumes that all ideas originate from sense experiences. But how do our experiences of various colors, shapes, odors, and sounds allow us to arrive at more complex ideas? Consider, for example, the concept of a car. If someone says the word *car,* you have an idea of what the thing may look like, what it is used for, and how you might feel if you sat in it. Where do all these ideas come from just given the sound of the letters *c, a,* and *r*? The British empiricists proposed that simple sensations were combined into more complex ideas by associations. Because you have heard the word *car* when you saw a car, considered using one to get to work, or sat in one, associations may have become established between the word *car* and various aspects of cars. The British empiricists considered such associations very important in their explanation of how the mind works. They therefore devoted considerable effort to detailing the rules of associations.

The British empiricists accepted two sets of rules for the establishment of associations, one primary and the other secondary. The primary rules were originally set forth by the ancient Greek philosopher Aristotle. He proposed three principles for the establishment of associations—contiguity, similarity, and contrast. Of these, the contiguity principle has been the most prominent in considerations of associations. It states that if two events repeatedly occur together, they will become associated. Once this association has been established, the occurrence of one of the events will evoke a memory of the other event. The similarity and contrast principles state that two things will become associated if they are similar in some respect or have some contrasting characteristics (one might be strikingly tall and the other strikingly short, for example). The various secondary laws of associations were set forth by the empiricist philosophers. Thomas Brown (1778–1820), for example, proposed that a number of factors influence the formation of associations, including the intensity of the sensations and the frequency and recency of their pairing. In addition, whether one event becomes associated with another was considered to depend on the number of other associations in which each event was already involved and the similarity of these past associations to the current one being formed.

The British empiricists discussed rules of associations as a part of their philosophical discourse. They did not perform experiments to determine which rules were correct and which ones were incorrect or the circumstances in which one rule was more important than another. Empirical investigation of the mechanisms of associations did not begin until the pioneering work of the 19th-century German psychologist Hermann Ebbinghaus (1850–1909). Ebbinghaus invented **nonsense syllables** to use in his experiments. The nonsense syllables were meaningless three-letter combinations (a consonant followed by a vowel and another consonant) so that their meaning could not influence how they were learned. Ebbinghaus presented lists of these nonsense syllables to himself and measured his ability to remember the syllables under various experimental conditions. With this general method he was able to answer experimentally such questions as how the strength of an association improves with increased training, whether syllables that appear close together in a list are associated more strongly with one another than syllables that are farther apart, and whether a syllable becomes more strongly associated with the next one on the list than with the preceding one.

Historical developments in the study of reflexes

The concept of reflex action, introduced by Descartes, greatly advanced our understanding of behavior. However, Descartes was mistaken in his assumptions about how reflexes are produced. He believed that sensory messages going to the brain and motor messages going to the muscles traveled along the same nerves. The nerves were thought to be hollow tubes. The pineal gland was thought to release substances called "animal spirits," which flowed down the tubes and entered the muscles, causing them to swell and create a movement. Finally, Descartes considered all reflexive movements to be innate and to be fixed by the anatomy of the organism.

Experimental observations after Descartes showed that he was wrong about the anatomy of the reflex arc and the mechanism of neural conduction. Later research also indicated that not all reflex responses are innate. The anatomy of the reflex arc was established in experiments performed by Charles Bell (1774–1842) in England and Francois Magendie (1783–1855) in France. They discovered that separate nerves are used to transmit sensory information from sense organs to the central nervous system and motor information from the central nervous system to muscles. If a sensory nerve is cut, the animal remains capable of muscle movements, and if a motor nerve is cut, the animal remains capable of registering sensory information. Establishing the mechanisms of neural conduction involved much more extensive experimentation. The idea that animal spirits were involved in neural transmission was disproved soon after the death of Descartes. In 1669 Swammerdam (1637–1680) showed that mechanical irritation of a nerve is sufficient to produce a muscle contraction. Thus, infusion of animal spirits from the pineal gland was not necessary. In other studies Francis

Glisson (1597–1677) demonstrated that muscle contractions are not produced by a swelling of the muscle by the infusion of some fluid, as Descartes thought. Glisson had people submerge one arm in water and observed that the water level did not change when they were asked to make a muscle contraction. Such experiments indicated that neural conduction did not occur by the mechanisms Descartes proposed. However, positive evidence of what was involved in neural conduction had to await the great advances that occurred in the understanding of electricity and chemistry in the 19th century. According to contemporary thinking, neural conduction involves a combination of chemical and electrical events.

Better understanding in the 19th century of the physiological processes responsible for reflexive behavior was accompanied by a liberalization of the restricted role of reflexes in the explanation of behavior. Descartes and most philosophers after him assumed that reflexes were responsible only for simple reactions to stimuli. The energy in a stimulus was thought to be translated directly (reflected) into the energy of the elicited response by the neural connections. The more intense the stimulus, the more vigorous the resulting response. This view of reflexes is consistent with many casual observations. If you touch a stove, the hotter the stove is, the more quickly you withdraw your finger. However, reflexes can also be more complicated.

Two Russian physiologists, Sechenov (1829–1905) and Pavlov (1849–1936), were primarily responsible for extending the concept of reflexes to explain more complex behaviors. Sechenov proposed that in some cases the effect of a stimulus is not to elicit a reflex response directly. Rather, a stimulus may release a response from inhibition. Sexual responses, for example, are suppressed in most social situations. These responses may be released between lovers by the stimuli of their private bedroom. With this type of mechanism the intensity of a stimulus does not necessarily become translated into the intensity of the elicited response. In our example, it is not the vividness of the stimuli in one's bedroom that determines the vigor of the sexual behavior. The sexual behavior is simply released from inhibition by the bedroom cues, and how passionate the behavior is

depends on other factors, such as how long it has been since the lovers were together. If the intensity of a stimulus does not determine the vigor of the elicited response in every case, it is possible for a very faint stimulus to produce a large response. Sechenov took advantage of this type of mechanism to provide a reflex analysis of voluntary behavior. He suggested that complex forms of behavior (actions or thoughts) that occur in the absence of an obvious eliciting stimulus are in fact reflexive responses. It is simply that in these cases the eliciting stimuli are so faint that we do not notice them. Thus, according to Sechenov, voluntary behavior and thoughts are actually elicited by inconspicuous, faint stimuli.

Sechenov's ideas about voluntary behavior represent a major extension of the use of reflex mechanisms to explain a variety of aspects of behavior. However, his proposition was a philosophical extrapolation from the actual research results he obtained. In addition, Sechenov did not address the question of how reflex mechanisms can explain the fact that the behavior of animals and people is constantly changing, depending on their experiences. From Descartes through Sechenov, reflex responses were considered to be innate—fixed by the anatomy of the organism's nervous system. They were thought to depend on a prewired neural connection between sense organs and the relevant muscles. According to this view, a given stimulus is expected to elicit the same response throughout the organism's life. Although this is true in some cases, there are also many examples in which the response to a stimulus changes. Explanation of such cases by reflex processes had to await the experimental and theoretical work of Ivan Pavlov. Pavlov showed experimentally that not all reflexes are innate. New reflexes can be established to stimuli through mechanisms of association. Pavlov's role in the history of the study of reflexes is comparable to the role of Ebbinghaus in the study of the mind. Both were concerned with establishing the laws of associations through empirical research.

Charles Darwin and the concept of evolution

Another very important historical antecedent of the type of study of behavior we will describe is the work of the 19th century British biologist Charles Darwin (1809–1882). Darwin was concerned with figuring out why various species and subspecies of animals have different characteristics. On the basis of extensive observation of various types of animals, he formulated his theory of evolution. He recognized that each member of a species is slightly different from other members. These individual variations, he thought, occurred randomly through unspecified processes. Some rabbits, for example, can run slightly faster than others, and some birds have slightly better eyesight than others. These features may make it more likely for these individuals to survive in nature than individuals without these characteristics. The ability to run fast helps rabbits escape from predators, and exceptionally good eyesight enables birds to detect food from a distance. Individuals whose skills best match the challenges to survival posed by the environment will be most likely to survive and pass on these characteristics to their offspring. This process is repeated over and over again across generations, with the result that more and more members of a group of animals will have the particular traits that promote survival in their environment. The process is called **evolution through natural selection.**

Through the process of evolution, one set of organisms can have descendants after many generations that bear little resemblance to their ancestors. Darwin proposed that evolution was responsible for the appearance of new species and saw no reason that unique human characteristics could not have developed from other types of organisms in the same way. He believed in a continuity of species that included human beings. No species was considered fundamentally different from any other. One species may simply be further along in the course of evolution than another. The belief in a continuity of species provides a strong rationale for the study of animals as a way to gain insights into human beings. If human beings in fact evolved from other animal forms, then information gained about animals could very well provide important information about human nature.

Darwin's scientific observations were concerned with behavioral characteristics as well as with physical traits of animals. Darwin did not restrict his theory of evolution to explaining physical character-

istics. He believed that behavioral characteristics, emotional expressions, and intelligence can evolve in the same way that physical traits evolve. If this assumption is true, then the detailed investigation of animal behavior should be very relevant to the understanding of human behavior.

The behavioral approach viewed in historical context

The behavioral approach to the study of psychology can be viewed as the modern extension of the study of reflexes started by Descartes. The behavioral approach uses the methods of scientific observation, focuses on aspects of behavior that are caused by environmental events, and is devoted to the study of small units of behavior before the investigation of complex psychological processes. However, the behavioral approach is not rooted entirely in the reflexology tradition. Some aspects of it can be traced to earlier philosophical debates about the nature of the mind. The nativism/empiricism controversy, for example, has had its counterpart in the development of behavioral psychology in the 20th century. The first and most vigorous advocate of the behavioral approach was the American psychologist John B. Watson (1878–1958), who believed that behavior was almost infinitely malleable by experience. In a famous statement, he once said:

> Give me a dozen healthy infants, well-formed, and my own specified world to bring them up in and I'll guarantee to take anyone at random and train him to become any type of specialist I might select—doctor, lawyer, artist, merchant-chief and, yes, even beggar-man and thief, regardless of his talents, penchants, tendencies, abilities, vocations, and race of his ancestors [Watson, 1924, p. 104].

Watson acknowledged that this statement was an exaggeration. However, the view that behavior is highly malleable can be considered analogous to the empiricism advocated by Locke in the 17th century. As we shall see in the following chapters, contemporary investigations of behavior are much more respectful of the fact that organisms are born with strong innate tendencies. It is now widely accepted that what organisms can learn through experience is limited by inherited behavioral characteristics. Thus, contemporary investigations of behavior have more of a nativist flavor.

Other respects in which the behavioral approach can be traced to earlier philosophical discussions about the mind include the concept of hedonism and the great importance placed on associations in the explanation of behavior. Hobbes proposed in the 17th century that the mind works by way of the pursuit of pleasure and the avoidance of pain. Many contemporary investigations can be viewed as experimental analyses of the role of pleasure and pain in the control of behavior (see Chapters 5–10). The concept of associations has been an even more pervasive influence in behavioral investigations. Most experiments conducted within the framework of the behavioral approach have been concerned in one way or another with the role of associations in the control of behavior.

Finally, the behavioral approach was greatly influenced by the ideas of Charles Darwin and the concept of evolution. Much of the research conducted in the behavioral tradition has been performed with animal subjects. Many of these experiments would not have been done if the investigators had not believed that the study of animal behavior can provide important insights into human behavior. This view is not as fervently held today as it was before about 1970. However, many animal experiments are still conducted with the intent of developing models and theories that are also applicable to human behavior. The concept of evolution is also important because it has made investigators sensitive to the fact that behavior in a given situation is determined not only by the stimuli animals encounter there but also by their inherited behavioral tendencies.

Learning and the Study of Behavior

The behavioral approach has been applied to the study of a variety of aspects of psychology, including abnormal behavior, speech, and personality. However, it has been used most extensively in the study of learning and conditioning mechanisms, and this as-

pect of the behavioral approach will provide the focus of our book.

Learning is one of the biological processes that are crucial for the survival of many forms of animal life. The integrity of life depends on a variety of biological functions. Animals have to take in nutrients, eliminate metabolic wastes, and otherwise maintain proper balance in internal functions. Through evolution, a variety of biological systems have emerged to accomplish these tasks. Many of them are primarily physiological, such as systems involved in respiration, digestion, and excretion. However, finely tuned internal physiological processes are often not enough to maintain the integrity of life. Animals and people live in environments that are constantly changing because of climatic changes, changes in food resources, the coming and going of predators, and other factors. Adverse effects of these changes often have to be minimized by behavioral adjustments. Animals have to know, for example, how to find and obtain food as food sources change, avoid predators as new ones enter their territory, and find new shelter when storms destroy their old homes. Accomplishing these tasks obviously requires motor movements, such as walking and manipulating objects. These tasks also require the ability to predict important events in the environment, such as the availability of food in a particular location and at a particular time. Acquisition of new motor behavior and new anticipatory reactions involves learning. Thus, animals learn to go to a new water hole when the old one dries up and learn new anticipatory reactions when new sources of danger appear. These learned adjustments to the environment are no less important for survival than internal physiological processes such as respiration and digestion.

The definition of learning

Most people automatically associate learning with the acquisition of new behavior. That is, learning is identified by the gradual appearance of a new response in the organism's repertoire. This is the case when people learn to read, ride a bicycle, or play a musical instrument. However, the behavior change involved in learning can just as well consist in the decrease or loss of some behavior in the organism's repertoire. A child, for example, may learn not to cross the street when the traffic light is red, not to grab food from someone else's plate, and not to yell and scream when someone is trying to take a nap. Learning to withhold responses is just as important as learning to make responses, if not more so.

We often think of learning as a complex process that requires extensive specialized practice and results in sophisticated and impressive forms of behavior. Numerous instances of learning are of this sort. Learning calculus, figure skating, championship swimming, or a foreign language involves extensive specialized practice and enables a person to perform in ways that seem incredible to those who do not have these skills. Learning is also involved in much simpler response systems. Investigators of learning have devoted a great deal of effort to studying the mechanisms of learning in simple response systems in the hope that knowledge obtained from such investigations will lead to the formulation of general principles of learning. Research on simple response systems is also expected to provide background information that is necessary for the study of more complex forms of learning.

A universally accepted definition of learning does not exist. However, many critical aspects of the concept of learning are captured in the following statement: *Learning is an enduring change in the mechanisms of behavior that results from experience with environmental events.* Several aspects of this definition are important. First, learning is said to be a change in the mechanisms of behavior—not a change in behavior itself. Why should we define learning as a change in the *mechanisms* of behavior? The main reason is that behavior is determined by many factors in addition to learning. Consider, for example, eating. Whether you eat something depends on how hungry you are, how much effort you have to expend to get to the food, how much you like the food, and whether you know where the food is. Of all these factors, only the last one necessarily involves learning. This example illustrates the importance of the distinction between learning and performance.

Performance refers to an organism's actions at a particular time. Whether an organism does something or not (its performance) depends on many things. Even the occurrence of a simple response such as pushing a shopping cart down an aisle is multiply determined. Whether or not you perform this response depends on the availability of a shopping cart, your motivation to use the cart, your ability to reach the cart handle, your physical capacity to push the cart, your ability to see ahead of the cart, and your learned knowledge of how shopping carts work. Performance is determined by opportunity, motivation, and sensory and motor abilities, in addition to learning. Therefore, a change in performance cannot be automatically considered to reflect learning.

The definition stated above identifies learning as a change in the mechanisms of behavior to emphasize the distinction between learning and performance. However, investigators cannot observe mechanisms directly. Rather, a change in the mechanisms of behavior is inferred from changes in behavior. Thus, the behavior of an organism (its performance) is used to provide evidence of learning. However, because performance is determined by many factors in addition to learning, one must be very careful in deciding whether a particular aspect of performance does or does not reflect learning. Sometimes evidence of learning cannot be obtained until special test procedures are set up. Children, for example, learn a great deal about driving a car just by watching others drive, but this learning is not apparent until they are permitted behind the steering wheel. In other cases (see below), a change in behavior is readily observed but cannot be attributed to learning, either because it is not sufficiently long-lasting or because it does not result from experience with environmental events.

Distinction between learning and other sources of behavior change

Evaluating various situations in terms of the abstract definition of learning stated above may be difficult because some aspects of the definition are rather imprecise. It is not specified exactly how long behavioral changes have to last to be considered instances of learning. It is also sometimes hard to decide what constitutes sufficient experience with environmental events to classify something as an instance of learning. Therefore, it is useful to distinguish learning from other known mechanisms that can produce changes in behavior.

Several mechanisms produce changes in behavior that are too short-lasting to be considered instances of learning. One such process is **fatigue.** Physical exertion may result in a gradual weakening in the vigor of a response because the subject becomes tired or fatigued. This type of change is produced by experience. However, it is not considered an instance of learning, because the decline in responding disappears if the subject is allowed to rest and recover. Behavior may also be temporarily altered by a *change in stimulus conditions.* If birds that have been housed in a small cage are suddenly set free, for example, their behavior will change dramatically. However, this is not an instance of learning, because the birds are likely to return to their old style of responding when returned to their cage. Another source of temporary changes in behavior that is not considered learning is *alterations in the physiological or motivational state* of the organism. Hunger and thirst induce responses that are not observed at other times. Changes in the level of sex hormones will cause temporary changes in responsiveness to members of the other sex. Short-lasting behavioral effects may also accompany the administration of psychoactive drugs.

Other mechanisms produce persistent changes in behavior but without the type of experience with environmental events that satisfies the definition of learning. The most obvious process of this type is **maturation.** A child will be unable to reach a high shelf until he or she grows tall enough. However, the change in behavior in this case would not be considered an instance of learning, because it occurs with the mere passage of time. One does not have to be trained to reach high places as one becomes taller. Maturation can also result in a loss of certain responses. For example, shortly after birth, touching an infant's feet results in foot movements that resemble walking, and stroking the bottom of the foot causes the toes to fan out. Both these reflex reactions are lost as the infant gets older.

Generally, the distinction between learning and maturation is based on the importance of special experiences in producing the change in behavior. However, the distinction has become blurred in instances in which exposure to stimuli has been found to be necessary for developmental changes that originally were thought to involve experience-independent maturation. For example, the visual system of cats will not develop sufficiently for them to be able to see horizontal lines unless they are exposed to such stimuli early in life (see, for example, Blakemore & Cooper, 1970). The appearance of sexual behavior at puberty was originally also thought to depend on maturation. However, experiments suggest that successful sexual behavior may require social contact early in life (for example, Harlow, 1969).

So far we have discussed mechanisms that create changes in behavior during the lifetime of the organism. Changes in behavior may also occur across generations through **evolutionary adaptation.** Individuals possessing genetic characteristics that promote their reproduction are more likely to pass these characteristics on to future generations. Adaptation and evolutionary change produced by differential reproductive success can lead to changes in behavior just as they lead to changes in the physical characteristics of species. Evolutionary changes are similar to learning in that they are also related to environmental influences. The characteristics of individuals that promote their reproductive success depend on the environment in which they live. However, evolutionary changes occur only across generations and are therefore distinguished from learning. (For a discussion of the relation between learning and evolution, see Plotkin & Odling-Smee, 1979.)

Although learning can be distinguished from maturation and evolution, it is not independent of these other sources of behavioral change. Whether a particular learning process occurs or how it operates depends on the subject's maturational level and evolutionary history. The dependence of learning on maturation is obvious in certain aspects of child rearing. For example, no amount of toilet training will be effective in a child until the nerves and muscles have developed sufficiently to make bladder control possible. The dependence of learning on evolutionary history can be seen by comparing learning processes in various types of animals. For example, fish and turtles appear to learn differently than rats and monkeys in instrumental conditioning situations (Bitterman, 1975). We will have more to say about the interaction of evolutionary history and learning processes in later chapters.

Use of Animals in Research on Learning

The study of learning can be conducted by investigating the behavior of either human beings or other animals. The scientific study of behavior is not restricted to any part of the animal kingdom. Nevertheless, most of the experiments we will be considering have been conducted with nonhuman animals. A variety of animals have been used, including rats, mice, rabbits, fish, pigeons, and monkeys.

Practical advantages of the use of animals

Use of animals rather than humans in research on learning has several important advantages, many of which involve practical problems encountered in research. It is much easier to control the past experience of animals than that of people. Ethical considerations, for example, preclude raising human beings in totally controlled environments. There are also important ethical restrictions on the conduct of animal research, and laboratory animals are generally much better cared for than animals in the wild. Without imposing the kind of hardship that animals have to live with in the wild, one can easily design laboratory environments in which many of the things animals experience are highly regulated.

Another practical advantage afforded by the study of animals in laboratory settings is that the genetic history of the subjects can be controlled, making it much easier to evaluate the contribution of genetic factors to behavior than with human beings. Use of animals also makes it easier to control the experimental situation. Experimental chambers can be smaller and do not need as many costly comforts, such as carpeting and furniture. Animals can also be subjected to such procedures as food or water deprivation with much less trouble than would be involved with human subjects. Finally, because animals rarely have a choice in whether they will participate in an experiment, investigations are not limited to those individuals who volunteer, and so it is more likely that subjects in animal experiments will be representative of their species. Ethical considerations often limit human research to those individuals who choose to participate in the experiment. For some kinds of studies (for example, those that involve a great deal of time and effort or include some kind of aversive stimulation), people who volunteer may not be representative of all humans.

Conceptual advantages of the use of animals

In addition to practical considerations, use of animals in the study of behavior has possible conceptual advantages. There is the hope that processes of learning may be simpler in animals reared in controlled laboratory situations than in people, whose backgrounds are much more varied. One cannot tell at present all the respects in which learning in animals is simpler than in humans. However, it is agreed that most animal behavior is not complicated by the linguistic processes that have a prominent role in certain kinds of human behavior. One of the most exciting contemporary areas of research is the study of linguistic abilities in primates (see Chapter 12). However, there is no evidence that learning processes of the sort we will discuss in most of this book involve linguistic functions.

Another important advantage of using animals is that one does not have to be concerned with the demand characteristics of the experiment. In many forms of research with people, one has to make sure their actions are not governed by their efforts to please (or displease) the experimenter. People serving in experiments often try to figure out what the purpose of the study is and what they are "supposed" to do. Whether or not they identify the purpose of the experiment correctly, their actions may be motivated by their wish to "do well" in the experiment rather than by the stimuli and the experimental conditions that were set up. Consequently, a person may react to circumstances in the laboratory very differently than he or she would respond to the same circumstances outside the laboratory. Such problems are not likely to arise in research with animals such as rats and pigeons. There is no reason to suspect that the actions of rats and pigeons in the laboratory are determined by their desire to please the experimenter or to do well in the experiment to avoid embarrassment.

Laboratory animals and normal behavior

Some have suggested that domesticated laboratory strains of animals may not provide useful information because such animals have degenerated in various ways as a result of many generations of inbreeding and long periods of captivity (for example, Lockard, 1968). However, this idea is probably false. In an interesting test, Boice (1977) took five male and five female albino rats of a highly inbred laboratory stock and housed them in an outdoor pen in Missouri without artificial shelters. All ten rats survived the first winter with temperatures as low as $-22°$ F. The animals reproduced normally and reached a stable population of about 50 members. Only three of the rats died before showing signs of old age during the 2-year period. Given the extreme climatic conditions, this level of success in living outdoors is remarkable. Furthermore, the behavior of these domesticated rats in the outdoors was very similar to the behavior of wild rats observed in similar circumstances.

The vigor of inbred laboratory rats in outdoor living conditions indicates that they are not inferior to their wild counterparts. Domesticated rats act similarly to wild rats in other tests as well, and there is some indication that they perform better than wild rats in learning experiments (see, for example, Boice, 1973, 1981; Kaufman & Collier, 1983). Therefore, one should not dismiss the results we will be describing in this book simply because many of the experiments were conducted with domesticated animals. In fact, it may be suggested that laboratory animals are preferable in research to their wild counterparts. Human beings in civilized society are raised and live in somewhat contrived environments. Therefore, research with animals may prove most relevant to the human case if the animals are domesticated and live in artificial laboratory situations. As Boice (1973,

p. 227) has commented, "The domesticated rat may be a good model for domestic man."

Generality of animal learning results

One of the most salient characteristics of animals is their diversity. Some animals are large, others are small; some live in the water, others live on land; some prefer humid places, others prefer dry places; some consist of only a few cells, others are complex multicellular organisms; some have only a rudimentary nervous system, others have a highly organized, complex nervous system. Most investigators of learning focus their efforts on one or a small number of species. To what extent will their findings be applicable to other species? Various species of animals differ in the motor movements they are able to perform and in the types of stimuli they are able to detect. Differences in motor and sensory capacity make for differences in what various species can learn to do. A dog, for example, can easily learn to climb stairs, but no amount of training will teach a fish to do the same. Differences in motor and sensory capacity lead to differences in what various species can learn—differences in the content of learning. However, differences in the content of learning do not necessarily imply differences in learning mechanisms or principles.

The same mechanisms or principles of learning can often be used to learn different content materials. Consider, for example, learning information for a sociology course and for a psychology course. Despite the difference in the content of the learning, you may use the same learning techniques: first survey a chapter, think up questions about it, read it, and then rehearse and review it. In a similar manner, the same learning mechanisms and principles may be involved in learning of different responses to diverse stimuli in various species of animals. For example, research has shown that in many respects the same principles are involved when pigeons learn to predict food on the basis of a visual signal and when rats learn to predict pain on the basis of an auditory cue. The critical issue in considering the generality of learning is the generality of learning mechanisms and principles—not the generality of the contents of learning. The contents of learning will certainly vary from one situation to another and from one species to another, but the principles and mechanisms may not.

The available evidence suggests that elementary principles of learning of the sort that will be described in this book have considerable generality. Most research on animal learning has been performed with pigeons, rats, and rabbits. However, some of the principles of learning observed with these vertebrate species have also been demonstrated in newts (Ellins, Cramer, & Martin, 1982), fruit flies (Platt, Holliday, & Drudge, 1980), honeybees (Couvillon & Bitterman, 1980, 1982; Menzel, 1983), terrestrial mollusks (Sahley, Rudy, & Gelperin, 1981), and the marine mollusks *Hermissenda crassicornis* (Farley & Alkon, 1980), *Aplysia californica* (Carew, Hawkins, & Kandel, 1983), and *Aplysia fasciata* (Susswein & Schwarz, 1983). Studies with organisms like *Hermissenda* and *Aplysia* are particularly exciting because the simplicity of the nervous system of these species has permitted investigators to identify the physiological mechanisms responsible for the learning (for example, Farley, Richards, Ling, Liman, & Alkon, 1983; Hawkins, Abrams, Carew, & Kandel, 1983; Hawkins & Kandel, 1984; Kandel, 1976; Kandel & Schwartz, 1982).

The assumption that general principles and mechanisms of learning exist has been a cornerstone in the study of learning since its inception. Scientists, in contrast to engineers, are always motivated by a search for generality. An engineer is faced with a particular problem—how to harden a plastic, for example. The engineer is successful if she finds a solution to the problem, whether or not the solution involves a generally applicable procedure. The task of the scientist is more difficult. It is to look for general solutions, general principles. Whether a general solution is found often depends on the level of analysis that is pursued. For example, by the 19th century, chemists knew many specific facts about what would happen when various chemicals were combined. However, a general account of chemical reactions had to await the development of the periodic table of the elements, which described chemical elements in terms of their constituent atomic components. In an analogous fashion, a general account of learning principles and processes requires a fairly

molecular level of analysis of the roles of stimuli and responses in learned behavior (Domjan, 1983).

About 15 years ago, several investigators argued that the laws of learning lacked generality because several phenomena were discovered that were contrary to learning principles that were generally accepted at the time (for example, Rozin & Kalat, 1971; Shettleworth, 1972). However, the discovery of exceptions to a general law does not imply that generality does not exist. It simply indicates that we have not found the correct general principle. The principles of learning are continually being modified in light of new findings. Discovery of exceptions to a rule simply requires that the rule be modified. New general principles have been formulated in light of new data during the past 15 years. The pursuit of general principles of learning is an ongoing enterprise as the science of behavior continues to progress.

The Behavioral Approach and Other Aspects of Psychology

There are probably few aspects of nature more complicated and difficult to study than behavior. One result of this complexity is that it is difficult to decide how to go about the investigation. Scientists do not agree on how to define the subject matter, what kinds of behavior to study first, and how long to pursue one approach before proceeding to the next stage of analysis. The absence of obvious answers to such questions has created a great deal of diversity in the way psychologists pursue their work. Some areas of psychology can be obviously differentiated from others by what aspect of behavior is being investigated. Sensory psychologists, for example, investigate the processes involved in sensation and perception, cognitive psychologists are interested in the processes of thinking and information processing, and clinical psychologists are interested in abnormal behavior. Another way to categorize various approaches to the study of behavior is by the complexity of the behavior under investigation. Psychologists interested in personality and intelligence, for example, study very complex behavioral systems. They do not investigate individual responses but, rather, response styles and aggregates of behavior that are organized in complex ways. A high score on a test of intelligence or a test of masculinity, for example, does not refer to a particular response. Rather, such scores identify a complex constellation of response tendencies of varying degrees of strength.

The behavioral approach can be distinguished from other approaches in psychology both by the aspect of behavior it focuses on and by the level of complexity of the behavior. As we have already noted, many experiments using this approach are concerned only with aspects of behavior that can be observed directly and involve discrete responses, small units of behavior instead of response styles and constellations of response tendencies. It is assumed that complex behavioral systems consist of the combined action of simpler responses. Therefore, the understanding of simple responses is viewed as a prerequisite for the study of complex psychological processes. The information gained from studying simpler responses is assumed to be useful in the design of studies of more complex systems.

The behavioral approach is part of a comprehensive position in psychology identified as behaviorism.

Many diverse ideas are subsumed under this philosophical position. Some have argued, for example, that the behavioral approach is the only one that is likely to be fruitful in the study of psychology (Watson, 1913). Such a radical behavioristic position is not advocated in this book. Given the complexity of behavior and given that there is no way to know at this point what is the best way to study it, the variety of approaches used in contemporary psychology is justified. The study of behavior can be profitably conducted at several levels of complexity simultaneously. Information gained in the various approaches can then be exchanged back and forth in the development of a complete description of behavior. Each level of analysis plays an integral role in such a multifaceted and integrated study. Thus, studies of physiological bases of behavior, simple responses, and complex response systems (as in personality variables) all make important contributions to a complete understanding of behavior. Our purpose in advocating this integrated approach is not to denigrate the importance of the behavioral approach but to allow the reader to better relate the information provided by this text to information about behavior presented in other discussions of psychology.

CHAPTER 2
Elicited Behavior, Habituation, and Sensitization

We begin our discussion of the principles of learning and behavior in the present chapter by describing elicited behavior—behavior that occurs in reaction to events in the environment. Numerous aspects of behavior are elicited by environmental events, and some of the most extensively investigated response systems involve elicited behavior. Our discussion will progress from a description of the simplest form of elicited behavior—reflexive behavior—to a discussion of complex emotional responses elicited by stimuli. Along the way we will describe two of the simplest and most common forms of behavioral change—habituation and sensitization. Habituation and sensitization can occur in a wide variety of response systems and are therefore fundamental properties of behavior.

The Nature of Elicited Behavior
  The concept of the reflex
  The nature of response-eliciting stimuli
  The role of feedback in elicited behavior
    Elicited behavior independent of feedback stimuli
    Presence or absence of the eliciting stimulus as feedback
    Responses elicited and guided by different stimuli
Effects of Repeated Stimulation: Three Examples
  Sucking in human infants
  Startle response in rats
  Mobbing in chaffinches
The Concepts of Habituation and Sensitization
  Adaptiveness and pervasiveness of habituation and sensitization
  Neural analysis of habituation and sensitization
    Distinctions among habituation, sensory adaptation, and response fatigue
    Dual-process theory of habituation and sensitization
Characteristics of Habituation and Sensitization
  Time course of habituation and sensitization
    Time course of sensitization
    Time course of habituation
  Stimulus specificity of habituation and sensitization
  Effects of strong extraneous stimuli
  Effects of stimulus intensity and frequency
Changes in Complex Emotional Responses
  The opponent-process theory of motivation
  Mechanisms of the opponent-process theory
  Examples of opponent processes
    Love and attachment
    Skydiving
    Drug addiction
Concluding Comments

The Nature of Elicited Behavior

It is a commonplace observation that organisms react to events in their environment. This is true for all animals, including human beings. The calls of an intruder elicit territorial defensive responses in white-crowned sparrows. The odor of a sexually receptive female dog or cat elicits approach and sexual behaviors in male dogs and cats. If something moves in the periphery of your vision, you are likely to turn your head in that direction. A particle of food in the mouth elicits salivation. Exposure to a bright light causes the pupils of the eyes to constrict. The pain of touching a hot surface elicits a quick withdrawal response. Irritation of the respiratory passages causes sneezing and coughing. These and numerous similar examples illustrate that much of behavior occurs in response to stimuli—it is elicited.

Elicited behavior has been the subject of extensive investigation. Many of the chapters of this book deal, in one way or other, with elicited behavior. We begin our discussion of elicited behavior by describing its simplest form, reflexive behavior. We will then discuss the nature of stimuli that trigger elicited behavior and the role of feedback cues in elicited behavior.

The concept of the reflex

A light puff of air directed at the cornea makes the eyes blink. A tap on a certain part of the knee causes the leg to kick. A loud noise causes a startle reaction. These are all examples of reflexes. A reflex involves two closely related events. One is the *eliciting environmental stimulus;* the other is a *specific response.* The stimulus and response are closely linked in a special way: the occurrence of the stimulus generally leads to the occurrence of the response, and the response rarely occurs in the absence of the stimulus. For example, salivation occurs when food is presented and rarely occurs in the absence of food.

The specificity of the relation between a particular type of stimulus and a particular reflex response reflects the organization of the nervous system. In vertebrates (including humans), simple reflexes are mediated by a minimum of three neurons. Figure 2.1 shows the neural organization of simple reflexes. The environmental stimulus for a reflex activates a **sensory, or afferent, neuron,** which transmits the sensory message to the spinal cord. Here the neural impulses are relayed to the **motor, or efferent, neuron,** which creates the observed reflex response. However, sensory and motor neurons do not communicate directly. Rather, the impulses from one to the

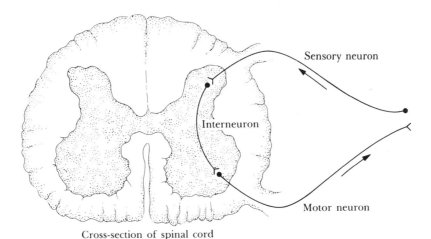

Cross-section of spinal cord

FIGURE 2.1.   Neural organization of simple reflexes. The environmental stimulus for a reflex activates a sensory neuron, which transmits the sensory message to the spinal cord. Here the neural impulses are relayed to an interneuron, which in turn relays the impulses to the motor neuron. The motor neuron activates muscles involved in movement.

other are relayed through an **interneuron.** Interneurons are located in such a way that one set of sensory neurons is connected to only one set of motor neurons. Because of this restrictive connection between particular sensory and motor neurons, the reflex response is elicited only by a restricted set of stimuli. The afferent neuron, interneuron, and efferent neuron together constitute what is called the **reflex arc.**

The reflex arc in vertebrates represents the fewest neural connections that are necessary for reflex action. Additional neural structures are often involved in the elicitation of reflexes. The sensory messages are often also relayed to the brain, which may influence the course of the reflex in various ways. For example, arousal mechanisms in the brain may influence the excitability of the interneurons. If you are highly aroused by a good horror movie, for example, you may startle more easily when someone taps you on the shoulder. We will discuss this type of effect in greater detail later in the chapter. For now, it is important to keep in mind that the occurrence of even simple reflexes can be influenced by higher nervous-system functions.

Reflexes have, no doubt, evolved to provide rapid behavioral adjustment to environmental events. Most reflexes promote the well-being of the organism in obvious ways. For example, in many animals painful stimulation of one limb causes withdrawal, or flexion, of that limb and extension of the opposite limb (Hart, 1973). Thus, if a dog stubs a toe while walking, it will automatically withdraw that leg and simultaneously extend the opposite leg. This combination of responses removes the first leg from the source of pain and at the same time allows the animal to maintain balance. The same sequence of reflex responses, however, would not benefit the two-toed sloth, a mammal that spends much of its time hanging upside down on branches. Consider what would happen if it responded to pain in the same way as the dog. If it flexed the injured limb and extended the opposite limb, it would end up putting most of its weight on the injured foot. As you might suspect, the sloth has evolved with a different sequence of responses. It extends the injured foot, thereby removing that foot from the branch it is on, and flexes the opposite foot, thereby putting more of its weight on

that leg, as shown in Figure 2.2 (Esplin & Woodbury, 1961).

Innate reflexes constitute much of the behavioral repertoire of newborn infants. Because newborn infants have not had much time to learn how to respond to environmental events, they have to survive with mainly inborn reactions to stimuli. Some of these reflexes can be a source of enjoyment for the parents. For example, newborn babies reflexively clench their fingers around anything that is placed in their hand. Another prominent reflex probably evolved to facili-

FIGURE 2.2. Painful stimulation of one leg of a dog causes withdrawal (flexion) of that leg and extension of the opposite leg. In contrast, painful stimulation of one leg of a sloth causes extension of that leg and flexion of the opposite leg. *(After Hart, 1973.)*

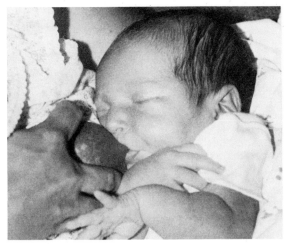

FIGURE 2.3.   Sucking is one of the prominent reflexes in infants.

tate finding the nipple: if you touch an infant's cheek with your finger, the baby will reflexively turn her head in that direction, with the result that your finger will probably fall in the baby's mouth. When an object is in the infant's mouth, she will reflexively suck. The more closely the object resembles a nipple, the more vigorous the elicited sucking behavior.

Although reflex responses are usually beneficial to the organism, the organization of reflex behavior can also lead to unexpected difficulties. The head-turning and sucking reflexes make it easy for newborn babies to get fed. However, sometimes another important reflex, the respiratory occlusion reflex, gets in the way. The respiratory occlusion reflex is stimulated by a reduction of air flow to the baby, caused by, for example, a cloth covering the face or an accumulation of mucus in the respiratory passages. When confronted with a reduction of air flow, the baby's first reaction is to pull her head back. If this does not remove the eliciting stimulus, the baby will move her hands in a face-wiping motion. If this also fails to remove the eliciting stimulus, then the baby will begin to cry. Crying involves vigorous expulsion of air, which is often sufficient to remove whatever was obstructing the air passages. The respiratory occlusion reflex is obviously essential for survival. If the baby does not get enough air, she may suffocate. The problem arises when the respiratory occlusion reflex is triggered during nursing. While nursing, the baby

can get air only through the nose. If the mother presses the baby too close to the breast during feeding so that the baby's nostrils are covered by the breast, the respiratory occlusion reflex will be stimulated. The baby will attempt to pull her head back from the nipple, may paw at her face to get released from the nipple, and may begin to cry. Thus, successful nursing requires a bit of experience. The mother and child have to adjust their positions so that nursing can progress without stimulation of the respiratory occlusion reflex (Gunther, 1961).

The nature of response-eliciting stimuli

In each of the examples of reflexes described above, the eliciting stimulus is fairly obvious. However, this is not true of all elicited behavior. In many situations a response is elicited by a complex sequence of events or stimuli, and it is not easy to tell exactly which features of the situation are critical for the occurrence of the response. Consider, for example, the sequence of events during the feeding of herring-gull chicks. The chicks remain in the nest after hatching and are entirely dependent on food brought to them. When the parent returns from a feeding trip, the baby chicks peck at the tip of its bill (see Figure 2.4). This causes the adult to regurgitate. The parent then picks up

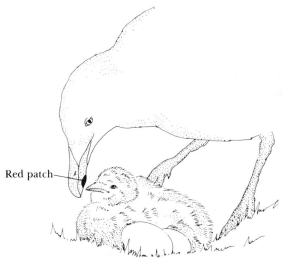

Red patch

FIGURE 2.4.   Feeding of herring-gull chicks. The chicks peck a red patch near the tip of the adult's bill, causing the adult to regurgitate food for the chicks.

some of the vomitus in its bill. As the chicks continue to peck at the bill, they manage to get some of the regurgitated food, and this provides their nourishment.

One of the critical aspects of this feeding sequence is how the chicks peck at the parent's bill to stimulate the parent to regurgitate. This is an elicited innate behavior. However, from casual observation of the situation, one cannot easily identify the critical stimulus features for eliciting the pecking behavior. Herring gulls have a long, yellow bill with a striking red patch near the tip. Pecking in the chicks may be elicited by movements of the parent, the color, shape, or length of its bill, the noises the parent makes, or some other stimulus. To isolate which of these features are important for the pecking response, Tinbergen and Perdeck (1950) tested herring-gull chicks with various artificial models instead of live adult gulls. From this research they concluded that a model had to have several characteristics to strongly elicit pecking. It had to be a long, thin, moving object that was pointed downward and had a contrasting red patch near the tip. These experiments suggest that the yellow color of the adult's bill, the shape and coloration of its head, and the noises it makes are all unimportant for eliciting pecking in the gull chicks. The specific features that were found to be required to elicit the pecking behavior are called the **sign stimulus** or **releasing stimulus** for this behavior.

Various sign stimuli have been identified in investigations of elicited behavior. A classic example is provided by the stimuli that elicit aggression or courtship in the three-spined stickleback, a small fish that breeds during the spring. During the breeding season, the male stickleback establishes and defends a territory. If another male intrudes into its territory, the intruder is attacked. In contrast, if a female stickleback enters, it is courted. How does the occupant of the territory distinguish between fish it should attack and fish it should court? A male intruder has several stimulus characteristics—a particular movement pattern, pattern of coloration, size, shape, and so on. To isolate the critical stimulus features, male sticklebacks were tested with various cardboard models (Tinbergen, 1951). This research showed that to elicit aggression, the model had to have a red underside. Movement was also relevant.

The model was more likely to be attacked if it was presented in a head-down posture similar to that of a threatening live fish. In contrast, the critical stimulus feature to avoid attack and possibly elicit courtship was a rounded, "swollen" underside similar to that of female sticklebacks holding many eggs.

The role of feedback in elicited behavior

Responses usually produce specific stimulus consequences. This is true for all behavior, including responses elicited by environmental events. When your pupils constrict in bright light, for example, less light reaches the retina as a result. The salivation elicited by food in the mouth makes the food softer and less concentrated. Coughing and sneezing in response to irritation of the respiratory passages produce loud noises and rapid expulsion of air and usually remove the irritant. A specific stimulus that results from a particular response is called a **feedback stimulus** for that response. A consideration of the role of feedback stimuli provides important insights into behavior. The present section will consider the role of feedback in the control of innate elicited behavior. Later chapters will discuss the importance of feedback in the control of learned responses.

Feedback stimuli may arise from sources internal or external to the organism. Internal feedback cues are provided by sensory neurons that allow the animal to feel the muscle and joint movements involved in making the response. If someone tapped your knee in the appropriate place and elicited the knee-jerk reflex, you would feel your leg kick. You would know when you made the response even if you closed your eyes, because of sensations provided by sensory neurons in the leg muscles and knee joint. Such internal feedback cues are called **proprioceptive stimuli.** The movement of most skeletal muscles provides proprioceptive sensations. However, not all reflex responses are accompanied by proprioceptive cues. For example, constriction of the pupils creates few internal sensations. Rather, the feedback that results from pupillary constriction occurs because less light reaches the retina. This feedback changes the external stimuli to which the organism is exposed. We will discuss the role of only such external feedback cues in elicited behavior. Some response patterns are largely independent of external feedback cues. In other cases, the behavior is almost exclusively controlled by feedback.

Elicited behavior independent of feedback stimuli.   Once some responses are initiated, they go to completion largely independent of the consequences of the behavior. Because of the fixed nature of such responses, they are called **fixed action patterns.** There are numerous instances of fixed action patterns in animal behavior. Some familiar examples can be observed in common pets. When eating, cats, for example, often take a bite, shake their heads slightly, and then proceed to chew and swallow. The shaking response is very useful when the cat is about to eat a live mouse because it helps to kill the mouse. This part of the fixed action pattern continues to occur even when the food does not have to be killed. Another commonly observed fixed action pattern in domestic cats is seen when they use the litter box. Elimination in cats ends with their scratching the dirt to cover up their waste. However, this scratching response is independent of its stimulus consequences. Cats scratch for a while after eliminating whether or not the dirt they scratch covers up their waste. In fact, sometimes they scratch on the side of the litter box and do not even move any dirt.

A dramatic example of a fixed action pattern is the cocoon-spinning behavior of the spider *Ciprennium salei* (see Eibl-Eibesfeldt, 1970). The spider begins by spinning the bottom of the cocoon; then it spins the sides. It lays its eggs inside the cocoon and then spins the top of the cocoon, thereby closing it. This response sequence is remarkable because it occurs in the specified order even if the usual outcome of the response is altered by an experimenter. For example, the spider will continue to spin the sides of the cocoon and lay the eggs even if the bottom of the cocoon is destroyed and the eggs fall through the cocoon. If the spider is placed on a partly completed cocoon, it will nevertheless begin the spinning response sequence as if it had to start an entirely new cocoon. Another remarkable aspect is that the spinning responses occur in much the same way even if the spider is unable to produce the material with which to con-

struct the cocoon. Thus, although the spider appears to go through the spinning movements in order to have a place to lay its eggs, the consequences of the behavior do not control its occurrence. (For additional examples of fixed action patterns, see Barnett, 1981.)

Presence or absence of the eliciting stimulus as feedback.   Fixed action patterns like those described above are generally elicited by discrete releasing stimuli. In other situations, responses are elicited by events that may be present for a long time. In some of these cases, the elicited response may either maintain the animal in contact with the eliciting stimulus or remove the animal from the stimulus. Which of these feedback events takes place strongly determines the future occurrence of the response. If the reflex response maintains the animal in contact with the eliciting stimulus, the response will persist. In contrast, if the behavior removes the animal from the eliciting stimulus, the response will cease.

We have already encountered reflex systems in which the response feedback is provided by the presence or absence of the eliciting stimulus. Consider, for example, the sucking reflex of newborn babies. When presented with a nipple, the baby begins to suck. This response serves to maintain contact between the baby and the nipple. The continued contact, in turn, elicits further sucking behavior. In other cases, the outcome of the reflex response removes the eliciting stimulus. Reflexive sneezing and coughing, for example, usually result in removal of the irritation in the respiratory passages that originally elicited the behavior. When the irritation is removed, the sneezing and coughing cease.

Feedback involving the presence or absence of the eliciting stimulus is very important in controlling reflexive locomotor movement in many animals. In one type of reflexive locomotion, the eliciting stimulus produces a change in the speed of movement (or the speed of turning) irrespective of direction. Any such movement is called a **kinesis.** The behavior of woodlice provides a good example. The woodlouse (*Porcellio scaber*) is a small isopod usually found in damp areas, such as under rocks, boards, and leaves. From a casual observation of the places in which woodlice are found, one might be tempted to conclude that they move toward damp places because they prefer such areas. However, their tendency to congregate in damp places is a result of a kinesis. Low levels of humidity elicit locomotor movement in the lice. As long as the air is dry, the lice continue to move. When they reach more humid places, a higher proportion of them are found to be inactive. Thus, they tend to congregate in areas of high humidity not because they prefer such areas and "voluntarily" seek them out but because in damp places the stimulus for movement is absent (Fraenkel & Gunn, 1961).

Kinesis determines the resting location of other types of animals as well. In contrast to the woodlice, both adult and larval grasshoppers are more active in moist areas and quiescent in dry places (Riegert, 1959). This response increases the likelihood that they will remain in dry areas. In flatworms kinesis is controlled by illumination rather than humidity. Several types of flatworms are more likely to stop in dark than in well-lit places (Walter, 1907; Welsh, 1933). Another interesting kinesis controlled by light is found in the larvae of the brook lamprey (*Lampetra planeri*). When exposed to light, they wriggle around with the head pointed downward. The greater the illumination, the greater the activity. On a muddy substrate, the wriggling movement results in the animal's burrowing into the ground. The burrowing persists until the light receptors at the tip of the tail become covered up with mud (Jones, 1955).

Kinesis produces movements toward (or away from) particular stimuli as an indirect result of changes in the rate of movement triggered by the stimuli. In another type of reflexive locomotion process, the stimulus directly creates movements toward or away from it. This type of mechanism is called a **taxis** (plural, *taxes*). A taxis is identified by the nature of the eliciting stimulus and whether the movement is toward or away from the stimulus. Earthworms tend to turn away from bright light (Adams, 1903). This is an example of a negative phototaxis. The South American bloodsucker orients and goes toward warm bodies (Wigglesworth & Gillett, 1934). In the laboratory, for example, the bloodsucker will go toward a test tube of warm water. This is an example of a positive thermotaxis. The tree

snail exhibits a negative geotaxis (Crozier & Navez, 1930). Pulling of the shell in one direction causes the snail to move in the opposite direction. In nature the result is that the snail climbs trees because gravity pulls its shell toward the ground. The direction of flight in many insects is controlled by taxes. Locusts, for example, have small tufts of hair on the front of the head. The animals always orient their flight in such a way that the hairs are bent straight back (Weiss-Fogh, 1949). Changes in flight orientation produce feedback in the form of changes in the hair tufts, and this feedback stimulates further changes in orientation that make the locust fly directly into the wind.

Taxes and kineses are remarkable because they illustrate how responses that appear to be goal-directed and volitional can be produced by relatively simple and mechanistic reflex processes. To explain the behavior of woodlice, for example, it is not necessary to postulate that they enjoy and seek out damp places. Similarly, it is not necessary to postulate that locusts seek to fly into the wind or enjoy doing so. Rather, these apparently goal-directed movements can be explained in terms of reflex responses controlled by feedback cues involving the presence or absence of the eliciting stimulus. The locomotor/orientation movement will persist as long as the response feedback involves continued contact with the eliciting stimulus and will cease when other types of feedback cues occur.

Responses elicited and guided by different stimuli. So far we have discussed elicited behavior that is largely independent of the feedback cues and elicited behavior that is controlled by feedback involving the presence or absence of the eliciting stimulus. There are also innate responses that are elicited by one stimulus and guided by feedback involving a second stimulus. A good example is provided by the mouthbreeding cichlid (*Tilapia mossambica*), a bass-like fish that incubates its eggs in its mouth. After hatching, the young remain close to the mother for a number of days. The approach of a large object or turbulence in the water causes the young to swim toward the mother. More specifically, they approach her lower parts and dark areas. When they reach the mother, they push on the surface and penetrate into holes, and hence many of them end up in the mother's mouth. If the mother is replaced by a model, the young also approach its lower parts and dark patches and push against these areas (Baerends, 1957). The stimulus that elicits the entire response sequence is the approach of a large object or water turbulence. However, the behavior is guided by other cues—the lower side of the mother (or model) and dark patches.

Certain aspects of the egg-retrieval response of the greylag goose also illustrate how one stimulus may be responsible for eliciting a behavior and another involved in guiding it (Lorenz & Tinbergen, 1939). Whenever an egg rolls out of the nest, the goose reaches out and pulls the egg back with side-to-side movements of its beak. This behavior has two components. One involves extending the body to reach the wayward egg and then moving the beak back toward the nest. The other component is the side-to-side adjustments of the beak involved in rolling the egg. The first component is a pure fixed action pattern. Once elicited, it goes to completion regardless of the response feedback that occurs. After the goose has extended its body to reach the egg, it pulls its beak all the way back to the nest even if the egg rolls out from under the beak somewhere along the way. In contrast, the side-to-side movements of the beak occur only if the goose is pulling back a rounded, egg-shaped object. If a straight pipe is substituted that does not wobble, the side-to-side movements do not occur. These movements are closely governed by response feedback. If the egg wobbles in one direction, the goose will move its beak more to that side to support it. This movement may cause the egg to wobble in the other direction, producing another side-to-side adjustment. The sequence of responses guided by feedback continues until the goose has pulled its beak all the way back.

Effects of Repeated Stimulation: Three Examples

Because elicited behavior involves a close relationship between an environmental event and a resulting response, elicited behavior is often considered invariant. We tend to assume that an elicited response—particularly a simple reflex response—will occur the same way automatically every time the eliciting stimulus is presented. We assume, for example, that a baby will suck with invariant vigor every time a nipple is presented. If elicited behavior did occur the same way every time the stimulus was presented, however, it would be of limited interest, particularly for investigators of learning. Learning is identified by changes in behavior that result from experience. If elicited behavior were invariant, it would not be of much relevance to the study of learning.

Contrary to common assumptions about reflexive and elicited behavior, such behavior is not invariant. One of the most impressive facts about behavior is its plasticity. Even simple elicited responses do not occur the same way each time the eliciting stimulus is presented. Our discussion of the role of feedback cues in elicited behavior indicated that in some cases the nature of the behavior is altered by the feedback cues that result from responding. Alterations in the nature of elicited behavior often also occur simply as a result of repeated presentations of the eliciting stimulus. The following examples illustrate several ways in which elicited behavior can change as a result of repeated stimulation.

Sucking in human infants

One of the most important reflexes in the human newborn is sucking. As we noted earlier, infants suck when something such as a nipple, finger, or pacifier is placed in the mouth. Several investigators have shown that this response does not always occur in the same way when the eliciting stimulus is presented. In one experiment (Lipsitt & Kaye, 1965), reflexive sucking of a baby-bottle nipple was compared with sucking of a piece of 1/4-in. rubber tubing. The stimuli were repeatedly presented to newborn infants. Each stimulus presentation lasted 10 sec, and 30 sec elapsed between successive presentations. Tests with the tube and nipple were alternated so that the babies received five trials with one stimulus followed by five trials with the other, and so on. Figure 2.5 shows the number of sucking responses observed on each trial.

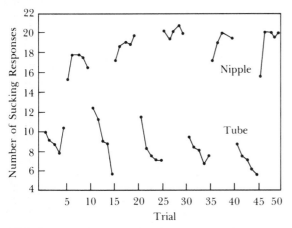

FIGURE 2.5. Number of sucking responses by human newborns during successive trials. A rubber nipple and a rubber tube served as stimuli in alternate five-trial blocks. *(After Lipsitt & Kaye, 1965.)*

The results shown in Figure 2.5 have several noteworthy aspects. First, we see that the initial amount of sucking differed for the two stimuli. The babies sucked the nipple more than the rubber tube. This is not surprising, because the nipple no doubt more closely resembles the natural stimulus for sucking (the mother's nipple) than the tube. Second, there were systematic differences in the patterns of responses to repeated presentations of the two stimuli. Generally, as the nipple was repeatedly introduced, the babies sucked more and more vigorously. The overall level of sucking was higher in the fifth series of five trials than in the first series. In addition, within each series of five nipple trials, the babies usually increased their sucking from the first to the fifth trial. The opposite trends occurred when the babies were tested with the tubing. Here, the overall level of sucking was lower during the fifth series of five trials than during the first, and the babies usually decreased their sucking from the first to the fifth trial within each series.

Startle response in rats

Variations in elicited behavior of the type that occur when a stimulus is repeatedly presented to elicit sucking can also be observed in many other response systems. The startle reaction of rats provides another illustration. The startle response is a sudden jump or tensing of the muscles when an unexpected stimulus is presented. You can be tremendously startled, for example, when a friend unexpectedly comes up behind you and taps you on the shoulder. In rats, the reaction can be measured by placing the animal in a stabilimeter chamber (see Figure 2.6). A stabilimeter is a small enclosure held in place by several springs. When startled, the animal jumps, producing a bouncing movement of the stabilimeter chamber. Sudden movements of the chamber can be precisely measured to indicate the vigor of the startle reaction.

The startle reaction can be elicited in rats by all sorts of stimuli, including brief tones and lights. In one experiment, Davis (1974) investigated the startle reaction of rats to presentations of a brief (90-millisecond) loud tone (110 decibels [dB], 4000 cycles per sec). Two groups of rats were tested. Each group received 100 successive tone trials separated by 30 sec. In addition, a noise generator provided background noise that sounded something like water running from a faucet. For one group, the background noise was relatively quiet (60 dB); for the other, the background noise was rather loud (80 dB).

The results of the experiment are shown in Figure 2.7. As was true of the sucking reflex, repeated presentations of the eliciting stimulus (the 4000-

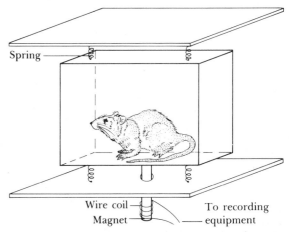

FIGURE 2.6. Stabilimeter apparatus to measure the startle response of rats. A small chamber is balanced on springs between two stationary platforms. A magnet, surrounded by a wire coil, is fixed to the bottom of the chamber. Sudden movements of the rat result in movements of the chamber that produce an electrical current in the wire coil. *(After Hoffman & Fleshler, 1964.)*

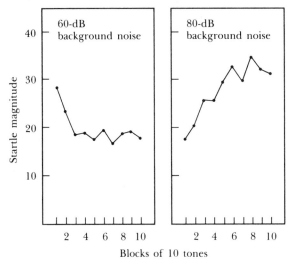

FIGURE 2.7. Magnitude of the startle response of rats to successive presentations of a tone with background noise of 60 and 80 dB. *(From Davis, 1974.)*

cycles-per-sec tone) did not always produce the same startle response. For subjects tested in the presence of the soft background noise (60 dB), repetitions of the tone resulted in smaller and smaller startle reactions. This outcome is similar to what was observed when the rubber tube was repeatedly presented to elicit sucking in babies. In contrast, when the background noise was loud (80 dB), repetitions of the tone elicited progressively larger and more vigorous startle reactions. This outcome is comparable to what was observed when sucking was repeatedly elicited by the nipple. Thus, as with sucking, repeated elicitations of the startle reflex produced a decrease in the startle reaction in some circumstances and an increase in others.

Mobbing in chaffinches

In the examples described above, repeated presentations of the eliciting stimulus produced either a decline or an increase in the elicited response. There are many examples of such one-directional changes in responsiveness with repeated stimulation. However, in numerous other circumstances, a combination of these two types of changes occurs. Repeated stimulation may at first produce an increase in responsiveness, which is followed by a decrease. To

illustrate the diversity of response systems in which such changes in responsivity occur, we shall describe the mobbing behavior of chaffinches.

Mobbing directed toward a potential predator occurs in a variety of small birds. When it is sufficiently vigorous, the mobbing behavior may cause the predator to leave the area. Chaffinches, for example, will mob a live owl or a stuffed model of an owl. When the owl first appears, the birds become agitated and begin to move their heads and then their bodies and tails. If the owl remains, the vigor of these movements increases, and the birds begin to make the "mobbing call." If there are enough chaffinches in the area, the mobbing call can become very loud and may scare the owl away.

In a classic experiment, Hinde (1954) measured the mobbing calls of individual chaffinches in response to a stuffed owl that was presented continuously for 30 min. Figure 2.8 shows the calls of three of the birds during the 30-min period. The presence

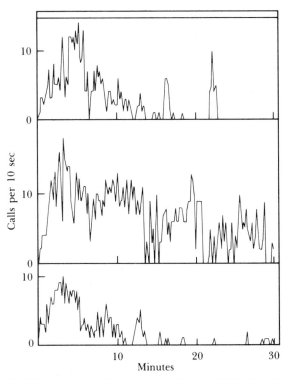

FIGURE 2.8. Mobbing calls of three individual chaffinches when exposed to a stuffed owl for 30 min. *(From Hinde, 1954.)*

of the stuffed owl initially resulted in a progressive increase in the mobbing call. However, as the owl stimulus remained, the intensity of calling gradually declined. The mobbing call stopped almost entirely in the first and third birds by the end of the 30-min test period. The second chaffinch continued to make the mobbing call for 30 min. However, the intensity of its call also decreased with prolonged exposure to the stuffed owl.

The pattern of responding shown by the chaffinches is observed with a wide variety of species in a variety of situations (see Thompson, Groves, Teyler, & Roemer, 1973, for a review). Responding first increases and then declines with repeated presentations (or one prolonged presentation) of the eliciting stimulus. The opposite type of bidirectional change in responsiveness, an initial decline in responding followed by an increase, does not occur.

The Concepts of Habituation and Sensitization

The three studies described above show that both decreases and increases in responding can occur with repeated (or continuous) presentation of an eliciting stimulus. Decreases in responsiveness produced by repeated stimulation are examples of **habituation.** Increases in responsiveness are examples of **sensitization.** Habituation and sensitization represent the most fundamental changes in behavior that result from experience.

Adaptiveness and pervasiveness of habituation and sensitization

At any moment, there are always many stimuli impinging on the organism. Habituation and sensitization processes help organize and focus behavior so that it can be effective in this sea of stimulation. Even such a simple situation as sitting at a desk involves a myriad of sensations. There are the color, texture, and brightness of the paint on the walls, sounds of the air conditioning system, noises from the other room, the smell of the air, the color and texture of the table, the tactile sensations of the chair against your legs,

seat, and back, and so on. If you were to respond to all the stimuli in the situation, your behavior would be disorganized and chaotic. Habituation and sensitization mechanisms help reduce reactivity to irrelevant stimuli and channel behavior into organized and directed actions in response to only some of the stimuli you experience.

Habituation and sensitization processes are so fundamental to the adjustment of organisms to the environment that they occur in nearly all species and response systems (see Peeke & Petrinovich, 1984, for a recent review). We have discussed three examples in some detail. There are also numerous instances of habituation and sensitization in common human experience. For example, most people who own a grandfather clock do not notice each time it chimes. They have completely habituated to the clock's sounds. In fact, they are more likely to notice when the clock misses a scheduled chime. In a sense, this is unfortunate, because they may have purchased the grandfather clock specifically for the beauty of its sound. Similarly, people who live on busy streets, near railroad tracks, or close to an airport may become entirely habituated to the noises that frequently intrude into their homes. In contrast, visitors are much more likely to respond to, and be bothered by, such sounds.

Driving a car involves exposure to a large array of complex visual and auditory stimuli. As a person becomes an experienced driver, he or she habituates to the numerous stimuli that are irrelevant to driving, such as details of the color and texture of the road, what kind of telephone poles line the sides of the road, certain tactile sensations of the steering wheel, and certain sounds from the engine. Habituation to irrelevant cues is particularly prominent during long driving trips. If you are driving continuously for several hours, you are likely to become oblivious to all kinds of stimuli that are irrelevant to keeping the car on the road. If you then come across an accident or arrive in a new town, you are likely to "wake up" and again pay attention to various things that you had been ignoring. Passing a bad accident or coming to a new town is an arousing stimulus that changes your state and sensitizes various orientation responses that were previously habituated.

If you ever had a cat or dog that you brought home when it was young, chances are the animal was extremely agitated and cried a great deal during the first few days. This occurs because most of the stimuli in the animal's new environment are effective in eliciting responses. As the cat or dog gets used to its new home—that is, as it becomes habituated to many of the stimuli in the situation—it stops being agitated and becomes generally less active. Humans experience similar effects. If you visit a new place or encounter people you have never dealt with before, you are likely to pay attention to all sorts of stimuli that you ordinarily ignore. If you are in a new building, for example, you are likely to study every sign on the walls in an effort to find where you have to go. You fail to respond to such details in places that are highly familiar, so much so that you may not be able to describe certain salient features, such as the color of certain walls or the type of knob that is attached to a door you use every day.

Neural analysis of habituation and sensitization

Because habituation and sensitization involve the simplest types of modification of elicited behavior, these phenomena have attracted the attention of many investigators interested in the neural basis of learning. We will describe one of the prominent neurophysiological models of habituation and sensitization. However, before doing so, it is important to distinguish between habituation and other processes that can also decrease the likelihood that a stimulus will elicit a response.

Distinctions among habituation, sensory adaptation, and response fatigue. As noted above, in many situations the response initially elicited by a stimulus ceases to occur when the stimulus is frequently repeated. This decline in responding is one of the identifying characteristics of habituation. However, not all instances in which repetitions of a stimulus result in a decline in responding represent habituation. As we discussed earlier, three types of events take place whenever a stimulus elicits a response. First, the stimulus activates one of the sense organs of the body, such as the eyes or ears. This process generates sensory neural impulses that are relayed to the central nervous system (the spinal cord and brain). Here the sensory messages are relayed to motor nerves. The neural impulses in motor nerves in turn activate the muscles that create the observed response. The elicited response will not be observed if for some reason the sense organs become temporarily insensitive to stimulation. You may be temporarily blinded by a bright light, for example, or suffer a temporary hearing loss because of repeated exposures to a loud noise. Such decreases in sensitivity are called **sensory adaptation.** The reflex response will also fail to occur if the muscles involved become incapacitated by fatigue. Sensory adaptation and response

---

BOX 2.1.   Habituation of obsessional ruminations

The principle of habituation is often used in behavior therapy to treat recurrent problematic thoughts. Many people are disturbed by their own "bad" thoughts, such as blasphemous ideas or images of another person's ill fate. Such thoughts tend to elicit great anxiety. Rachman (1978) has proposed that these obsessional ruminations can be regarded as noxious stimuli to which the individual has not habituated. The treatment, then, is to have the individual think the "bad" thoughts continuously until the anxiety response habituates. Procedures that accomplish this are often called "prolonged-exposure treatments" because the client, with the help of the therapist, exposes himself to the problematic ideas for long periods. Initially, the procedure results in an elevation of anxiety. As exposure continues, anxiety as rated by the client decreases (see Emmelkamp, 1982b). On the basis of a number of comparative outcome studies, Emmelkamp (1982a) has concluded that the prolonged exposure treatment is, by and large, successful for obsessional ruminations.

fatigue are impediments to the elicited response that are produced outside the nervous system, in sense organs and muscles.

The likelihood of a response will also be changed if the neural processes involved in the elicited behavior are altered. Various types of changes in the nervous system can hinder or facilitate transmission of neural impulses from sensory to motor neurons. Habituation and sensitization are assumed to involve such neurophysiological changes. Thus, habituation is different from sensory adaptation and response fatigue. In habituation, the subject ceases to respond to a stimulus even though it remains fully capable of sensing the stimulus and of making the muscle movements required for the response. The response fails to occur because for some reason the sensory neural impulses are not relayed to the motor neurons.

Dual-process theory of habituation and sensitization.   Different types of underlying neural pro-

cesses are assumed to be responsible for increases and decreases in responsiveness to stimulation. One category of changes in the nervous system involves reductions in the ability of a stimulus to elicit a response. Such a change is called a **habituation process.** Another category of changes in the nervous system produces increases in responsiveness. Such a change is called a **sensitization process.** These two types of processes may occur simultaneously in a given situation. The results observed will depend on which process is stronger. The left-hand graph in Figure 2.9 illustrates a hypothetical situation in which repetitions of a stimulus strengthen the habituation process more than the sensitization process. The net effect of these changes is a decline in the elicited response across trials (a habituation effect). The right-hand graph illustrates the opposite outcome: repetitions of a stimulus strengthen the sensitization process more than the habituation process, and the result is an increase in the elicited response across trials (a sensi-

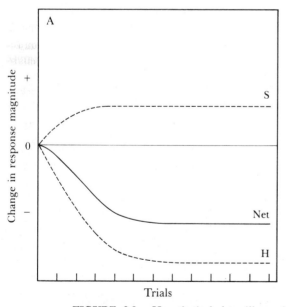
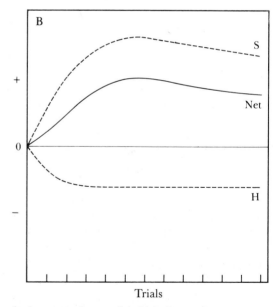

FIGURE 2.9. Hypothetical data illustrating the dual-process theory of habituation and sensitization. The dashed lines indicate the strength of the habituation (H) and sensitization (S) processes across trials. The solid line indicates the net effects of these two processes. In the left panel (A), the habituation process becomes stronger than the sensitization process across trials, and this leads to a progressive decrement in responding. In the right panel (B), the sensitization process becomes stronger than the habituation process across trials, and this leads to a progressive increase in responding.

tization effect). Thus, the changes in the elicited behavior that actually occur in a particular situation represent the net effect of habituation and sensitization processes.

On the basis of neurophysiological research, Groves and Thompson (1970; see also Thompson et al., 1973) suggested that habituation and sensitization processes occur in different parts of the nervous system. Habituation processes are assumed to occur in what they call the **S-R system.** This system consists of the shortest neural path that connects the sense organs stimulated by the eliciting stimulus and the muscles involved in making the elicited response. (The S-R system may be viewed as the reflex arc.) In contrast, sensitization processes are assumed to occur in what is called the **state system.** This consists of other parts of the nervous system that determine the organism's general level of responsiveness, or readiness to respond. The state system is relatively quiescent during sleep, for example. Drugs such as stimulants or depressants may alter the functioning of the state system and thereby change responsiveness. The state system is also altered by emotional experiences. The jumpiness that accompanies fear is caused by sensitization of the state system. The state system thus determines the animal's readiness to respond, whereas the S-R system enables the animal to make the specific responses elicited by the stimuli in the situation. The behavioral changes that are observed reflect the combined actions of these two systems.

The examples of habituation and sensitization described at the beginning of the chapter can be easily interpreted in terms of the dual-process theory. First consider the results with the sucking reflex (Figure 2.5). Repeated presentations of the 1/4-in. tubing produced a decrement in responding. This may be explained by assuming that the tube stimulus influenced only the S-R system and hence activated habituation processes. The interpretation of the results with the nipple stimulus is a bit more involved. The nipple was a much more powerful stimulus for the babies than the 1/4-in. tubing; it elicited much more vigorous sucking even at the beginning of the experiment. The increases in sucking that occurred with repeated presentations of the nipple can be explained by assuming that the nipple stimulus not only in-volved the S-R system but also activated the state system. Because a nipple is a very significant stimulus for babies, presentations of the nipple increased the babies' alertness and readiness to respond, and this effect presumably produced the progressive increments in sucking. Such sensitization did not occur with the 1/4-in. tube; this stimulus evidently does not increase babies' alertness and arousal.

The dual-process theory is also consistent with the habituation and sensitization effects we noted in the startle reaction of rats (Figure 2.7). When subjects were tested with a relatively quiet background noise (60 dB), there was little in the situation to arouse them. Therefore, we can assume that the experimental procedures did not produce changes in the state system. Repeated presentations of the startle-eliciting tone merely activated the S-R system and resulted in habituation of the startle response. However, the opposite outcome occurred when the animals were tested in the presence of a loud background noise (80 dB). In this case increased startle reactions occurred to successive presentations of the tone. Because the identical tone was used to elicit the startle response for both groups, differences in the results cannot be attributed to the tone. Rather, one has to assume that the loud background noise increased arousal or readiness to respond. This sensitization of the state system was presumably responsible for the increase in startle reaction.

Interpreting the changes in mobbing calls made by chaffinches to a stuffed owl requires the sensitization as well as the habituation process. The birds first increased and then decreased their mobbing calls. Apparently, the stuffed owl first increased the chaffinches' arousal or readiness to respond. However, the stuffed owl was not a strong enough stimulus to produce prolonged sensitization, and the mobbing calls habituated with continued exposure to the owl.

The above analyses of sucking, startle, and mobbing highlight several important features of the dual-process theory. As we have seen, the state and S-R systems are differently activated by repeated presentations of a stimulus. The S-R system is activated every time a stimulus elicits a response, because it is the neural circuit that conducts impulses from sensory input to response output. The state system becomes involved only in special circumstances. First, some extraneous event (such as an intense background noise) may increase the subject's alertness and sensitize the state system. Second, the state system may be sensitized by the repeated stimulus presentations if the stimulus is sufficiently intense or significant for the subject (a nipple as opposed to a rubber tube, for example). If the intense stimulus is presented often enough so that successive presentations occur while the subject remains sensitized from the preceding ones, progressive increases in the response will be observed.

The dual-process theory of habituation and sensitization has been very influential in the study of the plasticity of elicited behavior, although it has not been successful in explaining all habituation and sensitization effects. One of the important contributions of the theory has been the assumption that elicited behavior can be strongly influenced by neurophysiological events that take place outside the reflex arc directly involved in a particular elicited response. In dual-process theory, the state system is assumed to modulate the activity of reflex arcs. The basic idea that certain parts of the nervous system serve to modulate S-R systems that are more directly involved in elicited behavior has been developed further in other, more recent models of habituation and sensitization (for example, Davis & File, 1984). (For a detailed discussion of several recent theories of habituation, see Stephenson & Siddle, 1983.)

Characteristics of Habituation and Sensitization

Much research has been performed to determine how various factors influence habituation and sensitization processes. The characteristics of habituation and sensitization are not perfectly uniform across all species and response systems. However, there are many commonalities; we will describe some of the most important.

Time course of habituation and sensitization

Most of the forms of behavior change we will describe in later chapters are retained for long periods

(one or more years). In fact, this is one of the defining characteristics of learning phenomena (see Chapter 1). Instances of habituation and sensitization do not always have this characteristic, and therefore not all instances of habituation and sensitization are properly considered examples of learning.

Time course of sensitization. Sensitization processes generally have temporary effects. Although in some instances sensitization persists for several weeks (for example, Kandel, 1976), in most situations the increased responsiveness is short-lived. In fact, the temporary nature of an increase in responding can be used to identify the phenomenon as a sensitization effect. Different sensitization effects may persist for different amounts of time. Davis (1974), for example, investigated the sensitizing effect of a 25-min exposure to a loud noise (80 dB) in rats. As expected, the loud noise sensitized the startle response to a tone. However, this increased reactivity persisted for only 10–15 min after the loud noise was turned off. In other response systems, sensitization dissipates much more rapidly. For example, sensitization of the spinal hindlimb-flexion reflex in cats persists for only about 3 sec (Groves & Thompson, 1970). However, in all response systems the duration of sensitization effects is determined by the intensity of the sensitizing stimulus. More intense stimuli produce larger increases in responsiveness, and the sensitization effects persist longer.

Time course of habituation. Habituation also persists for varying amounts of time. With sensitization, differences in the time course of the effect usually reflect only quantitative differences in the same underlying mechanism. In contrast, there appear to be two *qualitatively* different types of habituation effects. One type of habituation is similar to most cases of sensitization in that it dissipates relatively quickly, within seconds or minutes. The other type is much longer-lasting and may persist for many days. These two types of habituation were nicely illustrated in an experiment on the startle response of rats (Leaton, 1976). The test stimulus was a high-pitched, loud tone presented for 2 sec. The animals were first allowed to get used to the experimental chamber without any tone presentations. Each rat then received a single test trial with the tone stimulus once a day for 11 days. Because of the long (24-hour) interval between stimulus presentations, any decrements in responding produced by the stimulus presentations were assumed to exemplify the long-lasting habituation process. The transient (short-lasting) habituation process was activated in the next phase of the experiment by giving the subjects 300 closely spaced tone presentations (every 3 sec). Finally, the animals were given a single tone presentation 1, 2, and 3 days later, to measure recovery from the short-term habituation.

Figure 2.10 shows the results. The largest startle reaction was observed the first time the tone was presented. Progressively smaller reactions occurred during the next 10 days. Because the animals were tested only once every 24 hours in this phase, the progressive decrements in responding indicate that the habituating effects of the stimulus presentations persisted throughout the 11-day period. This long-lasting habituation process did not result in complete loss of the startle reflex. The animals still reacted a

little even on the 11th day. In contrast, startle reactions quickly ceased when the tone presentations occurred every 3 sec in the next phase of the experiment. However, this loss of responsiveness was only temporary. When the animals were tested with the tone 1, 2, and 3 days later, the startle response recovered to the level of the 11th day of the experiment. This recovery occurred simply because the tone was not presented for a long time (24 hours) and is called **spontaneous recovery.** Spontaneous recovery is the identifying characteristic of the short-term, or temporary, habituation effect.

Repeated presentations of a stimulus do not always result in both long-lasting and short-term habituation effects. With the spinal leg-flexion reflex in cats, for example, only the short-term habituation effect is observed (Thompson & Spencer, 1966). In such cases, spontaneous recovery completely restores the animal's reaction to the eliciting stimulus if a long enough period of rest is permitted after habituation. In contrast, spontaneous recovery is never complete in situations that also involve long-term habituation

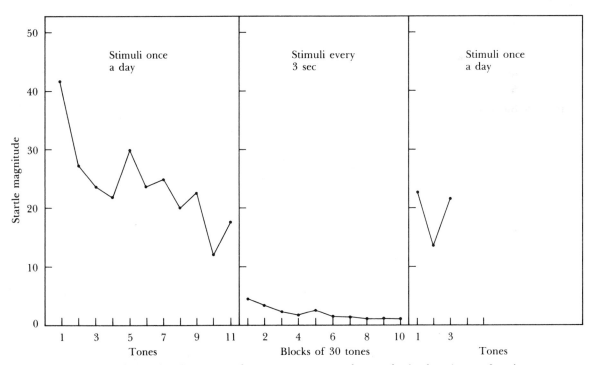

FIGURE 2.10.   Startle response of rats to a tone presented once a day in phase 1, every 3 sec in phase 2, and once a day in phase 3.   *(From Leaton, 1976.)*

effects, as in Leaton's experiment. As Figure 2.10 shows, the startle response was restored to some extent in the last phase of the experiment. However, even here the animals did not react as vigorously to the tone as they had the first time it was presented.

Few theories can explain the qualitative differences between the short- and long-term habituation effects. The dual-process theory described above was formulated primarily to account for only the temporary aspects of habituation and sensitization. Differences in the mechanisms of the short- and long-term habituation effects are detailed in a recent behavioral theory of information processing (see Whitlow & Wagner, 1984).

Stimulus specificity of habituation and sensitization

Habituation processes are assumed to be highly specific to the repeated stimulus. A response that has been habituated to one stimulus can be evoked in full strength by a new eliciting stimulus. After you have become completely habituated to the chimes of your grandfather clock, for example, if the clock malfunctions and makes new sounds, your attention to the clock is likely to become entirely restored. After complete habituation of the orienting response to one stimulus, the response is likely to occur in its normal strength if a sufficiently novel stimulus is presented. Stimulus specificity characterizes all examples of habituation and has therefore been considered one of the defining characteristics of habituation (Thompson & Spencer, 1966).

Although habituation effects are always stimulus-specific, some generalization of the effects may occur. If you have habituated to a particular clock chime, you may also not respond to another clock chime that is only slightly different from the old one. This phenomenon is called **stimulus generalization** of habituation. As the new stimulus is made increasingly different from the habituated stimulus, the subject's reaction will increasingly resemble the response in the absence of habituation.

In contrast to habituation processes, sensitization is less stimulus specific. If an animal becomes aroused or sensitized for some reason, its reactivity will increase to a range of cues. Pain induced by footshock, for example, increases the reactivity of laboratory rats to both auditory and visual cues. However, the range of stimuli to which an animal may become

---

BOX 2.2. Sexual responsiveness and stimulus change

Sexual intercourse is often followed by a temporary decrease in sexual responsiveness. Male rats and guinea pigs, for example, are not sexually aroused by a female just after they have mated with her. However, this decrease in responsiveness is specific to the female involved in the mating. If a new female is introduced, the male is again likely to engage in sexual activity. This effect is sometimes called the "Coolidge effect," after an anecdote involving President Coolidge and his wife. The story is that President and Mrs. Coolidge were taking a tour of an egg farm in separate parties. When Mrs. Coolidge saw one of the roosters, she asked her guide how many times the rooster mated each day. Impressed with the large number she was given, she asked one of her aides to make sure President Coolidge was told about this fact. When President Coolidge heard about the frequent sexual activity of the rooster, he asked whether the rooster always mated with the same female. He was told that of course it was often a different hen. Satisfied with the answer, the President asked that Mrs. Coolidge be also informed of this.

The fact that sexual responsiveness returns when a new female is introduced has applications in animal husbandry. For artificial insemination of cattle, for example, it is desirable to obtain large quantities of semen from bulls. The responsiveness of bulls declines if they are repeatedly presented with the same cow or cow model. Much more semen can be collected if several cows or models of cows are used (Hale & Almquist, 1960).

sensitized by footshock is not unlimited. Shock sensitization does not increase the reactivity of rats to novel taste stimuli. Reactivity to novel tastes is sensitized by internal malaise as opposed to cutaneous pain (Miller & Domjan, 1981). Separate sensitizations systems appear to exist for exteroceptive and interoceptive stimulation.

Effects of strong extraneous stimuli

As noted above, changing the nature of the eliciting stimulus can produce recovery of a habituated response. However, this is not the only way to quickly restore responding after habituation. The habituated response can also be restored by sensitizing the subject with exposure to a strong extraneous stimulus. This phenomenon is called **dishabituation.** The results of one dishabituation experiment are shown in Figure 2.11. The startle reaction of rats was repeatedly elicited by brief presentations of a tone. The animals' reaction to the tone at first increased and then habituated as the tone was repeatedly presented. (We saw a similar pattern of response changes in mobbing calls in chaffinches, Figure 2.8). The process of habituation appeared to be finished by the 8th tone trial. Just before the 15th trial, half the rats were sensitized by exposure to a brief, bright flashing light,

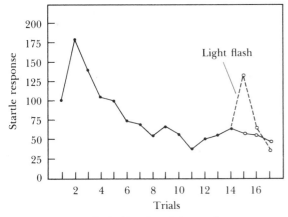

FIGURE 2.11. Dishabituation of the startle response to a tone. The response was first habituated by repeated presentations of the tone (trials 1–14). A brief flashing light was presented to half the subjects before the 15th tone trial, causing a temporary recovery of the startle reaction to the tone (see trial 15). *(From Groves & Thompson, 1970.)*

resulting in a substantial recovery of the habituated startle reaction. The animals responded much more to the tone on trial 15 than on the preceding trials. However, the sensitization effect was short-lasting. Responding to the tone returned to the habituated level on trials 16 and 17.

It is important to keep in mind that *dishabituation* refers to recovery in the response to the *previously* habituated stimulus. Figure 2.11 shows only the animals' reactions to repeated presentations of the tone. Whatever responses the animals made to the dishabituating stimulus (the flashing light) are not of interest. The purpose of the experiment was to see how exposure to the dishabituating flashing light changed the animals' response to the original tone stimulus.

Effects of stimulus intensity and frequency

Habituation and sensitization effects are closely related to the intensity and frequency of the eliciting stimulus. (The frequency of a stimulus is the number of presentations in a given amount of time, such as a second.) Because of the importance of stimulus intensity and frequency for habituation and sensitization, many investigators have been concerned with these variables. Studies have provided a rather complex pattern of results. The outcomes observed depend on the response system investigated and the types of stimuli and test procedures used. Generally, an increase in responding (sensitization) is more likely if the repeatedly presented stimulus is very intense. Furthermore, with intense stimuli, more sensitization occurs as the frequency of the stimulus is increased (for example, Groves, Lee, & Thompson, 1969). In contrast, habituation effects predominate if the repeated stimulus is relatively weak. Furthermore, the rate of habituation increases as the frequency of the weak stimulus is increased, because more frequent presentations of the weak stimulus permit summation of the short-term habituation process (see Figure 2.10). Long-term habituation processes are not facilitated by increasing the frequency of stimulus presentations. In fact, there is some evidence that less long-term habituation occurs with more frequent stimulations (for example, Davis,

1970). Because repeated presentations of a stimulus can activate sensitization as well as short-term and long-term habituation processes, the effects of stimulus intensity and frequency in any given situation will depend on the combined effects of these various processes. For this reason, it is often difficult to predict what effects changes in stimulus intensity and frequency will have in any particular situation.

Changes in Complex Emotional Responses

So far we have discussed how repetitions of an eliciting stimulus produce changes in relatively simple response systems. However, many stimuli produce much more complex effects on organisms than such responses as startling or orienting. A stimulus may evoke love, fear, euphoria, terror, satisfaction, uneasiness, or a combination of these emotions. In this section we will describe the standard pattern of emotions that is evoked by complex emotion-arousing stimuli and how this pattern of emotional responses is altered by repetitions of the stimulus. These issues have been most systematically addressed by the **opponent process** theory of motivation proposed by Solomon and his collaborators (Hoffman & Solomon, 1974; Solomon, 1977; Solomon & Corbit, 1973, 1974). We will describe the theory and its implications.

The opponent-process theory of motivation

What happens when an emotion-arousing stimulus is presented and then removed? Consider the reactions of a teenager who is given a car to drive for the first time. Initially, she will be extremely excited and happy. This excitement will subside a bit as time passes. Nevertheless, the car will continue to make her happy. If after a day or two the car becomes no longer available, the teenager's emotions will not simply return to neutrality. Rather, for a while after surrendering the car, she will have a longing for it. This longing will then gradually dissipate.

Obviously, different emotion-arousing stimuli

elicit different types of emotional responses. However, the patterns of the emotional changes appear to have certain common characteristics. Solomon and his associates have called these characteristics the **standard pattern of affective dynamics** (Solomon & Corbit, 1974). The key elements of the pattern are shown in Figure 2.12. The onset of the emotion-arousing stimulus, such as receipt of a car, elicits a strong emotional response (happiness) that quickly reaches a *peak*. This peak reaction is followed by an *adaptation phase* during which the emotional response subsides a bit until it reaches a *steady state*. The stimulus (the car) continues to elicit the emotion (happiness) during the steady state. When the stimulus ceases (the teenager has to surrender the car), the emotional state quickly changes to feelings that are opposite to those that occurred in the presence of the stimulus. (Now the teenager feels unhappy and has a longing for the car.) This reversal of the emotional state, called the **affective after-reaction,** gradually decays as the subject returns to her normal state.

How will a teenager react to getting a car once such an experience has become routine? If a person has had access to a car many times before, receipt of the car will not elicit the same intense happiness that

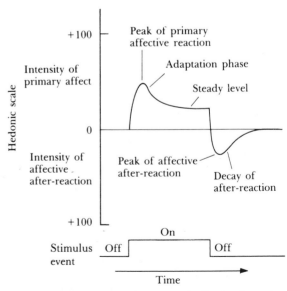

FIGURE 2.12. Standard pattern of affective dynamics. *(After Solomon & Corbit, 1974.)*

was experienced the first time. Getting the car is likely to produce only a mild reaction. However, this time, if the car becomes unavailable, the unhappiness and longing for it that result will be much more intense than the first time. Once a person has become accustomed to having a car, losing access to the car creates intense unhappiness. Thus, the pattern of emotional changes to a habituated emotion-arousing stimulus is different from the standard pattern of affective dynamics. This habituated pattern is shown in Figure 2.13. The stimulus elicits only a slight emotional response. However, the affective after-reaction is much stronger than in the standard pattern.

Mechanisms of the opponent-process theory

What underlying mechanisms produce the standard pattern of affective dynamics and modifications of this pattern with habituation to the emotion-arousing stimulus? The opponent-process theory of motivation assumes that neurophysiological mechanisms involved in emotional behavior act to maintain emotional stability. Thus, the opponent-process the-

ory is a *homeostatic* theory. It assumes that an important function of mechanisms that control emotional behavior is to minimize deviations from emotional neutrality or stability. (The concept of homeostasis has been very important in the analysis of behavior. We will discuss other types of homeostatic theories in later chapters.)

How might neurophysiological mechanisms maintain emotional stability or neutrality? Maintaining any system in a neutral or stable state requires that a disturbance that forces the system away from neutrality be met by an opposing force that counteracts the disturbance. Consider, for example, trying to keep a seesaw level. If something pushes one end of the seesaw down, the other end will go up. To keep the seesaw level, a force pushing one end down has to be met by an opposing force that keeps that end up. The concept of opponent forces or processes serving to maintain a stable state is central to the opponent-process theory of motivation. The theory assumes that an emotion-arousing stimulus pushes a person's emotional state away from neutrality. This shift away from emotional neutrality is assumed to trigger an opponent process that counteracts the shift. The patterns of emotional behavior observed initially and after extensive experience with a stimulus are attributed to various features of the opponent process and when it occurs in relation to when the primary emotional disturbance occurs. Basically, the opponent process is assumed to be a bit inefficient. It lags behind the primary emotional disturbance and becomes effective in substantially counteracting the primary disturbance only after repeated practice.

The opponent-process theory assumes that the presentation of an emotion-arousing stimulus initially elicits what is called the **primary process,** or **"a" process,** which is responsible for the quality of the emotional state (happiness, for example) that occurs in the presence of the stimulus. The primary, or *a*, process is assumed to elicit, in turn, an **opponent process,** or **"b" process,** that generates the opposite emotional reaction (unhappiness, for example). The emotional changes observed when a stimulus is presented and then removed are assumed to reflect the net result of the primary and opponent processes. The strength of the opponent process sub-

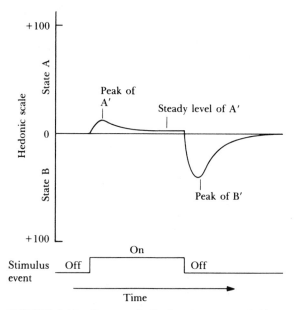

FIGURE 2.13.   Pattern of affective changes to a habituated stimulus.   *(After Solomon & Corbit, 1974.)*

tracts from the strength of the primary process to provide the emotions that actually occur.

Figure 2.14 shows how the primary and opponent processes determine the standard pattern of affective dynamics. When the stimulus is first presented, the *a* process occurs unopposed by the *b* process. The primary emotional reaction can therefore reach its peak quickly. The *b* process then becomes activated and begins to oppose the *a* process. The *b* process reduces the strength of the primary emotional response and is responsible for the adaptation phase of the standard pattern. The primary emotional response reaches a steady state when the *a* and *b* processes have each reached their maximum strength during the stimulus presentation. When the stimulus is withdrawn, the *a* process is quickly terminated, but the *b* process lingers for a while. Thus, the *b* process now has nothing to oppose. Therefore, the emotional responses characteristic of the opponent process become evident for the first time. These emotions are typically opposite to those observed during the presence of the stimulus.

The summation of primary and opponent pro-

cesses provides a good explanation for the standard pattern of affective dynamics. How do these underlying processes change during the course of habituation to an emotion-arousing stimulus? As we saw in Figure 2.13, after extensive exposure to the emotion-arousing stimulus, the stimulus ceases to elicit strong emotional reactions, and the affective after-reaction becomes much stronger when the stimulus is terminated. The opponent-process theory explains this outcome by assuming simply that the *b* process becomes strengthened by repeated exposures to the stimulus. The strengthening of the *b* process is reflected in several of its characteristics. The *b* process becomes activated sooner after the onset of the stimulus, its maximum intensity becomes greater, and it becomes slower to decay when the stimulus ceases. In contrast, the *a* process is assumed to remain unchanged. Thus, after habituation, the primary emotional responses are more strongly opposed by the opponent process. This effect of habituation reduces the intensity of the observed primary emotional responses during presentation of the emotion-arousing stimulus. It also leads to the excessive affective after-reaction when the stimulus is withdrawn (see Figure 2.15).

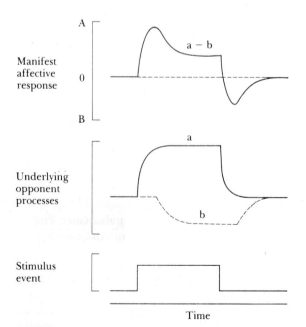

FIGURE 2.14. Opponent-process mechanism that produces the standard pattern of affective dynamics. *(From Solomon & Corbit, 1974.)*

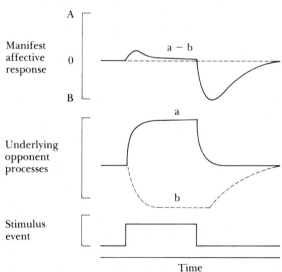

FIGURE 2.15. Opponent-process mechanism that produces the affective changes to a habituated stimulus. *(From Solomon & Corbit, 1974.)*

Examples of opponent processes

Love and attachment. The reactions of a teen-ager to getting a car for a few days, described above, are just one example of opponent-process mechanisms. Human couples may experience corresponding changes. Newlyweds are usually very excited about each other and are very affectionate whenever they are together. This primary emotional reaction habituates as years go by. Gradually, the couple settle into a comfortable mode of interaction that lacks the excitement of the honeymoon. However, this habituation of the primary emotional reaction is accompanied by a strengthening of the affective after-reaction. The more time a couple have spent together, the more unhappy they become when separated for some reason, and this unhappiness lasts longer. ("Absence makes the heart grow fonder.") After a couple have been together for several decades, the death of one partner is likely to cause a very extensive grief reaction in the survivor. The intense grief may last several years and sometimes also hastens the death of the surviving partner. This strong affective after-reaction is remarkable, considering that by this stage in their relationship the couple may have entirely ceased to show any overt signs of affection.

Similar emotional effects occur between children and their parents. Many children who have lived with their parents for a long time cease to show much love or affection toward them. When older teenagers or young adults are ready to leave home, they are more likely to complain about their parents than to praise them. This emotional state represents habituation of the primary affective reaction. Despite their lack of overt affection for their parents, when the children move away, they are likely to become homesick. The parents will also miss the children. This state represents the affective after-reaction. For both children and parents, many years of living together serve to strengthen the affective after-reaction that accompanies a separation.

The predictions of the opponent-process theory for human love and attachment have not been tested experimentally. However, animal research provides strong support for the theory in the area of attachment and separation (see Hoffman & Solomon, 1974;

Mineka, Suomi, & DeLizio, 1981; Starr, 1978; Suomi, Mineka, & Harlow, 1983).

Skydiving. Skydiving is an unusual sport intensely enjoyed by some people. Those who do not practice the sport are often puzzled about why others find it enjoyable. Indeed, there is little to enjoy in one's first jump. Inexperienced people are invariably scared of jumping from an airplane. Studies have shown that they exhibit extreme physiological arousal, and their facial expressions indicate that they are terrified. This is the primary emotional reaction to jumping. With repeated jumps, the primary affective reaction habituates as the opponent process is strengthened. Since the primary emotional reaction is terror, the opponent response is elation. In highly experienced jumpers, the primary process is canceled out by the opponent process, and they are not terrified by the jump. The strengthened opponent reaction is also evident in their affective after-reaction when they reach the ground. Experienced jumpers are exuberant and exhilarated when they land, and this good feeling may last several hours. In fact, the affective after-reaction is much more pleasant than the jump itself and may constitute most of the pleasure derived from jumping (Epstein, 1967).

Drug addiction. Many drugs are taken mainly for their emotional effects. The emotional changes that result from initial and later drug administrations are accurately described by the opponent-process theory of motivation in many cases (Solomon, 1977). The opponent-process theory predicts that psychoactive drugs will produce a biphasic emotional effect the first few times they are taken. One set of emotional responses is experienced when the drug is active (the primary affective response), and the opposite emotions occur when the drug has worn off (the affective after-reaction). Such biphasic changes are evident with a variety of psychoactive drugs, including alcohol, opiates (such as heroin), amphetamine, and nicotine. The sequence of effects of alcohol is very familiar. Shortly after taking the drug, the person becomes mellow and relaxed because the drug is basically a sedative. The opponent after-reaction is evident in headaches, nausea, and other symptoms of a hangover. With amphetamine, the presence of the drug creates feelings of euphoria, a sense of well-being, self-confidence, wakefulness, and a sense of control. After the drug has worn off, the person is likely to be fatigued, depressed, and drowsy.

The opponent-process theory predicts that, with repeated frequent uses of a drug, the primary emotional response will weaken and the opponent after-reaction will strengthen. Habituation of the primary drug reactions is an example of **drug tolerance,** in which the effect of a drug declines with repeated doses. Habitual users of alcohol, nicotine, heroin, caffeine, and other drugs are not as greatly affected by the presence of the drug as naive drugtakers. An amount of alcohol that would make a casual drinker a bit tipsy is not likely to have any effect on a frequent drinker. Frequent drinkers have to consume much more alcohol to have the same reactions as a naive drinker. Because of this tolerance, habitual drug users sometimes do not enjoy taking the drug as much as naive users. People who smoke many cigarettes, for example, rarely derive much enjoyment from doing so. Accompanying this decline in the primary drug reaction is a growth in the opponent after-reaction. Accordingly, habitual drug users experience much more severe "hangovers" on termination of the drug than naive users. Someone who stops smoking cigarettes, for example, will have headaches, will become irritable, anxious, and tense, and will feel generally dissatisfied. When a heavy drinker stops taking alcohol, he or she is likely to experience hallucinations, memory loss, psychomotor agitation, delirium tremens, and other physiological disturbances. For a habitual user of amphetamine, the fatigue and depression that follow the primary effects of the drug may be so severe as to cause suicide.

If the primary pleasurable effects of a psychoactive drug are gone for habitual users, why do they continue to take the drug? Why are they addicted? The opponent-process theory suggests that drug addiction is mainly an attempt to reduce the aversiveness of the affective after-reaction to the drugs—the bad hangovers, the amphetamine "crashes," the irritability that comes from not having the usual cigarette. There are two ways to reduce the aversive opponent after-

reactions of drugs. One is to simply wait long enough for them to dissipate. This is what is known as "cold turkey." For heavy drug users, cold turkey may take a long time and may be very painful. The opponent after-reaction can be much more quickly eliminated by taking the drug again. This will reactivate the primary process and stave off the agonies of withdrawal. Many addicts are not "trapped" by the pleasure they derive from the drug directly. Rather, they take the drug to reduce withdrawal pains.

Concluding Comments

Animals and people do not live in isolation. They live in a complex physical and social environment that determines nearly every aspect of their functioning. The quality of life and survival itself depend on an intricate coordination of behavior with the complexities of the environment. Elicited behavior represents one of the fundamental ways that the behavior of animals and people is adjusted to environmental events.

As we have seen, elicited behavior takes many forms, ranging from simple reflexes mediated by just three neurons to complex emotional reactions. Although elicited behavior occurs as a reaction to a stimulus, it is not rigid and invariant. In fact, one of the remarkable features of elicited behavior is that its form is often altered depending on the situation. Some instances of elicited behavior are guided by response feedback cues. If an eliciting stimulus does not arouse the organism, repeated presentations of the stimulus will evoke progressively weaker responses. This pattern represents the phenomenon of habituation. If the eliciting stimulus is particularly intense or of great significance to the subject, repeated presentations will arouse the organism and lead to progressively stronger reactions. This pattern represents the phenomenon of sensitization.

Any environmental event will activate habituation and sensitization processes to varying degrees. The strength of the responses that are observed reflects the net effect of habituation and sensitization. Therefore, if one does not know the past experiences of the organism, it is impossible to predict how strong a reaction will be elicited by a particular stimulus presentation.

Repeated presentations of an eliciting stimulus produce changes in simple responses as well as in more complex emotional reactions. Organisms tend to minimize changes in emotional state caused by external stimuli. According to the opponent-process theory of motivation, emotional responses stimulated by an outside event are counteracted by an opposing process in the organism. This compensatory, or oppo-nent, process is assumed to become stronger each time it is elicited, leading to a reduction of the primary emotional responses if the stimulus is frequently repeated. The strengthened opponent emotional state is evident when the stimulus is removed.

Habituation, sensitization, and changes in the strength of opponent processes are the simplest mech-anisms whereby organisms adjust their reactions to environmental events on the basis of past experience.

CHAPTER 3

Classical Conditioning: Foundations

The goal of Chapter 3 is to introduce the fundamental concepts and procedures involved in another basic form of learning, classical conditioning. Investigations of classical conditioning began with the work of Pavlov. Since then the research has been extended to a variety of organisms and response systems. We will describe several important procedures for studying classical conditioning and introduce the concept of a signal relation. Some classical conditioning procedures result in the learning of new responses to a stimulus, whereas others result in learning to withhold, or inhibit, responses. We will describe both types of procedures and also discuss how the learning can be extinguished. Finally, we will discuss various examples and applications of classical conditioning.

We began our discussion of the principles of behavior in the preceding chapter by describing elicited behavior and the modification of elicited behavior through sensitization and habituation. These relatively simple processes permit organisms to adjust their behavior to a wide range of environmental challenges. However, if animals had only the behavioral mechanisms described in Chapter 2, they would remain rather limited in the kinds of things they could do. They could not, for example, learn to make entirely new responses to stimuli, responses that would never occur as innate reactions to these cues. They also could not learn about relations between stimuli in their environment.

Learning to make new responses to stimuli obviously can be of great advantage. The world is always changing in various ways, and innate response mechanisms are not as flexible in meeting these challenges as learning mechanisms are. Animals can often benefit from learning to respond in new ways as they encounter new stimuli or familiar stimuli in novel contexts. Being able to learn about relations between stimuli is equally important. Events in the world do not take place in isolation or at random with respect to other events. Cause/effect relationships in the environment ensure that certain events reliably precede others. Your car's engine does not run unless the ignition has been turned on; you cannot walk through a doorway until you have opened the door; it does not rain unless there are clouds in the sky. Social institutions and customs also ensure that events occur in a predictable order. Classes are scheduled at predictable times; you can count on being allowed to pick out what you want to buy in a store before having to pay for it; you can predict whether someone will engage you in conversation by the way she greets you. Learning to predict events in the environment and learning to respond on the basis of such predictions constitute a very important aspect of behavioral adjustment to the environment. Imagine how much trouble you would have if you could never predict how long something would take to cook, when stores would be open, or whether your car would start in the morning.

The simplest mechanism whereby organisms learn to make new responses to stimuli and learn about relations between stimuli is **classical conditioning.** Classical conditioning enables animals to take advantage of the orderly sequence of events in the environment and learn which stimuli tend to go with which other events. On the basis of this learning, animals come to make new responses to stimuli. For example, classical conditioning is the process whereby animals learn to approach signals for food and to salivate when they are about to be fed. It is also integrally involved in the learning of emotional reactions such as fear and pleasure to stimuli that initially do not elicit these emotions. Before discussing further the role of classical conditioning in animal and human behavior generally, we will first describe some of the kinds of detailed experimental investigations that have provided us with what we know about classical conditioning.

Pavlov and the Early Years of Classical Conditioning

Even today, 50 years after his death, classical conditioning is intimately associated with the name and work of Ivan P. Pavlov. Pavlov began his investigations in the late 19th century in Russia. The phenomenon of classical conditioning was also independently discovered by Edwin B. Twitmyer in 1902 in a Ph.D. dissertation submitted to the University of Pennsylvania (see Twitmyer, 1974). However, Twitmyer did not conduct an extensive research program, and his findings were ignored for many years. Although Pavlov's writings were widely disseminated in the United States, the most thorough scholarly criticism and tests of his ideas were first performed by Konorski and his associates in Poland (see Konorski, 1948).

Pavlov's investigations of classical conditioning were an extension of his research on the processes of digestion. Much of his work on conditioning involved the actions of the salivary glands. Most people associate digestion primarily with activities of the stomach and intestines. However, digestion begins in the mouth, where food is chewed and mixed with saliva. Thus, the salivary glands are the first digestive glands involved in the breakdown of foods. They are large glands and have ducts that are close to the surface and can be easily observed. For example, the ducts of the submaxillary glands run along each side of the bottom of the mouth, coming together and releasing saliva near the lower front teeth. (You can readily see these ducts under your tongue with a mirror.) The submaxillary duct can be easily separated from the surrounding tissue, brought out through an incision in the bottom of the mouth, and secured with stitches to the outside skin surface. With this surgical modification, secretions of the gland can be collected, measured, and analyzed (see Figure 3.1).

Pavlov's initial interest in digestive functions was concerned with purely physiological matters. He was interested in the neural systems responsible for food-elicited salivation in dogs. However, he found that dogs that had served in several experiments did not wait to salivate until food was placed in their mouth: they began to salivate as soon as they saw the food. This anticipatory salivation made it difficult to study salivation in response to the food. If the dog was already salivating before the food was presented, one could not easily attribute its salivary secretion to the food presentation. Confronted with such a problem,

scientists less astute than Pavlov might have restricted their investigation to animals that were more naive to the experimental situation and did not engage in anticipatory salivation. Instead, Pavlov redefined the goals of his research and began an extensive investigation of what controls anticipatory salivation (Pavlov, 1927).

Why did experienced dogs start to salivate before receiving food? One of the first of Pavlov's students who worked on this problem, Anton Snarsky, suggested that the sight of food made the dogs think about food and that resulted in the anticipatory salivation. Pavlov rejected this interpretation because it was mentalistic and instead considered anticipatory salivation as the manifestation of a new reflex response elicited by food stimuli. (For a more detailed account of the discovery of the conditioned response, see Boakes, 1984.)

If one assumes that experienced dogs salivate in anticipation of food as a reaction to stimuli that have been paired with food presentation, then numerous experimental questions arise. What kinds of stimuli can come to elicit salivation; how do stimuli gain the ability to elicit salivation; do stimuli that come to elicit anticipatory salivation ever lose this function;

BOX 3.1.   I. P. Pavlov: Biographical sketch

Born in 1849 into the family of a priest in Russia, Pavlov spent a life dedicated to scholarship and discovery. He received his early education in a local theological seminary and planned a career of religious service. However, his interests soon changed, and at 21 he entered the university in St. Petersburg, where his studies focused on chemistry and animal physiology. After obtaining the equivalent of a bachelor's degree, he entered the Imperial Medico-Surgical Academy in 1875 to further his education in physiology. Eight years later, he received his doctoral degree for his research on the efferent nerves of the heart and then began investigating various aspects of digestive physiology. In 1888 he discovered the nerves that stimulate the digestive secretions of the pancreas, and this finding initiated a series of experiments for which he was awarded the Nobel Prize in Physiology in 1904.

Pavlov did a great deal of original research while a graduate student as well as after obtaining his doctoral degree. However, he did not have a faculty position or his own laboratory until 1890, when he was appointed professor of pharmacology at the St. Petersburg Military Medical Academy. In 1895 he became professor of physiology at the same institution. Much of the research for which he is famous today was performed after he received the Nobel Prize. Thus, unlike many scientists, who have their most creative periods early in their career, Pavlov remained very active in the laboratory until close to his death in 1936.

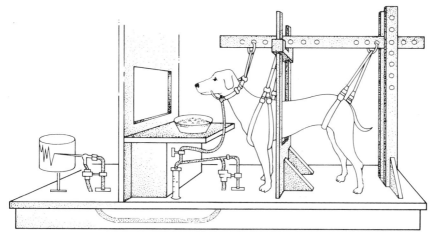

FIGURE 3.1.   Diagram of the Pavlovian salivary conditioning preparation. A cannula attached to the animal's salivary duct conducts drops of saliva to a data-recording device.   *(After Yerkes & Morgulis, 1909.)*

can animals learn to inhibit, or withhold, salivation in response to a stimulus in the same way that they can learn to produce salivation? The latter part of Pavlov's scientific career was devoted to answering questions such as these, and in the process he discovered a great deal about the mechanisms of classical conditioning.

The Classical Conditioning Paradigm

Most people are familiar with the type of procedure Pavlov eventually used to study anticipatory salivation. The procedure typically involved two stimuli of importance. One of these was a noise or the onset of a light. On its first presentation, this stimulus might have elicited an orienting response, but it did not elicit salivation. The other stimulus in the situation was food or the taste of a sour solution placed in the mouth. In contrast to the first stimulus, this second one elicited not only orientation movements but also vigorous salivation, even the first time it was presented. Pavlov referred to the tone or light as the **conditional stimulus** because the ability of this stimulus to elicit salivation depended on (was conditional on) pairing it with food presentation several times. In contrast, the food or sour-taste stimulus was called the **unconditional stimulus** because its ability to elicit salivation was not dependent on any prior training of the subjects. The salivation that eventually came to be elicited by the tone or light was called the **conditional response,** and the salivation that was always elicited by the food or sour taste was called the **unconditional response.** Thus, stimuli and responses whose properties and occurrence did not depend on prior training were called "unconditional," and stimuli and responses whose properties and occurrence depended on special training were called "conditional."

In the first English translation of Pavlov's writings, the term *unconditional* was erroneously translated as *unconditioned,* and the term *conditional* was translated as *conditioned.* The *-ed* suffix was used exclusively in English writings for many years. However, the term *conditioned* does not capture Pavlov's original meaning of "dependent on" as well as the term *conditional* (Gantt, 1966). The words *conditional* and *unconditional* are more common in modern writings on classical conditioning and are now used interchangeably with *conditioned* and *unconditioned.* Because the terms *conditioned (unconditioned) stimulus* and *conditioned (unconditioned) response* are frequent in discussions of classical conditioning, they are often abbreviated. *Conditioned stimulus* and *conditioned response* are abbreviated **CS** and **CR**, respectively. *Unconditioned stimulus* and *unconditioned response* are abbreviated **US** and **UR**, respectively.

Experimental Situations

Classical conditioning has been investigated in a large variety of situations involving a variety of species. Pavlov did most of his experiments with dogs using the salivary-cannula technique. However, this kind of research is rather costly. Therefore, most contemporary experiments on Pavlovian conditioning are carried out with domesticated rats, rabbits, and pigeons. Some of the more popular techniques are described below.

Eyeblink conditioning of rabbits

The rabbit eyeblink conditioning paradigm was developed by I. Gormezano (see Gormezano, 1966; Gormezano, Kehoe, & Marshall, 1983). Large albino rabbits are typically used. Gormezano chose to investigate the eyeblink response because in the absence of special training, rabbits rarely blink their eyes. Therefore, if the animal is observed to blink after the presentation of a stimulus, one can be quite certain that the response occurred because of the stimulus and would not have occurred otherwise. In eyeblink conditioning experiments, a rabbit is placed in a plastic holder, as shown in Figure 3.2. The animal's head protrudes from the holder, and one end of a fine string is attached to the upper lid of one eye. The other end of the string is tied to a small potenti-

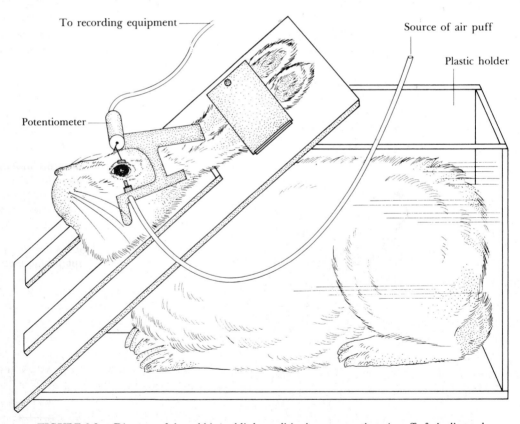

FIGURE 3.2. Diagram of the rabbit eyeblink conditioning preparation. A puff of air directed at the eye or a mild shock to the skin below the eye serves as the US. Eyeblinks are detected by a potentiometer.

ometer. Eyelid movements produce movements in the potentiometer, and these are translated into electrical signals that allow precise recording of the eyelid responses. The unconditioned stimulus is either a puff of air to the surface of the eye or a brief shock (.1 sec, for example) to the skin below the eye. Animals rapidly blink in response to the US. Various stimuli have been used as conditioned stimuli, including lights, tones, or vibration of the animal's abdomen with a hand massager.

In the typical conditioning experiment, the conditioned stimulus is presented for 500 msec and ends in the delivery of the unconditioned stimulus. The unconditioned stimulus elicits a rapid and vigorous eyelid closure. As the CS is repeatedly paired with the US, the eyeblink response also comes to be made to the CS. In the usual procedure, investigators record whether an eyeblink occurs during the CS, before the US is presented, on each trial. The data are presented in terms of the percentage of trials on which a CR is observed in blocks of trials.

Eyelid conditioning is often a relatively slow process, and even with extensive training subjects do not make a conditioned response on every trial. Figure 3.3 shows a typical learning curve for eyelid conditioning. The animals received 82 conditioning trials each day. By the eighth day of training (656 trials), conditioned responses occurred on about 70% of trials. When the conditioned response was made, it occurred very soon after the start of the CS (within 525 msec). Control groups in such experiments, which do not receive the CS paired with the US, typically blink on fewer than 5% of trials.

Fear conditioning

The conditioning of fear is typically studied with the use of rats and sometimes dogs. In most experiments the aversive unconditioned stimulus is shock to the feet delivered through a metal grid floor. The level of shock is considerably more intense than that used in eyelid conditioning. The conditioned stimulus is often a tone or the turning on of a light, and conditioned fear is measured indirectly by measuring how the conditioned fear stimulus alters the animal's ongoing activity.

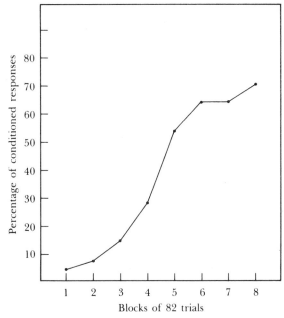

FIGURE 3.3. A typical learning curve for eyelid conditioning. *(From Schneiderman, Fuentes, & Gormezano, 1962.)*

One technique for indirect measurement of conditioned fear is called the **conditioned emotional response** (or **conditioned suppression**) procedure, abbreviated **CER.** This procedure, devised by Estes and Skinner (1941), has since been used extensively in the study of Pavlovian conditioning (Kamin, 1965). Rats are most often used in conditioned suppression experiments. The animals are first trained to press a response lever for food reward in a small experimental chamber (see Figure 3.4). After sufficient lever-press training, they come to press the lever at a steady rate, earning a food reward every 2–3 min. The classical conditioning phase of the experiment is instituted once the lever-press responding has been well established. The duration of the CS is usually longer than in rabbit eyelid conditioning (3 min, for example), and the shock US is typically also longer (.5 sec, for example). The typical conditioning procedure involves presentation of the shock US at the end of the conditioned stimulus. The intertrial interval is usually 15–30 min.

The progress of fear conditioning is evident from

(A)

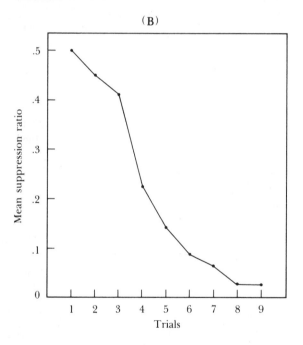

(B)

FIGURE 3.4.   (A) A rat pressing a response lever for food reward in a conditioned suppression experiment. (B) Sample results of a conditioned suppression experiment with rats (from Domjan, unpublished). Three conditioning trials were conducted on each of three days of training. The CS was an audiovisual stimulus, and the US was a brief shock through the grid floor. A suppression ratio of .5 indicates that subjects did not suppress their lever pressing during the CS. A suppression ratio of 0 indicates total suppression of responding during the CS.

the disruption of the food-rewarded lever pressing by the conditioned stimulus. If subjects have never encountered the conditioned stimulus before, the first time it is presented, a slight disruption of lever pressing may occur. If the CS is not paired with shock, this initial slight response suppression habituates: within 3–4 trials the CS has no effect whatever on the rats' behavior. However, if the CS is paired with footshock, it soon becomes conditioned to the shock, and the animals suppress their lever-press response when the CS is presented. Within 3–5 conditioning trials with an effective shock intensity, the conditioned suppression of lever pressing can become complete (Kamin & Brimer, 1963). The animals may not press the lever at all when the CS is presented. The response suppression, however, is specific to the CS. Soon after the CS is turned off, the animals resume the food-rewarded behavior.

Freezing, or becoming motionless, is one of the innate reactions of rats to fearful and aversive stimuli (Bolles, 1970). The CER procedure is designed to provide a sensitive measure of the response suppression induced by fear (Bouton & Bolles, 1980; Mast, Blanchard, & Blanchard, 1982). Because the animals are first trained to press a response lever at a steady rate for a food reward, deviations from this baseline of responding can be easily measured. The quantitative measure of the degree of response suppression produced by the conditioned stimulus is usually calculated by dividing the number of lever-press responses the subject makes during the CS by the sum of the number of responses it makes during the CS and during an equally long period preceding presentation of the CS. The formula is

$$\text{Suppression ratio} = \frac{\text{CS response}}{\text{CS response} + \text{pre-CS response}}$$

This index has a value of zero if the subject suppresses lever pressing completely during the CS, because the numerator of the ratio is zero. At the other extreme, if the rat does not alter its rate of lever pressing at all when the CS is presented, the index takes on the value of .5. You can confirm this by considering some hypothetical cases. For example, assume that the CS is presented for 3 min and that in a typical 3-min period the rat makes 45 responses. If the CS does not disrupt lever pressing, the animal will make 45 responses during the CS, so that the numerator of the ratio will be 45. The denominator will be 45 (CS responses) + 45 (pre-CS responses), or 90. Therefore, the ratio will be .5. Values of the ratio between 0 and .5 indicate various degrees of response suppression, or conditioned fear.

Figure 3.4 shows sample results of a conditioned suppression experiment with rats. Three conditioning trials were conducted on each of three days of training. Very little response suppression occurred the first time the CS was presented, and not much acquisition of suppression was evident during the first day of training. However, a substantial increase in suppression occurred from the last trial on day 1 (trial 3) to the first trial on day 2 (trial 4). With continued training, responding gradually became more and more suppressed, until the animals hardly ever pressed the response lever when the CS was presented.

Sign tracking

Pavlov's research concentrated on response systems such as salivation that may be characterized as highly reflexive. In such systems a distinctive unconditioned response occurs invariably following presentations of the unconditioned stimulus and comes to be also elicited by the conditioned stimulus as the CS and US are repeatedly paired. Because of Pavlov's work, for many years it was believed that classical conditioning procedures could produce learning only in highly reflexive systems. Studies of eyeblink conditioning exemplify this approach. In fact, because the eyeblink response occurs with shorter latencies and shows less variability than salivation, some considered this an even better paradigm for investigations of classical conditioning than salivary conditioning (Amsel, 1972). This restrictive conceptualization of classical conditioning procedures is not characteristic of all contemporary approaches. The conditioned suppression procedure, which was popularized as a technique for investigations of classical conditioning in the 1960s, is partly responsible for less restrictive approaches. Another contemporary procedure for the study of classical conditioning that has greatly broad-

ened our perspective of classical conditioning is called **sign tracking** or **autoshaping** (Hearst, 1975; Hearst & Jenkins, 1974).

Animals tend to approach and contact stimuli that signal the availability of food. In the natural environment, the availability of food is usually indicated by some aspect of the food itself. By approaching and contacting the food signals, animals in effect come in contact with the food. For a predator, for example, the sight, movements, odor, and perhaps noises of the prey are cues indicating the possibility of a meal. By tracking these stimuli, the predator is likely to catch its prey.

Sign tracking can be investigated in the laboratory by presenting a discrete, localized stimulus just before each delivery of a small amount of food. The first experiment of this sort was performed by Brown and Jenkins (1968) with pigeons. The animals were placed in an experimental chamber that had a small circular key which could be illuminated and which the pigeons could peck (see Figure 1.1). Periodically, the animals were given a small amount of food. The key light was illuminated for 8 sec immediately before each food delivery. The pigeons did not have to do anything for the food to be presented. The food was automatically delivered after each illumination of the response key no matter what the animals did. Since the animals were hungry, one might predict that when they saw the key illuminated, they would go to the food dish and wait for the forthcoming food presentation. Interestingly, however, that is not what happened. Instead of using the key light to find out when to go to the food dish, the pigeons started pecking the key itself. This behavior was remarkable because they were not required to peck the response key to get food at that point in the experiment.

Since its discovery, many experiments have been done on the sign-tracking phenomenon using a variety of species and unconditioned stimuli (see, for example, Locurto, Terrace, & Gibbon, 1981). We will describe some of these in coming pages and chapters. These experiments have shown that sign tracking is a very useful technique for the investigation of how associations are learned between one stimulus and another. In pigeon sign-tracking experiments, the conditioned stimulus is illumination of the response key, and the unconditioned stimulus is presentation of food. As in other conditioning procedures, learning proceeds most rapidly when the CS is presented just before the US, and learning does not occur if the CS and US are presented at random times in relation to each other (Gamzu & Williams, 1971, 1973).

The tracking of signals for a food reward is dramatically illustrated by instances in which the signal is located far away from the food delivery site. In one such experiment (see Hearst & Jenkins, 1974), pigeons were placed in a 6-ft (182-cm) alley that had a food dish in the middle (see Figure 3.5). Each end of the alley had a circular disk that could be illuminated. Presentation of food was always preceded by illumination of the disk at one end of the alley. The visual stimulus at the opposite end was uncorrelated with food. One other aspect of the experiment is important to point out. The food was available for only 4 sec each time it was presented. Therefore, if the animal did not walk to the food cup within 4 sec, it did not get any food on that trial.

After illuminations of the light at one end of the alley had been paired with delivery of food a number of times, the pigeons started doing a most remarkable thing. As soon as the light came on, they would run to that end of the alley, peck the illuminated disk, and then run to the center of the alley to get the food. Because the alley was very long, the pigeons did not always get back to the food dish in the middle before the food was removed. This sign-tracking behavior was amazing because it was entirely unnecessary.

The animals did not have to peck the lighted disk to get the food reward. They could have sat in the middle of the alley and just waited for the food on each trial. The fact that they did not is evidence of the compelling attraction of classically conditioned signals for food reward. In contrast, the subjects did not consistently approach the light at the other end of the box, which was uncorrelated with food presentations (see also Boakes, 1979).

Sign tracking is also evident in human behavior. While riding in an elevator, many people look up at the numbers above the door that indicate which floors the elevator is passing. Staring at the floor numbers does not make the elevator reach its destination faster, just as pecking the food signal in the long-box experiment does not produce food sooner. The floor numbers are signs of when the elevator doors will open. They stimulate "tracking" behavior because of this informational significance. People "track" stimuli that provide information about important upcoming events in the same sense that pigeons track a key light that signals presentation of food.

Taste-aversion learning

Another popular procedure for investigating classical conditioning involves taste-aversion learning. Although this learning phenomenon has been known for more than 30 years (see Richter, 1953; Rzoska, 1953), it did not become a popular technique for the study of classical conditioning until the 1970s as the

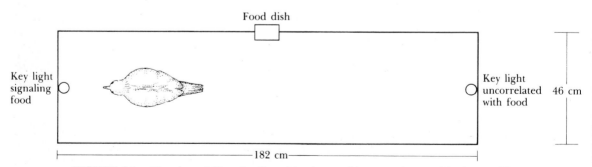

FIGURE 3.5. Top view of "long box" used in sign-tracking experiment with pigeons. The conditioned stimulus is illumination of the key light at one end of the experimental chamber, and food is delivered in the middle of the chamber. *(Based on Jenkins, personal communication, 1980.)*

work of John Garcia, James Smith, Paul Rozin, Sam Revusky, and others became well known (see Barker, Best, & Domjan, 1977; Milgram, Krames, & Alloway, 1977). In the taste-aversion conditioning technique, animals are given a flavored solution to drink and are then made to feel sick by injection of a drug or exposure to aversive radiation. As a result of the experience of ill effects after the taste exposure, the animals acquire an aversion for the taste. Their preference for and voluntary ingestion of the taste solution are suppressed by the conditioning treatment.

Taste-aversion learning is a result of the pairing of the CS (in this case a taste) and the US (drug injection or radiation exposure) in much the same manner as in other examples of classical conditioning. When taste-aversion learning was not yet well understood, it was believed that this type of conditioning was governed by some unique laws of learning that did not apply to conditioning situations such as eyelid and salivary conditioning (see Rozin & Kalat, 1971, for example). Many of the reasons for maintaining this belief are not compelling in light of more recent research (see Domjan, 1980, 1983). However, taste-aversion learning differs from other conditioning situations in some important respects. First, strong taste aversions can be learned in one pairing of the flavor and illness. Although one-trial learning is also observed in fear conditioning, one-trial learning is rarely, if ever, observed in eyelid conditioning, salivary conditioning, or sign tracking. The second unique feature of taste-aversion learning is that learning is evident even if the animals do not get sick until several hours after exposure to the novel taste. The interval between the CS and the US in eyelid conditioning, for example, is usually less than 1 sec because very little, if any, conditioning occurs when longer delays separate the two events. In contrast to the short CS-US intervals that are necessary in salivary, fear, and sign-tracking conditioning situations, animals will learn an aversion to a flavored solution even if the unconditioned stimulus is not presented for several hours (Garcia, Ervin, & Koelling, 1966; Revusky & Garcia, 1970).

A dramatic example of long-delay taste-aversion learning in rats is provided by an experiment by Smith and Roll (1967). The animals were first adapted to a water-deprivation schedule so that they would readily drink when a water bottle was placed on their cage. One day when they were thirsty, the animals were allowed to drink a novel .1% saccharin solution for 20 min. At various times after the saccharin presentation ranging from 0 to 24 hours, independent groups of animals were exposed to radiation from an X-ray machine. Animals serving as controls were also taken to the X-ray machine but were not irradiated. They were called the sham-irradiated rats. Starting 24 hours after the radiation or sham treatment, each rat was given a choice of saccharin solution or plain water to drink for 2 days. The preference of each group of animals for the saccharin solution is shown in Figure 3.6. Animals exposed to radiation within 6 hours after tasting the saccharin solution showed a profound aversion to the saccharin flavor in the postconditioning test. They drank less than 20% of their total fluid intake from the saccharin drinking tube. Much less of an aversion was evident in animals irradiated 12 hours after the saccharin exposure, and hardly any aversion was observed in rats irradiated 24 hours after the taste exposure. In contrast to this gradient of saccharin avoidance observed in the irradiated rats, all the sham-irradiated groups highly preferred the saccharin solution. They

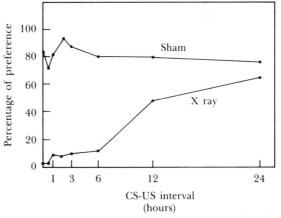

FIGURE 3.6.   Mean percent preference for the CS flavor after pairings with X irradiation or sham irradiation with various CS-US intervals. Percent preference is the percentage of a subject's total fluid intake (saccharin solution plus water) that saccharin constituted. *(After Smith & Roll, 1967.)*

drank more than 70% of their total fluid intake from the saccharin drinking tube.

Taste-aversion learning attracted a great deal of attention when it was first discovered that the learning could occur in one trial with very long delays between CS and US. On further reflection, however, one would be more surprised if taste-aversion learning did not have these characteristics. Taste-aversion learning plays a critical role in food selection. If animals encounter and eat poisonous food, they become sick. By learning an aversion, they can avoid the poisonous food in subsequent meals. To provide much protection, however, this learning has to occur over long CS-US intervals. Toxic materials in food often do not have their bad effects until the food is digested, absorbed in the blood, and distributed to various body tissues. This process takes time. Therefore, if animals were not able to associate the taste of bad foods with delayed ill effects, they would not be able to learn to avoid eating toxic materials. Poison-avoidance learning is especially important for such animals as the rat. Rats eat a large variety of foods and are therefore highly likely to encounter toxic materials.

Excitatory Pavlovian Conditioning

The type of Pavlovian conditioning we are most familiar with is technically known as **excitatory conditioning.** All the examples described above constituted excitatory conditioning. During excitatory conditioning, subjects learn a new response to the conditioned stimulus that is congruent with the unconditioned stimulus. Dogs learn to salivate in response to a bell that precedes food, rabbits learn to blink in response to a tone that precedes brief irritation to the skin surrounding the eye, rats learn to freeze in response to a light or tone that precedes painful shock, pigeons learn to approach and peck a key light that precedes food delivery, and rats learn to avoid drinking saccharin that precedes sickness. In all these cases, the conditioned stimulus came to energize or "excite" a conditioned response that was consistent with the US as a result of pairings of the CS with the US.

Excitatory conditioning procedures

One of the most important factors that determine the course of classical conditioning in each of the situations described above is the relative timing of the conditioned stimulus and the unconditioned stimulus. Seemingly small and trivial variations in how a CS is paired with a US can have profound effects on the rate and extent of classical conditioning. Five classical conditioning procedures that have been frequently investigated are diagramed in Figure 3.7. The horizontal distance in each diagram represents the passage of time, and vertical displacements represent the onset and termination of a stimulus. Each configuration of CS and US represents a single presentation of each stimulus—that is, one **conditioning trial.** In the typical classical conditioning experiment, numerous such trials may be presented in one or more training sessions. The interval between conditioning trials is

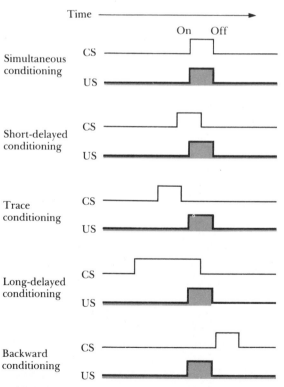

FIGURE 3.7. Five frequently investigated classical conditioning procedures.

called the **intertrial interval.** In contrast, the interval between the start of the CS and the start of the US within a conditioning trial is called the **interstimulus interval** or **CS-US interval.** The interstimulus interval is always much shorter than the intertrial interval. In many experiments the interstimulus interval is less than 1 min, whereas the intertrial interval may be 5 min or more.

1. *Simultaneous conditioning.* Perhaps the most obvious way to expose subjects to the CS paired with the US is to present the two stimuli at the same time. This procedure, called "simultaneous conditioning," is the first procedure depicted in Figure 3.7. The critical feature of this procedure is that the conditioned and unconditioned stimuli are presented concurrently.

2. *Short-delayed conditioning.* The CS can be presented slightly before the US. This procedure, called "short-delayed conditioning," is the most frequently used technique. The critical feature of this procedure is that the onset of the CS precedes the onset of the US by a short period (less than 1 min), and the US is presented either during the CS or immediately afterward.

3. *Trace conditioning.* The trace conditioning procedure is similar to the short-delayed procedure except that the US is not presented until after the CS has ended. The interval between the end of the CS and the beginning of the US is called the **trace interval.**

4. *Long-delayed conditioning.* This procedure is also similar to the short-delayed conditioning procedure in that the CS precedes the US. However, in this case the CS remains present much longer (5–10 min) before the US is delivered.

5. *Backward conditioning.* The last procedure depicted in Figure 3.7 differs from the other procedures in that the CS is presented shortly *after,* rather than before, the US. This technique is called "backward conditioning."

Measurement of the conditioned response

Pavlov and others after him have conducted systematic investigations of procedures of the type depicted in Figure 3.7 to find out how the conditioning

of the CS depends on the temporal relation between the CS and US presentations. To make comparisons of how learning proceeds with various procedures, one has to devise some method of measuring conditioning to the CS. Furthermore, this method should be equally applicable to all the procedures. One technique involves measuring how soon the conditioned response occurs after presentation of the conditioned stimulus. This measure of the strength of the response is called the **latency of the conditioned response.** Latency is the amount of time that elapses between presentation of the conditioned stimulus and occurrence of the conditioned response.

Measurement of response latency can tell us about the course of conditioning only if the conditioned response occurs before the US in a particular conditioning procedure. This can be the case in the short-delayed, long-delayed, and trace conditioning procedures because in all these cases the conditioned response can begin before the unconditioned stimulus is presented. However, the latency of the response in the simultaneous and backward conditioning procedures cannot be used as an index of conditioning. In these cases, the behavior observed during the CS is not clearly due just to the presence of the CS alone. This is particularly true for simultaneous conditioning. Any behavior observed during the CS in that procedure could have been elicited by the US rather than the CS, because the US is present at the same time. In backward conditioning, behavior observed during the CS may have been elicited by the US, which occurred before the CS. Measures of the latency of the response in the short-delayed, long-delayed, and trace conditioning procedures similarly may not indicate what learning has taken place if the conditioned response happens to be delayed until after the unconditioned stimulus is presented.

One way to avoid the problems described above is to test for conditioning by presenting the CS by itself (without the US) periodically during training. Responses elicited by the CS can then be observed without contamination from responses elicited by the US. Such CS-alone trials introduced periodically to measure the extent of learning are called **test trials.**

Test trials permit measurement of not only latency but also other aspects of the conditioned response.

When studying salivation, for example, Pavlov often measured how many drops of saliva were elicited. Such measures of response strength are said to reflect the **magnitude** of the response. One may also calculate the percentage of CS-alone test trials on which a conditioned response is observed. This provides an index of the **probability** of the conditioned response.

Effectiveness of excitatory conditioning procedures

Using test trials and measures of response latency, magnitude, or probability, one can compare the effectiveness of the various procedures depicted in Figure 3.7. Rarely have all five procedures been compared in the same experiment. Furthermore, the results of the comparisons that have been performed sometimes differ depending on the type of response that is conditioned. However, some generalizations can be made on the basis of the available evidence.

Simultaneous conditioning. Presenting the CS at the same time as the US is seldom effective in establishing the conditioned response. Some investigators have reported successful conditioning of fear after small numbers of simultaneous conditioning trials (for example, Burkhardt & Ayres, 1978; Mahoney & Ayres, 1976). However, simultaneous conditioning is not as effective in conditioning fear as short-delayed conditioning (Heth & Rescorla, 1973). Furthermore, in other types of classical conditioning experiments, simultaneous conditioning has been found entirely ineffective (for example, Bitterman, 1964; Smith, Coleman, & Gormezano, 1969).

Short-delayed conditioning. In many situations, the short-delayed conditioning procedure is most effective in producing excitatory conditioning. As we noted earlier, the interval between the start of the CS and the start of the US is called the interstimulus or CS-US interval. The CS-US interval is 0 sec in simultaneous conditioning. Generally, as the CS-US interval is increased, conditioning improves up to a point and then declines (for example, Ost & Lauer, 1965; Schneiderman & Gormezano, 1964).

Trace conditioning. In the short-delayed pro-

cedure, the CS is presented just before the US and persists until the US occurs on each trial. The trace conditioning procedure is similar in that here the CS is also presented shortly before the US (see Figure 3.7). However, in the trace procedure the CS is terminated for a short time before the US occurs. Whether there is a trace interval between the CS and the US has a significant effect on learning. The trace procedure is often less effective than the delayed procedure in producing excitatory conditioning (for example, Ellison, 1964; Kamin, 1965), and under certain circumstances the trace procedure teaches subjects to inhibit, or hold back, the conditioned response rather than to perform the CR (Hinson & Siegel, 1980; Kaplan, 1984).

Long-delayed conditioning. With the short-delayed and trace conditioning procedures, as training progresses, the magnitude of the conditioned response increases and its latency decreases. Interestingly, however, this does not happen if a longer CS-US interval is used. With long-delayed conditioning, as the animal begins to learn the conditioned response, the latency becomes shorter only up to a point. After extensive experience with the procedure, the animal appears to learn that the US is not presented for some time after the beginning of the CS, and it starts to delay its conditioned response until the presentation of the US. Pavlov referred to this withholding of the conditioned response at the start of the CS in long-delayed conditioning as *inhibition of delay.* Inhibition of delay has been observed in several response systems, including salivary and fear conditioning (for example, Pavlov, 1927; Rescorla, 1967a; Williams, 1965). However, it has not been investigated in some of the more recently developed classical conditioning preparations, such as sign tracking and taste-aversion learning.

Backward conditioning. Results of studies using the backward conditioning procedure have been mixed. Some investigators have reported that excitatory conditioning occurs with backward pairings of CS and US (see Shurtleff & Ayres, 1981; Spetch, Wilkie, & Pinel, 1981). Other investigators have failed to find excitatory conditioning, and some, in fact, have reported that animals learn to suppress, or inhibit, their behavior in backward conditioning (for example, Maier, Rapaport, & Wheatley, 1976; Moscovitch & LoLordo, 1968; Siegel & Domjan, 1971). Some of the discrepancy in results seems to be related to the number of conditioning trials conducted. Excitatory conditioning is more likely to be observed after small numbers of conditioning trials, and inhibitory conditioning is likely to be observed after more extensive backward conditioning (Heth, 1976; see also Wagner & Larew, 1985). We will have much more to say about the conditioning of inhibitory response tendencies later in the chapter.

Control procedures in classical conditioning

All the procedures shown in Figure 3.7 involve exposing subjects to both the conditioned and the unconditioned stimuli. The fact that they produce learning at different rates indicates that classical conditioning does not result from mere exposure to the CS and US. Learning occurs only if there is a special arrangement of presentations of the conditioned and unconditioned stimuli, as in the short-delayed conditioning procedure. Actual experiments on classical conditioning rarely include all the procedures described in Figure 3.7. Rather, the common practice is to choose just one procedure (usually short-delayed) that is sure to work. However, if subjects increase their responding under these circumstances, one cannot be sure that the increase is a result of the *association* of the CS and US. As we saw in our discussions of sensitization in Chapter 2, presentations of a powerful stimulus such as shock or some other US can increase the behavior elicited by a more innocuous stimulus, such as a CS, without an association being established between the two stimuli (see, for example, the phenomenon of dishabituation, discussed under "Characteristics of Habituation and Sensitization" in Chapter 2). Therefore, increases in responding observed with repeated CS-US pairings can sometimes result from just exposure to the US. Instances in which exposure to the US itself produces responses to the CS that mimic the CR are called **pseudoconditioning.** Control procedures have to be evaluated to ensure that responses that develop to the

CS during classical conditioning represent an association between the CS and US and not sensitization effects of exposure to the conditioned and unconditioned stimuli.

Investigators have debated at great length about what are proper control procedures for classical conditioning. One important control procedure involves repeatedly presenting subjects with both the conditioned and the unconditioned stimuli but arranging the schedule so that the two stimuli occur at random times with respect to each other (Rescorla, 1967b). This **random control procedure** appears to work well provided that there are numerous presentations of both the CS and the US. However, if only a few trials of each are given, there may be evidence of conditioning in the random control groups (Benedict & Ayres, 1972; Kremer & Kamin, 1971; Quinsey, 1971). In experiments calling for few trials, it is preferable to use control groups that receive only the CS, only the US, or both the CS and the US but never paired with each other. If resources prevent testing all three of these control procedures, the procedure involving unpaired presentations of the CS and US is recommended. (For a further discussion of control methodology, see Gormezano et al., 1983.)

Contiguity and Signal Relations between Conditioned and Unconditioned Stimuli

What determines the effectiveness of various procedures in conditioning a new response to the CS? Why are some procedures much more successful than others in producing excitatory classical conditioning? These questions are fundamental to the analysis of classical conditioning and have preoccupied investigators for decades. The simplest idea is that excitatory classical conditioning is produced by experience of the CS and the US at the same time. This is the principle of **stimulus contiguity.** Two events are said to be contiguous if they occur at the same time. The assumption that contiguity is critical for the learning of an association between two stimuli (the CS and US, for example) is one of the earliest and most frequently recurring ideas in the analysis of classical conditioning (see Gormezano & Kehoe, 1981). However, review of the excitatory conditioning procedures we described earlier shows that a simple notion of stimulus contiguity does not provide an adequate account of classical conditioning. Presentation of the CS and US at the same time, as in the simultaneous conditioning procedure, is not particularly effective in producing excitatory conditioning. Rather, the most successful procedure for excitatory classical conditioning is the short-delayed conditioning procedure, in which the CS is initiated slightly before presentation of the US. This is just one of many findings that are inconsistent with a simple stimulus contiguity principle of association learning. Because of such results, the principle of contiguity has undergone various reformulations and refinements to better explain results of classical conditioning experiments. We will discuss some of these theoretical developments in Chapter 4.

Problems with a simple contiguity principle have also encouraged the development of alternative ideas about the mechanisms of classical conditioning. One of the most prominent of these is based on the notion that classical conditioning involves the learning of a signal relation between the conditioned and unconditioned stimuli. According to this idea, organisms are most likely to learn to make the conditioned response to a CS if occurrences of the CS can be used as a signal of the forthcoming presentation of the US. Procedures in which the CS cannot be used as a basis for predicting the US often do not promote rapid acquisition of the conditioned response.

Examples of signal relations

One can easily assess how useful the conditioned stimulus is for predicting the unconditioned stimulus by thinking about real-world situations in which signals are used. There are many such situations. One involves sirens that ordinarily signal the approach of an emergency vehicle, such as an ambulance or fire truck. The purpose of the siren is to get people to make way for the emergency vehicle. The siren is analogous to the conditioned stimulus, and the arrival of the emergency vehicle is analogous to the unconditioned stimulus. If you always heard the siren just before the ambulance arrived, you would

quickly learn to get out of the way. In this case, the siren would be a good predictor, or signal, for the coming ambulance. Such a procedure is analogous to the short-delayed conditioning procedure, in which the CS is a good predictor of the US. In contrast, if you never heard the siren until the ambulance was on the scene, you would have no reason to react to the siren. The siren would not provide useful information about the coming of the ambulance. You could simply get out of the way when the ambulance arrived. This case is analogous to the simultaneous conditioning procedure, in which the signal relation between the CS and the US is not very good. You would have even less reason to get out of the way when the siren sounded if you always heard the siren only after the ambulance had already left. This case is comparable to the backward conditioning procedure. If you learned anything under these circumstances, it would be that the siren indicates the departure of the ambulance.

The analysis is a bit more complicated if the relation between the sounding of the siren and the presence of the ambulance is comparable to the trace conditioning procedure. In this case, the siren would stop before the ambulance arrived. Therefore, the presence of the siren would indicate that the ambulance was not to arrive for a while yet. The coming of the ambulance would be best indicated by the termination of the siren. Thus, with a trace procedure, you would be most likely to make way for the ambulance when the siren ended.

If you experienced something comparable to the long-delayed conditioning procedure, you would always hear the siren for a long time before the arrival of the ambulance. In this case, you would learn to ignore the siren when you first heard it, and you would worry about getting out of the way only after the siren had been on for a while. Most people's experience with sirens and emergency vehicles is closest to the long-delayed conditioning procedure. Perhaps this is why people rarely respond immediately when they hear a siren while driving.

CS/US contingency

One can often figure out whether one stimulus (for example, the CS) serves as a good signal for the forthcoming presentation of another event (for example, the US) by reflecting on common experience. However, this decision can be made more precisely with the use of formal definitions. A highly influential treatment of signal relations in classical conditioning was presented by Robert Rescorla (1967b). His discussion was important not only because of its precision but also because he pointed out certain aspects of signal relations that previously were not considered in classical conditioning. Rescorla pointed out that the extent to which one stimulus signals another depends not only on the way the two events are paired but also on the number of times each of the two events occurs by itself. In fact, the number of times the CS and US occur by themselves may be more important in determining the strength of conditioning than how the two are paired when they occur together. A second important idea that Rescorla emphasized is that signal relations need not always be positive: they can also be negative. That is, one stimulus can signal the absence of another stimulus, in much the same way that one stimulus can signal the forthcoming presence of another event.

Rescorla's ideas about signal relations were formally summarized in his concept of the **contingency between the conditioned and unconditioned stimuli.** The contingency between CS and US is determined from a comparison of two probabilities, the probability that the US will occur with the CS, symbolized as $p(US/CS)$, and the probability that the US will occur in the absence of the CS, symbolized as $p(US/noCS)$. If the US is presented only with the CS and the CS is never presented alone, as in the short-delayed conditioning procedure, occurrences of the US can be perfectly predicted from occurrences of the CS. This illustrates a perfect **positive contingency** between CS and US. In terms of the two probabilities that define contingency, the US is absolutely certain to occur given that the CS has occurred. Thus, $p(US/CS) = 1.0$. In contrast, the US is absolutely certain not to occur given that the CS has not occurred. Thus, $p(US/noCS) = 0$. These two probabilities define a perfect positive contingency.

Whenever one can predict occurrences of the US from the presence of the CS, a positive contingency exists between the two stimuli. The perfect positive contingency described above illustrates an extreme case. One can predict the US from the CS whenever the US is more likely to occur with the CS than without it. Thus, a positive contingency between CS and US is said to exist whenever $p(US/CS)$ is greater than $p(US/noCS)$. Deer hunters, for example, make use of an imperfect positive contingency when they predict the presence of deer from seeing deer droppings. One does not invariably see deer when deer

---

BOX 3.2.   A local paper features the headline MR. P KILLED AS TRAIN HITS CAR

An investigation of the accident revealed that the signal lights and bells at the crossing were working properly. Mr. P was said to be in fine physical and mental condition, and he had not been drinking. What happened? Why did Mr. P drive his car onto the tracks when the signals, both visual and auditory, clearly indicated the approach of a train? One possible explanation is that the warning signals were not arranged in a temporal relation with the coming of the train to make them effective. Often the warning bells and lights start going long before the train is at the crossing, and often they continue for some time after the train has left. Because of this ineffectual arrangement, if one arrives at a crossing when the warning signals are on, one cannot be sure whether a train is about to come or whether it has just passed. Therefore, drivers invariably approach the railroad tracks slowly when the warning signals are on, look both ways to see the train, and try to get off the track quickly if they see the train. Some of them do not make it in time, like Mr. P. A much more effective arrangement would be to have the warning signals start very shortly before the train was to reach the crossing and go off as soon as the train had passed. People could then be sure that the train would soon arrive when they saw the warning lights and bells, and they would not be tempted to take their lives in their hands by venturing onto the tracks to find out where the train is.

droppings are found. However, there is a positive contingency between these two events because deer are more likely to be located in areas where there are droppings than in other places.

In contrast to the positive contingency, which allows for prediction of one event on the basis of the occurrence of another stimulus, such a prediction is not possible when the contingency between two stimuli is zero. A **zero contingency** between CS and US is said to exist if the US is just as likely to occur with the CS as without the CS. Thus, in a zero contingency, $p(US/CS) = p(US/noCS)$.

A zero contingency can exist even if on some occasions the conditioned and unconditioned stimuli occur together. For example, even though some warm days begin with a clear sky, one cannot predict that it will be warm just because it is clear in the morning. Some days that start out with clear skies turn out to be cold, and some warm days begin with cloudy skies. Thus, the occasional coincidence of warm days following clear mornings is not sufficient to associate clear skies with warm weather.

Contingencies also exist in which the CS predicts the *absence* of the US. This is the case if the US is more likely to occur in the absence of the CS than in the presence of the CS. Such cases illustrate a **negative contingency** between CS and US. In a negative contingency $p(US/CS)$ is less than $p(US/noCS)$.

A CS that is in a negative contingent relation with the US provides as much information about the US as a CS that is related to the US according to a positive contingency. The only difference is that a negative contingent CS signals the absence of the US, whereas a positive contingent CS signals the presence of the US. We have already seen an example of a negative contingency in backward conditioning procedures. Here the US is presented before the CS on every trial, so that the CS comes to signal the absence of the US during the forthcoming intertrial interval (Moscovitch & LoLordo, 1968). There are also many instances of negative contingencies in common experience. For example, if you just had a test in a college course, that is a good indication that you will not have another test in that class for the next several class periods. Doctors use such symptoms as normal weight, normal blood pressure, and normal heart rate

to predict the absence of illness because illness is much less likely in such people than in people whose weight, blood pressure, and heart rate are abnormal.

By specifying that learning depends on the contingency between CS and US, the contingency model emphasizes that the pairing of CS and US is not sufficient to produce classical conditioning. One cannot predict what the animal will learn, if anything, from being exposed to the CS paired with the US on a number of occasions. For example, suppose that a dog is presented with a tone 100 times, and a random 50 of these tone presentations are immediately followed by the presentation of food. On the basis of this information, we cannot predict what the dog will learn, because we do not know what its probability is of getting food in the experimental situation when the tone is absent. If the animal is never given food in the absence of the tone, a weak positive contingency will exist between the tone and food. Under these conditions the dog will learn to salivate to the tone. However, if the dog is fed as often in the absence of the tone as it is immediately after the tone, the contingency between CS and US will be zero. In this case the dog may learn not to do anything in response to the tone. Finally, if the dog is fed more often in the absence of the tone than it is immediately after the tone, there will be a negative contingency between CS and US, and the dog may learn to treat the tone as a weak signal for the absence of food.

Inhibitory Pavlovian Conditioning

As noted above, stimuli can become conditioned to signal the forthcoming absence of the unconditioned stimulus just as well as to signal its forthcoming presence. Learning that a stimulus signals the absence of the US is called **inhibitory conditioning.** Although inhibitory conditioning was discovered by Pavlov along with excitatory conditioning, it did not command serious attention among American psychologists until the mid-1960s (Boakes & Halliday, 1972; Rescorla, 1969b). This relatively long neglect of inhibitory conditioning processes is puzzling. Conditioned inhibition teaches animals to inhibit, or hold back, a conditioned response. The inhibition of conditioned responding is as important in the organization of behavior as the ability to make conditioned responses. Furthermore, signals that indicate what unconditioned stimuli will not occur provide as much information about the world as signals that tell organisms what will occur. We have noted briefly that inhibitory conditioning involves the learning of a negative signal relation between CS and US. We will now discuss some of the important procedures for producing conditioned inhibition. We will also discuss how animals react to conditioned inhibitory stimuli. (For a review of recent research on conditioned inhibition, see Miller & Spear, 1985.)

Procedures for inhibitory conditioning

An important prerequisite for conditioning a stimulus to signal the absence of some US is that the US be periodically presented in that situation. There are many signals for the absence of events in our daily lives. Signs such as "Closed," "Out of Order," and "No Entry" are all of this type. However, these signs provide meaningful information and influence what we do only if they indicate the absence of something we otherwise expect to see. For example, if we encounter the sign "Out of Gas" at a gas station, we may become frustrated and disappointed and will not enter the station. The sign "Out of Gas" provides important information here because we ordinarily expect service stations to have gas. However, the same sign does not tell us anything of interest if it is put up in front of a jewelry store, and it is not likely to discourage us from going into the store to look at jewelry. This example illustrates the general rule that inhibitory conditioning and inhibitory control of

behavior occur only if there is an excitatory context for the unconditioned stimulus in question (for example, Baker & Baker, 1985; Fowler, Kleiman, & Lysle, 1985; LoLordo & Fairless, 1985). This principle makes inhibitory conditioning very different from excitatory conditioning, which is not as dependent on a special context in the same way.

Standard procedure for conditioned inhibition. Pavlov recognized the importance of an excitatory context for the conditioning of inhibitory response tendencies and was careful to provide such a context in his standard procedure for conditioning inhibition (Pavlov, 1927). The technique, diagramed in Figure 3.8, involves two conditioned stimuli and two kinds of conditioning trials repeated in random order. The unconditioned stimulus is presented on some of the trials. Whenever the US occurs, it is announced by one of the conditioned stimuli, the CS+ (a tone, for example). On the other type of trial, the CS+ is presented together with the second conditioned stimulus, the CS− (a light, for example). The US does not occur on these trials. As the animal receives repeated trials of CS+ followed by the US and CS+/CS− followed by no US, the CS− gradually becomes a signal for the absence of the US (for example, Marchant, Mis, & Moore, 1972). The trials in which the CS− and CS+ are presented without the US are the inhibitory conditioning trials. The excitatory context for this conditioning is provided by the presence of the CS+ on the inhibitory conditioning trials. Because the CS+ is paired with the US on some of the trials, the CS+ becomes conditioned to elicit an expectancy of the US. The absence of the US on the inhibitory conditioning trials

FIGURE 3.8.   Standard procedure for conditioned inhibition. On some trials the CS+ is paired with the US. On other trials the CS+ is paired with the CS− and the US is not presented. The procedure is effective in conditioning inhibitory properties to the CS−.

therefore occurs in a context in which the subject expects the US. This expectancy makes the absence of the US an important event and results in inhibitory conditioning of the CS−.

The standard conditioned inhibition procedure is analogous to situations in which something is introduced that prevents an outcome that is otherwise highly likely. A red traffic light at a busy intersection is a signal (CS+) of potential danger (the US). However, if a police officer indicates that you should cross the intersection despite the red light (perhaps because the traffic lights are malfunctioning), you will probably not have an accident. The red light (CS+) together with the gestures of the officer (CS−) are not likely to be followed by danger. The gestures act like a CS− to inhibit, or block, your hesitation to cross the intersection because of the red light.

Differential inhibition. Another frequently used procedure for conditioning inhibition is called **differential inhibition.** This procedure is very similar to the standard procedure described above. As in the standard procedure, the US is presented on some trials, and its occurrence is always announced by the presentation of the CS+. On other trials, the US is not presented, and animals experience only the CS−. Thus, the differential inhibition procedure involves two types of trials, CS+ followed by the US and CS− followed by no US (see Figure 3.9). As in the standard procedure, the CS− becomes a conditioned inhibitory stimulus (for example, Rescorla & LoLordo, 1965).

The differential inhibition procedure is analogous to having two traffic lights at an intersection, one red

and one green. The red light (CS+) signals danger (US) when crossing the intersection, whereas the green light (CS−) signals the absence of danger (no US). If you cross the intersection during the green light (CS−), you can be reasonably confident that you will not be involved in an accident.

It is not as obvious what provides the excitatory context for the conditioning of inhibition in the differential conditioning procedure as in the standard procedure. In the standard procedure, the presence of the CS+ leads to some expectation of the US on the initial inhibitory conditioning trials. The CS+ is not present on the inhibitory conditioning trials of the differential conditioning procedure. In fact, this is the only important difference between the two procedures. However, there is another factor that may produce an excitatory context during the inhibitory conditioning trials (CS−, no US) in the differential conditioning procedure. Because the US is periodically presented, the stimuli of the experimental situation may become conditioned by the US so that the animal has some expectation of the US whenever it is in this situation. Thus, the contextual cues of the experimental situation may provide the excitatory context for the learning of inhibition in the differential inhibition procedure. However, this does not always happen, and therefore the differential inhibition procedure is not always as effective in producing conditioned inhibition as the standard procedure (see LoLordo & Fairless, 1985, for an extensive discussion of this issue).

Negative CS/US contingency. Both the standard procedure and the differential procedure for producing conditioned inhibition involve a negative

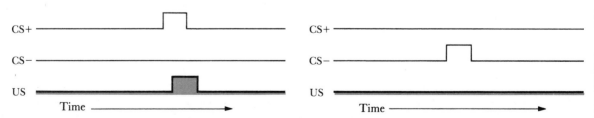

FIGURE 3.9. Procedure for differential inhibition. On some trials the CS+ is paired with the US. On other trials the CS− is presented alone. The procedure is effective in conditioning inhibitory properties to the CS−.

contingency between the conditioned inhibitory stimulus (CS−) and the unconditioned stimulus. In both procedures the probability of getting the US with or shortly after the presentation of the CS− is zero. The probability of getting the US when the CS− is not present is greater than zero. Thus, $p(US/noCS-)$ is greater than $p(US/CS-)$. Both procedures also involve excitatory conditioning of an explicit CS+. This second aspect of the procedures is not absolutely necessary for the occurrence of conditioned inhibition. Subjects do not have to be exposed to an explicit CS+ paired with the US in order to acquire inhibitory tendencies to the CS−. The only thing that is critical is that there be a negative contingency between the inhibitory CS and occurrences of the US. Therefore, conditioned inhibition can also result from procedures in which there is only one explicit conditioned stimulus, provided that this CS is presented in a negative signal relation to the US. That is, the probability that the US will occur has to be greater in the absence of the CS than in the presence of the CS or immediately after the CS occurs. A sample arrangement that meets this requirement is diagramed in Figure 3.10. The US is periodically presented by itself. However, each occurrence of the CS is followed by a predictable absence of the US.

Conditioned inhibition is reliably observed in procedures in which the only explicit conditioned stimulus is in a negative contingent relation to the US (Rescorla, 1969a). What provides the excitatory context for this inhibition? Since there is no explicit CS+ that predicts occurrences of the US in this procedure, the US is presented in the experimental situation without being signaled. The environmental cues of the experimental chamber therefore become conditioned to predict occurrences of the US. Thus, as in differential inhibition, the excitatory context for the inhibitory conditioning is provided by the contextual cues of the experimental situation (Dweck & Wagner, 1970).

Measuring conditioned inhibition

Once an animal learns that a stimulus signals the forthcoming absence of an unconditioned stimulus, what does it do with this information? How are conditioned inhibitory processes manifest in behavior? For conditioned excitation, the answer to the corresponding questions is straightforward. Stimuli that have become conditioned to predict the occurrence of a US usually come to elicit behaviors that were not evident in the presence of these stimuli before conditioning. Thus, conditioned excitatory stimuli come to elicit new responses such as salivation, approach, or eye blinking, depending on what the unconditioned stimulus is. One might expect that conditioned inhibitory stimuli would elicit the opposites of these reactions—namely, suppression of salivation, approach, or eye blinking. How are we to measure these response opposites?

Bidirectional response systems.   Identification of opposing response tendencies is very easy with response systems that can change in opposite directions from baseline (normal) performance. This is characteristic of many physiological responses. Heart rate, respiration, and temperature, for example, can either increase or decrease from normal. Certain behavioral responses are also bidirectional. For example, animals can either approach or withdraw from a stimulus, and their rate of lever pressing for a food reward can either increase or decrease. In these

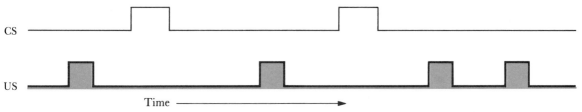

FIGURE 3.10.   Negative CS-US contingency procedure for conditioning inhibitory properties to the CS.

cases, conditioned excitation results in a change in behavior in one direction, and conditioned inhibition results in a change in behavior in the opposite direction. The sign-tracking procedure has been most often used to provide evidence of inhibitory conditioning through bidirectional responses. As noted earlier, pigeons approach visual stimuli that signal the forthcoming presentation of food. If an inhibitory conditioning procedure is used instead, so that the visual stimulus becomes a signal for the absence of food, the pigeons withdraw from the CS (Hearst & Franklin, 1977; Wasserman, Franklin, & Hearst, 1974). Evidence of inhibitory conditioning through bidirectional responses has also been obtained with the conditioned suppression technique with rats. As we saw, stimuli that have been conditioned to signal forthcoming shock suppress the rate of food-rewarded lever pressing in rats. In contrast, stimuli that have been conditioned to signal the forthcoming

absence of shock increase the rate of food-rewarded lever pressing (Hammond, 1966; see also Wesierska & Zielinski, 1980). Another good example of bidirectionality involves taste preference. We noted that animals reduce their preference for a taste that has been paired with sickness. However, animals increase their preference for tastes that have been conditioned to predict the absence of sickness (Batson & Best, 1981; Best, 1975).

It is important to note that the simple observation of a response opposite to the reaction to a conditioned excitatory stimulus is sometimes not sufficient to conclude that inhibitory conditioning is involved. One must make certain that the topography, or form, of the opposing response was due to the negative contingency between CS and US. Mere exposure to the CS sometimes results in a reaction to the CS that is opposite to what is typically observed with conditioned excitatory stimuli. This is true, for example,

---

BOX 3.3. Conditioned inhibition and protection from ulcers

Exposure to unpleasant and aversive situations can result in various physiological symptoms of stress, including stomach ulcers. One important factor that determines the severity of stress symptoms is the extent to which occurrences of the aversive stimulus are signaled and therefore predictable to the individual. In many cases stress symptoms are much less severe if aversive stimuli are signaled than if they are unpredictable (for example, Weiss, 1970). For example, rats exposed to signaled shock develop fewer and milder ulcers than rats exposed to unsignaled shock (Seligman, 1968; Weiss, 1971). In addition to the reduced gastric pathology, signaled shock produces less chronic fear or anxiety than unsignaled shock (for example, Hymowitz, 1979; Seligman, 1968; Seligman & Meyer, 1970).

An interesting explanation called the "safety-signal hypothesis" attributes these findings to conditioned inhibition (Seligman, 1968; Seligman & Binik, 1977). The presence of a shock signal obviously allows animals to predict when the aversive event will occur. The safety-signal hypothesis points out that shock signals also allow subjects to predict when shocks will not occur, because shocks never occur when the signal is absent. Therefore, the absence of the shock signal serves as a conditioned inhibitory stimulus and indicates periods of safety from shock. According to the safety-signal hypothesis, animals exposed to signaled shock develop fewer ulcers and have less anxiety because they experience such safe periods. Animals for which the shocks are not signaled can never be sure when the shock will or will not be presented and therefore never experience periods of safety.

The research findings suggest that psychosomatic illnesses caused by exposure to aversive events can be substantially reduced by introducing conditioned inhibitory stimuli that signal safe periods and allow subjects to relax. The implication is that an executive bothered by ulcers does not necessarily have to quit his or her job. The symptoms of stress can be reduced if the person learns to relax periodically during a hectic day.

for taste preferences. Mere exposure to a flavor often increases preference for it (Domjan, 1976). Inhibitory conditioning with poisoning also increases taste preference (Best, 1975). Therefore, inhibitory conditioning has to produce higher taste preferences than are observed with mere taste exposure before one can be sure that conditioned inhibition is responsible for the outcome.

Compound-stimulus, or summation, test.

Inhibitory conditioning can be investigated directly in bidirectional response systems. However, many responses cannot change in both directions. Eye blinking in rabbits is a good example. In the absence of an eliciting stimulus, rabbits rarely blink. If a stimulus had been conditioned to inhibit the eyeblink response, we would not observe eyeblinks when this stimulus was presented. The problem is that the animal also would not blink when the stimulus was absent. Therefore, we could not be sure whether the lack of responding reflected an active suppression of blinking or merely the low baseline level of this behavior in the absence of any stimulation. More sophisticated techniques have to be used before one can conclude that a stimulus actively inhibits blinking. The most versatile procedure for assessing inhibition is the **compound-stimulus test, or summation test.** This procedure was particularly popular with Pavlov (for example, Pavlov, 1927) and is becoming regarded as the most acceptable procedure for the measurement of conditioned inhibition in contemporary research (see Miller & Spear, 1985).

Difficulties created by low baseline levels of responding are overcome in the compound-stimulus test by presenting an excitatory conditioned stimulus that elicits the conditioned response. Conditioned inhibition is then measured in terms of the reduction or inhibition of this conditioned responding. Thus, the test involves observing the effects of an inhibitory CS— *in compound with* an excitatory CS+. Another way to think about the procedure is that it involves observing the *summation* of the effects of an inhibitory stimulus (CS—) and an excitatory stimulus (CS+).

An experiment by Reberg and Black (1969) illustrates the use of the compound-stimulus test to evalu-

ate inhibition in a conditioned suppression experiment. Subjects in the conditioned inhibition group received differential conditioning in which a CS+ was periodically presented ending in a brief shock and a CS— was periodically presented in the absence of shock. (Visual and auditory stimuli were used as CS+ and CS—.) The comparison group received only the CS+ paired with shock during this part of the experiment, so that for them the CS— did not become a signal for the absence of shock. Then, both groups received two types of test trials. During one test trial, only the CS+ was presented, to determine the degree of response suppression the animals learned to this stimulus. During the other test trial, the CS+ was presented simultaneously with the CS—. The results are summarized in Figure 3.11. For the conditioned inhibition group less response suppression occurred when the CS— was presented simultaneously with the CS+ than when the CS+ was presented alone. This outcome occurred because

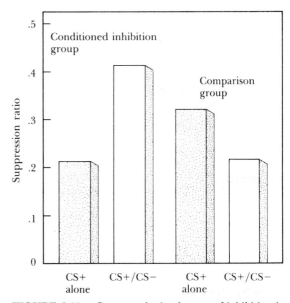

FIGURE 3.11. Compound-stimulus test of inhibition in a conditioned suppression experiment. For the conditioned inhibition group, the CS— was a predictor of the absence of shock. For the comparison group, the CS— was a novel stimulus. The CS— reduced the degree of response suppression produced by a shock-conditioned CS+ in the conditioned inhibition group but not in the comparison group. *(After Reberg & Black, 1969.)*

the CS— had become a signal for the absence of shock. Thus, the CS— inhibited the response suppression produced by the CS+. Such an inhibition effect did not occur in the comparison group. For these subjects, the CS— had not been conditioned to signal the absence of shock. In fact, the CS— was presented for the first time during the test trials. The presence of the CS— did not inhibit the response suppression produced by the CS+ in the comparison group.

Retardation-of-acquisition test. Another frequently used indirect test of conditioned inhibition is the **retardation-of-acquisition test** (for example, Hammond, 1968; Rescorla, 1969a). The rationale for this test is also rather straightforward: if a stimulus actively inhibits a particular response, then it should be unusually difficult to condition that stimulus to elicit the behavior. In other words, the rate of acquisition of a particular conditioned response should be retarded if the stimulus initially elicits an inhibition of the response.

Although the retardation-of-acquisition test has been frequently employed in research on conditioned inhibition, recent studies suggest that it is not as useful for the assessment of conditioned inhibition as the compound-stimulus test. One serious difficulty is that many factors can slow down the course of excitatory classical conditioning. We will discuss some of these factors in Chapter 4. The existence of numerous sources of retardation of acquisition makes it difficult to identify a particular instance of retarded acquisition as due to conditioned inhibition (see, for example, Baker & Baker, 1985). Another difficulty is that the retardation-of-acquisition test fails to detect certain forms of conditioned inhibition (for example, Holland, 1985).

Extinction

So far our discussion of classical conditioning has centered on various aspects of the acquisition of new responses to stimuli, be they excitatory or inhibitory. It would be maladaptive, however, if once stimuli became conditioned, the animal's response to these stimuli remained fixed for the rest of its life. Just as it is useful for animals to learn new responses to stimuli, it is also adaptive for them to lose this behavior once the circumstances no longer require it. One process whereby conditioned responses to stimuli are decreased is called **extinction.** The procedure for extinguishing a conditioned stimulus is to repeatedly present the CS without the unconditioned stimulus or in the absence of any kind of signal relation with the US. If the animal has been conditioned to salivate in response to a bell, for example, and the bell is then repeatedly presented in the absence of food, salivation to the bell will gradually decline.

A note on terminology: extinction procedures are said to extinguish responses and/or conditioned stimuli, not organisms. Animals do not die when they are exposed to extinction procedures. Another important definitional comment is that the loss of the conditioned response that is produced by extinction is not the same as the loss of behavior that may occur because of **forgetting.** In extinction, the repeated presentations of the CS by itself are responsible for the gradual decline of the conditioned response. Forgetting, in contrast, is a decline in the strength of the conditioned response that may occur simply because of the passage of time. Extinction involves a particular experience with the conditioned stimulus. Forgetting occurs with prolonged absence of exposure to the conditioned stimulus.

Extinction and habituation

The procedure for extinction of conditioned stimuli is very similar to the procedures we discussed in Chapter 2 for producing habituation. Both extinction and habituation involve repeated presentation of a stimulus. The critical difference between them is that in extinction the stimulus involved was previously conditioned. An earlier phase of conditioning is not required for habituation. Because of the similarity in the procedures for extinction and habituation, one might expect that there would also be similarities in the results observed. Research is beginning to uncover such similarities. Recent studies have shown, for example, that effects of the interval between successive presentations of a stimulus are similar in habituation and extinction paradigms (Westbrook, Smith, & Charnock, in press).

Another important characteristic of habituation is that the habituated stimulus recovers its ability to evoke the response with the passage of time. This phenomenon is called the "spontaneous recovery" of habituation. A similar effect is observed with extinguished stimuli and/or responses. If, after a series of extinction trials, the animal is given a period of rest away from the experimental environment, spontaneous recovery of the extinguished response may occur (Pavlov, 1927). Less spontaneous recovery would be expected after successive series of extinction trials, as was true in habituation. Eventually, there would be no recovery after rest periods.

Habituation and extinction are also similar in the effects of novel stimuli on the loss of responsiveness. As we noted in Chapter 2, presentation of a novel stimulus often results in recovery of the response elicited by the habituated stimulus (dishabituation). A comparable effect occurs in extinction. If, after a series of extinction trials, a novel stimulus is presented, recovery may occur in the response to the extinguished CS (Pavlov, 1927). This recovery in the conditioned response produced by novelty is called **disinhibition.** It is important to differentiate disinhibition from spontaneous recovery. Even though both processes are forms of recovery of the conditioned response, in spontaneous recovery the recovery occurs simply because of the passage of time, and in disinhibition it occurs because of the presentation of a novel stimulus.

What is learned in extinction

The phenomenon of extinction fits our definition of learning in that it involves a change in behavior (loss of responsiveness to a stimulus) as a result of experience (repeated presentations of the CS). However, one may wonder what is actually learned. One obvious answer is that extinction does not involve the learning of something new but, rather, just the unlearning of the previously conditioned response tendency. According to this view, the gradual decline in the conditioned response in extinction simply reflects

the loss of whatever was learned earlier. Rather than adopt this view of extinction, Pavlov (1927) suggested that during extinction animals learn to actively inhibit making the conditioned response in the presence of the CS. According to this interpretation, extinction of a conditioned response does not involve any loss of the original learning but, rather, the learning of a new antagonistic, or inhibitory, response tendency. This conditioned inhibition then prevents the appearance of the conditioned response.

The primary evidence for the conditioned inhibition interpretation of extinction was provided by the phenomenon of disinhibition. Pavlov reasoned that if extinction involved learning to inhibit the conditioned response to the CS, then the response should recover if this inhibition was disrupted by some treatment. Presentation of a novel stimulus presumably disrupts the inhibition, thereby producing the recovery of the conditioned response in the disinhibition phenomenon.

The phenomenon of disinhibition provides some support for the idea that extinction involves the conditioning of inhibition to the CS. Extinction, however, does not appear to involve the same type of inhibition that animals learn from a negative contingency between CS and US (Rescorla, 1969b). As noted above, evidence of conditioned inhibition resulting from negative CS-US contingencies can be provided in three ways. One possibility is that responses elicited by the inhibitory CS will be opposite to those elicited by an excitatory conditioned stimulus in bidirectional response systems. Other types of evidence are provided by a retardation of excitatory conditioning with the inhibitory CS and attenuation of the conditioned responses elicited by excitatory conditioned stimuli in compound tests. According to each of these three types of evidence, an extinguished CS is not inhibitory. Extinguished conditioned stimuli have not been observed to elicit responses opposite to those elicited by excitatory conditioned stimuli in bidirectional response systems. In fact, after extinction the CS is not likely to elicit any change in behavior from the baseline conditions. An extinguished conditioned stimulus is also no more difficult to condition than a novel stimulus. Indeed, the opposite result is usually observed: conditioning proceeds more rapidly with previously extinguished conditioned stimuli than with novel stimuli (Konorski & Szwejkowska, 1950, 1952). Finally, an extinguished stimulus does not inhibit the conditioned responses elicited by an effective conditioned stimulus in a compound test. Rather, it is not unusual to observe some facilitation of responding when the extinguished CS is presented together with an effective CS (Reberg, 1972).

The evidence summarized above indicates that extinction does not produce the same kind of inhibition of behavior that is learned in conditioned inhibition procedures. Evidently extinction procedures produce suppression of behavior through some other type of response-inhibiting mechanism. The precise nature of that mechanism is not yet understood (see Bouton & Bolles, 1985, for one proposal). However, extinction clearly does not involve the unlearning of a conditioned response and the return of the subject to its previously naive state.

Applications of Classical Conditioning

Classical conditioning is typically investigated in contrived laboratory situations. However, one does not have to know much about classical conditioning to realize that it often occurs outside the laboratory and is applicable to a wide range of situations. Classical conditioning is most likely to develop when one event reliably precedes another in a short-delayed CS-US pairing or in situations with a strong contingency. These conditions are met in many aspects of life. As we mentioned at the beginning of the chapter, stimuli in the environment occur in an orderly temporal sequence. One reason is the physical constraints of causation: some events simply cannot happen before other events have taken place. Social institutions and customs are also usually arranged to make things happen in a predictable order. Because of these factors, in many situations certain stimuli reliably precede others, and whenever that is the case, classical conditioning may take place.

We will describe a variety of examples and applications of classical conditioning in concluding the present chapter. Paying tribute to Pavlov's background as a physiologist, we will begin with several illustrations of the role of classical conditioning in the control of physiological processes. We will then describe some interesting examples of classical conditioning in human behavior.

Digestion

One clear example of a temporal sequence of events necessitated by the physical arrangement of causes and effects is the digestive system. Food does not enter the mouth until the subject has seen it, approached it, smelled it, and put it in the mouth. Food is not swallowed until it is chewed, and it does not appear in the stomach until it has been swallowed. Similarly, it does not enter the small intestine until it has been in the stomach, and it does not enter the large intestine until it has been in the small intestine. This sequence of events makes the digestive system a prime candidate for the involvement of classical conditioning.

Although not all the conditioning processes involved in digestion have been experimentally verified, it is not difficult to speculate about the role of classical conditioning in digestion. We know that different types of food require secretion of different combinations of digestive juices into the alimentary canal. It takes certain combinations and amounts of stomach and intestinal secretions to digest a large, tasty steak, and it takes other combinations and amounts to digest scrambled eggs. Because food always passes through the alimentary canal in the same sequence (mouth to stomach to small intestine to large intestine), one may speculate that the stimuli involved in one stage of the process become signals for where the food will be and what will happen in the next stage. In this way, the relevant digestive juices can be secreted in each part of the alimentary tract in anticipation of the arrival of food there. Thus, the stomach can begin to secrete the relevant digestive materials when the food is in the mouth or when the subject first smells the food. Similarly, the small intestine can become prepared for the arrival of food on the basis of the stimuli provided by food in the mouth and stomach. If such anticipatory secretions occurred (and there is no reason to believe they do not), they would substantially speed up the digestive process.

One example of a digestive conditioned response that has been investigated is the release of insulin in response to sweet tastes. Insulin is involved in the digestion of sugars. It is released by the pancreas as an unconditioned response to the presence of sugar in the digestive tract. The presence of sugar in the stomach and small intestine is always preceded by the taste of sugar in the mouth. Therefore, the taste of sugar can become conditioned to stimulate the release of insulin as an anticipatory conditioned response. After such conditioning, insulin may also be released as an anticipatory response when subjects taste artificial sweeteners, such as saccharin. If a real sugar is ingested (sucrose or glucose, for example), the released insulin is used up in the digestion of the sugar. However, if the subject ingests only saccharin, the released insulin is not used up, because there is no sugar to digest. Therefore, ingestion of saccharin results in excessive amounts of circulating insulin. This causes a drop in blood sugar level and is responsible for the "heady" feeling people sometimes get after having a diet drink on an empty stomach. Interestingly, the drop in blood sugar level elicited as a conditioned response by the taste of sweets can become extinguished if the subject receives extensive exposure to an artificial sweetener (Deutsch, 1974). Because insulin is not required for the digestion of saccharin, the release of insulin following ingestion of saccharin becomes extinguished with extensive exposure to saccharin.

Control of pain sensitivity

A second physiological system that can be influenced by classical conditioning is the neural mechanisms involved in pain perception. In Chapter 4 we will describe results of classical conditioning experiments in which painkilling drugs such as morphine are used as unconditioned stimuli. Pain sensitivity can also be reduced by exposure to stressful or painful events. The brain contains its own painkiller substances, called "endorphins," which are released by exposure to stress (for example, Willer, Dehen, & Cambier, 1981). Interestingly, the release of these

endogenous, or internal, painkillers can be classically conditioned to stimuli that signal presentation of an aversive stimulus. Fanselow and Baackes (1982), for example, administered shock to rats in a distinctive chamber and then measured conditioned fear (as indexed by the rats' becoming motionless) and pain sensitivity when the rats were exposed to this environment again. Exposure to the shock-conditioned stimuli elicited both fear and reduced pain sensitivity. Such results were not obtained when the rats were exposed to stimuli that had not been conditioned with shock. Subsequent research indicated that the reduction of pain sensitivity stimulated by exposure to a fear-conditioned stimulus was probably caused by the same neurophysiological processes that are activated by an injection of morphine (see also Chance, 1980; MacLennan, Jackson, & Maier, 1980; Oliverio & Castellano, 1982).

Suppression of the immune system

The immune system is involved in mobilizing physiological defenses against germs and other foreign substances that sometimes enter the body so that these substances do not cause disease. Traditionally, the immune system has been regarded as independent of the nervous system. That is, the production and release of antibodies were assumed to be the result of chemical and hormonal reactions, not neural activity. This view of the immune system as autonomous of the nervous system is being challenged by recent research indicating that the presentation of a conditioned stimulus can influence the immune system. Since conditioned stimuli act through the nervous system, these results suggest that the immune system is subject to neural control.

Research on conditioned modifications of the immune system developed from work on taste-aversion conditioning. As we noted earlier, taste aversions are conditioned by exposing animals to a novel taste, followed by an aversive experience. Injection of a wide variety of drugs can provide the aversive experience (Gamzu, 1985). One drug that is particularly effective in producing conditioned taste aversions in rats is cyclophosphamide. An important physiological effect of cyclophosphamide is that it suppresses the immune system, making subjects more prone to disease by interfering with the production of antibodies. In an elegant series of experiments, Robert Ader and his associates have shown that this suppression of the immune system can also be elicited as a conditioned response to a taste stimulus previously conditioned with cyclophosphamide (see Ader, 1985, for a review). In one experiment (Ader, Cohen, & Bovbjerg, 1982), for example, rats were first permitted to drink a novel saccharin solution and then injected with cyclophosphamide. Several days later, the animals were injected with a foreign tissue (blood cells from sheep), and the production of antibodies was measured in response to the introduction of these "germs." If the rats were reexposed to the saccharin conditioned stimulus, their immune response to the foreign tissue was suppressed. The conditioned stimulus suppressed the production of antibodies to combat the foreign blood cells. Other research demonstrated that such conditioned immunosuppression effects could be extinguished using the usual Pavlovian extinction procedure of repeatedly presenting the flavor CS by itself without the drug US (Bovbjerg, Ader, & Cohen, 1984). (For another interesting application of conditioned immunosuppression, see Ader & Cohen, 1982.)

Human food aversions

Taste-aversion and taste-preference learning as examples of Pavlovian conditioning have been extensively investigated in various animal species (see Riley & Tuck, 1985). A growing body of evidence indicates that many human taste aversions are also the result of Pavlovian conditioning. Much of the evidence of human taste-aversion learning has been provided by the results of questionnaire surveys (Garb & Stunkard, 1974; Logue, Ophir, & Strauss, 1981; Logue, 1985). Many people report having acquired at least one food aversion during their lives. Interestingly, the reported circumstances of food-aversion learning in people are often comparable to circumstances that have been shown to facilitate aversion learning in animals. For example, the aversions are more likely to have resulted from a forward pairing of the food with subsequent illness than from simultaneous or backward pairings. As in the animal experiments, the aversions are often learned in one trial, and learning can occur even if illness is delayed several hours after ingestion of the food. Another interesting aspect of the results is that in a sizable proportion of instances (21%) the subjects were certain that their illness was not caused by the food they ate. Nevertheless, they learned an aversion to the food. This finding indicates that food-aversion learning in people can be independent of rational thought processes and can go against a person's conclusions about the causes of his illness. (For a recent experimental demonstration of flavor-aversion learning in humans, see Cannon, Best, Batson, & Feldman, 1983.)

The fact that food aversions can be acquired to novel foods eaten prior to illness even if the illness is not caused by the food can create serious problems. One common form of treatment of cancer is chemotherapy, which involves taking strong doses of debilitating drugs. Chemotherapy procedures often cause nausea as a side effect. This raises the possibility that chemotherapy procedures might condition aversions to food ingested before a therapy session even though the patients realize that their illness is not caused by the food. Recent research indicates that this indeed happens. Both child and adult cancer patients have been shown to acquire aversions to a particular flavor of ice cream when this flavor was ingested before a chemotherapy session (Bernstein, 1978; Bernstein & Webster, 1980). These results suggest an explanation for the lack of appetite commonly found among chemotherapy patients. The lack of appetite, or anorexia, may reflect aversions learned to foods eaten before therapy sessions. This Pavlovian conditioning analysis suggests that some of the anorexia may be prevented by changing the schedule of meals relative to therapy sessions and by using foods that are highly familiar and bland so that they are not likely to become associated with subsequent illness (see Chapter 4).

Alcohol-aversion therapy

As research on taste-aversion learning indicates, people can acquire strong aversions to the flavor of a particular food if that flavor is paired with subsequent illness. Such aversion learning can be problematic, as in chemotherapy patients. Aversion conditioning can also be beneficial. One important therapeutic application of aversion conditioning is alcohol-aversion therapy. Conditioned aversion treatment of alcoholism became available in 1935 in Shadel Hospital in Seattle, Washington (see Lemere & Voegtlin, 1950). However, not until the last ten years has the procedure come to be widely used (see Elkins, 1975, for a review).

The basic procedure for alcohol-aversion therapy is to pair the taste and smell of alcohol with nausea. The nausea is caused by an injection of a drug (usually emetine). Just before the onset of nausea, the patient is asked to smell and taste various alcoholic beverages. In a typical procedure, five conditioning trials are conducted, with one day of rest separating successive treatments. The client is asked to return for a booster conditioning trial 2–3 weeks after the initial trials. Further trials are periodically conducted during the next year as required by the client's progress.

Aversion conditioning has been remarkably successful in the treatment of excessive alcohol ingestion, but it does not work for everyone seeking help. Lemere and Voegtlin (1950) reported that 60.5% of patients remained abstinent for 1 year and 38.5% remained abstinent for 5 years or more. In a more recent evaluation (Wiens & Menustik, 1983), 63% were found to remain abstinent for a year and about a third for 3 years. Males and females respond equally well to treatment, and success does not depend on educational level, employment status, type of employment, or prior history of treatment for alcoholism. However, older male patients are more likely to show improvement than younger male patients, and married males respond to treatment better than single males. (For experimental studies of alcohol-aversion therapy, see, for example, Boland, Mellor, & Revusky, 1978; Cannon & Baker, 1981.)

Emotional behavior

One area of interest in which classical conditioning has had a prominent role is the study of emotional behavior. In fact, for some time classical conditioning was considered to be exclusively involved in the learning of glandular and emotional responses. Recent research on phenomena such as sign tracking has broadened our conceptions of classical conditioning. Nevertheless, the idea that classical conditioning is important in emotional behavior has persisted. If you have a good time with someone, the sight of that person or the sound of his voice may come to elicit pleasant emotional reactions. If you are bitten by a dog, the sight or sound of dogs may come to elicit fear and unpleasant emotions.

The principles of classical conditioning have laid the foundation for much of clinical research on problematic emotional responses. Classical conditioning has had a fundamental role in two aspects of the psychopathology of emotions. First, classical conditioning is often assumed to be the underlying process responsible for acquisition of pathological fears, phobias, and hostilities. Second, it is often used as a basis for the development of treatment procedures. If problematic fears and phobias are indeed conditioned responses, then we should be able to apply learning principles to modify them. (For more detailed discussions of the role of classical conditioning in psychopathology, see Levine & Sandeen, 1985; O'Leary & Wilson, 1975.)

Classical conditioning and the development of phobias.   A phobia is an intense fear for which, generally, there is no rational basis. A person may experience intense fear on seeing a caged snake. No real danger exists, but the sensation of fear may be as intense as in a truly threatening situation. Such irrational fear can be extremely debilitating. Some people are so fearful of leaving their homes (agoraphobia), for example, that they remain housebound for years.

In 1920 Watson and Raynor showed that an "irrational" fear, or phobia, could be conditioned in an 11-month-old child, known as Little Albert. They paired a loud noise with the presentation of a white rat. Initially, only the loud noise elicited fear and crying in Little Albert. After seven pairings, Little Albert also appeared fearful at the sight of the rat. Since that simple demonstration, many researchers have been interested in documenting the role of classical conditioning in the development of phobias (see Emmelkamp, 1982a, for a review). Several investigators have tried to condition fears in much the same way as Watson and Raynor did but have had mixed success. For obvious reasons, this has not been a very popular experimental method. Few undergraduates tend to volunteer to become phobic!

A second approach that has been used to study the role of classical conditioning in phobias is to examine the backgrounds of people who have phobias for evidence of an incident favoring classical conditioning. The results of this type of research have also been mixed. Often an event can be identified that appears to have precipitated the phobia. Levine and Sandeen (1985), for example, describe a man who acquired an intense fear of high places. His job required that he work on beams high off the ground. His phobia interfered with his work and also prevented him from taking vacations because he was afraid to cross bridges or fly in airplanes. The man's phobia appeared to have resulted from an accident in which he almost fell off a high beam. He was able to climb back on the beam but only after he had hung about 100 feet above the ground. In another study, Goldstein and Chambless (1978) examined 36 phobic subjects and found that their phobias could be traced to an identifiable event favoring classical conditioning in only 17 cases. Thus, in many instances conditioning experiences related to a phobia cannot be identified. However, as we shall see, this does not necessarily mean that classical conditioning is unimportant in these cases.

A third approach to examining the role of classical conditioning in the acquisition of phobias is to investigate real-life situations in which fears or phobias might develop. Lewis (1942), for example, studied the incidence of neurotic illnesses after air raids in England. In another study, Parker (1977) looked for storm phobias among people who had experienced a cyclone disaster. Such studies indicate that a traumatic event is not sufficient for the acquisition of a phobia. By and large, the majority of individuals in these traumatic-event studies did not develop debilitating phobias.

The research described so far has provided equivocal evidence of the role of classical conditioning in the acquisition of phobias. In some instances, classical conditioning has been strongly implicated. However, not all instances of phobia could be traced to a conditioning experience, and not all traumatic events led to the acquisition of phobias. These results, by and large, are not surprising given the nature of classical conditioning and the problems of collecting reliable information from phobic patients. As we will see in Chapter 4, not all stimuli paired with a US come to elicit the conditioned response. Many other factors also govern classical conditioning. In Chapter 4 we will describe some such factors that have been identified in animal research. Research with human subjects has identified several other factors important for the acquisition of phobias. Hugdahl, Fredrickson, and Ohman (1977) suggested that individuals with high overall arousal are more likely to develop phobias than those with lower arousal levels. Other researchers have proposed that susceptibility to phobias is related to cognitive factors. That is, certain individuals become phobic because of the way they interpret events in their environment (see Ellis, 1962; Galassi, Frierson, & Sharer, 1981). These considerations suggest that the development of phobias is a multifaceted phenomenon (Mineka, in press).

Another major problem in documenting classical conditioning effects is that phobic individuals sometimes have great difficulty remembering the important events. The man with a fear of heights we described did not recall his very frightening accident until he was well into therapy. The incident was repressed, so that the man was unable to discuss it openly until some of his anxiety had been relieved. Several recent studies have documented similar crippling effects of trauma. Resick (1983) describes research with rape victims. Rape victims frequently become fearful of being alone, of darkness, of strange men, and of specific stimuli such as an odor or a colored shirt associated with their assault. Studies of rape victims document severe traumatic effects involving many facets of emotional and social behavior over a period of months and sometimes years. Initially, the terror and depression can be so strong that therapy may be ineffective in bringing relief. Only after several months do anxiety management therapies prove helpful. Kidd and Chayet (1984) have suggested that this emotional crippling may be a factor in the failure of women to report assaults to the authorities. To what extent this type of repression of a traumatic incident is a problem for studies looking for classical conditioning as a cause of phobia is difficult to determine.

Behavior therapy for fears and anxiety. We previously described one therapeutic application of classical conditioning, alcohol-aversion therapy. In alcohol-aversion therapy, the goal is to condition a negative response to alcohol. In the procedures we will describe here, the goal is to eliminate or at least reduce emotional responses of anxiety or fear. If a particular conditioned stimulus elicits an intense fear response, a conceptually simple approach to reducing this response would be to extinguish the CS. This idea underlies **flooding** therapy. Flooding basically requires that the phobic individual be exposed to the fear-eliciting stimulus in the absence of any danger. If the individual is safely exposed to the stimulus for an extended period, extinction should occur. An individual who is afraid of heights, for example, may be led onto a bridge and required to remain there for a while. In a variant of the flooding procedure, the individual is exposed to the fear stimuli gradually. An agoraphobic (a person who is afraid to leave her house), for example, may at first just stand outside the front door. Next she may venture out to the sidewalk and later down the street. A final phase of the procedure might involve having the client visit a crowded public place, like a circus.

A second technique for reducing fear and anxiety, **systematic desensitization,** is probably the most prominent behavior-therapy procedure developed. The method was originally conceived by its founder, Joseph Wolpe, as an instance of counterconditioning, a form of conditioning we will describe in Chapter 4. Basically, the idea is to condition responses to fear-eliciting stimuli that are incompatible with fear. Typically, these are relaxation responses. The client is first trained to relax. When he is able to relax easily at will, the fear-eliciting stimuli are presented in a hierarchical fashion. Stimuli that only slightly elicit fear are presented first and repeated until the client remains completely relaxed in their presence.

For example, to desensitize a person of a snake phobia, a stylized picture of a snake from a child's picture book may be presented first. A more realistic picture may be presented next. Then the size and vividness of the snakes may be increased. After the person has learned to relax in the presence of these stimuli, a real snake may be presented.

Systematic desensitization and flooding are typically conducted using imagined rather than actual environmental stimuli. That is, the client is asked to imagine the various fear-eliciting stimuli while remaining relaxed. Desensitization and flooding with real-life stimuli, or *in vivo,* as this is called, frequently present logistic problems. If the procedures are performed with imagined stimuli, the therapist and client do not have to visit zoos, bridges, tall buildings, and so forth. Although imagined stimuli can be used with considerable success, recent research shows that *in vivo* procedures are far more effective (see, for example, Emmelkamp & Wessels, 1975; Sherman, 1972).

Systematic desensitization and flooding have been found extremely useful in treating anxiety and fear. Systematic desensitization is perhaps the most extensively investigated psychotherapeutic procedure in current clinical use. Research indicates that the success of desensitization and flooding is due to specific components of the procedures, not to some general therapeutic effect (see Rachman & Wilson, 1980). Why the procedures are effective, however, is not fully understood. For example, some have questioned that systematic desensitization in fact involves the conditioning of relaxation responses to fear-eliciting stimuli and have suggested that the therapeutic outcome is a result of simple extinction of fear (see Emmelkamp, 1982a, for a more detailed discussion). Nevertheless, systematic desensitization and flooding are important therapeutic procedures that were inspired by the classical conditioning paradigm.

Concluding Comments

As we have seen, classical conditioning processes are involved in a wide variety of important aspects of behavior. Depending on the procedure used, the learning may occur quickly or slowly. With some procedures, excitatory response tendencies are learned, whereas with other procedures subjects learn to inhibit a particular response in the presence of the conditioned stimulus. Both types of learning involve the signal relation between the conditioned and unconditioned stimuli. Organisms can learn that a CS signals the impending presentation of the US or the absence of the US for a while. Finally, if the CS is repeatedly presented without the US after conditioning, it will become extinguished and lose most of its response-evoking properties.

CHAPTER 4
Classical Conditioning: Mechanisms

Chapter 4 is devoted to describing in greater detail the factors that influence the formation of an association between two stimuli. The discussion is organized in three parts. First, we will describe what makes environmental events effective as conditioned and unconditioned stimuli. Then we will discuss what determines the nature of the responses that become conditioned in classical conditioning. The third and final section will describe mechanisms involved in the formation of associations between conditioned and unconditioned stimuli.

What Makes Effective Conditioned and Unconditioned Stimuli?

Perhaps the most basic question to ask about classical conditioning is what makes some stimuli effective as conditioned stimuli and what makes others effective as unconditioned stimuli. Traditionally, Western investigators have been concerned mainly with how classical conditioning is influenced by various temporal arrangements and signal relations between conditioned and unconditioned stimuli. The issue of what makes stimuli effective as CSs and USs was originally addressed by Pavlov and is also increasingly attracting the attention of contemporary researchers.

Initial response to the stimuli

Pavlov provided a partial answer to the question of what makes effective conditioned and unconditioned stimuli in his definitions of the terms *conditioned* and *unconditioned*. According to these definitions, the conditioned stimulus is one that does not elicit the conditioned response initially but begins to do so with training. In contrast, the unconditioned stimulus is one that is effective in eliciting that response without any special training experiences. It is important to note that these definitions are stated in terms of the elicitation of a particular response, the one to be conditioned. The conditioned stimulus is usually not entirely ineffective before conditioning. It elicits orientation and perhaps other responses as well. However, initially it does not elicit the response to be conditioned.

Because Pavlov defined conditioned and unconditioned stimuli in terms of the elicitation of a particular response, identifying potential CSs and USs involves comparing the responses elicited by each before conditioning. Such a comparison makes the identification of CSs and USs a relative matter. A particular stimulus may serve as a CS relative to some stimuli and as a US relative to other stimuli. Consider, for example, a palatable saccharin solution for thirsty rats. This stimulus may serve as a *conditioned* stimulus in a taste-aversion experiment with illness serving as the US. In this case, conditioning trials would consist of exposure to the saccharin flavor followed by injection of a drug that induces malaise, and animals would learn to stop drinking the saccharin solution. A palatable saccharin solution may also serve as an *unconditioned* stimulus, in a sign-tracking experiment, for example. The conditioning trials in this case might involve the illumination of a light just before each presentation of a small amount of saccharin. After a number of trials of this sort, the animals would begin to approach the light CS. Thus, whether the saccharin solution is considered a US or a CS depends on its relation to other stimuli in the situation. In the sign-tracking experiment, the saccharin solution serves as the US because it elicits the response in question (approach) without conditioning. In the taste-aversion experiment, the saccharin solution serves as the CS because it elicits the conditioned response (withdrawal or aversion) only after pairings with sickness.

Novelty of conditioned and unconditioned stimuli

Whether a stimulus elicits the response of interest at the start of conditioning is only one of several factors that determine the effectiveness of conditioned and unconditioned stimuli. As we saw in studies of habituation, the behavioral impact of a stimulus is very much dependent on its novelty. Highly familiar stimuli often do not elicit as vigorous reactions as novel stimuli do. Novelty is also very important in classical conditioning. If either the conditioned or the unconditioned stimulus is highly familiar, Pavlovian conditioning proceeds much more slowly than if the CS and US are novel.

Investigations of the role of novelty in classical conditioning are usually conducted in two phases. In experiments that address the issue of CS novelty, for example, animals are first given repeated exposure to the stimulus that is later to be used as the CS. During this initial phase of the experiment, the CS-to-be is always presented by itself. After this stimulus familiarization, the CS is paired with an unconditioned stimulus using conventional classical conditioning procedures. Animals that have received preconditioning exposures to the CS are usually slower to learn the conditioned response than animals for which the CS is novel. This phenomenon is called the **CS preexposure** or **latent inhibition effect** (Lubow & Moore, 1959). Experiments that address the issue of US novelty are conducted in a manner similar to the CS preexposure experiments. In the first phase of the study, animals are given repeated exposures to the unconditioned stimulus presented alone. The US is then paired with a conditioned stimulus, and the progress of learning is monitored. Animals familiarized with an unconditioned stimulus are slower to associate the US with a conditioned stimulus than animals for which the US is novel during classical conditioning. This result is called the **US preexposure effect** (Baker, Singh, & Bindra, 1985; Randich & LoLordo, 1979; Randich & Ross, 1985).

The mechanisms of CS and US preexposure effects have been the subject of extensive research and debate. Although several mechanisms have been proposed, two are especially prominent. One focuses on the fact that during preexposure subjects are repeatedly exposed to the CS or the US in the presence of particular background cues (cues of the experimental chamber, for example). The hypothesis assumes that presentations of the CS or the US in a particular situation result in the learning of an association between the CS or US and the background cues of that situation. This association is then assumed to interfere with the subsequent learning of an association between the CS and the US (for example, Wagner, 1976). Thus, this first mechanism attributes the CS and US preexposure effects to the learning of interfering associations during preexposure. The second mechanism focuses on the fact that preexposure to the CS or US involves repeatedly presenting this stimulus by itself. Because the preexposed stimulus is presented by itself, subjects are assumed to learn that the CS or US is not related to anything of significance. This learning of irrelevance is then assumed to disrupt subsequent learning that the CS signals the US (for example, Baker & Mackintosh, 1977). Evidence in support of both the associative interference and learned irrelevance accounts of CS and US preexposure effects has been obtained, suggesting that both processes are involved (for example, Baker & Mercier, 1982; Baker, Mercier, Gabel, & Baker,

1981; Channell & Hall, 1983; Hinson, 1982; Randich, 1981).

CS and US intensity

Another important stimulus variable for classical conditioning is the intensity of the conditioned and unconditioned stimuli. Most biological and physiological effects of stimulation are directly related to the intensity of the stimulus input. This is also true for conditioning. The association of a CS with a US occurs more rapidly, and the final amount of conditioning achieved is greater, when more intense stimuli are used (for example, Kamin & Brimer, 1963; Kamin & Schaub, 1963). This relation is observed over a broad range of stimulus intensities. However, if the CS or US intensity is too high, conditioning may be disrupted, probably because very intense stimuli elicit strong unconditioned reactions that may make it difficult for the animal to engage in the conditioned response. Experiments on classical conditioning rarely involve such extreme CS and US intensities.

The fact that conditioning is facilitated by increasing the intensity of the CS and US may be related to the novelty of the conditioned and unconditioned stimuli. Animals and people rarely encounter stimuli that are very intense. Therefore, high-intensity conditioned and unconditioned stimuli may be more novel than lower-intensity stimulation. Novelty may be at least partly responsible for the stimulus-intensity effects in classical conditioning (see Kalat, 1974).

CS/US relevance, or belongingness

We noted earlier that whether a stimulus can serve as a CS is often relative to what stimulus serves as the US and vice versa. The relation we discussed earlier involved initial responses to the CS and US. Another relation that governs the rate of classical conditioning is the relevance, or belongingness, between the CS and US. It seems that certain conditioned stimuli are more easily associated with certain types of unconditioned stimuli, whereas other types of CSs are more easily associated with other USs. Apparently, some CSs are more relevant to, or belong better with, certain USs.

Stimulus relevance in aversion conditioning.
The phenomenon of CS/US relevance was first clearly demonstrated by Garcia and Koelling (1966) in one of the classic experiments in conditioning. They used two types of CSs (tastes and audiovisual cues) and two types of USs (shock and sickness). The experiment, diagramed in Figure 4.1, involved having rats drink from a drinking tube before administration of one of the unconditioned stimuli. The drinking tube was filled with water flavored either salty or sweet. In addition, each lick on the tube activated a brief audiovisual stimulus (the click of a relay and a flash of light). Thus, the conditioned stimulus was complex, involving both taste and audiovisual components. After exposure to this complex CS, the animals either received shock through the grid floor or were made sick with radiation exposure or drug injections.

Because all the unconditioned stimuli used were aversive, it was expected that the animals would learn some kind of aversion. The experimenters measured the response of the animals to the taste and audiovisual stimuli separately after conditioning. During tests of response to the taste CS, the water was flavored as before, but now licks did not activate the audiovisual stimulus. During tests of response to the audiovisual CS, the water was unflavored, and the audiovisual stimulus was briefly turned on whenever the animal drank. The degree of conditioned aversion to the taste or audiovisual CS was inferred from the amount of suppression of drinking.

The results of the experiment are summarized in Figure 4.2. Before this experiment was performed, there was no reason to expect that one of the unconditioned stimuli would be more effective than the other in conditioning an aversion to one aspect of the conditioned-stimulus complex. However, that is precisely what happened. Animals conditioned with shock subsequently suppressed their drinking much more when tested with the audiovisual stimulus than when tested with the taste CS. The opposite result occurred when animals were conditioned with sickness. These rats suppressed their drinking much more when the taste CS was present than when drinking produced the audiovisual stimulus. Thus, stronger aversions were conditioned to audiovisual cues than to taste cues when the US was shock, and stronger aversions were conditioned to tastes than to audiovisual cues when the US was internal malaise.

Garcia and Koelling's experiment demonstrates the principle of CS/US relevance, or belongingness. Conditioning in this experiment was governed only by the combination of the CS and US involved in the association. The audiovisual CS, for example, was not generally more effective than the taste CS. Rather, the audiovisual CS was more effective only when shock served as the US. Correspondingly, the shock US was not generally more effective than the

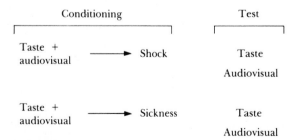

FIGURE 4.1. Diagram of Garcia and Koelling's (1966) experiment. A compound taste/audiovisual stimulus was first paired with either shock or sickness. The subjects were then tested with the taste and audiovisual stimuli separately.

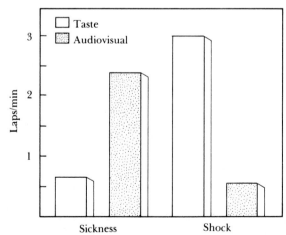

FIGURE 4.2. Results of Garcia and Koelling's (1966) experiment. Rats conditioned with sickness learned a stronger aversion to taste than to audiovisual cues. In contrast, rats conditioned with shock learned a stronger aversion to audiovisual than to taste cues.

sickness US. Rather, shock conditioned stronger aversions than sickness only when the audiovisual cue served as the CS. The only way to explain the results Garcia and Koelling observed is to acknowledge that certain combinations of conditioned and unconditioned stimuli (tastes with illness, audiovisual cues with shock) are more easily associated than other combinations (tastes with shock, audiovisual cues with illness).

The CS/US relevance effect demonstrated by Garcia and Koelling has since been observed in numerous experiments (see Domjan, 1983, for a recent review). Some have suggested that the effect occurs only when subjects receive exposure to the taste and the audiovisual stimuli simultaneously before the US during conditioning trials. However, the phenomenon is apparent even if the animals are exposed to only one or the other CS, not both, during conditioning (for example, Domjan & Wilson, 1972). The phenomenon also occurs in rats 1 day after birth

(Gemberling & Domjan, 1982). This last finding indicates that extensive experience with tastes, sickness, audiovisual cues, and peripheral pain is not necessary for the stimulus relevance effect. Rather, the phenomenon appears to reflect a genetic predisposition for the selective association of certain combinations of CSs and USs.

The stimulus relevance relation observed by Garcia and Koelling is also evident in human behavior. Surveys of the conditions under which people learn food aversions indicate that they usually learn such aversions as a result of illness, not as a result of accidents like breaking an arm or scraping a knee. Furthermore, illness is much more likely to condition aversions to foods than to nonfood stimuli such as the location where the food was eaten (Garb & Stunkard, 1974; Logue et al., 1981).

It is important to note that the CS/US relevance principle identified by Garcia and Koelling does not mean that associations between CSs and USs that are

---

BOX 4.1. Stimulus relevance and the modification of cigarette smoking

To quit smoking is a difficult task for habitual smokers. Cigarette smoking has been notoriously resistant to modification. Attempts to condition aversions to smoking stimuli with various aversive agents have not yielded particularly good results. An exception is a procedure developed by Lichtenstein and his associates (Schmahl, Lichtenstein, & Harris, 1972). The procedure is consistent with the principle of stimulus relevance in that it takes advantage of natural aversive consequences of smoking to condition an aversion. The smoker is asked to smoke rapidly and excessively until smoking becomes physically unpleasant. He is instructed to puff and inhale once every 6 seconds until another puff on the cigarette would cause vomiting, dizziness, and choking. Given that these unpleasant feelings result directly from smoking, one would expect rapid aversion conditioning to the taste of cigarette smoke (Erickson, Tiffany, Martin, & Baker, 1983). Some investigators have found up to a 60% success rate for abstinence 3 months after treatment (Bernstein & McAlister, 1976; Lichtenstein & Danaher, 1976). Although not perfect, the results are encouraging.

Erickson et al. (1983) found that success in therapy was at least partly determined by the degree of malaise (US intensity) produced. They compared the effects of rapid smoking and rapid puffing (without inhaling). Puffing produces less malaise than smoking but still maintains the same smoke-in-mouth CS. Rapid smoking was more successful in conditioning an aversion. Furthermore, the outcome of the therapy was correlated with the subjects' ratings of the malaise.

The aversive physical reactions caused by excessive and rapid smoking are probably due to a mild form of nicotine poisoning, which might be hazardous. At present there are no known problems with using the procedure, over and above the usual hazards of normal cigarette smoking. Nevertheless, the procedure should not be undertaken without the approval of one's physician.

not relevant to each other are impossible. The Garcia/Koelling experiment and similar studies do not purport to show that rats cannot learn aversions to tastes paired with shock or to exteroceptive cues paired with sickness. In fact, both these types of associations have been demonstrated (for example, Best, Best, & Henggeler, 1977; Krane & Wagner, 1975; but see Hankins, Rusiniak, & Garcia, 1976). Rather, stimulus relevance rests on the demonstration that associations are learned *more easily* between the CSs and USs that are relevant to each other than between other combinations of CSs and USs.

Generality of stimulus relevance. For several years, the stimulus relevance effect described above was the only known instance of CS/US relevance in classical conditioning. Consequently, some theorists suggested that the relevance of tastes to toxicosis and of audiovisual cues to foot shock in rats is an adaptive specialization of learning (for example, Rozin & Kalat, 1971). However, recent research has uncovered other stimulus relevance relations. For example, LoLordo and his associates found that pigeons associate visual cues with food much more easily than they associate auditory cues with food. In contrast, if the conditioning situation involves shock, auditory cues are more effective as the CS than visual cues. Thus, visual cues are relevant to food and auditory cues are relevant to shock for pigeons (see LoLordo, Jacobs, & Foree, 1982; Shapiro, Jacobs, & LoLordo, 1980; Shapiro & LoLordo, 1982). Another interesting stimulus relevance relation involves excitatory versus inhibitory fear conditioning in rats. A tone is much more effective in excitatory conditioning than a visual CS, whereas a visual CS is much more effective in inhibitory conditioning than a tone (Jacobs & LoLordo, 1980; LoLordo & Jacobs, 1983).

Importance of CS/US similarity. Although there is no doubt that CS/US relevance is a major factor in classical conditioning, at present it is not known what makes a CS relevant to a US. One promising answer is that similarity in the time course of conditioned and unconditioned stimuli is important (Testa, 1974). This idea explains the results of the Garcia/Koelling experiment by assuming that tastes and illness have similar time courses, as do audiovisual cues and shock. Tastes are generally considered long-duration stimuli because even if presented briefly, they often leave a slow-fading aftertaste or trace. This is particularly true of certain tastes, such as garlic and onion. One often continues to feel the taste of fresh onions long after eating them. Malaise induced by radiation or drug treatment is also lengthy. The similarity in the length of taste and sickness experiences may be critical to their rapid association. The relevance between audiovisual cues and shock may be explained in comparable terms. Audiovisual cues are typically short-lasting and do not have long traces. The foot shock used in these experiments was also brief, and that is perhaps why audiovisual cues became rapidly associated with shock.

The CS/US similarity hypothesis has been difficult to test in aversion conditioning experiments because of difficulties in specifying and experimentally manipulating the time course of taste and illness stimuli. Although we are probably correct in assuming that tastes and sickness are both long-lasting, we do not know exactly how long they are in particular cases. Good evidence for the CS/US similarity hypothesis has been obtained in other conditioning situations (for example, Rescorla & Cunningham, 1979; Rescorla & Furrow, 1977; Rescorla & Gillan, 1980). However, the applicability of these results to stimulus relevance in aversion learning remains a subject for speculation.

The concept of biological strength

In all the examples of classical conditioning discussed so far, prior to conditioning the CS did not elicit as strong responses as the US. The familiar example of salivary conditioning is a good case in point. In this situation, the conditioned stimulus (a bell) initially elicits only orientation movements. In contrast, the US (food) elicits vigorous approach, ingestion, salivation, chewing, swallowing, and so on. Pavlov was aware of this large difference in the "biological strength" of conditioned and unconditioned stimuli before the start of training and considered the difference necessary for the selection of conditioned and unconditioned stimuli (Pavlov, 1927). Pavlov suggested that for a stimulus to become conditioned, it had to be a weaker biological stimulus than the unconditioned stimulus with which it was to be paired. By "weaker biological stimulus" he meant one that initially elicited fewer and weaker responses.

Higher-order conditioning. One implication of Pavlov's criteria for conditioned and unconditioned stimuli is that a stimulus may serve in the role of an unconditioned stimulus after it has become conditioned. Consider, for example, a tone that is repeatedly paired with food. After a sufficient number of trials, the tone will come to elicit salivation. Because of its association with food, the tone will also result in stronger biological reactions than novel tones or lights. It will elicit orientation movements and approach responses, and the animal will become generally aroused when the tone is presented. According to Pavlov, the tone should be effective in conditioning salivation to other stimuli that do not initially elicit salivation. Pairings of the previously conditioned tone with a novel light, for example, should gradually result in the conditioning of salivation to the light. This result is often observed and is called **higher-order conditioning.** Figure 4.3 diagrams the sequence of events that brings about higher-order conditioning.

As the term *higher-order conditioning* implies, conditioning may be considered to operate at different levels. In the example above, conditioning of the tone with food is considered first-order conditioning. Conditioning of the light with the previously conditioned tone is considered second-order conditioning. If the conditioned light were then used to condition yet another stimulus—say, an odor—that would be third-order conditioning. Although there is no doubt that second-order conditioning is a robust phenomenon (for example, Rescorla, 1980a), little research has been done to evaluate the mechanisms of third and higher orders of conditioning. However, even the existence of second-order conditioning is of considerable significance because it greatly increases the range of situations in which classical conditioning can take place. With higher-order conditioning, classical conditioning can occur without a primary unconditioned stimulus. The only requirement is that a previously conditioned stimulus be available.

Counterconditioning. Many instances of association learning, including higher-order conditioning, satisfy the criterion of differential biological strength. However, this criterion is not met in all situations that permit the learning of associations between stimuli. Two stimuli can become associated with each other even though initially they both elicit strong responses or are both of considerable biological strength. One situation in which this can occur is called **counterconditioning.** In counterconditioning the response an animal makes to one stimulus is reversed, or "countered," by associating this stimulus with a second one that elicits opposite reactions. For example, counterconditioning would be implicated if an animal is trained to approach a stimulus that initially elicits withdrawal. Some counterconditioning experiments have involved pairs of stimuli that are ordinarily considered unconditioned. Sexual-aversion conditioning is often of this type. If a male rat is presented with a receptive female and is then shocked, it may learn an aversion to the female. Although a new response is learned to the female, it is difficult to argue that this learning occurs because the biological strength of the shock is greater than the biological strength of the female rat. Both stimuli initially elicit very vigorous unconditioned responses. Furthermore, the responses elicited are very different (chasing, sniffing, and mounting for the female-rat stimulus and startle, jumping, and possibly aggression for the shock stimulus). Therefore, it is impossible to decide whether the initial responses to the

FIGURE 4.3. Procedure for higher-order conditioning. CS_1 is first paired with the US and comes to elicit the conditioned response. A new stimulus (CS_2) is then paired with CS_1 and also comes to elicit the conditioned response.

female rat are stronger (or weaker) than the responses to the shock.

Sensory preconditioning. Counterconditioning involves the learning of an association between two stimuli each of which elicits a vigorous response before conditioning. Associations can also be learned between two stimuli each of which elicits only a mild orienting response before conditioning. One situation in which this type of learning is often investigated is called **sensory preconditioning.** Figure 4.4 shows the sensory preconditioning procedure. Animals first receive repeated exposures of two biologically weak stimuli presented together. The stimuli may be two visual cues, the triangle presented close to a square, for example. No response conditioning is evident in this phase of training. Neither the triangle nor the square comes to elicit new responses. Response conditioning takes place in the second phase of the experiment, in which a triangle is now paired with an unconditioned stimulus, such as food. An approach response becomes conditioned to the triangle as a result of this conditioning with food. The significant finding is that once the triangle elicits sign tracking, the square also elicits this response because of its prior association with the triangle. Thus, the association of the two innocuous visual cues with each other becomes evident when one of the stimuli is conditioned to elicit a vigorous response.

Differential biological strength as an aid to measuring learning rather than producing it. The example of sensory preconditioning suggests that differential biological strength may be important in instances of association learning because it permits observing the effects of learning more easily—not because it actually facilitates the learning process. The phenomenon of sensory preconditioning indicates that organisms are fully capable of learning to associate two innocuous stimuli, CS_1 and CS_2, with each other. However, this learning is not directly evident. The association is behaviorally silent until

---

BOX 4.2. Counterconditioning and the pain of childbirth

Many expectant parents today are receiving training to deal with the discomforts of childbirth without the use of anesthesia. One popular technique was developed by a French physician, Dr. Lamaze, after observing the practice of Russian obstetricians. The Lamaze method, as it has come to be called, was developed by Russian physicians as an application of counterconditioning. Childbirth involves a series of uterine contractions that become stronger and stronger until the baby is born. Women in labor frequently become fearful, tense, and panicky in response to this increasing discomfort. The tension elicited by the contractions only makes the situation worse, by increasing the discomfort. The Lamaze training technique is intended to countercondition the contraction sensations so that they will elicit a new response that is incompatible with tension. The woman is first given relaxation training. She then learns a set of breathing patterns to perform at the onset of each contraction. These breathing patterns require a good deal of concentration, which distracts the woman from the discomfort and thereby inhibits tension. Thus, instead of eliciting tension, the labor contractions elicit a complicated breathing pattern.

Although the Lamaze technique was originally based on the concept of counterconditioning, it is not entirely clear that the mechanisms responsible for the pain reduction are really those of counterconditioning. The technique varies from standard laboratory procedures in that the training is done almost entirely with mock contractions. Little direct conditioning with a true labor contraction is done. However, whether or not Lamaze training is a valid example of counterconditioning, it illustrates how laboratory principles can lead to beneficial applications. Many women today deliver their babies with less discomfort than before and avoid painkilling drugs that may be harmful to the infant.

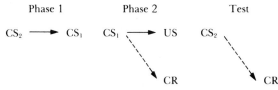

FIGURE 4.4. Procedure for sensory preconditioning. CS_2 is first paired with CS_1 without an unconditioned stimulus in the situation. CS_1 is then paired with a US and comes to elicit a conditioned response. In a later test session, CS_2 is also found to elicit the conditioned response, even though CS_2 was never paired with the US.

one of the stimuli (CS_1) is made to elicit a strong response—until one of the stimuli is made biologically strong, in Pavlov's terminology. The association can then be seen by a corresponding response being elicited by the second stimulus (CS_2).

The somewhat roundabout method used to give behavioral expression to a learned association in the sensory preconditioning procedure is not necessary in other procedures we have considered because in these other procedures cues are associated with stimuli that already elicit strong responses. In standard first-order conditioning (salivary conditioning, for example), an innocuous stimulus (CS) is associated with a biologically strong event (US); by virtue of this association, the CS comes to elicit a response corresponding to US. Higher-order conditioning is similar in that an initially "neutral" stimulus becomes associated with one that already elicits stronger responses. In counterconditioning, the associated stimulus is likewise biologically strong, so that associations with it result in an observable change in elicited behavior.

Differences in learning mechanism related to biological strength. The above discussion indicates that the biological strength of stimuli entering into an association is important for obtaining evidence of learning—for giving behavioral expression to a learned association. Is the biological strength of stimuli also important to the nature of the learning that takes place? This question has not been considered by many investigators. However, currently available evidence suggests that the answer is yes. Associations between two biologically weak stimuli (two visual cues, for example) appear to be learned

somewhat differently than associations between a weak and a strong stimulus (a tone and food, for example). We noted in Chapter 3, for instance, that in common Pavlovian conditioning procedures simultaneous presentation of the CS and US is not as effective in producing learning as presenting the US immediately after the CS. The reverse is true if the association is being formed between two biologically weak stimuli, as in a sensory preconditioning procedure. In this case, simultaneous conditioning is more effective than successive presentations of the stimuli to be associated. (For additional differences between conventional classical conditioning and learning of associations between two biologically weak stimuli, see Rescorla & Durlach, 1981.) Future research will have to define more precisely the conditions under which these "special" rules of learning apply.

What Determines the Nature of the Conditioned Response?

In the present and preceding chapters, we have described numerous examples of classical conditioning. In all of our discussion, conditioning was identified by the development of new responses to conditioned stimuli. We have described a large variety of responses that can become conditioned, including salivation, eye blinking, fear, locomotor approach and withdrawal, and aversion responses, as well as physiological processes involved in digestion, pain sensitivity, and immunological defense. However, we have not yet considered explicitly why one set of responses becomes conditioned in one situation and other responses become conditioned in other circumstances. What factors determine what responses are acquired during the course of classical conditioning? Several answers to this question have been suggested. We will describe some of the important models and discuss what evidence supports or contradicts each.

The stimulus substitution model

The oldest idea about what animals learn in classical conditioning is based on a model of conditioning proposed by Pavlov. As noted in Chapter 3, Pavlov was primarily a physiologist. Not unexpectedly, therefore, his model of conditioning has a decidedly physiological orientation. For purposes of theorizing, Pavlov viewed the brain as consisting of discrete neural centers (see Figure 4.5). He suggested that one brain center was primarily responsible for processing the unconditioned stimulus, and a different center was primarily responsible for processing the conditioned stimulus. A third brain center was assumed to be responsible for generating the unconditioned response. Because the unconditioned response occurred whenever the unconditioned stimulus was presented, Pavlov assumed that there was a neural connection between the neural center for the US and the neural center for the UR (see Figure 4.5). Furthermore, because the reaction to the US was not learned, the functional pathway between the US and UR centers was assumed to be innate (see Figure 4.5).

According to Pavlov's model, the learning of conditioned responses takes place through the establishment of new functional neural pathways. During the course of repeated pairings of the conditioned and unconditioned stimuli, a connection develops between the brain center for the CS and the brain center for the US. Presentation of the conditioned stimulus then results in excitation of the US neural center by way of this new neural pathway. Excitation of the US center in turn generates the unconditioned response because of the inborn connection between the US and UR

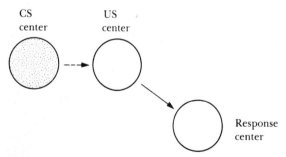

FIGURE 4.5. Diagram of Pavlov's stimulus substitution model. The solid arrow indicates an innate neural connection. The dashed arrow indicates a learned neural connection. The CS comes to elicit a response by activating the US center, which innately elicits the response.

centers. Therefore, conditioning enables the conditioned stimulus to elicit the unconditioned response. The response to the conditioned stimulus may not always be identical to the response to the unconditioned stimulus. Differences between the two may occur if, for example, the conditioned stimulus is not as intense as the unconditioned stimulus and therefore produces less excitation of the UR center. However, the Pavlovian model predicts that the general nature and form of the conditioned response will be similar to those of the unconditioned response. Because of the new functional pathway established between the CS center and the US center, the conditioned stimulus comes to have similar effects on the nervous system to the effects of the unconditioned stimulus. In a sense the CS becomes a surrogate US, a substitute for the US. That is why the model is called **stimulus substitution.**

The US as a determining factor for the CR. According to the stimulus substitution model, each unconditioned stimulus is assumed to have its own unique brain center, which is connected to a unique unconditioned response center. If conditioning turns a CS into a surrogate US, the model predicts that CSs conditioned with different USs will come to elicit different types of conditioned responses. This is obviously true. Animals learn to salivate when conditioned with food and to blink when conditioned with a puff of air to the eye. Salivation is not conditioned in eyeblink conditioning experiments, and eyeblink responses are not conditioned in salivary conditioning experiments.

The above comparison of salivary and eyeblink conditioning provides evidence that different unconditioned stimuli lead to different conditioned responses. The stimulus substitution model also predicts that the form of the conditioned response will be similar to the form of the unconditioned response. In some situations this prediction is also confirmed. Consider, for example, conditioning with food and water in pigeons. Food and water are both ingestible, rewarding stimuli. However, the unconditioned response in pigeons (and many other animals) is very different for these two stimuli. A pigeon eating grain makes rapid, hard pecking movements directed at the grain with its beak slightly open at the moment of contact. In contrast, it drinks by lowering its beak into the water, sucking up some water, and then raising its head gradually to allow the water to flow down its throat. Thus, the unconditioned responses of eating and drinking differ in both speed and form.

Jenkins and Moore (1973) compared sign tracking in pigeons with food and with water as the unconditioned stimulus. In both experimental situations, the conditioned stimulus was illumination of a small disk or response key for 8 sec before delivery of the unconditioned stimulus. With repeated pairings of the key light with presentation of grain, the pigeons gradually started pecking the illuminated key. Pecking also developed with repeated pairings of the key light with presentation of water. However, the form of the conditioned response was very different in the two situations. In the food experiment, the pigeons pecked the response key as if eating: the pecks were rapid with the beak slightly open at the moment of contact. In the water experiment, the pecking movement was slower, made with the beak closed, and was often accompanied by swallowing. Thus, the form of the conditioned response was determined by and resembled the form of the unconditioned response. Eating-like pecks occurred in conditioning with food, and drinkinglike pecks occurred in conditioning with water. These findings provide strong support for the stimulus substitution model. (For additional examples of conditioned responses determined by the nature of the US, see Davey & Cleland, 1982; Davey, Cleland, Oakley, & Jacobs, 1984; Pelchat, Grill, Rozin, & Jacobs, 1983; Peterson, Ackil, Frommer, & Hearst, 1972.)

Difficulties with the stimulus substitution model. Doubts arose about the stimulus substitution model very early in American investigations of classical conditioning. The problem was that in many situations the forms of the conditioned and unconditioned responses are significantly different. Hilgard reviewed several examples many years ago (Hilgard, 1936). He noted, for example, that whereas the unconditioned response to shock is an increase in respiration rate, the conditioned response to a CS paired with shock is a decrease in respiration. Detailed study

of the form of conditioned eyeblink responses also showed that humans blink differently in response to conditioned and unconditioned stimuli. In other research of this type, Zener (1937) carefully observed both salivation and motor responses to a bell that had been paired with food in dogs. The unconditioned response to food always involved lowering the head to the food tray and chewing one or more pieces of food. After conditioning, the bell rarely elicited chewing movements, and if chewing occurred, it was not sustained. The conditioned response to the bell only sometimes included orientation to the food tray. On some trials the dog looked toward the bell instead. On other trials the dog's orientation vacillated between the food tray and the bell, and on still other occasions the dog held its head between the food tray and the bell when the bell sounded. Thus, the conditioned responses elicited by the bell were often different from the unconditioned responses elicited by the food.

Modern approaches to stimulus substitution. Because the form of the conditioned response is not invariably similar to the form of the unconditioned response, some researchers have become skeptical about the stimulus substitution model. In addition, modern theorists believe that neural mechanisms of learning are much more complex than the stimulus substitution model implies. Nevertheless, the unconditioned stimulus appears to be very important in determining characteristics of the conditioned response other than its form. Manipulations that directly influence the unconditioned response have an impact on the conditioned response as well. Some modern theorists have therefore proposed a variant of the stimulus substitution model. This model retains the idea that the conditioned response is elicited by way of a US "center" of some sort. However, in an effort to avoid misleading implications about neural mechanisms, the contemporary view does not make reference to the nervous system. Rather, it is stated in more abstract language. The new model states that animals learn two things from repeated pairings of a CS with a US. First, they learn an association between the CS and the US. Second, they form an image, or representation, of the unconditioned stimulus. According to the model, the conditioned response depends on both these factors. The CS elicits the CR because of its association with the US representation. If either the CS/US association or the US representation is weak, the conditioned response will not occur.

Strong evidence for the importance of the US representation in classical conditioning is provided by experiments in which the US representation is manipulated without changing the CS/US association. One set of these studies involved reducing the value of the US representation after conditioning. The basic strategy and rationale involved in one experiment (Rescorla, 1973) are illustrated in Figure 4.6. During phase 1 of the experiment, both the experimental and the control groups received conventional conditioned suppression training with a loud noise as the unconditioned stimulus. This phase of the procedure was assumed to establish an association between the CS and the US for both groups as well as to lead the subjects to form a representation of the loud-noise US. In the next phase of the experiment, the experimental group received a treatment designed to devalue the US representation. The loud noise was repeatedly presented to reduce (habituate) subjects' response to the US. The control group was not exposed to the noise during this phase. Thus, the US representation was assumed to remain intact for the control group (see Figure 4.6). The effects of the devaluation of the US representation were then measured by testing subjects with the conditioned stimulus. The experimental group suppressed its responding during the CS significantly less than the control group. Thus, the US-devaluation treatment reduced the power of the CS to elicit the conditioned suppression response. This experiment shows in an ingenious way that the conditioned response is elicited by way of a US representation.

The effects of US devaluation on elicitation of the conditioned response have also been investigated in classical conditioning with food. However, because animals do not become habituated to food in the same way that they become habituated to loud noises, other techniques had to be used to devalue the US representation. Two such procedures have been tested. One was to satiate the animals with food. The other was to condition an aversion to the food by pairing the food with sickness induced either by rapid rotation of the animals on a platform or by injection of a drug. Both the satiation and food-aversion procedures reduced the extent to which a food-conditioned

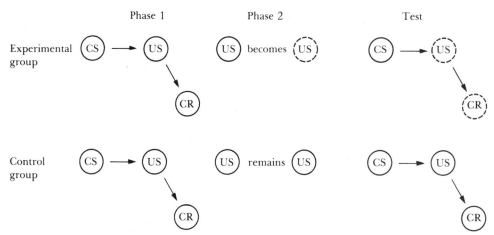

FIGURE 4.6.   Basic strategy and rationale involved in US-devaluation experiments. In phase 1 the experimental and control groups receive conventional conditioning to establish an association between the CS and the US and to lead subjects to form a representation of the US. In phase 2 the US representation is devalued for subjects in the experimental group. The US representation remains unchanged for subjects in the control group. If the conditioned response (CR) is elicited by way of the US representation, devaluation of the US representation in the experimental group is expected to reduce responding to the CS.

stimulus elicited the conditioned response (Cleland & Davey, 1982; Holland & Rescorla, 1975a; Holland & Straub, 1979).

The experiment described above, together with other research (for example, Bouton, 1984; Rescorla, 1974; Rescorla & Cunningham, 1977; Rescorla & Heth, 1975), shows that the status of the US representation can be very important in classical conditioning. In the situations described above, subjects learned an association between the CS and a representation of the US, and the conditioned response was elicited by way of the US representation.

S-S versus S-R learning.   In the examples described above, whether or not the conditioned stimulus elicited a CR critically depended on the status of the US representation. Classical conditioning did not result in the formation of a new reflex connection between the CS and CR such that the CR was elicited whenever the CS was presented. Rather, conditioning in these cases resulted in an association between the CS and a representation of the US. Presentation of the CS elicited the US representation, and the CR was simply a reflection of this US representation. This type of outcome is called stimulus-stimulus learning, or **S-S learning.** In S-S learning subjects learn an association between two stimuli (the CS and the US, for example), and the conditioned response is only an indirect reflection of this stimulus-stimulus association. Whether the conditioned response occurs depends on the behavioral impact of the associated stimulus (the US) at the time. If the associated stimulus is reduced in behavioral impact (by habituation, for example), the elicited conditioned response will also be reduced.

The examples of US devaluation described above provide one type of evidence for S-S learning. We previously encountered evidence of S-S learning in a different type of conditioning situation, sensory preconditioning (see Figure 4.4). In sensory preconditioning, subjects first learn an association between two innocuous stimuli, CS_2 and CS_1. Whether CS_2 elicits an observable conditioned response as a result of this association depends on the behavioral impact of the associated stimulus, CS_1. If the behavioral impact of the associated stimulus is increased (by pairing CS_1 with a biologically strong US), a condi-

tioned response to CS_2 appears. In sensory preconditioning experiments, the behavioral impact of the associated stimulus is increased. In US-devaluation experiments the behavioral impact of the associated stimulus is decreased. Both types of experiments illustrate S-S learning because in both cases the conditioned response is elicited by way of the behavioral impact of the associated stimulus.

Although evidence of S-S learning is available from a variety of classical conditioning situations, not all instances of classical conditioning involve S-S learning. In some cases subjects appear to learn a direct association between a CS and a CR. This type of learning is called stimulus-response learning, or **S-R learning.** Some evidence for S-R learning is available from studies of second-order conditioning.

S-S versus S-R learning in second-order conditioning.   How might we test whether second-order conditioning involves the learning of S-S or S-R associations? Recall that, in second-order conditioning, learning occurs because of the pairings of a novel second-order stimulus, CS_2, with a previously conditioned stimulus, CS_1 (see Figure 4.3). The relation of CS_2 and CS_1 in second-order conditioning is procedurally comparable to the relation of CS_1 to the US in first-order conditioning. If second-order conditioning involved S-S learning, CS_2 would evoke a conditioned response by way of the representation of CS_1. This possibility is illustrated on the left side of Figure 4.7. If CS_2 evoked a conditioned response by way of the associated representation of CS_1, then changing the behavioral impact of CS_1 should also change the re-

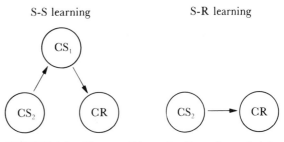

FIGURE 4.7.   Two possible mechanisms of second-order conditioning. In S-S learning, the conditioned response is elicited by way of the representation of CS_1. In S-R learning, the conditioned response is elicited directly by CS_2.

sponse evoked by CS_2. The behavioral impact of CS_1 can be altered simply by extinguishing CS_1. According to the S-S learning interpretation, extinguishing CS_1 after second-order conditioning should also weaken the subjects' response to CS_2.

If second-order conditioning involved S-R learning, CS_2 would elicit the conditioned response directly. This possibility is illustrated on the right side of Figure 4.7. If CS_2 came to elicit the conditioned response directly through an S-R association, then once this association had been established, changes in the behavioral impact of CS_1 should have no effect on the response to CS_2. Thus, according to the S-R learning interpretation, extinguishing CS_1 after second-order conditioning should not weaken the subjects' response to CS_2.

Studies of the effects of extinguishing CS_1 following second-order conditioning have provided a diversity of outcomes. In some situations, second-order conditioning has been shown to involve S-R learning (Archer & Sjoden, 1982; Holland & Rescorla, 1975a, 1975b; Rizley & Rescorla, 1972). In other cases, evidence indicates that second-order conditioning involves S-S learning (Hittesdorf & Richards, 1982; Leyland, 1977; Rashotte, Griffin, & Sisk, 1977; Rescorla, 1979). We are starting to gain insights into the conditions under which one type of learning predominates over the other (for example, Nairne & Rescorla, 1981; Rescorla, 1982). Future research on this question is bound to reveal important fundamental facts about learning processes.

The compensatory-response model

As we have seen, Pavlov's idea that conditioning involves stimulus substitution has not proved useful in light of modern research. The CS does not become a substitute for the US in that it always elicits a response like the unconditioned response. The closest that modern conceptions of classical conditioning come to the idea of stimulus substitution is that the CS activates a representation of the US, and the conditioned response is an indirect reflection of this US representation. However, the US-representation view does not specify what form the conditioned response will take. Several other ideas have been

proposed to explain the nature of conditioned responses. One of the most radical of these, the **compensatory-response model,** is based on extensive research with drug unconditioned stimuli.

In many classical conditioning situations involving drugs as unconditioned stimuli, the form of the conditioned response is opposite the form of the unconditioned response. For example, epinephrine causes a decrease in gastric secretion as an unconditioned response. In contrast, the response to a CS for epinephrine is increased gastric secretion (Guha, Dutta, & Pradhan, 1974). Dinitrophenol causes increased oxygen consumption and increased temperature. The response to a CS for dinitrophenol involves decreased oxygen consumption and decreased temperature (Obál, 1966). These and many similar examples (see Siegel, 1977b) have provided the impetus for the compensatory-response model. The model has been most often discussed in reference to drug conditioning situations. According to the model, responses conditioned by drug unconditioned stimuli are expected to be compensatory for the unconditioned responses elicited by the drug. Thus, if the drug causes a change in behavior in one direction, the model predicts that CSs for the drug will result in changes in behavior in the opposite direction.

The compensatory-response model has attracted a great deal of attention because it has been used as the basis for an innovative explanation of the development of drug tolerance. Tolerance to a drug is said to develop when repeated administrations of the drug have progressively less effect. Development of drug tolerance is often a serious problem in the use of drugs because progressively higher doses are required to produce a given effect. Traditionally, drug tolerance has been considered to result from pharmacological processes. In contrast to this traditional approach, Shepard Siegel has proposed a model of drug tolerance based on classical conditioning (see Siegel, 1983, for a recent review). The model assumes that, with repeated presentations of a drug, the stimuli that always accompany drug administrations will become conditioned by the drug. These stimuli might be the time of day, the sensations involved in preparing a syringe, or the stimuli involved in getting out a pill to swallow. The conditioned drug-administration cues are assumed to elicit conditioned responses that are opposite to the unconditioned reactions to the drug. Because the conditioned responses compensate for the effects of the drug itself, those responses reduce the reaction otherwise elicited by the drug. Therefore, the response to the drug is attenuated when the drug is taken in the presence of these conditioned stimuli (see Figure 4.8).

The conditioning model of drug tolerance attributes tolerance to compensatory responses conditioned to environmental stimuli paired with drug administration. If the model is correct, then manipulations of the external environment should influence the effectiveness of drugs. Various aspects of this prediction have been confirmed by Siegel and his colleagues in experiments with opiates, such as morphine and heroin (Siegel, 1975b, 1976, 1977a, 1978; Siegel, Hinson, & Krank, 1978). Morphine has a long history of medical use as a painkiller. However, patients quickly develop tolerance to it, so that a given amount of the drug becomes progressively less effective in reducing pain. The analgesic effects of the drug may

be restored if the usual drug-administration cues are removed, as by administering the drug with a novel procedure or in a new room. Drug tolerance is also less likely if subjects are made highly familiar with the drug-administration stimuli before being treated with the drug, because such CS familiarity interferes with conditioning. Finally, drug tolerance can be reversed by extinguishing the drug-administration cues by repeatedly presenting the cues without the drug. (For additional recent research on the conditioning model of drug tolerance, see, for example, Crowell, Hinson, & Siegel, 1981; Dafters, Hetherington, & McCartney, 1983; Poulos & Hinson, 1982; Shapiro, Dudek, & Rosellini, 1983; Tiffany & Baker, 1981).

The conditioned-compensatory-response model of drug tolerance has provided an important new perspective on the mechanisms of tolerance development and shows the power of classical conditioning in regulating drug responses. However, it has not provided an entirely satisfactory general account of the form of classically conditioned responses. The problem is that not all conditioned responses are opposite to the apparent effects of the unconditioned stimulus. For example, amphetamine causes increased activity as an unconditioned response, and this behavior can be conditioned to stimuli that reliably precede the presence of amphetamine (Pickens & Dougherty, 1971). Insulin causes decreased activity, convulsions, and unresponsiveness to applied stimulation; this pattern of behavior also occurs in response to a CS for insulin (Siegel, 1975a). In yet other cases, measurement of several response systems indicates that some conditioned responses are similar to the unconditioned response and others are opposite to it. For example, after conditioning with anticholinergic drugs, the conditioned stimulus elicits pupillary dilation and increased salivation (Korol, Sletten, & Brown, 1966; Lang, Brown, Gershon, & Korol, 1966). The pupillary dilation CR is similar to the unconditioned response to the drugs, whereas the increased salivation is opposite to the direct effects of the anticholinergic agents. These diverse findings make the compensatory-response model inadequate as a general account of the form of classically conditioned responses. (For recent proposals concerning what determines the

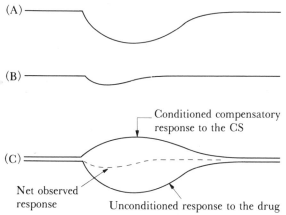

FIGURE 4.8. Diagram of the Pavlovian-conditioning model of drug tolerance. The strength of the drug reaction is represented by deviations from the horizontal line. (A) Reaction to the CS plus the drug before conditioning, illustrating the unconditioned response to the drug. (B) Attenuated reaction to the CS plus the drug after extensive experience with the drug, illustrating drug tolerance. (C) Components of the reaction after conditioning, showing that the net attenuated drug response is due to a compensatory conditioned response to the CS that counteracts the unconditioned response to the drug.

form of drug-conditioned responses, see Eikelboom & Stewart, 1982; Matysiak & Green, 1984).

The CS as a determinant of the form of the CR

According to the models of conditioning we have considered so far, the form of the conditioned response is determined by the unconditioned stimulus or its representation. The compensatory-response model assumes that the CR will "compensate" for the effects of the US. The US-representation model is not as specific about the form of the CR, but it also assumes that the nature of the conditioned response will depend on the US and its representation. Although these models have identified important influ-

ences on the nature of the conditioned response, they are incomplete because recent research indicates that the form of the CR also depends on the nature of the conditioned stimulus.

Earlier in this chapter we discussed how the speed of learning of the conditioned response is influenced by various aspects of the conditioned stimulus. The *rate* of learning depends on the intensity and novelty of the CS and the relevance of the CS to the US. Aspects of the conditioned stimulus also influence the *form* of the conditioned response. In an unusual experiment, for example, Timberlake and Grant (1975) investigated classical conditioning in rats with food as the unconditioned stimulus. One side of the experimental chamber was equipped with a sliding

---

BOX 4.3. Heroin overdose from the absence of drug-conditioned stimuli

Heroin overdose is a leading cause of death among heroin users. It is also one of the most perplexing causes of death. Victims rarely take more heroin before they die than they usually use. On occasion, death occurs while the syringe is still in the victim's arm—before he or she has finished injecting the intended amount. Therefore, heroin-related deaths are rarely caused by excessive amounts of the drug. Why do the addicts die, then? One answer is suggested by the conditioning model of drug tolerance. Long-term users of heroin have a set ritual they go through when taking the drug. They may use the drug only at certain times, only in the company of certain people, or only in special locations. These drug-related stimuli are expected to become conditioned by the heroin use. The conditioning model predicts that heroin-compensatory physiological reactions will come to be elicited by the usual drug-administration ritual. If experienced users take heroin at an unusual time, with a new group of people, or in a new place, the conditioned compensatory responses will not occur. Hence, the usual amount of heroin will have a much larger physiological effect than it has ordinarily. This unexpectedly large drug effect may be sufficient to cause physical complications and death.

Not all people who experience heroin overdose die. Prompt medical attention can be a lifesaver. Interviews with survivors of heroin overdose indicate that the adverse reaction to the drug often occurs when the heroin is taken in unusual circumstances. Animal research also indicates that the absence of drug-conditioned stimuli places subjects at increased risk of heroin-induced death (Siegel, Hinson, Krank, & McCully, 1982). Rats in this research first received several heroin injections in connection with a distinctive set of environmental stimuli. The animals were then given a higher test dose of the drug. For some subjects the test dose was administered in the presence of the usual drug-administration stimuli. For another group, the drug was given in an environment where the subjects had never received heroin before. The test dose of heroin resulted in a greater proportion of deaths among animals that received the drug in the absence of the drug-conditioned environmental cues. These findings support an explanation of the heroin-overdose phenomenon in terms of the conditioning model of drug tolerance. (For additional applications of conditioning theory to problems of drug addiction and treatment, see Poulos, Hinson, & Siegel, 1981.)

platform that could be moved in and out of the chamber through a flap door (see Figure 4.9). Instead of using a conventional light or tone as the conditioned stimulus, the experimenters restrained a live rat on the stimulus platform. Ten seconds before each delivery of food, the platform was moved into the experimental chamber, thereby transporting the stimulus rat through the flap door. The stimulus rat was withdrawn from the chamber at the end of the trial. Thus, presentation of the stimulus rat served as the conditioned stimulus for food.

The stimulus substitution model predicts that the experimental subjects will come to respond to the CS for food as they respond to food. Therefore, they are expected to gnaw or bite the stimulus rat that serves as the CS. It is unclear what the compensatory-response model predicts in this situation. In fact, as the CS rat was repeatedly paired with food, the CS came to elicit orientation, approach, and sniffing movements, as well as social contacts. Such responses did not develop if the CS rat was not paired with food

or was presented at random times with respect to food. This outcome does not support any model that explains the form of the conditioned response solely in terms of the unconditioned stimulus used. The pattern of conditioned responses, particularly the social behavior elicited by the CS rat, was no doubt determined by the unusual conditioned stimulus used in this experiment (see also Timberlake, 1983a). Other kinds of food-conditioned CSs elicit different conditioned responses. For example, Peterson et al. (1972) inserted an illuminated response lever into the experimental chamber immediately before presenting food to rats. With the protruding metal lever as a conditioned stimulus, the conditioned responses were "almost exclusively oral and consisted mainly of licking . . . and gnawing" (Peterson et al., 1972, p. 1010).

One of the most careful and systematic investigations of the role of the conditioned stimulus in determining the nature of the conditioned response was performed by Holland (1977). He compared visual and auditory stimuli in experiments involving a food

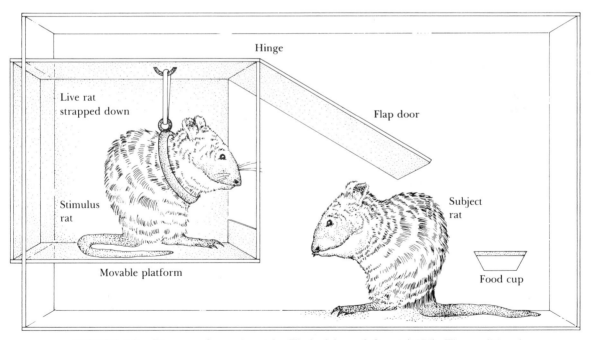

FIGURE 4.9. Diagram of experiment by Timberlake and Grant (1975). The conditioned stimulus for food is presentation of a stimulus rat on a movable platform through a flap door on one side of the experimental chamber. *(Based on W. Timberlake, personal communication, 1980.)*

US in rats. Conditioned auditory cues of various types invariably resulted in head-jerk and startle movements and standing by the food dish. The conditioned head-jerk and startle reactions were not evident with visual conditioned stimuli. When diffuse light was paired with food, the predominant conditioned response was standing by the food dish. When the conditioned visual stimuli was localized at the top of the experimental chamber, conditioned rearing on the hind legs was also often observed (see also Holland, 1980; Sigmundi & Bolles, 1983).

The CR as an interaction between conditioned and innate behavioral processes

Although a comprehensive performance model does not exist for all classically conditioned responses, a model of conditioned overt skeletal movements is beginning to take shape in contemporary thinking. The basic idea is that the effects of a conditioned stimulus on behavior result from an interaction between the conditioned properties of the stimulus and the innate behavior repertoire or tendencies of the organism. Such stimuli as lights, tones, and tastes all elicit innate responses in the absence of conditioning. Animals also have innate reactions to the expectation of significant biological events, such as food, water, or cutaneous pain. When such stimuli as lights, tones, and tastes become conditioned, the responses they come to elicit represent the integration of the original innate responses to these stimuli and the innate responses to the *expectancy* of the unconditioned stimulus. This view of the conditioned response emphasizes that the form of the CR is determined both by the nature of the conditioned stimulus and by the nature of the unconditioned stimulus. The nature of the CS is important because animals have different innate reactions to various stimuli before conditioning, and different stimuli are capable of supporting different responses. The nature of the unconditioned stimulus is important because it in part determines what animals learn to expect on the basis of the CS, and different expectancies are assumed to elicit different innate responses or response tendencies.

The interaction between conditioned and innate behavioral processes in determining the form of the conditioned response is nicely illustrated by an experiment on the conditioning of baby chicks with heat as the unconditioned stimulus. When baby chicks are cold and seek warmth in their natural environment, they approach the mother hen, peck at the feathers on the underpart of her body, and snuggle up to her (rub and push their heads up into her feathers). In contrast, the presence of heat elicits reduced locomotion, extension of the wings, twittering, and eye closure in the chicks. Wasserman (1973) used a small lighted disk as the conditioned stimulus and paired it with brief exposure to heat in young chicks. As the lighted disk became conditioned, the chicks started to approach and peck it. Later the pecking responses became less forceful as the chicks pushed the disk and shook their heads in a snuggling type of movement. These conditioned responses were very different from the reactions to the heat unconditioned stimulus itself. However, they are nicely predicted from what the chicks do naturally when they expect to receive heat from the mother hen. Because of the conditioning procedure, the naturally occurring heat-seeking response came to be directed toward the conditioned stimulus (see also Hogan, 1974; Jenkins, Barrera, Ireland, & Woodside, 1978; Timberlake, 1983a, 1983b; Wasserman, 1974, 1981b).

The idea that conditioned responses represent an interaction between conditioned and innate behavioral processes is a promising development in behavior theory. However, much still remains to make the hypothesis useful in predicting the form of conditioned responses. In many cases we do not know exactly what the animal's innate responses to the expectancy of a particular unconditioned stimulus are. The hypothesis also does not specify how innate reactions to the expectancy of a significant biological event become "integrated" with the innate reactions to the stimulus that is to serve as the CS. Further research is required on the relation between instinctive behavior and conditioning processes for these details to be worked out.

A functional/adaptive approach to the CR

The models of the conditioned response we have considered so far have provided suggestions about the mechanisms of conditioned behavior and have identified individual factors that determine the form of the conditioned response. However, they have not addressed explicitly the issue of why these mechanisms exist—why these mechanisms shape the form of conditioned behavior rather than some others. This issue is the focal point of a functional/adaptive approach to the conditioned response (see Hollis, 1982, 1984b; Shettleworth, 1983a).

Casual reflection reveals that classically conditioned responses are often of benefit to the subject. Anticipatory salivation speeds up digestion, aversion learning to poisonous food reduces subsequent intake of the harmful food, conditioned analgesia reduces the discomfort from a painful stimulus, and conditioned compensatory drug responses reduce the physiological disturbance caused by the administration of a drug. The beneficial effects of conditioned responses have been evident for a long time, as the following quotation reveals:

> [Without a signal] the animal would still be forced to wait in every case for the [shock] stimulus to arrive before beginning to meet it. The veil of the future would hang just before his eyes. Nature began long ago to push back the veil. Foresight proved to possess high survival-value, and conditioning is the means by which foresight is achieved. Indeed, this provision gave the distance-receptors most of their value. Neither sight nor sound of an approaching enemy is intrinsically hurtful; without conditioning, these exteroceptors would have lost their phylogenetic significance [Culler, 1938, p. 136].

According to this interpretation, animals have evolved to make conditioned responses because these responses allow them to become prepared for the unconditioned stimulus. Conditioning allows animals to "make preparatory adjustments for an oncoming stimulus" (Culler, 1938, p. 136).

Why should animals make "preparatory adjustments"? As the preceding quotation implies, the biological "benefits" of conditioned responses are measured by their contribution to fitness and reproductive success. By responding in a particular way to the impending delivery of an unconditioned stimulus, subjects increase the likelihood that they will survive to reproduce and pass their genes on to future generations. Thus, the form of the conditioned response is assumed to be adaptive and to contribute to the biological fitness of the organism.

It is important to note that the functional/adaptive approach is not an alternative to determinants of the conditioned response we discussed previously. The claim that conditioned responses are adaptive does not specify how the form of the conditioned response is determined by various antecedent factors such as the nature of conditioned and unconditioned stimuli. In a sense, the functional/adaptive approach specifies the biological uses that conditioned responses can serve (fitness)—not the mechanisms that create conditioned responses. An analogy to an automobile may clarify this distinction. The function of an automobile is to transport people and goods. However, specifying this function does not tell us about the mechanisms of the automobile—whether it has a diesel or a gasoline engine, for example.

Because the functional/adaptive view focuses on the functions of conditioned responses rather than on the mechanisms that produce CRs, it addresses the issue of conditioned behavior from a different perspective than other models we have considered. This new perspective can lead to innovative investigations of conditioning. Shettleworth (1983a) has suggested that a consideration of the functions of learning may provide suggestions about possible mechanisms involved in its production. Consideration of the functions of conditioned responses has also stimulated studies of interesting new forms of conditioning. Hollis (1984b), for example, has found that territorial male fish (gouramis) are more successful in defending their territory if an intruder is signaled by a CS than if the intruder appears without warning. Courtship behavior in males of this species is also more likely if presentation of a female is signaled by a CS than if the female is unexpected. The reproductive advantage provided by conditioned responses is also evident in work on classical conditioning of reproductive behavior in rats. Graham and Desjardins (1980) have shown that an odor CS paired with presentation of a sexually receptive female elicits the release of the sex hormone testosterone in male rats as a conditioned response. This conditioned hormone release can have significant impact on reproductive outcome because testosterone facilitates the reflexes that are involved in successful transmission of sperm from male to female (Hart, 1983).

The above examples illustrate how classically conditioned responses can contribute to fitness. These examples are consistent with accepted theories of conditioned behavior. They do not require modifications of theories of learning but simply illustrate the uses that conditioned responses can serve. However, a consideration of the functions of behavior can also lead to unexpected results that do have important implications for the mechanisms of learning. A recent example involves a consideration of how rodents learn aversions to odor stimuli. Odors can provide a variety of types of information for rats. Odors can identify, for example, a male intruder, a receptive female, a particular place, or a poisonous food. If a rat gets sick after eating a poisonous smelly food, how will it know to associate the odor with sickness? How will it know that the odor was a food-relevant stimulus and not a stimulus relevant to other rodents or particular places? One possibility is that an odor is identified as relevant to food if it is experienced in conjunction with a novel taste. Food tastes uniquely identify foods. Therefore, odors that are experienced in conjunction with a food taste are likely to be food odors. These functional considerations suggest that the presence of a novel taste should facilitate the association of odor stimuli with sickness. Experimental investigations have confirmed this prediction (for example, Palmerino, Rusiniak, & Garcia, 1980; Rusiniak, Hankins, Garcia, & Brett, 1979). The presence of a novel taste facilitates, or potentiates, the conditioning of an olfactory stimulus with poisoning. This phenomenon is called "potentiation." (For additional examples of potentiation, see, for example, Galef & Osborne, 1978; Kucharski & Spear, 1984; Lett, 1980; Rusiniak, Palmerino, & Garcia, 1982; Rusiniak, Palmerino, Rice, Forthman, & Garcia, 1982.)

The potentiation phenomenon is an effective way to solve a challenge to survival. By using food taste to identify odors to associate with poisoning, rats are less likely to learn useless and possibly maladaptive aversions to nonfood odors. Furthermore, by learning an aversion to food odors, they can avoid a poisonous food on the basis of its odor alone without having to taste the food. Thus, they do not have to take in any of the toxic material to avoid ingesting the bad food.

Although the potentiation effect functions well to solve a problem in poison avoidance, the effect was not expected on the basis of traditional learning theory. In the potentiation phenomenon, an effective cue (taste) facilitates the conditioning of another cue that is usually not as easily conditioned (odor). In many conventional classical conditioning situations, when an effective CS is presented together with a less effective one, the first CS interferes with conditioning of the second (for example, Kamin, 1969; Pavlov, 1927). This phenomenon is called "overshadowing." The phenomenon of potentiation is just the opposite of overshadowing and illustrates how functional considerations can lead to the discovery of a new phenomenon that is entirely unexpected from more traditional theoretical considerations.

As we noted earlier, a functional analysis does not substitute for investigations of the mechanisms of behavior. Although the functions of the potentiation effect are clear, its mechanisms are not. In fact, considerable controversy has surrounded the analysis of the potentiation phenomenon (for example, Durlach & Rescorla, 1980; Lett, 1982), and as yet we do not have a clear understanding of why one CS potentiates the conditioning of a second CS in some situations and overshadows the conditioning of a second CS under other circumstances.

How Do Conditioned and Unconditioned Stimuli Become Associated?

We have described numerous situations in which classical conditioning occurs and discussed various factors that determine what responses result from this learning. However, we have yet to address in detail the critical issue of how conditioned and unconditioned stimuli become associated. What are the mechanisms of association learning—the underlying processes that are strongly activated by conditioning procedures that produce rapid learning and weakly activated by procedures that are less effective in producing learning? We commented briefly on mechanisms of learning in the preceding chapter when we noted that classical conditioning is not produced merely by contiguous presentations of the CS and US. Rather, the signal relation, or contingency between the CS and US, is critical in producing learning. How are these signal relations detected by the organism, and how do they influence the learning of associations? These and related questions have been the subject of intense scholarly effort during the past 20 years. Many new ideas have emerged from this effort, and our conceptions of classical conditioning have changed radically as a result. The evolution of theories of classical conditioning continues today as investigators strive to formulate comprehensive accounts of the mechanisms of association learning that can embrace all the diverse research results.

Two views of the acquisition process

One of the fundamental facts about classical conditioning is that not every pairing of the CS with the US produces the same increase in the performance of the conditioned response. Figure 4.10 shows a hypo-

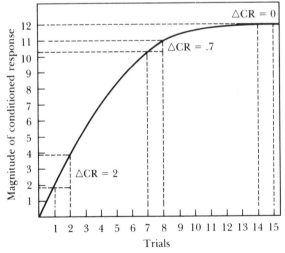

FIGURE 4.10. Idealized learning curve. The magnitude of the conditioned response increased 2 units ($\Delta CR = 2$) between the first and second conditioning trials, .7 unit ($\Delta CR = .7$) between the seventh and eighth trials, and 0 unit ($\Delta CR = 0$) between the fourteenth and fifteenth trials.

thetical learning curve in classical conditioning. The first few pairings of the CS and US produce large increases in performance of the conditioned response. Thus, initially each point on the learning curve is much higher than the previous point. These changes in the conditioned response are represented by ΔCR in Figure 4.10. (The symbol Δ, delta, is used to represent change.) As conditioning proceeds, the increases in the performance of the conditioned response become much smaller after each CS-US pairing. The value of ΔCR becomes less and less. With sufficient training, a stable level of responding is reached, and ΔCR is close to zero. This part of the learning curve is called the **asymptote.**

Why do early conditioning trials produce much larger increases in the performance of the conditioned response than later trials? One cannot attribute this effect to fatigue or decreases in motivation, because similar results are obtained even if subjects receive only one trial per day. There are two plausible explanations. One of these analyzes the learning curve in terms of changes in the ability of the conditioned stimulus to become associated with the US or gain associative strength. According to this view, the CS gradually loses its ability to become associated with the US during the course of conditioning. Initially, the CS is assumed to be highly associable with the US. However, the more conditioned the CS becomes, the more difficult it becomes for the CS to enter into further association with the US. This idea may be called the **CS-reduction hypothesis.** As conditioning proceeds, the ability of the CS to gain further associative strength is reduced. As the associability of the CS is gradually reduced, increments in the conditioned response become progressively smaller until the asymptote of conditioning is reached and no further learning occurs.

A second approach to the analysis of acquisition assumes that there are changes in the ability of the unconditioned stimulus to produce learning. According to this idea, the unconditioned stimulus is fully effective during the first few conditioning trials and therefore produces large increments in the conditioned response. However, as training progresses, the US gradually loses this ability to produce conditioning in the situation, and increases in the conditioned response become smaller and smaller. At asymptote, the US is assumed to be entirely incapable of producing further conditioning, and ΔCR is zero. This view may be called the **US-reduction hypothesis.** As conditioning proceeds, the effectiveness of the US gradually becomes reduced, and progressively less conditioning occurs.

Contemporary theories of learning differ in how they view the acquisition process. Some contemporary theories emphasize changes in the CS during the course of classical conditioning, whereas other theories emphasize changes in the US. We will begin our discussion of theories of association learning by exploring the idea that the ability of the US to produce new learning is altered as a result of conditioning. This idea was stimulated by investigations of the blocking effect in Pavlovian conditioning. Because of the central role that the blocking effect has had in contemporary theoretical developments, we turn to it next.

The blocking effect

Animals conditioned outside the laboratory typically encounter numerous stimuli. Events that signal danger, for example, may involve multiple visual, auditory, and olfactory stimuli. It is advantageous for the organism to use only those cues that signal danger most effectively. Other cues that either do not signal danger consistently or are redundant are best ignored. Otherwise, the organism might be in a constant state of alertness or tension, ready to flee or fight unnecessarily. The US-reduction hypothesis suggests how uninformative and redundant stimuli may be prevented from becoming conditioned. Conditioning one CS with a particular US to asymptote reduces the ability of the US to produce further conditioning in that situation. Therefore, if a new CS is added to the situation, little, if any, conditioning of the new stimulus should occur. This implication has been borne out in a series of experiments on what has come to be called the **blocking effect.** These experiments, initiated by Leon Kamin, delineate specific instances in which conditioning procedures fail to produce conditioning.

The blocking effect has been most extensively in-

vestigated using the conditioned suppression procedure with rats (Kamin, 1968, 1969). The basic procedure involved three phases (see Figure 4.11). In phase 1 the experimental group received repeated pairings of conditioned stimulus A with the unconditioned stimulus. This phase of training was continued until stimulus A was conditioned to asymptote, when animals completely suppressed their lever-press responses as stimulus A was presented. The conditioning of stimulus A presumably reduced the effectiveness of the unconditioned stimulus. To evaluate the loss in US effectiveness, an attempt was made to condition a new stimulus, B, with the same US. In phase 2 of the procedure, stimuli A and B were presented simultaneously and paired with the US. After several such conditioning trials, stimulus B was presented alone in a test trial to see to what degree the animals learned to suppress their behavior in the presence of stimulus B. The control group was given the same phase 2 training with stimulus B as the experimental subjects, but for them stimulus A was not conditioned in phase 1. Therefore, the US presumably was not reduced in effectiveness in phase 2. The US-reduction hypothesis predicts less conditioning of stimulus B in the experimental group than in the control group. Tests with stimulus B presented alone at the end of the experiment confirmed this result. In many replications of the experiment, stimulus B invariably produced less conditioned suppression of behavior in the experimental group than in the control group.

The blocking effect is a remarkable result because

Group	Phase 1	Phase 2	Test
Experimental	A → US	[A + B] → US	B
Control		[A + B] → US	B

FIGURE 4.11. Diagram of the blocking procedure. During phase 1, stimulus A is conditioned with the US in the experimental group, while the control group does not receive conditioning trials. During phase 2 both the experimental and control groups receive conditioning trials in which stimulus A is presented simultaneously with stimulus B and paired with the US. A later test of response to stimulus B alone shows that less conditioning occurs to stimulus B in the experimental than in the control group.

it is not predicted by any informal, common-sense notions about classical conditioning. For example, the blocking effect clearly indicates that classical conditioning does not occur merely because of the presentation of a CS together with a US. During phase 2 of the blocking experiment (see Figure 4.11), stimulus B is paired with the US in an identical fashion for the experimental and the control groups. If pairing of CS and US were sufficient for conditioning, stimulus B should become conditioned in both groups. The fact that stimulus B becomes conditioned only in the control group is strong evidence that pairing of a CS with a US is not enough to produce learning. What else is required is a fundamental question in classical conditioning.

In addition to demonstrating the blocking effect, Kamin (1968, 1969) performed many experiments to find out what aspects of this procedure were responsible for interference with the conditioning of stimulus B in the experimental group. These and other experiments have shown that the conditioning of stimulus B will be blocked if stimulus B is redundant—that is, if B adds no new information about the US. Two aspects of the blocking procedure are critical in meeting this requirement. First, stimulus A must be present together with stimulus B. Second, stimulus A has to be an adequate predictor of the US during the conditioning trials for stimulus B. These features ensure that stimulus A alone is sufficient to signal the US, and B is redundant (unnecessary). If the conditions that make stimulus B redundant are not met, blocking will not occur. For example, stimulus A does not block the conditioning of stimulus B if stimulus A is not present during phase 2 (see Figure 4.11). Blocking also does not occur if stimulus A is not conditioned with the US during phase 1 or if the conditioned properties of stimulus A are extinguished between phases 1 and 2. In both these cases, the result is that stimulus A does not signal occurrences of the US during phase 2, and therefore stimulus B is not redundant. These findings indicate that the conditioning of stimulus A to asymptote does not reduce the effectiveness of the unconditioned stimulus in all circumstances. Rather, US effectiveness is reduced only in those situations in which the unconditioned stimulus is signaled by stimulus A. When stimulus A

is absent or after extinction of stimulus A, when it no longer signals the US, the effectiveness of the unconditioned stimulus is in full force.

Why is it that a redundant stimulus does not become conditioned by the US? The presence of stimulus A during the conditioning trials for stimulus B in phase 2 of the blocking procedure makes the US entirely expected. Thus, the US is not surprising in phase 2. These considerations suggested to Kamin that the unconditioned stimulus has to be *surprising* to produce conditioning. If the unconditioned stimulus is not surprising, it does not startle the animal and stimulate the "mental effort" that is required for the formation of an association. Expected events do not require new adjustments by the organism and therefore do not stimulate new learning. By definition, unexpected events are stimuli to which the organism has not yet adjusted. Therefore, unexpected events are much more likely to create new learning.

The Rescorla/Wagner model of conditioning

The idea that the unconditioned stimulus has to be surprising to promote classical conditioning is a central concept in contemporary theories of conditioning. One of the first and most systematic developments of this idea into a theory of conditioning was provided by Robert Rescorla and Allan Wagner (Rescorla & Wagner, 1972; Wagner & Rescorla, 1972). These investigators formulated a mathematical model of the concept of US surprisingness. The mathematical model provides two important advantages over earlier verbal descriptions of the idea. First, it is a highly precise treatment of the concept of US surprisingness. Second, with the use of mathematical derivations and computer simulations, the implications of the concept of US surprisingness can be extended to a wide variety of conditioning phenomena. Consequently, the Rescorla/Wagner model dominated research on classical conditioning for about ten years after its formulation. We will not describe details of the mathematical treatment Rescorla and Wagner provided but will describe the conceptual basis and implications of the theory.

How might we measure the surprisingness of an unconditioned stimulus? What does it mean to say that something is surprising? By definition, an event is surprising if it is different from what we expected. A big difference between what you expect and what occurs makes the outcome very surprising. If you expect a small gift for your birthday, and you receive a car, you will be very surprised. In contrast, if the difference between what is expected and what occurs is small, the outcome is not very surprising. If you expect to receive a small gift and that is what you get, you will not be greatly surprised. Rescorla and Wagner formalized these notions in the assumption that the surprisingness and hence the effectiveness of a US depend on how different the US is from what the subject expects. Furthermore, they assumed that expectation of the US is based on prior learning. The expectation of the US is assumed to be a reflection of how well the CS has become conditioned—a reflection of the associative strength of the CS.

Let us consider how these relatively simple ideas can account for a typical learning curve in classical conditioning (Figure 4.10). On the first conditioning trial, the subject has no reason to expect the US, because it has not yet learned that the US will follow the CS. Therefore, the US is highly surprising and produces a lot of learning. Because of this learning, the subject acquires some expectation that the US will occur after the CS, and this makes the US less surprising on subsequent trials. Therefore, less new learning occurs on subsequent trials. This process continues until the US is perfectly predicted from the CS, at which point the US has no surprise value. No further learning occurs, and the asymptote is reached.

As this example illustrates, the Rescorla/Wagner model views learning as the adjustment of expectations to what actually happens. If current expectations do not accurately predict the US that is presented, the expectations will be readjusted. This readjustment of expectations will continue until the expectations perfectly match the outcome of conditioning trials. Learning ceases when discrepancies between expectations and outcomes no longer exist. If you can predict a US from a CS perfectly, you have acquired perfect knowledge of the signal relation between the CS and US, and no further learning of an association between the two stimuli will occur.

The basic ideas of the Rescorla/Wagner model

also predict the blocking effect, provided the important additional assumption is made that expectation of the US is based on all the cues available to the subject. The experimental group in the blocking design first receives extensive conditioning of stimulus A so that it acquires a perfect expectation that the US will occur whenever it encounters stimulus A (see Figure 4.11). In phase 2, stimulus B is presented together with stimulus A, and the two CSs are followed by the US. According to the Rescorla/Wagner model, no conditioning of stimulus B occurs in phase 2, because the US is fully expected in phase 2 on the basis of the presence of stimulus A. Subjects in the control group receive the identical training in phase 2, but the presence of stimulus A does not lead to an expectation of the US for them. Therefore, the US is surprising for the control group and produces new learning.

Although the Rescorla/Wagner model is consistent with fundamental facts of classical conditioning such as acquisition and the blocking effect, much of the importance of the model has come from its unusual predictions about learning. It predicts, for example, that under certain circumstances conditioned stimuli will lose associative strength despite continued pairings with the US. How might this happen? Recall that the model views learning as the adjustment of expectancies to outcomes. At the start of conditioning, for example, the CS fails to predict the US that occurs. Thus, the subject receives *more* of a US than what is expected, and the resulting adjustment is an *increase* in expectation of the US. The opposite result occurs if the subject receives *less* of a US than what is expected. In this case the resulting adjustment is a *decrease* in US expectation or associative strength. This can occur even if the US continues to be presented, as in the experiment outlined in Figure 4.12.

The experiment outlined in Figure 4.12 involves two phases. In phase 1 subjects receive conditioning trials in which stimulus A is paired with the US and trials in which stimulus B is paired with the same US (one pellet of food, for example). The conditioning of stimuli A and B on separate trials continues in phase 1 until both stimuli have been conditioned to asymptote—until both stimuli predict perfectly the one-

Phase 1	Phase 2
A → US	
	[A + B] → US
B → US	

FIGURE 4.12. Loss of associative strength despite continued presentations of the US. Stimuli A and B are conditioned separately to asymptote in phase 1 so that each CS perfectly predicts the US. In phase 2, stimuli A and B are presented simultaneously and paired with the same US that was used in phase 1. This produces an overexpectation of the US. Because the US is surprisingly small at the start of phase 2, the associative strengths of stimuli A and B decrease until the simultaneous presentation of the two CSs no longer produces an overexpectation.

food-pellet US. Phase 2 is then initiated. In phase 2 stimuli A and B are presented simultaneously, followed by the same US, one food pellet. The question is what happens to the individual associative strengths of stimuli A and B as a result of the phase 2 training. Note that the same US that was used in phase 1 continues to be presented in phase 2. Given that there is no change in the US, informal reflection suggests that the associative strengths of stimuli A and B should also remain unchanged during phase 2. In contrast to this common-sense prediction, the Rescorla/Wagner model predicts that the associative strengths of the individual stimuli A and B will decrease in phase 2.

As a result of training in phase 1, stimuli A and B both come to predict the one-food-pellet US. When stimuli A and B are presented simultaneously for the first time, in phase 2, the expectations based on each are assumed to add together, with the result that subjects expect a two-food-pellet US. This is an overexpectation because the US remains only one food pellet. Thus, there is a discrepancy between what is expected and what occurs. At the start of phase 2, subjects find the US surprisingly small. To bring their expectations of the US in line with what actually occurs in phase 2, subjects have to decrease their expectancy of the US based on stimuli A and B. Thus, stimuli A and B are predicted to lose associative strength despite continued presentations of the same US. The loss in associative strength is predicted to continue until A and B presented together predict

only one food pellet. The predicted loss of conditioned response to the individual stimuli A and B in this type of procedure is highly counterintuitive but has been verified experimentally (see Kremer, 1978).

The Rescorla/Wagner model stimulated a great deal of research and led to the discovery of many important phenomena of classical conditioning that probably would not have been investigated without guidance of the theory. However, the model has not been entirely successful. First, the model is concerned primarily with signal relations (expectancies of the US based on the presence of a CS) and therefore cannot address other aspects of classical conditioning. For example, the model says nothing about what determines the form of classically conditioned responses. It also does not address instances of classical conditioning that do not involve signal relations, such as sensory preconditioning using simultaneous presentations of the stimuli to be associated (see p. 80). The Rescorla/Wagner model has also encountered some difficulties explaining certain phenomena that presumably involved signal relations. In particular, it has had difficulty explaining certain results in inhibitory conditioning (for example, Zimmer-Hart & Rescorla, 1974).

Alternative US-reduction models

Difficulties with the Rescorla/Wagner model, as well as new ideas from other areas of investigation, have stimulated alternative US-reduction models of classical conditioning. These have not been as extensively tested yet as the Rescorla/Wagner model, but they provide promising new directions in which to search for mechanisms of associative learning. One of these, the **conditioned opponent theory** (Schull, 1979), is based on the opponent-process theory described in Chapter 2 and is in some ways an extension of the compensatory-response model of classical conditioning described earlier in the present chapter. This theory assumes that when a CS is paired with a US, it comes to elicit a number of conditioned responses, one of which involves physiological changes that oppose, or compensate for, the effects of the US. As conditioning proceeds, the CS becomes increasingly effective in eliciting this conditioned opponent response (the compensatory physiological response). Because this conditioned response compensates for the effects of the US, it serves to reduce the impact of the unconditioned stimulus. The impact of the US becomes reduced more and more as conditioning proceeds. At asymptote, the conditioned opponent response is assumed to be strong enough to entirely eliminate the impact of the US, and no further increments in conditioning occur. Thus, the conditioned opponent theory explains the typical course of acquisition in classical conditioning in terms of reductions in US effectiveness. Unlike the Rescorla/Wagner model, it assumes that the US is reduced because the CS elicits a strong conditioned opponent response—not because the CS makes the US no longer surprising.

The conditioned opponent theory predicts many of the same phenomena as the Rescorla/Wagner theory. For example, it is just as successful in explaining the blocking effect as the Rescorla/Wagner theory. Recall that to produce the blocking effect, one first gives subjects conditioning of stimulus A to asymptote. Stimulus A is then presented together with stimulus B, and the two cues together are followed by the US. The presence of stimulus A during this second phase blocks the conditioning of stimulus B. The conditioned opponent theory explains this result by assuming that, because of its prior conditioning, stimulus A comes to elicit a strong conditioned opponent response. The impact of the US is therefore reduced when stimuli A and B are paired with the US, and the reduced impact of the US is responsible for lack of conditioning of stimulus B. (For additional implications of the conditioned opponent theory, see Schull, 1979.)

The conditioned opponent theory is a promising development because it integrates several lines of theorizing (opponent-process theory, compensatory-response theory, and the Rescorla/Wagner model). However, in its original formulation it was too vague to permit precise experimental evaluation. The key ideas of the theory have been developed further in a precisely stated mathematical theory of conditioning recently proposed by Wagner (1981; see also Donegan & Wagner, 1981; Mazur & Wagner, 1982; Wagner & Larew, 1985).

CS-modification models

Investigators have also explored the possibility that various classical conditioning phenomena reflect changes in the ability of the CS to enter into association with the US, rather than changes in the ability of the US to produce conditioning. CS-modification models emphasize that for conditioning to take place, the conditioned stimulus has to be noticeable, or salient; it has to attract the subject's attention. The salience of a CS on a conditioning trial is assumed to determine how much conditioning takes place on that trial. If a stimulus has lost its salience and is no longer noticeable, subjects will not learn much that is new about it.

CS-modification models differ in their assumptions about what determines the salience, or noticeability, of the CS on a given trial. Pearce and Hall (1980; see also Hall, Kaye, & Pearce, 1985), for example, assume that how well subjects pay attention to the CS on a given trial is determined by how surprising the US was on the preceding trial. Subjects have a lot to learn in situations where the US is surprising. Therefore, if a CS is followed by a surprising US, the subjects will pay closer attention to that CS on the next trial. A surprising US is assumed to increase the salience of the CS. In contrast, if a CS is followed by an expected US, the subjects will pay less attention to that CS on the next trial. An expected US is assumed to decrease the salience of the CS.

The Pearce and Hall model is consistent with many common findings in classical conditioning. For example, it explains the typical course of acquisition of a conditioned response (Figure 4.10) by assuming that the surprisingness of the US at the start of conditioning makes subjects pay close attention to the CS, and this results in large increments in conditioning. As learning proceeds, the US becomes less surprising. This reduces the amount of attention subjects pay to the CS, with the result that less learning takes place. The asymptote, or limit, of conditioning is reached when the US is perfectly predicted, because perfect predictability completely reduces the salience of the CS.

The Pearce/Hall model also predicts some unusual results. Consider, for example, the following conditioned suppression experiment. During phase 1 subjects receive conditioning in which a tone CS is paired with a weak-shock US. They then receive pairings of the same tone CS with a strong-shock US in phase 2. How will conditioning the tone with a weak shock in phase 1 affect the ability of the tone to become conditioned in phase 2? The Pearce/Hall model predicts that weak-shock training will disrupt conditioning of the tone with the strong shock. The model assumes that the salience of a CS is reduced if that CS is followed by a predicted US. The weak shock will have become entirely predictable during the phase 1 training. The predictability of the US during phase 1 will reduce the salience of the tone CS, and that will disrupt conditioning of the tone when it is paired with a stronger shock in phase 2. Experimental results confirm this prediction (Hall & Pearce, 1979).

CS-modification models of conditioning differ from US-reduction models not only in their emphasis on changes in the salience of the CS but also in that the surprisingness of the US on a given trial is assumed to have an effect only on what happens on the next trial. If trial 10, for example, ends in a surprising US, that outcome increases the salience of the CS on the next trial, trial 11. The surprisingness of the US on trial 10 is not assumed to determine what is learned on trial 10. How much attention the CS attracts on trial 10 is assumed to have been determined by events prior to trial 10. Thus, US surprisingness is assumed to have only a prospective influence on conditioning. This is an important contrast to US-reduction models, in which the surprisingness of the US determines what is learned on the same trial that the US is presented. The assumption that the US on a given trial influences only what is learned on the next trial has permitted CS-reduction models to explain certain special results (for example, Mackintosh, Bygrave, & Picton, 1977) but has made it difficult for the models to explain other findings (for example, Balaz, Kasprow, & Miller, 1982; Dickinson, Nicholas, & Mackintosh, 1983). Neither CS-reduction nor US-reduction theories have proved to be capable of explaining all experimental results, a fact that suggests that both types of processes can be involved in classical conditioning.

Concluding Comments

Traditionally, classical conditioning has been regarded as a relatively simple and primitive type of learning that is involved only in the regulation of glandular and visceral responses, such as salivation. The establishment of CS-US associations was assumed to occur fairly automatically with the pairing of a CS and a US. Given the simple and automatic nature of the conditioning and its limitation to glandular and visceral responses, it was not viewed as very important in explaining the complexity and richness of human experience. This view of classical conditioning is no longer tenable.

The research reviewed in Chapters 3 and 4 has shown that classical conditioning is a rather complex process and is involved in the conditioning of a wide variety of responses, including not only glandular secretory responses but also emotional behavior and locomotor movements. The learning does not occur automatically with the pairing of a CS with a US. Rather, it depends on the subject's prior experience with each of these stimuli, the presence of other stimuli during the conditioning trial, and the extent to which the CS and US are relevant to each other. Furthermore, the processes of classical conditioning are not limited to CS-US pairings. Learned associations can occur between two biologically weak stimuli (sensory preconditioning), in the absence of an unconditioned stimulus (higher-order conditioning), or in the absence of conventional conditioned stimuli (counterconditioning).

Given these and other complexities of classical conditioning processes, it is a mistake to disregard classical conditioning in attempts to explain complex forms of behavior. The richness of classical conditioning mechanisms makes them potentially quite relevant to the richness and complexity of human experience. Tremendous advances have occurred in the understanding of classical conditioning processes during the last 20 years. It will be interesting to see how this new knowledge comes to be used in the analysis of complex forms of human and animal behavior.

CHAPTER 5
Instrumental Conditioning: Foundations

In Chapter 5 we will begin a discussion of instrumental conditioning and goal-directed behavior. In this type of conditioning, presentations of stimuli depend on the prior occurrence of designated responses. We will first describe origins of research on instrumental conditioning and then investigative methods used in contemporary research. Four basic types of instrumental conditioning procedures will then be described. We will end the chapter with a discussion of three fundamental elements of the instrumental conditioning paradigm: the instrumental response, the goal event, and the relation between the instrumental response and the goal event.

In the preceding chapters we discussed various aspects of how responses are elicited by discrete stimuli. Studies of habituation, sensitization, and classical conditioning are all concerned mainly with analyses of the mechanisms whereby stimuli trigger responses. Because of this emphasis, experiments on habituation, sensitization, and classical conditioning use procedures in which animals have no control over the stimuli to which they are exposed. Certain events, such as CSs and USs, are periodically introduced into the situation according to a schedule determined by the experimenter.

The procedures for studying and modifying elicited behavior mimic many situations in the lives of both animals and people. There are many occasions when an organism has no control over the events or stimuli that it encounters. However, there are also many circumstances in which events are a direct result of the individual's behavior. By studying hard, a student can learn the material in a course and get a good grade; by turning the car key in the ignition, a driver can start the engine; by putting a coin in a vending machine, a child can obtain a piece of candy. In all these instances, some aspect of the subject's behavior is instrumental in producing a consequent stimulus. Furthermore, the behavior occurs because of the consequences it produces. Students would not study if studying did not result in the learning of interesting information or in good grades; drivers would not turn the ignition key if this did not start the engine; and children would not put coins in a candy machine if they did not get something in return. Responses that occur mainly because they are instrumental in producing certain consequences are called **instrumental behavior.**

Because instrumental behavior is governed mainly by the events it produces, such behavior can be characterized as goal-directed. Instrumental responses occur because the goal would not be reached without them. Goal-directed behavior represents a large proportion of all animal and human behavior. Consider a morning routine. One gets out of bed in order to go to the bathroom and get cleaned up. One gets cleaned up to be ready to get dressed. One gets dressed to keep warm and avoid social embarrassment. The next step

may involve making breakfast to reduce hunger. Then the person may drive a car to get to work. On the job, one performs various tasks to receive praise and a salary. One's daily life is filled with actions, large and small, that are performed to produce certain consequences.

The fact that the consequences of an action can determine future occurrences of that action is obvious to everyone. If you happen to find a dollar bill as you are walking looking at the ground, you will keep looking. How such consequences influence future behavior is not so readily apparent. Much of the remainder of this book is devoted to a discussion of the mechanisms responsible for the control of behavior by its consequences. In the present chapter, we will describe some of the history, basic techniques, procedures, and issues in the experimental analysis of instrumental, or goal-directed, behavior.

How might we investigate instrumental behavior? One way would be to go to the natural environment and look for examples of goal-directed behavior. However, this approach is not likely to lead to definitive results, because factors responsible for goal-directed behavior are difficult to isolate without experimental manipulation. Consider, for example, a dog sitting comfortably in its yard at home. When an intruder approaches, the dog starts to bark vigorously, with the result that the intruder goes away. Because the dog's barking has a clear consequence (departure of the intruder), we may conclude that the dog barked in order to produce this consequence—that barking was goal-directed. However, an equally likely possibility is that barking was elicited by the novelty of the intruder and persisted as long as the eliciting stimulus was present. The response consequence—departure of the intruder—may have been incidental to the dog's barking. Deciding between these two alternatives is very difficult without experimental manipulations of the relation between barking and its consequences.

The type of research we will discuss brings instrumental behavior into the laboratory. The idea, as with elicited behaviors, is to study representative instrumental responses in the hope of discovering general principles. However, as we shall see, the task is complicated by a number of factors.

Elicited behavior is relatively simple to produce for investigation. One has only to select a stimulus that elicits the response of interest. Getting an instrumental response to occur for investigation can be considerably more difficult because the goal that motivates the behavior occurs *after* the response has been made. Accordingly, the experimenter first has to induce the organism to make the response so that the consequences of the behavior can occur and gain control of its future occurrence. In this sense instrumental behavior is voluntary, or, as Skinner (1953) suggests, it is *emitted* rather than elicited. We can do things to increase or decrease the likelihood that the response will occur. However, the ultimate initiation of the response belongs with the organism. Because instrumental behavior is emitted, laboratory investigations of it require providing a situation in which the behavior will be likely to occur.

Early Investigations of Instrumental Conditioning

Laboratory and theoretical analyses of instrumental conditioning began in earnest with the work of E. L. Thorndike. Thorndike's original intent was to study animal intelligence (Thorndike, 1898). The publication of Darwin's theory of evolution had led people to speculate about the extent to which human intellectual capacities, such as reasoning, are present in animals. (As we shall see in Chapter 12, such questions continue to interest contemporary researchers.) Thorndike investigated animal intelligence by devising a series of puzzle boxes. He would place a hungry cat (or dog or chicken) in the puzzle box with some food left outside in plain view. The task for the cat was to learn to escape from the box and obtain the food.

Different puzzle boxes required different responses by the cat to get out. Some were easier than others. In the simplest boxes, the cat's random movements initially led to escape and access to food. With repeated trials the cat escaped more and more quickly. In more complicated boxes, such as Box K, shown in Figure 5.1, escape also improved with practice, but more slowly. In Box K the cat had to pull a string, depress a pedal, and open one of two latches to get out. Figure 5.1 shows the median times for escape for five cats. None of the cats escaped on the first trial in the 10-min maximum time that was allowed. The cats' performance improved on later trials; toward the end of the experiment they escaped in 2–3 min.

BOX 5.1. Edward Lee Thorndike

Thorndike was born in 1874 and died in 1949. As an undergraduate at Wesleyan University, he became interested in the work of William James, then at Harvard. Thorndike himself entered Harvard as a graduate student in 1895. During his stay he began his research on instrumental behavior. He started out using chicks as subjects. Since there was no laboratory space at Harvard at that time, he set up his project in William James' cellar. After a short time, he was offered a fellowship at Columbia University. This time his laboratory was located in the attic of psychologist James Cattell. Thorndike received his Ph.D. from Columbia in 1898 for his work entitled "Animal Intelligence: An Experimental Analysis of Associative Processes in Animals." This included the famous puzzle-box experiments. Thorndike stayed on in New York at Columbia University Teachers College, where for many years he served as professor of educational psychology. Among other things, he attempted to apply to children the principles of trial-and-error learning he found with animals. He also became interested in psychological testing and became a leader in this newly formed field. Several years before his death, Thorndike returned to Harvard as the William James Lecturer, a fitting honor for this great psychologist.

Thorndike interpreted the results of his studies as reflecting the learning of an association. When a cat was initially placed in a box, it displayed a variety of responses that are typical of a confined animal. Eventually, some of these responses resulted in opening the door. Thorndike believed that such successful escapes led to the learning of an association between the stimuli inside the puzzle box and the escape responses. As the association, or connection, between the box and the successful responses became stronger, the cat came to make those responses whenever it was confined in the puzzle box. The consequence of the successful responses—escaping the box—strengthened the association between the box stimuli and those responses.

On the basis of his research, Thorndike formulated the **law of effect.** The law of effect states that *if a response in the presence of a stimulus is followed by a satisfying event, the association between the stimulus and the response is strengthened. If the response is followed by an annoying event, the association is weakened.* It is important to stress here that, according to the law of effect, animals learn an association between the response and the stimuli present at the time of the response. The consequence of the response is not involved in the association. The satisfying or annoying consequence simply serves to strengthen or weaken the bond, or association, between the response and the stimulus situation.

Modern Approaches to the Study of Instrumental Conditioning

Thorndike used 15 different puzzle boxes in his investigations, each requiring different manipulations for the cat to get out. As more and more scientists became interested in studying learning with animal subjects, the range of situations investigated became much smaller. Certain experimental situations became "standard" and have been used repeatedly to facilitate comparison of results obtained in different laboratories. Some popular contemporary techniques for studying instrumental behavior are similar to Thorndike's procedures in that they involve **discrete trials:** subjects are repeatedly placed in an apparatus and can perform the instrumental response only once with each placement. In contrast, other procedures involve the **free operant** method, in which the response of interest can occur repeatedly (freely) once the subject has been placed in the experimental chamber.

Discrete-trial methods

Discrete-trial investigations of instrumental behavior are often conducted in some type of maze. The use of mazes in investigations of learning was introduced at the turn of the 20th century by Small (1899,

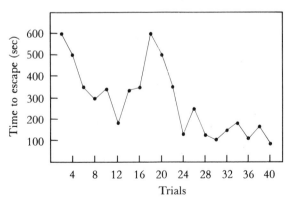

FIGURE 5.1.   Thorndike's puzzle box "K" and the median escape times of five cats tested in the box on 40 successive trials. The cats took less and less time to get out of the box with practice. *(After Thorndike, 1898, and Imada & Imada, 1983.)*

1900), an American psychologist. Small was interested in studying rats and was stimulated to use a maze by an article he read in *Scientific American* describing the complex system of underground burrows that kangaroo rats typically build in nature. Small reasoned that a maze would take advantage of the rat's "propensity for small winding passages."

Figure 5.2 shows two mazes frequently used in contemporary research. The **runway,** or straight-alley maze, contains a start box at one end and a goal box at the other. The rat is placed in the start box at the beginning of each trial. The movable barrier separating the start box from the main section of the runway is then lifted. The rat is allowed to make its way down the runway until it reaches the goal box, which usually contains a reward, such as food or water.

Improvement in the instrumental behavior is usually evaluated using a measure of response vigor. We can measure, for example, how long the animal takes to traverse the alley and reach the goal box. This is called the **running time.** With repeated trials, animals typically require progressively less time to get to the goal box. Some experimenters prefer measuring the **speed** at which the animals run down the alley. Running time can be easily converted to running speed by dividing the length of the runway by the running-time measure. Another common measure of behavior in runways and T mazes is the **latency of the running response.** The latency is how long the animal takes to leave the start box and begin moving down the alley. Typically, latencies become shorter as training progresses.

Another frequently used maze is the **T maze,** shown on the right side of Figure 5.2. The T maze consists of a start box and alleys arranged in the shape of a T. A goal box is located at the end of each arm of the T. Because it has two goal boxes, the T maze is well suited to studying instrumental *choice* behavior. For example, the experimenter may bait one goal box with plain food and the other goal box with food flavored with Nutrasweet. By repeatedly placing the rat in the T maze and seeing which arm it

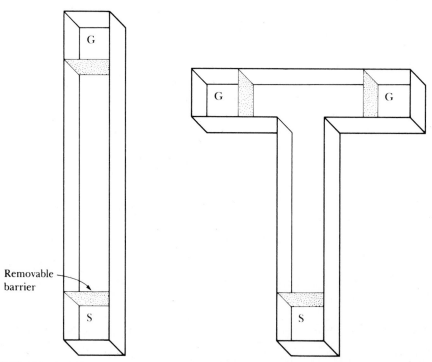

FIGURE 5.2.   Top view of a runway and a T maze. S is the start box; G, the goal box.

chooses, the experimenter can measure preference for one food over the other. The latency and speed of running down the stem of the T maze to the choice arms can also provide important information. If neither of the alternatives provided in the goal boxes is palatable, the rat may have a long latency to initiate running in the maze and may run slowly.

Free-operant methods

In a runway or a T maze, a subject has limited opportunities to respond. After reaching the goal box, the subject is removed for a while before being returned to the start box for another trial. In contrast, free-operant methods allow the subject to repeat the instrumental response "freely" over and over again. Free-operant methods were devised by B. F. Skinner (1938) to study behavior in a more continuous manner than is possible with mazes. Skinner was interested in the laboratory analysis of a form of behavior that is representative of all naturally occurring ongoing activity. However, before behavior can be experimentally analyzed, a measurable unit of behavior has to be defined. Casual observations of ongoing behavior indicate that behavior is continuous. One activity leads to another. Behavior does not fall neatly into units like molecules of a chemical solution. Skinner proposed the concept of the **operant** as a way of dividing behavior into meaningful and measurable units.

Figure 5.3 shows a typical **Skinner box** used to study free-operant behavior in rats. (A Skinner box used to study pecking in pigeons is presented in Figure 1.1.) The Skinner box is a small experimental chamber that contains something like a lever that the rat can manipulate. The chamber also has a mechanism that can deliver a reward, such as food or water. In the simplest experiment, a hungry rat is placed in the chamber. The lever is electronically connected to the food delivery system. When the rat depresses the lever, a pellet of food falls into the food cup.

Operant responses such as the lever press are defined in terms of the effect that they have on the environment. Activities that have the same effect on the environment are considered to be instances of the same operant. The critical thing is not the muscles

FIGURE 5.3.   A Skinner box equipped with a response lever and an automatic food delivery device. Electrical equipment is used to program procedures and record responses automatically.

that are involved in the behavior but how the behavior "operates" on the environment. For example, the lever-press operant response in rats is typically defined as a depression of the lever sufficient to cause the closure of a microswitch. The subject may press the lever with its right paw, its left paw, or its tail. All these different muscle responses constitute the same operant if they all depress the lever the required amount. Various ways of pressing the lever are assumed to be functionally equivalent because they all have the same effect on the environment—namely, closing the microswitch.

Most rats, when placed in a Skinner box, do not press the lever frequently. There are two preliminary steps for establishing the lever-press behavior. First the animals are taught when food is available in the food cup. This is done by repeatedly pairing the sound of the food delivery device with the delivery of a food pellet into the cup. After enough such pairings, the sound of the delivery of food comes to serve as a conditioned stimulus for the presence of food in the cup. This preliminary phase of conditioning is called **magazine training.**

After magazine training, the subject is ready to learn the required instrumental response. Most instrumental responses can be analyzed in terms of components. For example, lever pressing requires that the subject approach the response lever, raise its front paws above the lever, and then push down. To facilitate lever pressing, the experimenter may begin by giving the subject food for performing preliminary components of the lever-press response. Initially, the subject may be rewarded for just approaching the vicinity of the lever. Then, reward may be delivered only if the subject sniffs or touches the lever. Finally, reward may be delivered only if the animal actually presses down on the lever. Such a sequence of training steps is called **shaping by successive approximations.** The experimenter requires increasingly closer and closer approximations to the desired behavior before delivering the reward.

Response rate as a measure of operant behavior.

The major advantage of free-operant methods over discrete-trial techniques for studying instrumental behavior is that free-operant methods permit continuous observation of behavior over long periods. With continuous opportunity to respond, the subject rather than the experimenter determines the frequency of occurrence of the instrumental response. Hence, free-operant techniques provide a special opportunity to observe changes in the likelihood of behavior over time. How should we take advantage of this and measure the probability of an operant response? Measures of response latency and speed that are commonly used in discrete-trial procedures provide detailed information about individual responses but do not characterize the likelihood of repetitions of a response. Skinner proposed that the rate of occurrence of operant behavior (frequency of the response in a particular interval) be used as a measure of response probability. If the rate of responding is high, probability of the response is said to be high. If the rate of responding is low, probability of the response is said to be low.

The cumulative recorder.

Free-operant investigations are typically concerned with measuring the rate of behavior over time. Skinner devised a data-recording instrument—the **cumulative recorder**—that is ideally suited to recording and displaying such information. Figure 5.4 is a drawing of a cumulative recorder. The cumulative recorder consists of a rotating drum that pulls paper out of the recorder at a constant speed. A pen rests on the surface of the paper. If no responses occur, the pen remains stationary and makes a horizontal line as the paper comes out of the machine. If the animal performs a lever-press response, the pen moves one step vertically on the paper. Since each lever-press response causes the pen to move one step up the paper, the total vertical distance traveled by the pen represents the cumulative (total) number of responses the subject has made. Because the paper comes out of the recorder at a constant speed, the horizontal distance on the cumulative

---

BOX 5.2. Defining responses in behavior therapy

The concept of the operant is useful in defining behaviors in the clinic as well as the laboratory. A mother brings her child to the clinic complaining that the child is hyperactive or undisciplined. She describes her child with comments like "He wreaks havoc whenever he enters the room" or "He drives me crazy" or "He is completely uncontrollable." Similarly, a distraught husband and wife may seek help because they feel the love has disappeared from their marriage. Both the mother and the married couple describe their problem in general terms even though the difficulty comes from a series of specific responses. Treatment in many cases must start with a more precise definition of the activities that are problematic. What does the child actually do when he enters a room? What specific responses lead the husband and wife to conclude that love is lost? Sometimes defining the specific problem responses is enough to alleviate the difficulty. At other times the clinician has to help the clients find out what kinds of events or situations promote the problem responses. It may then be possible to change the environment in a way that encourages more desirable responses to replace the problematic activities.

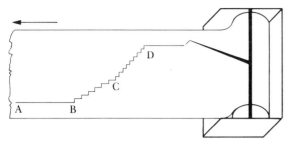

FIGURE 5.4. Cumulative recorder used for the continuous recording of behavior. The paper moves out of the machine toward the left at a fixed rate. Each response causes the pen to move up the paper one step. No responses occurred between points A and B. A moderate rate of responding occurred between points B and C, and a rapid rate occurred between points C and D.

record is a measure of how much time has elapsed in the session. The slope of the line made by the cumulative recorder represents the rate of responding.

The **cumulative record** provides a complete visual representation of when and how frequently the animal responds during a session. In the cumulative record shown in Figure 5.4, for example, the animal did not perform the response between points A and B. A slow rate of responding occurred between points B and C. Responses occurred more frequently between points C and D, and the animal quit responding after point D.

The behavioral-baseline technique. When a subject is first put in a Skinner box, it engages in a wide variety of activities. Each activity has a particular rate of occurrence before conditioning. A naive rat, for example, has a high rate of sniffing and a low rate of lever pressing. This initial rate of responding before the introduction of experimental manipulations is called the **free-operant baseline** or the **operant level.** The free-operant baseline can be used to assess the change in behavior that occurs when a conditioning procedure is introduced. Reinforcement of lever pressing, for example, will increase the rate of this response from its low operant level to a much higher rate.

The free-operant baseline, or operant level, is useful in revealing the effects of procedures such as reinforcement that *increase* the rate of responding.

However, if the operant level of a response is low to begin with, it cannot be used to detect the effects of experimental manipulations that might further *decrease* the rate of the behavior. In such cases, it is desirable to regularly reinforce the operant response so that it will occur at a stable rate higher than the operant level. This level of responding maintained by reinforcement is also called a baseline. The baseline rate of a reinforced operant response can be used to evaluate the effects of procedures, stimuli, or other manipulations that may either increase or decrease the rate of operant behavior. The effects of the experimental manipulations are revealed by changes in the baseline rate of the operant response.

In Chapter 3 we described the use of a **behavioral baseline** to evaluate the effects of aversive classical conditioning procedures. The technique, known as conditioned suppression or the conditioned emotional response procedure, first involves getting rats to lever-press for food reinforcement at a steady rate. A light or tone CS is then paired with shock. The effects of this classical conditioning are then evaluated by presenting the conditioned stimulus while the subject is pressing the response lever. As can be seen in Figure 5.5, the animal stops lever-pressing when the CS is presented. The cumulative record is flat during the CS. Before and after presentation of the CS, the animal presses the lever at a steady rate. Thus, the effects of the classical conditioning procedure are clearly evident in a change in the baseline rate of the operant behavior.

The behavioral-baseline technique popularized by Skinner and his students provides a novel method for the analysis of behavior because it permits evaluation of the effects of an experimental manipulation on the behavior of individual subjects (see Sidman, 1960). Until the behavioral-baseline technique was developed, studies of learning typically involved investigating large groups of subjects exposed to each experimental condition. The effects of these conditions were then evaluated by comparing the performance of subjects across groups. The results were based on the average performance of groups of subjects. Skinner objected to this group-statistical approach and advocated exposing individual subjects to the same reinforcement procedure until the behavior was

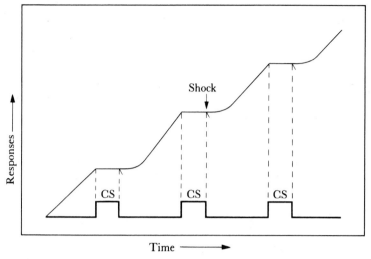

FIGURE 5.5. Cumulative record showing effects of conditioned emotional response training. Subjects are given a brief shock at the end of each CS presentation and consequently suppress their lever-press responding during the CS. (Hypothetical data.)

stable and predictable. He then observed how a manipulation influenced this stable baseline. As long as the baseline was indeed stable, the results of the experimental manipulation could be easily observed. Given that stable behavioral baselines can be produced, Skinner argued that large groups of subjects are unnecessary in behavioral research. The effects of experimental manipulations should be evident with individual subjects. As it has turned out, both the group-statistical and individual-subject approaches have their place in the experimental analysis of behavior. Some questions are more easily answered using a single-subject baseline technique. Other types of questions necessitate the use of groups of subjects. Throughout the remainder of the book we will discuss both types of research.

Instrumental Conditioning Procedures

In all instrumental conditioning situations, the subjects' behavior results in some type of environmental consequence. Instrumental conditioning procedures can be categorized according to the nature of the environmental event controlled by the behavior. The

event may be pleasant or unpleasant. A pleasant event is technically called an **appetitive stimulus.** An unpleasant event is technically called an **aversive stimulus.** Another factor that is important in the classification of instrumental conditioning procedures is the relationship, or contingency, between the response and the environmental event that it controls. The instrumental response may produce the event (in which case a positive contingency is said to be in effect) or eliminate it (in which case a negative contingency is said to be in effect). Table 5.1 describes four common instrumental conditioning procedures. The procedures differ in what type of stimulus (appetitive or aversive reinforcer) is controlled by the instrumental response and whether the response produces or eliminates the stimulus.

Positive reinforcement

The term **positive reinforcement** refers to a class of situations in which there is a positive contingency between the instrumental response and an appetitive reinforcing stimulus. In other words, if the subject performs the instrumental response, it receives the reinforcing stimulus; if the subject does not perform the response, the reinforcing stimulus is not pre-

TABLE 5.1. Types of instrumental conditioning procedures

Name of procedure	Effect of the instrumental response
Positive reinforcement	Response produces an appetitive stimulus that is not as likely to occur otherwise.
Punishment	Response produces an aversive stimulus that is not as likely to occur otherwise.
Negative reinforcement (escape or avoidance)	Response eliminates or prevents the occurrence of an aversive stimulus that is more likely otherwise.
Omission training	Response eliminates or prevents the occurrence of an appetitive stimulus that is more likely otherwise.

sented. Giving a hungry rat a food pellet whenever it presses a response lever but not when it does not press the lever is a laboratory example of positive reinforcement. There are many examples of positive reinforcement outside the laboratory. A father may give his child a cookie only when she puts away her toys; a teacher may praise a student only when the student hands in a good report; or an employee may receive a bonus check only when she performs well on the job. The intention of the father, the teacher, and the employer is to make sure that the instrumental response continues to occur and maybe even increases in frequency.

Sometimes continuous rewarding events are used in positive reinforcement procedures. In these cases, the rewarding event continues (or may even increase) as long as the instrumental response is being performed. If the instrumental response stops, the rewarding stimulus also stops or is decreased. In an interesting application of this type of positive reinforcement, infants were conditioned to kick in order to operate a mobile suspended over the crib (Rovee & Rovee, 1969). The harder they kicked, the more movement they could produce in the mobile. The infants showed a rapid and sustained increase in kicking under these circumstances.

Laboratory procedures in which a continuous reinforcing stimulus is used resemble situations outside the laboratory in which there is a direct mechanical connection between behavior and the environment. For example, as long as you pedal a bicycle, it continues to move; as long as you stoke a fire on a cold winter day, it continues to provide enjoyable warmth; as long as a child pumps her feet on a swing, she continues to enjoy the back-and-forth motion of the swing. Although these examples involve continuous reinforcers, they nevertheless represent positive reinforcement because there is a positive contingency in each case between the instrumental response and the reinforcer. As soon as the instrumental responses are terminated, the reinforcing stimuli are also terminated.

Punishment

The term **punishment** refers to a class of situations in which there is a positive contingency between the instrumental response and an unpleasant, or aversive, stimulus. If the subject performs the instrumental response, it receives the aversive stimulus; if it does not perform the instrumental response, the aversive stimulus is not presented. A mother may reprimand her child for running into the street but not for playing quietly in the yard; your boss may criticize you for being late to a meeting; your teacher may give you a failing grade for answering too many test questions incorrectly. Such procedures decrease the future likelihood of the instrumental response.

Laboratory experiments on punishment usually also involve some type of positive reinforcement to get the instrumental behavior to occur occasionally. The subject may be initially trained to make some response for positive reinforcement, such as pressing a lever or running down a runway for food. Once the lever response is established, an aversive stimulus, such as shock, may be presented after each lever press. In the runway, the subject may receive a brief shock in the goal box. The result is a decrease in lever pressing or running.

Negative reinforcement

The first two situations we described involved a positive contingency between the instrumental response and the reinforcer. If the response occurred, the reinforcer was delivered; if the response did not occur, the reinforcer was not delivered. In positive reinforcement, the reinforcer was a rewarding, or pleasant, stimulus; in punishment, the reinforcer was an unpleasant, or aversive, stimulus. We now turn to procedures that involve a **negative contingency** between the instrumental response and reinforcer. In a negative contingency the response turns off or prevents the presentation of the reinforcer. If the response occurs, the reinforcer is withheld; if the response does not occur, the reinforcer is delivered. Such a procedure increases the likelihood of behavior if the reinforcer is an aversive stimulus. Situations in which the occurrence of an instrumental response terminates or prevents the delivery of an aversive stimulus are called **negative reinforcement** procedures.

There are two types of negative reinforcement procedures. In one case the aversive stimulus is continuously present but can be terminated by the instrumental response. This type of procedure is called **escape.** Prisoners may escape the unpleasantness of a jail by breaking out. You may escape the unpleasant sounds of a radio that is receiving only static by turning it off. People may leave a movie theater to escape the experience of a bad movie. In the laboratory, a rat may be exposed to a continuous shock at the beginning of a trial. By jumping over a barrier or pressing a lever, the rat can escape the shock. In all these cases, the presence of the aversive stimulus sets the occasion for the instrumental response. The instrumental response is reinforced by termination of the aversive stimulus only if the response occurs during the aversive stimulus. If the rat presses the lever when the shock is not activated, the lever-press response is not reinforced by shock termination.

The second type of negative reinforcement procedure involves an aversive stimulus that is scheduled to be presented sometime in the future. In this case the instrumental response prevents delivery of the aversive stimulus. This type of procedure is called **avoidance.** There are many things we do to prevent the occurrence of something bad. Students often study before an examination to avoid receiving a bad grade; responding to a fire alarm may permit a person to avoid getting burned; people get their cars tuned up regularly to avoid unexpected breakdowns. In the laboratory, a rat may be scheduled to receive shock at the end of a warning stimulus. However, if it makes the instrumental response during the warning stimulus, the shock is not delivered. We will have much more to say about avoidance behavior in Chapter 9.

Omission training

Another type of situation that involves a negative contingency between the instrumental response and the reinforcer is called **omission training.** In this case, the instrumental response prevents the delivery of a pleasant event, or appetitive reinforcer. If the subject makes the instrumental response, the appetitive reinforcer is not delivered; if the subject does not respond, the appetitive reinforcer is presented. Thus, the reinforcer is delivered only if the subject withholds the instrumental response. As you might suspect, this type of procedure leads to a decrease in the likelihood of the instrumental behavior.

Omission training is often a preferred method of discouraging human behavior because it does not involve delivering an aversive stimulus (as punishment does). Omission training is being used when a child is told to go to his room after doing something bad. The parents are not introducing an aversive stimulus when they tell the child to go to his room. There is nothing aversive about the child's room. Rather, by sending the child to the room, the parents are withdrawing sources of appetitive reinforcement, such as playing with friends or watching television. Suspending someone's driver's license for drunken driving also constitutes omission training (withdrawal of the reinforcement or privilege of driving).

Omission training procedures are also sometimes called **differential reinforcement of other behavior,** or **DRO.** This term highlights the fact that in omission training the subject periodically receives the positive reinforcer provided it is engaged in behavior *other* than the response specified by the procedure. Making the target response results in omission of the reward that would have been delivered had the subject performed some "other" behavior. Thus, omission training involves the reinforcement of "other" behavior.

Final note on terminology

Often there is considerable confusion about the terms used to describe instrumental conditioning procedures. Several comments may help clarify matters. First, in the terms *positive* and *negative reinforcement, positive* and *negative* do not refer to pleasant and unpleasant outcomes. Rather, they refer to positive and negative contingencies between the instrumental response and its environmental consequence. Positive reinforcement involves a positive contingency between behavior and an environmental event (*presentation* of a rewarding stimulus), and negative reinforcement involves a negative contingency between behavior and an environmental event (*removal* of an aversive stimulus). The term *reinforcement* is used in both cases because both positive and negative reinforcement involve the strengthening (or reinforcement) of behavior.

Another common confusion involves negative reinforcement and punishment. An aversive stimulus is used in both procedures. However, the relation of the instrumental response to the aversive stimulus is drastically different in the two cases. In what is commonly called punishment, there is a positive contingency between the instrumental response and the aversive stimulus. (The response results in delivery of the aversive stimulus.) In contrast, in negative reinforcement, there is a negative response/reinforcer contingency. (The response either terminates or prevents the delivery of the aversive stimulus.) This difference in the contingencies produces very different outcomes. The instrumental response is decreased by the punishment procedure and increased by negative reinforcement.

Fundamental Elements of Instrumental Conditioning

As we shall see in the coming chapters, analysis of instrumental conditioning involves numerous factors and variables. However, the essence of instrumental behavior is that it is controlled by its consequences. Thus, instrumental conditioning fundamentally involves three elements: a response, an outcome (the reinforcer), and a relation, or contingency, between the response and the reinforcer. In the remainder of this chapter, we will discuss the effects that each of these fundamental elements has on instrumental conditioning.

The instrumental response

The outcome of instrumental conditioning procedures depends in part on the nature of the response being conditioned. Some responses are more easily modified by certain instrumental conditioning procedures than other responses are. In Chapter 9 we will describe how the nature of the response influences the outcome of negative reinforcement (avoidance) and punishment procedures. In the present section we will describe how the nature of the response determines the results of positive reinforcement procedures.

We have already described two contemporary techniques for the study of instrumental conditioning that involve different types of responses. In discrete-trial runway studies, subjects have to go from the start to the goal box in a runway to obtain the reinforcer. Subjects in these experiments do not have to learn the response involved in the task—locomotion. The animals used in these experiments are typically old enough that they are already able to walk and run. Runway studies involve teaching the animal where to run and what to run for.

In contrast to the runway situation, free-operant lever-press training does not involve a response already in the subjects' repertoire. Most of the rats that serve in lever-press experiments have never had the opportunity to press a lever before. Therefore, as we noted earlier, under "Free-Operant Methods," the lever-press behavior has to be shaped by the reinforcement of successive approximations. Exactly how is this shaping done and what does it accomplish? Although rats may come into a lever-press experiment never having pressed a lever before, they are not entirely inexperienced in the various behavioral components of pressing a lever. Lever pressing requires that the rat get up on its hind legs, that it reach out a paw, and that it press down with its paw. All these responses are likely to be already in the rat's repertoire. What, then, does a rat learn that is new? It learns to make various components of the lever-press behavior in a coordinated fashion so that the lever gets depressed and it earns the reward. Unless rearing, reaching out a paw, and pressing down occur in the correct sequence and in the correct place in the experimental chamber, these actions do not constitute pressing the lever. Thus, instrumental conditioning of lever pressing involves the rearrangement of components of the rat's behavior. Instrumental conditioning can lead to the *creation of a new behavioral unit defined by what is required to obtain the reinforcer* (see Schwartz, 1981, for a further discussion).

The runway and the lever-press examples illustrate that instrumental conditioning can act on already existing behavioral units and can result in the creation of new ones. What is the generality of these processes? Can instrumental conditioning control the frequency of all already existing behaviors? Are there any limits to the types of new behavioral units that instrumental conditioning can create? Answers to such questions are fundamental to evaluating the generality of instrumental conditioning.

Response constraints on instrumental conditioning.   During the past 25 years, numerous examples of response limitations on instrumental conditioning have been documented. In Chapter 4 we saw that classical conditioning occurs at different rates depending on the combination of CS and US that is used. Rats readily learn to associate tastes with sickness, for example, whereas associations between tastes and shock are not so easily learned. Such examples suggest that a CS has to "belong" with a US, or be "relevant" to the US, for conditioning to occur rapidly. Analogous belongingness, or relevance, relations occur in instrumental conditioning.

Thorndike was the first to observe differences in the conditionability of various responses with reinforcement. In many of the puzzle-box experiments, the cat had to manipulate a latch or string to escape from the box. However, Thorndike also tried to condition such responses as yawning and scratching. The cats could learn to make these responses. Interestingly, however, the form of the responses changed as training proceeded. At first, the cat would scratch itself vigorously to be let out of the box. On later trials, it would only make "aborted" scratching movements. It might put its leg to its body but would not make a true scratch response. Similar results were obtained in attempts to condition yawning. As training progressed, the animal might open its mouth to be let out of the box, but it would not give a *bona fide* yawn.

Thorndike proposed the concept of **belongingness** to explain the failures to train such responses as scratching and yawning. According to this concept, certain responses naturally belong with certain reinforcers because of the subject's evolutionary history. Operating a latch and pulling a string are manipulatory responses that naturally belong with release from confinement. In contrast, scratching and yawning have not evolved to help animals escape from confinement and therefore do not belong with release from the puzzle box. Presumably this is why scratching and yawning do not persist as vigorous *bona fide* responses when reinforced by release from the box.

The concept of belongingness in instrumental conditioning is nicely illustrated by the results of a study involving a fish called the three-spined stickleback (*Gasterosteus aculeatus*). During the mating season each spring, male sticklebacks establish territories from which they chase away and fight other males and court females. Sevenster (1973) used the presentation of another male or a female as a reinforcer in instrumental conditioning of a male stickleback. One group of subjects was required to bite a rod to obtain access to the reinforcer. Biting is a component of the aggressive behavior that occurs when a resident male encounters an intruder male. When the reinforcer was another male, biting behavior increased; access to another male was an effective reward for the biting response. In contrast, biting did not increase when it was reinforced with courtship opportunity. However, courtship opportunity was an effective reward for other responses, such as swimming through a ring. Evidently, a belongingness relation exists between biting and the consequent presentation of another male. In contrast, biting does not "belong with" presentation of a female, which typically elicits courtship instead of aggression.

Various limitations on instrumental conditioning

were also observed by Breland and Breland (1961), who encountered interesting difficulties in attempts to condition instrumental responses with food reinforcement in several species. Their goal was to train amusing response chains in animals with operant conditioning procedures for displays to be used in amusement parks and zoos. During the course of this work they observed dramatic behavior changes that were not consistent with the reinforcement procedures they were using. For example, they describe a raccoon that was reinforced for picking up a coin and depositing it in a coin bank:

> We started out by reinforcing him for picking up a single coin. Then the metal container was introduced, with the requirement that he drop the coin into the container. Here we ran into the first bit of difficulty: he seemed to have a great deal of trouble letting go of the coin. He would rub it up against the inside of the container, pull it back out, and clutch it firmly for several seconds. However, he would finally turn it loose and receive his food reinforcement. Then the final contingency: we [required] that he pick up [two] coins and put them in the container.
>
> Now the raccoon really had problems (and so did we). Not only could he not let go of the coins, but he spent seconds, even minutes, rubbing them together (in a most miserly fashion), and dipping them into the container. He carried on this behavior to such an extent that the practical application we had in mind—a display featuring a raccoon putting money in a piggy bank—simply was not feasible. The rubbing behavior became worse and worse as time went on, in spite of nonreinforcement [p. 682].*

The Brelands had similar difficulties with other species. Pigs, for example, also could not learn to put coins in a piggy bank. After initial training, they began rooting the coins along the ground. The Brelands called the development of such responses as rooting in the pigs and rubbing coins together in the raccoons **instinctive drift.** As the term implies, the extra responses that developed in these food-reinforcement situations were activities the animals instinctively perform when obtaining food. Pigs root along the ground in connection with feeding, and

---

*From "The Misbehavior of Organisms," by K. Breland and M. Breland. In *American Psychologist,* 1961, *16,* 682. Copyright 1961 by the American Psychological Association.

raccoons rub and dunk food-related objects. These innate food-related responses are apparently very strong and can take over to the extent that they compete with the responses required by the experimenter. The Brelands emphasized that such instinctive response tendencies have to be taken into account in the analysis of behavior.

Experimental analyses of response constraints on instrumental conditioning. Response limitations on the effectiveness of instrumental conditioning have attracted extensive experimental attention in recent years (see Domjan, 1983, for a recent review). This research has revealed a number of factors that determine how susceptible a particular response will be to modification through instrumental conditioning. One important factor is the *motivational state of the subject.* Instrumental conditioning involves motivating the subject in some way (depriving it of food, for example), and the subject's motivational state limits the types of activities it is likely to perform. In hamsters, for example, food deprivation decreases the probability of self-care responses such as face washing and scratching but increases the probability of environment-directed activities such as digging, scratching at a wall (scrabbling), and rearing on hind legs (Shettleworth, 1975). These changes in the likelihood of various responses induced by food deprivation are related to how readily the responses are increased by food reinforcement. Environment-directed responses (digging, rearing, scrabbling) that are increased by food deprivation are also readily increased by food reinforcement. In contrast, self-care responses (face washing, scratching) that are decreased by food deprivation are not readily strengthened by food reward (Shettleworth, 1975). These results suggest that some of the limitation on instrumental conditioning of certain responses is due to the fact that these responses are decreased by the motivational state (food deprivation) instituted during instrumental conditioning. Because animals are not likely to engage in self-care grooming responses when they are hungry, it is difficult to reinforce grooming with food (for further studies of reinforcement of grooming, see Charlton, 1983; Iversen, Ragnarsdottir, & Randrup, 1984).

BOX 5.3. Teaching violin playing

The research on response limitations in instrumental conditioning indicates that it is important to consider the subject's naturally occurring response tendencies in designing training procedures. This principle serves as the basis for a novel and highly successful method for teaching violin playing developed by the Japanese violinist Shinicki Suzuki. Traditional approaches to violin playing typically begin with teaching students to associate printed notes on a page with the position of their fingers on the violin. In addition, the students are required to draw the bow slowly across the strings to produce a smooth sound. Suzuki observed that neither of these tasks is close to naturally occurring response tendencies in young children. Instead, very young children find it much easier to associate the *sound* of a note with the position of their fingers on the violin. Suzuki likened this feature of learning to the way children naturally learn language. They initially learn meanings of words through listening, not through reading. Suzuki also observed that young children find it much easier to move the bow with quick, short movements over the strings than to draw the bow slowly. He successfully capitalized on these observations in his teaching method. With his method, which has been adopted in many parts of the world, children do not begin by learning to read music. Rather, they listen to recordings of their pieces and place their fingers on the violin so as to imitate these sounds. In addition, the beginning pieces use short, quick bowing movements exclusively. Long, smooth motions are not attempted until the child has considerable skill. The result is that many children have been taught highly complex violin-playing skills that teachers in the past thought were impossible at very young ages. Furthermore, because the technique makes use of responses that occur more naturally for the children, they can begin to play tunes early in their training and hence derive more enjoyment from their playing.

A second important variable in the susceptibility of various responses to instrumental conditioning is the presence of *supporting stimulation for the instrumental response*. As pantomime performers well know, it is difficult to go through the motions of climbing a ladder or hugging someone in the absence of a ladder to climb or someone to hug. Many instrumental responses, particularly ones that involve manipulating some aspect of the environment, require **supporting stimulation** to guide the response. The presence of supporting stimulation greatly facilitates performance of the behavior. Pearce, Colwill, and Hall (1978) obtained evidence that supporting stimulation can also facilitate instrumental learning. Their studies involved reinforcement of scratching in rats. They reasoned that scratching may be difficult to increase with food reinforcement because it is difficult to scratch without an itch. To provide an "itch," Pearce et al. fitted plastic collars around the rats' necks. The cutaneous stimulation provided by the collars greatly facilitated instrumental conditioning of scratching even after the rats had become fully accustomed to wearing the collars.

A third factor that potentially could create difficulties in the instrumental conditioning of a response is its *operant level*. As we noted earlier, the operant level is the rate of occurrence of a response before the instrumental conditioning procedure is introduced. Studies comparing the instrumental conditioning of responses like face washing, scratching, scrabbling, scent marking, rearing, and digging typically have not used shaping procedures. Therefore, investigators had to rely on the spontaneous occurrence of the responses before delivering the reinforcer. If a response had a very low operant level, it would not occur very often and therefore could not be reinforced often. The low frequency of reinforcement might then be responsible for lack of increase in the behavior. Plausible as such an account is, many of the response constraints on instrumental conditioning we have described cannot be attributed to low operant levels. In many studies, responses that were not increased by reinforcement were just as likely to occur prior to introduction of the conditioning procedures as more easily modified action patterns (see, for example, Annable & Wearden, 1979; Charlton

& Ferraro, 1982; Pearce et al., 1978; Shettleworth, 1975, 1978b).

The fourth and final factor we will consider that can influence whether a response is increased by reinforcement is the *intrusion of incompatible responses classically conditioned during the course of instrumental conditioning*. Instrumental conditioning procedures typically allow for the occurrence of classical conditioning. We will discuss interactions between instrumental and classical conditioning in greater detail in coming chapters. In the present context, classical conditioning is important in analyzing results first reported by Breland and Breland (1961). As we noted earlier, they found that a variety of species (raccoons and pigs, for example) have difficulty learning to pick up a coin and deposit it in a slot for food reinforcement. Instead of depositing the coins in the slot, the animals held them and manipulated them (see also Boakes, Poli, Lockwood, & Goodall, 1978). This persistent holding and manipulation was never explicitly reinforced and, in fact, resulted in loss of food reinforcement.

Recent research suggests that persistent holding and manipulation of coins reflects classical conditioning of the coins with food reinforcement (Timberlake, 1983b; Timberlake, Wahl, & King, 1982). When animals are reinforced with food for picking up a coin and putting it in a slot, they are experiencing more than just the pairing of particular instrumental responses with food reinforcement. Certain stimuli—namely, stimuli of the coin—are also being paired with food reinforcement, and this results in classical conditioning of the coin stimuli. Once the coin becomes conditioned with food, it comes to elicit food-related conditioned responses. These classically conditioned responses include holding and manipulating the food-signal object. The instrumental response of depositing the coin in the slot is disrupted by the occurrence of the classically conditioned holding and manipulating responses.

Holding and manipulating the coins was "maladaptive" in the Breland and Breland experiments because it prevented subjects from satisfying the requirements of the instrumental procedure and obtaining food reinforcement. What made the behavior maladaptive is that the food-signal object (the coin)

was different from the food object. Outside the laboratory, food-signal stimuli and the food itself often reside in the same object. Typically, the food signal is an aspect of the food that is evident from a distance. The sight of a mouse scurrying on the ground is a signal for food for hawks flying overhead. An unbroken nutshell is a signal of food for a squirrel. In such cases, approach and manipulation of the food signal help animals actually obtain the food. Thus, ordinarily classically conditioned responses of holding and manipulating a food-signal object are compatible with and facilitate the food-procurement instrumental response. The Breland and Breland experiment produced "maladaptive" behavior because it involved the unusual separation of the food signal from the food object.

Final comment on response limitations. Research on response constraints on instrumental conditioning has confirmed that some responses are more difficult to modify with instrumental conditioning than others. However, such limitations should not be interpreted as proof that instrumental conditioning is not a "general" process. All phenomena of nature are constrained by particular boundary conditions. Recent research on response limitations has helped to specify what those boundary conditions are for instrumental conditioning and thus has helped to specify in greater detail the generalizability of instrumental conditioning.

The instrumental reinforcer

The second fundamental element of instrumental conditioning we will consider is the reinforcer. Several aspects of a reinforcer determine its effects on the learning and performance of instrumental behavior. We will first consider the direct effects of the quantity and quality of a reinforcer on instrumental behavior. We will then discuss how response to a particular reward amount and type depends on the subject's past experience with other reinforcers.

Quantity and quality of the reinforcer. Many studies have evaluated the influence of the quantity and quality of the reinforcer in both reinforcement

and punishment situations. The basic finding in these experiments has been that the behavioral effect of the instrumental conditioning procedure increases as the quantity and quality of the reinforcer or punisher increase. For example, food-reinforced responding increases with increases in the amount or quality of food presented consequent to the response, and shock-punished responding is suppressed more as the intensity of the shock is increased.

Although the quantity and quality of the reinforcer are logically different characteristics, often it is difficult to separate them experimentally. A change in the quantity of the reinforcer may also make the reinforcer qualitatively different. An increase in shock intensity, for example, may result in a qualitatively different type of discomfort. In an interesting experiment involving positive reinforcement, Hutt (1954) tried to isolate the effects of quantity and quality on instrumental behavior. Nine groups of rats were trained to press a bar for a liquid reinforcer. The reinforcer was varied in both quantity and quality for the various groups. Three of the groups received a small amount of fluid, three a medium amount, and three a large amount. The fluid was a mixture of water, milk, and flour. One of the three groups given a particular amount of fluid received this basic mixture. For another group, the quality of the mixture was improved by adding saccharin. For the third group, the quality of the fluid was reduced by adding a small amount of citric acid. Figure 5.6 shows the average rate of bar pressing for each group. Increases in either the quality or the quantity of the reinforcer produced higher rates of responding.

Shifts in the quality or quantity of the reinforcer. In the study by Hutt (1954), a given subject received only one particular quantity and quality of food throughout the experiment. What would happen if subjects were shifted from one type of reward to another? This is a particularly interesting question because it raises the possibility that the effectiveness of a particular reinforcer depends not only on its physical properties but also on how the reward compares with others the subject has had. We saw in Chapter 4 that the effectiveness of an unconditioned stimulus in classical conditioning depends on how the

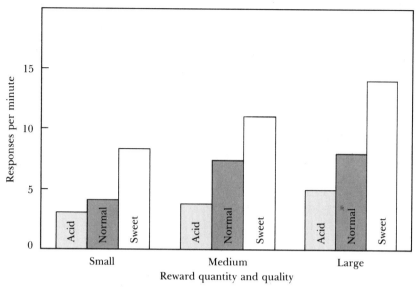

FIGURE 5.6. Average rates of responding in groups of subjects for which responding was reinforced with reinforcers varying in quantity and quality. *(After Hutt, 1954.)*

US compares with the subject's expectations based on prior experience. If the US is larger (or more intense) than expected, it will support excitatory conditioning. In contrast, if it is smaller (or weaker) than expected, the US will support inhibitory conditioning. Are there analogous effects of reward quantity and quality in instrumental conditioning? Evidently yes. Numerous studies have shown that the effects of a particular amount and type of reward on instrumental behavior depend on the quantity and quality of the reinforcer the subject previously experienced (see Flaherty, 1982, for a review). Speaking loosely, the research has shown that a good reward is treated as especially good after reinforcement with a poor reward, and a poor reward is treated as especially poor after reinforcement with a good reward.

Effects of a shift in the quantity of reward were first described by Crespi (1942). The basic results are also nicely illustrated by a more recent study by Mellgren (1972). Four groups of rats served in a runway experiment. During phase 1, two of the groups received a small reward (2 food pellets) each time they reached the end of the runway. The other two groups received a large reward (22 pellets) for each trip down the runway. (Delivery of the reward

was always delayed 20 sec after the subjects reached the end of the runway so that they would not run at their maximum speed.) After 11 trials of training in phase 1, one group of rats receiving each reward quantity was shifted to the alternate quantity. Thus, some rats were shifted from small to large reward (S-L), and others were shifted from large to small reward (L-S). The remaining two groups continued to receive the same amount of reward in phase 2 as they had received in phase 1. (These groups were designated as L-L and S-S.)

Figure 5.7 summarizes the results of the experiment. At the end of phase 1, subjects receiving the large reward ran slightly, but not significantly, faster than subjects receiving the small reward. For groups that continued to receive the same amount of reward in phase 2 as in phase 1 (groups L-L and S-S), instrumental performance did not change much when phase 2 was introduced. In contrast, significant deviations from these baselines of running were observed in groups of subjects that received shifts in reward magnitude with the start of phase 2. Subjects shifted from large to small reward (group L-S) rapidly decreased their running speeds, and subjects shifted from small to large reward (group S-L) soon increased their running speeds. The most significant finding was that, following a shift in reward magnitude, the subjects' behavior was not solely a function of the new reward magnitude. Rather, response to the new reward was enhanced by the subjects' previous history with a contrasting reward magnitude. Subjects shifted from a small to a large reward (group S-L) ran faster for the large reward than subjects that had always received the large reward (group L-L). Correspondingly, subjects shifted from a large to a small reward (group L-S) ran slower for the small reward than subjects that had always received the small reward (group S-S).

The results Mellgren obtained illustrate the phenomena of successive positive and negative behavioral contrast. **Positive behavioral contrast** refers to an outcome in which subjects respond more for a favorable reward if they previously received a less favorable reward than if they did not have this prior experience. In casual terminology, the favorable re-

ward looks especially good to the subjects in contrast to the worse reward they previously experienced. **Negative behavioral contrast** refers to an outcome in which subjects respond less for an unfavorable reward if they previously received a better reward than if they did not have this prior experience. In this case, the unfavorable reward looks especially bad to the subjects in contrast to the better reward they previously experienced.

Mellgren's results illustrate *successive behavioral contrast* effects because the two reward conditions were presented in different phases of the experiment, and only one shift in reward magnitude occurred for shifted groups. Positive and negative behavioral contrast are also obtained if reward conditions are shifted frequently, with some type of cue signaling each reward condition (see Williams, 1983, for a recent review). Such contrast effects are called *simultaneous behavioral contrast* because of the frequent reward shifts. The procedures used to produce simultaneous contrast are also called *multiple schedules of reinforcement*. We will consider multiple schedules further in Chapter 8.

Crespi (1942) suggested that positive and negative successive behavioral contrast phenomena reflect emotional reactions to the shift in reward conditions. A shift from small to large reward may create "joy," which facilitates instrumental responding. Correspondingly, a shift from large to small reward may create "anger" or frustration, which disrupts responding. Although various other approaches to the explanation of contrast effects have been pursued in recent years (see Flaherty, 1982), explanations that emphasize emotional reactions are still attractive. Details of an emotion-based account of positive behavioral contrast have not been well worked out yet. Much more information is available on the possible mechanisms of negative behavioral contrast.

Negative behavioral contrast may be explained in terms of the emotional effects of a downshift in reward conditions based on frustration theory, formulated by Abram Amsel (1958, 1962, 1967). Among other things, frustration theory provides a technical definition of frustration. The essence of the definition is that frustration occurs when subjects experience less reward than they expect. Frustration produced

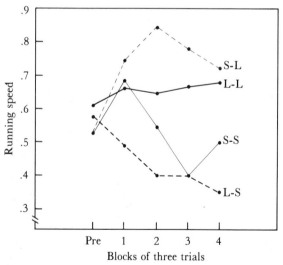

FIGURE 5.7. Running speeds of four groups of rats in blocks of three trials. Block "Pre" represents running speeds at the end of phase 1. Blocks 1–4 represent running speeds in phase 2. At the start of phase 2, groups S-L and L-S experienced a shift in amount of reward from small to large and large to small, respectively. Groups S-S and L-L received small and large rewards, respectively, throughout the experiment. *(After Mellgren, 1972.)*

by the encounter of less than an expected quantity or quality of reward is called **primary frustration.** Primary frustration is considered to be an unconditioned stimulus, much like other unconditioned stimuli we have encountered. Like other unconditioned stimuli, primary frustration elicits innate responses, which in this case consist in avoiding the goal area where the disappointing reward was encountered. How do these ideas help explain negative behavioral contrast? Negative behavioral contrast occurs when subjects are shifted from a large to a small reward (L-S). While they are reinforced with the large reward, subjects presumably learn to expect that particular type of reward. When they are then shifted to a small reward, the reward they encounter is smaller than what they expect, and therefore primary frustration is elicited. Primary frustration leads to avoidance of the goal box and hence slower running speeds. Such slow running speeds are not observed with subjects that are always given the small reward (S-S). These subjects never receive a large reward in the situation and therefore do not learn to expect one. Consequently, the small reward for them never constitutes less of a reward than what they expect, and hence they never experience frustration.

The response/reinforcer relation

As we have said, instrumental behavior produces and is controlled by its consequences. Animals and people perform all kinds of responses that have various consequences. In some cases, a direct relation exists between what a person does and the consequence that follows. If you put 50 cents into a coffee machine, you get a cup of coffee. As long as the machine is working, you will get a cup of coffee every time you put in the required 50 cents. In other cases, no relation may exist between behavior and an outcome. You may wear a red shirt to an examination and receive a good grade. However, you would not attribute your good grade to the wearing of the red shirt. In yet other instances, the relation between behavior and its consequences may be imperfect. An animal may search for food often but be successful only some of the time.

From the organism's point of view, figuring out the relation between its behavior and consequences of its behavior is an epistemological problem. Animals and people perform a continual stream of responses and experience all kinds of environmental events. You are continually doing something, even if it is just sitting still, and things are continually happening in your environment. For any organism, a critical problem is to figure out how its behavior is related to the environmental events it experiences. An organism must organize its behavior to meet various challenges, and it must do so in a way that makes the best use of its time and energy. To be efficient, an animal has to know the ways in which it can and cannot control its environment. There is no point in working hard to make the sun rise each morning, because that will happen anyway. It makes more sense to devote energy to building a shelter or hunting for food—things that do not become available without effort. You have to know what events are under your control to be able to distribute your efforts efficiently.

The relation between behavior and its consequences is one of the most important factors in the control of instrumental behavior. When we study the acquisition of instrumental behavior in the laboratory, we typically arrange for the instrumental response to produce the reinforcer without delay. If a pigeon pecks a key in the required fashion, it immediately receives grain; if a rat makes the correct turn in a T maze, it finds food right away. We casually think of such instrumental conditioning situations as involving cause and effect. Pecks cause delivery of grain, and correct turns cause access to food. In fact, however, two relations are involved in such situations. The first of these is a temporal relation between the instrumental response and the reinforcer. If the reinforcer is presented immediately after the response, we call this relation **temporal contiguity.** The second relation is the correlation between the instrumental response and the reinforcer, or the **response/reinforcer contingency.** The response/reinforcer contingency is the extent to which delivery of the reinforcer depends on the prior occurrence of the instrumental response. Investigators have been very much interested in analyzing the importance of both temporal contiguity and response/reinforcer contingency in instrumental conditioning.

Effects of temporal contiguity. The importance of temporal contiguity in instrumental conditioning has been investigated by systematically varying the delay between occurrence of the instrumental response and subsequent delivery of the reinforcer. Early investigations of the effects of delay of reinforcement on instrumental conditioning were conducted with the use of the T maze, in which the instrumental response was turning in a particular direction. Groups of rats were used, each receiving a different delay of reinforcement. Reinforcement was delayed by confining the rat to a compartment after it made its choice but before it was allowed to enter the goal box and gain access to the reinforcer. Figure 5.8 summarizes results from two such studies. In both experiments, learning was best with no delay of reinforcement and declined thereafter with increasing delays. The data from Wolfe (1934) show a much flatter gradient than the data from Grice (1948). Delays of reinforcement did not disrupt learning nearly as much in Wolfe's study as they did in Grice's. What accounts for this difference in results?

Unlike Wolfe's experiment, Grice's was specifically designed to eliminate cues other than the reinforcer that might signal to the rat that it had made the correct response and that food would be forthcoming. Food-associated stimuli that signal the forthcoming presentation of food are called **secondary** or **conditioned reinforcers.** A variety of cues can become conditioned as reinforcers. If the food reward is always given in the left arm of a T maze, for example, the left arm can become a conditioned reinforcer. Subjects that enter this arm will be immediately exposed to the conditioned reinforcer and therefore will not experience a delay of reward even if presentation of the food is delayed. Thus, conditioned reinforcers can enable subjects to "bridge" a delay between the instrumental response and delivery of the primary reinforcer (see Cronin, 1980; Winter & Perkins, 1982).

In Grice's experiment, the reinforced response was choosing the white arm of a T maze. However, the white arm was sometimes on the right and sometimes on the left. Therefore, secondary cues from turning right or left were not predictive of the food reward and did not become conditioned as reinforcers. The procedure ensured that groups of rats for which delivery of food was delayed after the choice response would not receive immediate feedback from conditioned reinforcers. Procedures like Grice's that minimize the possibility of immediate conditioned reinforcement typically result in a very steep delay-of-reinforcement gradient.

Grice showed that instrumental conditioning can be disrupted by delays of reinforcement as short as .5 sec. Why is instrumental conditioning so sensitive to a delay of reinforcement? A potential answer to this question is provided by realizing that behavior consists of an ongoing, continual stream of activities. When reinforcement is delayed after performance of a specified response R_A, the subject does not stop responding. After performing R_A, the subject performs other activities R_B, R_C, R_D, and so on. A

BOX 5.4.   Praise: Bridging the delay-of-reinforcement interval

Perhaps the greatest hindrance to the application of instrumental conditioning principles in various training situations is that it is often inconvenient to deliver reinforcers immediately after occurrences of the desired response. Trainers of animal circus acts often carry pieces of food with them during the performance to reinforce correct responses. However, they cannot always deliver the treats, because the animal may be too far away, or eating the treat may distract the animal from making the next response. Therefore, it is not uncommon for the trainers to use verbal praise. Words such as *good* and *nice* can be conditioned to serve as conditioned reinforcers for a variety of animals by saying the words whenever the animals are given pieces of food. The praise can then be used to provide immediate reinforcement and bridge the interval between performance of the desired response and actual delivery of the primary reward. This is one reason trainers frequently talk to their animals during a performance.

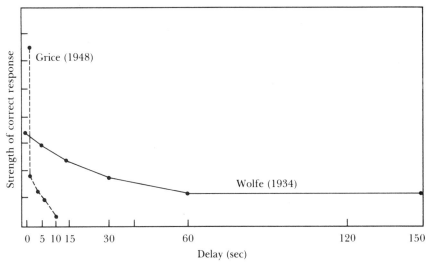

FIGURE 5.8. Strength of the correct response as a function of delay of reinforcement in two experiments (Wolfe, 1934; Grice, 1948).

delayed reward may be delivered immediately after response R_M. The problem for the subject then is to distinguish R_A, the target instrumental response, from other responses it performed during the delay interval. If the subject has no way of distinguishing R_A from its other actions, one of these other actions (probably the one closest to reward delivery) will become associated with the reinforcer.

The above considerations suggest that if the instrumental response were marked in some way to make it distinguishable from the ongoing stream of other actions of the subject, delay of reinforcement would not have such deleterious effects on instrumental conditioning. Lieberman, McIntosh, and Thomas (1979) tested this prediction in a study with rats, using the maze shown in Figure 5.9. After release from the start box, the rats had a choice between entering a white and a black side arm. Entering the white side arm was designated as the correct instrumental response and was reinforced with access to food in the goal box after a delay of 60 sec. The two groups were differentiated by what happened to them immediately after making the correct choice. Subjects in the "marked" group were picked up by the experimenter and placed in the delay box. In contrast, subjects in the "unmarked" group were undisturbed. After they

made the correct response, the door at the end of the choice alley was opened for them, and they were allowed to walk into the delay box. Thus, for them the correct choice response was not distinguished in a special way in their stream of other activities. Sixty seconds after the instrumental response, subjects in both groups were picked up and placed in the goal box to obtain the reinforcer. The same sequence of events occurred when the subjects made an incorrect response except that in these cases they were not reinforced at the end of the delay interval.

Results of the experiment are shown in the graph in Figure 5.9. Subjects in the marked group learned the instrumental response with the 60-sec delay of reinforcement much better than subjects in the unmarked group. At the end of 50 training trials, marked subjects were making the correct choice 90% of the time. In contrast, unmarked subjects were making the correct choice about 50% of the time, which is chance performance. In another experiment, Lieberman et al. demonstrated successful learning with delayed reinforcement when the instrumental response was marked by a brief, intense light or noise. These effects of marking cannot be explained in terms of secondary or conditioned reinforcement, because the marking stimulus was presented after

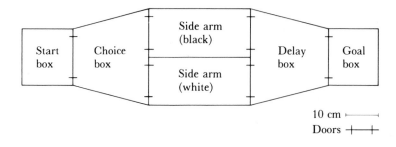

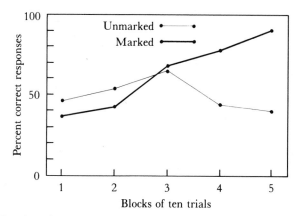

FIGURE 5.9. Top view of apparatus and results of an experiment to test the effects of marking an instrumental response on instrumental conditioning with reinforcement delayed 60 sec. Choosing the white side arm was designated as the correct instrumental response. Subjects spent the delay interval in the delay box. "Marked" subjects were placed in the delay box after each choice response. "Unmarked" subjects were allowed to walk into the delay box undisturbed. *(After Lieberman et al., 1979.)*

both correct and incorrect choice responses. Thus, the marking stimulus itself did not provide information that the subject had made a correct response (see also Thomas, Lieberman, McIntosh, & Ronaldson, 1983).

Studies of the effects of marking in delayed reinforcement situations are provocative but preliminary. Future research will have to document the range of situations in which marking facilitates delayed conditioning and what types of stimuli are effective markers and why.

The response/reinforcer contingency. We met the term *contingency* in Chapter 3 in our discussion of classical conditioning. In classical conditioning, *contingency* refers to the predictive relation between the conditioned and unconditioned stimuli.

In instrumental conditioning, *contingency* refers to the predictive relation between the instrumental response and the reinforcer. As discussed in Chapter 3, contingency is defined in terms of two probabilities. The response/reinforcer contingency is defined in terms of the probability that the reinforcer (S^{R+}) will occur given that the instrumental response (R) has been performed $[p(S^{R+}/R)]$ and the probability that the reinforcer will occur given that the instrumental response has not been performed $[p(S^{R+}/noR)]$. A perfect positive contingency exists if the reinforcer is delivered after each occurrence of the instrumental response $[p(S^{R+}/R) = 1.0]$ but is never delivered in the absence of the response $[p(S^{R+}/noR) = 0]$. A negative contingency exists if the reinforcer is more likely to occur when the instrumental response is not performed than when the response is performed

$[p(S^{R+}/noR) > p(S^{R+}/R)]$. Finally, a zero contingency exists if the reinforcer is equally likely whether or not the instrumental response has been performed $[p(S^{R+}/R) = p(S^{R+}/noR)]$.

The studies of delay of reinforcement reviewed above all involved a perfect positive contingency between response and reinforcement. Although reinforcement was delayed for some groups, the probability of reinforcement was always 1.0 given that the instrumental response occurred, and reinforcement was never provided if the instrumental response did not occur. Delaying the presentation of the reinforcer following the response did not change the fact that reinforcement was always entirely dependent on prior performance of the instrumental response. Studies of delay of reinforcement show that such a perfect contingency between response and reinforcer is not sufficient to produce instrumental conditioning. Even with total dependence of reinforcement on prior responding, conditioning typically does not occur if the reinforcement is delayed too long. Does this mean that the contingency between response and reinforcer is unimportant in instrumental conditioning?

Detection of causality.   Skinner (1948) was the first to investigate whether instrumental conditioning is possible in the absence of a positive response/reinforcer contingency. He placed several pigeons in separate experimental chambers and set the equipment to deliver a bit of grain every 15 sec irrespective of what the pigeons were doing. The birds were not required to peck a key or perform any other response to get the food. After a while, Skinner returned to see what the pigeons were doing. He described some of what he saw as follows:

> In six out of eight cases the resulting responses were so clearly defined that two observers could agree perfectly in counting instances. One bird was conditioned to turn counterclockwise about the cage, making two or three turns between reinforcements. Another repeatedly thrust its head into one of the upper corners of the cage. A third developed a "tossing" response, as if placing its head beneath an invisible bar and lifting it repeatedly. [Skinner, 1948, p. 168].

The pigeons appeared to Skinner to be responding as if their behavior controlled delivery of the reinforcer

when in fact the rewards were delivered independently of behavior. Accordingly, Skinner called this **superstitious behavior.**

Skinner's explanation of superstitious behavior rests on the idea of **accidental,** or **adventitious, reinforcement.** Animals are always doing something even if no particular responses are required to obtain reinforcers. Skinner suggested that whatever response a pigeon happens to make just before a reinforcer is delivered becomes strengthened and subsequently increases in frequency because of the reward. The accidental pairing of a response with delivery of the reinforcer is called *adventitious reinforcement.* One accidental pairing with a reinforcer increases the chance that the same response will occur just before the next delivery of reward. A second fortuitous response/reinforcer contiguity further strengthens the probability of the response. In this way, each accidental pairing helps to "stamp in" a particular response. After a while, the response will occur frequently enough to be identified as superstitious behavior.

Skinner's interpretation of his experiment was appealing and consistent with views of reinforcement that were widely held at the time. Impressed by studies of delay of reinforcement, theoreticians thought that temporal contiguity was the main factor responsible for learning. Skinner's experiment appeared to support this view and suggested that a positive response/reinforcer contingency is not necessary for instrumental conditioning.

Recent research has cast serious doubt on Skinner's conclusions. Although Skinner delivered food to his pigeons independently of their behavior, food deliveries were predictable because they occurred every 15 sec. Staddon and Simmelhag (1971) replicated Skinner's experiment and provided evidence that the "superstitious" behavior Skinner observed was generated by the predictability of food deliveries, not by adventitious reinforcement. They found that pigeons make different types of responses during short intervals between food presentations. Toward the end of the interval, for example, they all tend to perform food-related responses. These responses can become rather stereotyped, giving the impression that the pigeons are superstitious. (We will return to a more detailed discussion of the Staddon-Simmelhag experiment in Chapter 7.)

Skinner's analysis of "superstitious" behavior has also been called into question by recent evidence that animals are able to detect whether or not their behavior causes an environmental outcome. Killeen (1981; see also Killeen & Smith, 1984) devised an ingenious procedure for getting pigeons to tell him whether an outcome was caused by their behavior. The pigeons were placed in an experimental chamber with three pecking keys arranged in a row along one wall. Pecking the center key caused its light to go off 5% of the time. Occasionally, however, the center-key light was also turned off by signals from a computer independently of the pigeons' behavior. Each time the center key darkened, the pigeons were "asked" to report whether they or the computer had caused the light to go off. When the center key darkened, the two side keys were illuminated. If the pigeons had caused the light to go off, pecks at the left key were reinforced with food; if the computer had caused the center key light to go off, pecks at the right key were reinforced with food. Thus, by pecking on the left or right (the "I did it" or the "computer did it" side key), the pigeons could report on whether their behavior was responsible for the darkening of the center key.

The pigeons were remarkably accurate in their assessment of causality. They reported correctly 80–90% of the time. How they accomplished this was evident in some aspects of their behavior. For example, one bird pecked the center key in short quick bursts. If the light went off while it was pecking, it would choose the "I did it" side key. Between bursts of pecking on the center key, the pigeon stood in front of the "computer did it" side key. If the center light went off while the pigeon stood in front of the "computer did it" side key, it would peck that side key.

Effects of the controllability of reinforcers.

A strong contingency between an instrumental response and a reinforcer essentially means that the response controls the reinforcer. With a strong contingency, whether the reinforcer occurs depends on whether the instrumental response has occurred.

Studies of the effects of control over reinforcers have provided the most extensive body of evidence on the sensitivity of behavior to response/reinforcer contingencies. Although some of these studies have involved positive reinforcement (for example, Caspy & Lubow, 1981; Engberg, Hansen, Welker, & Thomas, 1972), most of the research has concerned the effects of control over aversive stimulation (see Alloy & Seligman, 1979; Maier & Seligman, 1976; Maier & Jackson, 1979; Seligman & Weiss, 1980).

Contemporary research on the effects of the controllability of aversive stimulation on learning originated with the pioneering studies of Seligman, Overmier, and Maier (for example, Overmier & Seligman, 1967; Seligman & Maier, 1967), who investigated the effects of exposure to uncontrollable shock on subsequent escape/avoidance learning. The typical finding was that exposure to uncontrollable shock disrupts subsequent learning. This phenomenon has come to be called the **learned-helplessness effect.** Learned-helplessness experiments are usually conducted in two phases with three groups of subjects. The various groups differ only in what happens to them in the first phase of the experiment. One group serves as an unstressed control group and receives no shocks during phase 1. The second group is exposed to a series of brief shocks that it can escape by performing a designated escape response, such as pressing on a panel. The third and most interesting group in the experiment receives shocks of the same intensity and duration as animals in the escape condition. However, for these subjects the shocks are uncontrollable—escape or avoidance responses are not available. All subjects then receive escape/avoidance training the next day in a new apparatus, such as a shuttle box. A shuttle box consists of two adjacent compartments separated by a low barrier (see Figure 9.4). Shocks are periodically presented, preceded by a signal. The animals can avoid shock by jumping over the barrier during the shock signal. If they fail to make the avoidance response in time, the shock is presented and jumping over the barrier to the other compartment serves as an escape response to turn off the shock.

The dramatic finding in experiments on the learned-helplessness effect is that exposure to uncontrollable shock during phase 1 produces a more severe deficit in subsequent escape/avoidance learning than exposure to escapable shocks of identical intensity and duration. A small deficit in learning is also observed in the escape group in comparison with subjects that received no shock during phase 1. However, this is not as severe as the deficit observed among animals exposed to inescapable shock. Thus, to a large extent the deficit in escape/avoidance learning in phase 2 is related to the controllability of the shocks received previously, not just to shock exposure. Recent research has shown that the detrimental effects of exposure to uncontrollable shock are also evident when subjects subsequently receive instrumental conditioning with food reinforcement (Caspy & Lubow, 1981; Rosellini & DeCola, 1981; Rosellini, DeCola, & Shapiro, 1982).

The fact that lack of control over shock creates a general deficit in subsequent instrumental behavior suggests that animals are sensitive to the contingent relation between their behavior and a reinforcer. Seligman and his associates proposed an explanation of the interference effect that emphasizes the detection of response/reinforcer contingencies. This account, known as the **learned-helplessness hypothesis,** assumes that during exposure to uncontrollable shocks animals learn that the shocks are independent of their behavior—that there is nothing they can do to control the shocks. This acquired expectation of a zero contingency between responding and shock interferes with learning that behavior can control presentations of a reinforcer during subsequent instrumental conditioning. The learned-helplessness explanation assumes that animals have two things to accomplish when they receive instrumental conditioning after exposure to inescapable shocks. They have to abandon their expectation of lack of control over reinforcers, and they have to learn what particular response is now required for reinforcement.

The learned-helplessness interpretation has gener-

BOX 5.5. Human applications of the concept of helplessness

The fact that a history of lack of control over reinforcers can severely disrupt subsequent instrumental performance has important implications for human behavior. The concept of helplessness has been extended and elaborated to a variety of areas of human concern, including depression, intellectual achievement, susceptibility to heart attacks, aging and death, and victimization and bereavement (see Garber & Seligman, 1980). An interesting aspect of these extensions is that with human beings the uncontrollability of aversive events is not sufficient to produce helplessness effects. How someone's behavior changes as a result of an unpleasant event depends on how the person interprets the causes of the bad event (Peterson & Seligman, 1984). Consider, for example, receiving a poor grade on a test. The extent to which this experience will make you lethargic and depressed will depend on what you think caused you to receive the bad grade. If you decide you received the bad grade because you are not very intelligent, you will become very discouraged in your studies and may drop out of college. Such an attribution is (1) global (being not very intelligent influences many of the things you do), (2) internal (it is something about yourself, not something about the situation you are in), and (3) stable (level of intelligence is difficult to change). Global, internal, and stable interpretations of the causes of aversive experiences tend to discourage instrumental behavior and lead to depression. Other types of interpretations do not have such deleterious effects. For example, if you attribute having received a poor grade to the fact that you were given the wrong test form or that the test was unfair, the poor grade is much less likely to make you depressed. These attributions are specific, external, and unstable. A wrong test form or a particular unfair test does not influence your behavior generally, does not indicate anything about you personally, and is not likely to recur every time you take a test.

ated considerable controversy (for example, Black, 1977; Levis, 1976). Research has shown that the deficit in instrumental learning that results from exposure to inescapable shock is not always due to the learning of an expectation of a zero contingency between responding and aversive stimulation. In some situations, inescapable shock produces a decrease in motor movement or response perseveration, and this is responsible for subsequent performance deficits (Anderson, Crowell, Cunningham, & Lupo, 1979; Anisman, de Catanzaro, & Remington, 1978; Anisman, Hamilton, & Zacharko, 1984; Irwin, Suissa, & Anisman, 1980). However, there are also situations in which effects on learning are not likely to be due to the suppression of movement caused by inescapable shock (for example, Jackson, Alexander, & Maier, 1980; Rosellini, DeCola, Plonsky, Warren, & Stilman, 1984). The diversity of findings suggests that exposure to uncontrollable aversive stimulation can activate several processes, including learned helplessness (Maier & Jackson, 1979).

One of the most exciting contemporary areas of investigation concerns the effects of escapable and of inescapable shock on endogenous opiates and pain sensitivity (see Maier, Drugan, Grau, Hyson, MacLennan, Moye, Madden, & Barchas, 1983). Exposure to stressful events stimulates recuperative processes, which include reduced sensitivity to pain (Bolles & Fanselow, 1980; Ross & Randich, 1984). Pain sensitivity is regulated in part by neurons in the brain that are activated by special neurotransmitter substances called "opiates." These neurons can be activated by opiates such as morphine and heroin that are introduced from outside the body. The neurons are also activated by opiates produced and released internally by the body as a part of normal physiological processes. These internally released opiates, called *endogenous opiates,* are involved in some of the changes in pain sensitivity that result from exposure to aversive events.

Maier and his associates have been investigating possible relationships among endogenous opiates, stress-induced analgesia (reduction in pain sensitivity), and learned-helplessness effects in rats. Jackson, Maier, and Coon (1979) showed that the type of shock exposure that produces learning deficits in

helplessness experiments also reduces pain sensitivity. Furthermore, lack of control over shock is critical for this stress-induced analgesia. Subsequent research has shown that the reduction in pain sensitivity is mediated by the opiate analgesia system (Maier et al., 1980; Maier, Sherman, Lewis, Terman, & Liebeskind, 1983). Analgesia does not occur with exposure to inescapable shock if subjects are injected with a drug (naltrexone) that prevents opiates from stimulating the relevant neurons. These results are very important because they show that neural systems involved in the control of pain are greatly influenced by "psychological" factors such as the controllability of the source of pain.

How stress-induced analgesia is related to learned-helplessness effects in rats has not yet been fully worked out. Evidence that the two types of phenomena are related is provided by the fact that shock procedures that produce learned-helplessness effects also produce analgesia (for example, Jackson et al., 1979) and shock procedures that eliminate helplessness effects also eliminate the analgesia effect (Moye, Coon, Grau, & Maier, 1981; Moye, Hyson, Grau, & Maier, 1983). Other research indicates that reductions in pain sensitivity are involved in response deficits produced by inescapable shock but may not be involved in association-learning deficits (Maier, Drugan, Grau, Hyson, MacLennan, Moye, Madden, & Barchas, 1983).

Research on the effects of the controllability of shock on stress-induced analgesia provides further evidence of the sensitivity of subjects to response/reinforcer contingencies. This work also illustrates some of the contributions of basic research on learning and behavior. Interest in the importance of response/reinforcer contingencies led to the discovery of the learned-helplessness effect. Because most of the research on the learned-helplessness effect in animals involved shock exposure, investigators became interested in how controllability of aversive stimulation influences pain perception. This research, in turn, led to investigations of the effect of controllability on neurophysiological pain mechanisms. Many landmark discoveries concerning the role of psychological factors in pain perception and the neurophysiology of pain might not have occurred without the earlier research on learning and behavior. Studies of learning and behavior established the basic behavioral phenomena that subsequent research sought to explain through other types of investigations.

Concluding comment.   As we have seen, organisms are sensitive to the contiguity as well as the contingency between an instrumental response and a reinforcer. Typically, these two aspects of the relation between response and reinforcer act jointly to produce learning (Davis & Platt, 1983). Both factors serve to focus the effects of reinforcement on the instrumental response. The dependency, or contingency, relation ensures that the reinforcer is delivered only after occurrence of the specified instrumental response, and the immediacy relation ensures that other activities do not intrude between the specified response and the reinforcer to disrupt conditioning.

CHAPTER 6
Schedules of Reinforcement and Choice Behavior

In Chapter 6 we will discuss further the importance of the response/reinforcer relation in instrumental behavior by describing effects of various schedules of reinforcement. Schedules of reinforcement are programs, or rules, that determine how instrumental behavior is related to reinforcement. We will begin by describing simple schedules and the effects of schedules of reinforcement on individual responses. We will then describe the importance of schedules of reinforcement in the analysis and control of choice behavior and will note that in some sense all behavior involves choice. The chapter ends with a discussion of how schedules of reinforcement in effect during the conditioning and maintenance of a response influence persistence of the behavior when extinction is introduced and reinforcement is no longer provided.

We ended Chapter 5 with a discussion of the importance of the response/reinforcer relation in instrumental conditioning. The present chapter is devoted to a further discussion of this fundamental element of instrumental conditioning. In describing various instrumental conditioning procedures in Chapter 5, we may have given the impression that every occurrence of the instrumental response results in delivery of the reinforcer in these procedures. Casual reflection suggests that such a perfect contingency between response and reinforcement is rare outside the laboratory. You do not get a high grade on a test every time you spend many hours studying. You cannot get on a bus every time you go to the bus stop. Inviting someone over for dinner does not always result in a pleasant evening. In fact, in most cases the relation between instrumental responses and consequent reinforcement is rather complex. Attempts to study how these complex relations control the occurrence of instrumental responses have led to laboratory investigations of schedules of reinforcement.

A **schedule of reinforcement** is a program, or rule, that determines how and when the occurrence of a response will be followed by a reinforcer. There are an infinite number of ways that such a program could be set up. The delivery of a reinforcer may depend on the occurrence of a certain number of responses, the passage of time, the presence of certain stimuli, the occurrence of other responses of the animal, or any number of things. One might expect that cataloging the behavioral effects produced by the various possible schedules of reinforcement would be a very difficult task. However, research so far has shown that the job is quite manageable. Reinforcement schedules that involve similar relations among stimuli, responses, and reinforcers usually produce similar patterns of behavior. The exact rate of responding may differ from one situation to another. However, the *pattern* of response rates is usually amazingly predictable. This regularity has made the study of the effects of reinforcement schedules both interesting and fruitful.

Schedules of reinforcement influence both how an instrumental response is learned and how it is then maintained by reinforcement. Traditionally, however, investigators of schedule effects have been most concerned with maintenance of behavior. Reinforcement schedules have been most extensively investigated in Skinner boxes that permit continuous observation of behavior so that fluctuations in the rate of responding can be readily observed and analyzed (for example, Ferster & Skinner, 1957). How the operant response is initially shaped and conditioned is rarely of interest. Often a given schedule of reinforcement will produce its characteristic pattern of instrumental behavior irrespective of how the operant response was originally learned. Thus, investigations of reinforcement schedules have provided a great deal of information about the factors that control the maintenance and performance, rather than the learning, of instrumental behavior.

Investigation of the mechanisms of reinforcement that maintain instrumental responding is just as important for the understanding of behavior as investigation of the mechanisms that promote the learning of new responses. More of an animal's behavior is devoted to repeating responses that were previously learned than to acquiring new responses. Humans also spend much of their day doing highly familiar tasks. Conditions of reinforcement that maintain behavior are of great concern to managers, who have to make sure their employees continue to perform the jobs they learned earlier. Even teachers are more often concerned with encouraging the occurrence of already learned responses than with teaching new responses. Many students who do poorly in school know how to do their homework and how to study but simply choose not to. Teachers can use information about the effects of reinforcement schedules to motivate more frequent studying.

Simple Schedules of Intermittent Reinforcement

Schedules of reinforcement are important in the analysis of instrumental behavior because they are largely responsible for variations in the frequency and pattern of instrumental responding. Schedules of reinforcement activate in different ways processes that organize and direct instrumental performance. The simplest schedule is a **continuous reinforcement schedule,** in which every occurrence of the instrumental response results in delivery of the reinforcer. Continuous reinforcement rarely occurs outside the laboratory because the world is not perfect. Pushing an elevator button usually brings the elevator, but all elevators occasionally malfunction so that nothing happens when you push the button. Instrumental behavior often results in reinforcement only some of the time. Situations in which responding is reinforced only some of the time are said to involve a **partial** or **intermittent reinforcement schedule.** There are many ways to arrange for responding to be reinforced intermittently. We begin with a discussion of intermittent schedules that use relatively simple rules for determining which responses will be reinforced.

Ratio schedules

The defining characteristic of **ratio schedules** of reinforcement is that reinforcement depends only on the number of responses the subject makes. The program relating responses to reinforcement requires merely counting the responses and delivering the reinforcer each time the required number is reached. One might, for example, deliver the reinforcer after every tenth lever-press response in rats. In such a schedule, there would be a fixed ratio between the number of responses the subject made and the number of reinforcers it got. (There would always be ten responses per reinforcer.) This makes such a procedure a **fixed-ratio schedule.** More specifically, the procedure would be called a fixed-ratio 10 schedule (abbreviated FR 10). Fixed-ratio schedules are found in daily life wherever a fixed number of responses are always required for reinforcement. The delivery person who always has to visit the same number of houses to complete his route is working on a fixed-ratio schedule. Piecework in factories is usually set up on a fixed-ratio schedule: workers get paid for every so many "widgets" they put together. Flights of stairs provide another example. In a given staircase, you always have to go up the same number of steps to reach the next landing.

Strictly speaking, a continuous reinforcement schedule is also a fixed-ratio schedule. Reinforcement depends only on the number of responses the subject makes. Furthermore, there is a fixed ratio of responses to reinforcements: one response per reinforcer. Therefore, continuous reinforcement is a fixed ratio of 1.

On a continuous reinforcement schedule, subjects typically respond at a steady and moderate rate. Only brief and unpredictable pauses occur. A rat, for example, will press a lever steadily at first and then slow down as it becomes satiated. A very different pattern of responding occurs when an intermittent fixed-ratio schedule of reinforcement is in effect. Figure 6.1 provides a sample cumulative record. The delivery of reward is indicated on the record by the small downward deflections of the pen, or hatch marks. As you can see, the animal stops responding after each reinforcement. However, when the subject resumes responding, it responds at a high and steady rate. Thus, responding on a fixed-ratio schedule has two characteristics. The zero rate of responding that occurs just after reinforcement is called the **postreinforcement pause.** The high and steady rate of responding that completes each ratio requirement is called the **ratio run.** If the ratio requirement is increased a little (from FR 15 to FR 30, for example), the rate of responding during the ratio run usually does not change. However, with higher ratio requirements the postreinforcement pause is longer. If the ratio requirement is suddenly increased a great deal (from FR 15 to FR 100, for example), the animal is likely to pause periodically before the completion of the ratio requirement. This effect is called *ratio strain.* In extreme cases ratio strain may be so great that the animal stops responding altogether. When training an organism, one must be careful not to raise the ratio (or, more generally, the difficulty of a task) too quickly, or ratio strain may occur and the organism may give up altogether.

The postreinforcement pause in fixed-ratio schedules is a result of the predictably large number of responses required for the next delivery of the reinforcer. Given enough experience with a fixed-ratio procedure, the subject learns that after reinforcement it always has to make a certain number of responses to receive the next reinforcer. This predictability can

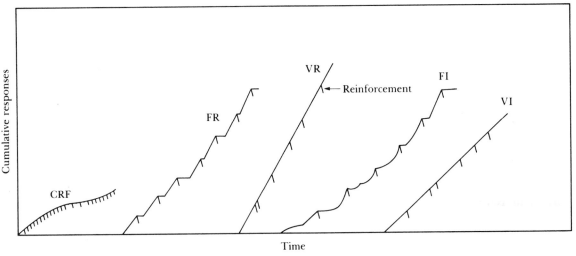

FIGURE 6.1. Sample cumulative records of lever pressing on various simple reinforcement schedules. Horizontal displacements in the records indicate passage of time. Vertical displacements indicate cumulative responses. Hatch marks indicate times when the reinforcer is delivered. CRF is continuous reinforcement; FR, fixed ratio; VR, variable ratio; FI, fixed interval; and VI, variable interval. (Hypothetical data.)

be disrupted by varying the number of responses required for reinforcement from one occasion to the next. Such a procedure is still a ratio schedule because reinforcement still depends on how many responses the subject makes. However, a different number of responses is counted for the delivery of each reward. Such a procedure is called a **variable-ratio schedule.** We may, for example, require the subject to make 10 responses to earn the first reward, 13 to earn the second reward, 7 for the next one, and so on. The numerical value of a variable-ratio schedule indicates the average number of responses required per reinforcement. Thus, our procedure would be a variable-ratio 10 schedule (abbreviated VR 10). Because the number of responses required for reinforcement is no longer predictable, there are no predictable pauses in the rate of responding on a variable-ratio schedule. Rather, the subject responds at a fairly steady rate until it becomes satiated (see Figure 6.1).

Variable-ratio schedules are found in daily life wherever an unpredictable amount of effort is required to obtain a reinforcer. Each time a custodian goes into a room on his rounds, he knows that some

amount of cleaning will be necessary, but he does not know exactly how dirty the room will be. Gamblers playing a slot machine are also responding on a variable-ratio schedule. They always have to play the machine several times to win. However, they never know how many plays will produce the winning combination. Variable-ratio schedules are also common in sports. A certain number of strokes are always required to finish a hole in golf, for example. However, players can never be sure how many strokes they will need to use when they start.

Interval schedules

Reinforcement does not always depend solely on the amount of effort or the number of responses the subject makes. Sometimes responses are reinforced only if they occur at certain times. **Interval schedules** of reinforcement illustrate this type of situation. In a simple interval schedule, a response is reinforced only if it occurs more than a set amount of time after the last reinforcer delivery. In a **fixed-interval schedule,** the set time is constant from one occasion to the next. Consider, for example, a fixed-interval

2-min schedule (FI 2 min) for lever pressing in rats. Animals exposed to this schedule always get reinforced for the first response they make after 2 min has passed since the last reward. Because responses that occur shortly after a reward are never reinforced, animals on a fixed-interval schedule learn to wait to make the instrumental response until near the end of the fixed 2-min interval (see Figure 6.1). Very few responses occur at the beginning of the interval after a reward. As the time for the availability of the next reinforcer draws closer, the response rate increases. The animal responds at a high rate at the end of the 2-min interval and therefore usually receives the reinforcer as soon as the 2 min is finished. There is a curve in the cumulative record as the animal speeds up responding toward the end of the interval. The pattern of response that develops with fixed-interval reinforcement schedules is accordingly called the **fixed-interval scallop.**

It is important to realize that a fixed-interval

BOX 6.1. The postreinforcement pause, procrastination, and cramming for exams

The postreinforcement pause that occurs in fixed-ratio and fixed-interval schedules is a very common human experience. In fixed-ratio schedules, the pause occurs because a predictably large number of responses are always required to produce the next reward. In a sense, the animal is "procrastinating" before embarking on the large effort necessary for reinforcement. Similar procrastination is legendary in human behavior. Consider, for example, a term in which you have several papers to write. You are likely to work on one term paper at a time. However, when you have completed one paper, you probably will not start working on the next one right away. Rather, there will be a postreinforcement pause. After completing a large project, people tend to take some time off before starting the next task. In fact, procrastination between tasks or before the start of a new job is the rule rather than the exception. Laboratory results provide a suggestion for overcoming such procrastination. Fixed-ratio-schedule performance in the laboratory indicates that once animals begin to respond on a ratio run, they respond at a high and steady rate until they complete the ratio requirement. This suggests that if somehow you got yourself to start on a job, chances are you would not find it difficult to keep working to finish it. Only the beginning is hard. One technique that works pretty well in getting started is to tell yourself that you will begin with only a small part of the new job. If you are trying to write a paper, tell yourself that you will write only one paragraph to start with. You may very well find that once you have completed the first paragraph, it will be easier to write the second one, then the one after that, and so on. If you are procrastinating about spring cleaning, do not think about doing the entire job. Instead, start with a small part of it, like washing the kitchen floor. The rest will then come more easily.

On a fixed-interval schedule, postreinforcement pauses may occur because once a reward has been delivered, there is no chance that another will be available for some time. Scheduling of tests in college courses has important similarities to the basic fixed-interval schedule. In many courses there are few tests, and the tests are evenly distributed during the term. There may be a midterm and a final exam. The pattern of studying that such a schedule maintains is very similar to what is observed in the laboratory. There is no studying at all at the beginning of the semester or just after the midterm exam. Many students begin to study only a week or so before each test, and the rate of studying rapidly increases as the day of the test approaches. Studying at the beginning of the term or after the midterm exam is not reinforced by the receipt of good grades on tests at that time. Therefore, students do not study at these points in the term. More frequent studying can be motivated by giving more frequent tests. The highest rate of responding would occur if unannounced tests were given at unpredictable times, in a manner analogous to a variable-interval schedule. This is the "pop quiz" technique.

schedule of reinforcement does not ensure that the animal will be reinforced at fixed intervals of time. Thus, rats on an FI 2-min schedule do not automatically receive the reinforcer every 2 min. Instrumental responses are required for the reinforcer in interval schedules, just as in ratio schedules. The interval only determines when the reinforcer becomes available. In order to receive the reinforcer when it becomes available, the subject still has to make the instrumental response.

Fixed-interval schedules are found in situations in which a fixed amount of time is required to prepare or set up the reinforcer. Consider, for example, washing clothes in an automatic washer. A certain amount of time is required to complete the wash cycle. No matter how many times you open the washing machine before the required amount of time has passed, you will not be reinforced with clean clothes. Once the cycle is finished, the reinforcer becomes available, and you can pick up your clean clothes any time after that. Making Jell-O provides another example. After the gelatin is mixed in hot water, it has to chill for a certain amount of time to gel. To be able to eat the Jell-O, you have to wait until it is ready. No matter how many times you check the refrigerator before the required amount of time has elapsed, the Jell-O will not have the proper consistency. If you are particularly eager to eat the Jell-O, the rate of your opening the refrigerator door will be similar to an FI scallop.

Like ratio schedules, interval schedules can be unpredictable. In a **variable-interval schedule,** the reinforcer is provided for the first response that occurs after a variable amount of time has elapsed since the previous reward. We may set up a schedule, for example, in which one reward is delivered when the animal makes a response more than 4 min after the last reward, the next reinforcer is given for the first response that occurs more than 5 min after that, and the next one is given for the first response that occurs at least 3 min later. In this procedure, the average interval that has to pass before successive rewards become available is 4 min. Therefore, the procedure is a variable-interval 4-min schedule, abbreviated VI 4 min. Like variable-ratio schedules, variable-interval schedules maintain steady and stable rates of responding without pauses (see Figure 6.1).

Variable-interval schedules are found in situations in which an unpredictable amount of time is required to prepare or set up the reinforcer. A mechanic who cannot tell you when your car will be fixed has imposed a variable-interval schedule on you. You have to wait a certain amount of time before attempts to get your car will be reinforced. However, the amount of time involved is unpredictable. A taxi dispatcher is also controlled by variable-interval schedules. After a cab has completed a trip, it is available for another assignment, and the dispatcher will be reinforced for sending the cab on another errand. However, once an assignment is made, the cab is unavailable for an unpredictable period, during which time the dispatcher cannot use the same cab for other trips.

In simple interval schedules, once the reward becomes available, the subject can receive the reward any time thereafter, provided it makes the required response. On a fixed-interval 2-min schedule, for example, reward becomes available 2 min after the previous reinforcement. If the animal responds at exactly this time, it will be reinforced. If it waits to respond for 90 min after the previous reinforcement, it will still get the reward. Outside the laboratory, it is more common for reinforcers to become available for only limited periods in interval schedules. Consider, for example, a dormitory cafeteria. Meals are served only at certain times. Therefore, going to the cafeteria is reinforced only if you wait long enough after the last meal. However, once the next meal becomes available, you have a limited amount of time in which to get it. This kind of restriction on how long reward remains available is called a **limited hold.** Limited-hold restrictions can be added to both fixed-interval and variable-interval schedules.

Comparison of ratio and interval schedules

There are striking similarities between the patterns of responding maintained by simple ratio and interval schedules. As we have seen, both fixed-ratio and fixed-interval schedules produce a predictable pause in responding after each reinforcement. In contrast, variable-ratio and variable-interval schedules both maintain steady rates of responding, without predictable pauses. Despite these similarities, there is a very important difference between ratio and interval schedules. This involves the extent to which the occurrence of responding determines how often the subjects are reinforced. A very strong and direct relation exists between the rate of response and the frequency of reinforcement in ratio schedules. Because the only thing that determines whether the subject will be reinforced is the number of responses it makes, the rate of responding totally determines the frequency of reinforcement. By responding more often, the subject can always earn the reinforcer more often. This relation makes ratio schedules extremely motivating. The subject is driven by the schedule to respond at high rates because each response gets it closer to the payoff.

In interval schedules the rate of response does not determine the frequency of reinforcement in the same manner as in ratio schedules. Consider, for example, a fixed-interval 2-min schedule. Each reward becomes available 2 min after the last reward. If the subject responds right away when the reward is set up, the reward is delivered and the next cycle begins. However, no matter how frequently the subject responds, it will never be reinforced any more often than once every 2 min. Therefore, the interval schedule sets a maximum limit on the frequency of reinforcers the subject can earn. In the FI 2-min example, the limit is 30 reinforcers per hour. If the subject does not respond as soon as each reward becomes available, it will not earn reinforcers as often as possible. Therefore, the rate of responding determines the frequency of reinforcement to some extent. However, the delivery of reward depends more on exactly *when* the subject responds than on how often it responds.

Because the rate of responding does not entirely determine the frequency of reinforcement in interval schedules, such schedules typically do not motivate as high response rates as ratio schedules, even if subjects receive the same number of reinforcements in the two types of schedules. In an important experiment on this topic, Reynolds (1968) compared the rate of key pecking in pigeons reinforced on variable-ratio and variable-interval schedules. Two pigeons were trained to peck the response key for food reinforcement. One of the birds was reinforced on a variable-ratio schedule. Therefore, for this animal the frequency of reinforcement was entirely determined by its rate of response. The other animal was reinforced on a variable-interval schedule. However, the availability of the reinforcer for this animal was controlled by the behavior of the other pigeon. Each time the variable-ratio pigeon was just one response short of the required number, the experimenter reinforced the next response that each subject made. Thus, the variable-ratio bird controlled the variable-interval schedule for its partner. This yoking procedure ensured that the frequency of reinforcement was virtually identical for the two subjects.

Figure 6.2 shows the pattern of responding exhibited by each subject. Even though the two subjects received the same frequency of reinforcers, they behaved very differently. The pigeon reinforced on the variable-ratio schedule responded at a much higher rate than the pigeon reinforced on the variable-interval schedule. The variable-ratio schedule motivated much more vigorous instrumental behavior (see also Peele, Casey, & Silberberg, 1984).

Ratio schedules motivate higher rates of responding than interval schedules outside the laboratory as well. Doctors, for example, usually work on a schedule that has very strong ratio characteristics. The more patients they see, the more money they make. Every patient whom they refuse to see represents the loss of a certain amount of income. This direct relation between rate of response and rate of reinforcement may contribute to their diligence. Because ratio characteristics in a schedule of reinforcement provide a strong impetus for responding, such schedules are usually strongly resisted by employees. In a labor/management negotiation, management is likely to want to build ratio characteristics into the contract, whereas representatives of labor will insist that interval-schedule characteristics be instituted.

Response-Rate Schedules of Reinforcement

As we have seen, ratio schedules of reinforcement encourage subjects to respond at higher rates than interval schedules. However, neither schedule re-

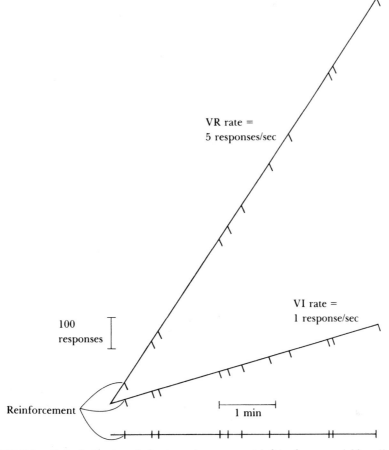

VR rate =
5 responses/sec

VI rate =
1 response/sec

100
responses

Reinforcement

1 min

FIGURE 6.2. Cumulative records for two pigeons, one reinforced on a variable-ratio (VR) schedule and the other yoked to it on a variable-interval (VI) schedule. Although subjects received the same reinforcements at about the same time, the VR bird responded five times as fast as the VI bird. *(From Reynolds, 1968.)*

quires that subjects perform at a specified rate in order to get reinforced. Therefore, differences in the rate of responding observed are indirect effects of the schedules. In contrast, other types of procedures specifically require that subjects respond at a particular rate to get reinforced. Such procedures are called **response-rate schedules** of reinforcement.

In response-rate schedules, whether a response is reinforced depends on how soon it occurs after the preceding response. The interval between successive responses is called the **interresponse time,** abbreviated **IRT.** A reinforcement schedule could be set up, for example, in which a response is reinforced only if it occurs sooner than 5 sec after the preceding response. If the subject makes a response every 5 sec, its rate of response will be 12 per min. Thus, the schedule provides reinforcement if the rate of response is 12/min or greater. The subject will not be reinforced if its rate of response is less than 12/min. As you might suspect, this procedure encourages responding at high rates. Therefore, it is called **differential reinforcement of high rates,** or **DRH.**

In DRH schedules, a response is reinforced only if it occurs *less than* a certain amount of time after the preceding response. The opposite result is achieved if a response is reinforced only if it occurs *more than* a certain amount of time after the previous response. This type of procedure is called **differential reinforcement of low rates,** abbreviated **DRL.** As you might suspect, DRL schedules encourage subjects to respond slowly.

Response-rate schedules are found outside the laboratory in situations that require particular rates of responding. An assembly line provides a good example. The speed of movement of the line dictates the rate of response for the workers. If an employee responds more slowly than the specified rate, he or she will not be reinforced and may, in fact, get fired. However, workers have to be careful not to work too rapidly, because of social pressure imposed by fellow workers. Those who respond at very high rates are likely to earn the enmity of their peers. Social pressure in some work situations differentially reinforces low rates of responding.

Concurrent Schedules: The Study of Choice Behavior

The reinforcement schedules we have discussed thus far have involved an analysis of the relation between occurrences of a particular response and reinforcement of that response. However, the study of situations in which only one response is being measured is not likely to provide us with a complete understanding of behavior. Animal and human behavior involves a great deal more than just the repetition of individual responses. Even in a simple situation such as a Skinner box, organisms engage in a wide variety of activities and are continually making choices among the various responses they are able to perform. Furthermore, the occurrence of a particular response very much depends on the availability of other re-

---

BOX 6.2.   Use of DRL schedules in neuropsychological assessment

Behavioral techniques developed in the course of research on animal learning are widely used in neurophysiological research. The psychological effects of various physiological treatments such as drug administration, brain lesions, brain stimulation, and dietary changes are often evaluated by the effects of these treatments on patterns of responding maintained by particular schedules of reinforcement. Oscar-Berman (1980), for example, used DRL schedules to evaluate neurophysiological deficits that occur in Korsakoff's disease. Korsakoff's syndrome is a complex of psychological and neurological disorders that can result from prolonged and excessive alcohol use in humans. The most obvious psychological deficit in Korsakoff patients is a disorder in memory for recent events. Oscar-Berman has been interested in the extent to which this memory deficit is secondary to other problems in Korsakoff patients. She hypothesized that the neurological deterioration in Korsakoff patients causes them to respond prematurely to incoming information—that Korsakoff patients "jump the gun." To evaluate this hypothesis, Oscar-Berman used a DRL schedule because reinforcement on a DRL schedule depends on waiting sufficiently between responses—not jumping the gun. Three groups of people were tested: normals, alcoholics who did not have Korsakoff's disease, and Korsakoff patients. The subjects were seated at a panel that had a protruding response lever. Lever presses were reinforced with pennies on various DRL schedules (DRL 3 sec, 6 sec, 12 sec, and 18 sec). Consistent with the prediction, Korsakoff patients were much less successful than normal people in waiting long enough to earn reinforcement on the DRL schedules. Another interesting finding was that the performance of alcoholics who were not considered to have Korsakoff's disease was intermediate between the performance of the other two groups. One possible interpretation of these results is that deficits in DRL performance are early warning signs of neural deterioration preliminary to Korsakoff's disease.

sponse alternatives. A teenager may trim the neighbor's grass for $25 if the sky is overcast and his friends are out of town. However, if the weather is good and his friends are home, he is more likely to spend the afternoon at the beach with them. We are constantly having to make choices about what to do. Should we go to the movies or stay at home and study? Should we go shopping tonight or watch television tonight and go shopping tomorrow? Understanding the mechanisms of response choice is fundamental to the understanding of behavior because the choices organisms make determine the occurrence of individual responses.

The choices available to animals and people can be very complex. For example, a person may have a choice of 12 different responses (reading the newspaper, watching television, going for a walk, playing with the dog, and the like), each of which produces a different type of reinforcer according to a different reinforcement schedule. Analyzing all the factors that control the individual's behavior in such a situation would be formidable, if not impossible. Therefore, psychologists have begun experimental investigations of the mechanisms of choice by studying simpler situations. The simplest choice situation is one in which the subject has two response alternatives and each response is followed by a reinforcer according to some schedule of reinforcement.

Historically, much of the research on choice behavior has been conducted using mazes, particularly the T maze. Choice can be measured by the frequency with which the subjects turn to the left or the right. In a classic paper entitled "The Determiners of Behavior at a Choice Point," Tolman (1938) advanced the argument that all behavior is essentially choice behavior. The choice may be one response or another or, more simply, responding or not responding (see Woodworth & Schlosberg, 1954, for a good review of the choice experiments using T mazes).

More recent approaches to the study of choice use Skinner boxes equipped with two manipulanda, such as two response levers. In the typical experiment, responding on each manipulandum is reinforced on some schedule of reinforcement. The two schedules are in effect at the same time, and the subject is free to switch from one manipulandum to the other. This type of procedure is called a **concurrent schedule of reinforcement.** Concurrent schedules of reinforcement allow for continuous measures of choice because the subject is free to change back and forth between the response alternatives. Preference (choice) is measured by the rates of response on each manipulandum or the time spent responding on each.

Figure 6.3 shows an example of a concurrent schedule for pigeons. The experimental chamber has two response keys. If the pigeon pecks the key on the left, it receives food reinforcers according to a variable-interval 60-sec schedule. Pecks on the right key produce food reinforcers according to a fixed-ratio 10 schedule. The animal is free to peck either response key at any time. The point of the experiment is to see how the animal distributes its pecks on the two keys and how the schedule of reinforcement on each key influences its choices.

On some concurrent schedules, particularly those involving interval-schedule components, the pigeon may be reinforced for the very first peck it makes after switching from one key to the other. This "accidental" reinforcement may encourage the subject to change frequently from one key to the other. To assess the effects of concurrent schedules without this

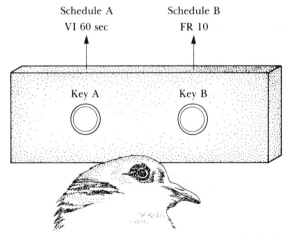

FIGURE 6.3. Diagram of a concurrent schedule. Pecks on key A are reinforced according to a VI 60-sec schedule of reinforcement. Pecks on key B are reinforced according to an FR 10 schedule of reinforcement.

reinforcement of switching, experimenters often add the constraint that the first one or two pecks after a switch will not be reinforced. This feature is called a **change-over delay (COD)** because it delays reinforcement after a change from one response key to the other.

Measures of choice behavior

The animal's choice in a concurrent schedule is reflected in the distribution of its behavior between two response alternatives. This can be measured in several ways. One common technique is to calculate the **relative rate of responding** on each alternative. The relative rate of responding on key A, for example, is calculated by dividing the response rate on key A by the total rate of responding (rate on key A plus rate on key B): $R_A/(R_A + R_B)$, where R_A is the rate of responding on key A and R_B is the rate on key B. If the subject pecks equally often on the two response keys, this ratio will be .5. If the rate of responding on key A is greater than the rate of responding on key B, the ratio will be greater than .5. If the rate of responding on key A is less than the rate of responding on key B, the ratio will be less than .5. The relative rate of responding on key B can be calculated in a comparable manner.

The matching law

As you might suspect, the distribution of the subject's behavior between the two response alternatives is greatly influenced by the reinforcement schedule for each alternative. For example, if the same variable-interval reinforcement schedule is available for each response alternative, as in a concurrent VI 60-sec VI 60-sec procedure, the pigeon will peck the two keys equally often. The relative rate of responding for pecks on each side will be .5. This result is intuitively reasonable. If the pigeon spent all its time pecking on one side, it would receive only the reinforcers programmed for that side. The subject can get more reinforcers by pecking on both sides. Since the VI reinforcement schedule available on each side is the same, there is no advantage in spending more time on one side than on the other.

By responding equally often on each side of a concurrent VI 60-sec VI 60-sec schedule, the subject will also earn reinforcers equally often on each side. The **relative rate of reinforcement** earned for each response alternative can be calculated in a manner comparable to the relative rate of response. For example, the relative rate of reinforcement for alternative A is the rate of reinforcement of response A divided by the total rate of reinforcement (the sum of the rate of reward earned on side A plus the rate of reward earned on side B). This is expressed in the formula $r_A/(r_A + r_B)$, where r_A and r_B represent the rates of reinforcement earned on each response alternative. On a concurrent VI 60-sec VI 60-sec schedule, the relative rate of reinforcement for each response alternative will be .5 because the subject earns rewards equally often on each side.

Effects of variations in the concurrent schedule. As we have seen, in the concurrent VI 60-sec VI 60-sec schedule, both the relative rate of responding and the relative rate of reinforcement for each response alternative are .5. Thus, the relative rate of responding is equal to the relative rate of reinforcement. Will this equality also occur if the two response alternatives are not reinforced according to the same schedule in the concurrent procedure? This important question was asked by Herrnstein (1961). Herrnstein studied the distribution of responses on various concurrent VI VI schedules in which the maximum total rate of reinforcement the subject could earn was 40 per hour. However, depending on the exact value of each VI schedule, different proportions of the total 40 rewards/hour could be obtained by each response alternative. For example, with a concurrent VI 6-min VI 2-min schedule, a VI 6-min schedule is in effect on the right key and a VI 2-min schedule on the left key. A maximum of 10 reinforcers per hour could be obtained by responding on the right, and a maximum of 30 reinforcers per hour could be obtained by responding on the left.

Herrnstein studied the effects of a wide variety of concurrent VI VI schedules. There was no constraint on which side the pigeons could peck. They could respond exclusively on one side if they chose, or they could distribute their pecks between the two sides in any proportion they chose. In fact, however, the pigeons distributed their responding in a uniform and predictable fashion. The results, summarized in Figure 6.4, indicate that the relative rate of responding on a given alternative was always very nearly equal to the relative rate of reinforcement earned on that alternative. If the pigeons earned a greater proportion of their reinforcers on alternative A, they made a greater proportion of their responses on alternative A. According to these results, *the relative rate of responding on an alternative matches the relative rate of reinforcement for that alternative.* This relation has been found in many situations and has been considered a law of behavior. It is called the **matching law** and is expressed symbolically as follows:

$$\frac{R_A}{R_A + R_B} = \frac{r_A}{r_A + r_B}$$

where R_A and R_B are the rates of responding on side A and side B, and r_A and r_B are the rates of reinforcement earned on each side. The matching law represents a fundamental fact about choice behavior and indicates that choices are not made capriciously but are a function of relative rates of reinforcement.

Conditions of matching. Relative rates of responding do not always perfectly match relative rates of reinforcement for response alternatives (for example, Baum, 1979; Wearden & Burgess, 1982), and much experimental and theoretical effort has been devoted to analyzing exceptional cases (see Williams, in press, for a review). Sometimes the preferred alternative is not preferred as strongly as the matching relation predicts. Such cases illustrate **undermatching.** In other instances, choice of the preferred

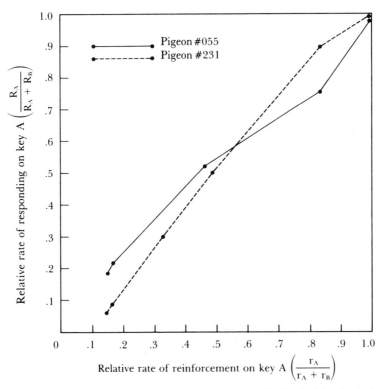

FIGURE 6.4. Results of two pigeons pecking on concurrent VI VI schedules. Each data point represents one combination of VI schedules whose combined reinforcement rate is 40 reinforcements per hour. Note that at each point the relative rate of responding nearly equals (matches) the relative rate of reinforcement. *(From Herrnstein, 1961.)*

alternative is stronger than the matching relation predicts. Such cases illustrate **overmatching.** Analysis of instances of undermatching and overmatching has helped to specify the conditions under which matching occurs.

One important variable for obtaining the matching relation is *independence of the two response alternatives*. Independence of the two responses is lost if subjects are reinforced (intentionally or otherwise) for a particular sequence of alternations between the two choices. A change-over delay can be used to eliminate such reinforcement of switching so that the two response alternatives do not become components of a single reinforced behavioral unit. A second important variable in matching is the *difficulty or travel time involved in going from one to the other response alternative*. If switching from one response to the other is difficult or takes long, subjects tend to overmatch—to exhibit an exaggerated bias for their preferred response alternative. A third critical factor for obtaining the matching relation is that the two response alternatives involve the *same response topography*. The matching relation is formulated for instances in which the subjects choose between two responses that are identical except for being reinforced according to different schedules of reinforcement. If the response alternatives are themselves different, the matching formula cannot be used directly because of complications involved in trying to find a common measure for the diverse behaviors. Despite these and some other limitations (see Williams, in press), the matching relation has been remarkably successful in describing choice behavior in a wide range of situations.

Extension of the matching law to simple reinforcement schedules.

If the matching law represents a fundamental fact about behavior, then it should also characterize responding on simple schedules of reinforcement. In a simple reinforcement schedule, only one response manipulandum is provided (such as a lever or a key), and the subject is reinforced for responses on this manipulandum according to some program. The matching law describes the distribution of responses among several alternatives. How can it be applied to single-response situations? As Herrnstein (1970) pointed out, even single-

response situations can be considered to involve a choice. The choice is between making the specified response (bar pressing or pecking a key, for example) and engaging in other possible activities (grooming, walking around, pecking the floor, sniffing holes in the experimental chamber). Subjects receive explicit reinforcers programmed for occurrences of the specific operant response. In addition, they no doubt receive intrinsic rewards for the other activities in which they engage. Hence, the total reinforcement in the situation has to be considered to include the programmed rewards and the intrinsic rewards. This type of analysis permits application of the matching law to single-response reinforcement schedules. Consider R_A to represent the rate of the specified operant response in the schedule, R_O the rate of the animal's other activities, r_A the rate of the explicit programmed reinforcement, and r_O the rate of the intrinsic reinforcement for the other activities. The matching law for single-response situations can be stated as follows:

$$\frac{R_A}{R_A + R_O} = \frac{r_A}{r_A + r_O}$$

By mathematically fitting a variation of this equation to single-response data, Herrnstein provides evidence that the matching law holds in such situations.

Matching and the concept of reinforcement value.

The distribution of responses that organisms make matches not only the relative rates of reinforcement they earn for the response alternatives but also other features of reinforcement. Catania (1963), for example, varied the *amount* of reinforcement available for responding on each of two alternatives in a concurrent schedule. He found that the relative rates of responding the subjects made on each alternative matched the relative magnitude of reinforcement they could earn on the alternatives. This relation can be expressed as

$$\frac{R_A}{R_A + R_B} = \frac{A_A}{A_A + A_B}$$

where R_A and R_B are the response rates on alternatives A and B, and A_A and A_B are the amounts of reward provided for responding on A and B, respectively. Matching has also been found with delays of reinforcement. Under certain circumstances, the relative rate of response for one of two alternatives matches the relative immediacy of reinforcement for responding on that alternative. The shorter the relative delay, the higher the relative rate of responding (Chung, 1965; Chung & Herrnstein, 1967; see also Dunn & Fantino, 1982; Gentry & Marr, 1980; Killeen, 1968).

Such features of reinforcers as amount and delay can be considered aspects of the quality, or value, of the reinforcer. We can assume that subjects prefer reinforcers that occur frequently, are of a large amount, and are delivered with short delays. Accordingly, we may think of the matching law more generally as the matching of relative rates of responding to the relative values of the alternative reinforcers. Furthermore, we could use relative rates of responding to measure the relative values of reinforcers. Let us suppose that we want to find out whether two reinforcers are equal in value to the subject. Does John like chocolate ice cream as much as he likes vanilla? To answer this question, we have to look at how frequently John eats each flavor when given a choice. If 50% of the time he eats the chocolate and 50% of the time he eats the vanilla, we can conclude that the two flavors are of equal value for John. Similarly, two reinforcement schedules are said to be of equal value if the subject chooses to respond 50% of the time on each alternative when the two schedules are simultaneously available in a concurrent procedure. Because the relative values of reinforcers are determined by relative response rates, the relative values of reinforcers cannot be used to *explain* why subjects distribute their responses between alternative reinforcers in particular ways. Relative rates of response and relative values of reinforcers are just two sides of the same coin. They are reflections of the same basic behavior process involved in making choices (see Killeen, 1972; Rachlin, 1971).

Mechanisms of the matching law

The matching law describes how subjects distribute their responses in a choice situation but does not explain what mechanisms are responsible for this response distribution. Relative rates of responding on two alternatives and relative rates of reward earned on those two response alternatives are both measures of the subject's behavior. What independent variable, or outside factor, is responsible for the choice behavior described by the matching law? This question has stimulated extensive experimentation and theoretical debate. Considerable progress has been made in recent years (see for example, Commons, Herrnstein, & Rachlin, 1982), but many important issues remain unresolved.

Matching and maximizing rates of reinforcement. The most extensively investigated explanations of choice behavior are based on the intuitively reasonable idea that animals distribute their actions among response alternatives so as to receive the maximum amount of reinforcement possible in the situation. According to this idea of **maximizing,** subjects switch back and forth between response alternatives so as to receive as many reinforcers as they possibly can. The idea that subjects maximize reinforcement has been used to explain choice behavior at two levels of analysis. *Molecular theories* use the idea of maximizing to explain behavior at the level of individual choice responses; *molar theories* use it to explain overall levels of responding rather than individual choice responses.

Molecular theories. According to molecular theories of maximizing, animals always choose whichever response alternative is most likely to be reinforced at the time. Shimp (1966, 1969) proposed an early version of molecular matching: that, in a concurrent schedule of reinforcement with two schedule alternatives, the subject switches from one schedule to the other as the probability of reinforcement for the other schedule increases. Consider, for example, a pigeon working on a concurrent VI VI schedule. As the pigeon pecks key A, the timer controlling reinforcement for key B is still operating. The longer the pigeon stays on key A, the greater is the probability that the requisite interval for key B will elapse and reinforcement will become available for pecking key B. By switching, the pigeon can pick up the reinforcer on key B. Now, the longer it continues to peck key B, the more likely key A will become set for reinforcement. Shimp proposed that the matching relation is a by-product of prudent switching when the probability of reinforcement on the alternative response key becomes greater than the probability of reinforcement on the current response key.

Detailed studies of the patterns of switching from one to another response alternative have not always supported the molecular maximizing theory proposed by Shimp. Some of these studies have also shown that matching is possible in the absence of momentary maximizing (for example, Nevin, 1969, 1979). Other experiments have provided strong evidence that momentary maximizing can occur in concurrent schedules (Hinson & Staddon, 1983a, 1983b). However, as Williams (in press) has pointed out, these experiments were conducted under circumstances that did not produce the matching relation. Therefore, the role of molecular maximizing in explaining the matching relation remains unresolved.

Molar theories. Molar theories of maximizing assume that animals and people distribute their responses among various alternatives so as to maximize the amount of reinforcement they earn over the long run (for example, Rachlin, Battalio, Kagel, & Green, 1981; Rachlin, Green, Kagel, & Battalio, 1976). How long is the "long run" is not clearly specified. However, in contrast to molecular theories, molar theories focus on aggregates of behavior over some

---

BOX 6.3.   The matching law, human behavior, and behavior therapy

The matching law and its implications have been found to apply to a wide range of human behavior situations, including pressing a button for monetary rewards, detecting signals on a screen in a vigilance task, conducting conversation with several persons in a group situation, and engaging in self-injurious behavior maintained by social reinforcement (see, for example, Baum, 1975; Conger & Killeen, 1974; McDowell, 1982). In addition, the matching law has important conceptual and technological implications for applications of reinforcement principles (McDowell, 1982). According to the matching law, the tendency to make a particular response depends not only on the rate of reinforcement for that response but also on the rates of reinforcement available for alternative activities. This implies that analysis of a problematic behavior (truancy from school, for example) has to include not only consideration of the rewards available for that particular behavior but also rewards the subject can obtain in other ways. Thus, the matching law suggests that accurate assessment of a behavior problem requires consideration of the subject's full range of activities and sources of reinforcement. The matching law also suggests novel techniques for decreasing a particular undesired behavior and increasing a particular desired one. According to the matching law, an undesired response can be decreased by increasing reinforcement for other activities or by simply increasing the rate of "free" reinforcements available to the subject. Conversely, the matching law implies that a desired response can be increased by decreasing the rate of reinforcement available otherwise.

Implications of the matching law for behavior therapy are illustrated by the treatment of a mildly retarded 22-year-old man to decrease his oppositional behavior (McDowell, 1981). The person periodically became very uncooperative, and his oppositional behavior sometimes escalated to the point of assault. Given the potential for aggression in the situation, punishment was judged to be an unsuitable technique for decreasing the oppositional behavior. The undesired behavior was successfully treated by introducing a system that permitted the subject to earn positive reinforcement by engaging in a variety of other activities. He could earn points for performing various personal hygiene, job, and educational tasks and then exchange the points for money. Increasing the rate of reinforcement for other activities significantly decreased the rate of oppositional behavior.

period of time rather than on individual choice responses. Molar maximizing theory was originally formulated to explain choice behavior in concurrent schedules involving ratio components. In concurrent ratio schedules, subjects rarely switch back and forth between response alternatives. Rather, they choose the ratio component that requires the fewest responses for reinforcement and respond only on this alternative. On a concurrent FR 20 FR 10 schedule, for example, the subject is likely to respond only on the FR 10 alternative. In this way it maximizes the rate of reinforcement it receives. Why should anyone work on the leaner FR 20 schedule if the same reinforcer can be earned with the same type of response on an FR 10 schedule?

Molar maximizing predicts that subjects will work to obtain the maximum possible amount of reinforcement in a situation. To determine whether they have achieved this requires determining what actually constitutes optimal performance. However, optimal performance is often difficult to determine. What constitutes optimal performance depends on how deliveries of the reinforcer are related to behavior, or, more generally, on the relation between behavior and the feedback consequences provided by the environment. This relation is called a **feedback function.** The relation between behavior and its consequences (the feedback function) is easy to specify in the case of ratio schedules. Consider, for example, a fixed-ratio 10 schedule of reinforcement. The subject receives the reinforcer for every tenth response. Therefore, the rate of reinforcement (environmental feedback) will be directly related to the rate of responding. More specifically, the rate of reinforcement will be equal to one-tenth the rate of responding. This equation describes perfectly the feedback function, the relation between behavior and the consequences provided by the environment. With feedback functions for various ratio schedules determined in a comparable manner, figuring out what response strategy provides the maximum amount of reinforcement is relatively easy for concurrent ratio schedules.

Whether subjects are obtaining the maximum possible reinforcement in the long run is much more difficult to determine in situations that involve complex relations between behavior and environmental feedback consequences. Consider, for example, fishing from a small pond—a fishing hole. What is the optimal rate of fishing? How frequently should you take fish out to obtain the maximum number of fish in the long run? To answer this question, we have to know the feedback function relating how many fish you can get to how rapidly you remove them. The feedback function is rather complicated and difficult to determine. If you remove fish at a high rate, you may soon deplete the pond, leaving no fish behind to breed and create the next generation. Therefore, a very high rate of fishing provides a limited rate of return in the long run. If you fish very slowly, you will not run into the problem of depletion, but you may also have a lower rate of return than what is optimally possible. An intermediate rate of fishing would produce the best outcome. The feedback function has to be known precisely to determine exactly which intermediate rate of responding provides the maximum rate of return.

Evaluations of molar maximizing have been complicated by the difficulty of specifying feedback functions for various schedules of reinforcement. On a variable-interval schedule, for example, reinforcement depends not only on the occurrence of a response but on *when* that response is made. If the subject makes a lot of responses just after each reward, it will receive few rewards for a high response rate. In contrast, if it waits after each reward and then spaces out its responding more evenly, it will earn many more rewards for the same overall response rate. Therefore, the temporal distribution of behavior is important in specifying the feedback function for interval schedules. The relation between responding and reinforcement is even more complicated in concurrent schedules. Here we have to consider the distribution of responses between the two alternatives in addition to their individual characteristics.

In many situations, molar maximizing and matching formulations predict the same type of choice behavior. However, certain aspects of choice behavior present difficulties for maximizing theories. One difficulty arises from results of concurrent VI VI schedules of reinforcement. On a concurrent VI VI schedule, subjects can earn close to all of the available rewards on both schedules provided they occasionally sample each alternative. Therefore, the total amount of reinforcement obtained on a concurrent VI VI schedule can be close to the same despite wide variations in how subjects distribute their behavior between the two alternatives. The matching relation is only one of many different possibilities that yield close to maximal rates of reinforcement. Because other response distributions can yield similar amounts of total reward, molar maximizing cannot explain why choice behavior is distributed so close to the matching relation on concurrent VI VI schedules and not in other equally effective ways (Heyman, 1983).

Another challenge for molar matching is provided by results of studies of concurrent variable-ratio and variable-interval schedules (see Prelec, 1982, for a detailed discussion of such schedules). On a variable-ratio schedule, the rate of reinforcement is directly related to the rate of responding. In contrast, on a variable-interval schedule, the subject has only to sample the schedule occasionally to obtain close to the maximum number of rewards. Given these differences in feedback relations for the two schedules, for maximum return on a concurrent VR VI schedule, subjects should concentrate their responses on the variable-ratio alternative and respond only occasionally on the variable-interval component. Evidence shows that animals do favor the VR component but not as strongly as molar maximizing would predict (for example, Baum, 1981; Herrnstein & Heyman, 1979).

Maximizing as goal rather than mechanism. As we have seen, in certain situations (concurrent VR VI schedules) choice behavior satisfies the matching law at the expense of maximizing the amount of reinforcement obtained. In other situations (concurrent VI VI schedules), choice behavior is consistent with both matching and maximizing formulations, but the matching law is more successful in predicting the distribution of choices that are made. These results suggest that maximizing is not the mechanism responsible for the matching relation (Mazur, 1981). Does this mean that maximizing has no role in choice behavior? Not necessarily. In certain situations animals distribute their choices so as to maximize rein-

forcement without satisfying the matching relation (Hinson & Staddon, 1983a, 1983b). Therefore, maximizing has to be considered in a complete account of choice behavior. Animals cannot be oblivious to maximizing reinforcement and survive for long in nature. Optimal performance has to be a *goal* in making response choices. However, it may not provide the *mechanism* of choice behavior (Staddon & Hinson, 1983). Figuring out what are the total possible benefits that can be obtained in the long run through various response alternatives can be a very difficult matter. Consider again, for example, how often you should remove fish from a small pond so as to maximize your yield. You may have maximizing as a goal, but to use maximizing as a mechanism governing your choice, you have to know a great deal about the natural history of the fish in question. You have to know what is the life span of the fish, how old they are when they breed, how many offspring they are likely to have, what types of food they eat and how their food supply is influenced by fish density, what predators prey on the fish and how loss to predation is related to fish density, and so forth.

Optimization may well be a goal in choice behavior even though subjects do not always meet this goal. Various factors can introduce "errors" that preclude optimal performance. Response biases, limitations of memory, and limitations in information-processing capability can all lead to inaccurate assessments of the optimal response strategy and failures to maximize earned reinforcement (for example, Staddon, 1980). Instances in which animals severely fail to maximize reinforcement (for example, Mazur, 1981) provide evidence against maximizing as a mechanism of choice behavior but do not invalidate maximizing as a goal of response choices.

Melioration.   If maximizing is to be considered more as a goal than as a mechanism of choice behavior, what mechanism *is* responsible for the distribution of choices specified by the matching law? Although a definitive answer is not yet available, a provocative suggestion known as **melioration** was recently made by Herrnstein and Vaughan (1980; see also Vaughan, 1981). *Melioration* refers to an act of bettering a situation. Herrnstein and Vaughan suggested that animals always switch to improve on the local rate of reinforcement they are receiving. Adjustments in the distribution of behavior between alternatives are assumed to continue until the subject is obtaining the same local rate of reward on all alternatives. It can be shown mathematically that when subjects distribute their responses so as to obtain the same local rate of reinforcement on each alternative, they are behaving in accordance with the matching law. Therefore, the mechanism of melioration results in matching.

To see how melioration works, consider a VI 1-min VI 3-min concurrent schedule. During the first hour of exposure to this schedule, the subject will switch back and forth between the two alternatives and may end up spending a total of 30 min responding on each component and earn all of the available rewards. On a VI 1-min schedule, 60 rewards are available in one hour. If the subject manages to get all of these during the course of spending a total of 30 min on the VI 1-min schedule, the local rate of reinforcement on the VI 1-min schedule will be 60 rewards for 30 min of responding, or 120/hour. On a VI 3-min schedule, 20 rewards are available in one hour. If the subject gets all of these during the course of spending a total of 30 min on the VI 3-min schedule, its local rate of reinforcement on the VI 3-min component will be 20 rewards in 30 min, or 40/hour. Since the local rate of reinforcement on the VI 1-min schedule is much higher (120/hr) than on the VI 3-min schedule (40/hr), the subject will shift its behavior in favor of the VI 1-min alternative. However, if it shifts too far and spends too much time on the VI 1-min schedule and samples the VI 3-min schedule only rarely, it may be rewarded every time it pecks the VI 3-min key. This would make the local rate of reward on the VI 3-min key higher than the local rate of reward on the VI 1-min alternative, with a resulting shift in favor of the VI 3-min schedule. Such shifts back and forth will continue until the local rates of reinforcement earned on the two alternatives are equal.

The melioration mechanism has not been extensively investigated yet but is consistent with a variety of aspects of choice behavior (McSweeney, Melville, Buck, & Whipple, 1983). Melioration is related to previous proposed mechanisms of the matching law in that it involves shifts in behavior to more favorable rates of return. It provides an analysis of choice behavior at a level somewhere between molecular and molar theories of maximizing. Molecular theories emphasize control by the probability of reinforcement at a given moment. If the momentary probability of reinforcement is higher on another alternative, the subject is assumed to switch to that alternative at that moment. Melioration is stated in terms of the *local rate of reinforcement* rather than in terms of momentary probability of reinforcement. Thus, it considers outcomes over a slightly longer term than molecular maximizing theories. But it is not concerned with overall rates of reinforcement, as molar theories of maximizing are.

Concurrent-Chain Schedules: The Study of Complex Choice

In the choice situations described above, animals had two response alternatives and could switch from one to the other at any time. Many choice situations outside the laboratory are of this type. If you are eating a dinner of roast beef, vegetables, and mashed potatoes with gravy, you can switch from one food to another at any time during the meal. You can similarly switch back and forth between radio stations you listen to or parts of the newspaper you read. However, other situations involve much more complex choices. Choosing one alternative may make other alternatives unavailable, and the choice may involve assessing complex, long-range goals. Should you go to college and get a degree in engineering or start in a full-time job without a college degree? One cannot switch back and forth between these two alternatives frequently. Furthermore, to make the decision, you need to consider more than merely whether you enjoy taking engineering courses more or less than you enjoy holding a job. This choice also involves long-range goals. A degree in engineering may enable you to get a higher-paying job eventually, but it may require significant economic sacrifices initially. Getting a job would enable you to make money sooner, but in the long run you might not be able to earn as much money.

Obviously, we cannot conduct experiments that directly involve complex choices such as choosing between college and employment. However, simplified analogous questions may be posed to laboratory animals. For example, does a pigeon prefer to work on an FR 10 schedule of reinforcement for 15 min, or does it prefer to work on a VI 60-sec schedule for the same amount of time? Answers to such questions can be obtained with the use of **concurrent-chain schedules of reinforcement.** A concurrent-chain schedule involves at least two components (see Figure 6.5). In the first component, the subject is allowed to choose between two alternatives by making one of two responses. In the example diagramed in Figure 6.5, the pigeon makes its choice by pecking either response key A or response key B. Pecking key A produces alternative A, the opportunity to peck key A for 15 min on an FR 10 schedule of reinforcement. If the pigeon pecks key B at the beginning of the cycle, it thereby produces alternative B, which is the opportunity to peck key B for 15 min on a VI 60-sec schedule. Responding on either key A or key B during the initial component of the schedule does not produce reinforcement. The opportunity for reinforcement

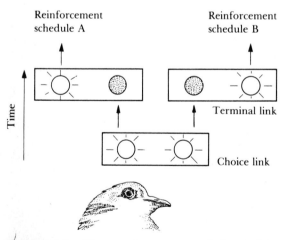

FIGURE 6.5. Diagram of a concurrent-chain schedule. Pecking key A in the choice link puts into effect reinforcement schedule A in the terminal link. Pecking key B in the choice link puts into effect reinforcement schedule B in the terminal link.

occurs only after the initial choice has been made and the pigeon has produced one or the other terminal component.

The pattern of responding that occurs in the terminal component of a concurrent-chain schedule is characteristic of whatever schedule of reinforcement is in effect during that component. In our example, if the pigeon has produced alternative A, its pattern of pecking during the terminal component will be similar to the usual response pattern in FR 10 schedules. If the pigeon has produced alternative B, its pattern of pecking during the terminal component will be characteristic of a VI 60-sec schedule.

The animal's choice between the schedules of reinforcement in effect in the terminal components of a concurrent-chain schedule is measured by the proportions in which it chooses key A and key B during the initial choice component. Research has shown that the choice behavior is largely determined by the overall reinforcement characteristics of each of the terminal components. The pigeon will show a preference for the terminal schedule that results in more frequent or greater reinforcement. In concurrent-chain schedules of punishment, the pigeon will prefer the terminal component that has the least frequent punishment. The concurrent-chain-schedule method can be used to determine how various aspects of reinforcement combine to influence choice behavior.

An interesting application of a concurrent-chain schedule is the experimental investigation of self-control. As every dieter knows, self-control is often a matter of choosing the greater delayed reward (being thin) over the immediate smaller reward (eating the piece of cake). When the piece of cake is there in front of you, it is very difficult to choose the delayed reward. Rachlin and Green (1972) set up a laboratory analog of self-control with pigeons. When given a direct choice between an immediate, small reward or a delayed, large reward, pigeons often chose the small, immediate reward. However, under certain circumstances they could be trained to exhibit self-control. The basic concurrent-chain schedule used in this research is shown in Figure 6.6. In the terminal components of the schedule, responding was rewarded by either immediate access to a small amount of grain (alternative A) or access to a large amount of grain that was delayed by 4 sec (alternative B). The pigeons could choose between these two alternatives by pecking either key A or key B during the initial component of the schedule.

Under what circumstances did the pigeons show self-control? Everyone who diets knows that it is easier to refuse a piece of cake that is to be eaten at tomorrow's luncheon than to refuse one that is to be eaten in the next few minutes. A similar effect occurred in the pigeons. The subjects were more likely to choose the delayed large reward over the immediate small reward if the terminal components of the concurrent-chain schedule were delayed after the pigeons made their initial choice. This was accomplished by requiring the subjects to respond 10 times

on the choice keys instead of only once during the initial component of the schedule.

The phenomenon of self-control as illustrated by the Rachlin and Green experiment has stimulated much research and theorizing. Numerous investigators have found, in agreement with Rachlin and Green, that preferences shift in favor of the more delayed large reward as subjects are made to wait longer to receive either reward after making their choice. If the rewards are delivered shortly after the choice response, subjects generally favor the closer small reward over the more delayed large reward. However, if a constant delay is added to the delivery of both rewards, subjects are more likely to show self-control and favor the more remote large reward. This

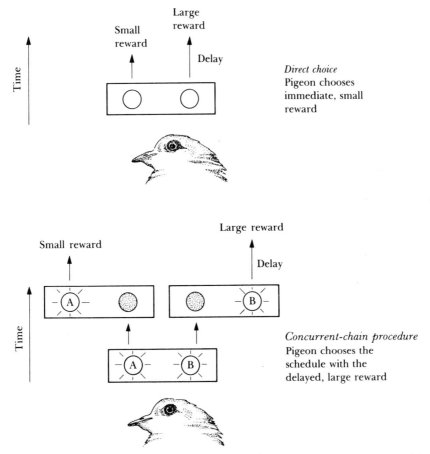

FIGURE 6.6. Diagram of the experiment by Rachlin and Green (1972) on self-control. Top panel shows the direct-choice procedure. Bottom panel shows the concurrent-chain procedure.

crossover in preference has been obtained in experiments with both people and nonhuman subjects and thus represents a general property of choice behavior (for example, Ainslie & Herrnstein, 1981; Solnick, Kannenberg, Eckerman, & Waller, 1980; see also Millar & Navarick, 1984).

Theoretical efforts to explain choice behavior in a self-control paradigm have been based on the assumption that the value of a reward decreases as a function of how long you have to wait to receive it. The longer subjects have to wait for a reward, the less valuable that reward is assumed to be. Figure 6.7 shows two hypothetical decay functions of this type, one for a small reward and the other for a large reward presented some time after the small reward. The figure also identifies two points in time, T_1 and T_2, before delivery of the small and large rewards. T_1 involves much less waiting time to reward delivery than T_2. The reward-value curves shown in Figure 6.7 predict the choice behavior that is typically observed in self-control experiments. When the waiting time for reward delivery is short (T_1 in Figure 6.7), the value of the small reward is greater than the value of the large reward. Hence, subjects will choose the small reward. In contrast, when waiting time is long (T_2 in Figure 6.7), the value of the large reward is greater than the value of the small reward, and the subject will choose the large reward. Thus, the model

depicted in Figure 6.7 predicts the crossover from preference for the small reward to preference for the more delayed large reward as the waiting time for both rewards is increased.

The results of self-control experiments are typically explained in terms of reward-value curves like those in Figure 6.7. However, the exact shape of the curves is in dispute. Some evidence is consistent with reward-value curves derived from the matching law (for example, Ainslie & Herrnstein, 1981; Logue, Rodriguez, Peña-Correal, & Mauro, in press). Other results are harder to explain in this way (for example, Snyderman, 1983), and alternative formulations for reward-value curves have been proposed (for example, Killeen, 1982).

The laboratory analog research suggests that dieting will be more successful if the dieter avoids confrontations with immediate small rewards. This is particularly true for dieting because being thin is a reward that is usually very delayed. One can add delay to the small immediate rewards of eating fattening foods by increasing the response requirement for obtaining food. If you do not have ready-to-eat foods in the house, the time and energy required to purchase and prepare the food may make it easier to forgo the small immediate reward of eating in favor of the delayed reward of being thin. (Interestingly, other lines of research also make this recommendation; see Schachter, 1971b.)

Extinction

So far we have discussed how organisms behave when their responses are reinforced according to various schedules of reinforcement. A related and very important issue concerns what responses occur when reinforcement is no longer available. Not many reinforcement schedules in nature remain in effect throughout the organism's lifetime. Responses that are successful in producing reinforcement at one time may cease to be effective as circumstances change. Children, for example, are praised for drawing crude representations of people and objects, but the same type of drawing is not considered good if made later in life. Dating someone may be extremely pleasant

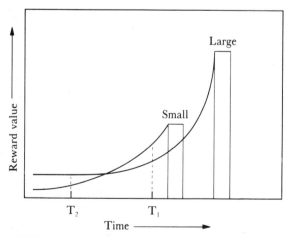

FIGURE 6.7. Hypothetical relations between reward value and waiting time to reward delivery for a small reward and a large reward presented some time later.

and rewarding until the person finds another special friend and no longer encourages your approaches. The nonreinforcement of a response that was previously rewarded is called **extinction.** We encountered extinction earlier in the book in connection with classical conditioning. There, *extinction* referred to the reduction in a response when the conditioned stimulus was no longer followed by the unconditioned stimulus. In instrumental conditioning, extinction is the reduction in an instrumental response when it is no longer followed by the reinforcer.

Effects of extinction procedures

Instrumental extinction procedures—withdrawal of reinforcement—have two important types of effects on the organism. First, of course, the procedure results in a gradual decrease in the rate of the instrumental response. During the first extinction session, the subject may respond rapidly at first and then gradually slow down until it stops making the instrumental response. If the subject is placed back in the experimental situation the next day, there may be a slight and temporary recovery in rate of responding. This is called **spontaneous recovery.** However, the amount of spontaneous recovery decreases with repeated extinction sessions, until the subject ceases to make the instrumental response altogether. Figure 6.8 shows the course of a response during the first two extinction sessions.

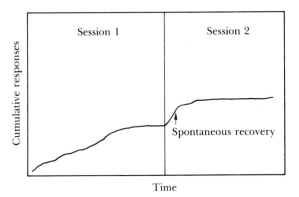

FIGURE 6.8. Cumulative record of responding during the first and second sessions of extinction. The burst of responding at the beginning of the second session is spontaneous recovery. (Hypothetical data.)

In addition to the expected decline in the instrumental response, extinction procedures also produce strong emotional effects and behavioral arousal. If the subject has become accustomed to receiving reinforcement for a particular response, it may become extremely upset and aggressive when rewards are no longer delivered. This emotional reaction induced by withdrawal of rewards is called **frustration.** Frustrative aggression induced by extinction procedures is dramatically demonstrated by experiments in which two animals (pigeons, for example) are placed in the same Skinner box (Azrin, Hutchinson, & Hake, 1966). One of them is initially rewarded for pecking a response key, while the other animal is restrained in a corner of the experimental chamber. The key-pecking bird largely ignores the other one as long as reinforcement is provided. However, when reinforcement ceases, the previously rewarded animal is likely to attack its innocent partner. Similar aggression occurs if a stuffed model instead of a real animal is placed in the Skinner box. (See Nation and Cooney, 1982, for an experimental study of extinction-induced aggression in human subjects.)

Frustrative reactions to withdrawal of rewards are also common outside the laboratory. When a vending machine breaks down and no longer delivers a soft drink or candy for the coins that are put into it, people often become abusive and pound and kick the machine. Vending machines have to be built very sturdily to withstand this frustrative aggression. Frustration is also common in interpersonal interactions when extinction is introduced by one of the parties. If a husband is accustomed to having his clothes always laundered, the first time his wife fails to do the laundry, he may become very angry. If a child is accustomed to being driven to school every day by her parents, she is likely to become upset if one day she has to walk or take the bus. If you and your special friend usually go on a date every Saturday evening, you will surely be very disturbed if unexpectedly your friend calls off the date.

Determinants of extinction effects

The most important variable that determines the magnitude of both the behavioral and emotional effects of an extinction procedure is the schedule of reinforcement in effect for the instrumental response before the extinction procedure is introduced. Various subtle features of reinforcement schedules can influence the subsequent extinction of instrumental responses. However, the dominant schedule characteristic that determines extinction effects is whether the instrumental response was reinforced every time it occurred (continuous reinforcement) or only some of the times it occurred (intermittent, or partial, reinforcement). Most of the schedules of reinforcement described earlier in the chapter involve partial reinforcement. We discussed these schedules in great detail because the pattern of responding that occurs when reinforcement is available closely depends on the special features of each schedule. However, the difference between continuous and partial reinforcement is much more important in the study of extinction effects than differences among the various possible partial reinforcement schedules. The general finding is that extinction is much slower and involves fewer frustration reactions if the subjects previously experienced a partial reinforcement schedule than if they previously experienced continuous reinforcement (see Figure 6.9). This phenomenon is called the **partial-reinforcement extinction effect**, or **PRE**.

The persistence in responding that is created by intermittent reinforcement can be remarkable. Aspiring actors and actresses study hard and persist in their eagerness to pursue an acting career even though they may get very few important roles. Habitual gamblers are similarly at the mercy of intermittent reinforcement. The few times they win big strongly encourage them to continue gambling during long strings of losses. Partial reinforcement also occurs often in interpersonal situations. If you are not really interested in dating someone who finds you extremely attractive, you may accept only a small proportion of his or her invitations. By doing this, you will be reinforcing the person intermittently and thus may make the person much more persistent in trying to win your favor. Intermittent reinforcement can also have undesirable consequences if parents give in to various demands from a child only after the child has made the request repeatedly. Consider, for example, a child riding in a grocery cart while the parent is

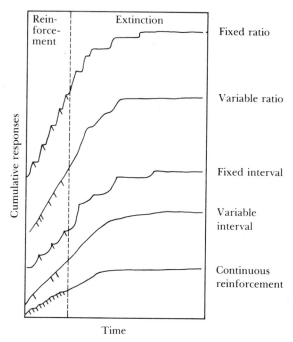

FIGURE 6.9. Cumulative records of extinction of instrumental behavior following various simple schedules of reinforcement. (Hypothetical data.)

shopping. The child asks the parent to buy a piece of candy. The parent says no. The child asks again and again and then begins to throw a temper tantrum because the parent continues to say no. At this point, the parent is likely to give in to avoid public embarrassment. By buying the candy, the parent will have reinforced the temper tantrum and also provided intermittent reinforcement for the repeated demands for candy. The schedule of reinforcement the parent used will make the child very persistent in making requests in the future and will also encourage tantrums.

Mechanisms of the partial-reinforcement extinction effect

Perhaps the most obvious explanation of the PRE is that animals continue responding more when reward is withdrawn after intermittent reinforcement than after continuous reinforcement because the withdrawal of reward is more difficult to detect in the former case. If the subject does not receive reward after each response during training, it may not notice right away when reward ceases. The change in reinforcement conditions is presumably much more dramatic if reward ceases after continuous reinforcement. This explanation of the partial-reinforcement extinction effect is called the **discrimination hypothesis.**

Although the discrimination hypothesis provides an intuitively satisfactory explanation of the PRE, the phenomenon is not so straightforward. In an ingenious test of the discrimination hypothesis, Jenkins (1962) and Theios (1962) first trained one group of animals with partial reinforcement and another group with continuous reinforcement. Both groups then received a period of continuous reinforcement before reinforcement for each group was withdrawn. Because the extinction procedure was introduced immediately after continuous reinforcement training for both groups, it was presumably equally noticeable or discriminable. Nevertheless, the subjects that initially received partial reinforcement training responded more during the extinction period. These experiments show that the advantage of partial reinforcement does not come from making the start of the extinction procedure more difficult to detect. Rather, it seems that subjects learn something important during partial reinforcement training that is not lost if they also receive continuous reinforcement before the extinction procedure.

What do organisms learn during partial reinforcement training that makes them respond more often when rewards are no longer available? Numerous complicated experiments have been performed in attempts to answer this question. These studies indicate that partial reinforcement training promotes persistence during extinction in two ways. One of the mechanisms of the partial-reinforcement extinction effect was proposed by Amsel (for example, 1958, 1962, 1967, 1979) and has come to be known as **frustration theory.** Frustration theory assumes that animals reinforced on an intermittent schedule go through several stages in their training. During the course of partial reinforcement, subjects receive some rewarded and some nonrewarded trials. Consequently, they develop conflicting expectations. Rewarded trials lead them to expect reinforcement and nonrewarded trials lead them to expect nonreinforcement. Initially, the anticipation of reward encourages the subjects to go ahead and make the instrumental response, whereas the anticipation of nonreinforcement discourages them from making the instrumental response. Thus, early in training the subjects are in a conflict about what to do. However, on some occasions when the subjects expect nonreward, performance of the instrumental response may in fact be followed by the reinforcer. Because of such experiences, performance of the instrumental response becomes conditioned to the expectation of nonreward. According to frustration theory, this is the key to persistent responding in extinction. Because animals learn to make the instrumental response in expectation of nonreward, subjects trained with intermittent reinforcement continue to make the response when extinction procedures are introduced. In contrast, there is nothing about the experience of continuous reinforcement that teaches animals to respond when they expect not getting rewarded. Therefore, these subjects stop responding much sooner in extinction.

The second prominent mechanism that explains responding in extinction after intermittent reinforcement was proposed by Capaldi (for example, 1967, 1971) and is known as **sequential theory.** Sequential theory relies heavily on memory mechanisms. It assumes that animals can remember very well whether or not they were reinforced for performing the instrumental response in the recent past. The theory assumes, further, that animals on a partial reinforcement schedule learn to make the instrumental response when they remember not having been rewarded on the preceding trials. Thus, the memory of not having been rewarded recently comes to motivate the subjects to perform the instrumental behavior. Precisely how this happens depends a great deal on the sequence of rewarded (R) and nonrewarded (N) trials that are administered in the intermittent reinforcement schedule.

Consider the following sequence of trials: RNNRRNR. In this sequence the subject is rewarded the first time it makes the instrumental response, not rewarded on the next two occasions, then rewarded twice, then not rewarded, and then rewarded again. The fourth and last trials are critical in this schedule. The subject is reinforced for responding on the fourth trial. It is assumed that on this trial the subject remembers not having been rewarded on the preceding two trials. Because of the reinforcement on the fourth trial, it is assumed, the subject learns that it will be reinforced for responding when its memory indicates that it was not rewarded on the preceding two trials. A similar mechanism is activated by the reinforcement on the last trial of the above sequence. Here the subject is rewarded for responding when its memory indicates that it was not reinforced on the single immediately preceding trial. With enough experiences of this type, subjects learn to respond whenever they remember not having been reinforced on the preceding trials. This learning, in turn, creates persistent responding in extinction after intermittent reinforcement. A continuous reinforcement schedule does not permit animals to learn such persistence. On a continuous reinforcement schedule, subjects are rewarded for every occurrence of the instrumental response. Therefore, they cannot learn that they will be rewarded for responding on occasions when they remember not having been reinforced on preceding trials. Nonreinforced trials during extinction therefore do not motivate them to continue responding.

Some have regarded frustration theory and sequential theory as competing explanations of the partial-reinforcement extinction effect. However, since the two mechanisms were originally proposed, a very large and impressive body of evidence has been obtained in support of each theory. Therefore, we cannot regard one of the theories as correct and the other as incorrect. Rather, the two theories point out two different ways in which partial reinforcement can promote responding during extinction. In some situations one or the other mechanism may be operative, and in other cases both processes could contribute to persistent responding in extinction.

Concluding Comments

The basic principle of instrumental conditioning is very simple: reinforcement increases (and punishment decreases) the future probability of an instrumental response. However, as we have seen, the experimental analysis of instrumental behavior can be rather intricate. Many important aspects of instrumental behavior are determined by the schedule of reinforcement. There are numerous schedules by which responses can be reinforced. Reinforcement can depend on how many responses have occurred, the passage of time, or the rate of responding, and more than one reinforcement schedule may be available to the subject at the same time. The pattern of instrumental behavior, as well as choices among various response alternatives, is strongly determined by the schedule of reinforcement that is in effect. Reinforcement schedules also determine the extent to which subjects persist in responding when rewards become no longer available. These various findings have told us a great deal about how reinforcement controls behavior in a wide variety of circumstances.

CHAPTER 7
Reinforcement: Theories and Experimental Analysis

Chapter 7 is devoted to a detailed discussion of the mechanisms whereby reinforcement increases the future probability of certain responses. We begin with a discussion of some fundamental issues in reinforcement theory. We then discuss three approaches to a theory of reinforcement. The first approach considers reinforcement to be the presentation of a special kind of stimulus and attempts to identify what are the special properties of reinforcing stimuli. The second approach views reinforcement as behavioral regulation and is concerned with identifying how instrumental contingencies produce a redistribution in the actions of the organism. The third approach views reinforcement as a process of the selection of a response from certain kinds of activities that are stimulated by periodic deliveries of a reinforcer.

Chapters 5 and 6 described how instrumental behavior is influenced by various kinds of experimental manipulations. This research has provided much information about the characteristics of instrumental behavior in a variety of circumstances. The present chapter will analyze in greater detail the mechanisms of reinforcement. We will consider why certain events are effective reinforcers and what organisms learn during the course of instrumental conditioning. The answers to these questions involve some of the most exciting and important aspects of behavior theory today.

We are witnessing a major reorientation in how theoreticians conceptualize the mechanisms of reinforcement. Early investigators followed Thorndike in assuming that reinforcement involved the strengthening of a particular response by the presentation of a certain kind of stimulus (a reinforcer) after occurrences of the response. Thus, the emphasis was on changes in a single response brought about by delivery of a particular type of stimulus. More recent conceptualizations of the reinforcement process take a broader view of the animal's behavior. They recognize that reinforcement involves much more than the presentation of a stimulus. Reinforcing stimuli must be consumed or used in some way. Consummatory responses (approach, chewing, and swallowing, for example, in the case of food) have a critical role in modern views of reinforcement processes. In addition, modern views are concerned not only with changes in the reinforced response that result from instrumental conditioning but also with changes in other activities of the subject. Thus, instrumental conditioning is viewed as creating a new distribution of activities, not just as strengthening a particular response. This shift in perspective has involved a change from thinking about reinforcement as a form of physiological regulation to thinking about reinforcement as a form of behavioral regulation.

Fundamental Issues in Reinforcement Theory

If we were to name all the stimuli that have been used

as reinforcers, we would have a very long list. Included would be the more popular stimuli, such as food, water, and sexual partners, and other diverse stimuli, such as oxygen, increases in atmospheric temperature, saccharin solution, and even electrical shock. The list would also include such activities as watching a moving electric train, playing pinball, and running in a running wheel. Finally, we might include reinforcers that are not always easily defined, such as the approval of others, self-satisfaction, and the like. What do all these stimuli have in common that makes them effective reinforcers? We might presume that where there is reinforcement, there is pleasure. Thorndike used a slightly different wording. In the law of effect he described what we now call reinforcing stimuli as events that produce "satisfying states of affairs." What, though, is a satisfying state of affairs? Or, what is pleasurable? It is tempting to define *pleasure* or *satisfying state of affairs* as any event or stimulus that the subject will work for—in other words, whatever will reinforce behavior. However, this makes the definition of a reinforcer circular. We cannot define a reinforcer as something that provides pleasure if we define something that provides pleasure as a reinforcer. What is needed is a definition of *pleasure* or *satisfying state of affairs* that is not stated in terms of a reinforcement effect.

One way out of the circularity in the answer to "What makes reinforcers reinforce?" is to restrict the scope of the question. Instead of trying to answer the question for all circumstances, we can try to provide an answer for only a particular reinforcing stimulus that is used to strengthen a particular response in a unique situation. For example, what makes food an effective reinforcer for lever pressing in rats placed in a Skinner box? A circular answer to this question would be that food reinforces lever pressing because it is a reinforcer in this situation. This is not an informative statement. Meehl (1950) suggested that the **principle of transsituationality** can be of help in cases like this. The principle of transsituationality assumes that reinforcers are effective in strengthening behavior in a variety of situations. Food, for example, is expected to reinforce not only lever pressing in a Skinner box but also running in a runway and swimming in a tank of water. Given this transsituationality, one can use the outcome of the effects of reinforcement in one situation to explain the effects in another. Thus, we can say that food strengthens behavior in a lever-press experiment because food has been identified as a reinforcer in a runway experiment. This explanation is not circular. The reinforcing properties of food are identified in a situation (the runway experiment) that is different from the situation in which we are trying to explain the reinforcement effect (the lever-press experiment).

Although the principle of transsituationality helps to avoid circularity, it is not entirely satisfactory. Assume that we use the fact that food is an effective reinforcer in a runway experiment to explain why food strengthens behavior in a lever-press experiment. Such an explanation would not provide much insight into behavior. The fundamental question of why reinforcers reinforce would remain unanswered until we knew why food is an effective reinforcer in a runway experiment. Another weakness of this approach is that reinforcers are not always effective across a broad range of situations. As we discussed in Chapter 5, there are serious constraints on operant conditioning. A reinforcer that is effective in strengthening one response may not be useful in reinforcing other types of behavior.

The theories of reinforcement that we will examine in the coming pages represent a more analytical approach to the question of what makes a reinforcer reinforce. Basically, there are two central problems in the analysis. One problem is to determine the essential characteristics of reinforcers. If these were known, one could identify reinforcers readily by the presence or absence of the critical characteristics. The second problem is describing the mechanism involved. That is, what does the reinforcer do, and how does it do it?

The theories of reinforcement we will discuss analyze the characteristics of reinforcers and the mechanisms of reinforcement in different ways. We will begin by discussing traditional and rather familiar ideas that conceptualize reinforcement as the presentation of special types of stimuli. Some theories of this type also view reinforcement as satisfying particular physiological needs. We will then discuss reinforcement conceptualized as behavioral regulation, contributing to the satisfaction of behavioral "goals" or "needs." The third and final approach to

reinforcement we will consider views reinforcement as a process of response selection.

Reinforcement as Stimulus Presentation

Traditionally, reinforcement has been viewed as the presentation of particular types of stimuli contingent on performance of a particular instrumental response. Various suggestions have been made about what special types of stimuli can serve as reinforcers. However, all theories of reinforcement that consider the reinforcer as a stimulus share the view that reinforcement "strengthens" the instrumental response. The various conceptions differ on how this is accomplished. Thorndike, for example, proposed that "strengthening" of the instrumental response is a secondary result of the formation of an association between stimuli present at the time of the response and the reinforcer. In contrast, Skinner placed much greater emphasis on the relationship between the instrumental response and the reinforcer. He suggested that reinforcement strengthens whatever behavior happens to occur just before delivery of the reinforcer.

Physiological homeostasis and drive reduction

In much of the research on instrumental learning, biologically important stimuli such as food and water are used as reinforcers. Subjects are first deprived of a substance such as food; the return of this substance then serves as the reinforcer. Because these stimuli are necessary to the animal's survival, many theories of reinforcement have emphasized physiological factors in reinforcement.

Some reinforcement theorists have described the procedures of deprivation and reinforcement as two opposing processes that alter the organism's physiological state. The concept of **physiological homeostasis** is useful here to describe the results of these two processes. By *physiological homeostasis* we mean that state of the organism in which all physiological systems are in proper balance. Deprivation procedures typically upset this balance. In contrast, reinforcement returns the organism to homeostasis, the balanced state. The motivation to perform the instrumental response is seen as the result of the loss of homeostasis. According to this view, reinforcement works because organisms always seek to return to homeostasis.

One of the first theorists to make extensive use of a physiological homeostatic mechanism was Clark Hull (see Amsel & Rashotte, 1984, for a contemporary review of Hullian theory). Hull believed that the deprivation procedures used in experiments that employ food and water as reinforcers create a biological drive state. Reinforcers were assumed to have the common characteristic of reducing this drive state. According to this hypothesis, the mechanism of reinforcement involves a homeostatic process. Each time the subject obtains the reinforcer, it moves a step closer to homeostasis. The inborn tendency of the organism to return to homeostasis is the motivation for the response. Therefore, according to Hull, the degree of drive determines (in part) the degree of responding.

Physiological needs or drives are assumed to be related to elements of the environment that are necessary for survival of the individual or the species. Therefore, need or drive states presumably can be identified with physiology experiments. Consistent with this view, food, water, oxygen, and temperature changes have all been successfully used as reinforcers.

Primary and incentive motivation

The drive-reduction hypothesis exemplifies the fact that the analysis of reinforcement is often cast as part of the broader field of motivation. Reinforcement is one way of forcing behavior to change. Where, though, does the force originate? Sometimes the force seems to lie within the organism as a drive state. Motivation induced by a drive state is called **primary motivation.** Motivation for behavior may also come from the reinforcer itself. Sometimes just the presence of food, water, or a sexual partner can trigger behavior. Such motivation created by the reinforcer itself is called **incentive motivation.** Large portions of food and more palatable foods can be more effective in reinforcing instrumental behavior than small portions and less palatable foods in

equally food-deprived animals. Given the equivalent levels of food deprivation, such results cannot be explained in terms of differences in drive level and illustrate the importance of incentive motivation.

We thus have two possible sources of motivation: (1) the drive state and (2) the incentive properties of the reinforcer. The role of each of these sources has been discussed at length in the psychology literature (see Bolles, 1975). At present it appears that reinforcement is neither solely drive reduction nor solely incentive motivation. Both aspects play a role. Miller and Kessen (1952), for example, compared the reinforcement effects of food delivered directly into the stomach through a fistula and food consumed in the normal fashion. They found that fistula feeding could serve effectively as a reinforcer. Drive reduction from fistula feeding appears to be sufficient. However, the effect was not as powerful as that produced by normal eating. Normal eating may have been more effective in increasing the instrumental response because it provided both drive-reduction reinforcement and incentive motivation.

At present, it is convenient to think of all sources of motivation as contributing to reinforcement effects. Modern research on brain stimulation, physiology, and biochemistry has made important contributions to our understanding of the motivational processes involved in reinforcement.

Sensory reinforcement

The distinction between primary and incentive motivation illustrates that drive-reduction mechanisms are not sufficient to explain all reinforcement effects. External stimuli also have an important role in the motivation of instrumental behavior. Other lines of evidence suggest that drive reduction may not even be necessary for reinforcement. Sheffield, Wulff, and Backer (1951), for example, demonstrated that a male rat will run down a runway in order to gain access to a female even though it is not allowed to ejaculate with the female. In this case, the instrumental behavior was performed to obtain a stimulus without drive reduction. In fact, the drive level or excitement of the male was probably increased by encounter with the female without copulation. Thus, a reinforcement effect was obtained in the face of an increase rather than a decrease in drive.

The lack of importance of drive reduction in reinforcement is also illustrated by numerous examples of the reinforcing effects of stimuli that are not biologically or physiologically significant in any obvious sense. One prominent reinforcement theorist has commented that "virtually anything can act as a reward in suitable circumstances" (Berlyne, 1969, p. 182). Activities such as watching a moving electric train can be used to reinforce the behavior of monkeys. Turning on a light, opportunity for exploration, and drinking a saccharin solution, which has no nutritive value and therefore does not reduce a physiological need, can also be effective rewards. Motivation of behavior by the sensory properties of stimuli is a common human experience. Fine works of art and music, for example, provide primarily sensory reinforcement.

To explain the effectiveness of sensory reinforcers, one might hypothesize the existence of corresponding drive states. For example, one might hypothesize the existence of a curiosity drive to explain the reinforcing effect of watching a moving electric train. However, this approach is not very productive. The only evidence for the existence of a curiosity drive is that moving trains and the like are effective reinforcers. This reintroduces the same type of circularity problem we discussed earlier. We would be saying that a moving train reinforces behavior because it reduces the curiosity drive and that we know that there is a curiosity drive because the sight of a moving train reinforces behavior. The drive-reduction theory compels us to add an item to our list of drives each time we find a reinforcer that does not satisfy a biological drive that has been identified by other means. However, if we do this, we will not have a way to identify reinforcers independently. Therefore, the drive-reduction hypothesis has not been entirely successful in specifying a common feature of reinforcers independent of their reinforcement effects.

Brain stimulation reinforcement and motivation

Two physiological psychologists, James Olds and Peter Milner, implanted electrodes in the septal area of the brain of rats. The rats were then observed in a large compartment where they were given brief, mild electrical pulses to the brain through the electrodes. The rats tended to move toward the area of the chamber where they had last received the brain stimulation. Olds and Milner then connected a response lever to the electrical stimulator and discovered that the rats would press the lever at extremely high rates for many hours to receive the brain stimulation. The phenomenon was called **intracranial self-stimulation** (Olds & Milner, 1954). Olds and Milner's study sparked interest in several areas. The implications of the research were tremendous. The prospects of having such a powerful reinforcer available raises moral as well as practical issues in the control of behavior (see Box 7.1). Reinforcement theorists, however, were interested in the less glamorous aspects of the phenomenon. The self-stimulation research raised hope that a mechanism common to all reinforcers could be analyzed on a physiological level.

The findings of Olds and Milner stimulated several lines of investigation. Many experiments were performed to map out the various areas of the brain that, when stimulated, yield a reinforcement effect. In addition, there have been neurochemical analyses of the various neural pathways involved. Another set of experiments has explored the similarity of self-stimulation to other types of reinforcers. One outstanding feature of self-stimulation is that it is persistent and the response rates are high compared with other types of instrumental responding. In other respects self-stimulation appears to be similar to the traditional reinforcers when the two are compared under carefully controlled situations (see Mogenson & Cioe, 1977, for a review). Thus, explanations for the effects of self-stimulation have followed the explanations for traditional reinforcers. In general, it is assumed that one physiologically based explanation can serve for both.

One early explanation of brain-stimulation reinforcement involved drive reduction. It was hypothesized that brain stimulation activated the neural circuits that are involved when drives are reduced by consummatory behavior. However, this explanation turned out to be simplistic. It was discovered that the same electrical stimulation of the brain that reinforces lever pressing can also elicit responses such as eating, drinking, and sexual behavior when the appropriate stimulus (food, water, or a sexual partner) is available (for example, Caggiula & Hoebel, 1966; Herberg, 1963; Hoebel & Teitelbaum, 1962; Margules & Olds, 1962; Mogenson & Stevenson, 1966). Thus, brain stimulation appears in part to *induce* rather than *reduce* drives. Deutsch (1960) concluded that reinforcement in general requires both drive induction and subsequent drive reduction. Glickman and Schiff (1967) offered a slightly different interpretation of the experiments. They suggested that the source of the reinforcement effect is the species-specific responses such as eating and drinking that help the organism adapt to its environment. Brain stimulation and instrumental deprivation/reinforcement procedures have the same effects on behavior

because they are simply two ways of eliciting these adaptive responses.

Other research suggests that self-stimulation involves incentive motivation. Pfaffman (1960) proposed that self-stimulation is the result of activating the pathways that generally transmit such sensations as the taste of food. According to this view, brain stimulation reinforces behavior for the same reason that saccharin is an effective reinforcer—not by drive reduction but through the sensations involved in the consummatory responses. Campbell (1971) found evidence in support of this hypothesis. He showed that brain-stimulation reinforcement can be produced by electrical stimulation of the peripheral neural pathways that are generally known to transmit sensations from natural reinforcers. Campbell proposed that the physiological basis for reward lies

---

BOX 7.1.   "Pleasure-seeking brains: Artificial tickles, natural joys of thought"

In an article with the above title, the physiologist H. J. Campbell (1971) has discussed the significance of self-stimulation research in light of evolutionary theory and what it means to be "human." Campbell's own research involves the natural stimulation of the limbic system of the brain. He proposes that for lower animals sensory stimulation leads to limbic-system stimulation. When animals are given the opportunity merely to stimulate themselves sensorily with an electric "tickler," they will do so in much the same way as they will self-stimulate more-central brain structures. The major difference is that sensory stimulation satiates or habituates whereas limbic-system stimulation does not. However, as Campbell notes, when one sensory system is satiated, the animal switches to another. It does not simply sit back and do nothing.

Campbell therefore suggests that the underlying principle of behavior is keeping the limbic system stimulated. Phylogeny determines the ways this can be done. We can assume that plants, unlike animals, do not have central pleasure centers. As we move along the phylogenetic scale, the interconnections between the limbic system and other neural systems become increasingly complicated. In lower animals the limbic system receives input primarily from sense organs. In people, however, neural connections involving the limbic system are more extensive and include the cortex of the brain. For this reason, complex cortical activities, such as thinking or problem solving, may stimulate the limbic structures. Thus, these activities help to keep our limbic system activated. Of course, the limbic system is also linked to sense organs in higher organisms as well. Behavior that we sometimes label subhuman or animalistic—vandalism for sheer pleasure, excessive eating, and the like—also is known to occur in humans. Campbell proposes that our social institutions exist to keep these forms of pleasure seeking under control and to promote higher intellectual forms of limbic stimulation. If the electrical circuitry that allows us to seek pleasure by intellectual pursuits is the result of evolution, in a flight of fantasy we can image that evolution may yet produce another creature capable of intellectual pleasures. Campbell's proposal gives us the possibility that in a million years the octopus may prove mathematical theorems!

in the activation of the central reward pathways by means of any one of several inputs. Generally we think of the inputs as triggered by exteroceptive stimuli, such as taste and smell. However, other types of inputs are possible. In the human brain, the pathways could presumably be activated by cognitive processes. This would explain why some people get pleasure from doing puzzles, studying mathematics, and the like and why those activities can sometimes serve as reinforcers.

As with traditional reinforcers, research on brain stimulation supports the idea that reinforcement is the result of both drive state and incentive motivation. Evidence for this point of view arises from the fact that the rate of self-stimulation can be enhanced or reduced by altering either the drive state or incentive stimuli. For example, a rat will self-stimulate faster if it is also food-deprived (Olds, 1958). If the site of stimulation also induces drinking, self-stimulation is enhanced if water is available (Mendelson, 1967; Mogenson & Kaplinsky, 1970; Mogenson & Morgan, 1967). If the water is made tastier by adding saccharin, the response rate is enhanced even more (Phillips & Mogenson, 1968). Results such as these have led theorists to conclude that reinforcement occurs when an external stimulus (such as water) is present in conjunction with an overall drive state (such as thirst). This is, of course, what happens in the typical instrumental situation. Both elements also appear to be present with brain stimulation, albeit artificially induced or mimicked. Several theorists have suggested mechanisms to describe these dual effects more precisely (for example, Bindra, 1969; Mogenson & Huang, 1973). We will briefly describe the model by Milner because it draws directly on both brain stimulation and conventional reinforcers.

Milner (1970) suggested that when an organism is deprived, general behavioral arousal ensues. Behavioral arousal is characterized by exploratory behavior and other increased motor responses. The organism's behavior involves switching from one response to another. If the organism finds an appropriate stimulus by making a particular response, a response-hold mechanism is activated. The animal no longer switches from one behavior to another. Rather, it remains locked into the response that keeps it in contact with the stimulus until the drive state is reduced. In the case of brain stimulation, Milner has proposed that some of the neural pathways are short-circuited. The response-switch mechanism may be inhibited for a long time, giving rise to the persistent self-stimulating behavior. Milner's model is bolstered by concurrent work on the catecholamine pathways in the brain. These pathways appear to be involved in brain stimulation and may exert the response-inhibiting processes Milner's model requires (Milner, 1976). A complete understanding of the workings of the neural mechanisms of reinforcement awaits further research.

Reinforcement as Behavioral Regulation

The stimulus theories of reinforcement we considered in the preceding section either were directly concerned with physiological mechanisms of reinforcement or were formulated in response to theories that viewed reinforcement as a mechanism for the regulation of internal physiological systems. The theories share the assumption that reinforced behavior is trained, or stamped into the organism's behavioral repertoire. The underlying assumption of the next set of theories we will consider is much different. These theories are not concerned with the physiological substrates of reinforcement. Rather, reinforcement is described in terms of how the organism must adjust its behavior to meet the demands of a particular situation. The effects of reinforcement are not viewed as the stamping in of a particular response but as the reorganization of behavior. The various theories describe different ways in which this reorganization may take place.

Homeostasis, as we have said, is a balanced physiological state of the organism. Homeostasis becomes relevant to reinforcement when deviations from the stable state occur and the organism attempts to rectify the situation. The behavioral regulation theories we will consider in this section assume that a similar homeostatic mechanism exists with respect to behavior. That is, we may consider the behaving organism as having a particular balance of responses to maintain. The organism has particular things to do: it must eat, breathe, drink, keep warm, exercise, entertain itself, and so on. All these activities have to occur in particular proportions. If the normal or optimal balance of activities is upset, behavior is assumed to change so as to correct the deviation from behavioral homeostasis. The actual behavioral balance may, in fact, serve to maintain physiological homeostasis. Eating, drinking, and exercise are all part of maintaining physiological homeostasis. However, behavior regulation theories of reinforcement are stated in terms of behavioral rather than physiological processes. Another major innovation of behavioral regulation theories is that they view reinforcement as involving changes in the opportunity to engage in particular responses rather than as the presentation of particular types of stimuli. The focus is on relations between the instrumental response and responses made possible by presentation of the "reinforcer."

Precursor of behavioral regulation theories

Behavioral regulation theories evolved from ideas about reinforcement formulated by David Premack in the mid-1960s. Premack developed the idea that opportunities to engage in particular types of responses can serve as reinforcers. The possibility that certain responses may serve as reinforcers was first seen by Sheffield and his co-workers, who formulated the **consummatory-response theory.** The consummatory-response theory was proposed in an effort to explain why particular incentive stimuli such as food are effective reinforcers. Most reinforcers have to be "taken in," consumed in some way, to be effective. There are many sensations involved in the process that may be important. This suggests that sensations produced by responses required to consume the reinforcer may be reinforcing. The consummatory-response theory asserts that consummatory behaviors—eating, drinking, and the like—are themselves the critical feature of reinforcers. Events such as drive reduction might follow a consummatory response but were not assumed to be important in reinforcement. Research on the consummatory-response theory

focused on demonstrations that consummatory responses could reinforce instrumental behavior in the absence of drive reduction. Famous experiments were performed showing that the artificial sweetener saccharin is an effective reinforcer for rats (for example, Sheffield, Roby, & Campbell, 1954). A mild solution of saccharin has a pleasant taste and stimulates consummatory behavior but is not nutritive and therefore presumably does not reduce a drive state.

Premack's theory of reinforcement

The consummatory-response theory represents a step away from stimulus theories of reinforcement in that it considers reinforcement as the opportunity to engage in a particular type of response. However, all these theories share the assumption that the responses that accompany reinforcing stimuli are fundamentally different in some way from responses that can serve as instrumental behavior. Consummatory responses (chewing and swallowing, for example) are assumed to be fundamentally different from various potential instrumental responses like running, jumping, or manipulating something. Premack took issue with this distinction and suggested that instrumental responses and responses accompanying reinforcing stimuli differ only in their likelihood of occurrence. He pointed out that responses involved with commonly used reinforcers are activities that the subject is highly likely to pursue. For example, animals in a food-reinforcement experiment are highly likely to engage in eating responses. Deprivation procedures serve to ensure that eating will be the most likely behavior in the situation. In contrast, instrumental responses are typically low-probability activities. An experimentally naive rat, for example, is quite unlikely to press a response lever. Premack (1965) proposed that this difference in response probabilities is critical for reinforcement. Formally, his reinforcement principle can be stated as follows: *Given two responses arranged in an operant conditioning procedure, the more probable response will reinforce the less likely behavior; the less probable response will not reinforce the more likely behavior.*

Eating will reinforce bar pressing because eating is typically more probable than bar pressing. Under ordinary circumstances, bar pressing cannot reinforce eating. However, Premack's theory suggests that if for some reason bar pressing became more probable than eating, it would reinforce eating. Thus, Premack's theory denies that there is a fundamental distinction between reinforcers and instrumental responses. The particular characteristic that makes a reinforcer act as such is not something intrinsic to the reinforcing response. Rather, the reinforcing response is simply a response that is more likely to occur than the instrumental response. Consequently, it is possible to use a wide variety of responses as reinforcers.

Experimental evidence. Premack and his colleagues conducted many experiments to test his theory (see Premack, 1965, 1971a). One of the early studies was a very simple test using young children. Premack first gave the children two response alternatives (eating candy and playing a pinball machine) and measured which response was more probable for each child. Some of the children preferred eating candy over playing pinball; others preferred the pinball. In a second phase of the experiment (see Figure 7.1), the children were tested with one of two procedures. In one procedure, eating was specified as the reinforcing response and playing pinball was the instrumental response. That is, the children had to play the pinball machine in order to get the opportunity to eat the candy. The question was whether all the children would increase their pinball playing. Consistent with Premack's theory, only those children who preferred eating to playing pinball showed a reinforcement effect under these circumstances. In the second procedure, the roles of the two responses were reversed. Eating was the instrumental response, and playing pinball was the reinforcing response. The children had to eat candy to get the opportunity to play pinball. In this situation only those children who preferred playing pinball to eating showed a reinforcement effect.

In another experiment, Premack (1962) altered the probabilities of the responses by changing deprivation conditions. Rats were tested using the responses of drinking and running in a rotating wheel. The experiment is diagrammed in Figure 7.2. In one study the rats were water-deprived but not deprived of the opportunity to run in the wheel. Under these circumstances drinking was more probable than running, and the opportunity to drink could be effectively used to reinforce running. In the second study, the rats were not deprived of water. Under these circumstances, they were more likely to run in the wheel than to drink. Now the opportunity to run in the wheel could be effectively used to reinforce drinking. However, drinking could no longer be used to reinforce running. Thus, running and drinking could be interchangeably used as instrumental and reinforcing responses, depending on the animal's state of water deprivation.

Measuring response probability. Both of the experiments described above had two parts. In the first part, behavior was measured in a situation in which the subject had unlimited opportunity to engage in either of the responses to be used later as the instrumental and the reinforcing responses. This situation is assumed to reveal the behavioral homeostatic balance of the organism in the absence of any constraints on responding. We call this the *baseline phase*. In the second part of the experiments, the

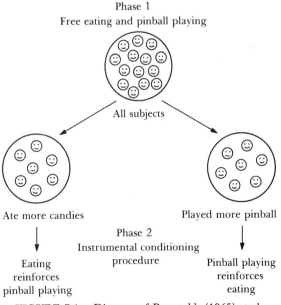

Phase 1
Free eating and pinball playing

All subjects

Ate more candies   Played more pinball

Phase 2
Instrumental conditioning
procedure

Eating
reinforces
pinball playing

Pinball playing
reinforces
eating

FIGURE 7.1.   Diagram of Premack's (1965) study.

Experiment 1

1. Rat is water deprived

2. Rat drinks more than it runs

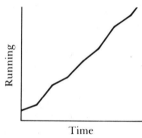

3. Drinking reinforces running

Experiment 2

1. Rat is not water deprived

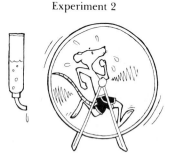

2. Rat runs more than it drinks

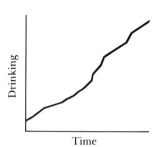

3. Running reinforces drinking

FIGURE 7.2.   When a rat is water-deprived (Experiment 1), it drinks more than it runs. Therefore, drinking reinforces running. When a rat is not water-deprived (Experiment 2), it runs more than it drinks. This time running reinforces drinking.   *(Based on Premack, 1962.)*

instrumental conditioning phase, the opportunity to engage in the high-probability reinforcer response was provided only when the subject made the lower-probability instrumental response. As we saw, what happened in the second phase depended on the relative probabilities of the two responses during the baseline phase. Therefore, before we can make precise predictions about how one response will (or will not) reinforce another, we must have some way to measure and compare the baseline probabilities of the two responses.

One possible measure of response probability is the frequency with which each response occurs in a set amount of time. This measure is fine as long as we are comparing responses that require similar amounts of time, such as pressing two alternative but otherwise identical response levers. What would we do, however, if we wanted to compare the probability of two very different responses, such as doing a crossword puzzle and eating? Comparing frequencies of response here would be very cumbersome and difficult. One would have to define what is an instance, or unit, of puzzle-solving behavior and what is an instance, or unit, of eating. Is completing one word in a crossword puzzle a unit of puzzle-solving behavior, or is completing all the items in a certain direction (horizontal or vertical) one unit of this behavior? Does a unit of eating mean taking one bite, completing one course, or eating an entire meal? We then have to decide which possible unit of puzzle solving should be considered equivalent to which unit of eating. Is each answer in a puzzle comparable to each bite of food?

As the above discussion suggests, it is difficult to formulate comparable units of behavior for diverse activities. However, a common dimension to all responses is *time.* Premack suggested that response probability may be measured in terms of the amount of time the subject spends engaged in the response in a specified period. We can express this idea in the following equation:

$$\text{probability of response} = \frac{\text{time spent on response}}{\text{total time}}$$

By this definition, responses taking up a greater proportion of the available time are considered more probable than responses on which the subject spends less time. If in an hour you spend 45 minutes eating and 15 minutes working on a puzzle, we would say that eating was more probable than working on the puzzle during this hour. Therefore, eating should reinforce working on the puzzle.

Although Premack's measure of response probability provides a means of comparing diverse responses, it is counterintuitive in some instances. Consider, for example, a comparison between sexual behavior and studying. A student may spend a good deal more time reading than engaging in sexual behavior. Nevertheless, most students would find sexual behavior more pleasant and reinforcing. This paradox may be resolved if we take into account the duration of the baseline observations. Given an unlimited choice between sex and reading in a two-hour period, sex will most likely predominate. However, over a two-year period, reading may be the more probable response. The baseline observation period is also critical for assessing the probability of responses that occur only periodically. For example, although you spend a good deal of time eating during a 24-hour period, eating is not uniformly distributed over the course of a day. Rather, it is highly likely only at certain times. In addition, the more time you devote to an activity such as eating, the less likely the response becomes for a while. After an hour has been spent in gastronomic pursuits, eating can become very *un*likely.

Because response probabilities vary with time itself, Premack further suggests that the more appropriate response measure is momentary probability. The use of this measure is illustrated in a hypothetical experiment using two responses whose frequencies change in different ways during a session. The experiment is summarized in Figure 7.3. Response A decreases in probability as the session progresses. In

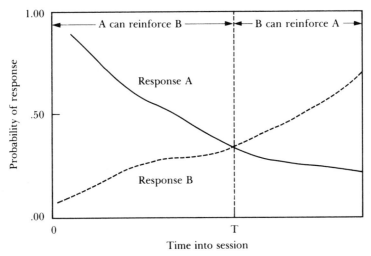

FIGURE 7.3.   Diagram of hypothetical response probabilities for two responses with different probabilities over time. At the beginning of the session (time = 0), response A has a greater momentary probability than response B. Hence response A can reinforce response B. At time T, response B becomes more probable than response A. From this point on, response B can reinforce response A.

contrast, the probability of response B increases. Over the entire session, the subject spends more time engaged in response A than in response B. However, response A can reinforce response B only during the first part of the session, because the momentary probability of response A is higher only during this time. During the second part of the session, response B has a greater momentary probability and therefore will effectively reinforce response A.

Response probability as a measure of response value.

Implicit in our discussion is the notion that more probable responses are more preferred or more valuable. Indeed, Premack suggests that value underlies all behavior. Organisms scale all response alternatives in terms of their value. At any given moment, the more valuable responses have more time allotted to them. If this is true, response probability should fit with other measures of value. In Chapter 6 we discussed concurrent schedules as a way of measuring reinforcement value. The matching law states that the relative rate of response equals the relative value of reinforcement. If we measure the time spent responding on an alternative rather than the response rate, we have

$$\frac{T_1}{\text{total time}} = \frac{V_1}{\text{total value}}$$
$$\text{and}$$
$$\frac{T_2}{\text{total time}} = \frac{V_2}{\text{total value}}$$

for each of two alternatives. Thus, Premack's measure of response probability can be used as a measure of value if we consider responding on schedule 1 as one behavior and responding on schedule 2 as a second behavior.

The idea that value underlies the time allocated to various responses is central to a homeostatic theory of reinforcement. The changes in behavior that we ordinarily attribute to motivational procedures can be considered to be reflected in changes in response value (Premack, 1971a). Hunger, thirst, and increased sexual arousal reflect increased values of eating, drinking, and sexual behavior. Any procedure (such as deprivation) that increases the value of a response relative to the instrumental behavior will enable this response to serve as a reinforcer. The actual reasons that the value has changed are not necessarily important for predicting reinforcement effects.

Momentary probability and restrictions on the reinforcing response.

In most instrumental conditioning procedures, the momentary probability of the reinforcing response is kept at a high level. This is generally accomplished by restricting the opportunity to engage in the reinforcing response. A rat lever-pressing for food, for example, typically comes into the experimental situation not having eaten much and does not receive a whole meal for each lever-press response. These limitations on the reinforcing response are very important. If we were to give the rat a full meal for making one lever-press, chances are we would not increase its rate of pressing very much. Restrictions on the opportunity to engage in the reinforcing response serve to increase its momentary probability. In general, we can characterize instrumental conditioning procedures as requiring the subject to do *more* of the instrumental response for less of the reinforcing response than it would do in an unrestricted situation.

Restrictions on the reinforcing response should be taken into account in measuring baseline response probabilities. That is, during the baseline session, the amounts of time spent engaged in various responses should be measured under the same constrained circumstances that will occur during the instrumental conditioning session. For example, the probability of eating should be measured in terms of the amount of time spent eating when food is periodically doled out in small pellets, as during instrumental conditioning.

The fact that the reinforcing response is restricted is a very important aspect of the instrumental learning situation. According to Premack (1965), it is one of the necessary conditions for reinforcement. Restriction of the reinforcer results in loss of behavioral homeostasis. That is, providing the reinforcer only when the instrumental response has occurred inflicts an imbalance on the natural flow of behavior. The subject cannot allocate time to the various responses in the way it would ordinarily. We may think, then, of the response restriction imposed by the instrumental procedure as giving rise to a kind of behavioral tension. Some degree of behavioral tension generated by behavioral deprivation may be necessary for even the smallest reinforcement effect.

Behavioral bliss points and behavioral regulation

Premack's principle of reinforcement was stated in terms of the relative probabilities of the instrumental and the reinforcing response. As we have seen, however, Premack was aware that the effectiveness of a response as a reinforcer depends on restricting opportunities to perform the response. This idea has been developed further in behavioral regulation theories of reinforcement (see Allison, 1983; Hanson & Timberlake, 1983; Timberlake, 1980, 1984; Timberlake & Allison, 1974). Behavioral regulation theories do not focus on the relative probabilities of the instrumental and reinforcing responses but on the extent to which an instrumental response/reinforcer contingency disrupts behavioral stability and forces the subject away from its behavioral "bliss point."

Every situation provides various response opportunities. In an experimental situation, for example, an animal can run in a wheel, drink, eat, scratch itself, sniff holes, or manipulate a response lever. Behavioral regulation theory assumes that if animals are free to distribute their responses among the available alternatives, they will do so in a way that is most comfortable or in some sense "optimal" for them. This response distribution can be considered to define a behavioral "bliss point." The particular distribution of activities that constitutes the bliss point will vary from one situation to another. For example, if the running wheel is made very difficult to turn or the subject is severely deprived of water, the relative likelihood of running and drinking will change. However, for a given circumstance, the behavioral bliss point, as revealed in unconstrained choices among response alternatives, is assumed to be fixed. Behavioral regulation theory assumes further that the behavioral bliss point will be defended against disruptions caused by limitations on the opportunity to engage in particular responses. Such limitations often result from instrumental conditioning procedures because instrumental procedures do not permit subjects access to the reinforcer response unless the subjects previously performed the instrumental response in the required fashion.

Behavioral regulation theory is similar in some respects to homeostatic physiological regulation. Consider, for example, homeostatic mechanisms for maintenance of body temperature. In humans, normal core body temperature is 98.6° F. This optimal temperature is defended against disruption by various homeostatic mechanisms. If you enter a walk-in freezer, your body temperature is defended by constriction of surface blood vessels, shivering, and the like. If you go into a sauna, your body temperature is defended by vasodilation and sweating. Usually, the homeostatic mechanisms defending body temperature are so successful that core body temperature does not change despite large variations in environmental temperature. A behavioral bliss point is analogous to optimal body temperature. It is defended against disruptions in the opportunity to engage in various responses. As we will see, however, unlike physiological homeostatic mechanisms that can successfully maintain a fixed optimal point, behavioral regulation cannot always get the animal back to its free-baseline behavioral bliss point in the face of disruptions caused by instrumental response/reinforcer contingencies.

The behavioral bliss point can be defined in terms of the relative frequency of occurrence of all the responses of an organism in an unconstrained situation. To simplify analysis, let us just focus on two responses, running and drinking, as in Premack's experiments illustrated in Figure 7.2. If no restrictions are placed on running and drinking, these activities may occur in any relation to each other. The animal may run a lot and drink a lot, run a lot and drink little, run little and drink a lot, or run little and drink little. Figure 7.4 represents amount of running on the horizontal axis and amount of drinking on the vertical axis. Without constraints, a subject's running and drinking could fall at any point on this set of axes. Let us assume that the subject's behavior in a free-baseline situation is represented by the open circle. The subject drinks for 15 sec and runs for 15 sec in our observation period. This defines the subject's behavioral bliss point in this situation. How would the introduction of an instrumental contingency between running and drinking disrupt the behavioral bliss? That depends on the nature of the contingency.

Figure 7.4 shows three possible contingent relations between running and drinking. These are represented by the solid lines emanating from the origin in the figure. These lines specify how much the animal has to run to obtain a particular amount of drinking time. Thus, these lines are feedback functions (see "Mechanisms of the Matching Law," Chapter 6). Line B represents a contingency in which one second of running is required for each second of

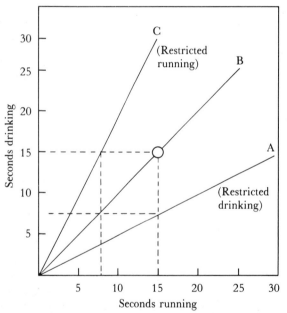

FIGURE 7.4. Allocation of behavior between running and drinking. The open circle shows the optimal allocation, or behavioral bliss point, obtained in a free-baseline session. Lines A, B, and C represent different contingent relations imposed between running and drinking. The contingency represented by line A restricts drinking by requiring twice as much running to maintain the optimal amount of drinking. The contingency represented by line C restricts running by requiring twice as much drinking to maintain the optimal amount of running. Line B, which passes through the bliss point, requires only that the organism does what it most prefers and therefore exerts no restriction.

drinking opportunity. Line B passes through the bliss point of running and drinking that was obtained in the free-baseline condition. This makes the contingency represented by line B rather special because it permits subjects to reach the behavioral bliss point and satisfy the response/reinforcer contingency at the same time. The contingencies represented by lines A and C do not allow that.

Line A specifies a contingency in which the subject has to run twice as much as it drinks. For 7.5 sec of drinking, it has to run for 15 sec. Because the behavioral bliss point is 15 sec of drinking for 15 sec of running, the contingency specified by line A involves a restriction of drinking. Line C represents a different kind of restriction. Here the subject has to drink twice as much as it runs. Thus, for 7.5 sec of running, it has to drink for 15 sec. In this case, the response/reinforcer contingency involves a restriction of running relative to the behavioral bliss point. Lines A and C represent instrumental conditioning procedures that challenge maintenance of the behavioral bliss point.

Behavioral regulation theory states that subjects will defend against challenges to the behavioral bliss point, just as physiological regulation involves defense against challenges to a physiological set point. However, the interesting thing is that the free-baseline behavioral bliss point cannot always be reestablished after an instrumental contingency is introduced. In our example, the behavioral bliss point was 15 sec of drinking and 15 sec of running in a standard observation period. Consider what is possible when the schedule of reinforcement represented by line C in Figure 7.4 is imposed on the free-response situation. Now the subject cannot achieve "bliss" with respect to running without strongly deviating from the optimal level for drinking, and vice versa. Since the line C contingency requires twice as much drinking as running, to achieve the optimal level of 15 sec of running, the subject would have to drink for 30 sec, twice its optimal level. Or if the subject achieved its optimal 15 sec of drinking, its running would be at 7.5 sec, half the optimal level. Line A represents similar problems in returning to the behavioral bliss point. The constraint of the response/reinforcer contingency prevents the subject from achieving "bliss" with respect to one response without strongly deviating from the optimal level for the other behavior.

Schedules of reinforcement like those represented by lines A and C in Figure 7.4 preclude subjects from returning to their behavioral bliss point. However, this does not mean that return to the behavioral set point is irrelevant in such cases; to the contrary, it is the force that drives motivated behavior. Behavioral regulation theory assumes that returning to the behavioral set point remains a goal of response allocation. When this goal cannot be reached, the redistribution of responses between the instrumental and contingent behaviors becomes a matter of compromise. Although the resulting distribution of behavior cannot be optimal for either response considered separately, it can be the optimal in terms of what is possible for both responses together given the constraints of the instrumental conditioning procedure. Staddon, for example, has proposed a **minimum-deviation model** of behavioral regulation (Staddon, 1979; see also Staddon, 1983). According to this model, introduction of a response/reinforcer contingency causes subjects to redistribute their behavior between the instrumental and contingent responses in a way that minimizes the total deviation of the two responses from the optimal point. For situations in which the free-baseline behavioral bliss point cannot be achieved, the minimum-deviation model provides one view of how subjects settle for the next best thing.

Factors that are relevant to response reallocations caused by schedules of reinforcement are also considered by economic theories of response allocation and theories of optimal foraging. We will discuss these in the coming sections.

How are reinforcement effects produced by behavioral regulation?

We have discussed behavioral regulation as the defense of a behavioral bliss point in the face of restrictions on response opportunities imposed by a response/reinforcer contingency and have noted that often this defense involves settling not for the free-baseline bliss point but for the next best thing possible in the situation. How do these mechanisms lead to increases in instrumental behavior in typical instrumental conditioning procedures? A reinforcement effect is identified by an increase in the occurrence of an instrumental response above levels that would occur in the absence of the response/reinforcer contingency. As Figure 7.4 illustrates, feedback functions that do not go through the behavioral bliss point invariably restrict access to a response below the level specified by the bliss point. In line A of Figure 7.4, for example, the subject's drinking is restricted relative to running. To move as close as possible to the behavioral bliss point, the subject has to increase its running so as to gain more opportunity to drink. This is precisely what occurs in typical instrumental conditioning procedures. Access to the reinforcer is restricted; to gain more opportunity to engage in the reinforcer response, the subject has to increase performance of the instrumental response. Increase in performance of the instrumental response (a reinforcement effect) results from behavioral regulatory mechanisms that function to minimize deviations from the behavioral bliss point.

Comparisons between behavioral regulation and traditional theories of reinforcement.

Behavioral regulation theory is a major departure from traditional notions of reinforcement. It is a revolutionary development in reinforcement theory. Several aspects of the theory contrast it with traditional theories of reinforcement. First, behavioral regulation theory does not regard reinforcement as the presentation of a special kind of stimulus or a special kind of response opportunity. Rather, according to behavioral regulation theory, reinforcement is the result of an interaction between the optimal allocation of behavior, as measured on a free-response baseline, and restrictions on response opportunities imposed by a schedule of reinforcement. Thus, reinforcement effects closely depend on free-baseline preference. One consequence is that reinforcement effects are specific to particular baseline conditions. Circumstances that change the baseline preference (introduction of new response possibilities, for example) are expected to change reinforcement effects. Thus, in contrast to drive-reduction theory, behavioral regulation theory does not assume that reinforcers that are effective in one situation will be effective in others.

BOX 7.2. Behavioral regulation and human behavior

Although most of the research on behavioral regulation theories of reinforcement has been performed with animal subjects, the principles also apply to human behavior. In a given situation, people also have a favorite, or what for them is an optimal, way to distribute their activities among the available alternatives. If a response/reinforcer contingency is introduced, they readjust their behavior to find the most comfortable new distribution of activities given the restrictions imposed by the instrumental procedure.

Bernstein and Ebbesen (1978) investigated response reallocation in three adults who were paid to live individually in a laboratory room 24 hours a day for several weeks. One subject was a 19-year-old female undergraduate, another was a 39-year-old homemaker, and the third was a 26-year-old unemployed construction worker. The laboratory provided all the amenities of a comfortable small apartment—tables, chairs, sofa, bed, refrigerator, bathroom with shower, cooking utensils, and so on. Subjects were observed from an adjacent room through a one-way-vision window. After observing the free-baseline distribution of behavior in the situation, the experimenters imposed a response/reinforcer contingency. Figure 7.5 shows the results of one such experiment involving sewing or knitting and studying Russian. The open circle represents the free-baseline levels of these activities. The subject spent much more time sewing and knitting than studying. An instrumental contingency was then imposed requiring the subject to spend a certain amount of time studying before gaining the opportunity to sew or knit. The solid line in Figure 7.5 illustrates the contingency. The contingency placed a restriction on sewing and knitting. If the subject studied as much as during the free-baseline condition, she could sew and knit far less than during baseline. The filled circle in Figure 7.5 illustrates the reallocation of behavior that resulted from the contingency. The subject increased her studying but not quite enough to be able to spend as much time sewing and knitting as during the baseline phase. Thus, the instrumental contingency produced a shift in both responses: the low-probability behavior (studying) increased, and the high-probability behavior (sewing and knitting) decreased.

Another fascinating observation in the experiment was that subjects redistributed their behavior in accordance with an instrumental contingency even though they resented the contingency and sometimes tried to resist complying with it. One subject attempted to resist the schedule of reinforcement by not using up the opportunity that she had earned to sew. After not sewing for 11 hours, she finally gave in and did some sewing, whereupon she quickly returned to the instrumental response. Apparently, the prospect of life without sewing was worse than giving in to the response limitations imposed by the schedule of reinforcement.

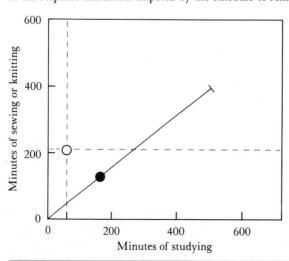

FIGURE 7.5. Allocation of behavior between studying Russian and sewing or knitting in the free-baseline condition and under the instrumental contingency imposed by the experimenters (solid line). The open circle represents the free-baseline levels observed; the filled circle represents the levels observed after the contingency was imposed. *(From Allison, 1983, as adapted from Bernstein & Ebbesen, 1978.)*

A second major difference is that behavioral regulation theory does not view instrumental conditioning procedures as "stamping in" instrumental behavior. Rather, instrumental conditioning is seen as creating a new distribution, or allocation, of responses. A third major difference is that behavioral regulation theory does not assume any distinctions between instrumental and reinforcer responses. Reinforcer responses are not assumed to be more likely than instrumental responses, to provide any special physiological benefits, or to have any inherent characteristics that make them different from instrumental responses. Rather, instrumental and reinforcer responses are distinguished only by the roles assigned to them by an instrumental contingency. The instrumental contingency requires less-than-baseline levels of the reinforcer response unless the subject performs more-than-baseline levels of the instrumental response. Finally, behavioral regulation theory views reinforcement effects as just one manifestation of how animals strive to distribute their responses among alternatives so as to make the best of their opportunities. Thus, behavioral regulation is a part of an organism's overall adaptation to its environment (see Staddon, 1983, for a comprehensive treatment of instrumental behavior as adaptation).

Economic concepts and behavioral regulation

Behavioral regulation theories involve an interplay between the subject's preferences and restrictions imposed by a schedule of reinforcement. As we have seen, schedules typically do not allow the subject to achieve its preferred distribution of behaviors (the bliss point). Psychologists have been interested in discovering principles that describe how behavior changes as a result of schedule constraints. Students who have studied economics may recognize a similarity here to problems of labor supply and consumer demand in microeconomics. Economists, like psychologists, strive to understand changes in behavior in terms of preferences and restrictions on fulfilling those preferences. Some psychologists have become interested in this commonality of concerns. It is appealing to "borrow" economic ideas in the analysis of behavior because economics provides highly developed theories and mathematical models. We will consider how economic ideas have influenced reinforcement theories, specifically behavioral regulation. For the sake of simplicity, we will concentrate on the basic ideas that have had the most impact on understanding reinforcement. (For further details, see Allison, 1983; Lea, 1978; Staddon, 1980).

Labor supply. In 1953 Skinner suggested that schedules of reinforcement are similar to human labor for wages. For example, one can think of a rat's bar-press response as a way to earn food, just as piecework in a factory is a way to earn money. The number of bar presses required per food pellet is then analogous to the rate of pay, or wage rate. Economists have studied how various wage rates influence the amount a person will work (the labor supply). The relationship between how much work is performed at various wage rates and the total amount earned at those wage rates is called a **labor supply curve.** Figure 7.6 shows a theoretical labor supply curve. Each of the lines radiating from the origin represents a different wage rate. Line 1 (L_1), for example, represents a high wage rate because here earnings increase quickly with only small increases in labor. Line 5 (L_5), in contrast, represents very poor wages. Here very little additional money is earned for even large increases in work. The points on each line represent the total amount earned at each wage rate. These points connected together constitute a labor supply curve.

Let us consider what happens according to a theoretical labor supply curve as we move from high to low wages (as we go from L_1 to L_5 in Figure 7.6). Going from a high wage rate (L_1) to a slightly lower rate (L_2), we see that people presumably try to maintain their total earnings by working more (increasing total work performed). As wage rates continue to fall (L_2 to L_4), people continue to increase their work output to offset the lower rates of pay. However, the increased effort is not sufficient to maintain total earnings at the original level. When wage rates are made very low (line 5 in Figure 7.6), total work performed no longer increases to compensate for the low wages. In fact, just the opposite happens. Total work performed decreases for the first time. Thus, decreases in wage rates are assumed to result in increases in total work performed up to a point (L_1 to

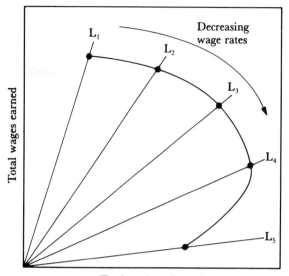

Decreasing wage rates

L_1

L_2

L_3

L_4

L_5

Total wages earned

Total work performed

FIGURE 7.6. An idealized standard labor supply curve showing total work that someone would be willing to perform and total wages earned as a function of different wage rates (represented by the straight lines radiating from the origin). Line L_1 represents the highest wage rate, line L_5 the lowest.

L_4), after which total work performed decreases (L_5). Because of this reversal, the labor supply curve is characterized as "backward-bending."

Backward-bending labor supply curves, like the one in Figure 7.6, are predicted by microeconomic theory. Such curves have also been obtained in instrumental conditioning research with animal subjects. Kelsey and Allison (1976), for example, performed an experiment with rats pressing a bar for sucrose reward. "Wage rate" was varied by changing the number of lever presses that were required to obtain ten licks of sucrose. As the lever-press requirement was increased, the total number of lever presses (total work performed) increased at first but then declined, as in backward-bending labor-supply curves.

Why does the labor-supply curve bend backward? Economists tell us that this effect has to do with the preference people have for work and its rewards compared with desire for leisure. At different wage rates, different amounts of money and leisure are possible. When wage rates are high, workers happily have a

good deal of both earnings and leisure. As the wage rate decreases, workers have to give up more and more leisure time for work to maintain reasonable earnings. When the rate of return for work effort becomes very low, people become less willing to forgo leisure for work, and total work performed declines. At this point the labor supply curve bends backward. The actual reversal point depends on how much someone values leisure compared with monetary earnings.

Instrumental conditioning experiments may be interpreted in a similar manner. In the study by Kelsey and Allison (1976), for example, rats allocated their time between leisure and lever pressing for sucrose. Leisure activities in a Skinner box include sniffing, exploring, grooming, and the like. When the number of lever presses required to obtain sucrose became too high, leisure activities predominated and the rats decreased their bar pressing.

Like other rules for behavioral regulation, labor supply theory incorporates the organism's preferences with schedule restrictions. However, this approach differs in a fundamental way from others we have described. Previously we have been concerned only with the instrumental and reinforcer responses involved in an instrumental conditioning procedure. With labor supply, we introduce a third type of behavior, leisure activity.

Consumer demand. In the previous section we made use of economic theory by making an analogy between instrumental behavior and labor. Another approach makes an analogy between instrumental behavior and the consumption of goods. The theory of consumer demand describes factors that influence how much a person will spend on various commodities. In borrowing from consumer demand theory, psychologists have equated time spent responding (or number of responses performed) with money. In this analogy, total time available to respond or the total number of responses the subject can make is analogous to income—the total amount of money someone has available to spend. The "price" of a reinforcer is the time or number of responses required to obtain it as specified by the instrumental conditioning procedure. The goal is to determine how instrumental behavior ("spending") is controlled by instrumental contingencies ("prices").

The relation between how much of some commodity is purchased and its price is expressed as a **demand curve.** Sometimes the consumption of a commodity is very easily influenced by its price. If the price of "penny candy" increases, you may buy less of it. Other commodities are less responsive to price changes. The degree to which price influences consumption is called **elasticity of demand.** Demand for penny candy is elastic. The more penny candy costs, the less candy you will buy. Demand for water, however, is inelastic. You will continue to purchase water even if its price increases a great deal. We can think of demand for reinforcers as being elastic or inelastic in an analogous fashion. If we increase the number of lever presses required to obtain food and find that a rat simply increases its responding, this shows that demand for food is inelastic. Demand for food does not decrease as a function of the price. Performance of other behaviors, such as running in a wheel, may be more elastic.

What determines the elasticity of demand? Economists have identified three factors. One is your income. If you are very wealthy, you may continue to purchase balloons even if the price skyrockets. A second factor is the price itself. Demand for so-called penny candies may be inelastic at prices under 25 cents but elastic over one dollar. The third and most important factor for our purposes is the availability of substitutes.

Substitutability.   Many people find tea a good substitute for coffee. Therefore, when the price of coffee increases, people tend to decrease their consumption of coffee and switch to tea. However, if you happen to dislike tea, you may continue to buy coffee at the higher prices. Your demand for coffee would be inelastic. Analogously, if a rat can obtain its daily food only by bar-pressing for food pellets, its demand for food pellets will probably be inelastic (see Lea, 1978, for a review). If, however, another food source is also available and on an easier schedule of reinforcement, the demand for food pellets will show

---

BOX 7.3.   The token economy as an economic laboratory: Contingencies that "backfire"

Instrumental conditioning principles have been extensively applied in psychiatric hospitals through token economies. The goal of token economies is to get low-functioning patients more fully engaged in the activities of daily living (eating properly, cleaning themselves, dressing, and so on). This is done by reinforcing targeted behaviors with tokens. The tokens can then be redeemed for primary reinforcers—cigarettes, privileges, better eating and sleeping accommodations, and the like.

Aside from their therapeutic value (for example, Ayllon & Azrin, 1968; Kazdin, 1977), token economies provide a laboratory for studying behavioral economics (see Winkler, 1980). In one study, the shape of the labor supply curve was an important factor for understanding token effects (Battalio, Kagel, & Winkler, 1975). In this study, the wage rate (in tokens) for toothbrushing was manipulated from zero to five tokens while wages for other activities remained constant. As would be predicted, toothbrushing increased as the wage rate increased. The interesting part of the study, however, was that, at the higher wage rates, the overall behavior changed depending on the patient's income level. Patients who initially had low income levels because they did not work at other tasks increased their total income by toothbrushing. The high-income patients, however, did not get richer. Their income remained constant. With high wage rates for toothbrushing, they stopped earning tokens with other activities. As the labor supply curve predicts, they substituted "leisure" for the lower-paying tasks. Looking at the total situation, the therapeutic effect was compromised in this group by the high wage rates for toothbrushing. Although these patients were brushing their teeth, they engaged in other target behaviors at the low rates they had shown before the reinforcement procedures were introduced.

greater elasticity, or responsiveness to schedule changes (Lea & Roper, 1977).

Two experiments performed by Kagel et al. (1975) nicely illustrate the effects of substitutability. Rat subjects lived in Skinner boxes with two levers. Each rat was allowed a fixed number of lever presses it could perform, or "spend," each day (daily income). In the first experiment, pressing one lever produced dry food pellets whereas pressing the other lever produced water. In the second study, lever presses could be "spent" on two sweet drinks. Food pellets and water are poor substitutes for each other. In fact, these commodities are probably complementary. That is, the more dry food pellets one eats, the more one needs to drink. In contrast, the two sweet drinks used in the second study were presumed to be good substitutes. In each experiment, the "price" of one of the reinforcers was increased by increasing the schedule requirement. In the first experiment, changes in "price" were not accompanied by changes in food consumption. The rats did not substitute the "cheaper" water for the more "expensive" food. Demand for food was inelastic. In contrast, substitution occurred in the second experiment. As the price of one sweet drink increased, the rats spent more of their responses obtaining the other drink. Demand for the sweet drinks was elastic. (For a study of substitutability in instrumental conditioning with children, see Burkhard et al., 1978.)

Importance of economic models for behavioral regulation.   As we have seen, economic theory has provided psychologists with new ways of analyzing behavioral regulation. Like other approaches to behavioral regulation, economic models assume that behavior changes so that something is maximized. What that "something" is depends on what we are looking at. In the labor supply analogy, the distribution of earnings and leisure is maximized. In the consumer demand analogy, the value of total behavioral output is maximized. Economic theory has provided new and precise ways of describing constraints that various instrumental conditioning procedures impose on the organism's repertoire of behavior. More important, it suggests that instrumental behavior cannot be described in a vacuum.

Rather, the entire repertoire of the organism at a given time has to be considered as a system (Rachlin, 1978; Rachlin & Burkhard, 1978). Changes in one part of the system influence changes in other parts. Constraints imposed by instrumental procedures are more or less effective depending on the characteristics of the nonconstrained behavior. Psychologists are just beginning to document substitutability effects and other interactions in behavioral systems.

Optimal foraging theory and behavioral regulation

One area in which a system of behaviors has been extensively studied is foraging. **Foraging** refers to behaviors involved in the search for and procurement of food. Foraging is a rather complex system of behaviors that may involve specialized perceptual mechanisms for recognizing foodstuffs, motor responses for getting to the food and handling it, memory mechanisms for remembering which food sources have already been depleted or locations where food might have been stored, and social behavior such as avoidance of competitors and predators or defense of a feeding area (for example, Kamil & Sargent, 1981). In Chapter 11 we will discuss some special memory mechanisms involved in the foraging behavior of hoarding birds. The aspect of foraging that is relevant to analyses of instrumental behavior is the relation between effort expended and food obtained. Optimal foraging theory states that, given the constraints of their environment, animals forage in such a way as to maximize energy intake per unit time or per unit energy expended in foraging (see Krebs, Houston, & Charnov, 1981, and Krebs & McCleery, 1984, for overviews of optimal foraging theory). In general terms, this statement of optimization is similar to molar maximizing theories of response choice (see Chapter 6), behavioral regulation in defense of a "bliss" point, and economic analyses that assume maximum return for time or effort (discussed in the previous section). However, unlike these other formulations, optimal foraging theory has been restricted to analyses of behavior involved in obtaining food. This emphasis makes details of the theory different from those of optimization theories that treat other circumstances.

In principle, optimal foraging theory can be studied outside the laboratory. However, obtaining enough and sufficiently detailed data to evaluate specific theoretical predictions has proved difficult. One of the problems is that field situations are often so complex that figuring out what would be optimal performance can be very difficult, if not impossible. Without a precise prediction of optimal performance, particular behavioral observations cannot be used to evaluate optimal foraging theory. These problems have encouraged some investigators to develop laboratory analogues of foraging situations (for example, Krebs, Erichsen, Webber, & Charnov, 1977; Krebs, Kacelnik, & Taylor, 1978; Krebs, Ryan, & Charnov, 1974; Mellgren, 1982).

Behavior involved in obtaining food can be broken down into several components. Foraging starts with *search* behavior—behavior involved in locating a food source. Before a squirrel can eat nuts, for example, it has to locate some. Once an animal has located a food source, it has to engage in *procurement* behavior, getting the food from its location. After finding some nuts, the squirrel has to pick them up and shell them to get the food out. Search and procurement involve different degrees of effort as a function of time and place. The squirrel may not have to go very far to reach some sources of nuts, and some nuts are easier to shell than others.

George Collier and his associates (for example, Collier, 1983) have devised a laboratory model for the study of foraging in rats that is illustrated in Figure 7.7. The experimental chamber has a response lever on each end wall. The lever on the right is designated as the "search" bar. Responses here are analogous to searching for a patch of food. When the required search behavior has been completed, cue lights on the opposite end wall are illuminated, signaling that a "prey," or source of food, has been found. The particular configuration of cues near the procurement bar indicates how many responses the subject has to perform to obtain the "prey." At this point the subject is free to perform the required procurement responses, or it can return to the "search" bar in hopes of finding a "prey" that will be easier to procure.

The laboratory model shown in Figure 7.7 permits studying a variety of factors of potential importance in foraging situations. For example, "search" behavior (responding on the "search" bar) can be investigated as a function of search cost (ratio schedule programmed on the "search" bar), procurement cost, relative abundance of meals of low and high procurement cost, or the value of the food source that can be obtained. One can also examine factors that influence procurement cost. Studies of foraging with this laboratory method have shown that rats and other species generally defend their food intake in a way that maximizes caloric gain relative to response cost over a wide range of circumstances. For example, as the costs of procuring a "prey" increase, subjects become less likely to expend the required effort to procure the food and are more apt to return to searching for another prey item. However, this effect of procurement cost depends in part on the costs of searching. As search costs become greater, animals become more likely to procure whatever food the search behavior locates (see Collier, 1983, for more details and other examples).

Foraging theory deals with some of the same issues that are highlighted by other analyses of response allocation we have considered. For example, one of the prominent issues in foraging theory is when an animal will move from one source of food to another. For many animals, food is distributed in the environment in discrete patches (clumps of flowers for a honeybee, for example). The longer an animal feeds at a given patch of food, the more depleted that patch will become, and the more difficult finding food there will become. This pattern is similar to the principle of diminishing marginal utility proposed by economic theorists. When an animal will switch from feeding at one patch to feeding at another is predicted to depend on the effort involved in going to the new patch in comparison with the effort involved in obtaining food from the current patch. An animal is predicted to stay at a given patch until the effort to obtain food there increases to equal the effort required to switch to the next patch (see Krebs & McCleery, 1984).

Although in some respects foraging theory deals with the same issues as other theories of response allocation, it provides a much more biological per-

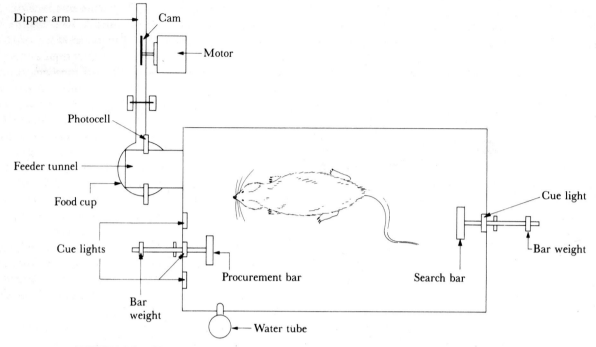

FIGURE 7.7.   The experimental cage in which animals live around the clock. The animal searches for a food item by completing the operant requirement on the "search bar," which is active when the cue light mounted above it is illumined. That a food item has been encountered as a result of search is signaled by the illumination of a pattern of cue lights at the opposite end of the cage, the particular pattern of lights indicating the cost to the animal of procuring the item that has been encountered. The animal identifies the nature of the prey encountered in terms of its cost and either procures it by completing the prescribed number of presses on the "procurement bar" or renews searching on the "search bar," which may result in the encounter of a less costly food item. When the item has been procured, the door to the feeder tunnel opens and the animal is free to eat a meal of any size (that is, for as long as it "wishes"), the feeder door closing only after the animal has remained out of the feeder tunnel for ten or more consecutive minutes. Water is continuously available, and weights can be placed on either bar in order to manipulate the energetic cost of foraging independent of the time required to complete the bar-press requirement.   *(From Collier, 1983.)*

spective on the problem. Foraging theory is basically concerned with how animals obtain their food in nature. As such, foraging theory provides an interdisciplinary bridge between field and laboratory studies performed by zoologists and ethologists and psychological investigations of the problem of response allocation (Kamil & Yoerg, 1982; Shettleworth, 1984). One contribution of this biological perspective is that it raises questions about the comparative performance of diverse species. Foraging behavior occurs in

diverse forms in the animal kingdom. Some types of animals feed only in certain seasons. Deer and moose, for example, feed a lot in the spring and summer to build up adipose and mineral reserves for winter. Animals that eat only plants (herbivores) have to eat a great deal to obtain enough nutrition from their relatively poor-quality food. The response cost of procuring plants to eat is usually low, but animals have to eat frequent meals. In contrast, animals that hunt and eat only other animals (carnivores) can get by with far less food because the nutritional quality of their food is so much better. However, their procurement costs (effort required to capture a prey) may be very great. Foraging theory, with its biological perspective, highlights the fact that a complete theory of response allocation will have to address the diversity of ways in which animals obtain food in nature.

Reinforcement as Response Selection

The theories of reinforcement we considered in the preceding section were based on the premise that the allocation of behavior in the face of a restriction imposed by a response/reinforcer contingency can be construed as a "rational" process of maximizing benefits. The underlying assumption was that if we could clearly determine costs and benefits of various possible ways of allocating responses in a particular situation, we could predict behavior perfectly. Although such "rational behavior" analyses go a long way toward explaining various effects of instrumental conditioning procedures, some effects of reinforcement are "irrational" by all appearances. They do not help get behavior back to a free-baseline bliss point. In addition, they are not required by the instrumental contingency and therefore involve unnecessary and seemingly purposeless expenditures of effort.

Schedule-induced adjunctive behavior

Most research on instrumental behavior is performed in laboratory situations devoid of many response options. The reason, of course, is to minimize variability in the data. When the environment is made just a little more complicated, dramatic effects are sometimes observed. For example, Falk (1961) added a water bottle to Skinner boxes in which rats were reinforced with food for pressing a response lever on a variable-interval schedule. Although the animals were not water-deprived, they consumed huge quantities of water. In some instances, the fluid intake during a 3-hour session was nearly half the rat's body weight! This excessive drinking is called **schedule-induced polydipsia.** Schedule-induced polydipsia is particularly curious because it has defied various traditional physiological and behavioral explanations. It does not involve known physiological mechanisms of thirst. Nor does it seem to be the result of accidental reinforcement, classical conditioning, or mediating responses for the instrumental response (see Cohen & Looney, 1984; Roper, 1981; Wetherington, 1982, for recent reviews).

Drinking is not the only kind of "extra" behavior that develops in reinforcement situations. Schedule-induced aggression has been observed in a number of animals (see Looney & Cohen, 1982, for a recent review). Monkeys will bite a rubber hose after reinforcement (Hutchinson, Azrin, & Hunt, 1968). Pigeons will attack another pigeon or a stuffed model of a pigeon (for example, Campagnoni, Cohen, & Yoburn, 1981; Gentry, 1968). Monkeys and rats will chew on wood (for example, Roper, Edwards, & Crossland, 1983; Villareal, 1967), and rats will run in a running wheel (Levitsky & Collier, 1968) or lick a stream of air (Mendelson & Chillag, 1970) when these response alternatives are available in the experimental situation.

Falk (1972) has suggested that the above responses be classified together as **adjunctive behavior** because they have certain similar characteristics. First, they all develop during exposure to schedules of intermittent reinforcement even though these responses are not involved in obtaining or consuming the reinforcer. They all tend to be excessive and to occur shortly after reinforcement. In addition, although adjunctive behavior is observed with response-dependent instrumental conditioning procedures, the response requirement does not seem to be necessary. Intermittent food delivery is sufficient to produce adjunctive behavior without any response requirement for obtaining the reinforcers. Finally, the magnitude of adjunctive behavior is related to the interval between successive food presentations. Figure 7.8 shows the level of adjunctive drinking and aggression as a function of time between reinforcers. Adjunctive behavior first increases and then decreases as a function of the interreinforcement interval.

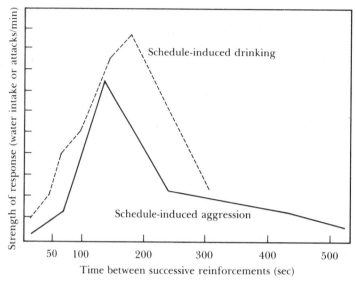

FIGURE 7.8. Amount of adjunctive behavior as a function of the interreinforcement interval. [Schedule-induced-drinking data are adapted from Falk (1972). Schedule-induced-aggression data are adapted from Flory (1969).]

BOX 7.4. Schedule-induced human behavior

Excessive behavior that is not task-oriented but is, rather, an *adjunctive by-product of a task* has also been observed in humans (for example, Cantor, Smith, & Bryan, 1982; Cherek, 1982; Kachanoff, Leveille, McClelland, & Wayner, 1973; Wallace, Singer, Wayner, & Cook, 1975). Cantor (1981) noted that, during activities such as reading, writing, and watchkeeping, people frequently engage in "bad habits" such as nailbiting, hair twirling, fidgeting, snacking, smoking, and head scratching (the latter especially when the task is difficult). Such activities are analogous to adjunctive behavior in animals that are responding on schedules of intermittent reinforcement.

Cantor and Wilson (1984) have identified several employment situations that stimulate excessive adjunctive behavior because the work involves periods of high concentration followed by periods of waiting (as in intermittent reinforcement schedules). Working at a computer terminal is an example. Periods of concentrated data entry, programming, or error correction are punctuated with short waits while the computer processes the information or waits its turn in a time-sharing system. Those waiting periods are often filled with fidgeting, eating, smoking, or scratching.

Adjunctive behavior is also evident in people working in telephone sales. Here again, periods of concentrated activity (presenting the sales pitch to the customer) are interspersed with waiting periods (for the phone to be answered or for the person's spouse to be asked). Dr. Michael Cantor has observed that many people working in telephone sales engage in adjunctive behavior such as smoking, snacking, and coffee drinking during the waits. One worker drank more than 20 cups of coffee a day!

Interim and terminal responses

The occurrence of schedule-induced adjunctive behavior often depends on the presence of objects that provide supporting stimulation for the schedule-induced behavior: a water bottle for drinking, a block of wood for chewing, a model of another animal for aggression, a running wheel for running, and the like. Periodic presentations of reinforcement can also induce distinctive response patterns in the absence of special supporting stimulation. These types of behaviors were first noted by Staddon and Simmelhag (1971) during an experiment intended to study in greater detail the development of "superstitious" behavior previously described by Skinner (1948). You may recall from Chapter 5 that Skinner fed pigeons every 15 sec irrespective of what they were doing. The subjects were not required to peck a key or perform any other response to get the food. (This kind of schedule is called a "fixed-time [FT] schedule of reinforcement.") After a while, Skinner returned to see what the pigeons were doing and reported that they had developed distinctive "superstitious" response patterns.

Staddon and Simmelhag (1971) repeated Skinner's superstition experiment with more extensive and systematic observations. They compared the behavior of pigeons on three schedules of food reinforcement. In two of the schedules, food was presented periodically irrespective of the pigeons' behavior. One of these schedules involved a fixed amount of time between successive reinforcers. Another was a response-independent variable-time schedule. The third schedule was a standard fixed-interval schedule in which the pigeons were required to peck a response key for reinforcement.

Staddon and Simmelhag carefully observed the total behavior of the pigeons throughout the experiment. They defined and measured the occurrence of many responses, such as orienting responses to the food hopper, pecking the response key, wing flapping, turning in quarter circles, and preening. The frequency of each response was recorded according to when it occurred during the interval between successive deliveries of the reinforcer. Figure 7.9 shows data for several responses for one pigeon. The figure

shows that some of the responses occurred predominantly toward the end of the interval between successive reinforcers. For example, R_1 and R_7 (orienting to the food magazine and pecking at something on the magazine wall) were much more likely to occur at the end of the interreinforcement interval than at other times. Staddon and Simmelhag called these **terminal responses.** Other activities increased in frequency

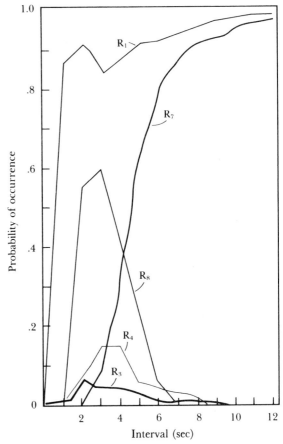

FIGURE 7.9. Probability of several responses as a function of time between successive deliveries of a food reinforcer. R_1 (orienting toward the food magazine wall) and R_7 (pecking at something on the magazine wall) are terminal responses, having their highest probabilities at the end of the interreinforcement interval. R_3 (pecking at something on the floor), R_4 (a quarter turn), and R_8 (moving along the magazine wall) are interim responses, having their highest probabilities somewhere near the middle of the interreinforcement interval. *(From Staddon & Simmelhag, 1971.)*

after the delivery of a reward and then decreased as the time for the next reward drew closer. The pigeons were most likely to engage in R_8 and R_4 (moving along the magazine wall and making a quarter turn) somewhere near the middle of the interreinforcement interval. These activities were called **interim responses.** Which actions were terminal responses and which were interim responses did not vary very much from one pigeon to another. The terminal responses by and large appeared to include activities that are parts of the pigeon's natural eating pattern—pecking, putting head in food hopper, and so on. In contrast, activities not related to eating, such as preening and turning, tended to make up the interim-response category.

Distinctive interim and terminal responses developed with all three reinforcement schedules tested. The results of the response-dependent schedule differed from the results of the response-independent schedules (fixed time and variable time) only in that key pecking was always a strong terminal response on the response-dependent schedule. This outcome suggests that a response/reinforcer contingency facilitates the selection of one particular terminal behavior from the set of all possible terminal responses. Furthermore, Staddon and Simmelhag failed to find evidence of accidental reinforcement effects. Responses did not always increase in frequency merely because they occurred coincidentally with food delivery. Food delivery appeared to influence only the strength of terminal responses, even in the initial phases of training.

Later research has provided much additional evidence that periodic presentations of food result in two categories of behavior, terminal responses that increase as the next reward delivery becomes more imminent and interim responses that occur earlier in the interreinforcement interval (see Anderson & Shettleworth, 1977; Innis, Reberg, Mann, Jacobson, & Turton, 1983; Innis, Simmelhag-Grant, & Staddon, 1983; Reberg, Innis, Mann, & Eizenga, 1978; Reberg, Mann, & Innis, 1977). Rather than showing idiosyncratic response patterns like those Skinner (1948) reported, all subjects show this distribution of behavior into terminal and interim responses. The inconsistency between contemporary observations of interim and terminal responses and Skinner's observations of "superstitious" behavior remains puzzling. Skinner may have observed distinctive stereotyped responses in his subjects because he focused on different aspects of behavior in different subjects. He may have focused on a terminal response in one subject, for example, and different interim responses in others. In any event, contemporary research has failed to confirm his observations and has called into question his suggestion that mere pairing of a response with a reinforcer is sufficient to strengthen that response. Recent evidence indicates that a contingent relation between response and reinforcement is also necessary for instrumental conditioning (see Chapter 5).

Evolutionary response-selection model of reinforcement

Research on schedule-induced adjunctive behavior and interim and terminal responses indicates that animals do many things during the course of intermittent reinforcement that cannot be construed as goal-directed "rational" behavior designed to obtain the greatest return for invested effort. Strong terminal responses and adjunctive behavior develop with periodic presentations of a reinforcer even though such responses are not necessary for reward delivery. Furthermore, similar terminal responses and adjunctive behavior develop whether or not a response/reinforcer contingency is imposed (for example, Anderson & Shettleworth, 1977; Staddon & Simmelhag, 1971). These results suggest that the development of terminal responses and adjunctive behavior during an instrumental conditioning procedure has little to do with the response/reinforcer contingency. Therefore, the theories of reinforcement we have considered so far cannot explain these behaviors.

Staddon and Simmelhag (1971) proposed an alternative model of reinforcement to embrace not only goal-directed aspects of instrumental behavior but also other observations that have been problematic for more traditional theories. This model, like the multiple-response approaches we considered in the preceding section, takes an all-encompassing view of the animal's behavior. Reinforcement is viewed as one way in which particular responses are selected out of the animal's repertoire to predominate at certain times and places.

One set of observations embraced by the Staddon/Simmelhag model involves belongingness and instinctive drift, described in Chapter 5. You will recall that these observations indicate that some responses are amenable to reinforcement whereas others defy or compete with reinforcement effects. A second set of observations incorporated into the Staddon/Simmelhag model concerns the adjunctive-behavior phenomena described earlier in this chapter. Traditional accounts of behavior have not been successful in explaining these "extraneous" schedule effects. A third area of research incorporated into the model involves the phenomenon of sign tracking, described in Chapter 3. You may recall that pigeons will come to peck a key that is illuminated just before each periodic delivery of food. This phenomenon was problematic for theories of operant conditioning when it was discovered, because up to that time it was believed that pecking could be strengthened only with operant conditioning procedures. Finally, the Staddon/Simmelhag model is concerned with the superstition experiment and interim and terminal responses. What do all these areas of research—interim and terminal responses, adjunctive behavior, sign tracking, and belongingness—have in common? They all involve responses to periodic delivery of reinforcement, and many of them appear to be biologically determined. The Staddon/Simmelhag model describes how intermittent reinforcement reorganizes behavior.

The model of behavior Staddon and Simmelhag proposed is fashioned after Darwin's theory of evolution. Darwin saw the emergence of particular physical characteristics in a species as the result of an interplay between two processes, variation and selection. Individuals of a species vary naturally in many of their characteristics (for example, height, hair color, and agility). Characteristics that facilitate the transmission of genes from one generation to the next are selected out as individuals bearing maladaptive characteristics fail to reproduce or have unhealthy offspring.

Staddon and Simmelhag proposed that processes of variation and selection analogous to those entertained by Darwin are at work with behavior. There are always variations in behavior. Organisms in nature do not persist in doing the same thing for very long. Behavior is forever changing because of experience and learning, transitory changes in physiological state, variations in the stimulus environment, and the like. Certain events or characteristics of the environment are assumed to select from the variability in behavior certain responses that come to predominate at particular times and in particular situations. One of these selection mechanisms is provided by the delivery of a reinforcer, whether the reinforcer is response-contingent or response-independent. According to this point of view, reinforcement does not "stamp in" particular responses. Rather, it limits behavioral variability at particular times. The subject is not victimized by accidental response/reinforcer pairings. Rather, the subject does what it usually does with the particular reinforcer; if the reinforcer is grain, we expect responses such as pecking to emerge in pigeons. If the reinforcer comes on a periodic or intermittent schedule, the subject simply shifts its pattern of behavior to accommodate this schedule. When a particular reinforcer is not likely to be delivered, there is more variability in behavior, or responses are selected out by other reinforcers.

According to the Staddon/Simmelhag model, superstitious behavior and sign tracking are products of the same process. Both are considered to emerge as terminal responses. In sign tracking, the behavior is directed to the lighted key. The selective feature of reinforcement is also consistent with the belongingness and instinctive-drift phenomena. Each reinforcer is assumed to give rise to its own set of terminal responses. Hence, responses and reinforcers have a special relation to each other. Instinctive drift is apt to occur when the response required for reinforcement is not one of the terminal responses for that reinforcer.

Reinforcement as response selection explains the operation of reinforcement outside the laboratory as well. Consider, for example, starting an old car on a cold morning. Each time you turn the key in the ignition, you will undoubtedly go through a number of responses, such as pulling out the choke, pressing the accelerator down, and turning the ignition key for sometimes long and sometimes short periods. You may also engage in such responses as sneezing, wrapping your scarf more tightly around your neck, or making a rash of verbal reprimands at the jalopy. Let us assume the car finally starts. The start of the engine is far more likely to reinforce activities related to the ignition than the other responses you performed just before the car started. We might think of the ignition-related responses as terminal responses for getting the car started. All the things you do related to the ignition may not in fact be necessary for getting the engine started. Jiggling the key in the ignition, for example, may not actually help. However, it is unlikely that you will ever limit your responses to only those actions that are absolutely necessary to get the car started. Rather, you will probably repeat the entire pattern with superfluous responses. In contrast, nonterminal responses, such as fixing the scarf, sneezing, or making verbal reprimands, will not be reinforced by the start of the engine and will not necessarily occur the next time you try to start the car.

Concluding Comments

We have presented research and theories about reinforcement representing several points of view. No one approach is comprehensive. Each approach starts from a particular set of ideas about what a reinforcer is. Whether one regards a reinforcer as a stimulus or as a response leads one, as we have seen, in different directions. In fact, a reinforcer in most cases involves both stimuli and responses. Determining a common feature for all reinforcers is therefore an extremely complex task.

Explaining the mechanism of reinforcement likewise rests on a set of starting assumptions about instrumental behavior. The instrumental response was originally viewed as a single behavior that increases in frequency with reinforcement. Drive-reduction theorists suggested a physiologically based mechanism to account for this "stamping in" effect. However, with more research it became clear that the motivating circumstances are not so simple. Drive states and incentive stimuli interact in complex and not completely understood ways. Behavioral theories tend to view instrumental behavior as a by-product of a total reorganization of behavior under less than optimal conditions. The idea of maximizing behavioral value plays a central role in these models. Subjects reallocate their time to various responses so as to maximize behavioral value. Most comprehensive approaches in the future may well follow in the direction proposed by Staddon and Simmelhag. This type of model may bring together the biological approaches with the behavioral. Terminal behaviors do seem to have a "stamped in" quality that may be better called "selected." This selection, however, is going on within the framework of a reallocation of time to various responses within the constraints of an instrumental conditioning procedure.

CHAPTER 8
Stimulus Control of Instrumental and Classical Conditioning

Chapter 8 is devoted to a discussion of how the processes of instrumental and classical conditioning can be brought under the control of particular stimuli that are present when a response is reinforced or a CS is paired with a US. Because stimulus control of instrumental conditioning has been investigated much more extensively than stimulus control of classical conditioning, we will discuss stimulus control of instrumental behavior in much more detail. We begin by defining stimulus control and describing how it can be measured. We then describe in detail various important factors that determine the stimulus control of instrumental behavior and theoretical interpretations of the effects of these factors. Stimulus control of the processes of classical conditioning is described at the end of the chapter.

Stimulus Control of Instrumental Behavior

In our discussion of instrumental behavior so far, we have emphasized the relation between the instrumental response and the reinforcer. As we have seen in Chapters 6 and 7, the response/reinforcer relation is a very important aspect of instrumental conditioning. However, responses and reinforcers do not occur in a vacuum. Animals typically experience particular stimuli when they perform the instrumental response, as illustrated in Figure 8.1. Consider, for example, the reinforcement of lever pressing in rats with pellets of food. The lever-press response (R) is made in the presence of many ambient stimuli (S_A), such as the sight, smell, and sounds of the experimental chamber, and is followed by presentation of the reinforcer (S^{R+}). Therefore, the instrumental conditioning situation is properly considered to contain three fundamental elements, the ambient stimuli S_A, the instrumental response R, and the reinforcer S^{R+}. The stimuli S_A, which are present when the instrumental response is reinforced, can have a very important role in the control of instrumental behavior. The sight, smell, and sounds of the experimental chamber (stimuli S_A) provide the stimulus context for the instrumental behavior. Because the instrumental response is rewarded in the presence of these cues, these stimuli can come to control occurrences of the response.

Stimulus control of instrumental behavior is evident in many spheres of life outside the laboratory. For most students, for example, studying is under the strong control of school-related stimuli. College students who have fallen behind in their work often make determined resolutions to do a lot of studying when they return home during the Thanksgiving, Christmas, or spring vacation. However, not much work gets accomplished during these holidays. The

$$\begin{bmatrix} S_A \\ R \rightarrow S^{R+} \end{bmatrix}$$

FIGURE 8.1. Diagram illustrating that an instrumental response (R) typically occurs in the presence of particular stimuli (S_A) and is followed by the reinforcer (S^{R+}).

stimulus context of the holidays is usually very different from the stimuli experienced when classes are in session. Therefore, the holiday stimuli do not evoke effective studying behavior. Traveling businesspeople often have a similar problem. They may find it difficult to get much work done on airplanes because the stimulus context of an airplane is too different from the stimuli of their offices.

Stimulus control of behavior is an important aspect of behavioral adjustments to the environment. The survival of animals in the wild frequently depends on their ability to perform responses that are appropriate to the stimulus circumstances. With seasonal changes in their food supply, for example, animals may have to adopt different foraging responses to obtain food. Within the same season, one type of behavior is required in the presence of predators or intruders, and other types of responses are reinforced in the absence of nearby danger. In cold weather, animals may seek comfort by going to areas warmed by the sun; on rainy days they may seek comfort by going to sheltered areas. To be effective in obtaining comfort and avoiding pain, animals always have to behave in ways that are appropriate to their changing circumstances.

Performance of instrumental responses appropriate to the stimulus situation is so important that failure to do this is often considered abnormal. Many instrumental acts that are evident in psychologically disturbed persons are pathological only in that they occur in situations where they should not. Getting undressed, for example, is acceptable instrumental behavior in the privacy of your bedroom. The same behavior on a public street is considered highly abnormal. Staring at a television set is considered appropriate if the set is turned on. Staring at a blank television screen may be a symptom of behavior pathology. If you respond in a loving way in the presence of your spouse or other family members, your behavior generally has positive consequences. The same behavior directed toward strangers on the street can have quite different effects. Yelling and screaming are reinforced by social approval at football games. The same responses are frowned on if they occur in a church, a classroom, or a supermarket.

As we noted above, reinforcement of an instrumental response typically occurs in the presence of particular stimuli, and these stimuli may come to control the performance of the instrumental behavior. How can we tell that instrumental behavior has come under the control of such stimuli? How do stimuli gain control over instrumental behavior? In what sense do these stimuli control behavior, and what do subjects learn about the stimuli? Questions such as these have been extensively discussed and investigated. We will review some of the highlights of this research.

Differential responding and stimulus discrimination

The first problem that has to be solved in an investigation of stimulus control is how to identify and measure instances of it. How can we tell that an instrumental response has come under the control of certain cues? Consider, for example, a pigeon pecking for food on a variable-interval reinforcement schedule in a Skinner box. While in the Skinner box, the pigeon is exposed to a wide variety of stimuli, including the color and texture of the walls of the chamber, the sight of the nuts and bolts holding the chamber together, the odor of the chamber, and the noises of the ventilating fan. In addition, let us assume that the circular response key in the box is illuminated by a pattern consisting of a white triangle on a red background. The pigeon in this situation is probably also stimulated by internal sensations provided by its degree of food deprivation and its general physical well-being. How can we determine whether these external and internal stimuli control the pigeon's key-pecking behavior?

Reynolds (1961a) conducted an experiment using stimuli similar to those described above. Two pigeons were reinforced on a variable-interval schedule for pecking a circular response key. Reinforcement for pecking was available whenever the response key was illuminated by a visual pattern consisting of a white triangle on a red background (see Figure 8.2). The stimulus on the key thus had two components, the white triangle and the red color of the background. Reynolds was interested in finding out which of these stimulus components gained control over the pecking behavior. Therefore, after the pigeons learned to peck steadily at the triangle on the red background,

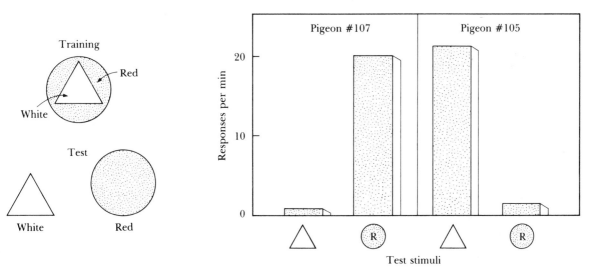

FIGURE 8.2. Summary of procedure and results of experiment by Reynolds (1961a). Two pigeons were first reinforced for pecking whenever a compound stimulus consisting of a white triangle on a red background was projected on the response key. The rate of pecking was then observed in each subject when the white triangle and the red background stimuli were presented separately.

Reynolds measured the amount of pecking that occurred when only one of the component stimuli was presented. On some of the test trials, the white triangle was projected on the response key without the red color. On other test trials, the red background color was projected on the response key without the white triangle.

The results are summarized in Figure 8.2. One of the pigeons pecked a great deal more when the response key was illuminated with the red light than when it was illuminated with the white triangle. This outcome shows that its pecking behavior was much more strongly controlled by the red color than by the white triangle. In contrast, the other pigeon pecked a great deal more when the white triangle was projected on the response key than when the key was illuminated by the red light. Thus, for this subject, the pecking behavior was more strongly controlled by the triangle than by the color stimulus.

Reynolds' experiment illustrates several important ideas. First, it shows how we can experimentally determine whether instrumental behavior has come under the control of a particular stimulus. *Stimulus control of instrumental behavior is demonstrated by differential responding in the presence of different stimuli.* If a subject responds in one way in the presence of one stimulus and in a different way in the presence of another stimulus, we can conclude that its behavior has come under the control of the stimuli involved. Such differential responding was evident in the behavior of both the pigeons Reynolds tested. Both animals responded more frequently in the presence of one of the stimuli (red color or triangle) than in the presence of the other.

Differential responding to two or more stimuli also indicates that the subjects are discriminating among the stimuli—that they are treating each stimulus as different from the other cues. Such stimulus discrimination does not always occur. If the pigeons had ignored the visual cues projected on the response key or had been blind, they would have responded the same way to the white triangle and the red background. The fact that they responded differently to the two stimuli shows that they discriminated between the two cues. Thus, *stimulus discrimination exists whenever subjects respond differently to different stimuli.* Stimulus discrimination and stimulus control are two ways of considering the same phenomenon. One cannot have one without the other. If a subject does not discriminate between two stimuli, its behavior is not under the control of those cues.

Another interesting aspect of the results was that the pecking behavior of each animal came under the control of a different stimulus component. The behavior of one bird came under the control of the red color, and the behavior of the other came under the control of the triangle. The procedures used in the experiment did not direct the animals to attend especially to either the red light or the triangle. Therefore, it is not surprising that different stimuli came to control pecking behavior in the two subjects. The experiment was comparable to showing a group of schoolchildren a famous picture in a beautiful gold frame without telling them what to look at. Some of the children may become captivated by the beauty of the frame, others by the beauty of the picture. In the absence of special procedures of the sort we will discuss below, one cannot always predict which of the various stimuli that an organism experiences will gain control over its instrumental behavior.

Although only one of the stimulus components evoked much pecking in each of the pigeons, one cannot conclude from this information that the other stimulus had no effect whatever. Perhaps measurement of some other response to the stimuli or some other aspect of key pecking, such as its duration, would have provided evidence of control by both stimulus components. As the experiment was conducted, it yielded information only about the stimulus control of the rate of key pecking. The conclusions that can be reached from the study are also limited to the stimulus features that were varied in the tests. The fact that one pigeon responded more frequently to the white triangle than the red background allows us to conclude only that some property or properties of the triangle were important. It does not tell us that the shape of the triangle was the critical feature of the stimulus. The pecking behavior may have been controlled instead by the color or brightness of the triangle. Further tests are required to identify exactly which of these stimulus characteristics controlled the pecking behavior. These considerations indicate that *the conclusions that can be reached about stimulus control are limited to the particular responses and stimuli used in a particular test procedure.*

Stimulus generalization

In our discussion so far, we have treated stimuli as if they were clearly identifiable and distinguishable entities in the world. However, identifying and differentiating various stimuli is not a simple matter. Stimuli may be defined in all kinds of ways. Sometimes widely different objects or events are considered instances of the same stimulus because they all share the same function. A wheel, for example, may be small or large, may be spoked or not spoked, may be made of wood, rubber, or metal, and may or may not have a tire on it. In contrast, in other cases stimuli are identified and distinguished in terms of precise physical features such as the frequency of sound waves or the wavelength of light. The color red, for example, refers to a small range of wavelengths of light. Light that fails to fall within this restricted range (reddish orange, for example) is not considered red even if it misses the criterion range only slightly.

Psychologists and physiologists have long been concerned with how organisms identify and distinguish different stimuli. We will address some aspects of this problem in our discussion of concept formation in Chapter 12. The problem is also related to the issue of stimulus control. As we will see, numerous factors are involved in identification and differentiation of stimuli. Experimental analyses of the problem have depended mainly on the phenomenon of **stimulus generalization.** In a sense, stimulus generalization is the opposite of differential responding, or stimulus discrimination. Stimulus generalization is said to exist *whenever the subject fails to respond differentially to various stimuli*—whenever the same level of behavior is observed in the presence of different stimuli.

The phenomenon of stimulus generalization was first observed by Pavlov. He found that after a particular stimulus was conditioned, subjects would also make the conditioned response to other, similar stimuli. That is, they failed to respond differentially to stimuli that were similar to the original conditioned stimulus. Stimulus generalization has also been investigated in instrumental conditioning. In a landmark experiment, Guttman and Kalish (1956) first reinforced pigeons on a variable-interval schedule for pecking a response key illuminated by a light whose wavelength was 580 nanometers (this has a yellowish-orange color). After training, the animals were tested with a variety of other colors projected on the response key, and the rate of responding in the presence of each color was recorded. The results of the experiment are summarized in Figure 8.3. The highest rate of pecking occurred in response to the original 580-nm light. The subjects also made substantial numbers of pecks when lights of 570 and 590 nm wavelength were tested: the responding generalized to the 570-nm and 590-nm stimuli. However, as the color of the test stimuli became increasingly different from the color of the original training stimulus, progressively fewer responses occurred. The results show a gradient of responding as a function of how similar each test stimulus was to the original training stimulus. This type of outcome is called a **stimulus generalization gradient.**

Stimulus generalization gradients as a measure of stimulus control. Stimulus generalization

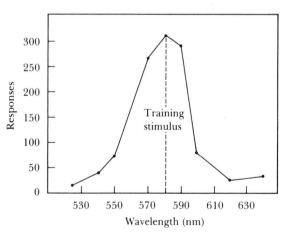

FIGURE 8.3. Stimulus generalization gradient for pigeons that were trained to peck in the presence of a colored light of 580 nm wavelength and then tested in the presence of other colors. *(After Guttman & Kalish, 1956.)*

gradients are often used to evaluate stimulus control because they provide information about how sensitive the subject's behavior is to variations in a particular aspect of the environment. With the use of stimulus generalization gradients, we can determine exactly how much the environment has to be changed to produce a change in behavior. Consider, for example, the gradient in Figure 8.3. Subjects responded much more when the original 580-nm training stimulus was presented than when the response key was illuminated by lights whose wavelengths were 520, 540, 620, and 640 nm. Thus, differences in color controlled different levels of responding. However, this control was not very precise. Responding to the 580-nm color generalized to the 570- and 590-nm stimuli. The wavelength of the 580-nm training stimulus had to be changed by more than 10 nm before a decrement in performance was observed. This aspect of the stimulus generalization gradient provides precise information about how much the wavelength of the light had to be changed for the pigeons to treat the colors as different from the training stimulus.

The fact that substantial rates of responding oc-curred in the presence of stimuli between 570 and 590 nm indicates that the color of the response key did not have to have a wavelength of exactly 580 nm to evoke the pecking response. How do you suppose pigeons would have responded in this experiment if they had been color-blind? If the subjects had been color-blind, they could not have distinguished lights of different wavelengths. Therefore, they would have responded in much the same way regardless of what color was projected on the response key. Figure 8.4 presents hypothetical results of an experiment of this sort. If the pigeons did not respond on the basis of the color of the key light, similar high rates of responding would have occurred as different colors were projected on the key. Thus, the stimulus generalization gradient would have been flat.

A comparison of the results obtained by Guttman and Kalish and our hypothetical experiment with color-blind pigeons indicates that *the steepness of a stimulus generalization gradient can be used as a measure of the extent to which the stimulus feature being varied controls the behavior of the subjects.* A flat generalization gradient (Figure 8.4) is obtained if

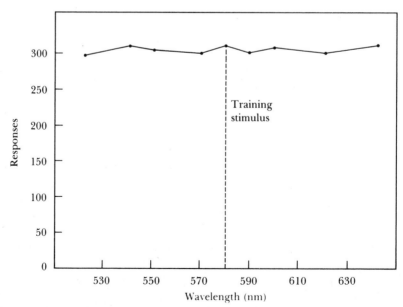

FIGURE 8.4. Hypothetical stimulus generalization gradient for color-blind pigeons trained to peck in the presence of a colored light of 580 nm wavelength and then tested in the presence of other colors.

subjects respond the same way to a variety of stimuli. This lack of differential responding shows that the stimulus feature that is varied in the generalization test does not control the instrumental behavior. In contrast, a steep generalization gradient (Figure 8.3) is obtained if subjects respond more to some of the test stimuli than to others. This differential responding is evidence that the instrumental behavior is under the control of the stimulus feature that is varied among the test stimuli. We may think of generalization and differential responding as opposites. If a great deal of generalization occurs, there is little differential responding. If responding is highly differential to stimuli, little generalization is obtained.

Mechanisms of stimulus generalization.   The phenomenon of stimulus generalization is remarkable because it shows that responding can occur with stimuli that have never been presented or paired with reinforcement during training. Why should new stimuli that have not occurred in training evoke the conditioned behavior? The first person to suggest an answer to this question was Pavlov. Pavlov observed stimulus generalization effects in his classical conditioning experiments. He noted, for example, that if a tactile stimulus applied to one part of the skin was conditioned with a US, tactile stimuli applied to nearby areas of the skin would also elicit the conditioned response. However, the strength of the conditioned response was less as the test stimuli were applied to areas farther and farther from the location of the original CS. From such observations, Pavlov formulated a model of stimulus generalization based on the **irradiation of excitation.**

Pavlov assumed that every stimulus produces excitation in a particular area of the cortex, and similar stimuli activate physically adjacent areas. He proposed that when a CS is presented and paired with reinforcement, excitation occurs in the brain locus corresponding to the CS, and this excitation irradiates to adjacent brain locations, much as circular waves irradiate from the point of contact when a pebble is tossed into a calm lake. The irradiation of excitation was assumed to be progressively weaker with increasing distance from the center of excitation. You may recall from Chapter 4 that simultaneous

excitation of the CS and US centers was assumed to result in an association between the two stimuli. Because of the irradiation of excitation, whenever the CS was presented, nearby areas also became activated, and Pavlov assumed that these nearby areas of the brain also became associated with the US center. Thus, during the course of conditioning, the US was assumed to become associated not only with the CS but also with stimuli that were similar to the CS.

The neural mechanism Pavlov proposed to explain stimulus generalization was greeted with skepticism, but the basic idea that effects of training spread to stimuli similar in some way to the training cues was adopted by major behavior theorists, such as Hull and Spence. However, some psychologists argued that even this formulation was unacceptable. Consider, for example, our hypothetical experiment on stimulus generalization in color-blind pigeons. We suggested that such animals would respond equally to stimuli of various colors. They would show perfect stimulus generalization. Such a result could not be explained in terms of the spread of effect of excitation, because in color-blind animals the presentation of a particular color during training presumably does not produce excitation of a brain area corresponding to that color. A much more reasonable explanation of our results with color-blind subjects is that they responded similarly to all the colors because they could not distinguish differences among them. This type of alternative account of stimulus generalization was proposed by Lashley and Wade (1946) in a spirited attack on the irradiation-of-excitation hypothesis. Lashley and Wade suggested that the generalization of a conditioned response from one stimulus to another reflects a failure of subjects to discriminate differences between the stimuli. They suggested that animals have to learn to treat stimuli as similar to or different from one another. Thus, in contrast to Pavlov, they considered the shape of a stimulus generalization gradient to be determined entirely by the subject's previous sensory experiences rather than by the physical properties of the stimuli tested. Experimental investigations have not confirmed all of Lashley and Wade's ideas. As we shall see, however, there is ample evidence that the shape of stimulus generalization gradients depends a great deal on the subjects' previous experiences with the stimuli involved. (For a recent review of theory and methodology based on stimulus generalization gradients, see Honig & Urcuioli, 1981.)

Acquisition of stimulus control: The pairing hypothesis

Having defined what constitutes stimulus control and how it can be measured, we can begin to discuss how stimuli come to control behavior. The first analyses of stimulus control were based on what can be called the **pairing hypothesis.** According to this idea, the mere presence of a stimulus when a response is reinforced is sufficient for that stimulus to gain control over the behavior. We have noted that the instrumental conditioning situation is made up of three elements, the ambient stimuli S_A in the presence of which instrumental conditioning is conducted, the instrumental response R, and the response consequence, or reinforcer, S^{R+} (see Figure 8.1). The pairing hypothesis states that stimuli S_A gain control over performance of the instrumental response merely because these ambient stimuli are present when the response is reinforced. This relatively simple idea has had an important and enduring influence on thinking about the mechanisms of stimulus control.

In early analyses of instrumental behavior, such as those of Thorndike and Guthrie, the ambient stimuli that are present when the response is reinforced were thought to have a very important role in the control of the behavior. The ambient stimuli were assumed to become conditioned to elicit the instrumental response in much the same way that a classically conditioned stimulus elicits a conditioned response. For example, in his law of effect, Thorndike stated that if a response in the presence of a stimulus is followed by a satisfying event, the association between the stimulus and the response is strengthened (see Chapter 5). Because of this association, the instrumental response comes to be controlled by the stimulus. The only requirement for the formation of such a stimulus-response association was considered to be *contiguity* of the stimulus with the reinforced response. Thus, stimuli were thought to gain control over behavior simply by being present when the behavior was reinforced.

Despite its simplicity, the pairing hypothesis has been remarkably successful in its prediction that seemingly incidental stimuli present during instrumental conditioning can gain control over the performance of the instrumental response. Riccio, Urda, and Thomas (1966), for example, conditioned pigeons to peck an illuminated response key on a variable-interval schedule. No special effort was made to call attention to the orientation of the floor of the experimental chamber during training of the key-peck response. After conditioning, subjects received a stimulus generalization test in which the floor was tilted various amounts away from its original position. Consistent with the pairing hypothesis, the stimulus generalization test revealed that the orientation of the floor had gained control over the instrumental response. The highest rate of pecking occurred when the floor was in the same orientation as during training; various degrees of tilt away from this training value produced corresponding decrements in the instrumental behavior.

Although the pairing hypothesis has met with considerable success, it has not always dominated thinking about the acquisition of stimulus control. Shift in interest away from the pairing hypothesis has been stimulated by the recognition of numerous other factors also important in the acquisition of stimulus control that set limits on the operation of the pairing hypothesis. We will discuss these alternative processes next. However, we will return to findings consistent with the pairing hypothesis when we consider recent research on the role of contextual stimuli in the control of learned behavior at the end of the chapter.

Effects of sensory capacity and orientation on stimulus control

Two factors that set important limits on what aspects of the environment can gain control over behavior are the organism's sensory capacity and orientation. These two factors help determine how the environment looks to the organism. Presentation of an environmental event with certain features of interest to us does not guarantee that the subject will respond to these same features. One must always consider the subject's perspective in an analysis of stimulus control. We cannot simply note certain features of the events we present to an organism and assume that the subject will perceive the cues as we do. Rather, we have to let the subject tell us by its behavior what it perceives of the events we present.

One of the most obvious determinants of how the subject perceives its environment is the organism's sensory capacities. A subject's behavior can come under the control of a particular stimulus only if the organism is sensitive to that stimulus. Events outside the range of what the subject can detect with its sense organs simply do not exist for that individual unless the stimuli are amplified or transduced into something the organism can detect. People, for example, cannot detect sounds whose pitch is above about 20,000 cycles per second. Such stimuli are called "ultrasounds" because they are outside the range of human hearing. Because ultrasounds are inaudible to people, such sounds cannot come to control human behavior. Other species, however, are able to hear ultrasounds. Dogs, for example, can hear whistles outside the range of human hearing and therefore can be trained to respond to such sounds.

Limitations on what stimuli can come to control behavior are also set by whether the subject comes in contact with the stimulus. Consider, for example, a child's crib. Parents often place mobiles and other decorations on and around the crib to provide interesting stimuli for the child to look at. The crib shown in Figure 8.5 is decorated with such a mobile. The mobile consists of several thin needlework animal figures mounted on cardboard (including a giraffe, a seal, and a lion). Which aspects of this stimulus complex can potentially control the child's behavior? To answer this question, one first has to consider what the child sees about the mobile rather than what the mobile looks like to adults. From the child's vantage point under the mobile, only the bottom edges of the animal figures are visible. The shapes of the animals and surface decorations cannot be seen very well from below. Therefore, these other features are not likely to gain control of the child's looking behavior. These considerations illustrate that the subject's orientation with respect to the various features of its environment greatly influences what stimuli can gain control over its behavior. (For research findings illustrating the importance of orientation for the acquisition of stimulus control, see, for example, Gillette, Martin, & Bellingham, 1980.)

Effects of experience on stimulus control

One of the most important determinants of stimulus control is the subject's past experience. Encouraged in part by Lashley and Wade's proposals, investigators have been very much interested in this variable. Lashley and Wade assumed that animals learn to distinguish similarities and differences among stimuli by experiencing natural variations of the stimuli. Exposure to various colors during one's normal course of activities, for example, was assumed to produce discriminations among colors. If this is true, then animals exposed to very few colors from birth should not respond differentially when tested with various colors later in life. Several experimental tests of this prediction have been conducted. Peterson (1962), for example, raised ducks in cages illuminated by a sodium light that provided little if any

FIGURE 8.5.   An infant looking up at a mobile.

variation in color. The ducks were then conditioned to peck a response key of a particular color. A control group of animals that had been raised in normal light and exposed to various colors in the usual manner received the same kind of key-peck training. Both groups were then tested in the presence of various colors for stimulus generalization. Consistent with Lashley and Wade's prediction, the ducks reared in the monochromatic sodium light showed a flat generalization gradient. They responded approximately equally to all the colors presented during the generalization test. In contrast, the normally reared ducks showed the more familiar bell-shaped gradient, indicating differential responding to the various colors. From the difference in these generalization gradients, one can conclude that color controlled the pecking behavior of only the normally reared ducks.

Peterson's findings clearly indicate that previous experience is important for stimulus control. However, the results have not been widely replicated. In addition, it is not clear what aspect of the experimental group's abnormal experience was responsible for the results. Raising ducks without exposure to various colors may alter the development of the visual system. Proper development of various parts of the eye and brain involved in color vision may require exposure to different colors early in life.

Stimulus discrimination training. A possible reason that ducks raised without normal exposure to various colors sometimes do not respond differentially to colors is that they have not had different types of experiences with color stimuli. For example, color cues have not distinguished various objects in the environment for them. This possibility can be tested by exposing subjects to a situation in which differences in color signify something important. This can be done in laboratory experiments using **stimulus discrimination procedures.** In a stimulus discrimination procedure, the subject is exposed to at least two different stimuli—let us say a red and a green light. However, reinforcement for performing the instrumental response is available only in the presence of one of the colors. For example, the subject could be reinforced for responding on trials when the red light is on but not when the green light is on. In

---

BOX 8.1.   Perception of pictures

Pictures are among the most frequently used educational materials. Teachers can greatly extend the exposure of children to various elements of their environment as well as the world at large with the use of pictures. Pictures are used extensively with very young children and retarded individuals to facilitate language acquisition. In all these cases, the assumption is that the child can perceive that the picture represents something in the real world. A study by Lois Dixon (1981) questions the validity of this simple assumption when working with severely retarded individuals. She first trained severely retarded adolescents on a discrimination problem called "matching to sample." The child was first shown an object (the sample), such as a banana. Then the child was shown two additional objects (choice objects), each in a separate box. One of the choice objects was the same as the sample and one was different. The child was to put the sample object in the same box as the matching choice object. Correct matches were reinforced. (For a more detailed discussion of matching-to-sample procedures, see Chapter 11.) Later, the samples and objects were photographs, and finally photographs and objects were used together. The test was to see whether the children could match the photograph of an object with the object itself. Only one of the five children tested could do this. Further work suggested that the failures were due in part to the physical properties of the photographs. In particular, the failures seemed to be related to the fact that the photographs were flat and rectangular. When the object image was cut out of the photographs, performance improved. It appears that shape was a more prominent feature for these children than the likeness of a photographic image to a physical object.

this procedure, diagrammed in Figure 8.6, the red light signals the availability of reinforcement for responding. The green light signals that responding will not be reinforced. The stimulus that signals the availability of reinforcement is often called the **S+** or **S^D** (pronounced "ess dee"). In contrast, the stimulus that signals the lack of reinforcement is often called the **S−** or **S$^\Delta$** (pronounced "ess delta").

With sufficient exposure to a discrimination procedure, subjects will come to respond whenever the S+ is presented and withhold responding whenever the S− is presented. The acquisition of this pattern of responding is illustrated in the graph in Figure 8.6. Initially, subjects respond similarly in the presence of the S+ and the S−. However, as training progresses, responding in the presence of the S+ persists and responding in the presence of the S− declines. The fact that the subjects respond much more to the S+ than to the S− indicates differential responding to the S+ and S− stimuli. Thus, stimulus discrimination procedures establish control by the stimuli that signal when reinforcement is and is not available. Once S+ and S− have gained control over the

subject's behavior, they are called **discriminative stimuli.** S+ is a discriminative stimulus for performing the instrumental response, and S− is a discriminative stimulus for not performing the response.

The procedure diagramed in Figure 8.6 is the standard procedure for stimulus discrimination training in instrumental conditioning. Stimulus discriminations can be also established with the use of classical conditioning procedures. In this case one CS (the CS+) is paired with the unconditioned stimulus and another CS (the CS−) is presented in the absence of the US. With repeated pairings of the CS+ with the US and presentations of the CS− by itself, subjects will gradually learn to make the conditioned response to the CS+ and inhibit the conditioned response when the CS− is presented. (We discussed this procedure in Chapter 3; see Figure 3.9.) Instrumental stimulus discrimination procedures are different from classical conditioning procedures only in that the subject has to perform the instrumental response in the presence of the S+ in order to receive reinforcement. Thus, the S+ does not signal that reinforcement will be automatically provided. Rather,

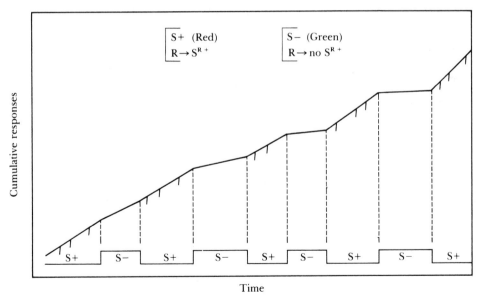

FIGURE 8.6. Procedure and hypothetical results (presented as a cumulative record) of stimulus discrimination training. Responding is reinforced in the presence of the S+ (a red light) and is not reinforced in the presence of the S− (a green light). Differential responding gradually develops to the two stimuli. (Hatch marks on the cumulative record indicate reinforcements.)

the S+ indicates that performance of the instrumental response will be reinforced.

Multiple schedules of reinforcement. The stimulus discrimination procedure shown in Figure 8.6 is just one way that differential responding can be established. Differential responding to two (or more) stimuli can develop whenever each stimulus signals a different schedule of reinforcement for the instrumental response. For example, we could reinforce responding in the presence of a red light on a variable-ratio 5 schedule of reinforcement (VR 5) and reinforce responding in the presence of a green light on a fixed-interval 1-min schedule (FI 1 min). Such a procedure is diagramed in Figure 8.7. You may recall from Chapter 6 that a variable-ratio schedule maintains a stable rate of responding. In contrast, on a fixed-interval schedule subjects pause just after each reinforcement and gradually increase their rate of responding after that until the next reinforcement (producing a scalloped pattern). In a multiple sched-

ule, subjects will gradually come to perform the appropriate pattern of instrumental behavior in the presence of each stimulus. Whenever the red light is on, a steady rate of responding will occur, corresponding to the variable-ratio schedule; whenever the green light is on, a scalloped pattern will be evident, corresponding to the fixed-interval schedule. This outcome is illustrated in Figure 8.7. The different patterns of responding that occur in the presence of the red and green lights indicate that these stimuli control differential responding. To conclude that there is differential responding to stimuli, one does not necessarily have to see responding to one stimulus and no responding to a different stimulus.

A procedure of the sort shown in Figure 8.7 is called a **multiple schedule of reinforcement.** In a multiple schedule, different schedules of reinforcement are in effect consecutively in the presence of different stimuli. Stimulus discrimination procedures are a special type of multiple schedule in which the reinforcement schedule provided in the presence of

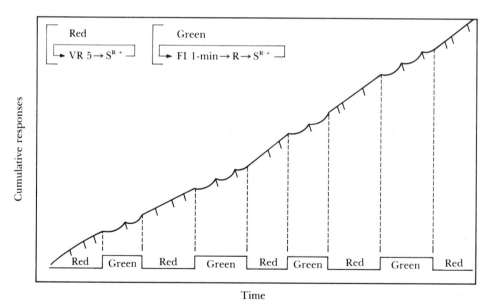

FIGURE 8.7. Procedure and hypothetical results (presented as a cumulative record) of a multiple schedule of reinforcement. Responding is reinforced on a variable-ratio 5 schedule in the presence of a red light and is reinforced on a fixed-interval 1-min schedule in the presence of a green light. A steady rate of responding characteristic of a VR 5 schedule occurs during the red light, and a scalloped pattern of responding characteristic of an FI 1-min schedule occurs during the green light. (Hatch marks on the cumulative record indicate reinforcements.)

one of the stimuli is extinction. The general result with multiple schedules is that the pattern of responding that occurs in the presence of a particular stimulus corresponds to whatever reinforcement schedule is in effect with that stimulus. Multiple schedules illustrate that the patterns of responding produced by various schedules of reinforcement can come under the control of stimuli present when each schedule is in effect.

Stimulus discrimination and multiple schedules outside the laboratory.   Nearly all reinforcement schedules that exist outside the laboratory are in effect only in the presence of particular stimuli. Playing a game yields reinforcement only in the presence of enjoyable or challenging partners. Hurrying is reinforced in the presence of stimuli that indicate that you will be late and is not reinforced in the presence of stimuli that indicate that you will not be late. Driving rapidly is reinforced when you are on the highway but not when you are on a city street. Loud and boisterous discussions with your friends are reinforced at a party Saturday night. The same type of behavior is not reinforced during a sermon in church. Eating with your fingers is reinforced when you are on a picnic but not when you are in a fine restaurant. Getting dressed in your best clothes is reinforced when you are going to the senior prom but not when you are preparing to paint the garage. One's daily activities typically consist in going from one situation to another (to the kitchen to get breakfast, to the bus stop, to your office, to someone else's office, to the grocery store, and so on), and in each situation reinforcement is provided on different schedules.

Effects of discrimination training on stimulus control.   We have noted that discrimination training brings the instrumental response under the control of the stimuli used. We reached this conclusion because discrimination training produces differential responding to the S+ and S− stimuli. How precise is the control that S+ acquires over the instrumental behavior, and what factors determine the precision of the stimulus control that is achieved? To answer such questions, it is not enough to note differential responding to S+ versus S−. One must also find out how steep the generalization gradient is when subjects are tested with stimuli that systematically vary from the S+ along some stimulus dimension. Furthermore, one must find out what aspect of the discrimination training procedure is responsible for the type of stimulus generalization gradient obtained. These issues were first addressed in classic experiments by Jenkins and Harrison (1960, 1962).

Jenkins and Harrison investigated how auditory stimuli of different frequencies (pitches) come to control the pecking behavior of pigeons reinforced with food. They measured how pigeons responded to tones of various frequencies after three types of training procedures. One group of subjects was reinforced during training for pecking in the presence of a 1000-cycle-per-second tone and received no reinforcement when the tone was off. Therefore, for these subjects the 1000-cps tone served as the S+ and the absence of tones served as the S−. A second group of pigeons also received discrimination training. The 1000-cps tone again served as the S+. However, for the second group the S− was a 950-cps tone. Thus, these pigeons were reinforced for pecking whenever the 1000-cps tone was presented and were not reinforced whenever the 950-cps tone was presented. The third group of pigeons served as a control group and did not receive discrimination training. The 1000-cps tone was continuously activated for these animals, and they could always receive reinforcement for pecking in the experimental chamber.

After the training procedures described above, each pigeon was tested for pecking in the presence of tones of various frequencies to see how precisely pecking was controlled by the pitch of the tones in each group. Figure 8.8 shows the generalization gradients obtained in the experiment. The control group, which had not received discrimination training, responded nearly equally in the presence of all the test stimuli: the pitch of the tones did not control behavior. Each of the other two training procedures produced control over the pecking behavior by the frequency of the tones. The strongest stimulus control (steepest generalization gradient) was observed in animals that had been reinforced for responding in the presence of the 1000-cps tone (S+) and not for responding to the 950-cps tone (S—). Subjects that received discrimination training between the 1000-cps tone (S+) and the absence of tones (S—) showed an intermediate degree of stimulus control by tonal frequency.

Jenkins and Harrison's experiment shows that *discrimination training increases the stimulus control of instrumental behavior.* Furthermore, a particular stimulus dimension, such as tonal frequency, is most likely to gain control over responding if the S+ and S— stimuli used in the discrimination procedure differ along that stimulus dimension. The most precise control by tonal frequency was observed in subjects that had received discrimination training in which the S+ was a tone of one frequency (1000 cps) and the S— was a tone of another frequency (950 cps). Discrimination training did not produce as strong control by pitch if the S+ was a 1000-cps tone

and the S— was the absence of tones. In this case subjects learned a discrimination between the presence and absence of the 1000-cps tone and could have been responding in part on the basis of the loudness or timbre of the tone in addition to its frequency.

Some investigators have used results of the sort obtained by Jenkins and Harrison to argue that stimuli come to control instrumental behavior only if subjects experience differential reinforcement in connection with the stimuli (for example, Terrace, 1966b). According to this suggestion, if subjects are not exposed to different reinforcement schedules in the presence of different stimuli, these stimuli will not gain control over their behavior.

In analyzing why a particular type of stimulus has gained control over instrumental behavior, it is important to consider not only what differential reinforcement is provided during an experiment but also

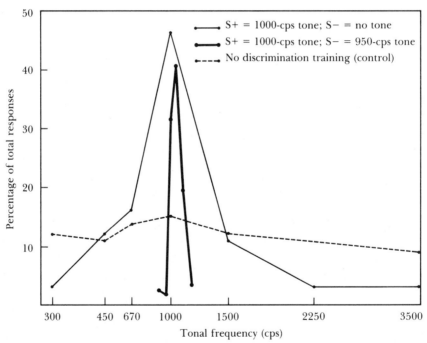

FIGURE 8.8. Generalization gradients of response to tones of different frequencies after various types of training. One group received discrimination training in which a 1000-cps tone served as the S+ and the absence of tones served as the S—. Another group received training in which a 1000-cps tone served as the S+ and a 950-cps tone served as the S—. The control group did not receive discrimination training before the generalization test. *(After Jenkins & Harrison, 1960, 1962.)*

what differential reinforcement may occur outside the experimental context. Thomas, Mariner, and Sherry (1969), for example, replicated the control group tested by Jenkins and Harrison and confirmed that the generalization gradient for tonal frequencies is flat when subjects do not receive discrimination training. They also tested a second group of pigeons that had received experience with a 1000-cps tone in the home cage. For these subjects the 1000-cps tone was sounded every time food was delivered in the home cage. Key-peck training in the experimental chamber was conducted in the same way for these animals as for the control group. Tests of stimulus generalization using tones of various frequencies resulted in a steep generalization gradient for the group that had experienced the tone paired with food delivery. Thus, the effects of differential training conducted in the home cage with the 1000-cps tone transferred to the experimental chamber and resulted in greater stimulus control of pecking by the frequency of the tones.

The idea that differential reinforcement is necessary for the development of stimulus control is intuitively attractive. However, the hypothesis is also nearly impossible to refute with experimentation. Any time we find a case in which stimulus control occurs in the absence of explicit differential training, one can always postulate a possible source of inadvertent differential training that might have occurred outside the experimental situation. The mere fact, for example, that different responses are required to obtain food in a Skinner box than in the home cage may be sufficient to produce control by the stimuli in the Skinner box.

Range of possible discriminative stimuli. Discrimination procedures can be used to bring a subject's instrumental behavior under the control of a wide variety of stimuli. Discrimination training has been successfully conducted with all sorts of discriminative stimuli. For example, Eslinger and Ludvigson (1980) used the odors left by rewarded versus nonrewarded rats as discriminative stimuli for other rats. Spetch and Wilkie (1981) used 10-sec versus 5-sec presentations of food as discriminative stimuli for pigeons. Capaldi, Nawrocki, and Verry (1984)

showed that internal cues of recently having been rewarded or not rewarded can serve as discriminative stimuli for future instrumental responses. D'Amato and Salmon (1982) used two different tunes as discriminative stimuli for rats and monkeys, and Porter and Neuringer (1984) showed that pigeons are able to discriminate the music of Bach from that of Stravinsky and generalize this discrimination to music of other composers from the same periods in musical history. The fact that stimulus discrimination procedures can be used to bring animals' behavior under the control of a wide variety of stimuli makes discrimination procedures powerful tools for the investigation of how animals process information. We will describe some fascinating fruits of this research in our discussions of animal cognition in Chapters 11 and 12.

What is learned in discrimination training?

As we have seen, if the instrumental response is reinforced in the presence of one stimulus (S+) and not reinforced in the presence of another stimulus (S−), these stimuli will come to control occurrences of the instrumental behavior. Because of the profound effect that discrimination training has on stimulus control, investigators have been interested in what subjects learn during discrimination training. Consider the following relatively simple situation: responses are reinforced whenever a red light is turned on (S+) and not reinforced whenever a loud tone is presented (S−). What strategies could the subject use to make sure that most of its responses were reinforced in this situation? One possibility is that the subject will learn simply to respond whenever the S+ is present and will not learn anything about the S−. If it followed the rule "Respond only when S+ is present," the subject would end up responding much more to S+ than to S− and would obtain the available reinforcers. Another possibility is that the subject will learn to not respond during S− but will not learn anything about S+. This would constitute following the rule "Suppress responding only when S− is present." If the subject followed this rule, it would also end up responding much more to S+ than to S−. A third possibility is that the subject will learn both to respond to S+ and to not respond to S−. Thus, it may learn something about the significance of both the stimuli in the discrimination procedure.

Spence's theory of discrimination learning.
One of the first and most influential theories of discrimination learning was proposed by Kenneth Spence in 1936. Spence advocated the third of the possibilities described above. According to his theory, reinforcement of a response in the presence of the S+ conditions excitatory properties to the S+ that come to evoke the instrumental behavior on future presentations of this stimulus. In contrast, nonreinforcement of responding during presentations of S− is assumed to condition inhibitory properties to S− that serve to inhibit the instrumental behavior on future presentations of S−. Differential responding to S+ and S− is assumed to reflect the excitation and inhibition that become conditioned to S+ and S−, respectively.

How can we experimentally evaluate the excitation/inhibition theory of discrimination learning? As noted above, mere observation that subjects respond more to S+ than to S− is not sufficient to argue that they have learned something about both these stimuli. More sophisticated experimental tests are required. One possibility is to use stimulus generalization gradients. If an excitatory tendency has become conditioned to S+, then stimuli that increasingly differ from S+ should be progressively less effective in evoking the instrumental response. In other words, we should observe a steep generalization gradient, with the greatest amount of responding occurring to S+. Such an outcome is called an **excitatory stimulus generalization gradient.** If an inhibitory tendency has become conditioned to S−, then stimuli that increasingly differ from S− should be progressively less effective in inhibiting the instrumental response. Such an outcome is called an **inhibitory stimulus generalization gradient.**

Behavioral techniques were not sufficiently sophisticated when Spence proposed his theory to allow direct observation of the kind of excitatory and inhibitory stimulus generalization gradients his theory assumed. However, experimental tests conducted

decades later proved that his ideas were substantially correct. In one important experiment, two groups of pigeons received discrimination training with visual stimuli before tests of stimulus generalization (Honig, Boneau, Burstein, & Pennypacker, 1963). One group of subjects was reinforced for pecking when the response key was illuminated by a white light that had a black vertical bar superimposed on it (S+) and was not reinforced when the white light was presented without the vertical bar (S−). The second group of animals received the same type of discrimination training. However, for them the S+ and S− stimuli were reversed: the black vertical bar served as the S−, the white key without the bar as the S+. After both groups learned to respond much more to S+ than to S−, Honig et al. conducted tests of stimulus generalization to see how much control the vertical bar had gained over the instrumental behavior in the two groups. The test stimuli consisted of the black bar on a white background, with the bar tilted at various angles away from the vertical position.

The results of the experiment are summarized in Figure 8.9. Let us first consider the outcome for group 1. Recall that for this group the vertical bar served as the S+ during discrimination training. Therefore, these subjects came to respond in the presence of the vertical bar. During the generalization test, the highest rate of responding occurred when the bar was presented in the original vertical position, and progressively less responding was observed when the bar was tilted farther and farther away from the vertical. These results indicate that the position of the vertical bar gained control over the pecking behavior when the stimulus served as S+. Let us consider next the results for group 2. For these subjects the vertical bar had served as the S− during discrimination training. At the end of discrimination training, these subjects did not peck when the vertical bar was projected on the response key. Results of the generalization test indicated that this failure to respond to the vertical bar was due to active inhibition of the pecking behavior in response to the position of the vertical bar. As the bar was tilted farther and farther away from the original vertical position, progressively more pecking occurred. Stimuli that were increasingly different from the original S— produced progressively less inhibition of the pecking behavior.

This experiment shows that discrimination training can produce both excitatory conditioning to S+ and inhibitory conditioning to S—. An excitatory stimulus generalization gradient around the vertical bar was obtained when the bar served as the S+, and an inhibitory gradient of generalization around the vertical bar was obtained when the bar served as the S—. The excitatory gradient had an inverted-U shape, with greatest responding occurring to the original S+. The inhibitory gradient had the oppo-site shape, with the least responding occurring to the original S—. The fact that gradients of excitation and inhibition can occur around S+ and S— provides strong support for Spence's theory of discrimination learning.

Errorless discrimination training. The results reviewed above show that discrimination training can result in excitatory tendencies conditioned to the S+ and inhibitory tendencies conditioned to the S—. However, this experiment does not tell us whether all discrimination training procedures pro-

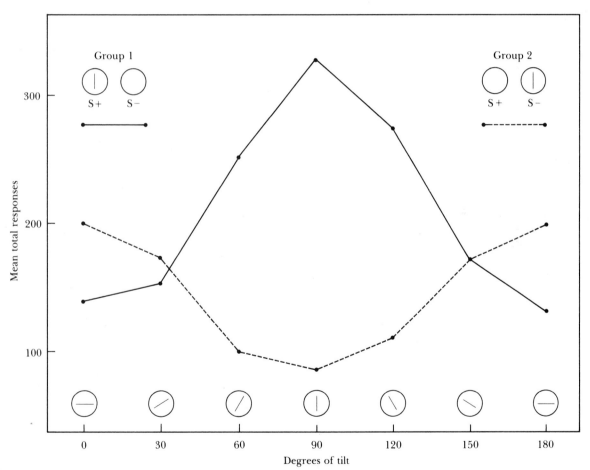

FIGURE 8.9. Stimulus generalization gradients for line-tilt stimuli in two groups of subjects after discrimination training. For group 1 a vertical black bar on a white background served as the S+ and the white light without the bar served as the S—. For group 2 the functions of the stimuli were reversed. *(After Honig, Boneau, Burstein, & Pennypacker, 1963.)*

duce both kinds of learning. In fact, subsequent research has shown that discrimination training does not always result in inhibitory tendencies conditioned to the S−. In the typical discrimination procedure, the S+ and S− stimuli remain unchanged during the course of training. Initially, subjects respond during both presentations of the S+ and presentations of the S− (see Figure 8.6). However, because reinforcement is not available during S−, responding during S− gradually becomes extinguished. In a series of important experiments, Terrace (1964, 1966b) investigated whether subjects can learn a discrimination without ever making a response to S− and experiencing the fact that responses are not reinforced during S−.

Terrace developed a novel discrimination procedure in which subjects make very few if any responses during S− ("errors"). The technique involves gradually fading in the S− stimulus. Let us assume that we wish to train pigeons to peck when the response key is illuminated by a red light and to not peck when the key is illuminated by a green light. If we used a standard discrimination procedure, we would present the red and green stimuli on alternate trials and reinforce the pecking response only during the red light. The intensity and duration of the S+ and S− stimuli would remain the same during the course of training. In Terrace's errorless discrimination procedure the S+ is presented at the same intensity and duration on every S+ trial throughout training (for example, Terrace, 1972). However, this is not true for the S−; the S− is gradually faded in. During the initial trials of the discrimination procedure, the S− is presented so briefly and at such a low intensity that the subject does not respond to it. The duration and intensity of the S− are gradually increased in small steps on successive S− trials as discrimination training progresses. If these fading steps are small enough, subjects may never respond to the S−. Thus, the fading procedure enables the discrimination to be learned without errors.

Early results suggested that errorless discrimination training leads to fundamentally different types of reactions to S− than more standard discrimination techniques. As we have seen, during the course of conventional discrimination training, the S− comes to actively inhibit the instrumental response (see Figure 8.9). The S− also becomes aversive to the subject and may elicit aggressive responses and attempts to escape and avoid the S−. Another possible result of conventional discrimination training is the peak-shift effect, described in the following section. Terrace found that, after errorless discrimination training, the S− does not come to actively inhibit responding or produce aggression or escape and avoidance attempts, and the peak-shift effect does not occur. He therefore proposed that the performance of nonreinforced responses to S− ("errors") during the course of discrimination training is necessary for the S− to actively inhibit responding and produce the various other side effects of conventional discrimination training (for example, Terrace, 1972). However, subsequent research has shown that the absence of errors is probably not the critical factor. Rather, the fading technique used to introduce the S− in the errorless procedure may be what prevents the S− from becoming conditioned to actively inhibit responding and produce the other emotional effects of more conventionally trained S− stimuli (Rilling, 1977).

Effects of intradimensional discrimination training

So far we have discussed general characteristics of stimulus discrimination training that can be found with any combination of stimuli serving as the S+ and the S− in a discrimination procedure. In addition to the effects already described, certain special problems and phenomena arise if the S+ and S− in a discrimination procedure differ from each other in only one stimulus characteristic, such as color, brightness, or pitch. Instances in which the S+ and S− are identical except in one stimulus characteristic are called **intradimensional discrimination** procedures. Consider, for example, discrimination training in which the S+ and S− are identical in every respect except color. What effect will the similarity in the colors of S+ and S− have on the control of S+ over the instrumental behavior? Will the rate of response to S+ be determined mainly by the availability of reinforcement in the presence of S+, or will the rate of response to S+ also be influenced by how similar the color of S+ is to the color of S−?

BOX 8.2. Applications of errorless discrimination procedures in education

Educators have taken an interest in the procedures used by Terrace to teach discriminations without errors. Programmed textbooks rely heavily on fading techniques. The idea is to present unknown material in small enough steps so that the individual builds up an understanding of the material easily. Information is usually presented in a question-and-answer format. The questions are designed so that the student makes few errors in answering. Anyone who has worked through a programmed textbook knows that it is indeed possible to learn in an errorless fashion. Unfortunately, the small steps in which the information is presented can make working on a programmed textbook tedious and boring.

In another application, Gary La Vigna (1977) developed an errorless discrimination program to teach autistic children a written language system for communication. All the children were initially mute and displayed a variety of psychotic symptoms typical of autism. The immediate goal was to teach the children to identify objects with printed labels. In the part of the program we will describe, the children learned to identify three types of candy (mints, gumdrops, and candy corn) with printed cards. If the child identified the candy with the correct card, he got to eat the candy. The number of identifying cards and the printing on the cards were faded in as in errorless discrimination training. Figure 8.10 shows a series of sample trials. On the first trial to teach "mint," only one label card was presented. On the second trial, the correct label and a blank card were presented. Gradually, the printing on the second card was faded in. At this point the gumdrop was presented. As in the first trial, only one answer card was available at first. Then the "drop" and "mint" cards were presented together. Gradually a third card was added in a similar fashion. Eventually, the children learned to identify all three candies with the correct labels and did so with very few errors.

Errorless discrimination procedures have been found very useful in a variety of special education settings, such as the training of mentally retarded individuals. One important advantage is that minimizing errors in learning minimizes the frustrations and disappointments that result from mistakes, thus making the learning situation more pleasant and encouraging.

Step number	Actual candy present	Available labels (printed cards)		
1	Mint	**mint**		
2	Mint	**mint**	(blank)	
3	Mint	**mint**	drop	
4	Mint	**mint**	drop	
⋮	⋮	⋮	⋮	
9	Mint	**mint**	**drop**	
⋮	⋮	⋮	⋮	
12	Gumdrop	**drop**	(blank)	
13	Gumdrop or mint	**drop**	**mint**	
14	Gumdrop or mint	**drop**	**mint**	(blank)

8.10. Candy stimulus and available labels for sample steps in a language program. *(After La Vigna, 1977.)*

199

The peak-shift phenomenon.   In an important experiment, Hanson (1959) investigated the effects of intradimensional discrimination training on the extent to which various colors controlled the pecking behavior of pigeons. All the subjects in the experiment were reinforced for pecking in the presence of a light whose wavelength was 550 nanometers. Thus, the S+ was the same for all animals. The groups differed in how similar the S− was to the S+. One group, for example, received discrimination training in which the S− was a color of 590 nm wavelength. For another group the S− was much more similar to the S+; the wavelength of the S− was 555 nm, only 5 nm away from the S+. The performance of these subjects was compared with the behavior of a control group that did not receive discrimination training but was also reinforced for pecking in the presence of the 550-nm S+ stimulus. After these different types of training, all subjects were tested for their rate of pecking in the presence of stimuli of various wavelengths.

The results are shown in Figure 8.11. Let us consider first the performance of the control group. These animals showed the highest rates of response to the S+ stimulus, and progressively lower rates of responding occurred as the subjects were tested with stimuli increasingly different from the S+. Thus, the control group showed the usual excitatory stimulus generalization gradient around the S+. Animals that had received discrimination training with the 590-nm color as S− yielded slightly different results. They also responded at high rates to the 550-nm color that had served as the S+. However, these subjects showed much more generalization of the pecking response to the 540-nm color. In fact, their rate of response was slightly higher to the 540-nm color than to the original 550-nm S+. This shift of the peak responding away from the original S+ was even more dramatic in subjects that had received discrimination training with the 555-nm color as S−. These subjects showed much lower rates of responding to the original S+ (550 nm) than either of

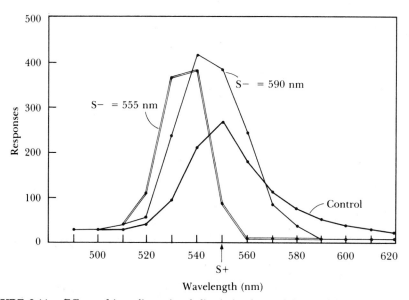

FIGURE 8.11.   Effects of intradimensional discrimination training on stimulus control. All three groups of pigeons were reinforced for pecking in the presence of a 550-nm light (S+). One group received discrimination training in which the S− was a 590-nm light. Another group received discrimination training in which the S− was a 555-nm light. The third group served as a control and did not receive discrimination training before the test for stimulus generalization. *(After Hanson, 1959.)*

the other two groups. Furthermore, their highest response rates occurred to colors of 540 and 530 nm wavelength. This shift of the peak of the generalization gradient away from the original S+ is remarkable because in the earlier phase of discrimination training, responding was never reinforced in the presence of the 540-nm or 530-nm stimuli. The highest rates of pecking occurred to stimuli that had never even been presented during the original training.

The shift of the peak of the generalization gradient away from the original S+ is called the **peak shift** phenomenon. The results of Hanson's experiment indicate that the peak-shift effect occurs following intradimensional discrimination training. A shift in the peak of the generalization gradient did not occur in the control group, which had not received discrimination training. The peak of the generalization gradient is shifted away from S+ in a direction opposite the stimulus that was used as the S− in the discrimination procedure. In addition, the peak-shift effect was a function of the similarity of the S− to the S+ used in discrimination training. The greatest shift in peak responding occurred in subjects for which the S− had been very similar to the S+ (555 nm, compared with 550 nm). The peak-shift effect was much less for subjects that had received discrimination training with more widely different colors (590 nm, compared with 550 nm). (For more recent examples of the peak-shift effect, see Moye & Thomas, 1982; Weiss & Schindler, 1981.)

Transposition and relational learning. The peak-shift effect is remarkable because it shows that the only stimulus in whose presence responding is reinforced (the S+) is not necessarily the stimulus that evokes the highest rate of responding after intradimensional discrimination training. This kind of outcome can also be observed in choice situations. Köhler (1939), for example, exposed chickens to a choice between two stimuli differing in brightness. Both stimuli were gray, but one was a slightly lighter gray than the other. The subjects were reinforced for choosing the lighter of the two stimuli (see Figure 8.12); the lighter stimulus was the S+. After the subjects learned to select the lighter stimulus, Köhler introduced an interesting test. He presented the origi-

nal S+, but this time the alternative was a stimulus that was even lighter than the old S+. Thus, the relation between the stimulus alternatives was the same during the test as it had been during original training: one stimulus was lighter than the other. The test stimuli involved a transposition of the "lighter than" relation between the original S+ and S−. Would the chickens pick the S+ that they had been reinforced for picking during training, or would they pick the new, lighter alternative stimulus? Remarkably, the chickens picked the lighter alternative: they responded more to the new stimulus, the lighter gray, than to the medium shade of gray that they had learned to pick during the initial phase of the discrimination training. This phenomenon is called **transposition.**

Köhler explained his findings in terms of the concept of **relational learning.** He proposed that, during training with stimuli that differ on a particular stimulus dimension, subjects learn to respond on the basis of the relation between the stimuli rather than on the basis of their absolute stimulus characteristics. Thus, in his experiment the chickens presumably learned to respond on the basis of the relation between the brightness of the two stimuli present on a given trial: they learned to pick the lighter of the two cues available. During the test session, the lighter of the two stimuli was one they had never encountered before. However, because the subjects were responding on the basis of the relative brightness of the stimuli, they again chose the lighter stimulus, even though this meant rejecting the original S+.

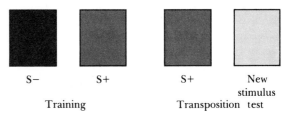

S−   S+   S+   New
                                 stimulus
  Training   Transposition test

FIGURE 8.12.   The phenomenon of transposition. During training the subject is reinforced for choosing the lighter of two shades of gray. During the test session, the subject is given a choice between the original S+ and a new stimulus that is a lighter shade of gray than the S+. The new stimulus is chosen during the test session.

The test stimuli consisted of a transposition of the original stimuli in such a way that the relation that existed between the two cues during training (one being lighter than the other) was maintained during the test session. The presence of the original relation in the test stimuli presumably controlled the choice behavior.

Relational versus stimulus learning in intradimensional discrimination.   The phenomena of peak shift and transpositional choice seem to challenge the idea that the absolute stimulus features of events that signal the availability of reinforcement acquire control over the instrumental response. These phenomena also appear to be inconsistent with the notion that discrimination learning involves the learning of excitatory tendencies surrounding S+ and inhibitory tendencies surrounding S−. Can the phenomena of peak shift and transposition be explained in terms of the excitatory and inhibitory gradients that we have assumed develop as a result of discrimination training, or do we have to accept different mechanisms, such as relational learning? In an ingenious analysis, Spence (1937) suggested that excitatory and inhibitory gradients may in fact produce the peak-shift and transposition phenomena.

His analysis is particularly remarkable because it was proposed more than 20 years before the peak-shift effect was experimentally demonstrated.

Spence's explanation of peak shift and transposition is based on two assumptions. First, Spence assumed that intradimensional discrimination training produces excitatory and inhibitory stimulus generalization gradients centered at S+ and S−, respectively, in much the same way as other types of discrimination training. Second, he assumed that the tendency to respond to a particular stimulus is determined by the generalized excitation to that stimulus *minus* the generalized inhibition to that stimulus. By subtracting the assumed gradient of inhibition centered at S− from the assumed gradient of excitation centered at S+, Spence was able to predict the phenomena of both peak shift and transposition.

Consider, for example, two gray stimuli that are very similar except that one is somewhat lighter. Let us assume that the lighter stimulus serves as S+ in a discrimination procedure and the darker gray shade serves as S−. What is learned about the S+ and S− stimuli will presumably generalize along the dimension of shades of gray. Figure 8.13 shows the excitatory and inhibitory generalization gradients that will presumably develop around the S+ and S−

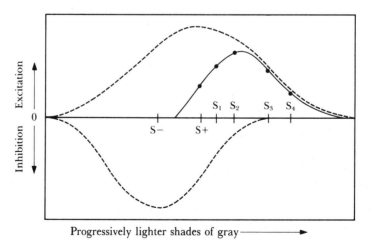

FIGURE 8.13.   Spence's model of intradimensional discrimination learning. Excitatory and inhibitory stimulus generalization gradients (dashed curves) are assumed to become established around S+ and S−, respectively. The subject's behavior is predicted from the net generalization gradient (solid curve), which is calculated by subtracting the inhibitory gradient from the excitatory gradient.

stimuli. Notice that because S+ and S− are close together on the stimulus dimension, the excitatory and inhibitory gradients overlap to some extent. To predict the level of response that will occur to various shades of gray, one has simply to subtract the level of inhibition that is assumed to be generalized to a particular stimulus from the level of excitation generalized to that stimulus. The inhibitory gradient in Figure 8.13 does not extend to stimuli S_3 and S_4. Therefore, no generalized inhibition is subtracted from the generalized excitation for these test stimuli. The greatest amount of inhibition is subtracted from the generalized excitatory strength of stimulus S−, with lesser amounts subtracted from the S+ and test stimuli S_1 and S_2. The dots connected with a solid line in Figure 8.13 represent the net excitatory strength of S−, S+, and test stimuli S_1 through S_4.

The net excitatory gradient in Figure 8.13 is a prediction of the subject's behavior. This prediction is consistent with the phenomena of both peak shift and transposition. Note that the peak of the net generalization gradient calculated in Figure 8.13 is not at the S+ but is displaced away from S+ in a direction opposite S−. This is precisely what is observed in peak-shift experiments (see Figure 8.11). The net generalization gradient also predicts transposition if subjects are given a choice between two stimuli within a certain range of shades of gray. If subjects are given a choice between the original S+ and the S−, they will choose S+ (the lighter of the two stimuli) because greater net excitatory strength is associated with S+. If the subjects are given a transpositional choice between S+ and a new stimulus S_1 that is a lighter shade of gray than S+, they will choose the new stimulus because S_1 has a greater net excitatory strength than S+. According to the data in Figure 8.13, the lighter of the two stimuli will also be selected if subjects are given a choice between S_1 and S_2. Thus, the transposition phenomenon is predicted between stimuli S− and S_2 along the dimension of shades of gray. However, if the subjects are tested with stimuli S_2 and S_3, they will no longer choose the lighter cue. Instead, in this choice test, Spence's model predicts that they will select the darker of the two stimuli (S_2) because S_2 has a greater net excitatory strength than S_3. Thus, Spence's model of intra-

dimensional discrimination learning not only predicts that transposition will take place but also indicates that the phenomenon is limited to stimuli that are close to S+ and S− on the stimulus dimension. Subsequent experimental work has confirmed that the phenomenon of transposition breaks down when subjects are tested with stimuli that are too far from original training stimuli (for example, Kendler, 1950; Spence, 1937).

Precise predictions from Spence's model depend on the exact shape of the excitatory and inhibitory gradients that are assumed to exist around S+ and S−, respectively. At the time that Spence proposed his model, experimental techniques were unavailable to obtain direct evidence of excitatory and inhibitory gradients and their net effects. However, more recent research conducted with modern operant conditioning techniques has provided impressive evidence for the types of generalization gradients Spence assumed served as the basis for peak shift and transposition (see Hearst, 1968, 1969; Klein & Rilling, 1974; Marsh, 1972). Thus, tests of stimulus generalization have typically provided supportive evidence for Spence's model. However, the model has been less successful with data on how subjects choose among stimuli. The model has particular difficulty in explaining results with the intermediate-choice problem.

In the intermediate-choice problem, subjects are reinforced for selecting the intermediate stimulus in a group of three. During initial training, subjects may be exposed to three squares of different sizes, for example, and reinforced for selecting the mid-size square (see Figure 8.14). Subjects can learn a discrimination like this without too much difficulty. Notice that in this case there are two incorrect (S−) stimuli, one on each side of the correct stimulus (S+), along the dimension of size. Spence would predict that inhibitory generalization gradients will develop around each S− stimulus and an excitatory gradient will develop around S+ (see Figure 8.14). If the inhibitory gradients are subtracted from the excitatory gradient, the net result is an excitatory gradient that remains centered at the original S+ (see Figure 8.14). The original S+ has the greatest net excitation associated with it. Therefore, Spence's model predicts that if the subjects are tested with a new group of three stimuli, they will always choose whichever stimulus is most similar to the original S+, whether or not this is the intermediate-size stimulus. Contrary to this prediction, however, research has shown that subjects sometimes will continue to pick the intermediate-size stimulus when tested with new sets of three stimuli (for example, Gonzalez, Gentry, & Bitterman, 1954). Thus, in the intermediate-choice problem, subjects can respond on the basis of the relation among the stimuli rather than the absolute feature of the S+.

Where does all this evidence leave interpretations of the effects of intradimensional discrimination training? Clearly, the relational-learning account is not entirely correct or entirely incorrect. Similarly, an analysis in terms of learning about specific stimulus features is also not entirely correct or entirely incorrect. The evidence indicates that animals can learn to respond on the basis of the relation between reinforced and nonreinforced stimuli. They can also learn to respond on the basis of the absolute features of the S+ and S− stimuli. It may be that different aspects of their learning are measured by stimulus generalization and transpositional-choice tests. In stimulus

generalization tests, the results no doubt reflect what animals have learned about specific stimulus features. Subjects cannot respond on the basis of a relation between stimuli in a generalization test because they are exposed to only one stimulus at a time. In contrast, choice tests are likely to reflect both stimulus learning and relational learning. The results indicate that both types of learning can occur.

A multiple-response approach to discrimination learning

The theoretical perspectives on discrimination learning that we have discussed so far have analyzed discrimination learning in terms of only the response conditioned to the S+. The theories have differed in assuming that subjects respond to S+ on the basis of its absolute stimulus characteristics or on the basis of relational features between S+ and S−, but they agreed that the presence or absence of the reinforced instrumental response is the major issue in the analysis of stimulus control. The lack of responding to S− was treated as a reflection of the inhibition of the reinforced instrumental response. Thus, all the various phenomena of discrimination learning were ex-

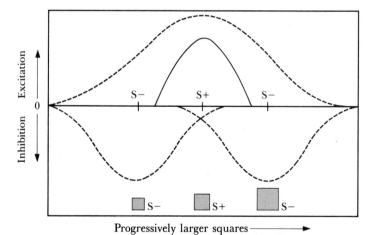

FIGURE 8.14. Analysis of the intermediate-choice problem in terms of Spence's theory of discrimination learning. Subjects are presented with three stimuli and are reinforced for choosing the intermediate one (for example, intermediate in size). An excitatory gradient is assumed to become established around the intermediate-size stimulus (S+), and inhibitory gradients are assumed to develop around the nonreinforced (S−) stimuli. (Dashed lines represent these gradients.) The net excitatory gradient (solid line) is centered at the original S+.

plained as resulting from differential excitation and inhibition of a single behavior by different stimuli.

Staddon (1983) recently described an important alternative approach to discrimination learning that considers not only the reinforced instrumental response but also other activities of the organism that are not related to the reinforcer. The theory treats the reinforced instrumental response and the other behaviors of the organism as two separate response categories and refers to these as terminal and interim responses. We encountered these response categories in our discussion of Staddon and Simmelhag's experiment on how pigeons respond to periodically presented food (see "Interim and Terminal Responses," Chapter 7). Terminal responses are activities like pecking that occur in anticipation of the reinforcer, and interim responses are activities like turning or walking that occur when food reward is unlikely. In an instrumental discrimination procedure, the terminal response is the reinforced instrumental response, and interim responses are other activities of the subject.

Staddon's theory assumes that the instrumental response becomes conditioned to $S+$ and interim responses become conditioned to $S-$. Both these response tendencies are assumed to generalize along a continuum of stimulus similarity. According to the theory, whether a given test stimulus will elicit the reinforcer-relevant instrumental response depends on how much competition the instrumental response receives from interim responses that may also be elicited by the test stimulus. If the instrumental response is elicited more strongly than interim responses, the instrumental response will be observed; if interim responses are elicited more strongly than the instrumental response, the instrumental response will be suppressed. Thus, suppression of the instrumental response in the presence of $S-$ is not viewed as caused by the inhibition of this behavior but as caused by strong competition from interim responses elicited by $S-$. This represents a sharp contrast to Spence's theory of discrimination learning. In contrast to Spence, Staddon does not rely on the concept of inhibition. The concept of inhibition is replaced by competition between instrumental and interim responses.

Staddon's conceptualization of discrimination learning predicts all the phenomena of stimulus discrimination and generalization we have discussed that are also predicted by Spence's theory. How successful Staddon's conceptualization will be in accurately predicting new findings remains to be seen. Evaluation of the theory will require measuring not only terminal instrumental responses but also interim responses. Such a multiple-response approach to discrimination learning is bound to reveal important information about the stimulus control of behavior. Animals obviously do something else when they do not perform the target instrumental response during $S-$. Better understanding of these other activities and the factors that determine their strength will lead to a more complete understanding of the effects of discrimination training. Just as multiple-response approaches have revolutionized our conceptions of reinforcement (see Chapter 7), those approaches may also come to revolutionize our conceptions of stimulus control.

Control by elements of a compound stimulus

So far in our discussion of stimulus control, we have addressed how organisms respond to individual stimuli—a red or a green light, for example, or a vertical or horizontal line. However, stimuli never occur individually. Even a simple stimulus like a circular pecking key illuminated with a red light is more appropriately considered a compound stimulus with various stimulus elements. These elements include, for example, the wavelength of the red light, its brightness, the shape of the response key, and the location of the key. Situations outside the laboratory can be even more complex. During a football game, for example, cheering is reinforced by social approval if the people near you are all rooting for the same team as you are. The discriminative stimulus for cheering consists of a rich array of visual stimuli indicating that your team has scored, the sound of the announcer stating the score, and the complex visual and auditory cues provided by others around you cheering. Most discriminative stimuli outside the laboratory are equally complex. Consider, for example, the discriminative stimulus that tells you that pushing your grocery cart up to the checkout counter is appropriate. The customer before you has to have finished checking out, the checkout counter has to be free of other carts, the checkout person is likely to say something like "Next," and if you hesitate, the people behind you in line are likely to have something to say also.

What determines which and how many of the elements of a compound stimulus gain control over the instrumental behavior? The pairing hypothesis assumes that all perceptible stimulus elements present at the time a response is reinforced gain control over that response. Although this may be true to some extent, certainly not all stimulus elements gain *equal* control over the instrumental response. Some elements come to exert much stronger influence on the instrumental behavior than others. In the present section we will consider some of the factors that determine which elements of a compound stimulus come to predominate in determining the occurrence of the instrumental behavior.

Compound stimuli as complex as those found at a football game or a checkout counter are difficult to analyze experimentally. Laboratory studies of how elements of a compound stimulus come to control instrumental behavior have been most often conducted with compounds that consist of only two simple elements, such as a light and a tone. Research has shown that which of the elements of a compound gains predominant control over the instrumental behavior depends on their relative effectiveness as signals for reinforcement, the type of reinforcement used, what responses subjects are required to perform for reinforcement, and the relative ease of conditioning of the stimulus elements.

Relative effectiveness of stimulus elements as signals for reinforcement.

We noted in the study of classical conditioning that the signal value of the CS is an important factor for conditioning. Simply pairing the CS with the US does not necessarily result in conditioning. If the US occurs both in the presence and in the absence of the CS, the CS may not become conditioned even though it is periodically paired with the US. Similar findings have been observed with discriminative stimuli. The procedures used in one such investigation (Wagner, Logan, Ha-

berlandt, & Price, 1968) are summarized in Figure 8.15. Two groups of rats were conditioned with a discrete-trial procedure in which the subjects were reinforced on 50% of the trials for pressing a lever in the presence of a compound stimulus consisting of a light and one of two tones. For both groups, one of the tones (tone 1) was presented simultaneously with the light on half of the trials, and the other (tone 2) was presented simultaneously with the light on the remaining trials. For group 1, responding was reinforced on 50% of the trials on which the light/tone-1 compound stimulus was presented and on 50% of the trials on which the light/tone-2 compound stimulus was presented.

Before describing the procedure for group 2, let us consider the relative predictive value of the two tones and the light stimulus in the procedure for group 1. Note that the subjects received reinforcement for responding 50% of the time that tone 1 was presented. The procedure also provided reinforcement

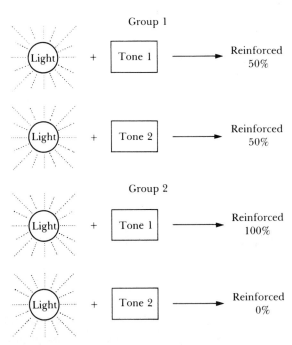

FIGURE 8.15. Diagram of experiment by Wagner, Logan, Haberlandt, and Price (1968). Relative to the two tones, the light was a better predictor of reinforcement for group 1 than for group 2. Consequently, subjects responded to the light more in group 1 than in group 2.

50% of the time that tone 2 was presented. Finally, the subjects were also reinforced 50% of the time that the light appeared, even though the light was presented on a greater total number of trials than the tones. Because reinforcement was delivered on 50% of the times that tone 1, tone 2, and the light were each presented, the three stimuli were equally good predictors of reinforcement in the situation.

The procedure for group 2 was similar to that for group 1 in many respects. Again tone 1 was presented with the light on half the trials, and tone 2 was presented with the light on the remaining trials. However, this time reinforcement was always available on trials with the light/tone-1 compound stimulus. In contrast, responses were never reinforced on trials with the light/tone-2 stimulus. This procedure ensured that, as in group 1, reinforcement was available 50% of the time that the light stimulus was presented. However, this time the light stimulus was not as good a predictor of the availability of reinforcement as tone 1. Of the three stimuli, tone 1 was the best predictor of reinforcement because subjects could obtain reinforcement on 100% of the trials on which tone 1 was presented. Tone 2 was the least valid predictor of reinforcement because subjects were never reinforced on tone-2 trials. The value of the light as a signal for reinforcement was intermediate between the two tones.

Relative to the tones in the experiment, the light stimulus was a better predictor of the availability of reinforcement for group 1 than for group 2. Therefore, if the relative predictive value of the cues is important in determining stimulus control, we would expect the light to have greater control over the behavior of the animals in group 1 than in group 2. This is precisely what Wagner and his associates observed. In tests with the light stimulus presented alone at the end of the experiment, subjects in group 1 responded much more than subjects in group 2. It is important to realize that this outcome cannot be explained in terms of the percentage of time that reinforcement was available when the light stimulus was presented. In both groups 1 and 2, subjects could obtain reinforcement on 50% of the trials on which the light was presented. The critical difference between groups 1 and 2 was that, relative to the other stimuli in the situation (tones 1 and 2), the light was a better predictor of reinforcement for group 1 than for group 2.

Results of the sort obtained by Wagner et al. (1968) clearly indicate that the pairing hypothesis is not sufficient to account for stimulus control. The two groups in the experiment received the same number of pairings of the light stimulus with reinforcement. The results suggest that discriminative stimuli have a powerful effect on behavior not only because they are paired with the reinforcement but because they signal how or when a reinforcer is to be obtained. Other things being equal, if a stimulus is a better predictor of the availability of reinforcement than another cue, it is more likely to gain control of instrumental behavior.

Effects of type of reinforcement on stimulus control. Stimulus control depends not only on the relative effectiveness of a stimulus as a signal for reinforcement but also on the nature of the reinforcer. Certain types of stimuli are more likely to gain predominant control over the instrumental response with positive than with negative reinforcement. This relation has been most clearly demonstrated in experiments with pigeons (see LoLordo, 1979, for a review). In one study, for example, two groups of pigeons were given discrimination training to press a foot treadle in the presence of a compound stimulus consisting of a red light and a 440-cps tone (Foree & LoLordo, 1973). Responses in the absence of the light/tone compound were not reinforced. For one group of animals, reinforcement for treadle pressing in the presence of the light/tone S+ stimulus consisted of food. For the other group, treadle pressing was reinforced by the avoidance of shock. If these subjects pressed the treadle in the presence of the S+, no shock was delivered on that trial; if they failed to respond during the S+, a brief shock was periodically applied until a response occurred. Both groups of pigeons learned the discrimination. The animals pressed the treadle much more frequently in the presence of the light/tone stimulus than in its absence. Once this occurred, Foree and LoLordo sought to determine which of the two components of the complex S+, the light or the tone, was primarily responsible for the response during the S+. Subjects received test trials in which the light or the tone stimulus was presented alone. Responding during these tests with the stimulus elements was then compared with the subjects' behavior when the light and the tone were presented simultaneously, as during the initial discrimination training.

The results are summarized in Figure 8.16. Pigeons that received discrimination training with food reinforcement responded much more when tested with the light stimulus alone than when tested with the tone alone. In fact, their rate of treadle pressing in response to the isolated presentation of the red light was nearly as high as when the light was presented simultaneously with the tone. We can conclude that the behavior of these subjects was nearly exclusively controlled by the red-light stimulus. A very different pattern of results occurred with the animals that had received discrimination training with shock-avoidance reinforcement. These animals responded much more when tested with the tone alone than when tested with the light alone. Thus, with shock-avoidance reinforcement the tone ac-

quired more control over the treadle response than the red light.

Similar results have been obtained in a variety of experiments (for example, Foree & LoLordo, 1975; LoLordo & Furrow, 1976; Schindler & Weiss, 1982; see also Shapiro, Jacobs, & LoLordo, 1980; Shapiro & LoLordo, 1982). These findings indicate that stimulus control of instrumental behavior is determined in part by the type of reinforcement used. Visual stimuli appear to be more likely to gain control over positively reinforced behavior than auditory cues, and auditory cues are more likely to gain control of negatively reinforced behavior than visual cues. This dependence of stimulus control on type of reinforcement is probably the result of the evolutionary history of pigeons. Responding to visual cues may be particularly useful for pigeons in seeking food, whereas responding to auditory cues may be particularly adaptive in avoiding danger. Unfortunately, we do not know enough about the evolutionary history of pigeons to be able to identify the evolutionary advantages of different types of stimulus control in different situations. We also do not know much about

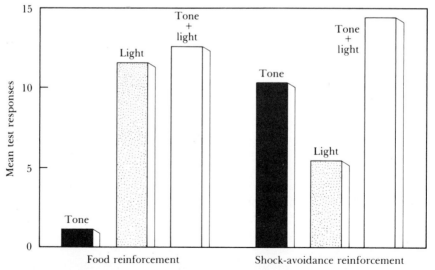

FIGURE 8.16.   Effects of type of reinforcement on stimulus control. A treadle-press response in pigeons was reinforced in the presence of a compound stimulus consisting of a tone and a red light. With food reinforcement, the light gained much more control over the behavior than the tone. With shock-avoidance reinforcement, the tone gained more control over behavior than the light.   *(After Foree & LoLordo, 1973.)*

how stimulus control varies as a function of type of reinforcement in other species. This question is a fertile area for future research.

Effects of type of instrumental response on stimulus control.

Another factor that can determine which of several components of a discriminative stimulus gains control over behavior is the nature of the response required for reinforcement. The importance of the instrumental response for stimulus control is illustrated by an experiment by Dobrzecka, Szwejkowska, and Konorski (1966). These investigators studied discrimination learning in dogs with auditory stimuli. The dogs were gently restrained in a harness, with a metronome placed in front of them and a buzzer placed behind them. The metronome and buzzer provided qualitatively different types of sounds: the metronome produced a periodic beat and

the buzzer produced a continuous rattle. The two stimulus sources also differed in location, one in front of and the other behind the animal. Dobrzecka et al. were interested in which of these two stimulus characteristics (quality of the sound or its location) would come to control behavior.

Two groups of dogs served in the experiment (see Figure 8.17). The two groups differed in what responses were required for reinforcement in the presence of the buzzer and the metronome stimuli. Group 1 received training on what can be called a right/left discrimination. When the metronome was sounded, subjects in this group were reinforced for raising the right leg; when the buzzer was sounded, they were reinforced for raising the left leg. Thus, the location of the response (right/left) was important for reinforcement in this group. Group 2 received training on what may be called a go/no-go discrimination. In this

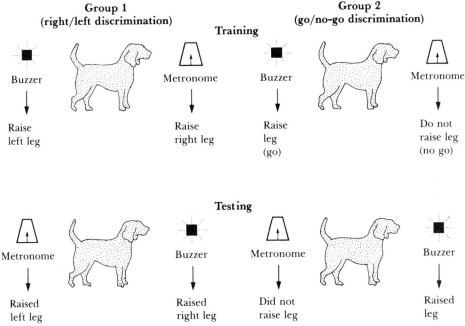

FIGURE 8.17. Diagram of experiment by Dobrzecka, Szwejkowska, and Konorski (1966). Dogs were conditioned in a left/right or go/no-go discrimination (groups 1 and 2, respectively) with auditory stimuli that differed both in location (in front or in back of the subjects) and in quality (the sound of a buzzer or a metronome). During testing the location of the two sounds was reversed. The results showed that the left/right differential response was controlled mainly by the location of the sounds, whereas the go/no-go differential response was controlled mainly by the quality of the sounds.

case the subjects learned to raise the right leg to the buzzer (S+) but to leave it down when the metronome (S−) was on. Thus, the quality of the response (go/no-go) was important for reinforcement for this group rather than its location.

What aspect of the sounds of the metronome and buzzer—quality or location—gained control over the instrumental behavior in the two groups of subjects? To answer this question, Dobrzecka et al. tested the animals with the positions of the metronome and buzzer reversed. During these tests, the buzzer was placed in front of the animals and the metronome behind them (see Figure 8.17). This manipulation produced very different results in the two groups. Subjects trained on the right/left discrimination (in which the location of the response was critical for reinforcement) had learned to respond mainly on the basis of the location of the auditory cues rather than their quality. Subjects in group 1 raised their right leg in response to sound from the front, regardless of whether the sound was made by the metronome or the buzzer. When the sound came from the back, they raised the left leg, again regardless of whether the sound was made by the metronome or the buzzer. Thus, the location of the sounds controlled their behavior much more than sound quality. The opposite outcome was observed in subjects trained on the go/no-go discrimination. These dogs responded mainly on the basis of the quality of the sound rather than its location. They raised a leg in response to the buzzer regardless of whether the sound came from the front or the back, and they did not raise a leg when the metronome was sounded, again irrespective of the location of the metronome.

These results indicate that responses that are differentiated by location (right/left) are more likely to come under the control of the location of discriminative stimuli. In contrast, responses that are differentiated by quality (go/no-go) are more likely to come under the control of the quality of discriminative stimuli. It is not known at present why such relations exist. However, the results clearly indicate that the activities required for reinforcement can determine which aspects of discriminative stimuli come to control the instrumental behavior.

Effects of relative ease of conditioning various stimuli.   Research on the effects of the type of reinforcement and the type of instrumental response on stimulus control has not been very extensive. Therefore, the range of discrimination situations in which these variables are important is not yet known. Another determinant of stimulus control, the relative ease of conditioning the various stimuli in the situation, has been known for a long time and is likely to be important in most instances of stimulus discrimination learning. As we noted in Chapter 4, Pavlov (1927) observed that if two stimuli are presented simultaneously, the presence of the stimulus that is easier to condition may hinder the conditioning of the other stimulus. This phenomenon is called **overshadowing.** The presence of the stimulus that becomes conditioned rapidly overshadows the conditioning of the other stimulus. In many of Pavlov's experiments the two stimuli were of the same modality (two tones, for example) but differed in intensity. Generally, more intense stimuli become conditioned more rapidly. Pavlov found that a low-intensity stimulus could become conditioned (somewhat slowly) if it was presented by itself and repeatedly paired with the US. However, much less conditioning occurred if the weak stimulus was presented simultaneously with a more intense stimulus. Later research has shown that overshadowing can occur between stimuli of different modalities as well, provided that one stimulus is more easily conditioned than the other (for example, Kamin, 1969).

Although the phenomenon of overshadowing was first discovered in classical conditioning, it also occurs in instrumental discrimination procedures (see Sutherland & Mackintosh, 1971, for a review). If a stimulus is composed of two components, acquisition of control by the weaker component may be disrupted by the presence of the more effective component. From the research of LoLordo and his associates, for example, we would expect that in food-reinforcement situations the acquisition of control by an auditory stimulus would be overshadowed by the presence of a visual stimulus. We previously discussed studies of auditory-stimulus control of food-reinforced pecking in pigeons by Jenkins and Harrison (1960, 1962).

The response key in these experiments was always illuminated with a white light, and unless one of the auditory cues was used as a discriminative stimulus, the pecking behavior did not come to be controlled by the auditory cues. This result was interpreted as showing that a stimulus must be an S+ in order to acquire control over behavior. However, a later experiment by Rudolph and Van Houten (1977) challenges this conclusion. They found steep auditory generalization gradients, indicating strong control by the auditory cues, provided that the pigeons pecked a dark key. This finding suggests that Jenkins and Harrison (1960, 1962) may not have found stimulus control of pecking by auditory cues in the absence of discrimination training (see Figure 8.8) because the response key they used was illuminated with a light. Perhaps the light overshadowed the auditory stimulus during training.

The phenomenon of overshadowing indicates that stimuli may, in a sense, compete for control over behavior. Two or more stimuli, each of which can gain control over behavior when presented alone, may not all come to control the instrumental response when they are presented simultaneously. Acquisition of control by less effective stimuli can be hindered by the presence of more easily conditioned stimuli. Some investigators believe that competition among stimuli is a major factor determining stimulus control (see Mackintosh, 1977). Organisms may have limits on their capacity to process various stimuli, or reinforcers may be effective in conditioning only a limited set of stimuli at the same time. In either case, only the "best" stimuli in a situation may acquire control over behavior. The problem is to determine what the "best" stimuli are for any given circumstance.

Conditional Stimulus Control in Classical Conditioning

Much of our discussion of stimulus control of instrumental conditioning focused on stimulus discrimination procedures and their effects. How organisms learn to discriminate stimuli is fundamental to a consideration of stimulus control because discrimination training is the most important learning influence on the stimulus control of instrumental behavior. In a discrimination procedure, subjects are reinforced for responding in the presence of S+ but are not reinforced in the presence of the S−. Thus, a discrimination procedure consists of three basic components, a cue (S+ or S−), a response, and a reinforcer. These three components are arranged in a special way so that the first component (the S+ or S−) signals the relation between the second and third events (the response and the reinforcer). Another way to think about this procedure is that the relation that exists between the response and the reinforcer is dependent, or conditional, on the presence of the S+ or S−. One response/reinforcer relation exists when the S+ is present (positive reinforcement), and a different relation exists when the S− is present (extinction). Thus, instrumental discrimination procedures in fact involve conditional control of the relation between the response and the reinforcer (Jenkins, 1977; Holman & Mackintosh, 1981).

Conditional control has also been investigated in classical conditioning. The fundamental concept of conditional control is that one event signals the relation between two other events. Classical conditioning is typically conceived as involving a relation between a conditioned and an unconditioned stimulus. The CS may be brief illumination of a localized response key with an orange light, and the US may be food. A strong relation exists between the CS and US if the food is presented immediately after each occurrence of the CS but not at other times. How could we establish conditional control over such a CS/US relation?

By analogy with instrumental discrimination procedures, we should have a third event indicate whether presentation of the key light will end in food. For example, we could use a noise stimulus, in the presence of which the key light would be followed by food. In the absence of the noise stimulus, the key light would not end with the food US. This procedure is diagramed in Figure 8.18. As in instrumental discrimination procedures, subjects receive both reinforced and nonreinforced trials. During reinforced trials, the noise stimulus is turned on for 15 sec. Ten seconds after onset of the noise, the orange key-light CS is turned on for 5 sec and is immediately followed by the food US. During nonreinforced trials, the noise stimulus is not presented. The key-light CS is simply turned on alone for 5 sec without the food US.

The procedure just described is similar to one that was recently tested in a sign-tracking (autoshaping) experiment with pigeons by Rescorla, Durlach, and Grau (1985). Rescorla et al. used the noise stimulus as the conditional cue on reinforced trials for half the pigeons. For the other half, a diffuse flashing light was used in place of the noise. The conditioned response that was measured was pecking the response key when it was illuminated with the orange key-light CS. Since pecking is not elicited by diffuse auditory or visual cues, the key-peck behavior could be interpreted as a response only to the orange key-light CS.

The results of the experiment are illustrated in Figure 8.19. Subjects pecked the orange key much more when it was presented in compound with a conditional cue than when it was presented as an isolated element. Thus, the presence of the conditional cue facilitated responding to the key-light CS. It is important to keep in mind that the conditional cues did not elicit pecking themselves, because pigeons do not peck in response to diffuse auditory and visual stimuli. Rather, the conditional cues increased the ability of the orange key-light CS to elicit pecking. The diffuse conditional cues had gained conditional control over the ability of the key-light CS to elicit the conditioned response. Just as a discriminative stimulus facilitates instrumental behavior, the diffuse conditional cues facilitated CS-elicited responding in the present study.

In instrumental discrimination procedures, the conditional cues (S+ and S−) are called "discrimi-

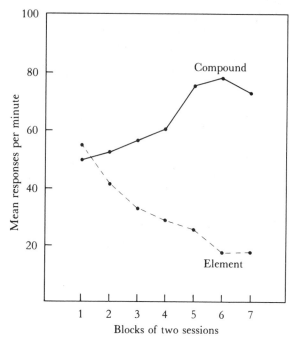

FIGURE 8.19. Acquisition of pecking to an orange key light in a study of conditional stimulus control of classically conditioned key pecking in pigeons. The orange key-light CS was paired with food in the presence of a diffuse auditory or visual stimulus (compound trials) and was presented without food in the absence of the diffuse auditory or visual stimulus (element trials). *(After Rescorla, Durlach, & Grau, 1985.)*

native stimuli." The conditional control of CS/US relations in classical conditioning has only recently become the focus of detailed experimental analysis, and a standard terminology is not yet available. Some investigators have referred to such conditional control as instances of **facilitation** because the conditional cue facilitates elicitation of the CR by the CS (Rescorla, 1985; Rescorla, Durlach, & Grau, 1985). In this terminology the conditional cue is called a **facilitator.** Others have preferred to call conditional control in classical conditioning **occasion setting** because the conditional cue sets the occasion for pairing of the CS with the US (Holland, 1985; Ross, 1983; Ross & Holland, 1981). In this terminology, the conditional cue is called an **occasion setter.** (For investigations of occasion setting in inhibitory classical conditioning, see Holland, 1985; Rescorla, 1985.)

Reinforced trials	Nonreinforced trials
Noise	No noise
Key light → food	Key light → no food

FIGURE 8.18. Procedure for establishing conditional stimulus control in classical conditioning. On reinforced trials, a noise stimulus is presented and a key-light CS is paired with food. On nonreinforced trials, the noise stimulus is absent and the key-light CS is presented without food.

Facilitation, or occasion setting, is an important aspect of classical conditioning not only because it illustrates that classical conditioning is subject to conditional control but also because it appears to involve different mechanisms of learning from those we have considered so far. As discussed in Chapter 4, during pairings of a CS with a US, subjects learn an association between the two events such that presentation of the CS comes to activate a representation of the US. We have referred to this kind of learning as the conditioning of excitation to the CS. Facilitation is a learned characteristic that is very different from conditioned excitation. In facilitation the cue does not activate a representation of another event (the US). Rather, it activates a representation of a relation between two other events (a CS and a US).

The most important challenge for research on facilitation is to document the ways in which facilitation differs from conditioned excitation and to specify the circumstances that lead to each type of learning. Evidence suggests that the two forms of learning are distinct and lead to separable effects on behavior even if the same stimulus is conditioned both as a facilitator and as a conditioned exciter (for recent reviews, see Holland, 1985; Rescorla, 1985). One of the most interesting differences between facilitation and conditioned excitation involves the effects of an extinction procedure. As we noted in Chapter 3, a conditioned excitatory stimulus that is repeatedly presented by itself gradually loses the capacity to elicit the conditioned response; it undergoes extinction. The same procedure applied to a facilitator has no effect. Once a stimulus has become established as a conditional cue signaling a CS/US relation, repeated presentations of the stimulus by itself do not reduce its ability to facilitate conditioned responding to the CS.

The difference in the effects of extinction on conditioned excitatory stimuli and facilitators may be related to what is signaled. A conditioned excitatory stimulus signals the forthcoming presentation of the US. The absence of the US during extinction is a violation of the expectancy conditioned to the CS. Hence, the signal value of the CS has to be readjusted in extinction to bring it in line with the new reality. Such a readjustment is not required by an extinction procedure for a facilitator stimulus. A facilitator signals a relation between two other events (a CS and a US). The absence of those events in extinction does not mean that the relation between them has changed. The information signaled by a facilitator is not proved incorrect by the stimuli (or lack of stimuli) that are presented during extinction. Therefore, the ability of the facilitator to promote responding elicited by another CS remains intact during extinction. These considerations suggest that the facilitating effect of a conditional stimulus will be altered only if the CS/US relation signaled by that facilitator is altered. Research on this and related issues will no doubt provide important new insights into the various mechanisms that bring behavior under the control of stimuli.

Stimulus Control outside the Laboratory

Self-control

Most people at some time in their lives experience problems with self-control. Students who wish to improve their grades have trouble improving their study habits; smokers who want to quit cannot resist a cigarette; people who want to lose weight have trouble controlling their food intake. Problems with self-control often involve behaviors occurring at inappropriate times and places that interfere with long-range goals. Behavior therapists, in helping people improve their self-control, have suggested techniques to limit the control that various stimuli have over certain behaviors (see Fox, 1966, for an examination of the problems). Some suggestions for improving study habits are as follows:

1. Select a suitable place for study, with adequate lighting and free from distractions.
2. Study at this place and only at this place. (Do not study on your bed, as this will probably lead to sleeping rather than studying.) Do not use the study area for other tasks, such as letter writing or drawing.
3. Remain at the study area only as long as you

are studying. If you begin to daydream, prepare to leave the area.

4. Before actually leaving the area, complete one small unit of work. Finish reading the page or complete one problem.

The goal of these suggestions is to establish the study area as a discriminative stimulus for concentrated study as opposed to other behaviors, such as letter writing, sleeping, or socializing. As in many cases of application, the laboratory principles are only loosely applied here. You may have noted that no true differential contingency is in effect here—the student is not actually constrained. The hope is, nevertheless, that by limiting the behavior that occurs in the presence of the study space, this stimulus situation will come to control the study behavior. In fact, many students find these suggestions quite helpful.

A similar approach has been taken in weight reduction programs. Weight reduction programs strive to reduce caloric intake through diet and increase caloric output through exercise. Many weight reduction programs now include a behavioral component as well. Research has shown that altering the conditions under which people eat helps to alter the amount eaten (see Stunkard & Mahoney, 1976). This occurs because eating is frequently triggered by stimuli when there is no real need for food. Eating may be triggered by such things as time of day, the presence of ready-made snacks, turning on the television, or sitting down to talk with a friend. Weight reduction programs try to counteract the effects of such stimuli by requiring participants to eat only in a limited setting. The dieter is instructed, for example, to eat only at a particular table with a proper table setting. The stimulus conditions can be made highly specific by using only a particular tablecloth and china. In addition, only food that is properly prepared and served is to be eaten. We must repeat here that these suggestions are only part of a total program for weight reduction. They are not sufficient in and of themselves. They are very useful in many cases because it is often easier to limit where one eats than how much one eats. Moreover, in restricting where one eats, one often reduces the amount eaten as well. For more details the interested reader may want to

consult a highly successful diet plan proposed by Stuart and Davis (1972) in a book entitled *Slim Chance in a Fat World*.

Social interactions

In our everyday social interactions, we provide and use many cues that can be described as discriminative stimuli. Facial expressions, for example, can serve as powerful discriminative cues. Children readily recognize "that look" from their mother that says "Do that one more time and you'll be in big trouble." If you meet a friend who is smiling and walking briskly, you will probably be inclined to greet that person warmly. Your social overtures are highly likely to be reinforced. The opposite is likely if the person's brow is furrowed and he is looking at the ground.

Different body postures also invite characteristic responses from others. Some postures are described as provocative, inviting sexual advances. Research on body postures and orientation has shown that "body language" can provide considerable information. For example, when an interaction is friendly, people tend to stand closer to each other, with direct body and head orientation (for example, Mehrabian, 1970; Mehrabian & Weiner, 1966).

In an interesting study, Murphy and Levine (1982) analyzed the body postures of boys who are physically and verbally abused by their peers. When trying to alleviate this kind of victimization, teachers and parents usually try to change the perpetrator's behavior rather than the victim's. The results of this study suggest that the victim may be a better target for intervention. The researchers videotaped peer-victimized boys as they interacted in a small-group setting. These boys maintained a greater distance from other members of the group than the nonvictimized children, and they oriented both body and head away from the group more frequently. These actions and body orientations may be signals (discriminative stimuli) that provoke victimization. Getting victimized children to remain closer to their peers and getting them to engage in body movements and orientations more indicative of group participation may help make these children more acceptable to their peers.

Sometimes social discriminative stimuli are provided by the role that an individual has in society. Police officers, teachers, and parents serve as powerful discriminative stimuli that signal that certain responses will be reinforced or punished. Encountering a police officer while driving on a highway makes you check your speedometer and otherwise take more care in following the rules of the road. Every elementary school child knows how the teacher's presence or absence determines the level of disruptive antics in the classroom. In a similar fashion, a parent's presence or absence can alter the probability of unruly behavior in children.

Stimulus control, or the lack of it, often creates problems in parent/child relations. Parents would ideally like their children to respect them by being reasonably obedient. One could ensure obedience in most children by always delivering severe punishers for transgressions or by reinforcing obedience with extraordinary rewards. However, few parents wish to deal with their children in such an authoritarian manner. Parents are inconsistent. Many times what they say does not really represent the actual relation between behavior and its consequences. Therefore, their words do not always serve as the discriminative stimuli they would like them to be. For example, Mom may say, "Johnny, if you hit your sister one more time, you can't watch TV today." Johnny hits his sister again and is deprived of his TV shows. However, about 4 P.M. Mom is tired of having Johnny underfoot all day and in desperation sets him in front of the TV. Given such occurrences, it is no wonder Johnny is not always obedient!

Sometimes problems in parent/child interactions can be understood in terms of the aversive nature of signals for nonreinforcement (S$-$s). Some children, for whatever reason, are more difficult to manage than others. The very presence of these children can serve as an S$-$ to their parents. The presence of a hyperactive child can signal to her father that his efforts at maintaining peace and harmony in the house will go unrewarded. Children who are hyperactive or are perceived by their parents to be difficult and hostile are more likely to be the target of child abuse than their siblings in abusive families (see, for example, Kempe & Kempe, 1978). This finding is consistent with experimental evidence that an S$-$ can be aversive and can elicit aggression.

Many parents of hyperactive children, even if they are not abusive, report that they feel angry toward their child. This anger was the subject of therapy for a group of parents reported by Levine and Sandeen (1985). The original goal of the group program was to teach parents better ways to handle their children, but after two sessions no one in the group reported any progress. It was discovered that the parents were simply too angered by the child's mere presence to try anything new. The group was then desensitized to the misbehaviors of the children. In the final item of the desensitization hierarchy, the parents were trained to remain relaxed as they imagined their child biting their leg as they served coffee to their clergyman. The parents were able to work with their children more successfully after this desensitization.

CHAPTER 9
Aversive Control: Avoidance and Punishment

In the present chapter we will discuss how behavior can be controlled by aversive stimulation. We will limit the presentation to two types of instrumental aversive control—avoidance and punishment. Avoidance conditioning increases the performance of a target behavior, whereas punishment decreases the target behavior. However, in both cases subjects learn to minimize their exposure to aversive stimulation. Because of this similarity, theoretical analyses of avoidance and punishment have some concepts in common. Nevertheless, experimental analyses of the two types of conditioning have proceeded largely independently of each other. We will describe the major theoretical puzzles and empirical findings in both areas of research.

Avoidance Behavior

Avoidance is a type of instrumental behavior in which the organism's responses prevent the occurrence of an aversive stimulus. Effective avoidance behavior is critical for survival. Animals have to avoid predators and exposure to extreme climatic conditions, as well as more mundane things, such as slipping and falling or running into objects. Avoidance also constitutes much of human behavior. Grabbing a handrail while walking on an uneven surface helps you avoid falling, holding your hands in front of you as you walk in a dark room helps you avoid bumping into things, and making adjustments in the position of the steering wheel as you drive helps you avoid driving off the road. These and numerous other activities constitute avoidance behavior because in each case the instrumental response is responsible for preventing an aversive situation that would otherwise occur.

In most cases the avoidance response is followed by nothing more than the absence of an aversive event. If you make the appropriate avoidance responses, you will not fall, bump into things, or drive off the road. No particular pleasure is derived from these experiences. You simply don't get hurt.

The absence of an aversive situation is presumably the reason that avoidance responses are made. However, how can the absence of something provide reinforcement for instrumental behavior? This is the fundamental question in the study of avoidance. Mowrer and Lamoreaux (1942, p. 6) pointed out some years ago that "not getting something can hardly, in and of itself, qualify as rewarding." Since then, much intellectual effort has been devoted to figuring out what else is involved in avoidance conditioning procedures that might provide reinforcement for the behavior. In fact, the investigation of avoidance behavior has been dominated by this theoretical problem.

Origins of the study of avoidance behavior

The study of avoidance behavior was initially closely allied to investigations of classical conditioning. The first avoidance conditioning experiments were conducted by the Russian psychologist Bechterev (1913) as an extension of Pavlov's research. Unlike Pavlov, however, Bechterev investigated conditioning mechanisms in human subjects. In one situation, participants were asked to place a finger on a metal plate. A warning stimulus (the CS) was periodically presented, followed by a brief shock (the US) through the plate. As you might suspect, the subjects quickly lifted the finger off the plate upon being shocked. With repeated conditioning trials, they also learned to make this response to the warning stimulus. The experiment was viewed as a standard example of classical conditioning. However, in contrast to the standard classical conditioning procedure, in Bechterev's method the subjects determined whether they were exposed to the US. If they lifted their finger off the plate in response to the CS, they did not experience the shock scheduled on that trial. This aspect of the procedure constitutes a significant departure from Pavlov's methods because in standard classical conditioning the delivery of the US does not depend on the subject's behavior.

The fact that Bechterev and others who followed his example did not use a standard classical conditioning procedure went unnoticed for many years. Starting in the 1930s, several investigators attempted to compare directly the effects of a standard classical conditioning procedure with the effects of a procedure that had the added instrumental avoidance component (for example, Schlosberg, 1934, 1936). One of the most influential of these comparisons was performed by Brogden, Lipman, and Culler (1938). They tested two groups of guinea pigs in a rotating wheel apparatus (see Figure 9.1). A tone served as the CS, and shock again served as the US. The shock stimulated the guinea pigs to run and thereby rotate the wheel. For one group of subjects, the shock was always presented 2 sec after the beginning of the tone (classical group). The second group (avoidance group) received the same type of CS-US pairings when they did not make the conditioned response (a small movement of the wheel). However, if these subjects moved the wheel during the tone CS before the shock occurred, the scheduled shock was omitted. Figure 9.2 shows the percentage of trials on which each group made the conditioned response. It is evident from the results that the avoidance group quickly learned to make the conditioned response and

FIGURE 9.1. Modern running wheel for rodents.

was responding on 100% of the trials within eight days of training. In contrast, the classical group never achieved this high level of performance, even though training was continued much longer for them.

These results show a big difference between standard classical conditioning and a procedure that includes an instrumental avoidance component. The avoidance procedure produced a much higher level of

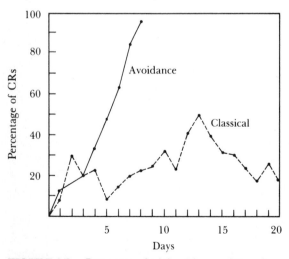

FIGURE 9.2. Percentage of trials with a conditioned response on successive days of training. The conditioned response prevented shock delivery for the avoidance group but not for the classical group. *(After Brogden, Lipman, & Culler, 1938.)*

responding than was observed with mere pairings of the CS with shock. This facilitation of behavior cannot be explained solely by what is known about classical conditioning. In fact, the results obtained by Brogden et al. are paradoxical when viewed just in terms of classical conditioning. For the avoidance group, the CS was often presented without the US because subjects often prevented the occurrence of shock. These CS-alone trials constitute extinction trials and hence should have attenuated the development of the conditioned response. In contrast, the classical group never received CS-alone trials, because it could never avoid shock. Therefore, if CS-US pairings were the only important factor in this situation, the classical group should have performed better than the avoidance group. The fact that the opposite result occurred indicates that analysis of avoidance behavior requires more than classical conditioning principles.

The discriminated avoidance procedure

Although avoidance behavior is not just another case of classical conditioning, the classical conditioning heritage of the study of avoidance behavior has greatly influenced its subsequent experimental and theoretical analysis. Investigators have been greatly concerned with the importance of signals for the aversive event in avoidance conditioning and with the relation of the warning signal to the instrumental response and the aversive US. Experimental questions of this type have been extensively investigated with procedures similar to that used by Brogden and his colleagues. This method is called **discriminated** or **signaled avoidance,** and its standard features are diagramed in Figure 9.3.

The first thing to note about the signaled avoidance technique is that it involves discrete trials. Each trial is initiated by the CS. The events that occur after that depend on what the subject does. There are two possibilities. If the subject makes the response required for avoidance during the CS but before the shock is scheduled, the CS is turned off, and the US is omitted on that trial. This is a successful **avoidance trial.** If the subject fails to make the required response during the CS-US interval, the scheduled

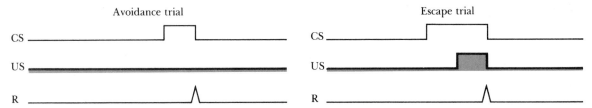

FIGURE 9.3. Diagram of the discriminated, or signaled, avoidance procedure. *Avoidance trial:* If the subject makes the response required for avoidance during the CS (the signal) but before the US (for example, shock) is scheduled, the CS is turned off, and the US is omitted on that trial. *Escape trial:* If the subject fails to make the required response during the CS-US interval, the scheduled shock is presented and remains on until the response occurs, whereupon both the CS *and* the US are terminated.

shock is presented and remains on until the response occurs, whereupon both the CS and the US are terminated. In this case, the instrumental response results in escape from the shock. Hence this type of trial is called an **escape trial.** During early stages of training, most of the trials are escape trials, whereas avoidance trials predominate once the avoidance response is well established.

Discriminated avoidance procedures can be conducted using a variety of experimental situations. One may, for example, use a Skinner box in which a rat has to press a response lever during a tone to avoid shock (Hoffman, 1966). Another experimental situation that has been extensively used in studies of discriminated avoidance is the shuttle box, an example of which is shown in Figure 9.4. The shuttle box consists of two compartments separated by a low barrier

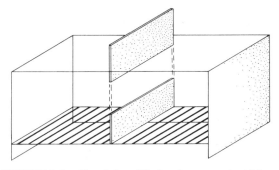

FIGURE 9.4. Shuttle box. The box has a metal grid floor and is separated into two compartments by a low barrier and a guillotine door. The door is raised at the start of each trial. The instrumental response consists in crossing from one side of the box to the other.

and a vertically sliding door. The animal is placed in one side. At the start of the trial, the CS is presented (a light or a tone, for example), and the door between the two compartments is opened. If the animal crosses over to the other side before the shock is scheduled, no shock is delivered, and the door is closed until the next trial. The next trial can be administered starting with the animal in the second compartment. With this procedure, the animal shuttles back and forth between the two sides on successive trials. The response is therefore called **shuttle avoidance.**

In the shuttle avoidance procedure, the animal can be shocked on either side of the apparatus. For example, if the subject is on the left side when a trial starts and it fails to make the shuttle response, it will receive shock there. If it is on the right side when a trial begins and it again fails to cross, it will receive shock on the right side. A variation of the shuttle avoidance procedure has also been extensively investigated in which the subject is always placed on the same side of the shuttle box at the start of each trial. For example, it may always be placed in the left compartment. In this case, the animal would have to run to the right compartment on each trial to avoid (or escape) shock. At the end of the trial it would be removed from the right compartment and replaced in the left compartment to start the next trial. Such a procedure is called a **one-way avoidance** procedure because the animal always has to cross in the same direction. An important aspect of the one-way procedure is that the animal can be shocked in only one of the two compartments (the one it is placed in at the start of each trial). This part of the apparatus is called the **shock compartment,** and the other side is called the **safe compartment.** Because there is a consistently safe compartment in one-way avoidance procedures, one-way avoidance behavior is usually learned more rapidly than shuttle avoidance.

Two-process theory of avoidance

It is clear from the results of experiments such as that by Brogden et al. (1938) that avoidance procedures can produce much more responding than procedures in which a warning signal is repeatedly paired with shock but avoidance is not possible. The avoidance contingency provides some kind of instrumental reinforcement for the avoidance response. Exactly what this source of reinforcement is has been the central question in investigations of avoidance learning. The first and most influential answer to the puzzle, proposed by Mowrer (1947) and elaborated by Miller (for example, 1951) and others, is known as the **two-process theory of avoidance.** In one form or another, this two-process theory has been the dominant theoretical viewpoint on avoidance learning for many years. As we shall see, the theory has some serious shortcomings, and it is no longer viewed as a complete explanation of avoidance learning. Nevertheless, it continues to be important, at least to the extent that it is the standard against which all other explanations of avoidance behavior are always measured.

As its name implies, two-process theory assumes that two mechanisms are involved in avoidance learning. The first is a classical conditioning process activated by pairings of the warning stimulus (CS) with the aversive event (US) on trials when the subject fails to make the avoidance response. As was common at the time, Mowrer assumed that classical conditioning occurs by stimulus substitution. Because the US was an aversive event, Mowrer assumed that it elicited fear. Through classical conditioning with the US, the CS presumably also comes to elicit fear. Thus, the first component of two-process theory is the *classical conditioning of fear to the CS.*

Fear is an emotionally arousing state that motivates the organism. It is also aversive, so that a reduction in fear can provide negative reinforcement. Since fear is elicited by the CS, termination of the CS presumably results in a reduction in the level of fear. The second process in two-process theory is based on these considerations. Mowrer assumed that the instrumental avoidance response became learned because it terminated the CS and thereby reduced the conditioned fear elicited by the CS. Thus, the second component is *instrumental reinforcement of the avoidance response through fear reduction.*

There are several noteworthy aspects of two-process theory. First, and perhaps most important, is that the classical and instrumental processes are not assumed to provide independent sources of support for the avoidance behavior. Rather, the two processes are very much interdependent. Instrumental reinforcement through fear reduction is not possible until fear has been conditioned to the CS. Therefore, the classical conditioning process has to occur first. After that, the instrumental conditioning process may create extinction trials for the classical conditioning process. This occurs because each successful avoidance response prevents the occurrence of the US. Thus, two-process theory predicts a constant interplay between classical and instrumental processes. Another important aspect of two-process theory is that it explains avoidance behavior in terms of escape from conditioned fear rather than in terms of the prevention of shock. The fact that the avoidance response prevents shock is seen as a by-product in two-process theory, not as the critical event that motivates avoidance behavior. Escape from conditioned fear provides the critical reinforcement for avoidance behavior. Thus, according to two-process theory, the instrumental response is reinforced by a tangible event (fear reduction) rather than merely the absence of something (aversive stimulation).

Experimental analysis of avoidance behavior

A great deal of research has been conducted concerning avoidance behavior, much of it stimulated in one way or another by two-process theory. We cannot review all the evidence. However, we will consider several important types of results that have to be considered in any effort to fully understand the mechanisms of avoidance behavior.

Acquired-drive experiments. In the typical avoidance procedure, classical conditioning of fear and instrumental reinforcement through fear reduction occur intermixed in a series of trials. However, if these two processes make separate contributions to avoidance learning, it should be possible to demonstrate their operation in situations in which the two types of conditioning are not intermixed. This is the goal of acquired-drive experiments. The basic strategy is to first condition fear to a CS with a "pure" classical conditioning procedure in which the organism's responses do not influence whether the US is presented. In the next phase of the experiment, the animals are periodically exposed to the fear-eliciting CS and allowed to perform an instrumental response that is effective in terminating the CS (and thereby reducing fear). No shocks are scheduled in this phase. Therefore, the instrumental response is not required to avoid shock presentations. If two-process theory is correct and escape from the fear-eliciting CS can reinforce instrumental behavior, then subjects should be able to learn the instrumental response in the second phase of the experiment. This type of experiment is called an **acquired drive** study because the drive to perform the instrumental response (fear) is learned through classical conditioning. (It is not an innate drive, such as hunger or thirst.)

One of the first and most famous acquired-drive experiments was performed by Miller (1948). However, because of certain problems with that study, we will describe a follow-up experiment by Brown and Jacobs (1949). Rats were tested in a shuttle box. During the first phase of the procedure, the door between the two shuttle compartments was closed. The rats were individually placed on one side of the apparatus and a pulsating-light/tone CS was presented, ending in shock through the grid floor. Twenty-two such Pavlovian conditioning trials were conducted, with the rats confined on the right and left sides of the apparatus on alternate trials. The control group received the same training except that no shocks were delivered. During the next phase of the experiment, each subject was placed on one side of the shuttle box and the center barrier was removed. The CS was then presented and remained on until the subject turned it off by crossing to the other side. The animal was then removed from the apparatus until the next trial. No shocks were delivered during this phase of the experiment, and a one-way procedure was used, with the animals placed on the same side of the apparatus at the start of each trial. The investigators were interested to see whether the rats would learn to cross rapidly from one side to the other when the only reinforcement for crossing was termination of the previously conditioned light/tone CS.

The amount of time each subject took to cross the shuttle box and turn off the CS was measured for each trial. Figure 9.5 summarizes these response latencies for both the shock-conditioned and the control group. The two groups had similar response latencies at the beginning of instrumental training. However, as training progressed, the shock-conditioned animals learned to cross the shuttle box faster (and thus turn off the CS sooner) than the control group. This outcome shows that termination of a fear-conditioned stimulus is sufficient to provide reinforcement for an instrumental response. Such findings have been obtained in a variety of experimental situations (for

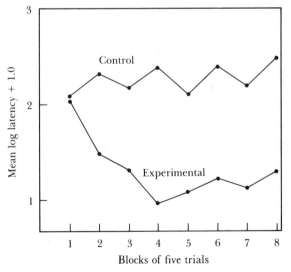

FIGURE 9.5. Mean latencies to cross from one side to the other in the shuttle box for control and experimental groups. The shuttle crossing resulted in termination of the CS on that trial. For the experimental group, the CS was previously conditioned with shock. Such conditioning was not conducted with the control group. *(After Brown & Jacobs, 1949.)*

example, Dinsmoor, 1962; McAllister & McAllister, 1971). In addition, other experiments have shown that delaying the termination of the CS after the instrumental behavior reduces the reinforcement effect, just as it does with instrumental responses maintained by positive reinforcement (for example, Delprato, 1969; Israel, Devine, O'Dea, & Hamdi, 1974; Katzev, 1967, 1972). These results provide strong support for two-process theory.

Independent measurement of fear during acquisition of avoidance behavior.

Another important strategy that has been used in investigations of avoidance behavior involves independent measurement of fear and instrumental avoidance responding during acquisition. If two-process theory is correct in assuming that fear provides the motivation for avoidance behavior, then the conditioning of fear and of instrumental avoidance responding should proceed together. Contrary to this prediction, conditioned fear and avoidance responding are not always highly correlated (see review by Mineka, 1979). Fairly early in the investigation of avoidance learning, it was noted that animals become less fearful as they learn the avoidance response (Solomon, Kamin, & Wynne, 1953; Solomon & Wynne, 1953). Since then, more systematic measurements of fear have been used. One popular behavioral technique for measuring fear involves the conditioned suppression procedure described in Chapters 3 and 5. In this technique, animals are first conditioned to make an instrumental response (such as lever pressing) for a food reward. A shock-conditioned CS is then presented while the subjects are responding to obtain food. Generally, the CS produces a suppression in the lever-press behavior, and the extent of this response suppression is assumed to reflect the amount of fear elicited by the CS. If the warning signal in an avoidance procedure comes to elicit fear, then presentation of that warning stimulus in a conditioned suppression experiment should result in suppression of food-reinforced behavior. This possibility was first investigated in a famous experiment by Kamin, Brimer, and Black (1963).

Kamin et al. initially trained their rats to press a response lever for food reinforcement on a variable-

interval schedule. The animals were then trained to avoid shock in response to an auditory CS in a shuttle box. Training was continued for independent groups of subjects until they successfully avoided shock on 1, 3, 9, or 27 consecutive trials. The animals were then returned to the lever-press situation. After their rate of responding had stabilized, the auditory CS that had been used in the shuttle box was periodically presented to see how much suppression in responding it would produce. The results are summarized in Figure 9.6. Lower values of the suppression index indicate greater disruptions of the lever-press behavior by the shock-avoidance CS. Increasing degrees of response suppression were observed among groups of subjects that had received avoidance training until they successfully avoided shock on 1 to 9 successive trials. With more extensive avoidance training, however, response suppression declined. Subjects trained

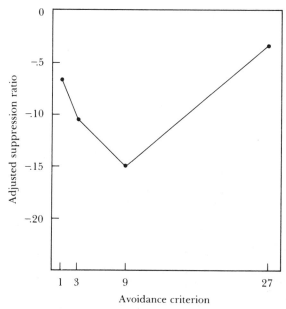

FIGURE 9.6. Suppression of lever pressing for food during a CS that was previously conditioned in a shock-avoidance procedure. Independent groups received avoidance training until they met a criterion of 1, 3, 9, or 27 consecutive avoidance responses. The suppression scores were adjusted for the degree of suppression produced by the CS before avoidance conditioning. Lower values of the adjusted ratio indicate greater suppression of lever pressing. *(After Kamin, Brimer, & Black, 1963.)*

until they avoided shock on 27 consecutive trials showed less conditioned suppression to the avoidance CS than subjects trained to a criterion of 9 consecutive avoidances. This outcome indicates that fear as measured by conditioned suppression decreases during extended avoidance training and is at a minimal level after extensive training (see also Linden, 1969; Starr & Mineka, 1977). However, the decrease in fear is not accompanied by a decrease in the strength of the avoidance response (Mineka & Gino, 1980).

The decline in fear to the CS with extended avoidance training provides a puzzle for two-process theory. If fear reduction is necessary to reinforce avoidance behavior, how can the behavior increase and persist in the face of declining CS-elicited fear? A recent study by McAllister, McAllister, and Benton (1983) provides a clue. They investigated the relative amounts of fear elicited by the CS and by background cues of the experimental chamber during the course of discriminated avoidance training in rats and found that the animals acquired substantial fear of both the CS and the background stimuli during initial stages of avoidance training. However, as training proceeded, the rats learned a discrimination between the CS and the background stimuli, and their fear of background stimuli was rapidly lost. Fear to the background stimuli declined more rapidly than fear to the CS. Consequently, CS termination could continue to result in fear reduction after extensive avoidance training.

According to two-process theory, the development of a discrimination between background stimuli and the CS can contribute to the persistence of avoidance responding in the face of declining fear to the CS. However, this mechanism may not provide a complete explanation for high levels of avoidance responding at asymptote. Lack of correspondence between independent measures of fear and avoidance responding has been an enduring problem for two-process theory (see Mineka, 1979). We will encounter further evidence of this dissociation in studies of the extinction of avoidance behavior.

Asymptotic avoidance performance. Two-process theory of avoidance not only specifies the mechanisms of the acquisition process for avoidance behavior but also makes predictions about the nature of performance once the response has been well learned. More specifically, it predicts that the strength of the avoidance response will fluctuate in cycles. Whenever a successful avoidance response occurs, the shock is omitted on that trial. This is assumed to be an extinction trial for the conditioned fear response. Repetition of the avoidance response (and thus the CS-alone extinction trials) should lead to extinction of fear. As the CS becomes extinguished, there will be less reinforcement resulting from the reduction of fear, and the avoidance response will also become extinguished. As this happens, the avoidance response will cease to occur in time to prevent the US. However, when shock is not avoided, the CS is paired with the US. This pairing should reinstate fear to the CS and reestablish the potential for reinforcement through fear reduction. Hence, the avoidance response should become reconditioned. Thus, the theory predicts that after initial acquisition the avoidance response will go through cycles of extinction and reacquisition. Although evidence of this sort has been observed on occasion (for example, Sheffield, 1948), avoidance behavior usually does not fluctuate in cycles. Rather, one of the most noteworthy aspects of avoidance behavior is that it is highly resistant to extinction when shocks no longer occur, as long as the response continues to be effective in terminating the CS. After shuttle avoidance conditioning with an intense shock in dogs, for example, the animals continue to make the avoidance response for hundreds of trials without receiving shock. One dog was observed to make the avoidance response on 650 successive trials after only a few shocks (Solomon et al., 1953). (For examples of similarly persistent avoidance behavior in rats, see Levis, 1981.)

The persistence of avoidance behavior is difficult to explain by two-process theory. Early attempts to modify the theory to accommodate such results (Solomon & Wynne, 1953) did not meet with much success (see Mineka, 1979). However, recent empirical findings suggest a clue if we focus on the role of response feedback stimuli in avoidance conditioning. In all avoidance conditioning procedures, the avoidance response is followed by a period free from shock. There are also always distinctive feedback stimuli that accompany the instrumental response. These may be provided by a change in location, as when a rat moves from one side to the other in a shuttle box; they may be tactile or other external stimuli involved in making the response, such as those provided by touching and manipulating a response lever. The response feedback stimuli may also be proprioceptive (internal) cues provided by the muscle movements involved in making the response. Regardless of what they are, because the instrumental response produces a period free from shock, the stimuli accompanying the response are negatively correlated with shock. As we discussed in Chapter 3, this is one of the circumstances that lead to the development of conditioned inhibition. Therefore, response feedback cues can become conditioned inhibitors of fear (for example, Morris, 1974; Rescorla, 1968).

The above analysis suggests that, after extensive avoidance training, subjects experience two conditioned stimuli in succession on each trial of a discriminated avoidance procedure: the fear-eliciting warning stimulus for shock (CS+), followed by fear-inhibiting feedback cues from the avoidance response (CS−). Therefore, asymptotic avoidance trials should not be viewed as extinction trials in which the CS+ is presented alone but as trials in which the CS+ is followed by fear-inhibitory response feedback cues. Recent evidence indicates that the presentation of fear-inhibiting stimuli following a CS+ can block extinction of the CS+ (Soltysik, Wolfe, Nicholas, Wilson, & Garcia-Sanchez, 1983). This type of blocking can be conceptualized in a manner analogous to the blocking of excitatory conditioning, discussed in Chapter 5. Because an inhibitory stimulus is a signal for the absence of shock, occurrence of the CS− makes the absence of shock on avoidance trials fully expected, and this protects the CS+ from any changes in associative strength. Another way to think about this effect is that the absence of shock on avoidance trials is attributed to the CS−. This makes reevaluation of the CS+ unnecessary, thus leaving its fear-eliciting properties unchanged. If response feedback cues protect the CS+ from extinction on avoidance trials, the CS+ can continue to elicit fear and motivate the avoidance response. Therefore, this mechanism makes the persistence of avoidance behavior in the face of numerous no-shock trials less puzzling in the context of two-process theory.

Extinction of avoidance behavior through response blocking and CS-alone exposure. As we noted above, if the avoidance response is effective in terminating the CS and no shocks are presented, avoidance responding persists for a long time. Is avoidance behavior always highly resistant to extinction, or are there procedures that result in fairly rapid extinction? The answer is very important not only for a theoretical analysis of avoidance behavior but also for extinguishing maladaptive or pathological avoidance responses in human patients. An effective and extensively investigated extinction procedure for avoidance behavior is called **flooding** or **response prevention** (Baum, 1970). It involves presenting the CS in the avoidance situation but with the apparatus altered in such a way that the subject is prevented from making the avoidance response. Thus, the subject is exposed to the CS without being permitted to terminate it. In a sense, it is "flooded" with the CS.

One of the most important variables determining the effects of a flooding procedure is the duration of the forced exposure to the CS. This is nicely illustrated in an experiment by Schiff, Smith, and Prochaska (1972). Rats were trained to avoid shock in response to an auditory CS warning stimulus in a one-way avoidance situation. After all the animals avoided shock on ten consecutive trials, the safe compartment was blocked off by a barrier, and subjects received various amounts of exposure to the CS without shock. Independent groups of subjects received 1, 5, or 12 blocked trials, and on each of these trials, the CS was presented for 1, 5, 10, 50, or 120 sec. The barrier blocking the avoidance response was then removed, and all subjects were tested for extinction. At the start of each extinction trial, the subject was placed in the apparatus, and the CS was presented until the animal crossed into the safe compartment. Shock never occurred during the extinction trials, and subjects were tested until they took 120 sec or longer to cross into the safe compartment on three consecutive trials. The strength of the avoidance response was measured by the number of trials subjects took to reach this extinction criterion.

As expected, blocked exposure to the CS facilitated extinction of the avoidance response. Furthermore, this effect was determined mainly by the total duration of exposure to the CS. The number of flooding trials administered (1, 5, or 12) facilitated extinction only because each trial added to the total amount of time the subjects were exposed to the CS without being allowed to escape from it. The results of the experiment are summarized in Figure 9.7. Increases in the total duration of blocked exposure to the CS resulted in more rapid extinction (see also Baum, 1969; Weinberger, 1965).

Two-process theory predicts that flooding will extinguish avoidance behavior because forced exposure to the CS is expected to produce extinction of fear. The fact that more extensive exposure to the CS results in more rapid extinction (for example, Schiff et al., 1972) is consistent with this view. However, detailed investigations of the role of fear in flooding procedures have also provided evidence contrary to two-process theory. Independent measurements of fear (with the conditioned suppression technique, for example) have shown that in some situations flooding

extinguishes avoidance behavior more rapidly than it extinguishes fear, whereas in other situations the reverse holds (see, for example, Coulter, Riccio, & Page, 1969; Mineka & Gino, 1979; Mineka, Miller, Gino, & Giencke, 1981). These results suggest that extinction of fear is only one factor responsible for the effects of flooding procedures. Other variables may be related to the fact that, during flooding, subjects not only receive forced exposure to the CS but are prevented from making the avoidance response. In certain situations, blocking of the avoidance response can contribute to extinction of the avoidance behavior independent of CS exposure. One demonstration of this fact was performed by Katzev and Berman (1974).

Katzev and Berman first conditioned rats to avoid shock in a shuttle box. Fifty extinction trials were then conducted. Pairs of subjects were set up for this phase of the experiment. For one subject of each pair, the shuttle response was not blocked during the extinction trials, so that the rat could turn off the CS by crossing to the other side. The other subject of each pair received the identical CS exposures that the first

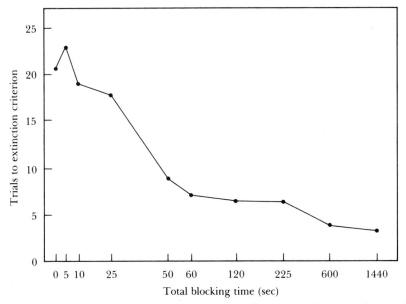

FIGURE 9.7.   Trials to extinction criterion for independent groups of animals that previously received various durations of blocked exposure to the CS.   *(From Schiff, Smith, & Prochaska, 1972.)*

rat received, except that the shuttle response was blocked by a barrier. Thus, CS exposure was equal for the two types of subjects, but only one of the subjects in each pair could terminate the CS by making the shuttle response. A third group of rats served as a control group and was not exposed to the CS (or the shuttle box) during this phase. All the subjects were then given a series of standard extinction trials. The barrier was removed altogether, and the CS was periodically presented until the subjects crossed to the other side of the apparatus. The results are summarized in Figure 9.8. The control group made the greatest number of shuttle crossings. The fewest responses occurred in subjects that had received blocked exposure to the CS. In fact, these animals were much less likely to respond than animals that had received the identical exposure to the CS but could always terminate the CS presentations by making the shuttle response. These results show that response blocking can facilitate extinction of avoidance behavior independent of variations in CS exposure. Thus, evidently the flooding procedure involves more than just Pavlovian extinction of the CS (see Baum, 1970; Mineka, 1979, for a more detailed discussion). Perhaps subjects learn a response that is incompatible with the avoidance behavior during blocked exposures to the CS, and this contributes to the observed loss of avoidance responding.

Nondiscriminated (free-operant) avoidance. As we have seen, two-process theory places great emphasis on the role of the warning signal, or CS, in

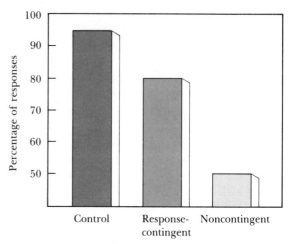

FIGURE 9.8. Percentage of shuttle responses that occurred during the first ten test trials. In the previous phase of the experiment, the control group was not exposed to the CS, the response-contingent group received CS exposures that could be terminated by a shuttle response, and the noncontingent group received yoked CS exposures independent of behavior. Initially all subjects received discriminated avoidance training. *(After Katzev & Berman, 1974.)*

avoidance learning. Could animals also learn to avoid shock even if there were no external warning stimulus in the situation? Within the context of two-factor theory, this would seem to be almost a heretical question. However, science often progresses when investigators ask bold questions, and Sidman (1953a, 1953b) did just that. He devised what has come to be known as the **nondiscriminated** or **free-operant avoidance** procedure. (It is also sometimes called **Sidman avoidance.**) In this procedure shock is scheduled to

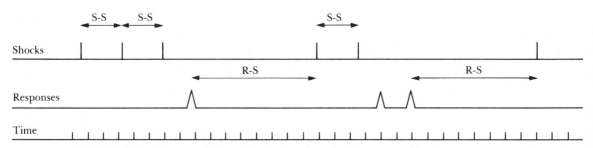

FIGURE 9.9. Diagram of the nondiscriminated, or free-operant, avoidance procedure. Each occurrence of the response initiates a period without shock, as set by the R-S interval. In the absence of a response, the next shock occurs a fixed period after the last shock, as set by the S-S interval. Shocks are not signaled by an exteroceptive stimulus and are usually brief and inescapable.

occur periodically without warning, let us say every 10 sec. Some behavior is specified as the avoidance response, and each occurrence of this response prevents the delivery of the scheduled shocks for a fixed period—say, 30 sec. Animals will learn to avoid shocks under these conditions even though there is no warning stimulus. The procedure is constructed from only two time intervals (see Figure 9.9). One of these is the interval between shocks in the absence of a response. This is called the **S-S** (shock-shock) **interval.** The other critical time period is the interval between the response and the next scheduled shock. This is called the **R-S** (response-shock) **interval.** The R-S interval is the period of safety created by the response. In our example, the S-S interval is 10 sec and the R-S interval is 30 sec.

BOX 9.1.   Two-factor theory and compulsive behavior

Two-factor theory has served as an important model in the analysis and treatment of obsessive-compulsive behaviors. Obsessive-compulsive behaviors can take several forms. Some people are obsessed with fears of contamination and expend a good deal of effort avoiding contamination or washing after contact with a feared object. Others are compulsive checkers: they spend excessive time checking objects in their environment or some aspect of their own behavior. One woman, for example, could not leave her home until every door was checked several times in a ritualistic fashion. Certain aberrant eating and exercise habits are also sometimes considered obsessive-compulsive behaviors. In all these cases, a real or imagined object or event induces anxiety, and the ritualistic behavior can be viewed as avoidance behavior reinforced by reduction of anxiety. Compulsive washers, for example, become anxious when they get near or touch the feared "contaminated" object. Extensive washing (in some cases including several showers and laundering each day) reduces the anxiety.

Research findings support the assumption that compulsive rituals reduce anxiety (see, for example, Hodgson & Rachman, 1972; Roper, Rachman, & Hodgson, 1973). In experimental investigations, compulsive behavior is provoked while anxiety is measured with self-reports, psychophysiological techniques, or other procedures. Such studies indicate that provoking the compulsion increases anxiety and performance of the ritualistic behavior decreases it.

Some therapeutic procedures for obsessive-compulsive behavior are based on two-factor theory and involve the avoidance extinction procedure of flooding, or response prevention. The compulsion is provoked, but execution of the ritual is prevented. The individual is "flooded" with the feared object or event. This is expected to produce extinction of the anxiety. Outcome research on this type of therapy has indicated that it is highly successful (see Emmelkamp, 1982a, for a review).

Two-factor theory has also been useful in understanding the eating dysfunctions of anorexia nervosa and bulimia nervosa. In anorexia nervosa, the individual eats very little and exercises excessively so that rapid weight loss ensues. In bulimia nervosa, the individual engages in cycles of excessive eating (binge eating) followed by vomiting. Rosen and Leitenberg (1982) describe both these disorders as stemming from a morbid fear of gaining weight. Eating—particularly binge eating—increases this anxiety. In anorexia nervosa, anxiety is reduced by avoiding food and exercising excessively. In bulimia nervosa, anxiety is reduced by vomiting. Leitenberg and his associates (Leitenberg, Gross, Peterson, & Rosen, 1984) successfully treated bulimic individuals through response prevention. The clients were required to eat until they felt the urge to vomit. They were then prevented from vomiting by the therapist and not released from supervision until the urge had completely subsided. As predicted, the clients reported an increase in anxiety and an increase in the urge to vomit as they ate. However, both of these decreased with repeated treatment sessions.

In addition to lacking a warning stimulus, the free-operant avoidance procedure differs from discriminated avoidance in allowing for avoidance responses to occur at any time. In discriminated avoidance procedures, the avoidance response is effective in preventing the delivery of shock only if it is made during the CS. Responses in the absence of the CS (the intertrial interval) have no effect. In fact, in some experiments (particularly those involving one-way avoidance), the animals are removed from the apparatus between trials. In contrast, in the free-operant procedure, an avoidance response occurring at any time will reset the R-S interval. If the R-S interval is 30 sec, shock is scheduled 30 sec after each response. However, by always responding just before this R-S interval is over, the subject can always reset the R-S interval and thereby prolong its period of safety indefinitely.

There are several striking characteristics of free-operant avoidance experiments. First, these studies generally involve much longer periods of training than discriminated avoidance experiments. It is rare, for example, for a discriminated avoidance experiment to be conducted long enough so that the animals receive 100 shocks. However, 100 shocks are not excessive in free-operant avoidance studies, in part because sometimes it takes a lot of experience with shock before subjects learn to make the avoidance response regularly. Extensive training is also often used because the investigators are specifically interested in what steady-state adjustment the animals will make to such schedules of aversive stimulation. Thus, in many cases the initial learning of the avoidance behavior is not the primary focus of the experiment. Another general characteristic of these experiments is that, even after extensive training, animals often never get good enough to avoid all shocks. Finally, subjects often differ greatly in how they respond to the identical free-operant avoidance procedure.

Figures 9.10 and 9.11 illustrate the kinds of results that can be obtained with free-operant avoidance training. Each figure shows cumulative records of lever pressing during successive 1-hour periods of the first time that two rats were exposed to the avoidance procedure. In the absence of lever presses, the sub-

jects received shock every 5 sec (the S-S interval). Each lever-press response initiated a 20-sec period without shocks (the R-S interval). Shocks are indicated by downward deflections of the cumulative-recorder pen. Rat H-28 (Figure 9.10) received a lot of shocks at first but started to press the lever even during the first hour of training. It responded a great deal during the second hour of the session and then settled down to a steady rate of lever pressing for the next 5 hours that the procedure was in effect. This was its stable response pattern under these conditions. Rat H-28 was a particularly fast learner. However, even at the end of the 7 hours of training it received more than 25 shocks/hour.

Rat O-10 (Figure 9.11) did not perform as well as rat H-28. It received a great many more shocks and never achieved a high rate of responding. Its stable pattern of behavior after several hours of training was always to wait for the shock to occur at the end of an R-S interval before responding again. It usually did not respond to reinstitute the R-S interval and did not obtain prolonged periods free from shock. Therefore, it received a shock about every 20 sec, as set by the R-S interval.

Numerous experiments have been conducted on free-operant avoidance behavior (see Hineline, 1977; Sidman, 1966). The rate of responding is controlled by the values of the S-S and R-S intervals. The more frequently shocks are scheduled in the absence of responding (the S-S interval), the more likely the animal is to learn the avoidance response. Increasing the periods of safety produced by the response (the R-S interval) also promotes the avoidance behavior. In addition, the relative values of the S-S and R-S intervals are important. For example, the animal is not likely to make the instrumental response if the R-S interval is shorter than the S-S interval.

Nondiscriminated avoidance behavior presents a challenge for two-process theory because there is no explicit CS to elicit conditioned fear and it is not clear how the avoidance response reduces fear. However, two-process theory has not been entirely abandoned in attempts to explain free-operant avoidance (see Anger, 1963). The S-S and R-S intervals used in effective procedures are usually rather short (less than 1 min). Furthermore, they remain fixed during

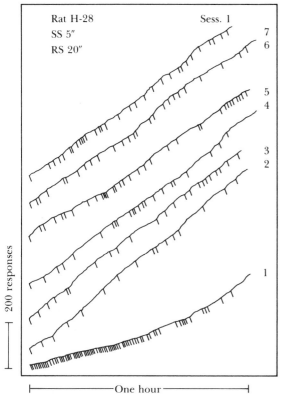

FIGURE 9.10. Cumulative record of lever pressing for a rat the first time it was exposed to a nondiscriminated avoidance procedure. Numerals at the right label successive hours of exposure to the procedure. Oblique slashes indicate delivery of shock. *(From Sidman, 1966.)*

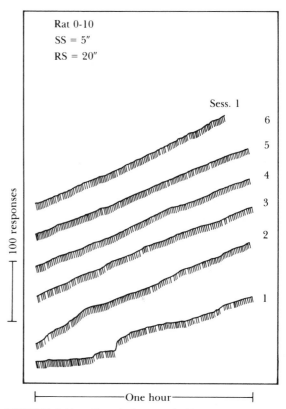

FIGURE 9.11. Cumulative record of lever pressing for a rat the first time it was exposed to a nondiscriminated avoidance procedure. Numerals at the right label successive hours of exposure to the procedure. Oblique slashes indicate delivery of shock. *(From Sidman, 1966.)*

an experiment, so that the intervals are highly predictable. Therefore, it is not unreasonable to suggest that the animals might learn to respond to the passage of time as a signal for shock. This assumption of temporal conditioning permits application of the mechanisms of two-process theory to free-operant avoidance procedures. The basic strategy is to assume that the passage of time after the last shock (in the case of the S-S interval) or after the last response (in the case of the R-S interval) becomes conditioned to elicit fear. Since the timing starts anew with each occurrence of the avoidance response, the response effectively removes the fear-eliciting temporal cues. Termination of these time signals can then reinforce the avoidance response through fear reduction. Thus,

the temporal cues involved in getting near the end of the S-S or R-S interval are assumed to have the same role that the explicit CS has in discriminative avoidance procedures.

The above analysis of free-operant avoidance in terms of two-process theory predicts that subjects will not distribute their responses randomly in time. Rather, they will be more likely to respond as the end of the R-S interval gets closer, because it is here that the temporal cues presumably elicit fear. Results consistent with this prediction have been obtained. However, many animals successfully avoid a great many shocks without distributing their responses in the manner predicted by two-process theory. Furthermore, the predicted distribution of responses often develops only after extensive training, after the subjects are avoiding a great many of the scheduled shocks (see Sidman, 1966). In addition, avoidance behavior has been successfully conditioned with the use of free-operant procedures in which the S-S and R-S intervals are varied throughout the experiment (for example, Herrnstein & Hineline, 1966). When the S-S and R-S intervals are of unpredictable duration, subjects are much less likely to be able to learn to use the passage of time as a signal for shock. It is therefore difficult to adapt two-process theory to explain their avoidance learning. These types of results have discouraged some investigators from accepting two-process theory as an explanation of free-operant avoidance learning (see Herrnstein, 1969; Hineline, 1977, 1981, for further discussion).

Alternative theoretical accounts of avoidance behavior

In the preceding discussion of experimental investigations of avoidance behavior, we used two-process theory to provide the conceptual framework. This was reasonable because many of the research questions were stimulated in one way or another by two-process theory. As we saw, however, the theory is not fully supported by the experimental evidence in every case. Accordingly, various modifications and alternatives to two-process theory have been proposed. We will discuss some of the more important of these. In two-process theory, reinforcement for the avoidance response is assumed to be provided by the reduction of fear. This is a case of negative reinforcement—reinforcement due to removal of an aversive state. Several recent theoretical treatments have proposed that avoidance procedures also provide for positive reinforcement of the avoidance response, whereas others have suggested that neither negative nor positive reinforcement is important in avoidance learning.

Positive reinforcement through conditioned inhibition of fear. As we noted earlier, performance of an avoidance response always results in distinctive feedback stimuli, such as spatial cues involved in going from one side to the other in a shuttle box or tactile and other external stimuli involved in pressing a response lever. Because the avoidance response produces a period of safety in all avoidance conditioning procedures, response feedback stimuli may acquire conditioned inhibitory properties and become signals for the absence of aversive stimulation. Since a shock-free period is desirable, a conditioned inhibitory stimulus for shock may serve as a positive reinforcer. In this way, the stimuli that accompany avoidance responses may provide positive reinforcement for avoidance behavior. (This hypothesis is also called the **safety-signal theory** of avoidance.)

In most avoidance experiments, no special steps are taken to ensure that the avoidance response is accompanied by vivid feedback stimuli that could become conditioned inhibitors. Spatial, tactile, and proprioceptive stimuli that are not specifically programmed but inevitably accompany the avoidance response serve this function. However, one can easily modify any avoidance procedure to provide a distinctive stimulus, such as a brief light or tone, after each occurrence of the avoidance response. The conditioned inhibition reinforcement model predicts that introducing an explicit feedback stimulus will facilitate the learning of an avoidance response. Numerous experiments have found this to be true (for example, Bolles & Grossen, 1969; D'Amato, Fazzaro, & Etkin, 1968; Keehn & Nakkash, 1959). Other studies have shown that, during the course of avoidance training, a response feedback stimulus becomes a conditioned inhibitor of fear (for example, Morris, 1974; Rescorla, 1968). Furthermore, there is also direct evidence that a feedback stimulus that has been conditioned to inhibit fear during avoidance training thereby becomes an effective positive reinforcer for new responses (Morris, 1975; Weisman & Litner, 1972; see also Dinsmoor & Sears, 1973). Thus, there is considerable evidence for the conditioned inhibition reinforcement factor in avoidance learning.

There are important similarities and differences between positive reinforcement of avoidance behavior through conditioned inhibition and the negative reinforcement process assumed by two-process theory. Both mechanisms involve a reduction of fear. However, how this occurs is different in the two cases. A conditioned inhibitor actively inhibits fear, whereas CS termination is assumed to lead to the passive dissipation of fear. Because both mechanisms involve fear reduction, the operation of both processes depends on the existence of fear. However, the conditioned inhibition reinforcement process is less restrictive about the source of the fear. In two-process theory, fear is assumed to be elicited by the explicit discriminative stimulus for shock—the CS. In contrast, fear may be elicited by other stimuli as well for conditioned inhibition reinforcement. For example, fear could be elicited by situational cues of the environment in which avoidance conditioning is conducted.

The fact that fear elicited by situational cues can provide the basis for conditioned inhibition reinforcement makes the safety-signal hypothesis particularly well suited to explain free-operant avoidance behavior. Subjects often experience numerous shocks during acquisition of free-operant avoidance behavior. This and the absence of an exteroceptive warning stimulus make it highly likely that the entire experimental situation becomes conditioned to elicit fear. Because shocks never occur for the duration of the R-S interval after a response is made, the proprioceptive and tactile stimuli that accompany the response can become conditioned inhibitors of fear. Thus, the response-associated feedback cues can come to provide positive reinforcement for the free-operant avoidance response (Dinsmoor, 1977; Rescorla, 1968).

It is important to realize that the conditioned inhibition reinforcement mechanism is not incompatible with or necessarily a substitute for the negative reinforcement process assumed by two-process theory. That is, negative reinforcement through CS termination and positive reinforcement through conditioned inhibitory feedback cues could well coexist and both contribute to the strength of the avoidance behavior (see Cicala & Owen, 1976; Owen, Cicala, & Herdegen, 1978).

Reinforcement of avoidance through reduction of shock frequency.

The conditioned inhibition reinforcement mechanism does not present a radical alternative to the two-process theory of avoidance. In contrast, another reinforcement mechanism, **shock-frequency reduction,** has been proposed as an alternative to two-process theory (deVilliers, 1974; Herrnstein, 1969; Herrnstein & Hineline, 1966; Hineline, 1981; Sidman, 1962). By definition, avoidance responses prevent the delivery of shock and thereby reduce the frequency of shocks the subject receives. The theories of avoidance we have discussed so far have viewed the reduction of shocks almost as an incidental by-product of avoidance responses rather than as an immediate primary cause of the behavior. In contrast, the shock-frequency-reduction position views avoidance of shock as critical to the motivation of avoidance behavior.

Shock-frequency reduction as the cause of avoidance behavior was first entertained by Sidman (1962) as a way of explaining results he obtained in a concurrent free-operant avoidance experiment. Rats were exposed to two free-operant avoidance schedules at the same time. Responses on one response lever prevented shocks on one of the schedules, and responses on the other lever prevented shocks on the second schedule. Sidman concluded that the subjects distributed their responses between the two response levers so as to reduce the overall frequency of shocks they received. The idea that shock-frequency reduction can serve to reinforce avoidance behavior was later encouraged by evidence of learning in a free-operant avoidance procedure specifically designed to minimize the role of fear-conditioned temporal cues (Herrnstein & Hineline, 1966). In addition, studies of the relative importance of various components of the discriminated avoidance procedure have also shown that the avoidance component significantly contributes to the learning (for example, Bolles, Stokes, & Younger, 1966; see also Bolles, 1972; Kamin, 1956).

Although the evidence cited above clearly indicates that avoidance of shock is important, the mechanisms responsible for these results are debatable. Several experiments have shown that animals can learn to make an avoidance response even if the response does not reduce the frequency of shocks delivered (for example, Gardner & Lewis, 1976; Hineline, 1970). Responding in these studies delayed the onset of the next scheduled shock but did not prevent its delivery. Thus, overall shock frequency was unchanged by the instrumental response. Such results can be explained in terms of the shock-frequency-reduction hypothesis by assuming that subjects calculate shock frequencies over only a limited period following an avoidance response. However, the hypothesis does not specify the duration of these intervals, leaving them to be determined experimentally (see, for example, Logue, 1982).

In evaluating the shock-frequency-reduction hypothesis, one must also consider the extent to which evidence consistent with the hypothesis can be explained in other ways—specifically, by means of conditioned inhibition reinforcement or by means of punishing effects of shocks in the absence of an avoidance contingency. If a response reduces the frequency of shocks, external and proprioceptive stimuli involved in making the response will come to signal the absence of shock and become a conditioned inhibitor. The conditioned inhibitory properties of these stimuli can then reinforce the behavior. This conditioned inhibition mechanism is a plausible alternative to the shock-frequency interpretation, particularly for free-operant avoidance experiments (for example, Herrnstein & Hineline, 1966). In fact, it is a more broadly applicable explanation. Unlike the shock-frequency hypothesis, the conditioned inhibition account can also explain the results reviewed in the preceding section concerning the properties of response feedback cues in avoidance experiments.

Avoidance behavior and species-specific defense reactions. The theories discussed so far have been concerned mainly with how the events that precede and follow the avoidance response control avoidance behavior. The exact nature of the instrumental response required to prevent scheduled shocks was not a primary concern of these theories. In addition, the reinforcement mechanisms assumed by the theories all required some time to develop. Before fear reduction could be an effective reinforcer, fear first had to be conditioned to the CS; before feedback cues could come to serve as reinforcers, they had to become signals for the absence of shock; and before shock-frequency reduction could work, subjects had to experience enough shocks to be able to assess shock fre-

quencies. Therefore, these theories tell us very little about what determines the organism's behavior during the first few trials of avoidance training. The lack of concern with what the subject does during the first few trials is a serious weakness. For an avoidance mechanism to be very useful to the subject in its natural habitat, the process has to generate successful avoidance responses very quickly. If an animal is trying to avoid being eaten by a predator, for example, it may not be alive to experience repeated training trials.

In contrast to the theories we considered earlier, the account of avoidance behavior we will discuss in the present section focuses on the specific nature of the instrumental response required to prevent shock and addresses what controls the subject's behavior during the early stages of avoidance training (Bolles, 1970, 1971). The theory starts by recognizing that aversive stimuli and situations elicit strong unconditioned, or innate, responses in animals. It is assumed that many of these innate responses have evolved because they enable the organism to cope with or obtain protection from aversive events. Therefore, Bolles has called these innate responses **species-specific defense reactions** (SSDRs). We have already seen some examples of SSDRs. The mobbing behavior of birds directed toward a potential predator (Chapter 2) is a particularly complicated social SSDR. Another example is the tendency of the young of mouthbreeding cichlids to swim toward dark areas when the water is disturbed (Chapter 2). In rats and many other animals, species-specific defense reactions include flight (running), freezing (immobility), fighting, and defensive burying. Which of these responses is observed depends on the circumstance. If there is an obvious way out of the situation, running may be the predominant response. When running is not possible, freezing may occur. If there is another animal in the situation, fighting may be the most likely behavior.

The SSDR account of behavior in avoidance situations states that species-specific defense reactions predominate during the initial stages of avoidance training. If the most likely SSDR is successful in preventing shocks, this behavior will persist as long as the avoidance procedure is in effect. If the first SSDR is not effective, it will be followed by shock, which will suppress the behavior through punishment. The animal will then make the next-most-likely SSDR. If shocks persist, this second SSDR will also become suppressed by punishment, and the organism will make the third-most-likely SSDR. The process will end when a response is found that is effective in avoiding shocks, so that the behavior is not suppressed by punishment. Thus, according to the SSDR account, punishment is responsible for the selection of the instrumental avoidance response from other activities of the organism. Furthermore, the range of responses available to the subject in an aversive situation is assumed to be restricted to its species-specific defense reactions. Reinforcement, be it positive or negative, is assumed to have a minor role, if any, in avoidance learning. The correct avoidance response is not strengthened by reinforcement. Rather, it occurs because other SSDRs are suppressed by punishment.

One obvious prediction of the SSDR theory is that some types of responses will be more easily learned in avoidance experiments than other types. Consistent with this prediction, Bolles (1969) found that rats can rapidly learn to run in a running wheel to avoid shock. In contrast, their performance of a rearing response (standing on the hind legs) did not improve much during the course of avoidance training. Presumably, running was learned faster because it was closer to the rat's species-specific defense reactions in the running wheel. In another study, Grossen and Kelley (1972) initially documented the subjects' responses to shock before selecting the avoidance response. The rats were placed on a large, flat grid surface. When shocked, the animals were highly likely to freeze near the side walls of the apparatus (thigmotaxis). A platform was then placed on the grid floor either in the center or near the side walls, and the animals were required to jump onto the platform to avoid shock. Faster learning occurred when the platform was near the sides of the apparatus than when it was in the center of the grid surface. Thus, the avoidance performance was accurately predicted from the subjects' innate reactions to shock. In an important follow-up experiment, Grossen and Kelley also showed that the position of the platform did not make any difference if the subjects were reinforced with food for making the jump response.

The consummatory-stimulus-reward hypothesis.

The SSDR theory differs from other theories of avoidance behavior we have considered not only in its emphasis on the form of the avoidance response but also in its concern for the contributions of innate behavioral tendencies to avoidance learning. Species-specific defense reactions are assumed to be adaptations that have evolved to promote survival in dangerous situations. The last mechanism of avoidance learning we consider, the **consummatory-stimulus-reward hypothesis,** is similarly sensitive to evolutionary contributions to avoidance behavior but focuses on stimulus rather than response aspects of defensive behavior. Masterson and Crawford (1982) noted that each species-specific defense response results in a particular constellation of consequent stimuli. Freezing, for example, results in a fixed configuration of proprioceptive, vestibular, and environmental stimuli as the animal stays still. In contrast, fleeing results in a host of rapidly changing visual, olfactory, vestibular, and proprioceptive cues. Because these stimuli result from the completion or consummation of defense responses, they are called "defense consummatory stimuli."

Masterson and Crawford proposed that aversive situations induce a defense motivation system that not only increases the likelihood of particular innate responses but also makes defense consummatory stimuli effective reinforcers. Defense consummatory stimuli are assumed to shape and positively reinforce behavior in aversive situations in a manner analogous to drive-reduction views of food reinforcement. Just as food deprivation is assumed to induce food-seeking responses and make food-related stimuli positively reinforcing, aversive stimuli are assumed to induce defensive behavior and make defense-related stimuli positively reinforcing. (For a different view of perceptual processes in defensive behavior, see Bolles and Fanselow, 1980.)

The consummatory-stimulus-reward hypothesis

predicts that animals will rapidly acquire various nonbiological defense responses in avoidance conditioning provided that these responses result in defense consummatory stimuli. Crawford and Masterson (1978) tested this prediction in a study with rats conditioned to press a response lever in a discriminated avoidance task. Two groups of subjects were reinforced for the lever-press avoidance response with defense consummatory stimuli associated with fleeing. One of these groups was allowed to run to a safe compartment on making the lever-press response; the second group was carried to the safe compartment contingent on lever pressing. A third group of rats served as controls and remained in the experimental chamber after each lever press. Consistent with the consummatory-stimulus-reward hypothesis, getting to the safe compartment contingent on lever pressing significantly facilitated the discriminated avoidance behavior. This was true whether the rats actually performed the flight response or were carried to the safe compartment by the experimenter. A second experiment (Masterson, Crawford, & Bartter, 1978) showed that remaining in the safe compartment between trials facilitated avoidance performance. However, getting to the safe area was sufficient to produce rapid avoidance learning even if subjects were returned to the shock box for most of the intertrial interval.

The consummatory-stimulus-reward hypothesis takes an interesting but largely untested approach to the analysis of avoidance learning. Further experimental tests of the theory will have to pay particular attention to the distinction between this hypothesis and the safety-signal hypothesis. We already know that introducing distinctive response feedback cues greatly facilitates avoidance learning because such stimuli become conditioned inhibitors of fear. The consummatory-stimulus-reward hypothesis assumes that certain types of feedback cues (those that result from innate SSDRs) are much more effective as reinforcers for avoidance behavior than arbitrary auditory and visual stimuli. In further contrast to the safety-signal hypothesis, it assumes that the positive reinforcing effect of these special stimuli is immediately instituted when an animal encounters an aversive situation and does not depend on a period of inhibitory conditioning. Future research will have to provide evidence relevant to these claims before consummatory reward stimuli can be accepted as yet another source of reinforcement for avoidance behavior.

The avoidance puzzle: Concluding comments

We have learned a great deal about avoidance behavior in the 40 years since Mowrer and Lamoreaux (1942) puzzled about how "not getting something" can motivate avoidance responses. As we saw, numerous ingenious answers to this puzzle have been provided. Two-process theory, conditioned inhibition reinforcement, shock-frequency reduction reinforcement, and consummatory-stimulus reward all provide different views of what happens after an avoidance response to reinforce it. In contrast, the SSDR account suggests a punishment alternative to reinforcement theories. None of these theories can explain all the data. However, each provides useful ideas in understanding various aspects of avoidance behavior. For example, none of the more recent formulations is as useful in explaining the acquired-drive experiments as two-process theory. The conditioned inhibition theory is particularly useful in explaining free-operant avoidance behavior, the results of studies of the role of response feedback stimuli in avoidance conditioning, and the maintenance of avoidance behavior in the absence of much fear elicited by a warning stimulus. In contrast, the SSDR and consummatory-stimulus-reward theories are very useful in considering what happens during early stages of avoidance training. They also provide important ideas about why certain responses are much more easily acquired than others in avoidance situations. Given the complexities of avoidance learning, the use of several conceptual frameworks to explain all the data may be inescapable.

Punishment

Although most of us engage in avoidance behavior of one sort or another every day, there is little public awareness of or concern about what is involved in making avoidance responses. This may be because avoidance conditioning is rarely used to control others' behavior. In contrast, the other aversive conditioning process we will discuss, punishment, has always been of great concern to people. In some situations punishment is used as a form of retribution or as a price for undesirable behavior. The threat of punishment is also frequently used to encourage adherence to religious and civil codes of conduct. Many institutions and rules have evolved to ensure that punishment will be administered in ways that are deemed ethical and acceptable to society. Furthermore, what constitutes justified punishment in the criminal justice system, in child rearing, in schools, and elsewhere is a matter of continual debate.

In contrast to societal concerns about punishment, for many years experimental psychologists did not devote much attention to the topic. On the basis of a few experiments, Thorndike (1932) and Skinner (1938, 1953) concluded that punishment is not a very effective method for controlling behavior and has only temporary effects at best (see also Estes, 1944). This claim was not seriously challenged until the 1960s, when punishment processes began to be much more extensively investigated (Azrin & Holz, 1966; Campbell & Church, 1969; Church, 1963; Solomon, 1964). We will describe the effects of punishment on positively reinforced instrumental behavior. In such situations punishment can be a very effective technique for modifying behavior. In fact, punishment often suppresses responding in just one or two trials. Thus, punishment typically produces a change in behavior much more rapidly than other forms of instrumental conditioning, such as positive reinforcement or avoidance.

Experimental analysis of punishment

The basic punishment procedure involves presenting an aversive stimulus after a specified response. The usual outcome of the procedure is that the specified response becomes suppressed. By not making the punished response, the subject avoids the aversive stimulation. Because punishment involves the suppression of behavior, it can be observed only with responses that are likely to occur in the absence

of punishment. To ensure occurrence of the behavior, experimental studies of punishment usually also involve reinforcement of the punished response with something like food or water. Therefore, the subjects frequently face a conflict between responding to obtain positive reinforcement and not responding to avoid punishment. The degree of response suppression that occurs is determined both by variables related to presentation of the aversive stimulus and by variables related to the availability of positive reinforcement.

Characteristics of the aversive stimulus and its method of introduction.   A great variety of aversive stimuli have been used in punishment experiments, including electrical shock, a blast of air, loud noise, a physical slap, and a cue previously conditioned with shock (Azrin, 1958; Hake & Azrin, 1965; Masserman, 1946; Skinner, 1938). Other response suppression procedures have involved the loss of positive reinforcement, time out from positive reinforcement, and overcorrection (Foxx & Azrin, 1973; Thomas, 1968; Trenholme & Baron, 1975). **Time out** refers to removal of the opportunity to obtain positive reinforcement. Time out is often used to punish children, as when a child is told "Go to your room" after doing something bad. **Overcorrection** involves requiring a person not only to rectify what was done badly but to overcorrect for the mistake. For example, a child who has placed an object in his mouth may be asked to remove the object and also to wash out his mouth with an antiseptic solution.

The response suppression produced by punishment depends in part on certain features of the aversive stimulus. The effects of various characteristics of the aversive event have been most extensively investigated with shock. The general finding has been that more intense and longer shocks are more effective in suppressing responding (see reviews by Azrin & Holz, 1966; Church, 1969; Walters & Grusec, 1977). Low-intensity aversive stimulation produces only moderate suppression of responding, and the disruption of behavior may recover with continued exposure to the punishment procedure (for example, Azrin, 1960). In contrast, if the aversive stimulus is sufficiently intense, responding may be completely suppressed for a long time. In one experiment, for example, high-intensity punishment completely suppressed the instrumental response for 6 days (Azrin, 1960).

Another very important factor in punishment is how the aversive stimulus is introduced. If a high intensity of shock is used when the punishment procedure is first introduced, the instrumental response will be severely suppressed. Much less suppression of behavior will occur if initially a mild punishment is used, with the shock intensity gradually increased during the course of continued punishment training (Azrin, Holz, & Hake, 1963; Miller, 1960; see also Banks, 1976). Thus, subjects can be protected from the effects of intense punishment by first being exposed to lower levels of shock that do not produce much response suppression. It appears that because a low intensity of punishment does not disrupt responding very much, subjects learn to persist in making the instrumental response in the presence of the aversive stimulation. This learning then generalizes to higher intensities of shock, with the result that the instrumental response continues to be made when the more aversive punishment is used.

The above findings suggest that subjects adopt a particular mode of responding during their initial exposure to punishment, and this type of behavior generalizes to new punishment situations (Church, 1969). This idea has an interesting implication. Suppose that subjects are first exposed to intense shock that results in a very low level of responding. The mode of behavior adopted during initial exposure to punishment is severe suppression of responding. If the shock intensity is subsequently reduced, the severe suppression of behavior should persist, resulting in less responding than if the mild shock had been used from the beginning. Results like this have been obtained by Raymond (reported in Church, 1969). Thus, initial exposure to mild aversive stimulation that does not disrupt behavior very much *reduces* the effects of later intense punishment. In contrast, initial exposure to intense aversive stimulation *increases* the suppressive effects of later mild punishment.

Response-contingent versus response-independent aversive stimulation.   Another impor-

tant variable that determines the extent to which aversive stimulation suppresses behavior is whether the aversive stimulus is presented contingent on a specified response or independently of behavior. Response-independent aversive stimulation can result in some suppression of instrumental behavior. However, the general finding is that significantly more suppression of behavior occurs if the aversive stimulus is produced by the instrumental response (for example, Azrin, 1956; Camp, Raymond, & Church, 1967; Frankel, 1975). In one experiment (Church, 1969), three groups of rats were reinforced for pressing a response lever on a variable-interval 1-min schedule of food reinforcement. Then punishment was introduced while the food reinforcement was continued. One group was never shocked. The second group received response-independent aversive stimulation. A brief shock was presented every 2 min, on the average, irrespective of the rats' lever pressing. The third group received response-contingent aversive stimulation. The brief shock became available on the average of every 2 min but was delivered to the subjects only if they made a lever-press response, at which time it was delivered immediately after the response. The results are summarized in Figure 9.12. The data are presented in the form of suppression ratios that compare the rate of responding during the punishment phase of the experiment with the rate observed before punishment was introduced. A score of .5 indicates no suppression of responding, and a score of 0 indicates complete suppression of the lever-press behavior. As you can see, the response-independent shocks produced a small suppression of responding that started to dissipate after the third session. In contrast, response-contingent shocks produced a severe and lasting suppression of lever pressing. Thus, response-produced aversive stimulation was much more effective in suppressing behavior than response-independent aversive stimulation. (See also Bolles, Holtz, Dunn, & Hill, 1980.)

Effects of delay of punishment.   In response-independent procedures, the aversive stimulus may occur immediately after the instrumental response on some occasions and a long time after the response on other occasions. Explicit investigation of the interval

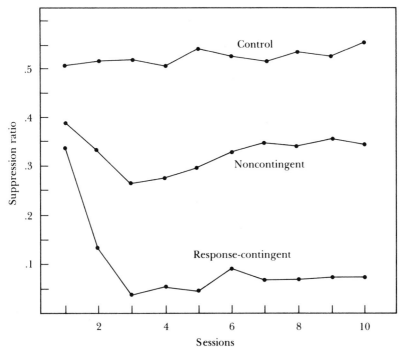

FIGURE 9.12.   Degree of response suppression observed during ten successive sessions. The control group did not receive shock. The noncontingent group received shocks independent of behavior, and the response-contingent group was shocked when it responded.   *(From Church, 1969.)*

between instrumental behavior and aversive stimulation has shown that this variable greatly influences the degree of response suppression. The general finding is that increasing the interval between the instrumental response and delivery of punishment results in less suppression of behavior (for example, Baron, 1965; Camp et al., 1967). This relation is particularly important in attempts to use punishment to modify behavior outside the laboratory. Inadvertent delays may occur if the undesired response is not detected right away, if it takes time to investigate who is actually at fault for an error, or if preparing the aversive stimulus requires time. Such delays can make punishment totally ineffective in modifying the undesired behavior.

Effects of schedules of punishment.   Just as positive reinforcement does not have to be provided for each occurrence of the instrumental response,

punishment may also be delivered only intermittently. For example, instead of punishing every occurrence of the instrumental response, punishment may be provided after a fixed number of responses. Such a procedure is called a "fixed-ratio punishment schedule." In one study of fixed-ratio punishment, pigeons were first reinforced with food on a variable-interval schedule for pecking a response key (Azrin et al., 1963). When the key-pecking behavior was occurring at a stable and high rate, punishment was introduced. Various fixed-ratio punishment procedures were tested while food reinforcement continued to be provided for the pecking behavior. The results are summarized in Figure 9.13. When every response was shocked (FR 1 punishment), key pecking ceased entirely. With the other punishment schedules, the rate of responding depended on the frequency of punishment. Higher fixed-ratio schedules allow more responses to go unpunished. Not surprisingly,

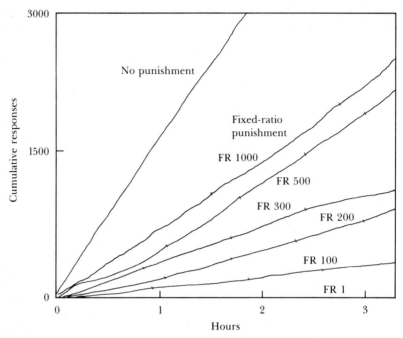

FIGURE 9.13.   Cumulative record of pecking when the response was not punished and when the response was punished according to various fixed-ratio schedules of punishment. The oblique slashes indicate the delivery of punishment. Responding was reinforced on a variable-interval 3-min schedule.   *(From Azrin, Holz, & Hake, 1963.)*

therefore, higher rates of responding occurred when higher fixed-ratio punishment schedules were used. However, some suppression of behavior was observed even when only every 1000th response was followed by shock.

Effects of schedules of positive reinforcement.

As we noted earlier, in most studies of punishment the instrumental response is simultaneously maintained by a positive reinforcement schedule so that there is some level of responding available to be punished. As it turns out, the effects of a punishment procedure are in part determined by this positive reinforcement. When behavior is maintained by either a fixed- or a variable-interval schedule of positive reinforcement, punishment produces a decrease in the overall rate of responding. However, the temporal distribution of the behavior is not disturbed. That is, during the punishment procedure, variable-interval positive reinforcement produces a suppressed but

stable rate of responding (see Figure 9.13), whereas fixed-interval positive reinforcement produces the typical scalloped pattern of responding (for example, Azrin & Holz, 1961). The outcome is considerably different if the behavior is maintained by a fixed-ratio positive reinforcement schedule. As we noted in Chapter 6, fixed-ratio schedules produce a pause in responding just after reinforcement (the postreinforcement pause), followed by a high and steady rate of responding to complete the number of responses necessary for the next reinforcement (the ratio run). Punishment usually increases the length of the postreinforcement pause but has little effect on the ratio run (Azrin, 1959). The initial responses of a fixed-ratio run are much more susceptible to punishment than later responses. Thus, shock delivered early in a ratio run increases the postreinforcement pause more than shock delivered later in the completion of the ratio (Dardano & Sauerbrunn, 1964; see also Church, 1969). Another important aspect of positive reinforcement schedules is the frequency of reinforcement provided. Generally, punishment has less effect on instrumental responses that produce more frequent positive reinforcement (for example, Church & Raymond, 1967).

Availability of alternative responses for obtaining positive reinforcement. In many experiments, the punished response is also the only response the subject can perform to obtain positive reinforcement, such as food. By decreasing its rate of responding, the subject may decrease the number of food pellets it receives. Therefore, the subject is in a conflict between suppressing its behavior to avoid punishment and responding to obtain positive reinforcement. This predicament does not exist if alternative responses for obtaining positive reinforcement are available. In this case, the subject can entirely cease making the punished response without having to forgo positive reinforcement. As one might expect, the availability of an alternative source of reinforcement greatly increases the suppression of responding produced by punishment. In one study, for example, adult males were seated in front of two response levers, and pressing either response lever was reinforced with a cigarette on a variable-interval schedule (Herman & Azrin, 1964). After the behavior was occurring at a stable rate, responses on one of the levers resulted in a brief obnoxious noise. In one experimental condition, only one response lever was available during the punishment phase. In another condition, both response levers were accessible, and responding on one of them was punished with the loud noise. Figure 9.14 shows the results. When the punished response was the only way to obtain cigarettes, punishment produced a moderate suppression of behavior. In contrast, when the alternative response lever was available, responding on the punished lever ceased altogether. Thus, the availability of an alternative response for obtaining positive reinforcement greatly increased the suppressive effects of punishment. Similar results have been obtained in other situations. For example, children punished for playing with certain toys are much less likely to play with these if they are allowed to play with other toys instead (Perry & Parke, 1975).

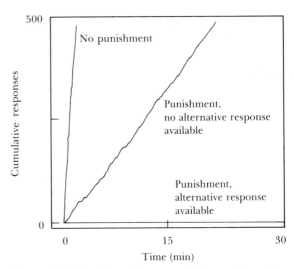

FIGURE 9.14. Cumulative record of responding when responses are not punished, when responses are punished and there is no alternative source of reinforcement, and when responses are punished but an alternative reinforced response is available. *(From Azrin & Holz, 1966; after Herman & Azrin, 1964.)*

Effects of a discriminative stimulus for punishment. As we saw in Chapter 8, if positive reinforcement is available for responding in the presence of a distinctive stimulus but is not available in its absence, the subject will learn to respond only when the stimulus is present. The suppressive effects of punishment can also be brought under stimulus control. This occurs if responding is punished in the presence of a discriminative stimulus but is not punished when the stimulus is absent. Such a procedure is called **discriminative punishment.** With continued exposure to discriminative punishment, the suppressive effects of punishment will come to be limited to the presence of the discriminative stimulus.

In one of the first experiments of this type, Dinsmoor (1952) reinforced rats with food on a variable-interval 2-min schedule for pressing a response lever. After responding had stabilized, successive 5-min periods of punishment were alternated with 5-min periods of no punishment. During the punishment periods, the lights in the experimental chamber were turned off, and each lever-press response resulted in a brief shock. During the safe periods, the lights were turned on and no shocks were delivered. (Food reinforcement continued during both the punishment periods and the safe periods.) The rats quickly learned to restrict their lever-press responses to the safe periods. When the lights were turned off, signaling that the punishment procedure was in effect, responding was suppressed. However, responding resumed whenever the lights were turned back on, signaling that responses would not be punished.

The fact that the suppressive effects of punishment can be limited to the presence of discriminative stimuli is often problematic in applications of punishment. In many situations, the person who administers the punishment also serves as a discriminative stimulus for punishment, with the result that the undesired behavior is suppressed only as long as he or she is present. If one teacher is more strict about discipline than another, children will learn to suppress their rambunctious behavior in that class more than in other classes. If one parent is stricter than another, children will be better behaved in the presence of the stricter parent. A Highway Patrol car is a discriminative stimulus for punishment for speeding. Drivers are more likely to obey speed laws in areas where they see many patrol cars than in unpatrolled stretches of highway.

Punishment as a signal for the availability of positive reinforcement.

Punishment does not always suppress behavior. In fact, in certain situations people seem to seek out punishment. Does this represent a breakdown of the normal mechanisms of behavior, or can such behavior be explained by the principles we have discussed so far? Experimental evidence suggests that conventional behavioral mechanisms may lead to such seemingly abnormal behavior. Punishment seeking can result from a situation in which positive reinforcement is available only when the instrumental response is also punished. In such circumstances, punishment may become a signal, or discriminative stimulus, for the availability of positive reinforcement. If this occurs, punishment will increase rather than suppress responding.

In one demonstration of the discriminative stimulus properties of punishment, pigeons were first trained to peck a response key for food reinforce-

ment on a variable-interval schedule (Holz & Azrin, 1961). Each response was then punished by a mild shock sufficient to reduce the response rate by about 50%. In the next phase of the experiment, periods in which the punishment procedure was in effect were alternated with periods in which punishment was not scheduled. In addition, the pecking response was reinforced with food only during the punishment periods. The punishment and safe periods were not signaled by an exteroceptive stimulus, such as a light or a tone. Therefore, the only way for subjects to tell whether reinforcement was available was to see whether they were punished for pecking. Under these circumstances higher rates of pecking occurred during punishment periods than during safe periods. Punishment became a discriminative stimulus for food reinforcement.

Other instances of self-punitive behavior.

Self-punitive behavior is of considerable interest because it occurs in many forms of human behavior pathology and sometimes is highly ritualized. During the Middle Ages in Europe, for example, Flagellants traveled from place to place beating one another to purge themselves of sin.

Making punishment a discriminative stimulus for positive reinforcement is one way to create self-punitive behavior. Self-punitive behavior can also result from prior escape training. This phenomenon, sometimes called **vicious-circle behavior,** has been extensively investigated in runway situations with rats. In a typical experiment, the animals are first given escape training in which the entire runway is electrified and they have to run the length of the alley to escape shock and reach a safe goal box. After the subjects have learned the runway escape response, an extinction procedure is introduced for control subjects; shock is no longer presented in any segment of the runway. For experimental subjects, a portion of the runway (say, the last third of the alley) remains electrified. Thus, the experimental subjects encounter shock if they run during extinction, whereas the control subjects do not receive punishment. The remarkable finding is that punishment increases the resistance to extinction of the running response in the experimental subjects. Instead of suppressing behavior, punishment of a conditioned escape behavior facilitates responding. (For a further discussion of this phenomenon, see Brown, 1969; Brown & Cunningham, 1981; Melvin, 1971.)

Response limitations on the effectiveness of punishment.   The vicious-circle behavior described above illustrates the resistance to punishment of a learned defensive response (a conditioned escape response). Other studies have provided evidence that unlearned, or innate, defensive responses are also somewhat resistant to punishment. Shettleworth (1978a, 1981), for example, investigated the suscepti-

bility to punishment of various response patterns in hamsters and found that open-rearing (rearing up on the hind legs without touching a wall of the experimental chamber) was significantly less susceptible to punishment than was scrabbling (rapid movements of the forepaws against a side wall of the experimental chamber, as in a digging motion). This difference appeared to be due to the fact that, unlike scrabbling, open-rearing is an innate defensive behavior in hamsters—it is increased by response-independent shocks. (For additional examples of the resistance of defensive behavior to punishment, see Melvin & Ervey, 1973; Walters & Glazer, 1971.)

BOX 9.2.   When punishment doesn't work

Sometimes children are brought to a therapist because their behavior is out of control. In a typical example the child is unruly and does not respond to the disciplinary practices of parents or teachers. Even punishment, used as a last resort, does not work. The parents or teachers complain that punishing the child only makes the behavior worse. It is not uncommon for children with a severe problem of this type to be diagnosed as hyperactive or emotionally disturbed. These labels suggest there is something fundamentally wrong with the child. Behavior therapists, however, have found that in some cases the problem may be nothing more than the result of mismanaged discipline. The parents or teachers may have inadvertently established punishment as a discriminative stimulus for positive reinforcement. Instead of decreasing some undesirable behavior, punishment increases it. How can this happen?

Let us take the hypothetical situation of Johnny, who lives in a home with two busy parents. Johnny, like most children, is rather active. If he is quietly playing in his room, the parents are likely to ignore him and engage in activities of their own. In contrast, if Johnny behaves badly or makes demands, the parents are forced to attend to him. The parents may be giving Johnny attention only when he is misbehaving or making demands. Any time he is not being a problem, the parents may be thankfully relieved to have a moment's peace. Thus, rather than reinforcing cooperative or peaceful behavior, the parents can come to ignore Johnny at these times. What we have then is a vicious cycle. The more Johnny misbehaves, the less attention he is given for nondisruptive behavior, because the parents come to cherish quiet moments as a chance to do something on their own. Misbehavior becomes his main means of obtaining attention. The punishments and reprimands that go with the behavior signal to the child that the parents are caring and attending.

In actuality the therapist does not have the opportunity to observe how behavior problems of this type originate. The "discriminative value of punishment" explanation is supported by the outcome of attempts to change the situation. The hypothesis suggests that if one changes the attention patterns, Johnny's behavior problem can be alleviated. Indeed, clinical psychologists often show parents how to attend to appropriate and constructive activities and to use punishment with as little attention as possible. In many cases dramatic improvement ensues when parents are able to positively reinforce cooperative behavior with their attentions and ignore disruptive activities as much as possible.

Punishment and response reallocation. In Chapter 7 we discussed how reinforcement of a particular response may cause a reorganization, or reallocation, of the organism's entire behavioral repertoire. Reinforcement often increases the future likelihood of the reinforced response and decreases some other activities the subject might perform. Punishment likewise produces a reallocation of the subject's behavior. Suppression of the punished response may be accompanied by increases in some other activities as well as, possibly, decreases in certain nonpunished responses. In one experiment, for example, thirsty rats were given access to a running wheel and a drinking tube at the same time (Dunham, 1972). The rats were then punished for drinking. As expected, punishment suppressed the drinking response. However, punishment also increased the amount of time the rats spent running in the wheel. Such compensatory increases in nonpunished responses have been observed in a variety of situations. Typically not all the animal's nonpunished responses increase when one response is selected out for punishment. Rather, it is often the most likely of the nonpunished responses that becomes increased (Dunham, 1971, 1978). Reorganization of the subject's response profile can also involve decreases in the rate of nonpunished responses. For example, in guinea pigs the punishment of certain responses (open-rearing, scrabbling, or face washing) results in an increase in freezing and a walk/sniff behavior as well as a decrease in unpunished wall-rearing and gnawing (Shettleworth, 1978a). Research on such reorganizations of behavior is still in its infancy, and it is not entirely clear precisely what mechanisms determine the outcome in punishment situations (see Dunham, 1978; Shettleworth, 1978a).

Theories of punishment

In contrast to the study of avoidance behavior, investigations of punishment, by and large, have not been motivated by theoretical considerations. Most of the evidence available about the effects of punishment has been the product of empirical curiosity. The investigators were interested in finding out how punishment is influenced by various manipulations rather than in testing certain theoretical formula-

tions. In fact, there are few systematic theories of punishment, and most of these were formulated in some form more than 30 years ago. We will describe three of the most prominent theories.

Conditioned emotional response theory of punishment. One of the first theories of punishment was proposed by Estes (1944) and is based on the observation by Estes and Skinner (1941) that a conditioned stimulus that has been paired with shock will suppress the performance of food-reinforced instrumental behavior. We discussed this conditioned suppression, or conditioned emotional response, procedure earlier in this chapter as well as in Chapters 3 and 5. The standard conditioned suppression experiment involves first conditioning animals to make an instrumental response, such as lever pressing, for food reinforcement. Classical conditioning is then conducted in which a CS (a tone or light, for example) is paired with a brief shock. The conditioned aversive stimulus is then presented while the animal is allowed to lever-press for the food reinforcement. The usual result is that responding is disrupted during presentations of the CS. This response suppression was originally interpreted as resulting from competing responses elicited by the CS. The basic idea was that the conditioned stimulus came to elicit certain emotional responses (such as freezing) by virtue of being paired with shock. These conditioned emotional responses were presumably incompatible with making the lever-press response (the rat could not freeze and press the lever at the same time). Therefore, the rate of lever pressing was suppressed during presentations of the CS.

Estes (1944) proposed that punishment suppresses behavior through the same mechanism that produces conditioned suppression to a shock-paired CS. In contrast to the conditioned suppression experiment, however, punishment procedures usually do not involve an explicit CS that signals the impending delivery of shock. Estes suggested that the various stimuli the subject experiences just before making the punished response serve this function. For example, just before the rat presses a response lever, it experiences the visual and other spatial cues that exist near the lever, the tactile cues of the lever, and perhaps proprioceptive stimuli that result from its posture just as it is about to make the lever press. When the response is punished, all these stimuli become paired with shock. With repetition of the punishment episode, the various preresponse stimuli become strongly conditioned by the shock. As these cues acquire conditioned aversive properties, they will come to elicit conditioned emotional responses that are incompatible with the punished behavior. Thus, the punished response will become suppressed.

The conditioned emotional response theory can explain a great many facts about punishment. For example, the fact that more intense and longer-duration shocks produce more response suppression can be explained by assuming that the stimuli conditioned by these aversive events elicit more vigorous conditioned emotional responses. The theory can also explain why response-contingent aversive stimulation produces more response suppression than response-independent delivery of shock. If shock is produced by the instrumental response, the stimuli that become conditioned by the shock are more likely to be closely related to performance of this behavior. Therefore, the conditioned emotional responses are more likely to interfere with the punished response.

In a reformulation of the conditioned emotional response theory, Estes (1969) has proposed an alternative account of the mechanisms of conditioned suppression. The new formulation may be paraphrased in motivational terms. The basic idea is that a shock-conditioned stimulus disrupts food-reinforced responding because it evokes an emotional or motivational state (let us say fear) that is incompatible with the motivation maintaining the food-reinforced behavior. The shock-conditioned stimulus is assumed to inhibit the motivation to respond based on positive reinforcement. This revision is compatible with modern two-process theory, which we will discuss in Chapter 10. As we shall see, modern two-process theory also assumes that motivational states elicited by a classically conditioned stimulus can interact with or influence the motivational state created by an instrumental conditioning procedure.

Avoidance theory of punishment. An ingenious alternative to the conditioned emotional response theory regards punishment as a form of avoidance behavior. This theory is most closely associated

with Dinsmoor (1954, 1977) and follows the tradition of the two-process theory of avoidance. Dinsmoor accepted the notion that the stimuli that set the occasion for the instrumental response become conditioned by the aversive stimulus when the response is punished. Thus, these stimuli were assumed to acquire conditioned aversive properties in much the same manner as stated in the conditioned emotional response theory. However, Dinsmoor added a second process to the mechanism of punishment. He proposed that subjects learn to escape from the conditioned aversive stimuli related to the punished response by engaging in some other behavior that is incompatible with the punished activity. Since this other behavior is incompatible with the punished response, performance of the alternative activity results in suppression of the punished behavior. Thus, the avoidance theory explains punishment in terms of the acquisition of incompatible avoidance responses.

The avoidance theory of punishment is an ingenious proposal. It suggests that all changes produced by aversive instrumental conditioning, be they increases or decreases in the likelihood of a response, can be explained by the same response-strengthening mechanisms. Suppression of behavior is not viewed as reflecting the weakening of the punished response. Rather, it is explained in terms of the strengthening of competing responses that effectively avoid the aversive stimulation. Thus, a single theoretical framework is used to analyze the outcomes of both punishment and avoidance procedures. Such economy has always been considered desirable in scientific explanations.

Despite its cleverness and parsimony, the avoidance theory of punishment is not uniformly applauded. First, because it explains punishment in terms of avoidance mechanisms, all the theoretical problems that have been troublesome in the analysis of avoidance behavior become problems that have to be solved in the analysis of punishment as well. Another challenge for the theory is that its critical elements are not stated in a way that makes them easily accessible to experimental verification (Rachlin & Herrnstein, 1969; Schuster & Rachlin, 1968). The stimuli that are assumed to acquire conditioned aversive properties are not under the direct control of the experimenter. Rather, they are events that one assumes the subject experiences when it is about to make the punished response. Similarly, the activities the subject learns to perform to avoid making the punished response are ill specified. The theory does not tell us what these responses will be in a given situation or how one might look for them. The theory also provides a rather cumbersome explanation of the outcome of experiments on concurrent-chain schedules of punishment (for example, Schuster & Rachlin, 1968). However, the theory has remained compatible with most of the facts about punishment, perhaps because it is stated in a way that makes experimental tests of it difficult.

Punishment and the negative law of effect. The third and last concept about punishment that we shall consider is also the oldest. Thorndike (1911) originally proposed that positive reinforcement and punishment involve symmetrically opposite processes. Just as positive reinforcement strengthens behavior, so punishment weakens it. In later years Thorndike abandoned the idea that punishment weakens behavior because he failed to find supporting evidence in some of his experiments (Thorndike, 1932). However, the belief that there is a negative law of effect that is comparable but opposite to the familiar positive law of effect has retained favor with some investigators (for example, Azrin & Holz, 1966; Rachlin & Herrnstein, 1969).

One approach to the analysis of the negative law of effect has been initiated by Premack and his colleagues. As we discussed in Chapter 7, Premack proposed that positive reinforcement occurs when the opportunity to engage in a highly valued activity is made dependent on the prior performance of an activity of lower value. The subject allocates time according to this restriction. The instrumental response is increased and the reinforcing behavior is decreased by the contingency. According to Premack, the punishment contingency reverses this relation. Here, a low-valued activity is made to occur contingent on the performance of a higher-valued behavior. Undergoing shock, for example, has a much lower probability than pressing a lever for food. Hence, shock can punish lever pressing.

Premack and his colleagues tested this idea about punishment using a motor-driven running wheel equipped with a drinking tube. In one experiment (Weisman & Premack, 1966), rats were deprived of water, so that drinking was more probable than running. Then a punishment procedure was introduced in which a bout of drinking was followed by a period of forced running. (The motor attached to the running wheel was turned on to force the rats to run.) Under these conditions, drinking was suppressed by running. Thus, a punishment effect was obtained. This and other experiments (see Premack, 1971a) illustrate that the punishing effects of forced running are similar to those of shock. The studies by Premack and his colleagues also illustrate the comparability of reinforcement and punishment. In the Weisman/Premack experiment, the same contingency (running after drinking) produced opposite effects depending on the relative values of running and drinking. When running was made more likely than drinking (by no longer water-depriving the rats), running reinforced drinking. Thus, running after drinking punished or reinforced drinking, depending on whether running was less or more valuable than drinking.

With a reinforcement procedure the instrumental response is increased and the reinforcing response is decreased relative to a baseline free-responding situation. With a punishment procedure the instrumental response is decreased and the reinforcing or punishing response is increased relative to a baseline condition. Moreover, in both cases the response that increases is the low-valued behavior and the one that decreases is the higher-valued behavior. Viewed in this way, the procedures of reinforcement and punishment produce the same effects. Operationally, there is only one significant difference. In punishment the subject has to be forced to engage in the lower-valued activity. Rats do not ordinarily apply electrical shocks to themselves or run more than they want. In reinforcement the subject is "induced" to engage in the lower-valued activity by the contingency itself.

The similarity between punishment and reinforcement described above was tested in an interesting experiment involving toy-playing behavior in children (Burkhard, Rachlin, & Schrader, 1978). In a baseline phase, children were observed playing with three toys. The toys were ranked high, medium, and low on the basis of how much time the children spent with each one. The children were assigned to reinforcement and punishment groups. For the reinforcement group 1 min of playing with the high-ranked toy was allowed after 1 min of play with the low-ranked toy. For the punishment group, 1 min of play with the low-ranked toy was required after 1 min of play with the high-ranked toy. In both cases the medium toy provided background activity and could be used freely. If Premack's punishment hypothesis is correct, the reinforcement and punishment procedures should produce the same new distribution of time among the three toys. This in fact was the result. The reinforcement and punishment groups were indistinguishable in how much time they ended up playing with each toy. Playing with the low-ranked toy increased and playing with the high-ranked toy decreased to comparable levels for the two groups.

Research along the lines Premack has proposed is continuing. As in the case of positive reinforcement, the work suggests that punishment imposes a restriction against which behavior has to be adjusted. The negative law of effect, in light of this approach, is a statement of the way behavior changes under these restrictions: a low-valued activity produces a decrease in a higher-valued activity. Economically minded theorists propose, as in the case of positive reinforcement (see Chapter 7), that the subject responds so as to maximize overall value. The maximization process, with both reinforcement and punishment procedures, involves an increase in a low-valued activity balanced against a decrease in a high-valued activity and may include effects on other behaviors as well.

Use of punishment outside the laboratory

Nowhere in the application of the principles of learning and conditioning is there more controversy than in the application of aversive control procedures. Books to guide parents in the use of discipline disagree on whether punishment is useful or should be used at all; controversy rages in the courts and on school boards over whether punishment may be used by teachers in the classroom and by therapists in hospitals; much debate has occurred over the centu-ries on the proper use of aversive control in the criminal justice system. What is the basis for all this debate? On closer inspection we see that the issues concern both the practical problems involved in the application of aversive control procedures and moral questions that arise when one person does harm to another.

Practical problems in the use of punishment. One argument that has been used against the application of punishment is that it does not work. However, this is likely to be true only if punishment is used inappropriately. The preceding review of research findings suggests a number of ways to maximize the effectiveness of punishment. Punishment should be made response-contingent and delivered immediately after the unwanted response. The aversive stimulus should be intense enough to suppress the behavior from the start of punishment training so that the subject does not learn to persist in responding in the face of punishment. Punishment should not be administered intermittently, and positive reinforcement for the unwanted response should be minimized; positive reinforcement should be provided for alternative responses rather than for the punished response. Punishment procedures should avoid providing discriminative stimuli for punishment and making punishment a discriminative stimulus for positive reinforcement. Finally, efforts should be made not to condition the punished response as a defensive behavior prior to the introduction of punishment. Applications of punishment outside the laboratory often violate one or another of these prescriptions for effective use.

Punishment has also been criticized on the grounds that it produces an overall suppression in the individual's behavior rather than just a suppression of the punished response. Some people claim that using punishment as a means of disciplining a child merely stifles the child's normal overall activity. Recent research, however, does not support this claim. Earlier in the chapter we reviewed evidence that punishment indeed suppresses particular responses. In addition, we know that punishment leads to a reallocation of behavior that often includes an increase in certain nonpunished responses (for example, Dunham,

1978). Some suppression of other nonpunished responses may also occur. However, this decrease is rarely as great as the suppression of the punished response (for example, Church, Wooten, & Matthews, 1970).

Another reservation about the use of punishment is that it has undesirable side effects, such as aggression, escape, and hostility. Some parents and teachers do not like to use punishment because the child may become hostile, throw tantrums, try to run away, or come to hate the parents, teachers, or school. The adult may find these side effects far more difficult to deal with than the original undesired responses. Advocates of criminal justice reform often cite the fact that a prison sentence frequently does not produce the hoped-for reform in the criminal. Rather, the convict may return to society with more hostility than before. This hostility, together with newly acquired antisocial skills learned from other prisoners, may be more detrimental to society in the long run than the original transgression.

Laboratory investigations have documented the undesirable side effects of punishment. Several investigators have studied behaviors elicited by aversive events used in punishment procedures. Shock, for example, can elicit aggression. If two animals are placed in an experimental chamber together and shocked, they will assume an attack posture and fight for the duration of the shock (for example, Ulrich, Hutchinson, & Azrin, 1965). Similarly, monkeys will bite a rubber hose (Hutchinson, Azrin, & Hake, 1966), and humans will show jaw-clenching movements when aversively stimulated. These elicited responses occur when aversive stimuli are presented contingent on an instrumental response, as in punishment (see Hutchinson, 1977). Hence, it is not surprising that children may turn and hit the parent after punishment or that a prisoner may strike out at available objects of aggression on being sentenced or incarcerated.

Punishment can also motivate escape from the punishment situation. Laboratory experiments have shown that rats and pigeons will learn an instrumental response whose only consequence is escape from a punishment situation (for example, Azrin, Hake, Holz, & Hutchinson, 1965; Hearst & Sidman, 1961).

Outside the laboratory such escape may present a serious problem because the goal of the application of punishment is rarely to drive the individual out of the situation. When we punish a child for not doing house chores or not doing homework, we do not want him to run away from home. When we punish a teenager for smoking in school, we do not want the student to drop out of school or escape the situation by taking psychoactive drugs.

Another undesirable side effect of punishment is that the motivating and eliciting properties of the aversive stimulus may become conditioned to other stimuli present in the situation by way of classical conditioning. Thus, a person administering punishment may become associated with the aversive stimulation. We know that stimuli conditioned by shock and other aversive USs themselves acquire aversive properties. Through this mechanism, the punished subject may come to dislike the teacher, playmate, or parent who delivered the punishment.

A final difficulty concerns the effects on the person who is delivering the aversive stimulus. Delivering punishment is often accompanied by certain reactions in the person who does the punishing. Parents become upset or angry with the undesired activities of their children. It is a rare parent or teacher who can deliver punishment in a purely detached manner. Delivery of punishment can be seen in many cases as an aggressive act elicited by the child's unruly behavior. As such, it may go out of control. Child abuse, battered adults, brutality by prison guards and prisoners are all examples in which punishment has gone out of control. Unfortunately, these are serious problems in our society that we do not understand very well or know how to deal with as yet.

Moral considerations.   It is a safe generalization that most people do not like to be punished. In addition, at least in our more relaxed moments we do not like to inflict punishment on others. Parents do not like to see their children unhappy, teachers do not want to be disliked or perceived as "executioners" by inevitably errant children, and judges do not want to see human life spent unproductively in jail. When we use punishment, we may be reminded of the baser side of human nature, revealed in torture, concentration camps, and the like. However, there are cases in which we purposefully inflict pain in order to prevent a greater pain. We do not think we are executioners if we recommend a trip to the dentist, a vaccination, or a spoon of codliver oil. We do not regard these practices as immoral, because even though they inflict discomfort, they are performed in pursuit of a greater good.

The same rationale is often used in advocating the use of punishment. Most parents do not feel that slapping a toddler for approaching a hot stove or touching an electrical wire is wrong. The overall safety of the child is at stake, and the pain of a slap is insignificant by comparison. Punishment has the tremendous advantage over other behavioral procedures that the suppression of behavior is sometimes immediate when the procedure is applied properly. With alternative methods, such as extinction, the response suppression usually takes longer. To ensure that a toddler will not get burned by a stove, for example, immediate suppression of the behavior is of paramount importance.

The moral dilemma of punishment can be illustrated by the controversy surrounding the use of punishment with autistic children. Autistic children frequently engage in self-injurious behavior, such as banging their heads against a wall, pulling out their hair, or biting themselves. Sometimes the self-injurious behavior is so severe that the child's hands must be bound together to prevent injury. In extreme cases, the child's hands and feet have to be tied to the corners of the bed. Lovaas and his colleagues studied self-injurious behavior in many children (see Carr & Lovaas, 1983; Lovaas & Newsom, 1976). They concluded that, in the cases they observed, the behavior was maintained largely by attention given to the children whenever they mutilated themselves. In attempting to soothe the children, caretakers appeared to be inadvertently reinforcing the self-injurious responses. When the caretakers ignored the behavior, the responses eventually extinguished. However, the extinction period could be long and sometimes began

with an initial increase in self-inflicted injury. In some cases to allow the child to go through extinction would have been very dangerous; the child could have severely injured himself during the extinction process. Lovaas and his colleagues turned to punishment to treat the severe cases. Each instance of self-mutilation was followed by a slap or a brief electrical shock. The result was a quick suppression of the self-injurious behavior.

Naturally, the punishment procedures that were used met with objections. It is our common belief that hitting or shocking children whom we regard as severely ill is fundamentally wrong. However, the research seems to show that our love and attention only serve to promote the self-injurious behavior. Lovaas and his colleagues suggest that the use of punishment with autistic children is a case of small pain inflicted for the greater good of the child. Ten or twelve 1-sec shocks can eliminate self-injurious behavior that otherwise might result in fingers being chewed off, eyes gouged out, noses broken, and the like. Suppressing these self-mutilating behaviors is only one step in the treatment procedure. The fact that the child is no longer engaging in this self-destructive compulsive behavior enables the therapist to go on and establish more socially appropriate behaviors through love and affection. However, the research has not yet elucidated all aspects of the punishment procedures. There are many unanswered questions about the long-range effects of punishing self-mutilation and the effects of this punishment on other behaviors. Such questions have to be answered before a fully informed decision on the therapy of choice can be made.

Although punishment can be effective in certain situations, it must be used with great care. The problems that go along with the use of punishment are very real. Punishment should never be used indiscriminately. However, when used properly in a morally justified situation, punishment can be a useful technique for the suppression of undesired activities.

CHAPTER 10

Interactions of Classical and Instrumental Conditioning

Chapter 10 is devoted to a general discussion of how classical and instrumental conditioning processes may interact. We begin with a description of experiments that have evaluated the possible role of instrumental reinforcement in classical conditioning procedures. We then describe some of the extensive theoretical and experimental work that has been done to assess the role of classical conditioning in instrumental conditioning situations.

Classical and instrumental conditioning are clearly distinguishable conceptually and according to the standard procedures used to investigate them. As we saw in Chapters 3 and 4, classical conditioning is assumed to involve the learning of relations, or associations, between stimuli (usually the CS and the US), and classical conditioning procedures focus on when the stimuli occur in relation to each other independent of what the animal does. In contrast, as we noted in Chapters 5-7, instrumental conditioning is assumed to involve the learning or redistribution of the animal's responses, and instrumental conditioning procedures focus on the relation between occurrences of a specified (instrumental) response and delivery of the reinforcer. Despite these conceptual and procedural distinctions between classical and instrumental conditioning, in practice most conditioning procedures involve instrumental as well as classical components. Conditioning procedures typically involve both stimulus-stimulus and response-outcome relations. Furthermore, isolating the effects of these components is often difficult and sometimes impossible.

We already saw examples of the interaction of classical and instrumental conditioning processes in analyses of discrimination learning (Chapter 8) and avoidance behavior and punishment (Chapter 9). In the present chapter we will consider the interaction of classical and instrumental conditioning more generally. We will first describe the potential role of instrumental conditioning processes in classical conditioning experiments and ways in which investigators have tried to rule out instrumental conditioning. We will then describe the potential role of classical conditioning processes in instrumental learning.

Special procedures have provided some evidence that classical conditioning may occur without much instrumental reinforcement. However, procedures do not exist that permit the occurrence of instrumental learning without the possibility of classical conditioning. Because of this, much theoretical and experimental effort has been devoted to elucidating the role of classical conditioning in instrumental learning situations.

Role of Instrumental Reinforcement in Classical Conditioning Procedures

In classical conditioning procedures, a conditioned stimulus is periodically presented, followed by an unconditioned stimulus. With repetitions of such CS-US trials, the subject comes to make a conditioned response to the CS, but the occurrence of the conditioned response does not determine whether the US is presented. The US is presented irrespective of the conditioned response. In fact, this aspect of classical conditioning is one of the primary bases for distinguishing classical from instrumental training procedures. Nevertheless, for a long time investigators of conditioning mechanisms have been concerned with the fact that an opportunity for instrumental reinforcement exists in many classical conditioning procedures, and this reinforcement may be partly responsible for the ensuing learning (Coleman & Gormezano, 1979; Gormezano & Coleman, 1973).

The potential for instrumental reinforcement in classical conditioning is most obvious in situations in which the subject makes anticipatory conditioned responses. Anticipatory conditioned responses occur before presentation of the unconditioned stimulus on a given trial. This pairing of the CR with the US provides at least two possible opportunities for instrumental reinforcement. First, if the US is a positive reinforcer, such as food, its presentation shortly after the CR may result in unintended reinforcement of the CR. Second, the occurrence of the CR may somehow alter the unconditioned stimulus so as to make the US either more rewarding or more effective in conditioning (for example, Hebb, 1956; Perkins, 1955, 1968). The possibility that conditioned responses may make the US more effective or rewarding was first recognized by Schlosberg (1937). He proposed, for example, that dogs may learn to salivate in a conditioning experiment using food as the US because anticipatory salivation makes it easier to dissolve and swallow dry food. Correspondingly, salivation may be learned in a classical conditioning situation with a drop of acid as the US because anticipatory salivation helps to dilute the aversive taste of the acid. Such instrumental modifications of the US can be postulated to occur in all classical conditioning experiments.

Two experimental strategies have been devised to evaluate the role of instrumental reinforcement in classical conditioning situations. One of these effectively eliminates the possibility of reinforcement of the conditioned response by presentation of the US. The other technique is designed to assess the role of modifications in the unconditioned stimulus caused by the occurrence of the CR, by specifically arranging for such changes in the US. Experiments using both strategies have indicated that instrumental reinforcement is not necessary for the learning that takes place in classical conditioning procedures. Consequently, classical conditioning can be observed even if the situation does not permit the occurrence of instrumental reinforcement.

The omission control procedure

As we noted above, if the US is a positive reinforcer, such as food, presentation of the US following the CR may result in unintended reinforcement of the CR. Investigators have attempted to rule out this kind of instrumental reinforcement by modifying the standard classical conditioning procedure. The modified technique, called the **omission control procedure,** is diagrammed in Figure 10.1. In the omission control procedure, presentation of the US on a given trial depends on whether the conditioned response of interest occurs. If the subject fails to make the conditioned response on a particular trial, the CS is followed by the US in the usual manner. In contrast, if the subject performs the conditioned response,

the US is omitted on that trial. The omission contingency ensures that the specified CR will not be followed by the US. This procedure is assumed to preclude instrumental reinforcement of the conditioned response.

The omission control procedure was introduced by Sheffield (1965) in the study of salivary conditioning in dogs. He tested dogs in conditioning with food and acid in the mouth as unconditioned stimuli. In both types of conditioning, omitting the US when a CR occurred did not prevent development of conditioned salivation. Acquisition of conditioned salivation was generally slower with the omission control procedure than with presentations of the US on all trials. Nevertheless, the omission procedure was remarkably effective. One dog, for example, continued to salivate on about 50% of trials after 800 trials on the omission control procedure.

Since its introduction by Sheffield, the omission control procedure has been tested in a variety of classical conditioning situations (for example, Gormezano & Hiller, 1972; Patten & Rudy, 1967). It has been perhaps most frequently used in studies of sign tracking (see Locurto, 1981, for a review). As we have noted, in sign tracking, animals come to approach and touch (peck, in the case of pigeons) stimuli that signal the delivery of a positive reinforcer, such as food. Investigations of omission control in sign tracking have provided inconsistent results (for example, Hursh, Navarick, & Fantino, 1974; Williams & Williams, 1969).

Peden, Browne, and Hearst (1977) provided one noteworthy demonstration of sign tracking in an omission control procedure. Pigeons were tested in an experimental chamber that had a food hopper built

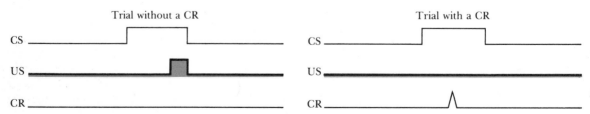

FIGURE 10.1.   Diagram of the omission control procedure. On trials without a conditioned response, the CS is followed by the US in the usual manner (left panel). On trials with a conditioned response, the US is omitted (right panel).

into one wall and a response key built into an adjacent wall 35 cm away. The key light was periodically illuminated for 8 sec, followed by access to grain for 5 sec. Approaching the key light was considered the conditioned response. In the first phase of the experiment (omission control), food delivery at the end of a trial was canceled if the pigeon approached within 20–25 cm of the key-light CS. In phase 2, food always followed illumination of the key light regardless of what the pigeons were doing. The investigators measured the percentage of trials on which the animals approached the light CS during each phase of the experiment.

The results are shown in Figure 10.2. The remarkable finding was that pigeons persisted in approaching the key-light CS during the first phase of the experiment even though such approach responses canceled the delivery of food. Fifty trials were conducted each day, and even after about 2000 trials, the pigeons were observed to approach the CS approximately 40% of the time. This occurred even when subjects were not in the vicinity of the response key at the start of the trial. Other research has shown that many fewer CS-approach responses occur if the CS and food are presented randomly so that the CS does not signal food (Peden et al., 1977, Experiment 2). Thus, as was true in Sheffield's (1965) experiment, an instrumental contingency was not necessary for the conditioned response to emerge.

In Sheffield's experiment with dogs, acquisition of conditioned salivation was slower with the omission control procedure than with a standard classical conditioning procedure. Peden et al. obtained similar results in sign tracking. In the second phase of their experiment, when every trial ended in food delivery, approach responses increased (see Figure 10.2). A higher performance level with standard classical conditioning than with the omission control procedure is a common finding in studies of this kind (for example, Schwartz & Williams, 1972).

The difference between omission control and standard classical conditioning procedures in sign-tracking experiments has been the subject of considerable debate (Jenkins, 1977; Locurto, 1981). Why do omission control procedures lead to lower levels of responding than standard classical conditioning? One

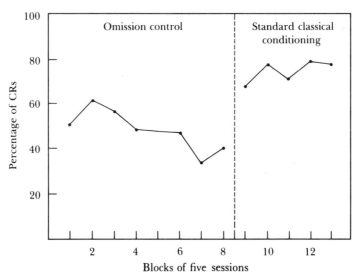

FIGURE 10.2.   Percentage of trials on which a conditioned response (approach to the CS) was observed during blocks of five sessions. Each session consisted of 50 trials. During the first eight blocks of sessions (2000 trials) an omission control procedure was in effect. During the remainder of the experiment a standard classical conditioning procedure was in effect. *(After Peden, Browne, & Hearst, 1977.)*

alternative emphasizes classical conditioning and explains the lower level of responding by pointing out that the US is not presented on every trial when occurrences of the CR are made to prevent US delivery in the omission control procedure. Classical conditioning generally leads to lower levels of performance if only some presentations of the CS end in delivery of the US. Other alternatives emphasize instrumental conditioning. Omission control procedures may produce lower levels of responding because they punish the conditioned response by withholding an expected reward. They may also lower the probability of the CR by providing reinforcement for activities incompatible with the target CR (since only non-CR responses can be followed by reward in omission training). Yet another possibility is that unintended instrumental reinforcement of the CR during standard classical conditioning elevates the level of responding in standard classical conditioning above what is observed with omission training. The omission control experiment does not enable us to decide among these alternatives.

A second part of the debate on the results of omission control procedures in sign tracking has focused on why responding persists in many, though not all, cases. Many authors (for example, Williams & Williams, 1969) have taken the persistence of responding as evidence that the behavior was learned and maintained by classical conditioning processes. Dissenters from this view consider sign tracking to be entirely the result of instrumental conditioning and attribute conditioned responding in omission training to generalization from other responses that are assumed to be inadvertently reinforced by delivery of the US in the omission control procedure (Dougan, McSweeney, O'Reilly, & Eacker, 1983). This response generalization account is consistent with the results of some studies of pigeon key pecking (for example, Barrera, 1974; Jenkins, 1981). However, the hypothesis may not be applicable to the results of omission training of other responses and of other species. In addition, the hypothesis cannot explain why certain responses are consistently acquired in sign tracking even though they are not required for obtaining reinforcement. Given these difficulties, we cannot reject classical conditioning as an important factor in sign tracking.

Conditioned response modifications of the US

A second experimental technique that has been used to evaluate the contribution of instrumental reinforcement to the learning that occurs in classical conditioning procedures has focused on possible modifications of the US caused by the conditioned response. Consider, for example, a classical conditioning situation in which the US is an aversive stimulus. Perhaps in such cases the subject learns to make the CR because the CR somehow reduces the aversiveness of the US. (Perhaps by making the CR, the subject "braces" itself against the US.) If this is true, then explicitly arranging for the intensity of the US to be reduced when the CR occurs should facilitate acquisition of the conditioned response.

The importance of CR modifications of the US was investigated in an experiment on the conditioning of the nictitating-membrane response in rabbits (Coleman, 1975). The CS was a tone, and the US was a brief shock to the skin near one eye. Retraction of the nictitating membrane over the eyes was measured as the conditioned (and unconditioned) response. Four groups of rabbits were tested. All groups received a 5.0-milliampere shock after the CS on trials in which a conditioned response did not occur. For group 5-5, the shock was also 5.0 ma when the rabbits made a conditioned response. For the other groups, the shock intensity was decreased when a conditioned response occurred. For group 5-3, the shock was decreased to 3.3 ma on trials when the CR occurred. For group 5-1, the CR decreased the shock intensity to 1.7 ma, and for group 5-0, the CR prevented delivery of the shock altogether (essentially, group 5-0 received an omission control procedure). If shock reduction provides important instrumental reinforcement for the conditioned response in this type of classical conditioning, better learning should occur in groups 5-3, 5-1, and 5-0 than in group 5-5.

The results are shown in Figure 10.3. Contrary to the instrumental reinforcement prediction, the speed and level of conditioning were not increased by reducing the shock intensity whenever the conditioned response occurred. Groups 5-3, 5-1, and 5-0 did not learn the nictitating-membrane response faster than group 5-5. In fact, the only difference evident among

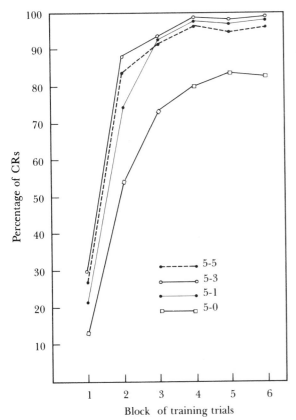

FIGURE 10.3. Percentage of conditioned responses in an experiment on nictitating-membrane conditioning with rabbits. The conditioned response resulted in reduction of the intensity of the shock US for groups 5-3 and 5-1 and omission of the US for group 5-0. In contrast, the conditioned response had no effect on the delivery of the US in group 5-5. *(From Coleman, 1975.)*

the groups was that completely reducing the shock intensity to 0 ma whenever the conditioned response occurred (group 5-0) resulted in a lower level of conditioning than in all other groups. This outcome probably reflects the fact that group 5-0 did not receive shock on every trial whereas the other groups did.

These results provide strong evidence that modifications of the US caused by the CR were not necessary for classical conditioning of the nictitating-membrane response and did not even facilitate learning. Thus, classical conditioning can occur in the absence of instrumental reinforcement. However, this does

not mean that instrumental reinforcement does not have a role in any classical conditioning procedure. The contribution of instrumental reinforcement has to be evaluated separately in each case with the techniques we have described.

Role of Classical Conditioning in Instrumental Conditioning Procedures

As we noted in Chapters 5 and 8, in an instrumental conditioning procedure the instrumental response occurs in the presence of certain distinctive stimuli and is followed by the reinforcer. This sequence of events is reviewed in Figure 10.4. S_A represents the stimuli that are present when the instrumental response is made, R represents the instrumental response, and S^{R+} represents the reinforcing stimulus. The wavy line between the response and the reinforcing stimulus signifies that the response causes the delivery of the reinforcer. This causal relation ensures that the reinforcer will be paired with the subject's exposure to stimuli S_A. The pairing of stimuli S_A with the reinforcer may result in classical conditioning, and an association may develop between stimuli S_A and the reinforcer.

In the preceding section we discussed ways in which instrumental reinforcement can be ruled out as a contributing factor in classical conditioning procedures. Unfortunately, analogous strategies do not exist for ruling out classical conditioning in instru-

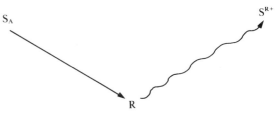

FIGURE 10.4. Relations that exist in instrumental conditioning. The instrumental response (R) occurs in the presence of distinctive stimuli (S_A) and results in delivery of the reinforcer (S^{R+}). The reinforcement of response R in the presence of stimuli S_A allows for the classical conditioning of S_A by the reinforcer.

mental procedures. To prevent classical conditioning, one cannot omit presenting the reinforcer after the animal's exposure to stimuli S_A, because this would also result in nonreinforcement of the instrumental response.

Specification of an instrumental response ensures that the animal will always experience certain distinctive stimuli (S_A) in connection with making the response. These stimuli may involve the place where the response is to be performed, the texture of the object the subject is to manipulate, or distinctive odor or visual cues. Whatever they may be, reinforcement of the instrumental response will inevitably result in a pairing between stimuli S_A and the reinforcer. The only way to prevent this pairing is not to present the reinforcer. However, this would also prevent instrumental conditioning. One cannot assume that pairings of stimuli S_A with the reinforcer will inevitably produce classical conditioning. As we noted in Chapters 3 and 4, the occurrence of classical conditioning depends on much more than just stimulus pairings. Nevertheless, pairings of stimuli S_A with the reinforcer provide the potential for the occurrence of classical conditioning. Consequently, many important theories have been concerned with the role of classical conditioning in the control of instrumental behavior.

The r_g-s_g mechanism

One of the earliest and most influential accounts of the role of classical conditioning in instrumental behavior was originally proposed by Clark Hull (1930, 1931) and was later elaborated by Kenneth Spence (1956). Essentially, Hull and Spence added a classical conditioning component to the mechanism of instrumental behavior proposed by Thorndike. You may recall from Chapter 5 that, according to Thorndike, reinforcement of an instrumental response increases the future likelihood of the behavior by establishing an association between the response and the stimuli present at the time the response is made. Using the symbols in Figure 10.4, Thorndike's view assumes that reinforcement establishes an association between S_A and R. Therefore, the presence of the stimuli S_A in the future directly triggers the occur-

rence of the instrumental response. This direct stimulation of the instrumental response is the instrumental conditioning process. Hull and Spence suggested that there is also a classical conditioning process that encourages or motivates the instrumental behavior. More specifically, they assumed that, during the course of instrumental conditioning, animals not only learn to make response R in the presence of stimuli S_A but also acquire an expectation that they will be rewarded. This reward expectancy is learned through classical conditioning and also motivates the instrumental response.

It seems intuitively reasonable that instrumental behavior occurs in part because organisms learn to expect reward. If you were to introspect about why you perform certain instrumental responses, the answer would probably be that you expect to be rewarded. You go to work because you expect to get paid; you study for a test because you expect that doing so will help you get a higher grade. To incorporate these ideas into a systematic account of instrumental behavior, one has to specify in greater detail what expectations are, how they are learned, when they occur in relation to the instrumental response, and how they motivate the instrumental behavior. The r_g-s_g mechanism provides answers to these questions.

Hull and Spence recognized that whenever the instrumental response R is followed by the reinforcer S^{R+}, the stimuli S_A present at the time of the response will become paired with the reinforcer. This pairing is assumed to result in the classical conditioning of stimuli S_A by the reinforcer S^{R+}. Hull and Spence believed that classical conditioning occurs by stimulus substitution. As we noted in Chapter 4, according to the stimulus substitution hypothesis, the conditioned stimulus is assumed to acquire properties of the unconditioned stimulus to some extent. In the instrumental conditioning paradigm, S_A acts in the role of the CS, and the reinforcer acts in the role of the US. Therefore, Hull and Spence assumed, S_A will come to elicit some of the same reponses that are elicited by the reinforcer. If the reinforcer is food, during the course of instrumental training, the animal will presumably come to salivate and perhaps make chewing movements when it experiences stimuli S_A. These classically conditioned responses are rarely as vigorous as the salivation and chewing elicited by the food itself, and they occur in anticipation of the food delivery. Therefore, they are called **fractional anticipatory goal responses.** The conventional symbol for such a response is r_g.

Anticipatory goal responses are also evident in some types of human behavior. Fingering a bus ticket in anticipation of getting on a bus, smacking one's lips in anticipation of a good meal, and "getting ahead of oneself" when talking are examples of goal-anticipatory responses.

The fractional anticipatory goal response is assumed to be similar to other types of responses. As noted in Chapter 2, responses typically produce some type of sensory feedback. That is, the act of making a response usually creates distinctive bodily sensations. The sensory feedback produced by the fractional anticipatory goal response is represented by the symbol s_g.

The fractional anticipatory goal response, with its feedback stimulus s_g, is assumed to constitute the expectancy of reward. Figure 10.5 illustrates the full sequence of events in the r_g-s_g mechanism. The fractional anticipatory goal response r_g is elicited by S_A before the instrumental response occurs. Thus, the instrumental response is made in the presence of the sensory feedback s_g from r_g. Because the instrumental response is reinforced when it is made after experience with s_g, a connection becomes established between s_g and the response R. The outcome of these events is that as instrumental conditioning proceeds, the instrumental response comes to be stimulated by two factors. First, the presence of S_A comes to evoke the instrumental response directly by association with R. Second, the instrumental activity also comes to be made in response to the expectancy of reward (r_g-s_g) because of an association between s_g and R (see Figure 10.5).

Functions of $\mathbf{r_g}$-$\mathbf{s_g}$. The fractional anticipatory goal response mechanism (r_g-s_g) is assumed to have two important functions. First, it is assumed to contribute to the general level of motivation of the animal and thereby enhance instrumental behavior. Second, it directs behavior. Because of the association of the

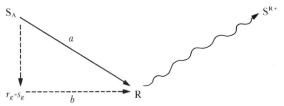

FIGURE 10.5. The r_g-s_g mechanism. During instrumental conditioning, the instrumental response R is followed by the reinforcer S^{R+}. Because this happens in the presence of distinctive situational cues S_A, an association is formed between S_A and R (arrow *a*). Delivery of the reinforcer following exposure to S_A results in the classical conditioning of S_A by the reinforcer. Therefore, S_A comes to elicit a classically conditioned fractional anticipatory goal response r_g with its feedback cues s_g. Because the instrumental response R is reinforced in the presence of s_g, an association also becomes established between s_g and R (arrow *b*).

instrumental response (R) with the stimulus feedback (s_g) from the fractional anticipatory goal response (see arrow *b* in Figure 10.5), the instrumental response is predicted to occur whenever the fractional anticipatory goal response is elicited. Once the instrumental response has been conditioned to s_g, it will occur in the presence of any stimulus that elicits the fractional anticipatory goal response. As we will see, the general motivational properties of r_g-s_g have been abandoned in contemporary theorizing. However, the second function of r_g-s_g—directing behavior—continues to be recognized.

The* $\mathbf{r_g}$-$\mathbf{s_g}$ *mechanism and positive instrumental reinforcement. The r_g-s_g mechanism is consistent with numerous aspects of positively reinforced instrumental behavior. It predicts, for example, that classical conditioning procedures will influence the performance of positively reinforced instrumental behavior in certain ways. Consider, for example, a discrimination procedure in which rats are reinforced for pressing a response lever in the presence of a tone (S+) and not reinforced in the absence of the tone. How might this discriminated lever pressing be influenced by classical conditioning procedures involving the tone? The r_g-s_g mechanism predicts that performance of the lever-press response in the presence of the tone will be facilitated by initially conducting classical conditioning in which the tone is repeatedly paired with food. The response lever can be removed from the experimental chamber during this phase to avoid accidentally reinforcing lever presses. Classical conditioning of the S+ with food should condition the fractional anticipatory goal response to the tone S+. Elicitation of r_g by the tone should increase motivation for the instrumental behavior and thereby increase lever pressing during the tone. In contrast, once the discriminated lever-press response has been established, extinguishing the fractional anticipatory goal response should produce a decrement in the instrumental behavior. Such extinction can be accomplished by removing the response lever from the experimental chamber and repeatedly presenting the S+ without food. Extinguishing the fractional anticipatory goal response is expected to reduce both its motivational and response-directing functions. Evidence consistent with these and similar predictions of the r_g-s_g mechanism has been obtained (for example, Trapold & Winokur, 1967).

Concurrent measurement of instrumental behavior and classically conditioned responses

The experiments reviewed above involved somewhat indirect predictions from the r_g-s_g mechanism. One direct implication is that classically conditioned responses develop during instrumental conditioning. In addition, the r_g-s_g mechanism specifies how these classically conditioned responses should be related to the occurrence of the instrumental response. The r_g-s_g mechanism treats classically conditioned responses as reflections of a reward expectancy that motivates the instrumental response. Therefore, the classically conditioned responses are predicted to begin before the instrumental behavior on any trial (see Figure 10.5).

Perhaps the simplest and most direct approach to investigating the role of classical conditioning in instrumental learning is to measure classically and instrumentally conditioned responses at the same time. This is the approach taken by **concurrent-measurement experiments.** Numerous investigations of this type have been carried out in positive and negative reinforcement situations (see Black, 1971; Rescorla & Solomon, 1967, for reviews). All these experiments provide evidence that classically conditioned responses are learned during instrumental conditioning. However, the relation between the two types of conditioned responses varies from one situation to another. Rather than summarize all the evidence, we will describe the results of a few important experiments with positive reinforcement to illustrate the kinds of outcomes that can be obtained.

Preinstrumental classically conditioned responses. In some experimental situations the relation between classically and instrumentally conditioned responses is as predicted by the r_g-s_g mechanism. That is, the classically conditioned responses begin before the instrumental activity. In one such demonstration, Miller and DeBold (1965) conditioned rats to press a response lever for water reinforcement. The water was squirted into each rat's mouth through a small metal tube permanently attached to the animal's head. In addition to recording occurrences of the lever-press response, Miller and DeBold measured how often the rats licked at the water delivery tube. It was assumed that licking was classically conditioned by the water reinforcement. Lever-press responses were almost always accompanied by licking behavior. The rats were also observed to lick the tube at other times. However, licking was much less vigorous when it occurred without lever pressing. The relation between licking and lever pressing is illustrated in Figure 10.6, which shows the rate of licking for 1/2-sec periods before and after lever-press responses. As you can see, the rate of licking gradually increased just before the lever-press response. The highest rate of licking occurred just after the response, when the reinforcer was ordinarily delivered, and licking subsided after that. Similar results have been observed by Shapiro (1962), using dogs reinforced for pressing a lever on a differential reinforcement of low rates (DRL) schedule. Salivation usually began just before the dogs pressed the response lever and continued for a little while after the response.

Coincidental classically conditioned responses. Contrary to the findings of Miller and DeBold (1965) and Shapiro (1962), in some cases classically conditioned responses coincide with occur-

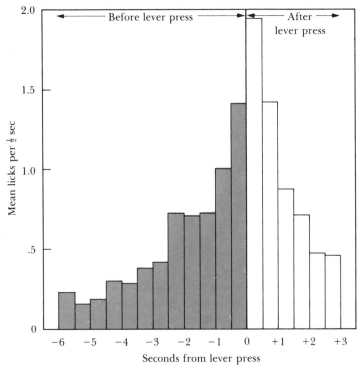

FIGURE 10.6.   Rate of licking a water tube for 1/2-sec periods before and after a lever-press response.   *(From Miller & DeBold, 1965.)*

rences of the instrumental behavior during instrumental conditioning. A good example is provided by the behavior of two dogs tested by Williams (1965). The animals were required to press a response lever on a fixed-interval 16-sec schedule for food reinforcement. The first response that occurred 16 sec or more after the last reinforcement was rewarded. As we noted in Chapter 6, a fixed-interval schedule typically produces a "scalloped" pattern of responding. The instrumental response occurs at a very low rate, if at all, at the beginning of the fixed interval. As the end of the interval (and the availability of the reinforcer) gets closer, the rate of the instrumental response gradually increases. In addition to recording the lever-press responses of the dogs, Williams measured their rate of salivation during the fixed interval. He was interested in whether the pattern of salivation during each trial would match the pattern of lever pressing.

The results are shown in Figure 10.7 for each dog.

The data represent the animals' performance after extensive training. Each graph shows the average number of lever-press responses and drops of saliva each dog produced during successive 1-sec periods of the 16-sec fixed-interval cycle. As you can see, at the beginning of the fixed-interval cycles, the dogs hardly ever pressed the response lever and salivated very little. However, as the end of the FI period approached, both lever pressing and salivation gradually increased. Furthermore, the general pattern of this increased responding toward the end of the interval was nearly indistinguishable for the instrumental (lever pressing) and classically conditioned (salivation) responses. This coincidence of salivation and instrumental responding on a fixed-interval schedule has also been observed by other investigators (Shapiro, 1960, 1961). In addition, Kintsch and Witte (1962) noted that the scalloplike temporal pattern of lever pressing is learned faster than the scalloplike pattern of salivation.

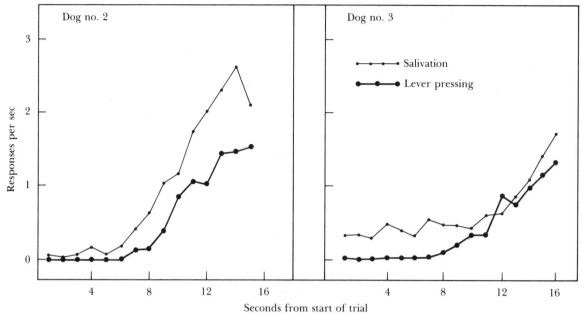

FIGURE 10.7. Rate of lever pressing and salivation by two dogs during successive 1-sec periods of a 16-sec fixed-interval trial. *(After Williams, 1965.)*

Postinstrumental classically conditioned responses. So far we have seen instances in which classically conditioned responses precede and/or coincide with instrumental behavior. In other situations, the classically conditioned responses occur after the instrumental response. This happens, for example, if the instrumental behavior is reinforced on a fixed-ratio schedule. You may recall from Chapter 6 that on a fixed-ratio schedule the only factor that determines the delivery of reward is how many responses the subject has made. When these responses occur does not matter. Williams (1965) reinforced dogs with food for pressing a lever on a fixed-ratio 33 schedule and also measured salivation during this instrumental conditioning. Figure 10.8 shows what he found with two of his subjects. Each graph presents the rates of lever pressing and salivation that occurred during successive seconds from the previous reward. For dog 4, data are shown for the first 13 sec after reinforcement; for dog 7, the first 23 sec. Each dog started lever-pressing within several seconds and achieved a stable rate of responding (between 1.5 and

2 responses per sec) by the fourth second. However, salivation did not appear until much later, when the animal was close to completing its ratio requirement. Dog 4 did not show substantial salivation until the 10th second after the previous reward, and dog 7 did not consistently increase its salivation until more than 18 sec had elapsed. A similar dissociation between instrumental behavior and conditioned salivation has been observed by Ellison and Konorski (1964).

Implications of concurrent-measurement experiments for the r_g-s_g mechanism. As we have seen, concurrent measurement of instrumental behavior and classically conditioned responses has failed to reveal a consistent pattern of results. In different situations classically conditioned responses may precede, coincide with, or follow the instrumental behavior. This varied pattern of results is not limited to classically conditioned salivation or positive reinforcement procedures (see Black, 1971; Rescorla & Solomon, 1967). Where does this leave the r_g-s_g mechanism? As we noted earlier, the r_g-s_g mecha-

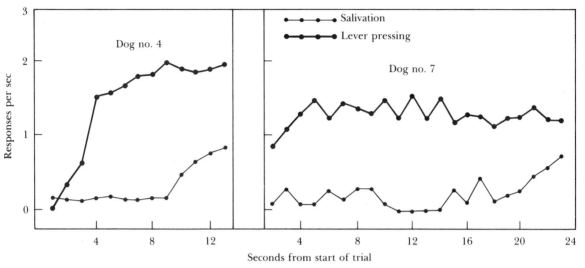

FIGURE 10.8. Rate of lever pressing and salivation by two dogs during successive 1-sec periods in a fixed-ratio trial. Lever pressing was reinforced on a fixed-ratio 33 schedule. *(After Williams, 1965.)*

nism predicts that classically conditioned responses will precede the instrumental response. However, sometimes the opposite is observed.

There are several possible reactions to this type of evidence. One is to maintain that the r_g-s_g mechanism provides a useful account of the relation between classical and instrumental conditioning but to claim that r_g does not represent a measurable classically conditioned response (Logan, 1959; MacCorquodale & Meehl, 1948). According to this approach, r_g is considered to represent a hypothetical construct, a theoretical entity, whose characteristics are governed by the rules of classical conditioning. It is assumed that r_g cannot be observed directly but may be inferred from certain aspects of instrumental behavior. If this approach is adopted, evidence from concurrent-measurement experiments cannot be used to disprove the r_g-s_g mechanism.

A second possible approach is to maintain that r_g is a measurable response but to suggest that it is only one of several classically conditioned responses that may be learned during instrumental training. Perhaps the experiments we cited did not measure the appropriate response as an index of r_g. However, if this alternative is accepted, it has to be accompanied by independent criteria for deciding in advance what

response will be a good measure of r_g in a particular situation.

A third possible approach to the inconsistent relations observed between classically conditioned responses and instrumental behavior is to abandon the r_g-s_g mechanism and consider alternative ways to conceptualize the relation between classical and instrumental conditioning. This is the approach adopted by modern two-process theory, to which we turn next. Modern two-process theory has been very influential in stimulating a great deal of research on the interaction of classical and instrumental conditioning. As we shall see, however, this theory has not been entirely successful, and it has turned out to be necessary to retain the response-directing functions of the r_g-s_g mechanism to fully account for the available evidence.

Modern two-process theory

The model of the interrelation of classical and operant conditioning we will discuss in this section was brought into focus in 1967 by Rescorla and Solomon. However, it was developed from ideas entertained as early as the 1940s, especially in connection with theorizing about the mechanisms of avoidance learning (see Mowrer, 1960; Rescorla & Solomon, 1967). We term the model "modern two-process theory" to distinguish it from the two-process theory of avoidance learning discussed in Chapter 9. Modern two-process theory is similar to the r_g-s_g mechanism in that it assumes that classical conditioning is important in motivating instrumental behavior. However, it adopts a different view of classical conditioning and a different view of the role of classical conditioning in motivation.

In contrast to the r_g-s_g mechanism, modern two-process theory does not regard classical conditioning as involving the learning of particular responses or as contributing to general motivation. Rather, it assumes that the primary outcome of classical conditioning is that a previously "neutral" stimulus comes to elicit a particular type of motivation, or **central emotional state.** The emotional state that comes to be elicited by a conditioned stimulus corresponds to the particular type of unconditioned stimulus that is used and is considered to be a characteristic of the central nervous system—a mood, if you will. Emotional states do not invariably lead to particular responses. On the contrary, they may be manifest in any one of a variety of actions. Anger, for example, may result in fighting, shouting, a frown, or refusal to acknowledge someone's presence, depending on the circumstances.

Because instrumental conditioning procedures allow for classical conditioning, modern two-process theory assumes that central emotional states are conditioned during ordinary instrumental training. These states become conditioned either to situational cues or to discriminative stimuli that accompany the reinforcement procedure. Furthermore, the emotional states are assumed to motivate the instrumental behavior. The fact that classically conditioned emotional states are not always manifest in the same responses makes modern two-process theory much less precise than the r_g-s_g mechanism. It also makes the concurrent measurement of instrumental behavior and classically conditioned responses irrelevant to evaluation of the theory. Because modern two-process theory does not specify what responses a conditioned emotional state will lead to, it cannot be disproved by the type of evidence concurrent-measurement experiments provide.

If modern two-process theory cannot be disproved by concurrent-measurement experiments, how can it be empirically tested? As it turns out, the theory makes one very important and unambiguous prediction about behavior—namely, that *the rate of an instrumental response will be modified by the presentation of a classically conditioned stimulus.* This prediction is based on the following considerations. During instrumental conditioning, a conditioned central emotional state is assumed to develop to motivate the instrumental response. Classically conditioned stimuli are also assumed to elicit central emotional states. Therefore, presentation of a classically conditioned stimulus to a subject while it is performing on an instrumental reinforcement schedule will alter the emotional state that was maintaining the instrumental response. This will be evident in a change in the rate of the instrumental behavior. We have already seen an example of this effect in the conditioned emotional response (CER) procedure, described in earlier chapters. You may recall that in the CER procedure animals are first trained to press a response lever for food reinforcement. A discrete stimulus, such as a light or a tone, is then repeatedly paired with shock. This classically conditioned fear stimulus is then presented to the animals while they are lever-pressing for food. Consistent with the prediction of modern two-process theory, presentation of the shock-conditioned CS produces a change in the rate of the lever-press response. The rate of lever pressing for food decreases.

Classically conditioned stimuli do not always suppress instrumental behavior, as in the CER procedure. According to two-process theory, the kind of changes that various kinds of classically conditioned stimuli will produce will depend on the emotional state created by these CSs and the emotional state created by the instrumental reinforcement schedule. If the classically conditioned stimulus produces emotions that are opposite to those that motivate the instrumental behavior, the rate of the instrumental response will decrease. This is presumably what happens in the CER procedure. The food-reinforcement schedule motivates lever pressing by way of a positive emotional state conditioned by food. This emotion is disrupted when the shock-conditioned CS is presented because the CS elicits an aversive emotional state. In other situations the classically conditioned stimulus may evoke an emotion that is similar to the emotional state created by the instrumental reinforcement schedule. When this occurs, the two emotions will summate, and the rate of the instrumental behavior will increase.

Specific predictions of modern two-process theory. Specific predictions about how classically conditioned stimuli will influence instrumental behavior can be made by considering the types of emotions that are elicited by various types of CSs and by instrumental reinforcement schedules. Borrowing language introduced by Mowrer (1960), Table 10.1 provides metaphorical labels for the emotional states that are presumably elicited by some common types of classically conditioned stimuli. Let us first consider classical conditioning with a positive (appetitive) unconditioned stimulus, such as food or water. If the stimulus is a CS+, meaning that it becomes associated with the impending presentation of the US, we may refer to the emotional state created by the CS as **hope.** In contrast, if the stimulus is a CS−, meaning that it has become associated with the removal or the absence of the appetitive US, we may refer to the emotional state created as **disappointment.** In the case of a CS+ for the impending presentation of an aversive US, such as shock, the conditioned emotional state is called **fear.** Finally, if the conditioned stimulus is a CS− associated with the removal or absence of an aversive US, we may presume that **relief** is elicited by presentations of the CS. Using this same terminology, we may assume that instrumental behavior reinforced by the presentation of food (or other appetitive reinforcers) is motivated by "hope" and that instrumental behavior reinforced by the avoidance or removal of shock (or other aversive events) is

motivated by "fear." It is important to note that these labels are used for convenience only and do not imply that the Pavlovian CSs involved necessarily elicit the same emotions that people experience when they describe their feelings using the terms *hope, disappointment, fear,* and *relief.*

If presentation of a classically conditioned stimulus alters instrumental behavior solely by changing the emotions that motivate the instrumental response, what should we expect in various situations? Table 10.2 lists the predicted outcomes when classically conditioned stimuli eliciting hope, disappointment, fear, and relief are presented to animals responding either to obtain food (positive reinforcement) or to avoid shock (negative reinforcement). These predictions are based on the assumption that hope and relief (both being positive emotions) and fear and disappointment (both being negative emotions) are compatible with each other (Goodman & Fowler, 1983). In contrast, hope and fear (and relief and disappointment) are assumed to be incompatible (Dickinson & Pearce, 1977).

Let us first consider predictions in the case of positive reinforcement (cells 1–4). The underlying emotional state created by positive reinforcement is hope. Hope is assumed to be incompatible with fear, and hence the rate of the instrumental response is expected to decline when a CS+ for an aversive US is presented (cell 1). Hope and relief are assumed to be compatible emotions. Therefore, we predict an increase in the positively reinforced instrumental behavior when a CS− for an aversive US is presented (cell 2). The classically conditioned stimulus is also predicted to facilitate the instrumental behavior in cell 3 because here the CS elicits hope, which is the same type of emotion as the motivational state created by the instrumental procedure. In contrast, the instrumental behavior is predicted to decrease when a CS− for food is presented (cell 4) because the disappointment it elicits is incompatible with the hope that motivates the instrumental behavior.

Cells 5–8 state the predictions when the instrumental procedure involves negative reinforcement, such as shock avoidance. The underlying emotion that motivates the instrumental behavior in this case is fear. This fear is enhanced when a CS is presented that also elicits fear (cell 5). Hence, an increase in the

TABLE 10.1.   Emotional states elicited by the CS after various types of classical conditioning

Conditioned stimulus	Unconditioned stimulus	
	Appetitive (such as food)	*Aversive (such as shock)*
CS+	Hope	Fear
CS−	Disappointment	Relief

TABLE 10.2.   Effects of classically conditioned stimuli on the rate of instrumental behavior

Instrumental schedule	Aversive US		Appetitive US	
	CS+ (fear)	CS− (relief)	CS+ (hope)	CS− (disappointment)
Positive reinforcement (procurement of food) (hope)	1 Decrease	2 Increase	3 Increase	4 Decrease
Negative reinforcement (avoidance of shock) (fear)	5 Increase	6 Decrease	7 Decrease	8 Increase

rate of the instrumental response is predicted. The fear is reduced by presentation of a CS that has been associated with the removal or absence of an aversive US (cell 6). Instrumental responding therefore declines. Fear is presumably also reduced when the classically conditioned stimulus elicits hope (cell 7) because fear and hope are incompatible emotions. Finally, performance of the instrumental response is expected to increase when a CS− for an appetitive US is presented (cell 8) because disappointment and fear are both aversive emotional states.

Results consistent with modern two-process theory.   We have already noted that the concurrent measurement of instrumental behavior and classically conditioned responses cannot be used to evaluate modern two-process theory. How, then, can the predictions in Table 10.2 be experimentally tested? The experiments that have been performed to evaluate modern two-process theory were modeled after the CER procedure and are called **transfer-of-control experiments.** Such experiments basically consist of three phases, as outlined in Table 10.3. Phase 1 involves instrumental conditioning of an operant response using some schedule of positive or negative reinforcement. In phase 2 the subjects are given classical conditioning in which an explicit CS is associated with either the presence or absence of an unconditioned stimulus. Phase 3 is the critical transfer phase. Here the animal is allowed to engage in the instrumental response, and the CS from phase 2 is periodically presented to see what effect it has on the rate of the instrumental behavior. In some applications of the transfer-of-control design, the classical

conditioning phase is conducted before instrumental conditioning. In some other experiments, phases 1 and 2 are conducted concurrently. That is, classical conditioning trials with the CS and US are periodically presented while the subject is being trained on the instrumental reinforcement schedule. These variations in the basic design are often unimportant to the results observed in phase 3, the critical transfer phase.

Modern two-process theory has stimulated a great deal of research testing predictions of the type in Table 10.2 using the transfer-of-control design. Many of the results of these experiments have been consistent with the predictions. We will not review all the evidence here but will cite some illustrative examples. Let us first consider the effects of classically conditioned stimuli on the performance of instrumental behavior maintained by positive reinforcement (cells 1–4 in Table 10.2). As we have already noted, cell 1 represents the conditioned emotional response procedure. The common finding is that a CS+ conditioned with an aversive US suppresses the rate of positively reinforced instrumental behavior (see reviews

TABLE 10.3.   Outline of transfer-of-control experiments

Phase 1	Phase 2	Phase 3
Instrumental conditioning of the baseline response	Classical conditioning of the CS	Transfer test: the CS is presented during performance of the baseline response

by Blackman, 1977; Davis, 1968; Lyon, 1968). The effects of a signal for the absence of an aversive US (a CS−) on positively reinforced responding (cell 2) have not been as extensively investigated. However, the available data are again consistent with the prediction. Hammond (1966), for example, found that lever pressing in rats reinforced by food increased when a CS− for shock was presented (see also Davis and Shattuck, 1980). In certain situations, food-reinforced instrumental behavior is also increased by presentation of a CS+ for food, consistent with the prediction in cell 3 (for example, Estes, 1943, 1948; LoLordo, 1971; Lovibond, 1983). Research on the effects of a signal for the absence of

an appetitive reinforcer (CS−) on positively reinforced responding (cell 4) has not been very extensively pursued. However, evidence consistent with two-process theory (a suppression of the instrumental response) has been observed in what studies there are (for example, Gutman & Maier, 1978; Hearst & Peterson, 1973).

Many experiments have been performed to determine how stimuli that signal an aversive US (CS+) or its absence (CS−) influence the rate of negatively reinforced instrumental behavior (cells 5 and 6). These studies generally support predictions of modern two-process theory. Numerous studies have shown that the rate of avoidance behavior is increased

---

BOX 10.1. Fear and relief conditioning: Behavior therapies

Mowrer's original two-factor theory is the historical basis for several behavior therapies. These therapies usually aim to modify complicated instrumental activities maintained by a variety of reinforcers not under the therapist's control. The goal in therapy is to condition (through classical conditioning) a central emotional state that will transfer to control the instrumental behavior in a variety of settings outside the clinic. Alcohol aversion therapy, described in Chapter 3, is of this type. In this case, the therapist does not directly modify the client's instrumental drinking behavior by providing reinforcement or punishment. Rather, some aspects of the alcohol (its smell and taste, for example) are paired with nausea. The hope is that an emotional state of aversion will be conditioned to stimulus aspects of the alcohol and will then inhibit instrumental approach and drinking of alcohol outside the clinic.

A similar therapy was developed by Feldman and MacCulloch (1971) for treating male homosexuals who wish to change their sexual orientation. Many homosexuals achieve satisfactory adjustment to their sexual orientation and have no inclination to become heterosexual. However, among those with adjustment problems, some seek to have their sexual orientation altered. Part of Feldman and MacCulloch's procedure involved administering an aversive stimulus (electrical shock) to the individual while he viewed photographs of nude males. A fear response was assumed to become conditioned that would inhibit sexual approach responses to males. In addition, on some of the conditioning trials, a picture of a female was presented at the moment the shock was terminated. The intent of this aspect of the procedure was to condition relief to some quality of "femaleness" presented in the photographs of females. This conditioned relief was assumed to enhance approach responses to females outside the clinic.

Results of initial work with homosexuals appeared to be quite promising. However, further outcome studies have not been so positive (see Rachman & Wilson, 1980). One of the major problems in this kind of behavior therapy is that every time the undesirable behavior occurs outside the clinic, the emotional state conditioned by shock (and relief from shock) undergoes extinction. Thus, it has been found that the conditioning becomes rapidly extinguished (see Rachman & Teasdale, 1969). Like therapy for excessive alcohol ingestion, therapy for changing sexual orientation requires treatment for various aspects of the behavior. Fear and relief conditioning constitutes one part in the overall program.

by the presentation of a CS+ for shock and decreased by the presentation of a CS− for shock (for example, Bull & Overmier, 1968; Desiderato, 1969; Rescorla & LoLordo, 1965; Weisman & Litner, 1969). Presentation of a signal for the presence of food (CS+) has also been noted to decrease the rate of instrumental avoidance behavior, as cell 7 predicts (for example, Bull, 1970; Davis & Kreuter, 1972; Grossen, Kostansek, & Bolles, 1969). The effects of a signal for the absence of food (CS−) on avoidance behavior (cell 8) have not been extensively investigated. One experiment that included a test of the prediction in cell 8 failed to find any effect on avoidance responding (Bull, 1970). However, in another study (Grossen et al., 1969), a classically conditioned CS− for food facilitated instrumental avoidance behavior, as predicted in cell 8.

Response interactions in the effects of classically conditioned stimuli on instrumental behavior

The evidence reviewed above provides many instances in which predictions of modern two-process theory have been confirmed. However, other studies have yielded results inconsistent with, and sometimes opposite to, predictions of modern two-process theory. This has been particularly true with the effects of a CS+ for food on positively reinforced instrumental behavior (cell 3 of Table 10.2). Modern two-process theory predicts an increase in the instrumental behavior in this case. However, many investigators have found suppressions of behavior instead, a phenomenon sometimes called *positive conditioned suppression* (for example, Azrin & Hake, 1969; Konorski & Miller, 1930; Meltzer & Brahlek, 1970; Miczek & Grossman, 1971). These contradictory findings suggest that the interaction of central emotional states is not the only factor determining the outcome of transfer-of-control experiments, and in certain situations it may not even have a critical role.

Classically conditioned stimuli elicit not only emotional states but also overt responses. Consequently, a classically conditioned stimulus may influence instrumental behavior through the overt responses it elicits. Consider, for example, a hypothetical situation in which the classically conditioned stimulus makes the animal remain still, and the instrumental response is shuttling back and forth in a shuttle box. In this case, presentation of the CS will decrease the instrumental response simply because the tendency to stop moving elicited by the CS will interfere with the shuttle behavior. An appeal to interaction between central emotional states elicited by the CS and the instrumental reinforcement schedule is not necessary to understand such an outcome. If the classically conditioned stimulus elicited overt responses that were similar to the instrumental behavior, presentation of the CS would increase responding because responses elicited by the CS would be added to the responses the animal was performing to receive instrumental reinforcement. Assumptions about central emotional states would again be unnecessary in explaining the results.

Investigators have been very much concerned with the possibility that the results of transfer-of-control experiments are due to the fact that Pavlovian CSs elicit overt responses that either interfere with or facilitate the behavior required for instrumental reinforcement. Various strategies have been used to rule out this possibility (see Overmier & Lawry, 1979, for a recent review). These efforts have been generally successful in showing that many transfer-of-control effects are not produced by interactions between overt responses (see, for example, Grossen et al., 1969; Lovibond, 1983; Overmier, Bull, & Pack, 1971; Scobie, 1972). However, overt classically conditioned responses can have an important role in some transfer-of-control experiments.

Response interactions are especially important to consider in two types of situations. One of these involves transfer-of-control experiments in which classical conditioning is conducted with an appetitive stimulus such as food or water that subjects have to obtain in a particular location—from a cup placed in a corner of the experimental chamber, for example. If subjects have to go to a particular location to obtain the US, a CS+ may suppress instrumental responding because it elicits approach to the site of US delivery (for example, Karpicke, 1978).

Response interactions are also very important to consider when the classically conditioned stimulus is a discrete localized stimulus (such as a spot of light) because such CSs elicit sign tracking. As we noted earlier, when a localized stimulus becomes a CS+ for food, animals tend to approach it. In contrast, if the stimulus becomes a CS+ for shock, it comes to elicit withdrawal, or *negative sign tracking* (for example, Leclerc & Reberg, 1980). Positive and negative sign tracking elicited by classically conditioned stimuli may increase or decrease the performance of a baseline instrumental response, depending on whether the sign tracking is compatible or incompatible with the instrumental behavior (for example, LoLordo, McMillan & Riley, 1974; Schwartz, 1976). This compatibility, in turn, often depends on the location of the classically conditioned stimulus relative to the location of the instrumental response.

A study by Karpicke, Christoph, Peterson, and Hearst (1977) nicely illustrates the role of positive and negative sign tracking in transfer-of-control experiments. Rats were trained to pull a chain suspended from the top of the experimental chamber for milk reinforcement. When the chain-pulling operant was occurring at a stable rate, classical conditioning trials were superimposed on the instrumental reinforcement schedule. These trials consisted in turning on a localized light CS shortly before the delivery of several drops of free milk. For one group of rats the light CS was close to the chain manipulandum; for another group it was located in another part of the experimental chamber. After conditioning, the light CS disrupted instrumental chain pulling in both groups. Therefore, the experimenters reported their results in terms of suppression ratios (see Chapter 3). The lower the value of this ratio, the more suppression in the instrumental response was produced by the CS. A score of .5 was achieved if presentation of the CS had no discernible effect on instrumental responding.

The results are summarized in the left portion of Figure 10.9. When the CS was located near the chain manipulandum, presentation of the CS had only a minor disruptive effect on instrumental chain pulling. In contrast, when the CS was located in another part of the experimental chamber, chain pulling was much more severely disrupted during the CS presentations. More-detailed observations of the animals

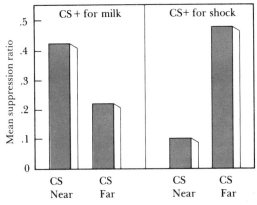

FIGURE 10.9. Suppression of chain pulling reinforced by milk in rats when a CS+ for milk or shock is presented. The CS was located either near or far from the chain manipulandum. (Lower values of the suppression ratio indicate greater disruptions of instrumental behavior.) *(After Karpicke, Christoph, Peterson, & Hearst, 1977.)*

indicated that the response suppression occurred because the animals tended to approach the CS. When the CS was located far from the chain manipulandum, approaching the CS took the rats away from the chain and thereby reduced their chain-pulling behavior.

Sign tracking elicited by the classically conditioned CS can also determine transfer-of-control effects when the CS is conditioned with an aversive rather than an appetitive US. As we noted earlier, if a localized CS+ is conditioned with an aversive stimulus, such as shock, animals will tend to move away from it (negative sign tracking). Karpicke et al. (1977) repeated the experiment described above, with a shock-conditioned CS+ that was either close to or far from the location where the instrumental response was performed. Rats again served as subjects and were first trained to pull a chain to obtain milk. When the chain-pulling operant was well established, classical conditioning trials were conducted in which presentation of a localized light ended in shock. For one group the light was near the chain manipulandum, whereas for a second group it was in another part of the experimental chamber. If animals tend to move away from a CS+ for shock, this should disrupt chain pulling more when the CS is near the chain manipulandum than when it is far away.

The results are summarized in the right panel of Figure 10.9. As predicted by the response-interaction hypothesis, the CS+ disrupted the instrumental chain-pulling response much more when it was close to the chain than when it was farther away. It is interesting to note that this effect is opposite to what occurred when the CS was conditioned with milk (left panel of Figure 10.9). In that case, the far CS disrupted chain pulling more than the near CS. Thus, the location of the CS is not the sole determinant of what effect the CS has on chain pulling. Rather, the transfer-of-control results depend on whether the CS is conditioned with a positive or negative reinforcer (milk or shock) and whether the sign tracking elicited by the CS makes the animal move away from the location where the instrumental response has to be performed.

Experiments on the role of sign tracking in transfer-of-control studies are significant because they show that the emotional interactions emphasized by modern two-process theory cannot explain all transfer-of-control results. However, it is important to keep in mind that transfer-of-control experiments do not invariably involve response interactions resulting from approach to or withdrawal from the CS or approach to the location where the US is presented. In a recent study with rabbits, for example, Lovibond (1983) eliminated approach to the site of US delivery by using as the US a sugar solution squirted directly into the animal's mouth through a cannula permanently implanted in the cheek. CS-directed responses can be similarly minimized by using stimuli that cannot be localized in the external environment (diffuse illumination of the entire experimental chamber, for example).

Discriminative stimulus properties of classically conditioned states

We have described the results of many experiments showing that classically conditioned stimuli can influence the performance of instrumental behavior. In analyzing these effects we have emphasized two aspects of classically conditioned stimuli: the emotional state or particular type of motivation evoked by the stimuli and the overt responses these stimuli elicit. However, explanation of all the ways that classically conditioned stimuli can influence instrumental behavior requires postulating a third variable as well. We must assume that classically conditioned stimuli evoke a theoretical state that has not only particular motivational and response-eliciting properties but also stimulus characteristics. The idea is that the state of neural excitation in the brain created by classically conditioned stimuli leads to particular sensations in addition to eliciting particular types of motivation (emotions) and overt responses. These sensations can come to serve as discriminative stimuli for the instrumental behavior and thereby influence instrumental performance.

How might classically conditioned states acquire discriminative stimulus properties? Theoretically the answer is rather straightforward. We know from Chapter 8 that a stimulus acquires discriminative control of behavior if responses in the presence of the stimulus are reinforced and responses in its absence are not reinforced. Therefore, stimulus features of a classically conditioned state should acquire discriminative control over instrumental behavior through differential reinforcement in the usual manner. However, this is easier to say than it is to prove experimentally. The experimental demonstration is complicated by the fact that we cannot directly manipulate the stimulus features of classically conditioned states; we cannot present and remove these stimuli at will the way we can turn a light or tone on and off.

One experimental approach to the study of discriminative stimulus properties of classically conditioned states involves an instrumental discrimination procedure. Consider, for example, the procedure diagramed in Figure 10.10. Subjects are placed in a two-way shuttle box and are reinforced with food for crossing from one side to the other when a clicker is sounded but are not reinforced in the absence of the clicker. Thus, the clicker becomes an appetitive S+. Because subjects receive food during the S+ (and not during its absence), the S+ also becomes classically conditioned by the food and presumably comes to elicit a classically conditioned state, denoted by the

Procedure

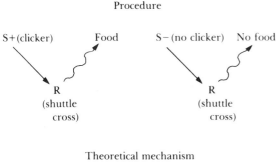

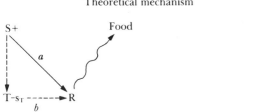

FIGURE 10.10. Procedure and theoretical mechanism for discrimination training of an instrumental shuttle response (R). Shuttle crossings are reinforced with food during a clicker (S+) and not reinforced in the absence of the clicker (S−). The S+ comes to elicit a classically conditioned state T with its stimulus properties s_T. The instrumental response can be evoked by the S+ either directly (arrow a) or by way of the discriminative stimulus properties of the classically conditioned state (arrow b).

symbol T in the lower part of Figure 10.10. The classically conditioned state T presumably has stimulus features, denoted by s_T in Figure 10.10. These sensations (s_T) are present when the instrumental response is reinforced because the classically conditioned state (T) is elicited by the S+. However, the s_T sensations are not present on nonreinforced trials because the S− is not conditioned to elicit the classically conditioned state T. The presence of s_T on reinforced but not on nonreinforced trials may enable these stimuli to serve as discriminative cues for the instrumental response, as denoted by arrow b in the lower part of Figure 10.10.

The schema presented in Figure 10.10 makes it plausible that during discrimination training the stimulus properties (s_T) of a classically conditioned state may acquire discriminative control over the instrumental behavior. However, according to the theoretical model outlined in Figure 10.10, there are two means whereby the S+ can come to evoke the instru-

mental response. The S+ may evoke the instrumental response directly, as denoted by arrow a in the lower part of the figure, or may evoke the response indirectly by way of the stimulus properties of the classically conditioned state (arrow b). Therefore, if we find that subjects make the shuttle response during the S+ and not during the S−, this does not tell us specifically that the stimulus properties s_T of the classically conditioned state have gained discriminative control over the behavior. Behavior elicited by the S+ could just as well have occurred because of a direct connection between the S+ and the response.

To prove that s_T can evoke the instrumental response by itself, we have to present s_T without the S+. In this case any shuttling that is observed can only be attributed to s_T. But how can this be done, since we do not have direct control over s_T? One possibility is to condition some stimulus other than the S+ to also elicit the classically conditioned state T. Let us add a second phase to the experiment we have been considering. After the discriminative shuttle-response training that we have conducted with the clicker as the S+, let us put the subjects in a distinctively different apparatus and conduct simple classical conditioning in which a pure tone (CS+) is paired with the presentation of food and a different pure tone (CS−) is given without food. This procedure, together with the first phase of the experiment we have been considering, is summarized in Figure 10.11. Keep in mind that the second phase of the experiment involves only classical conditioning. The subject is not required to perform any particular instrumental response for the food to be delivered. Shuttle responses are not reinforced in this phase of the experiment. In fact, the conditioning is carried out in an apparatus where the subject cannot make shuttle crossings. Thus, in the second phase, the only thing that happens is that one tone becomes a CS+ for food and another tone becomes a CS− for food.

Both phase 1 and phase 2 of the experiment shown in Figure 10.11 involve conditioning with food. Therefore, the pure tone CS+ presumably comes to elicit the same classically conditioned state T in phase 2 that was conditioned to the S+ in phase 1. We can assume that, after conditioning of the CS+, the CS+ will elicit the classically conditioned state T, with its

Phase 1
(shuttle box)

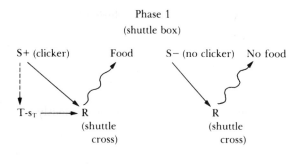

Phase 2
(classical conditioning box)

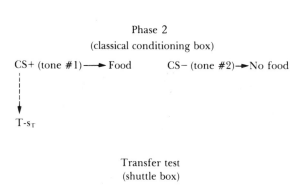

Transfer test
(shuttle box)

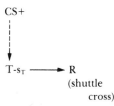

FIGURE 10.11. Outline of the experiment by Overmier and Lawry (1979). Instrumental discrimination training is conducted in a shuttle box in phase 1. Classical conditioning is then conducted in a separate apparatus that does not permit subjects to make the shuttle response. The CS+ is then tested in the shuttle box to see whether it increases shuttle responding. (See text for further details.)

accompanying stimulus properties s_T. This brings us to the most important aspect of this complicated experiment. Recall that we are trying to prove that the stimulus properties s_T of the classically conditioned state came to serve as discriminative stimuli for the shuttle response in phase 1 of the experiment. If this is true, then any time the subjects experience s_T in the shuttle box, shuttle crossings should increase. Therefore, presentation of the food-conditioned CS+

should evoke increased shuttle responding. Furthermore, this outcome is expected even if the subject is not responding for positive reinforcement at the time.

The experiment that we have been describing was carried out by Overmier and his associates (see Overmier & Lawry, 1979). Dogs served as subjects. In describing the study, we omitted several aspects to simplify the presentation. Between phases 1 and 2 of the experiment, subjects received free-operant avoidance training in the shuttle box in the presence of a bright light. (Each shuttle crossing here postponed the next scheduled shock by 30 sec.) This free-operant avoidance schedule was in effect during the final phase of the experiment when the food-conditioned CS+ was presented in the shuttle box. The point of interest was whether shuttle crossings would be increased by presentation of the CS+. The final transfer test also involved presentation of the food-conditioned CS−.

Figure 10.12 summarizes the results. The data are presented in terms of the percent change (increase or decrease) in shuttle responding caused by presentation of the food-conditioned CS+ and CS− stimuli. The free-operant avoidance schedule remained in effect for the shuttle behavior during these stimulus presentations.

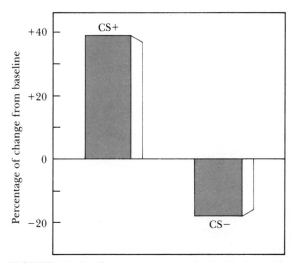

FIGURE 10.12. Percent change in shuttle shock-avoidance responding when a food-conditioned CS+ or CS− is presented. *(After Overmier & Lawry, 1979.)*

As Figure 10.12 shows, presentation of the food-conditioned CS+ increased shuttle responding. This is a very significant finding because it cannot be explained by either the emotional properties of the state elicited by the CS+ or the responses elicited by the CS+. Since the CS+ was conditioned with food, the emotional state it evoked (hope) should have subtracted from the emotion (fear) maintaining the baseline avoidance behavior, and there should have been a decrease in shuttle responding. The responses conditioned to the CS+ cannot explain the increased shuttle behavior, because the CS+ was conditioned in a classical conditioning procedure and special precautions were taken to make sure that the shuttle response would not become conditioned to the CS+ in the second phase of the experiment. The increased responding evoked by the CS+ is best explained by the discriminative stimulus properties (s_T) of the classically conditioned state (T) elicited by the CS+. These cues (s_T) presumably gained control over the shuttle response because of the training that subjects received in phase 1 of the experiment.

Let us next consider what happened when the food-conditioned CS− was presented in the transfer test. This time a small decrease in shuttle crossings occurred. This is an important control observation because it shows that not all stimuli will produce increases in shuttling in this situation. Therefore, we can be sure that the effect observed with the CS+ was due to the specific conditioning history of that stimulus.

Overmier and his colleagues have conducted several experiments of the sort that we have described (see Overmier & Lawry, 1979). These studies provide strong support for the idea that classically conditioned states have stimulus properties that can acquire discriminative control over instrumental behavior. Furthermore, the discriminative properties of classically conditioned states can override the emotional properties of the states, as in the experiment just described.

It is interesting to note that the present theoretical analysis in terms of discriminative stimulus properties of classically conditioned states (see Figure 10.10) is very similar to the r_g-s_g mechanism discussed earlier (see Figure 10.5). As in the r_g-s_g

mechanism, the stimuli present during instrumental conditioning (S+) are assumed to become classically conditioned, and the classically conditioned entity is assumed to have stimulus characteristics that come to serve as discriminative cues for the instrumental response. Thus, the present model has the same type of response-directing function that we previously discussed in connection with the fractional anticipatory goal response mechanism. However, the present account differs from the r_g-s_g mechanism in that a classically conditioned intervening state (T) is assumed to be acquired rather than a fractional anticipatory goal response (r_g). In addition, in the contemporary theoretical model, the classically conditioned entity elicited by the S+ is also assumed to have emotional properties that can add to or subtract from other elicited emotions, in accordance with the predictions of modern two-process theory.

Conditioned central emotional states or reward-specific expectancies?

Modern two-process theory assumes that classical conditioning mediates instrumental behavior through the conditioning of central emotional states like hope, disappointment, fear, and relief. However, a growing body of evidence indicates that in certain situations animals acquire specific reward expectancies instead of more general central emotional states during instrumental and classical conditioning (Peterson & Trapold, 1980). Baxter and Zamble (1982), for example, compared electrical stimulation of the brain (ESB) and food as rewards in transfer-of-control experiments with rats. Since both of these USs are positive reinforcers, they would be expected to condition the emotional state of hope. Baxter and Zamble found that a CS+ for brain stimulation increased instrumental lever pressing reinforced with ESB, and a CS+ for food increased lever pressing reinforced with food. However, a CS+ for ESB did not increase lever pressing conditioned with food reinforcement. Thus, a positive classically conditioned stimulus increased instrumental responding only if it signalled the same US that had been used to condition the instrumental response.

In another study, solid food pellets and a sugar

solution were used as USs in classical and instrumental conditioning of rats (Kruse, Overmier, Konz, & Rokke, 1983). The results showed that a CS+ for food had a much greater facilitory effect on instrumental responding reinforced with food than on instrumental behavior reinforced with the sugar solution. Correspondingly, a CS+ for sugar had a greater facilitory effect on instrumental behavior reinforced with sugar than on instrumental behavior reinforced with food pellets. Thus, as in the study by Baxter and Zamble (1982), expectancies for specific rewards rather than a more general central emotional state of hope determined the results (see also Hendersen, Patterson, & Jackson, 1980).

The studies described above clearly indicate that under some circumstances animals acquire reinforcer-specific expectancies rather than more general emotional states during instrumental and classical conditioning. Reinforcer-specific expectancy learning is a challenging alternative to modern two-process theory in explaining certain types of results. In particular, expectancy theory is more successful in explaining results of transfer-of-control experiments in which the USs used during classical and instrumental conditioning phases are of the same type—both aversive or both appetitive (cells 3, 4, 5, and 6 of Table 10.2). If the USs employed are identical in the two phases (classical and instrumental conditioning with the same type of food, for example), then predictions of expectancy and two-process theory are identical. If the USs are not identical but are of the same affective category (food pellets and sucrose, for example), the evidence we described above indicates that expectancy theory is more successful in explaining the results than two-process theory.

These considerations suggest that expectancy theory could replace modern two-process theory in explaining many findings. However, expectancy theory is not as successful as two-process theory in explaining effects of classical conditioning on instrumental performance when the USs used in the two types of conditioning are from opposite affective systems (food and shock, for example). (These instances are illustrated by cells 1, 2, 7, and 8 of Table 10.2.) For example, it is not clear on the basis of reinforcer-specific expectations why a CS− for food should facilitate shock-avoidance instrumental behavior (cell 8 of Table 10.2). The specific reinforcer expectancy elicited by a CS− for food is certainly not the same as the specific reinforcer expectancy presumably responsible for instrumental shock-avoidance behavior. However, the emotion elicited by a CS− for food (disappointment) is similar to the emotion presumably acquired during avoidance training (fear). Therefore, two-process theory is more successful in explaining such transfer results.

Concluding Comments

Classical and instrumental conditioning procedures are clearly different from each other. However, instrumental reinforcement can be involved in classical conditioning procedures, and classical conditioning processes can be involved in instrumental conditioning procedures. Experimental investigations have shown that classical conditioning can take place in the absence of the opportunity for instrumental reinforcement. However, comparable investigations cannot be conducted to show that instrumental conditioning is possible without the occurrence of classical conditioning.

All instrumental conditioning procedures allow for the occurrence of classical conditioning. Concurrent-measurement experiments confirmed that classically conditioned responses in fact develop during instrumental conditioning procedures. However, the concurrent measurement of classically and instrumentally conditioned responses has not proved to be very helpful in elucidating the interrelation of these two processes. Another experimental technique, the transfer-of-control design, has provided much more enlightening information. This type of experiment has confirmed in numerous instances the basic tenet of two-process theory—that classically conditioned stimuli can influence the performance of an independently established instrumental response. Research has shown that the transfer of control from Pavlovian conditioned stimuli to instrumental behavior is governed by several factors. One important factor is the nature of the central emotional state elicited by the

Pavlovian CS in comparison with the central emotional state that is established by the baseline instrumental reinforcement schedule. (This factor has been emphasized by modern two-process theory.) A second important variable is the overt responses elicited by the Pavlovian CS and the extent to which these are compatible or incompatible with the instrumental behavior. A third factor in transfer-of-control experiments is the discriminative stimulus properties of the classically conditioned states. (This factor has been emphasized by theories similar to the r_g-s_g mecha-

nism.) Finally, transfer-of-control experiments can also involve reinforcer-specific expectancies. Generally, particular transfer-of-control experiments have been designed to highlight the importance of a particular variable. Therefore, results of individual experiments often provide evidence consistent with one but not other perspectives on the interrelation of classical and instrumental conditioning. However, the totality of the evidence suggests that the interaction of classical and instrumental conditioning procedures is multiply determined.

CHAPTER 11
Animal Cognition: Memory Mechanisms

In Chapter 11 we will begin a consideration of a recent and rapidly developing area of research relevant to the study of learning and behavior—animal cognition. After defining animal cognition and describing reasons for studying it, we will discuss one of the most important aspects of cognition—memory. We will first describe working memory and experiential modifications of memory because the processes involved in these aspects of memory are distinct from learning. We will then end the chapter with a discussion of interactions between learning and memory.

One of the most prominent contemporary developments in the study of conditioning and learning is a renewed interest in cognitive processes in animal behavior (for example, Griffin, 1976, 1982; Hulse, Fowler, & Honig, 1978; Roitblat, Bever, & Terrace, 1984). Although cognitive issues were entertained in considerations of animal behavior decades ago (for example, Tolman, 1932), such concepts have not been extensively used in scientific analyses of animal behavior until recently. This resurgence of interest in cognitive concepts can be traced to two coincidental developments. First, research in animal behavior has shown that the strict S-R behaviorist approach does not provide an entirely adequate conceptual framework for certain aspects of animal behavior. Second, great advances have been made in the last 20 years in the development of a scientific approach to the study of human cognitive functions. The significant success that has been achieved in the experimental investigation of human cognitive behavior has encouraged similar investigations in animal behavior.

What Is Animal Cognition?

The word *cognition* comes from the Latin meaning "knowledge or thinking" and is used in common parlance to refer to thought processes. To most people, thought processes have two prominent characteristics. First, we tend to regard thinking as involving the voluntary, deliberate, and conscious consideration of some topic, usually with the use of language. Thus, thinking is informally considered to be a kind of "talking to oneself." The second prominent characteristic of thinking is that it can lead to actions that cannot be explained on the basis of the external stimuli the person happens to experience at the time. For example, on your way to work, you may remember that you did not lock up when you left home. This thought may make you return home and lock the door. Your returning cannot be explained by the external stimuli to which you are exposed as you go to work. You encounter these same stimuli every day, but they usually do not make you return home.

Rather, your behavior is attributed to the thought of the unlocked door.

In the scientific study of animal behavior, the term *cognition* is used in a more restricted sense than in common language. A clear consensus has not yet emerged concerning the definition of **animal cognition.** However, animal cognition is not defined as voluntary or conscious reflection about a topic. It does not refer to thinking in the ordinary sense. Rather, *animal cognition* refers to the use of *a neural representation, or model, of some past experience as a basis for action.* A neural representation ("mental" record or image, if you will) cannot be investigated directly by looking into the nervous system. Rather, it is inferred from behavior. Thus, an internal representation is a theoretical construct, in the same sense that gravity is a theoretical construct inferred from the behavior of, for example, falling objects (see Roitblat, 1982, for a more detailed discussion). Internal representations may encode various types of information such as particular features of stimuli or relations among previously experienced events. The concept of an internal representation is useful because it allows us to explain the occurrence of responses that are not entirely governed by external stimuli. Behavior can be guided by internal representations of events and relations rather than by concrete external stimuli. Consequently, cognitive mechanisms are often invoked when an animal's actions cannot be entirely explained in terms of the external stimuli the animal is exposed to at the time.

The assumption that animals possess cognitive processes should not be taken to mean that they also possess consciousness and self-awareness. As Terrace (1984, p. 8) has commented recently, "The rationale for the study of cognitive processes in animals requires no reference to animal consciousness." Research on animal cognition is concerned with questions such as how neural representations are formed, what aspects of experience they encode, how the information is stored, and how it is used later to guide behavior. These questions are investigated with the same experimental rigor as any other research question that involves making theoretical inferences from observed behavior.

Cognition is clearly involved in memory, which we

will discuss in this chapter, and in serial pattern learning, concept formation, reasoning, and language, which we will discuss in Chapter 12. However, cognition is also important in classical and instrumental conditioning. Much of our discussion of classical conditioning in Chapters 3 and 4 followed the strong cognitive orientation of contemporary research in this area. As we noted in Chapter 4, research on classical conditioning suggests that animals do not learn to make a particular response to the CS. Rather, they learn *an association between two stimuli, the CS and US (an S-S association)*. The S-S approach assumes that the conditioned response is not elicited directly by the CS. Rather, the CS elicits or activates a representation ("mental image") of the US, and the conditioned response is performed because of this representation. If the representation of the US is independently altered, the response elicited by the CS is thereby also altered (see "Modern Approaches to Stimulus Substitution" in Chapter 4).

We have also mentioned some cognitive mechanisms in instrumental conditioning. The learned-helplessness hypothesis, for example, is a cognitive formulation. As we noted in Chapter 5, according to the learned-helplessness hypothesis, subjects exposed to inescapable and unavoidable aversive stimulation learn that the aversive event is independent of their behavior. They acquire a representation or view of the environment according to which their behavior cannot have control over the aversive stimulation. The relational-learning hypothesis, discussed in Chapter 8, is also a cognitive mechanism. A particular relation between two stimuli (one being bigger than the other, for example) is not a physical attribute of either stimulus. To respond on the basis of a relation between two stimuli, subjects have first to abstract certain features of each stimulus (size, for example) and then to compare these features. Thus, relational learning requires the formation of representations of the stimuli in the situation.

Why Study Animal Cognition?

As we noted earlier, interest in cognitive processes in animal behavior followed great advances in the understanding of human cognitive functions. This raises an interesting question: If we already know a lot about human cognition, why study cognition in animals? There are several compelling reasons. First, although we know a lot about human cognition, we do not know how humans came to have their cognitive abilities—we do not know much about the evolution of cognition. Information about the evolution of cognition and thinking will come only from careful comparative animal research involving a variety of species. The current resurgence of interest in animal cognition reflects a resurgence of interest in comparative psychology and questions about the evolution of information processing, thinking, and the mind (Wasserman, 1981a). We often casually assume that humans possess unique abilities to form symbolic representations and use these in communicating and reasoning. In fact, we sometimes assume that our highly developed cognitive skills are what make us human. Study of the evolution of cognition through comparative work with animals is important in placing human cognitive behavior in proper biological perspective and may provide insights into how our cognitive abilities contribute to our humanity.

The study of animal cognition also promises to contribute to research on the neurophysiology of cognitive behavior. Neurophysiological interventions are often not possible with human subjects (nor should they be), for ethical reasons. Nevertheless, information about the neurophysiology of cognition is important to enable physicians to evaluate and treat cognitive disorders and to predict the potential effects of medications and medical procedures on cognitive functioning. To help fill this gap in knowledge, animal models have been developed and used in research on the neurophysiology of cognition (for example, Martinez, Jensen, & McGaugh, 1981; Pribram, 1984).

Another area to which the study of animal cognition may make an important contribution is the construction of inanimate thinking machines. The increasing automation and computerization of many forms of human work has been accompanied by increased interest in inanimate thinking machines (robots) and artificial intelligence. Given the complexities of the human nervous system, it is difficult to use it as a model for the design of artificial intelligence systems. However, inanimate thinking machines could be modeled after animals that have a much simpler nervous system. Studies of the cognitive abilities of such organisms could provide important information about how much can be accomplished with simpler systems.

Research on animal cognition is also useful in that it provides techniques that can be used to address certain questions about human cognition. One particularly fertile area in this regard is the study of cognitive processes in retarded people and prelinguistic human infants. Very young human infants cannot be tested with most of the procedures used in the study of adult human cognition. However, procedures developed in animal research can be adapted for this purpose, since animal research techniques typically do not depend on linguistic abilities (for example, Cohen, 1976; Rovee-Collier, 1983).

Finally, the study of animal cognition is important to the understanding of animal behavior. The information we will describe provides numerous insights into behavior. Without this information, we would be at a loss to explain many of the things that animals do.

Memory Mechanisms in Animal Behavior

Memory is one of the most extensively investigated cognitive processes. Much of the research and theorizing dealing with memory has been concerned with the performance of human subjects. However, investigators of animal behavior have also become very much interested in the study of memory mechanisms during the past 15 years (for example, Honig & James, 1971; McGaugh & Herz, 1972; Medin, Roberts, & Davis, 1976; Spear, 1978; Spear & Miller, 1981). In the present chapter we will describe some of the prominent techniques used in the study of animal memory and also discuss a few of the major theoretical issues in the field.

The term **memory** is commonly used to refer to the

BOX 11.1.   How well do human infants remember?

Until recently, research on infant memory indicated that very young babies do not remember their experiences for more than a few seconds or minutes. It has been suggested that an infant's ability to remember experiences develops around 8 or 9 months of age (see, for example, Kagan, 1979). Rovee-Collier (1983) suggests that these conclusions are counterintuitive and do not fit with other existing views of infant development. For example, it is commonly held that early infant experiences are very important for development. How could this be if the infant cannot remember experiences for more than a minute? In addition, it would seem unlikely that the complex behaviors an infant displays at 9–12 months could be attained without the cumulative effects of experience. Rovee-Collier further suggests that the problem is not that infants do not remember. Rather, the techniques that have been used to measure infant memory may not have allowed the very young infant to "show its stuff." Working with a 3-month-old infant requires special techniques because the infant is highly limited in the actions it can perform. It cannot walk in mazes, push buttons and levers, or do the myriad of other tasks we ask of our other nonverbal subjects. Rovee-Collier has developed a response/reinforcer system that permits investigation of memory processes early in life. The infant's leg is connected to a mobile with a ribbon in such a way that the mobile moves when the infant kicks its leg. Response-contingent movement of the mobile is reinforcing, and infants readily learn to kick in this situation. In one memory experiment, infants were first trained to kick to make the mobile move. After a retention interval during which no further training occurred, they were returned for a test session during which the mobile was disconnected (to prevent new learning). Rovee-Collier found that infants remembered the task (their kicking was above control levels) even after a retention interval of a week.

ability to reproduce or recount information that was experienced at an earlier time. Thus, we are said to remember what happened in our childhood if we can tell stories of childhood experiences. We are said to remember a phone number if we can state it accurately, and we are said to remember someone's name if we call her by the correct name. Unfortunately, similar tests of memory with animals are usually impractical. We cannot ask an animal to tell us what it did last week. Instead, we have to use the animal's overt responses as a clue to its memory. If your cat wanders far from the house and finds its way back home, you might conclude that it remembered where you live. If your dog has grown fond of a particular person and eagerly greets him after a long separation, you might conclude that it remembered that person. These and similar cases illustrate that *the existence of memory in animals is identified by the fact that their current behavior can be predicted from some aspect of their earlier experiences.* Any time the animal's behavior is determined by past events, we can conclude that some type of memory mechanism is involved in the control of that behavior.

You may notice that our definition of memory is very similar to the way we defined learning. In Chapter 1 we characterized learning as an enduring change in the mechanisms of behavior that results from prior exposure to environmental events. The major difference between the definitions of memory and learning is that *learning* refers to "enduring" effects of prior experience. In contrast, memory mechanisms do not preclude instances in which the control of behavior by past experiences is short-lasting. Things can be remembered for either short or long periods. We can say that something is remembered even if the memory lasts only briefly. All instances of learning involve memory. If the subject is incapable of remembering past events, past experiences cannot produce an enduring change in its behavior. However, not all instances of memory involve learning. Temporarily remembered experiences that influence an animal's actions involve memory but not learning.

Because the concepts of learning and memory are so similar, the concept of memory is superfluous in the interpretation of many learning experiments.

Consider, for example, salivary conditioning to a tone. With repeated pairings of a tone with food, the dog comes to salivate in response to the tone. After the conditioned response has been well established, we may wait for a month before testing the animal again. When the subject is returned to the experimental situation, chances are that it will again salivate in response to the tone. We do not need the concept of memory to explain this outcome. It would be sufficient to conclude that the subject's performance of the conditioned response after a month's rest simply indicated that it had learned the response to the tone. However, one cannot do without the concept of memory in explaining the control of behavior by past experiences in situations in which learning is not involved. The concept of memory is indispensable in at least two types of situations. One involves instances in which past events have only a short-lasting effect on the organism's actions, thus precluding a learning interpretation. Memory mechanisms are also required to explain cases in which responses to past events are changed by procedures that do not produce learning in and of themselves. We will describe examples of both temporary memory effects and modifications of memory by procedures that do not involve learning. Finally, we will discuss some theoretical issues concerning the interrelation of learning and memory.

Working and reference memory

As noted above, one aspect of behavior that involves memory and can be clearly distinguished from learning concerns short-lasting effects of past events. One of the earliest investigations of short-term memory effects was carried out by Hunter (1913), who was interested in the ability of animals to retain a "mental" representation of a stimulus. Hunter tested rats, dogs, and raccoons in a simple memory task. The apparatus consisted of a start area from which the animals could enter any one of three goal compartments. Only one of the goal compartments was baited with a piece of food on each trial, and the baited compartment was marked by illumination of a light bulb above that compartment at the start of the trial. Which compartment was baited (and illuminated) was varied from trial to trial.

After the subjects had learned to choose the illuminated compartment on each trial, Hunter made the task a bit more difficult. Now the light marking the baited compartment remained on for only a short time. After the signal was turned off, the subject was detained in the start area before being allowed to choose among the three compartments. Therefore, the animal had to remember somehow which compartment had been illuminated in order to find the food. The longer subjects were delayed before being allowed to make a choice, the less likely they were to go to the correct compartment. The maximum delay rats could withstand was about 10 sec. The performance of dogs did not deteriorate until the delay interval was extended to more than 5 min, and raccoons performed well as long as the delay was no more than 25 sec. The species also differed in what they did during the delay interval. Rats and dogs were observed to maintain a postural orientation toward the correct compartment during the delay interval. No such postural orientations were observed in the raccoons. Since the raccoons did not maintain a postural orientation during the delay interval, their behavior required some type of neural memory mechanism.

With the delay procedure, the animals had to remember which compartment had been illuminated at the start of that trial. However, once the trial was finished, this information was no longer useful because the food was likely to be in a different compartment on the next trial. Thus, memory of which compartment had been recently illuminated was required only to complete the work during a given trial. This type of memory is called **working memory.**

Working memory is operative when information has to be retained only long enough to complete a particular task, after which the information is best discarded because it is not needed or (as in Hunter's experiment) because it may interfere with successful completion of the next task. If you have to go to several stores in a shopping mall, for example, it is useful to remember which stores you have already visited as you select which one to go to next. However, this information is useful only during that

particular shopping trip. A mechanic changing the oil and lubricating a car has to remember which steps of the job she has already completed, but only as long as she is working on that particular car. In cooking a good stew, you have to remember what spices you have already put in before adding others, but once the stew is finished, you can forget this information. All these illustrate instances of working memory.

Working memory is often short-lasting. In Hunter's experiment, the memory lasted only 10 sec in rats and 25 sec in raccoons. However, as we shall see, in special situations working memory may last for several hours or days.

Examples of working memory illustrate the retention, for a limited duration, of recently acquired information. However, often such information is useful only in the context of more enduring knowledge. In Hunter's experiment, for example, remembering which compartment had been illuminated at the start of a trial was not enough to obtain food. This information was useful only in the context of enduring knowledge that the light marked the baited compartment. In contrast to information in working memory that was disposed of after each trial, information about the relation between the light and food had to be remembered on all trials. Such memory is called **reference memory** (Honig, 1978).

Reference memory is long-term retention of information necessary for successful use of incoming and recently acquired information. To shop efficiently in a shopping mall, you have to remember not only what stores you have already been to but also general information about shopping malls. Similarly, information about what a mechanic has done recently is useless unless the person generally knows how to lubricate a car and change the oil, and knowledge of what spices you have already added to a stew is useful only if you know which spices and how much of each to use. All successful uses of working memory require appropriate reference memories.

Investigations of working memory

Since Hunter's research, increasingly sophisticated techniques have been developed for the study of working memory. We will describe three situations that have provided important information about working memory. One of these, the delayed-matching-to-sample procedure, is a laboratory procedure that was developed without much regard for the innate behavioral predispositions of animals and can be adapted to the study of how animals remember any one of a variety of stimuli. The other techniques appear to be closely related to species-specific foraging strategies and illustrate some remarkable adaptive specializations in working memory for spatial stimuli.

Delayed matching to sample. The delayed-matching-to-sample procedure, one of the most versatile techniques for the study of working memory, is a substantial refinement of the technique that Hunter originally used. As in Hunter's procedure, the subject is exposed to a cue indicating which is the correct response on a particular trial. This stimulus is then removed before the animal is permitted to perform the designated behavior. In the typical experiment with pigeons, for example, the experimental chamber contains three response keys arranged in a row, as in Figure 11.1. The point of the study is to see whether

the pigeons can remember a sample stimulus long enough to pick it out when they are later given a choice between the sample and some other stimulus. The center key is used to present the sample stimulus, and the two side keys are later used to present the choice cues. The test stimuli might consist of an array of horizontal or vertical lines projected on the response keys from the rear. At the start of a trial, the center key is illuminated with a white light (see row A in Figure 11.1). After the pigeon pecks the white center key, one of the test stimuli—the horizontal array, for example—is projected on it (row B in Figure 11.1). This is the sample for that trial. Usually several pecks at the sample stimulus are required, after which the sample is turned off and the two side keys are lit up. One of the side keys is illuminated with the sample for that trial (horizontal), and the other key is illuminated with the alternative pattern (vertical) (row C in Figure 11.1). If the pigeon pecks at the pattern that matches the sample (in this case horizontal), the pigeon is reinforced. If it pecks the other pattern, no reward is provided. Thus, the reinforced response "matches" the sample. Which of the test stimuli serves as the sample is randomly varied from one trial to the next, and the matching stimulus is equally likely to be presented on the right or left key during the choice. Therefore, the pigeon can never predict which stimulus will be the sample on a given trial or where the matching stimulus will appear during the choice.

During the initial stages of matching-to-sample training, the sample stimulus remains visible until the subject has made the correct choice. Thus, in our example, the horizontal pattern on the center key would remain illuminated until the subject correctly pecked the horizontal side key. Such a procedure is called **simultaneous matching to sample** and does not require memory processes, because the cue for the correct response is visible when the response is made. Once subjects have mastered the simultaneous-matching procedure, the sample stimulus can be presented only briefly and removed before the choice stimuli are provided. Introduction of a delay between exposure to the sample stimulus and availability of the choice cues changes the procedure to **delayed matching to sample.**

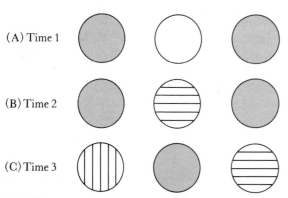

(A) Time 1

(B) Time 2

(C) Time 3

FIGURE 11.1. Diagram of the delayed-matching-to-sample procedure for pigeons. The experimental chamber has three response keys arranged in a row. At the start of a trial, the center key is illuminated with a white light (row A). After the pigeon pecks the white center key, the sample stimulus (horizontal) is projected on it (row B). This stimulus is then removed, and after a delay two choice stimuli (horizontal and vertical) are presented on the side keys (row C). Pecks at the choice stimulus that matches the sample are reinforced.

In most applications, as we mentioned, the matching stimulus is equally likely to appear on the left or the right choice key. Hence, subjects cannot make the correct choice by orienting to the right or left when the sample appears on the center key and holding this body posture until the choice stimuli are presented. Thus, in contrast to Hunter's procedure, simple postural orientations cannot be used to increase the likelihood of making the correct choice. Subjects are forced to use more sophisticated memory processes to obtain reinforcement in the delayed-matching procedure.

Procedural determinants of delayed matching to sample. The delayed-matching-to-sample procedure has been extensively used in research with a variety of species, including monkeys, pigeons, dolphins, goldfish, and rats (Blough, 1959; D'Amato, 1973; Herman & Thompson, 1982; Jarrard & Moise, 1971; Roberts & Grant, 1976; Steinert, Fallon, & Wallace, 1976; Wallace, Steinert, Scobie, & Spear, 1980), and the procedure has been adapted to investigate how animals remember a variety of stimuli, including visual shapes, numbers of responses performed, presence or absence of reward, and the spatial location of stimuli (for example, D'Amato, 1973; Maki, Moe, & Bierley, 1977; Wilkie & Summers, 1982). Three aspects of the matching-to-sample procedure are critical in determining the accuracy of performance. One of these is the nature of the stimulus that has to be remembered. In a recent study, for example, Wilkie and Summers (1982) tested the ability of pigeons to remember the spatial position of illuminated lights. Nine lights were arranged in an array of three columns and three rows. Three of the lights were illuminated on each trial. Memory for the position of the illuminated lights was much better if the three lights were in a straight line than when they formed a discontinuous pattern. (We will discuss the importance of patterns of stimulation further in Chapter 12.)

Two other factors that are important in determining the accuracy of delayed matching to sample are the delay interval and the duration of exposure to the sample stimulus at the start of the trial. In one experiment, for example, Grant (1976) tested pigeons in a standard three-key apparatus after they had received extensive training on delayed matching to sample with visual stimuli. Two pairs of colors—red/green and blue/yellow—served as sample and comparison stimuli on alternate trials. At the start of each trial, the center key was illuminated with a white light. When the subject pecked the center key, the sample color for that trial was presented on the center key for 1, 4, 8, or 14 sec. This was followed by delay intervals of 0, 20, 40, or 60 sec, after which the two side keys were illuminated, one with the sample-matching color and the other with the paired alternate color. After the subject made its choice, all the keys were turned off for a 2-min intertrial interval.

The results of the experiment are summarized in Figure 11.2. If subjects pecked the choice keys randomly, they would be correct 50% of the time. Higher scores indicate that subjects responded on the basis of their memory for the sample stimulus. For all the sample durations evaluated, the accuracy of matching decreased as longer delays were introduced between exposure to the sample and opportunity to make the choice response. In fact, if the sample was presented for only 1 sec and the opportunity to make a choice was delayed 40 sec or more, the pigeons responded at chance level. Performance improved if they were exposed to the sample for longer periods. When the sample was presented for 4, 8, or 14 sec, the subjects performed above chance levels even when the delay interval was as long as 60 sec. Thus, accuracy in the delayed-matching-to-sample procedure decreased as a function of the delay interval and increased as a function of the duration of exposure to the sample stimulus.

Response strategies in matching to sample. The matching-to-sample procedure is analogous to a discrimination problem in that the subject has to respond to a correct stimulus and not respond to an incorrect one to get reinforced. As we noted in discussions of discrimination learning in Chapter 8 (under "What Is Learned in Discrimination Training?"), such a two-alternative task can be solved by just responding to the correct choice, by just inhibiting behavior to the incorrect choice, or by using both these response strategies. Discrimination learning

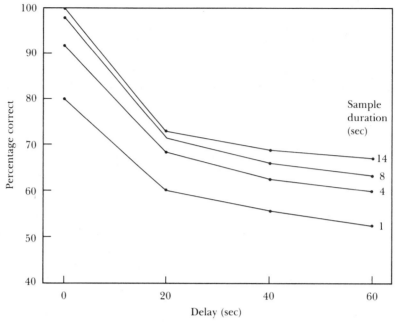

FIGURE 11.2.   Percentage of correct responses in a delayed-matching-to-sample task as a function of duration of presentation of the sample stimulus (1–14 sec) and delay between the sample and the choice stimuli (0–60 sec).   *(From Grant, 1976.)*

(which may be considered to involve the establishment of a reference memory) appears to involve the combined response strategy. In contrast, subjects in matching to sample appear to focus only on the correct choice. One interesting experiment supporting this conclusion used a three-key apparatus for pigeons that was specially constructed so that the stimulus projected on a response key was visible only if the pigeon was standing directly in front of that key (Wright & Sands, 1981). This apparatus enabled the experimenters to determine which response keys the pigeons looked at before making their choice responses in a matching-to-sample procedure. The results showed that the birds focused on the correct alternative. If they saw the matching stimulus, they pecked it without bothering to check what stimulus appeared on the other side key (see also Zentall, Edwards, Moore, & Hogan, 1981).

General versus specific rule learning.   The evidence reviewed above indicates that animals focus on the correct choice in matching to sample. What leads them to identify a stimulus as correct? One possibility is that they learn a general rule involving a comparison between the sample and choice stimuli. The rule may be, for example, "Choose the same as the sample." Another possibility is that animals learn a series of specific rules or stimulus-response relations. In the experiment by Grant (1976) described above, for example, pairs of colors were used—red/green and blue/yellow. The pigeons may have learned a series of specific stimulus-response relations: "Peck red after exposure to red," "Peck green after exposure to green," and so on. Most matching-to-sample procedures can be solved either by learning a general "same as" rule or by learning a series of specific stimulus-response relations, and no clear consensus has developed on which of these types of learning predominates (for example, Roitblat, 1984; Zentall, Hogan, & Edwards, 1984).

Evidence in support of one or the other alternative has been provided by studies of transfer of training. One type of transfer experiment involves first conducting matching-to-sample training with one set of stimuli and then conducting the same kind of training with a new set of stimuli. The hypothesis of specific stimulus-response learning predicts little positive (or negative) transfer of matching behavior to new stimuli because the new task requires learning a new set of stimulus-response relations. In contrast, the hypothesis of general rule learning predicts considerable positive carryover because the second matching-to-sample task involves the same general "same as" rule as the first one. Thus, in transfer of training from one matching-to-sample problem to another, the general-rule-learning hypothesis predicts better transfer performance than the specific-rule-learning hypothesis.

Evidence consistent with the general-rule-learning hypothesis has been obtained from transfer studies (see Zentall et al., 1984). However, some have argued that the magnitude of these effects has not been very large (see Roitblat, 1984). The preponderance of evidence suggests that both general rule learning and specific stimulus-response learning can occur (for example, Farthing & Opuda, 1974; Wilkie, 1983). A likely possibility is that the type of learning that occurs is related to the size of the stimulus set used in the matching-to-sample procedure. A study like that of Grant (1976), which used only four colors over and over again on successive trials, may favor learning of specific stimulus-response relations. In contrast, procedures that employ a large range of stimuli may favor learning of a more general rule. The extreme of this type of procedure is the *trials-unique procedure,* in which a different stimulus is used as the sample on each trial (for example, Overman, McLain, Ormsby, & Brooks, 1983).

Passive versus active memory processes. Another important issue in the analysis of delayed-matching-to-sample behavior concerns the type of memory involved. Results like those shown in Figure 11.2 have encouraged a **trace decay** interpretation of short-term memory (Roberts & Grant, 1976). This hypothesis assumes that presentation of a stimulus produces changes in the nervous system that gradually decrease, or decay, after the stimulus has been removed. The initial strength of the stimulus trace is assumed to reflect the physical energy of the stimulus.

Thus, longer or more intense stimuli are presumed to result in stronger stimulus traces. However, no matter what is the initial strength of the trace, it is assumed to decay at the same rate after the stimulus ends. The extent to which the memory of an event exerts control over the organism's actions depends on the strength of the stimulus trace at that moment. The stronger the trace, the stronger is the effect of the past stimulus on the subject's behavior. The trace-decay model predicts results of exactly the sort summarized in Figure 11.2. Increasing the delay interval in the matching-to-sample procedure reduces the accuracy of performance presumably because the trace of the sample stimulus is weaker after longer intervals. In contrast, increasing the duration of exposure to the sample improves performance presumably because longer exposures to the sample establish stronger stimulus traces.

The trace-decay hypothesis emphasizes the physical characteristics of the sample stimulus and is a passive memory mechanism. After the stimulus has been terminated, the decay of its trace is assumed to proceed automatically independent of further experiences. As the trace decays, information about the stimulus is assumed to become irretrievably lost. Contrary to the trace-decay hypothesis, various types of results suggest that working memory does not depend entirely on the physical features of the event to be remembered but involves active processes. For example, delayed-matching-to-sample performance improves with practice with the same types of stimuli. The learning history of a monkey named Roscoe provides a dramatic illustration. After 4500 training trials, Roscoe could not perform above chance level if a 20-sec interval was introduced between the sample and choice stimuli. However, after 17,500 trials he correctly matched the sample stimulus nearly 80% of the time with a 2-min sample-to-choice delay interval, and after approximately 30,000 trials his performance was better than chance with a 9-min delay interval (D'Amato, 1973). Another important determinant of working memory is the extent to which the stimulus is surprising. Several lines of investigation have shown that surprising events are remembered better than expected events (Maki, 1979; Terry & Wagner, 1975). The existence of active memory processes in working memory is also implicated by studies, discussed below, showing that memory processes can be brought under external stimulus control.

Spatial memory in a radial maze. The matching-to-sample procedure can be adapted to investigate how animals remember a variety of stimuli. The next technique we shall consider has more limited applicability but focuses on a very important type of memory—memory for places. To be able to move about their habitat efficiently, animals have to remember how their environment is laid out—where open spaces, sheltered areas, and potential food sources are located. In many environments, once food has been eaten at one location, it is not available there again for some time until it is replenished. Therefore, in foraging, animals have to remember where they last found food and avoid that location for a while. Such foraging behavior has been nicely documented (Kamil, 1978) in a species of Hawaiian honeycreeper, the amakihi (*Loxops virens*). These birds feed on the nectar of mamane flowers. After feeding on a cluster of flowers, they avoid returning to the same flowers for about an hour. By delaying their return to clusters they have recently visited, the birds increase the chance that they will find nectar in the flowers they search. They appear to remember the spatial location of recently visited flower clusters.

Memory for locations in space—**spatial memory**—has been studied in the laboratory with the use of complex mazes (for example, Olton, 1979). In one investigation, rats were tested in a maze similar to that shown in Figure 11.3 (Olton & Samuelson, 1976). The maze had eight arms radiating from a central choice area. A pellet of food was placed at the end of each arm. In each test, the rat was placed in the center of the maze and was free to enter each arm to obtain the food there. Once a food pellet had been consumed, that arm of the maze remained without food for the rest of the trial. How should the rat go about finding food in this situation? One possibility is to select randomly which alley to enter each time. Thus, the rat might enter an alley, eat the food there, return to the center area and then randomly select another arm of the maze to enter next, and so on.

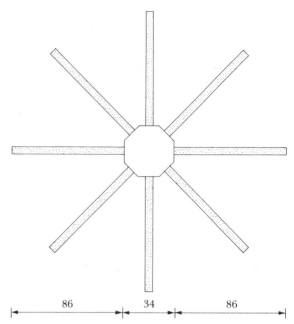

FIGURE 11.3. Top view of an eight-arm radial maze used in the study of spatial memory. Numbers indicate dimensions in centimeters. *(From Olton & Samuelson, 1976.)*

However, this might involve going down alleys from which the rat had already taken the food. A more efficient strategy would be to enter only those arms of the maze that the animal had not visited yet on that trial. This is in fact what most of the animals learned to do. Entering an arm that had not been visited previously (and therefore contained food) was considered to be a correct choice. Figure 11.4 summarizes the number of correct choices subjects made during the first eight choices of successive tests. During the first five test runs after familiarization with the maze, the rats made a mean of nearly seven correct choices during each test. With continued practice, the mean number of correct choices was consistently above seven, indicating that the subjects rarely entered an arm they had previously chosen in that trial.

Figure 11.4 illustrates that the rats did not require much training to come to perform efficiently in the radial maze. The radial maze task appears to take advantage of the inborn tendency of rats and other species to avoid recently visited places (for example,

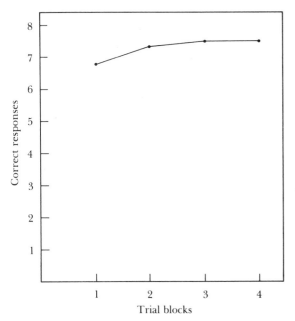

FIGURE 11.4.   Mean number of correct responses rats made in the first eight choices during blocks of five test trials in the eight-arm radial maze.   *(After Olton, 1978.)*

Haig, Rawlins, Olton, Mead, & Taylor, 1983). This may be related to the foraging strategies of the species or to exploratory behavior (Cole, Hainsworth, Kamil, Mercier, & Wolf, 1982; Gaffan & Davies, 1981).

Mechanisms governing radial maze performance. The fact that the rats in the study by Olton and Samuelson nearly always chose an arm from which they had not yet removed the food makes for efficient food gathering. However, this information is not enough to show that the animals were using some kind of spatial-memory mechanism. There are several ways in which they could have entered only previously unchosen arms without necessarily remembering the locations of all the arms they had already visited. For example, the rats might have been able to smell the food at the entrance to unvisited alleys. Another possibility is that the rats marked each arm they visited with something like a drop of urine and then just avoided arms of the maze that had this odor marker. Alternatively, the animals might have

learned a response chain of some sort, always selecting arms in a fixed sequence. For example, they might have learned to enter successive arms in a clockwise direction.

Numerous experiments have been done to determine whether the performance of rats in a radial maze is governed by spatial memory or some other mechanism. These studies have generally upheld the memory interpretation. One of these studies tested whether the rats were using the odor of food as a cue for entering an alley. The rats were allowed to remove food from six of the eight arms of the maze as usual. Before the subjects were permitted to make their remaining choices, those six arms were rebaited with food. If the rats were using the odor of food as a cue for entering an alley, replacing the food was expected to get them to reenter previously chosen alleys. However, this did not happen. Subjects did not return to previously chosen arms on their next two choices even if the arms were rebaited, and after that they were no more likely to enter rebaited arms than arms that did not have food (Olton & Samuelson, 1976).

In another study the maze was doused with aftershave lotion to mask any odor trails the rats might have made as they walked through the maze (Olton & Samuelson, 1976). In a related study, the animals' sense of smell was surgically disrupted (Zoladek & Roberts, 1978). Neither of these manipulations decreased the animals' performance. In another type of procedure, animals were allowed to enter several alleys during a test session. They were then confined to the center of the maze before being allowed to enter the remaining arms. During the confinement period, some of the arms of the maze were interchanged, or the entire maze was rotated 45°. The partitions blocking the entrances to the alleys were then removed, and the animals were free to make additional choices. The point of interest was whether the rats would reenter previously chosen arms if these were now in new locations or whether they would avoid the previously chosen arms regardless of where these arms were. The results indicated that the rats responded on the basis of spatial location rather than on the basis of the odor or other characteristics of the maze arms (Olton, Collison, & Werz, 1977; Olton &

Samuelson, 1976). Once subjects had removed food from an alley in a particular location, they avoided reentering that location even if a new maze arm was placed there. However, they did not avoid visiting old maze arms that were now in new locations.

The available evidence also indicates that rats in a radial maze experiment can perform efficiently without using response chains or entering maze arms in a fixed order from one trial to the next. As long as the central choice area is fairly small so that the rats can easily reach all the arms from anywhere in the central area, they do not choose arms in a fixed order (Olton & Samuelson, 1976; see also Olton et al., 1977). If the central area is made larger, the rats are more apt to select maze arms that are close by and enter adjacent arms on successive choices (Yoerg & Kamil, 1982). This response strategy serves to minimize their travel time for each pellet of food obtained and is predicted by optimal foraging theory.

The studies reviewed above have been important in ruling out various potential cues for radial maze performance and suggest that spatial stimuli are critical. What are spatial cues and how are they identified? Spatial cues are stimuli that identify the location of an object in the environment. Rats appear to use things like a window, door, corner of the room, or poster on the wall as landmarks of the experimental environment and locate maze arms relative to these landmarks. Movement of these landmarks relative to the maze causes the rats to treat the maze arms as being in new locations (Suzuki, Augerinos, & Black, 1980). Thus, spatial location is identified relative to distal room cues, not to local stimuli inside the maze (see also Morris, 1981). The distal environmental cues seem to be perceived visually (Mazmanian & Roberts, 1983).

Spatial map versus serial list memory. In what form do animals remember information about where they have been recently? One possibility is that animals remember a serial list of recently visited places. However, this seems unlikely given the remarkable capacity of spatial memory. For example, rats and gerbils have been observed to perform well in a radial maze with 17 arms (Olton et al., 1977; Wilkie & Slobin, 1983), and this probably does not represent

the limit of their spatial memory (Roberts, 1979). (Human beings are able to hold a serial list of only about seven items in working memory.) A more likely possibility is that animals form a spatial map that has previously visited locations marked (Roberts, 1984). One interesting implication of this hypothesis is that once animals have learned the location of something, they will be able to get there even from unpracticed start positions.

Morris (1981) tested the spatial map hypothesis with an innovative procedure that required rats to find the location of a slightly submerged platform in a water tank. Water in the tank was made opaque by adding milk so that the rats could not see where the platform was located. During training, the animals were always put in the water at the same place near the perimeter of the pool and quickly learned to swim from there directly to the platform. The interesting aspects of the study came during later tests when the animals were started from novel positions at the perimeter of the pool. If they had learned specific responses to get to the platform, they would not have been able to swim to the platform from new locations. However, results showed remarkably good performance on the test trials (see Figure 11.5). This finding suggests that the rats had formed a spatial map of the pool, with the position of the submerged platform marked on this mental map.

Duration and context specificity of spatial working memory. In addition to the large number of places animals remember at one time, the duration and context specificity of spatial working memory are also remarkable.

In an important test of the limits of spatial memory, Beatty and Shavalia (1980b) allowed rats to make four choices in the eight-arm radial maze in the usual manner. The subjects were then detained in their home cages for various periods up to 24 hours. After the delay interval, they were returned to the maze and allowed to make choices 5–8. An entry into an alley they had not previously chosen was considered a correct choice, and an entry into a previously used alley was considered an error. Figure 11.6 shows the percentage of correct choices as a function of the delay interval. A delay interval of up to 4 hours

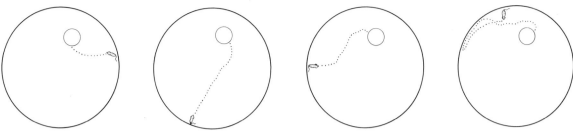

FIGURE 11.5.   Top views of a circular pool with a submerged (invisible) platform (small circle) placed in the northeast quadrant on four trials. At the start of each trial, a rat was placed in the tank at a different point on the perimeter of the pool. The lines from the perimeter to the platform show the tracks taken by the rat to get to the platform on each trial.   *(After Morris, 1981.)*

imposed after the first four choices did not disrupt performance. Longer periods of confinement in the home cage produced progressively poorer perfor-

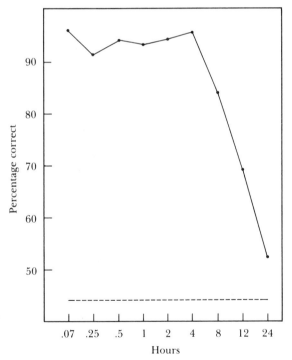

FIGURE 11.6.   Percentage correct responses on choices 5–8 in an eight-arm radial maze. Between choices 4 and 5 the animals were returned to their home cages for varying intervals ranging from .07 to 24 hours. The dashed line indicates chance performance (41%). *(After Beatty & Shavalia, 1980b.)*

mance. In fact, only one rat out of five showed significant retention of the first four choices after a 24-hour period. These data show that spatial memory is not permanent. However, it lasts at least several hours.

Other research has shown that spatial working memory is context-specific and therefore remarkably immune to disruption from other experiences. In one study (Beatty & Shavalia, 1980a), rats were trained on two identical eight-arm radial mazes located in different rooms. After completing four choices in one maze, they were taken to the other room and allowed to complete four choices in the other maze. Four hours after their choices in the first room, they were returned there to complete another four arm choices. The remarkable finding was that experiences in the second maze did not disrupt performance when the subjects were returned to the first maze, even though the two mazes were identical. The fact that the mazes were located in different rooms apparently served to segregate the memories of places visited in each room (see also, for example, Maki, Brokofsky, & Berg, 1979).

Species specificity of radial maze spatial memory. As we noted earlier, the radial maze task takes advantage of rats' innate tendency to avoid recently visited places. Their radial maze performance may also be related to the foraging patterns of rats in their natural habitat. These considerations suggest that rat spatial memory investigated in the radial maze may reflect a species-specific adaptation. Evidence relevant to this issue is inconclusive. The few studies that have been conducted with nonrodent species have suggested that spatial memory of Siamese fighting fish (*Betta splendens*) and pigeons is not nearly as good as that of rats (Bond, Cook, & Lamb, 1981; Roitblat, Tham, & Golub, 1982). However, others have presented evidence that the spatial memory of pigeons is, in many respects, comparable to that of rats (Olson & Maki, 1983). Further research will have to sort out these apparent contradictions. In particular, special attention will have to be devoted to designing mazes that are equally appropriate for the various species compared, since we know that certain apparatus features such as size of the central choice area can influence how a given species solves the radial maze problem (Yoerg & Kamil, 1982).

Spatial memory in cache recovery by birds.
Animals in a radial maze experiment have to recover food items that were previously stored in various locations by the experimenter. This situation is a laboratory analogue of many natural situations in which animals have no control over the location of food items. Another interesting spatial memory problem involves the recovery of food items that were stored in various places by the animal itself. Under these circumstances, the location of the food items is under the subject's own control. Several species of birds, for example, hoard food in various locations if they find more food than they need at the moment (see Shettleworth, 1983b). Later they revisit these caches to recover the stored food items. Such hoarding serves to hide food from competitors (other birds, ground squirrels, and so on) and provides the birds with a food supply when other food sources are not readily available.

The Clark's nutcracker (*Nucifraga columbiana*) provides a dramatic example. These birds live in alpine areas of the southwestern United States and harvest seeds from pine cones in late summer and early autumn. They hide the seeds in underground caches and recover them many months later in the winter and spring when other food sources are scarce. A Clark's nutcracker may store as many as 33,000 seeds in caches of four or five seeds each and recover several thousand of these during the next winter.

Memory has an important role in this behavior (for example, Balda & Turek, 1984).

Memory for the locations of hoarded food has also been studied in the marsh tit (*Parus palustris*), a small, lively bird found in England and related to North American chickadees. Shettleworth and Krebs (1982) tested marsh tits in a seminaturalistic environment consisting of tree branches distributed in an aviary (see Figure 11.7). The branches had about 100 small holes drilled in various locations, each just big enough to store a hemp seed. The holes were covered with small cloth flaps the birds had to lift in order to store a seed or look for one. In the first experiment, the birds were let into the aviary and permitted to store 12 seeds. They were then returned to a holding cage for 2–3 hours, after which they were let back into the aviary for a 12-min recovery period. On average, the birds recovered 8 of the 12 seeds during this time and made few errors in their search. They were particularly accurate in finding their first 5 seeds, making only about one error per seed. If they had been searching for the seeds randomly, they would have made about eight errors for each seed they found. Other evidence indicated that the birds could not detect the location of the seeds by smell. They were very inefficient in finding seeds stored in various holes by the experimenters rather than by the birds themselves.

The remarkably accurate performance of the marsh tits may have reflected memory for specific locations where the birds had stored the seeds. However, a prominent alternative possibility is that they had a number of favorite spots in the aviary and simply went to these first when storing and recovering the seeds. To decide between these alternatives, Shettleworth and Krebs conducted a second experiment in which the birds received two types of trials. On one type of trial (hoard-recovery), the birds were first allowed to store 8 seeds and then tested for recovery of these seeds 2.5 to 3 hours later. In the second type of trial (hoard-hoard-recovery), the first hoarding opportunity was followed 2.5–3 hours later by a second opportunity to hoard 8 more seeds. This was followed by a recovery test another 2.5–3 hours later. The hoard-hoard-recovery procedure was de-

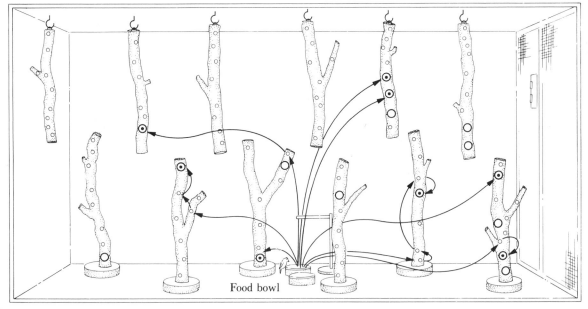

FIGURE 11.7.   Experimental environment for the study of spatial memory for hoarded food in marsh tits. Lines indicate flight paths and cache locations chosen by a marsh tit the second time it was permitted to hoard eight seeds. In choosing holes for the second batch of seeds (large circles with dots), it avoided the holes in which it had stored the first batch of seeds (large circles without dots). This indicates that it remembered the locations it had previously used to store seeds. *(After Shettleworth, 1983b.)*

signed to test the specific-memory hypothesis. If the birds remembered the specific holes where they previously stored food, they would stay away from these locations during the second hoarding opportunity because the holes were not big enough for two seeds. In contrast, if they always went to particularly favored holes, they would try to store seeds during the second hoarding opportunity in holes that already had seeds in them. The results clearly favored the specific-memory hypothesis (see Figure 11.7). The birds stayed away from filled holes during the second hoarding opportunity but visited these locations during recovery tests. Thus, instead of just going to the same favored holes each time, they appeared to remember which holes were filled with previously stored seeds. Because food-hoarding strategies are species-specific adaptations, memory processes involved in recovery of food stored in diverse locations may also reflect adaptive specializations.

Disruption and facilitation of memory

Examples of working memory illustrate the necessity of a distinction between learning and memory because they involve memory but not learning. The choice behavior of pigeons in a delayed-matching-to-sample task, for example, is a function of past experience (earlier exposure to the sample stimulus), but this influence is not long-lasting and therefore does not constitute what is usually considered to be learning. The concept of memory, as distinct from learning, is also necessary to explain instances in which the control of behavior by past experiences is either disrupted or facilitated by procedures that do not produce new learning in and of themselves. To explain such results, we assume that the subject's memory for the past experiences has been altered somehow. There are many ways that memories can be either disrupted or facilitated without producing new learning. You may, for example, tie a string around your finger to remind yourself to call someone. The string by itself does not tell you whom to call or what the person's phone number is. Rather, it facilitates your memory of a name and a phone number that you previously learned. In an analogous fashion, various manipulations can either disrupt or facilitate the memory of animals without producing new learning. Experiences before and after an event can influence how well the event is remembered. Memory can also be influenced by cues indicating whether it will be important to remember an event. Other factors that can modify actions based on memory include neurophysiological treatments and contextual cues present during acquisition of information. We will describe each of these various types of modifications of memory.

Proactive and retroactive interference.   Perhaps the most common source of memory disruption is exposure to prominent stimuli either before or after the event to be remembered. Consider, for example, a cocktail party. If the only person there you do not know is your neighbor's brother, chances are you will not have much trouble remembering who he is. However, if you are introduced to a number of new people before and/or after meeting your neighbor's brother, you may find it much harder to remember his name. There are numerous well-documented and analyzed situations in which memory is disrupted by exposure to a prominent stimulus prior to the event to be remembered. Because in these cases the interfering stimulus occurs *before* the target event, the disruption of memory is called **proactive interference.** In other instances memory is disrupted by exposure to a prominent stimulus after the event to be remembered. Because in these situations the interfering stimulus occurs *after* the target event, the disruption of memory is called **retroactive interference.** The mechanisms of proactive and retroactive interference have been extensively investigated in human memory (Postman, 1971; Slamecka & Ceraso, 1960; Underwood, 1957). Proactive and retroactive interference have also been investigated in animals with tasks involving delayed matching to sample (for example, Grant, 1975; Grant & Roberts, 1973, 1976) and spa-

tial memory (for example, Gordon, Brennan, & Schlesinger, 1976; Gordon & Feldman, 1978; Maki et al., 1979).

Proactive interference can be investigated in the delayed-matching-to-sample procedure by exposing subjects to an interfering stimulus just before presentation of the sample stimulus on each trial (see Grant, 1982a; Medin, 1980; Reynolds & Medin, 1981). In the standard matching-to-sample procedure, animals are given a sample (let us say S_1), followed by two choice stimuli (let us say S_1 and S_2), one of which (S_1) matches the sample. The subjects are reinforced only for responding to the matching stimulus. In one study of proactive interference with monkeys, illumination of stimulus panels with a red or a green light served as the S_1 and S_2 stimuli (Jarvik, Goldfarb, & Carley, 1969). The experimental chamber had three stimulus panels arranged in a row. The sample was always presented on the center panel. One second after presentation of the sample stimulus, the two side panels were illuminated with the choice stimuli. To investigate the effects of proactive interference, subjects were exposed to an interfering stimulus for 3 sec at various intervals ranging from 1 to 18 sec before presentation of the sample. The interfering cue was always the incorrect choice for that trial. If the sample on a given trial was the green color, the preceding interfering stimulus was exposure to the red color on the center key, and vice versa. Subjects also received control trials not preceded by exposure to an interfering stimulus.

The results are summarized in Figure 11.8. On control trials—that is, when no interfering cues were presented before exposure to the sample—the monkeys made the correct choice nearly 100% of the time. They responded less accurately when the sample stimulus was preceded by an interfering cue. Furthermore, greater disruptions of performance occurred when the interfering stimulus more closely preceded the sample stimulus. No proactive interference occurred if the interfering stimulus was presented more than 8 sec before the sample.

Retroactive interference can be studied in the delayed-matching-to-sample procedure by introducing an interfering stimulus between exposure to the sample and presentation of the choice stimuli. If

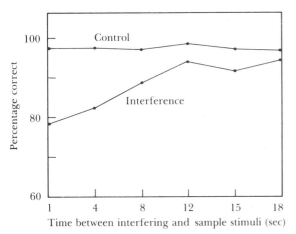

FIGURE 11.8. Percentage correct responses in a delayed-matching-to-sample task. On some trials an interfering stimulus was presented for 3 sec 1–18 sec before the sample stimulus. On control trials no interfering stimulus was presented.   *(After Jarvik, Goldfarb, & Carley, 1969.)*

the delayed-matching-to-sample task involves visual cues, memory for the sample is more likely to be disrupted by visual than by auditory cues presented during the delay interval (for example, Worsham & D'Amato, 1973; see also Thompson, Van Hemel, Winston, & Pappas, 1983). Perhaps the simplest way to present interfering visual stimuli is to turn on a light so that the animals can see various features of the experimental chamber. Several experiments have shown that illumination of the experimental chamber during the delay interval impairs memory for visual stimuli in a matching-to-sample task (for example, Grant & Roberts, 1976; Worsham & D'Amato, 1973). In one experiment, pigeons highly experienced in delayed matching to sample were tested with two visual cues as sample and choice stimuli (Roberts & Grant, 1978). The test cues, three vertical or horizontal white stripes on a black background, were projected on circular response keys in the usual three-key experimental chamber. The choice stimuli were presented 0–12 sec after exposure to the sample, and the experimental chamber was either illuminated or dark during the delay period. Figure 11.9 shows the results. Subjects correctly chose the matching stimulus more than 90% of the time when there was no delay after the sample stimulus. Accuracy decreased

as the interval between the sample and choice cues increased. However, this decrement in performance was much greater when the house lights were on during the delay interval. Thus, if subjects could see various features of the experimental chamber during the delay interval after exposure to the sample stimulus, their memory for the sample was impaired.

In trying to interpret deficits in performance observed in proactive and retroactive interference situations, one must consider whether the deficit reflects loss (forgetting) of information about the target stimulus or confusion about which stimulus was the target. The example of proactive interference described above (see Figure 11.8) may well have reflected confusion rather than forgetting. Here the monkeys were first exposed to the incorrect stimulus (green, for example) on a particular trial; they were then presented with the sample stimulus (red in this case), followed by a choice between the sample and the incorrect stimulus. The monkeys probably remembered having seen both the green and red stimuli but may have been confused about which one was the sample or which one had been presented first (D'Amato, 1973), and this confusion may have led to the proactive interference effect.

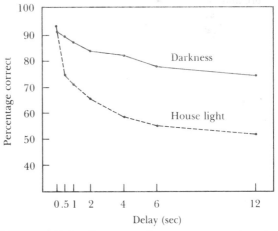

FIGURE 11.9. Percentage of correct responses in a delayed-matching-to-sample task as a function of increasing delays (0–12 sec) between the sample and the choice stimuli. On some trials the delay interval was spent in darkness. On other trials the house lights were on during the delay interval.   *(From Roberts & Grant, 1978.)*

Many studies of proactive interference can be explained in terms of some kind of confusion between the sample and the interfering stimulus rather than forgetting of the sample. One way to distinguish between these alternatives is to consider the importance of similarity between the interfering stimulus and the sample stimulus. According to the confusion hypothesis, similarity between the interfering and sample stimuli should be important in determining the degree of interference because the more similar these two events are, the more likely they are to be confused. Research has confirmed the importance of stimulus similarity in studies of proactive interference (for example, Reynolds & Medin, 1981). In contrast, studies of retroactive interference have favored a forgetting interpretation (Cook, 1980; Roberts & Grant, 1978; Thompson et al., 1983). Disruptions of performance have been observed in retroactive interference studies even if the interfering stimulus could not cause confusion errors (Wright, Urcuioli, Sands, & Santiago, 1981). Because the interfering stimulus occurs after the target stimulus in the retroactive interference procedure, it may cause forgetting by disrupting rehearsal of the sample stimulus.

Directed forgetting.   In proactive and retroactive interference situations, errors are an unintended result of exposure to the interfering stimuli and are penalized by nonreinforcement. In contrast, in **directed forgetting** procedures, forgetting is an intended result of cues indicating that the subject will not be required to remember a particular sample stimulus. Much research has been done indicating that human memory performance can be modified by instructions stating that something will or will not be important to remember (for example, Bjork, 1972). This research has sparked interest in finding analogous directed-forgetting effects in research with animal subjects. Investigators reasoned that if maintenance of information in working memory involved some type of rehearsal process (Wagner, 1976), this process might be subject to stimulus control, permitting the demonstration of directed forgetting in animal working memory. In recent years, directed forgetting has been demonstrated in pigeons, rats,

and squirrel monkeys (Grant, 1982b; Maki & Hegvik, 1980; Roberts, Mazmanian, & Kraemer, 1984; see Rilling, Kendrick, & Stonebraker, 1984, for a review).

In one experiment (Stonebraker & Rilling, 1981), a variation of the delayed-matching-to-sample procedure was used with pigeons. A circular pecking key was illuminated with either a red or a green light as the sample stimulus at the start of a trial. The first peck after 12 sec terminated the sample and instituted a 4-sec delay interval, after which the key light was again lit up either red or green. If the color after the delay interval matched the sample (red/red or green/green), pecks at the key were reinforced with food. If the color after the delay did not match the sample (red/green or green/red), pecks at the key did not end in reward. Thus, accurate performance required memory for the sample color that started each trial. However, unlike the matching-to-sample procedure we discussed earlier, in this procedure the matching and nonmatching comparison stimuli were not presented together at the end of the retention interval. This type of procedure is called **successive delayed matching to sample.**

Directed-forgetting training was instituted after subjects had learned to perform accurately on the delayed-matching-to-sample procedure. Arrays of black vertical and horizontal lines projected on the response key against a white background served as remember (R) and forget (F) cues. One or the other of these patterns was presented briefly (for 1/2 sec) immediately after the sample red or green color on each trial. On R-cue trials, memory was tested in the usual manner at the end of the delay interval—the red or green color was presented, and responding was reinforced only if the matching color appeared. (To make sure that the pigeons would look at the response key when the test stimulus was presented, a tone was briefly sounded with the test stimulus.) On F-cue trials, memory was not tested at the end of the delay interval; the trial simply ended after the F cue was presented. The pigeons soon learned that the F cue always ended without the opportunity for reinforcement and turned away from the response key on seeing the F cue.

The critical data of the experiment were obtained

on special test trials at the end of the directed-forgetting training. Test trials were like training trials except that memory for the sample stimulus was tested even when exposure to the sample was followed by the forget cue. Thus, test trials measured the accuracy of memory following both R and F cues to see whether memory would be worse after exposure to the forget cue. Another factor of interest was how much time elapsed between presentation of the sample stimulus and presentation of the remember or forget cue. On some test trials, the R and F cues were presented immediately after the sample stimulus. On other trials the R and F cues were presented 2 or 3.5 sec after the sample during the retention interval.

Figure 11.10 shows the results of the memory tests in terms of the percentage of the total number of pecks that were to the correct (matching) comparison stimulus during the memory tests. On remember-cue test trials, close to 90% of responses occurred to the correct stimulus regardless of when the remember cue was presented relative to the sample stimulus. Thus, the pigeons had learned to perform very well

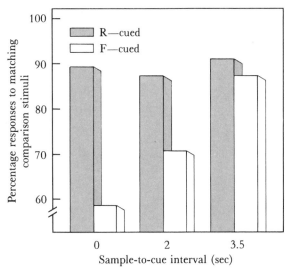

FIGURE 11.10. Percentage correct responses by pigeons in a successive-delayed-matching-to-sample procedure. On R-cued trials, a remember cue was presented 0–3.5 sec after the sample stimulus. On F-cued trials, a forget cue was presented after the sample stimulus. *(After Stonebraker & Rilling, 1981.)*

on the delayed-matching problem. Dramatically different results were obtained on forget-cue test trials. When the forget cue followed the sample stimulus immediately, performance on the memory test fell to below 60%. This is close to random performance (50%) in this task. Thus, the forget cue produced a substantial decrement in performance on the memory test. Progressively less disruption occurred when the forget cue was presented 2 sec or 3.5 sec after the sample stimulus.

Results like those presented in Figure 11.10 are consistent with a directed-forgetting interpretation. Pigeons may have performed less accurately on forget-cue test trials than on remember-cue test trials because the F cue disrupted information-storage mechanisms of working memory. Attractive as this interpretation may be, however, other alternatives also have to be evaluated. One important issue concerns the procedure that was used to train the forget cue. On forget-cue training trials, subjects were not tested for their memory of the sample stimulus and also could not earn reinforcement. The memory-disruption interpretation assumes that the absence of the memory test was critical. Several studies have shown that the absence of reinforcement on F-cue training trials is also important for directed-forgetting effects (Maki & Hegvik, 1980; Maki, Olson, & Rego, 1981). However, others have obtained directed-forgetting effects even when subjects were permitted to earn reinforcement on F-cue training trials (for example, Grant, 1982b). (This was accomplished by permitting subjects to earn reinforcement on a substitute task that did not require memory.) Thus, directed-forgetting effects do not require that the forget cue become conditioned as a signal for the absence of reinforcement.

Another important question is whether F cues disrupt working memory specifically or produce a more general disruption of discriminative instrumental behavior. Maki et al. (1981, Experiment 2) tested this possibility in pigeons by seeing whether an F cue would disrupt performance on a simultaneous discrimination task that did not require memory. Stimuli consisting of displays of vertical and horizontal lines were simultaneously projected onto two pecking keys, and pecking one of the patterns was reinforced.

Presentation of a forget cue did not significantly disrupt the simultaneous discrimination performance. This outcome indicates that F cues do not have a general disruptive effect on the stimulus control of instrumental behavior.

Finally, it is important to consider what type of information-retention mechanism is being disrupted by forget cues. One possibility is that the memory is some type of central process located somewhere in the brain. Alternatively, the information might be maintained in the animal's overt behavior. People, for example, sometimes repeat a phone number over and over to themselves to remember it long enough to dial the number. Some instances of directed forgetting may involve disrupting such overt response mediation during the delay interval. This may have been the case in the study by Stonebraker and Rilling (1981). Results of their tests of memory following R and F cues were summarized in Figure 11.10. Stonebraker and Rilling also measured the number of times the pigeons pecked the stimulus key during the retention interval between presentation of the sample and comparison colors. Figure 11.11 shows the rate of this retention-interval pecking for their various test conditions. The remarkable finding was that presentation of the F cue not only disrupted accuracy of memory (Figure 11.10) but also disrupted delay-interval pecking (Figure 11.11). In fact, the effects on memory accuracy and delay-interval pecking were strikingly similar. This raises the strong possibility that the directed-forgetting effects were due to disruption of overt mediational behavior. Further research is required to determine how such overt mediational behavior is involved in this and other examples of directed forgetting.

Neurophysiological means of disrupting memory. The disruptions of memory we have considered so far (proactive and retroactive interference and directed forgetting) were produced by events that were in no sense intrinsically disruptive. Factors extrinsic to the stimuli themselves made interfering events and forgetting cues disruptive. In proactive and retroactive interference, the extrinsic factors involved temporal and sequential relations of the interfering event to the information that was to be remembered; in directed forgetting, the extrinsic factor was that the forgetting cue was conditioned as a signal for the absence of memory testing. In contrast, the neurophysiological sources of memory disruption we will consider next are produced by events that are inherently disruptive, such as brain damage due to disease or accidental trauma. Someone who receives a strong blow to the head, for example, may suffer **amnesia** (loss of memory) as a result. The person is most likely to forget events that took place just before the injury and remember earlier experiences. Thus, the person may forget how the injury occurred, where the accident took place, or who else was there. However, the person will still remember more long-term information, such as his or her name and address and the names and ages of brothers and sisters. The first extensive study of memory loss following brain injury in humans was conducted by Russell and Nathan (1946). In general, they found that there is a temporal gradient of memory loss going back in time from the point of injury. The closer an episode is to the time of injury, the more likely the person is to forget that information. This phenomenon is called **retrograde amnesia**.

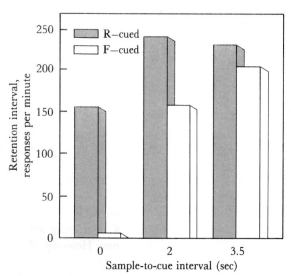

FIGURE 11.11. Rates of pecking by pigeons during the retention interval of a successive-delayed-matching-to-sample procedure. (For additional details, see Figure 11.10.) *(After Stonebraker & Rilling, 1981.)*

Retrograde amnesia has been extensively studied in animal laboratory experiments. The first studies of this sort used electroconvulsive shock (ECS) to induce amnesia. Electroconvulsive shock, introduced as a treatment for mental illness many years ago (Cerletti & Bini, 1938), is a brief electrical current passed through the brain between electrodes placed on each side of the head. It is not known exactly how ECS produces changes in disturbed patients. Investigators interested in memory started to study the effects of ECS because patients often reported amnesia after ECS treatment (for example, Mayer-Gross, 1943).

In the first laboratory investigation of the amnesic effects of ECS, Duncan (1949) trained rats to perform an instrumental response to avoid aversive stimulation. One conditioning trial was conducted on each of 18 days of training. All subjects except those in the control group received an electroconvulsive shock after each training trial. For independent groups of animals, the ECS was delivered at various times ranging from 20 sec to 4 hours after the training trials. The question of interest was whether and to what extent ECS would disrupt learning of the task. The results are summarized in Figure 11.12. Subjects treated with electroconvulsive shock 1 hour or more after each training trial performed as well on the avoidance task as the control group, which did not receive ECS. In contrast, the performance of the animals given ECS within 15 min of the training trials was disrupted. In fact, there was a gradient of interference: administration of ECS closer to the training trials resulted in poorer avoidance performance.

The pattern of results Duncan obtained is consistent with a retrograde-amnesia interpretation. Electroconvulsive shock is assumed to produce a gradient of amnesia such that events close to the ECS are not remembered as well as earlier events. Therefore, delivery of ECS shortly after a conditioning trial disrupts retention of that conditioning experience more than delivery of ECS at a longer period after the conditioning trial. It is possible to explain Duncan's results without the concept of amnesia (for example, Coons & Miller, 1960). However, numerous subsequent experiments have provided convincing evidence of experimentally induced retrograde amnesia in a wide variety of learning tasks (see McGaugh &

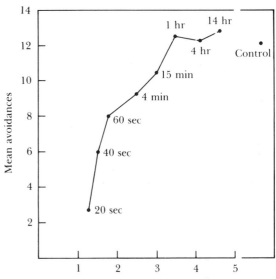

FIGURE 11.12. Mean number of avoidance responses for independent groups of rats given electroconvulsive shock (ECS) at various intervals after each avoidance trial. The control group was not given ECS. *(From Duncan, 1949.)*

Herz, 1972; Spear, 1978, for reviews). In addition, experiments have shown that retrograde amnesia can be produced by many treatments that affect the nervous system, including anesthesia (McGaugh & Petrinovich, 1965), temporary cooling of the body, or hypothermia (Riccio, Hodges, & Randall, 1968), and injection of drugs that inhibit protein synthesis (for example, Flexner, Flexner, & Stellar, 1963).

Why do treatments such as ECS produce a graded loss of memory? One explanation of retrograde amnesia is the *memory-consolidation hypothesis* (see McGaugh & Herz, 1972). This hypothesis assumes that when an event is first experienced, it is in a short-term, or temporary, state. While in short-term memory, the information is vulnerable and can be lost because of presentation of interfering stimuli or other disruptive manipulations. However, if the proper conditions are met, the information gradually becomes consolidated into a relatively permanent form. **Memory consolidation** is assumed to be some kind of physiological process that gradually puts information into a long-term or permanent state. Neu-

BOX 11.2. **Retrograde amnesia in Korsakoff patients**

In Box 6.2 we described some research on short-term memory problems of Korsakoff patients. Patients with alcohol-induced Korsakoff's syndrome also exhibit retrograde amnesia. That is, these individuals have difficulty remembering events in their past, particularly those events near the onset of their illness. For example, Butters and Cermak (1980) asked a newly diagnosed patient in 1975 whether the United States was still at war. "I think they have that war in Korea all wrapped up" was the reply, ignoring the more recent Vietnam war. Investigators have charted the gradient of memory loss for Korsakoff patients in several interesting ways. Figure 11.13 summarizes data from a study comparing normal people and Korsakoff patients (Albert, Butters, & Levin, 1979). In this study, each subject was asked to identify pictures of famous people. The people pictured were famous during one of five decades from the 1930s through the 1970s (for example, Tiny Tim, Rosemary Clooney). As shown in Figure 11.13, Korsakoff patients recognized fewer people than normal subjects did. More important, they showed a decline in recognition across the time period sampled. The closer someone's prominence was to the onset of illness in the Korsakoff patients, the worse was the patients' recognition memory. This gradient is indicative of retrograde amnesia. Studies such as this one are part of a growing body of research that advances our understanding of memory and memory deficits resulting from neurological damage.

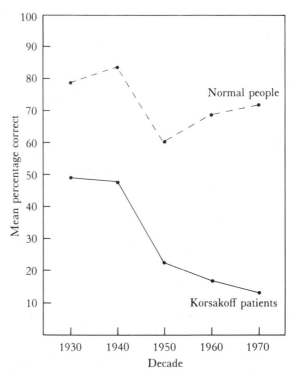

FIGURE 11.13. Mean percentage of photographs of people famous in various decades correctly identified by normal people and Korsakoff patients. *(After Albert, Butters, & Levin, 1979.)*

rophysiological disturbances such as electroconvulsive shock, anesthesia, body cooling, or inhibition of protein synthesis are assumed to interfere with the consolidation process and thereby disrupt the transfer of information to long-term memory. Disruption of consolidation produces amnesia only for information stored in short-term memory. Once information has been consolidated and transferred to long-term memory, it cannot be lost because of disruptions of consolidation. Amnesic agents presumably lead to loss of memory for recently experienced events but not earlier experiences because only the recent events are in short-term memory and thus are susceptible to disruptions of consolidation.

Disruptions of performance caused by amnesic agents can also be explained in a very different way. According to this alternative account, amnesia results not from loss of the memory but from inability to retrieve information from the long-term storage system (Lewis, 1979; Miller & Springer, 1973; Riccio & Richardson, in press; Spear, 1973). This explanation is called the *retrieval-failure hypothesis*. **Retrieval** refers to the recovery of information from long-term memory. The consolidation and retrieval-failure hypotheses can be highlighted by an analogy. To make sure that you do not lose the information in your grandfather's will, you may decide to put the will into a safe deposit box. Your grandfather dies some time later, and you find that you are unable to produce the will to see what is in it. Why might you be unable to gain access to the information in the will? One possibility is that the will never got put into the safe deposit box. Perhaps you lost it on the way to the bank. This type of loss is analogous to a failure of consolidation. The alternative is that the will is in fact in the safe deposit box but you lost the key to the box or do not remember where the box is located. This type of loss is analogous to a failure of retrieval.

A distinction between alternative theoretical explanations such as consolidation failure and retrieval failure is unimportant if we cannot find evidence to decide between the two. What kinds of experimental results would favor one explanation over the other? The consolidation-failure hypothesis states that once a memory is lost, it cannot be recovered. In contrast, the retrieval-failure view holds that amnesia can be reversed if the proper procedure is found to "remind" subjects of the memory. Thus, to decide between the alternatives, we have to find techniques that can reverse the effects of amnesic agents. Several such procedures have been developed, some of which are described in the next section. The fact that amnesia can be reversed makes it very difficult, if not impossible, to prove the memory-consolidation hypothesis. Given that many presumably "lost" memories have been reactivated by various reminder treatments, it is possible to argue that every loss of memory represents a failure of retrieval rather than a failure of consolidation (Miller & Springer, 1973). Even if one reminder treatment is found ineffective in reversing a case of amnesia, one can never be sure that some other reactivation treatment will not be successful. Thus, one can never be sure that a memory is irretrievable, as is required by the consolidation-failure position.

Facilitation of memory retrieval by "reminder" treatments. Numerous experiments have shown that memory for earlier conditioning trials can be reinstated by exposing subjects to some aspects of the stimuli that were present during the training trials (see reviews by Gordon, 1981; Spear, 1976, 1978). In early investigations of this phenomenon, exposure to the reinforcer independent of behavior was often used as the "reminder" treatment. In one experiment, for example, memory loss produced by electroconvulsive shock was counteracted by reexposing subjects to the aversive unconditioned stimulus before the retention test (Quartermain, McEwen, & Azmitia, 1970). However, experiments in which the "reminder" episode involves the unconditioned stimulus have been criticized on the grounds that such procedures permit new learning to occur (for example, Gold, Haycock, Macri, & McGaugh, 1973; Schneider, Tyler, & Jinich, 1974). If the "reminder" treatment produces new learning, the improved performance of subjects given this treatment may be due to the new learning rather than the reinstatement or retrieval of an old memory.

It is always important to consider the possibility of new learning when evaluating the effects of "reminder" treatments. However, many aspects of recent research on the facilitation of memory retrieval are difficult to explain using the new-learning hypothesis. Perhaps the most convincing way to make sure that a reminder treatment does not produce new learning is to use an extinction trial to reinstate the old memory. Improved performance after an extinction trial clearly cannot be attributed to new learning that is compatible with the old memory. Several experiments have demonstrated the facilitation of memory retrieval by an extinction trial. In one such study (Gordon & Mowrer, 1980), four groups of rats were conditioned to make a one-way avoidance response. The apparatus consisted of two compartments, one white and the other black. At the beginning of each trial, the subject was placed in the white compartment. Several seconds later the door to the black compartment was opened, simultaneously with the onset of a flashing light. If the subject crossed over to the black side within 5 sec, it avoided shock. If it did not cross in time, the shock was presented until the rat entered the black compartment. Subjects received repeated conditioning trials until they successfully avoided shock on three consecutive trials. Immediately after this training, two groups of rats were given electroconvulsive shock to induce amnesia.

Memory for the avoidance response was tested 72 hours after the end of training. During the retention test, subjects received five trials conducted the same way as during conditioning, except now the shock was never turned on no matter how long the rats took to cross to the black side. The most important aspect of the experiment involved giving an extinction ("reminder") trial to some of the subjects 15 min before the beginning of the retention test. This reminder treatment consisted in placing the rats in the white compartment of the apparatus for 60 sec with the flashing light turned on. No shock was delivered at the end of this stimulus exposure. Ordinarily we would expect such an extinction trial to decrease avoidance performance. The critical question was whether the extinction trial would also decrease the performance of rats made amnesic by electroconvulsive shock. If the extinction trial serves as a reminder treatment and facilitates retrieval of the memory of avoidance conditioning after ECS, it should facilitate avoidance behavior.

The results of the study are summarized in Figure 11.14. The data are presented in terms of the latency of avoidance responses during the retention test. Lower scores indicate that subjects performed the avoidance response faster. Higher scores indicate poorer performance. Let us first consider the two groups of rats that had not been given electroconvulsive shock. For these subjects, administration of the reminder extinction trial 15 min before the retention test resulted in slower avoidance behavior. This is the usual outcome of extinction. Let us next consider the results for subjects that had received ECS. Electroconvulsive shock in the absence of a reminder treatment (ECS, no reminder) resulted in the slowest avoidance responses. This outcome indicates that ECS produced amnesia for the prior avoidance training. However, if ECS-treated subjects were also given the extinction reminder trial before the retention test, their performance was much improved. In

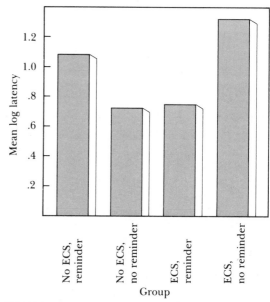

FIGURE 11.14. Latency of the avoidance response during a retention test for four groups of rats. Two of the groups were not given electroconvulsive shock (ECS) after training and were tested either after a reminder extinction trial or without the reminder trial. The other two groups were treated with ECS after training and were also tested either after a reminder extinction trial or without the reminder trial. *(After Gordon & Mowrer, 1980.)*

fact, the ECS rats given the reminder treatment responded as fast as subjects that had not received either ECS or the extinction trial. These results suggest that the reminder treatment fully restored the memory of the prior avoidance training. Thus, the amnesic effects of ECS were eliminated by exposing the subjects to the extinction trial. Since the extinction trial produced a decrement in performance in the absence of ECS, these results cannot be explained in terms of any new learning produced by the reminder treatment.

Much has been learned in recent years about facilitation of memory retrieval by reminder treatments (see Gordon, 1981; Spear, 1976, 1978, 1981). Various reminder procedures have been found to facilitate memory retrieval in addition to exposure to the reinforcer alone or the conditioned stimulus alone. Other effective reminder treatments have included exposure to the background stimuli of the experimental room (for example, Deweer, Sara, & Hars, 1980), exposure to lights and a tone in the experimental chamber (Thomas, McKelvie, Ranney, & Moye, 1981), exposure to interoceptive cues created by the injection of pentobarbital (Spear et al., 1980), and exposure to the nonreinforced stimulus in a discrimination procedure (Campbell & Randall, 1976). Memories retrieved by a reminder treatment are similar to memories retrieved directly by presentation of a conditioned stimulus. For example, cue-retrieved memories are remembered as long as or longer than memories retrieved by exposure to a conditioned stimulus (Rovee-Collier, Sullivan, Enright, Lucas, & Fagen, 1980; Spear, Hamberg, & Bryan, 1980). Another similarity is that cue-retrieved memories are also susceptible to disruption by amnesia-producing agents such as electroconvulsive shock or body cooling. Thus, administration of ECS or hypothermia after a reminder treatment will disrupt memory for the original conditioning experience (Mactutus, Ferek, George, & Riccio, 1982; Mactutus, Riccio, & Ferek, 1979; Misanin, Miller, & Lewis, 1968).

Finally, reminder treatments can be used to reverse many types of response decrements in addition to memory loss due to administration of amnesia-producing agents like ECS. Reminder treatments can, for example, facilitate memory retrieval from short-term memory (Feldman & Gordon, 1979). They can remind older animals (and babies) of forgotten early-life experiences (for example, Campbell & Randall, 1976; Fagen & Rovee-Collier, 1983; Haroutunian & Riccio, 1979; Richardson, Riccio, & Jonke, 1983). Reminder treatments can counteract stimulus generalization decrements that occur when learned behavior is tested in a new situation (Gordon, McCracken, Dess-Beech, & Mowrer, 1981; Mowrer & Gordon, 1983). Reminder treatments can also compensate for disruptions of performance typically observed with overshadowing and blocking classical conditioning procedures (Kasprow, Cacheiro, Balaz, & Miller, 1982; Schachtman, Gee, Kasprow, & Miller, 1983).

Interrelations of learning and memory

So far we have focused on various behavioral phenomena that involve manipulations of memory rather than learning. However, as we noted earlier, memory is obviously involved in learning. If organisms were incapable of remembering past events, learning could not take place. Advances in our knowledge of memory mechanisms in animals have been accompanied by increased interest in integrating this information with analyses of learning. We will consider two illustrations of this integration: an analysis of the role of retrieval practice in learning and an analysis of the role of rehearsal in learning and memory.

Reconsideration of the learning curve. In most learning tasks, the average performance of a group of subjects gradually improves during the course of training (see, for example, Figure 4.10). This gradual improvement is generally interpreted as reflecting the progressive acquisition of new knowledge—knowledge about the relation between a CS and a US or between a response and a reinforcer, for example. As the subjects acquire more and more knowledge, their performance gets progressively better. However, research on memory mechanisms suggests that, in addition to the acquisition of new knowledge, other processes may also contribute to improvements in performance as a function of training trials. Each conditioning trial involves more than just the information the subject is to learn. In a classical conditioning experiment, for example, each conditioning trial may involve exposure to the conditioned and unconditioned stimuli. As we have seen, exposure to the CS or the US can serve as an effective reminder, or retrieval cue for past conditioning trials. Therefore, a conditioning trial may not only convey new information to the subject but also remind the subject of earlier trials. Improvements in performance during acquisition may in part reflect the retrieval function of training trials.

In a study of maze learning in rats, Miller (1982) recently investigated the possibility that training trials contribute to improved performance because they serve as retrieval cues. Training occurred in a somewhat complex maze (the Lashley III maze), shown in Figure 11.15. To get from the start to the goal box, the rats had to learn to make a series of alternate left and right turns. Entries into dead ends were scored as errors. Subjects received one trial in the maze every other day. All the rats were thirsty at the time of each trial, and half of them were rewarded with access to a sugar solution for reaching the goal box. For the other half of the rats, the floor of the maze was electrified with a mild current at the start of each

trial, and shock escape served as the reinforcer. The point of primary interest in the experiment involved reminder treatments administered 24 hours after trials 3 and 4. The reminder treatments consisted in exposure to the USs (sucrose for sucrose-rewarded rats and shock for shock-escape rats) in a chamber distinctively different from the maze. Control subjects were just handled in place of the reminder treatments.

The results of the experiment are summarized in Figure 11.16. Exposure to the US alone in a distinctively different chamber after trials 3 and 4 significantly facilitated performance in the complex maze for both sucrose-rewarded and shock-escape-rewarded rats. Animals that received the reminder treatments made fewer wrong turns in the maze on

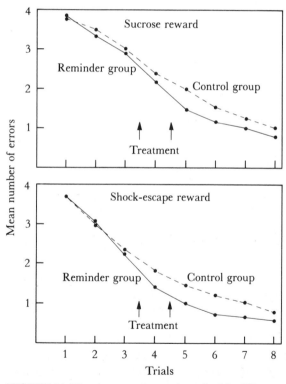

FIGURE 11.16. Accuracy in running a Lashley III maze for control and reminder groups reinforced with shock escape or sucrose. Subjects in the reminder groups received exposure to their reinforcer (shock or sucrose) in a distinctively different chamber after trial 3 and trial 4. *(After Miller, 1982.)*

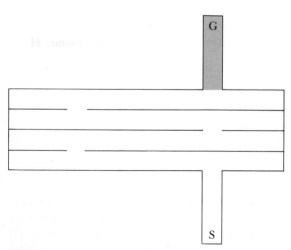

FIGURE 11.15. Top view of Lashley III maze used by Miller (1982). S, start box; G, goal box. The sides and partitions of the maze were constructed of wood.

average than animals that just received handling in place of the US-alone exposures. This facilitory effect of reminders is hard to explain in terms of new learning because the US-alone exposures were given in a chamber distinctively different from the maze. Subjects could not have learned to make correct maze turns in this other apparatus. The effect is also hard to explain in terms of increased motivation produced by the US-alone treatments because each reminder was administered 24 hours before the next training trial. In addition, Miller (1982) has shown similar effects with exposure to the start box of the maze as the reminder treatment, something that would not be expected to increase motivation. Miller's findings suggest that typical learning curves reflect not only the acquisition of new information but also improvements in how well the information is retrieved. Evidently, training trials function in part to provide retrieval practice.

Rehearsal theory. One of the most systematic efforts to integrate the study of memory with the study of learning has been pursued by Allan Wagner and his associates and has resulted in a theoretical model of memory, conditioning, and habituation known as *rehearsal theory* (Wagner, 1976, 1978, 1979; see also Wagner, 1981, for an elaboration and greater specification of the concepts in the form of a detailed mathematical model).

Rehearsal theory accepts the common assumption that there are two types of memory, long-term and short-term. Short-term memory (abbreviated STM) is assumed to have a limited capacity, so that presentation of a new stimulus may interfere with the processing of other events in STM. In contrast, the capacity of long-term memory is assumed to be much larger and is never exceeded in the usual experiment. All stimuli the subject is exposed to are first assumed to enter short-term memory. From here the information may simply be lost with the passage of time, or if a stimulus becomes associated with another stimulus, the information learned will be stored in long-term memory. The extent to which information in short-term memory influences the subject's behavior or leads to learning is assumed to depend on the extent to which the information is "rehearsed." **Rehearsal**

can be thought of as a means of maintaining the memory in an active state. The more vigorously a stimulus is rehearsed, the more likely it is to influence the subject's immediate behavior (elicit some response). Rehearsal is also important in conditioning and the transfer of information to long-term memory. It is assumed that two stimuli (a CS and a US, for example) will become associated with each other to the extent that they are simultaneously rehearsed in short-term memory. Once the association between the CS and the US has been established, presentation of the CS will result in retrieval of the memory of the US from long-term to short-term memory. Thus, the subject becomes "reminded" of the US when it experiences the CS after conditioning has taken place.

The concept of rehearsal has a critical role in the theory. Another important concept is **priming.** A stimulus is said to be primed in short-term memory if it is already being rehearsed. There are two ways a stimulus can come to be rehearsed in STM. First, it can be rehearsed because it was recently presented. This type of priming is called **self-generated priming**: the stimulus is primed by a prior presentation of itself. The second way a stimulus can come to be primed in STM is for the stimulus to be retrieved from long-term memory by an associated stimulus (such as a CS). For example, a US can become primed in STM by the prior presentation of a CS that was associated with the US. This type of priming is called **retrieval-generated priming.** This technical language may seem a bit burdensome. However, the ideas involved are not very obscure. If you are actively thinking of a stimulus, it is said to be primed. You can be thinking of a stimulus because it was recently presented (self-generated priming) or because you were exposed to another event that reminded you of the stimulus (retrieval-generated priming).

At this point we are ready to consider the most important aspect of rehearsal theory—the relation between priming and rehearsal. The critical assumption of the theory (the feature that leads to most of its interesting predictions) is that *priming of a stimulus in STM interferes with rehearsal of another presentation of the same stimulus.* Thus, an event will not receive much rehearsal if the same stimulus was presented in the recent past (self-generated priming) or if an associated stimulus was presented in the recent past (retrieval-generated priming). The assumption that priming blocks rehearsal has important implications for both the responses elicited by a stimulus and the new learning in which a stimulus may participate. Recall that the extent to which a stimulus influences the subject's behavior or leads to new learning depends on the extent to which the stimulus is rehearsed. Because priming disrupts rehearsal, the priming of a stimulus in STM reduces the extent to which that stimulus will elicit responses or will be involved in new learning. These implications of rehearsal theory are compatible with many findings in habituation and conditioning. We will describe some of the more important results below.

Priming and habituation phenomena. As we noted in Chapter 2, repeated presentations of a stimulus often result in reduction of the subject's response to the stimulus. There are two types of habituation effects. One is a short-term decrement in reactivity to a stimulus from which the subject recovers spontaneously if it is not exposed to the stimulus for some time. The second type of habituation is much more long-lasting and does not dissipate with a period of rest. Both these phenomena are consistent with rehearsal theory. The temporary loss of responsiveness to a stimulus may be explained in terms of self-generated priming (for example, Whitlow, 1975). Each presentation of a stimulus primes that stimulus in STM for a limited period. If the event is repeated while the subject is still rehearsing the previous stimulus presentation, the subject will not rehearse the new occurrence of the stimulus and therefore will not react to it. This decrement in reactivity will dissipate with time as the subject finishes rehearsing earlier stimulus presentations. Thus, response decrements due to self-generated priming will show spontaneous recovery.

Long-lasting habituation effects are explained in terms of retrieval-generated priming. The idea is that, during repeated presentations of a test stimulus in a particular situation, an association is established between background cues of the situation and the test stimulus. Because of this association, the subject is "reminded" of the test stimulus whenever it is in the experimental situation. Thus, the test stimulus is

primed by way of a retrieval-generated priming process. This retrieval-generated priming reduces the extent to which the subject will rehearse presentations of the test stimulus and therefore reduces the extent to which the subject will react to them. An interesting implication of this interpretation is that the decrement in responsiveness should be reversed by extinguishing the association between the background cues of the experimental situation and the test stimulus. This can be done by simply leaving the subject in the experimental situation for a long time without presentations of the test stimulus. After such an extinction experience, the background cues of the situation should no longer "remind" the subject of the test stimulus and therefore should no longer produce retrieval-generated priming. In confirmation of this predicted outcome, Whitlow and Pfautz (reported in Wagner, 1976) found that a rest period spent in the experimental chamber without stimulus presentations resulted in recovery from long-term habituation.

Priming and classical conditioning. The assumption that priming interferes with the degree of rehearsal a stimulus ordinarily elicits also has interesting implications for classical conditioning. Rehearsal theory assumes that an association will be established between the CS and the US to the extent that the two stimuli are simultaneously rehearsed in STM. This simultaneous rehearsal can be disrupted by the priming of either the CS or the US in STM before the conditioning trial. One way to accomplish this is to present either the CS or the US by itself shortly before the conditioning trial. Such a CS or US preexposure episode would produce self-generated priming of the CS or US, respectively, and should interfere with establishment of the CS-US association. Consistent with this prediction, several investigations have shown that presentation of the CS or the US by itself shortly before a conditioning trial interferes with conditioning (for example, Best & Gemberling, 1977; Domjan & Best, 1977; Terry, 1976).

Another way to disrupt conditioning by priming of either the CS or the US before the conditioning trial involves retrieval-generated priming. Retrieval-generated priming of the US can be accomplished by presenting a stimulus that was previously associated with the US. Thus, exposure to a previously conditioned stimulus should block the formation of an association between a new CS and the US. As we discussed in Chapter 4, this outcome, known as the blocking effect, has been demonstrated in many conditioning experiments. Retrieval-generated priming of the CS can be accomplished through the mechanisms we discussed above in connection with long-term habituation effects. Repeated presentations of the CS (without the US) in an experimental situation should establish an association between the CS and the background stimuli of the situation. These background cues will then prime the memory of the CS in STM, and this will interfere with establishment of a new association between the CS and a US. Evidence in support of this prediction has been obtained by Wagner, Pfautz, and Donegan (reported in Wagner, 1979) in both rabbit eyelid conditioning and fear conditioning in rats.

Concluding Comments

We have learned much about animal memory mechanisms in recent years. Several highly effective laboratory techniques have been developed for the study of working memory in animals, and the importance of working memory in the natural history of several species has been documented. Other studies have shown that memory can be disrupted by events that precede or follow the target information, by forget cues, and by certain neurophysiological treatments. However, in many cases failures of memory can be alleviated by exposure to some of the stimuli that were present during the original acquisition of the information. Our increased knowledge of animal memory mechanisms has stimulated considerations of the various ways in which memory mechanisms are involved in learning processes and phenomena.

CHAPTER 12
Animal Cognition: Diverse Information-Processing Mechanisms

In Chapter 12 we will describe a diversity of contemporary research areas in animal cognition involving the processing of various types of information. We will begin with a discussion of the processing of time and number information. We will then discuss processing of information about serial patterns, learning of concepts, reasoning in nonhuman primates, and the training of language in nonhuman primates. We will end the chapter by describing applications of language-training procedures to verbally handicapped children.

The various aspects of behavior we will discuss in this chapter—timing, counting, serial pattern learning, concept formation, reasoning, and language learning—have more apparent differences among them than similarities. They are not all reflections of a common underlying mechanism, nor are they all involved in the solution of a common behavioral problem or challenge to survival. However, they all involve contemporary areas of research in animal cognition that have stimulated a great deal of interest. This interest has come in part because until recently these cognitive processes were considered to be associated primarily with human behavior. The interest is also due to varying degrees of controversy that have met each of these areas of research. The controversies have centered on whether complex cognitive processes had to be postulated to explain the various behaviors that were observed. Opponents of cognitive interpretations have argued that the phenomena of timing, counting, serial pattern learning, concept formation, reasoning, and language learning could be explained by traditional learning principles. In contrast, proponents of cognitive interpretations have argued that cognitive mechanisms provide simpler explanations for the phenomena and are more productive in stimulating new research. Work in animal cognition has amply borne out this latter justification. Without a cognitive perspective, much of the research we will describe in this chapter would never have been done and many of the phenomena would never have been discovered.

Timing and Counting

Interest in whether animals can tell time and count has a long history filled with entertaining anecdotes. However, only recently have these areas of animal behavior come under experimental scrutiny (for example, Church, 1978; Davis & Memmott, 1982). Meck and Church (1983) have suggested simple definitions of timing and counting: animals are said to be timing if the duration of an event serves as a discriminative stimulus for them (a cue for responding one way rather than another). Correspondingly, animals are said to be counting if the number of events serves as a discriminative stimulus for them (see also Davis & Memmott, 1982). Although these definitions are pretty straightforward, experimental applications of them can be difficult. A critical methodological requirement in research on both counting and timing is to make sure no other environmental events are correlated with duration (in the case of timing) or number (in the case of counting). The task for the subject has to be set up carefully to eliminate correlated stimuli that could inadvertently "tip off" the subject and permit it to respond correctly without the use of some sort of internal timing or counting process. Eliminating such correlated cues is easier to accomplish with timing than with counting. We will first describe research on timing and will then describe a model that considers timing to be a variation of counting.

Techniques for the measurement of timing behavior

A variety of aspects of animal behavior reflect sensitivity to time (Richelle & Lejeune, 1980), and a variety of techniques have been used to investigate animal timing (for example, Mellgren, Mays, & Haddad, 1983). Some tasks involve duration estimation. For example, rats may be presented with either a .5-sec or an 8-sec burst of white noise on a given trial and required to make a discriminative response based on the duration of the signal. Immediately after presentation of the short or long noise, two response levers may be inserted into the experimental chamber. If the short noise was presented, a response on the left lever will be rewarded with a pellet of food; if the long noise was presented, a response on the right lever will be rewarded. Rats can learn to perform accurately in such a task without too much difficulty (for example, Church, Getty, & Lerner, 1976; see also Wasserman, DeLong, & Larew, 1984).

Another very fruitful technique for the study of timing has involved duration production instead of duration estimation. This technique, called the **peak procedure,** involves a discrete-trial variation of a fixed-interval schedule. Each trial is defined by the presentation of a noise or light. A specified duration after the onset of the trial stimulus, a food pellet is set up, or primed. Once the food pellet has been set up, the subject can obtain it by pressing a lever. A recent study by Roberts (1981) nicely illustrates the technique. Rats were tested in standard lever-press chambers housed in sound-attenuating enclosures to minimize extraneous stimulation. On some trials a light stimulus was presented, and on other trials a noise was presented. In the presence of one of the trial stimuli, food was primed after 20 sec; in the presence of the other stimulus, food was primed after 40 sec. Most of the trials ended when the subject responded and obtained the food pellet. However, a small proportion of the trials continued for a variable duration not less than 80 sec and ended without food reward. These extra-long trials were included to see how the subject would behave after the usual time of reinforcement passed.

Figure 12.1 presents the results of the experiment in terms of rates of responding at various points during a trial. The figure shows that during the 20-sec signal, the highest rate of responding occurred around 20 sec into the trial. In contrast, during the 40-sec signal, the highest rate of responding occurred around 40 sec into the trial. The incredible orderliness of the data and the correspondence of peak response rates to the times of food priming make this technique very useful in the analysis of animal tim-

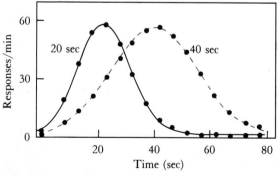

FIGURE 12.1. Rate of responding as a function of time during a signal in the presence of which food was primed after 20 sec (solid line) and during a different signal in the presence of which food was primed after 40 sec (dashed line). *(After Roberts, 1981.)*

ing. It should be noted, however, that these results were obtained only after extensive training. The data in Figure 12.1 were obtained during five daily 4-hour sessions after ten daily training sessions of 6 hours each. Behavior reflecting temporal discrimination developed slowly during the course of training. Early in training, animals did not show the distinctive peak responding that was evident later, as in Figure 12.1.

Results like those presented in Figure 12.1 illustrating behavioral control by the duration of a stimulus could arise in several ways. One possibility is that the onset of a stimulus initiates a fading neural trace whose strength is related to time since stimulus onset, and the subject learns to use a particular strength of the trace as a cue to respond to obtain reward. Another possibility is that the animal engages in some type of "pacing" behavior, and the amount of this behavior is somehow used to provide information about time. Yet another possibility is that animals have an internal clock that provides an internal representation of time, and they "read" this clock to cue their peak responding.

Why should we accept the internal clock interpretation instead of other possibilities? Church (1978) has suggested three reasons. First, the assumption of an internal clock may simplify explanation and discussion of instances of behavior under temporal control. Other alternatives are likely to be much more cumbersome to apply to a wide range of timing phenomena. Second, the concept of a clock is bound to stimulate questions about animal timing that we would not be likely to ask otherwise (see below). Finally, an internal clock may be a physiological reality, which we are more likely to find if we first postulate its existence and investigate its properties (Meck, Church, & Olton, in press).

Characteristics of the internal clock

If the concept of an internal clock is useful in explaining results in peak-response and other timing situations, we should be able to use the concept to generate interesting research questions. We may ask, for example, whether the clock can be temporarily stopped without loss of information about how much time has already elapsed. To answer this question,

Roberts (1981; see also Roberts & Church, 1978) interrupted a 40-sec time signal for 10 sec on selected test trials. During intertrial intervals, the experimental chamber was dark. Each trial was marked by presentation of a light; on most trials, food was primed 40 sec after the onset of the light. On special test trials without food reward, the light was turned off for 10 sec starting 10 sec after the start of the trial. Figure 12.2 shows the resulting distributions of response rates at various times during trials with and without this break. Introducing the 10-sec break simply shifted the peak response rate, by about 10 sec (13.3 sec, to be exact). These results suggest that, within a bit of error, the internal clock stops timing when a break is introduced and resumes timing without resetting at the end of the break.

Other research has shown that internal clocks have many of the same properties as a stopwatch. Internal clocks measure how much time has elapsed (as does a stopwatch) rather than how much is left before the end of the interval (as does an oven timer). Animals seem to use the same internal clock to measure the duration of stimuli from different modalities (visual and auditory); they also use the same clock and clock speed to measure intervals of different durations (Meck & Church, 1982; Roberts, 1981, 1982; Roberts & Church, 1978). Having worked out these basic behavioral characteristics of timing in normal subjects, investigators are starting to turn their attention to the physiology of timing and pharmacological ef-

fects on timing. For example, some drugs, like methamphetamine, have been observed to increase the speed of an internal clock, whereas other drugs, like haloperidol, have been noted to decrease clock speed (Maricq, Roberts, & Church, 1981; Meck, 1983). Such results can provide important insights into the effects of psychoactive drugs. Without the basic research on the behavioral mechanisms of timing, research on how various drugs influence the perception of time could not have been started.

A model of timing

So far we have considered the notion of an internal clock somewhat loosely. What might be the details of a mechanism that permits animals (and people) to respond on the basis of temporal information? Gibbon and Church (1984) have proposed an information-processing model of time estimation, which is diagramed in Figure 12.3 (see also Gibbon, Church, & Meck, 1984). The model assumes three independent processes: a clock process, a memory process, and a decision process. The clock process is activated by the start of the interval to be timed. Timing is assumed to be accomplished by having a pacemaker that generates impulses at a certain rate (something like a cardiac pacemaker). The pacemaker impulses are fed to a switch, which is turned on by the start of the interval to be timed. This allows the pacemaker impulses to go to an accumulator that counts the number that come through. When the interval to be timed ends, the switch closes, thereby blocking any further accumulations of pacemaker impulses. Thus, the accumulator accumulates information about elapsed time. This information is then fed to working memory, providing input about the current trial. The nervous system is also assumed to have information about the duration of similar stimuli in reference memory from past training. The contents of working and reference memory are compared in the decision process, and this comparison provides the basis for the animal's response. For example, in the peak-response procedure, if the time information in working memory matches the information in reference memory concerning availability of reward, the subject is encouraged to respond. If information in work-

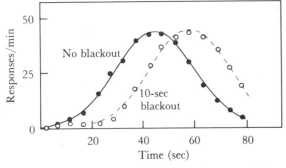

FIGURE 12.2. Rate of responding as a function of time during a signal in the presence of which food was primed after 40 sec. On some trials, the signal was interrupted for a 10-sec blackout period (dashed line). On other trials, no blackout occurred (solid line). *(After Roberts, 1981.)*

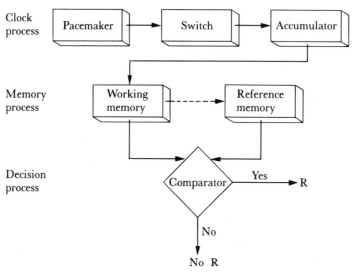

FIGURE 12.3.   Diagram of an information-processing model of timing.   *(After Gibbon &*
Church, 1984.)

ing and reference memory does not match closely
enough, the animal is not encouraged to respond.
This mechanism makes the peak rate close to the time
of priming of the reward.

Spelling out the details of a hypothetical model of
timing is helpful because it permits more detailed
analyses of various types of error that animals may
make in timing tasks (see Gibbon & Church, 1984).
Such analyses permit explanations of more detailed
aspects of timing behavior than would be possible
otherwise. The model also helps in indicating various ways in which timing behavior can be altered.
Recent evidence, for example, suggests that certain
drugs alter timing behavior by changing the speed of
the internal clock (altering the frequency of impulses
generated by the pacemaker). In contrast, other drugs
change timing behavior by altering the memory process, the remembered duration of past time intervals
(Meck, 1983). These contrasting influences on timing behavior would be difficult to interpret without a
model that distinguishes a clock process from a memory process.

Relation between timing and counting

The model of timing proposed by Gibbon and
Church (1984) and outlined in Figure 12.3 can be eas-

ily adapted for counting as well as timing. Whether
the system acts as a timer or a counter depends only
on how the switch operates that allows impulses to go
from the pacemaker to the accumulator (see Figure
12.3). The contrasting modes of switch operation that
result in timing and counting are displayed in Figure
12.4. In the timing mode, the switch stays open as
long as a stimulus is on and is closed when the
stimulus is turned off. With this arrangement, the
number of impulses allowed to go to the accumulator
provides information about how long the stimulus
was on, irrespective of how many times it was turned
on. In the counting mode, the switch is opened for a
brief, fixed duration each time a stimulus is presented, irrespective of the duration of the stimulus.
With this arrangement, the number of impulses al-

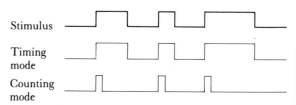

FIGURE 12.4.   Contrasting modes of switch operation
that result in timing or counting using the same pacemaker
and accumulator.   *(After Meck & Church, 1983.)*

lowed to go to the accumulator reflects the number of stimulus events—not their duration.

The above discussion raises the possibility that counting and timing are in many respects similar. This is an intriguing possibility that is attracting increasing research interest. The accumulating evidence suggests that the hypothesis may be correct. One way to assess similarity in timing and counting behavior is to compare the accuracy of rats in making judgments about differences in time with their accuracy in making judgments about differences in number. Provided that the ratio of long to short durations is the same as the ratio of large to small numbers (8 sec/2 sec, compared with 8 events/2 events, for example), accuracy in time estimation is remarkably similar to accuracy in number estimation. Similarity in the mechanisms of timing and counting is also suggested by the fact that methamphetamine has very similar effects on the two types of behaviors (Meck & Church, 1983).

Serial Pattern Learning

Stimuli in the environment rarely occur randomly and independently of each other. Rather, many aspects of the environment involve orderly patterns of stimulation. Behavior in response to serial patterns of stimuli has been extensively investigated in humans (for example, Jones, 1974; Restle & Brown, 1970; Simon & Kotovsky, 1963). Consider, for example, what you would do if you were asked to memorize the following list of numbers: 1234234534564567. You could learn the numbers by memorizing which number was in each of the 16 positions of the list. If you knew that 1 was in the first position, 2 in the second and fifth positions, 3 in the third, sixth, and ninth positions, and so on, you could recall the numbers in the correct order. However, this would be the hard way. A much simpler strategy would be to look for a pattern to the numbers. If you could figure out the pattern, you would have a rule that you could use to generate the sequence of numbers. The numbers listed above were generated by a relatively simple rule, which might be stated as follows: start counting

with the number 1, but every four numbers subtract 2. Memorizing this rule is much easier than learning what number is located in each of the 16 positions of the list.

Abstracting a rule from a sequence of stimuli involves responding to the pattern of the stimuli. It is clear that people respond on the basis of the patterns inherent in the stimuli they experience. Can animals also learn to respond on the basis of patterns in serially presented stimuli? This question is attracting increasing research interest (for example, Capaldi, Verry, Nawrocki, & Miller, 1984; Hulse, 1978; Hulse, Cynx, & Humpal, 1984; Straub & Terrace, 1981).

Experimental analysis of how animals respond to serial patterns of stimuli first requires selecting effective stimuli. Numerous investigations of serial pattern learning in animals have used a technique developed by Stewart Hulse and his colleagues in which different numbers of food pellets serve as stimuli. Hungry rats are tested in a runway and receive different numbers of food pellets in the goal box at the end of each run. In one experiment, for example, the goal box contained either 14, 7, 3, 1, or 0 food pellets. Subjects were given sets of five runs in the runway. In each series of five runs, one group of subjects received 14 food pellets on the first run, 7 pellets on the second run, 3 on the third, 1 on the fourth, and finally 0 on the fifth run. Thus, the sequence of stimuli these subjects experienced was 14-7-3-1-0. Running speed was used to measure response to the various food quantities. As training progressed, the rats learned to adjust their running speed to the amount of reward they were to receive for each run. In particular, they learned to run much slower on the fifth run of each series, which ended in 0 pellets, than on earlier runs, which ended in 1 to 14 pellets. Such slowing down on the fifth run could not be attributed to fatigue, because other research has shown that the rats would not have slowed down if they had received reward on the fifth run. Why did the slowdown occur? Hulse and his associates have proposed a **serial-pattern-learning hypothesis.** According to this interpretation, animals learn to respond to a series of stimuli (such as a series of food quantities) on the basis of the pattern, or structure, inherent in the series.

Implications of serial pattern learning

What sort of pattern could rats have extracted from the series of food quantities used in the above experiment, and how could we be sure they were responding to the pattern of the stimuli? The sequence 14-7-3-1-0 has a simple and easily identified pattern: the change from one food quantity in the series to the next is always of the same type—a decrease. A pattern in which succeeding elements of a series always involve changes in the same direction is called a **monotonic sequence.** A monotonic sequence of stimuli has a much simpler pattern than a sequence in which successive elements do not always involve the same type of change. For example, the series 14-1-3-7-0 is a **nonmonotonic sequence** because going from one element to the next involves both decreases (for example, 14-1) and increases (for example, 1-3). If rats respond to the pattern of a sequence of food quantities, then the simplicity of the pattern should facilitate learning. They should learn monotonic sequences more easily than nonmonotonic sequences.

The experiment described above also included a group of rats that received the nonmonotonic sequence of food quantities 14-1-3-7-0 during successive runs in the runway. Figure 12.5 shows the running times on each run of the 5-run sequence at the end of the experiment for groups of rats trained with the monotonic sequence (14-7-3-1-0) and the nonmonotonic sequence (14-1-3-7-0). Both groups took much longer to run down the alley on the nonreinforced (fifth) run of the sequence than on earlier runs. Other aspects of the results indicated that subjects exposed to the monotonic sequence learned this slowdown response with less training than subjects exposed to the nonmonotonic sequence. In addition, as Figure 12.5 shows, subjects in the monotonic group slowed down more on the fifth run than subjects in the nonmonotonic group. These results are consistent with a serial-pattern-learning interpretation (see also Fountain, Evensen, & Hulse, 1983).

The most important prediction of the serial-pattern-learning hypothesis is that subjects' response will depend on the kind of pattern a series of stimuli has. Hulse and his colleagues have tested this pre-

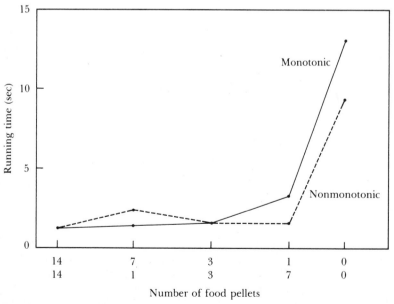

FIGURE 12.5. Asymptotic running times on five successive runs reinforced by different numbers of food pellets. One group of rats received a monotonic, decreasing series of food quantities (14-7-3-1-0 pellets). The other group received a nonmonotonic series of food quantities (14-1-3-7-0 pellets). *(From Hulse, 1978.)*

diction in various ways (for example, Fountain & Hulse, 1981; Hulse & Dorsky, 1979). In one study, for example, they compared learning of a strongly and a weakly monotonic sequence of food quantities, 14-7-3-1-0 and 14-5-5-1-0 (Hulse & Dorsky, 1977, Experiment 2). Both sequences involved decreasing quantities of food across the five runs. However, the weakly monotonic sequence (14-5-5-1-0) included a temporary interruption of the decreasing pattern (both the second and third runs were reinforced with 5 pellets). The strongly monotonic sequence had a more easily discerned pattern. If rats respond on the basis of the pattern of reinforcement, we may expect more appropriate performance with the strongly monotonic sequence than with the weakly monotonic sequence. The results confirmed this prediction.

In another study, the difficulty of learning the pattern of a long sequence was manipulated by introducing phrasing cues (Fountain, Henne, & Hulse, 1984). Research with human subjects has shown that learning of a long sequence is facilitated by subdividing the sequence into smaller units that have their own consistent internal structure. (This process is sometimes called *chunking*.) For example, the numbers 214325436547 are difficult to memorize as such. The task is made much easier if the numbers are grouped as 214 325 436 547. In this case the spaces between successive triplets of numbers act as phrasing cues to chunk the entire series into four smaller groupings. Phrasing cues facilitate learning only if they break a series into units that have their own internal structure. If the phrasing cues are placed at inappropriate points in the series, they may not help at all or may even hinder learning because they will obscure the pattern of the series. For example, the pattern of the above series would be obscured by the phrasing 2143 2543 6547.

Fountain et al. (1984) tested rats in a T maze with food quantities serving as stimuli arranged in a serial pattern. Only one side of the T maze was open on a given run. Each rat received the rewards 14-7-3-1-0 five times each day. Thus, the total series of food quantities consisted of 25 elements made up of five repetitions of the subsequence 14-7-3-1-0. For one group of rats (group N), no phrasing cues were provided; the subjects received 25 consecutive runs to the same goal box, and repetitions of the subsequence on

a given day were not marked in any way. For a second group (group E), phrasing cues were introduced by changing the available goal box in the T maze from one side to the other after each completion of a subsequence—each run to 0 pellets of food. The phrasing cues were provided for the first 7 days of the experiment and were removed when the subjects were tested on day 8.

Figure 12.6 summarizes the results of the experiment, showing running times to various numbers of food pellets on days 7 and 8 for group E and on day 8 for group N. Group N (which did not receive any phrasing cues) ran equally rapidly for all food quantities, including 0 pellets, on day 8. This indicates that without phrasing the subjects did not learn to respond appropriately to the food quantity stimuli in the eight days of training—they did not slow down on zero-pellet runs. In contrast, group E, which received a phrasing stimulus during training, tracked the food quantities very well on day 7, when phrasing was still in effect; subjects in group E ran much slower on zero-pellet runs than on other runs. The subjects continued to track the sequence (though not as well) when the phrasing stimulus was removed on day 8, indicating that some of what they had learned about

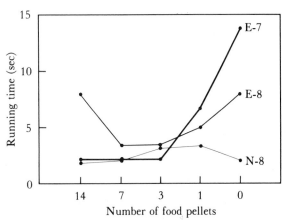

FIGURE 12.6. Running times of rats on five successive runs reinforced by different numbers of food pellets. Curve N-8 was obtained on day 8 from subjects that were never provided with phrasing cues between repetitions of the five-run sequence. Curves E-7 and E-8 were obtained from subjects trained with phrasing cues. The phrasing cues were present on day 7 (curve E-7) but were absent on day 8 (curve E-8). *(After Fountain, Henne, & Hulse, 1984.)*

the pattern persisted in the absence of phrasing. These results are consistent with the interpretation that animals can respond to the formal structure of a serial pattern.

The results presented in Figure 12.6 for group N deserve further comment. Why did these subjects do so poorly? After all, they received the same strongly monotonic sequence (14-7-3-1-0) that we previously described as producing good tracking of the serial pattern (see Figure 12.5). Two factors were probably responsible for this discrepancy. The monotonic group in the earlier study received phrasing cues at the end of each completion of the 14-7-3-1-0 series, in the form of an extended time interval before being put back into the runway for the next series of five runs. Research has shown that an extended interval between runs can serve as an effective phrasing cue (Fountain et al., 1984). In addition, the data for the monotonic group in Figure 12.5 were obtained after more extensive training than the data for group N in Figure 12.6. Group N eventually also learned the serial pattern, but not until day 13 of training.

Alternatives to serial pattern learning

The types of experiments we have described can also be analyzed using theoretical concepts that do not assume pattern learning (see Hulse & Dorsky, 1977, 1979). The most prominent alternative view is based on sequential associations and assumes that the learning of a list of items involves formation of associations between successive pairs of items (Capaldi & Molina, 1979; Capaldi, Nawrocki, & Verry, 1982; Capaldi, Verry, & Davidson, 1980). We discussed an application of this theory to instrumental behavior during extinction in Chapter 5. The theory assumes that subjects can remember the reward outcome of the preceding run over long intervals. This memory is then assumed to become associated with the outcome of the next run. Whether the memory of a prior outcome stimulates (or inhibits) the instrumental response depends on whether it has become associated with reinforcement (or nonreinforcement). Consider, for example, the sequence 14-7-3-1-0. In this sequence the subjects are reinforced for responding (on the second run) when they remember having received

14 pellets on the preceding run (S^{14}). They are also reinforced for responding (on the third and fourth runs) when they remember having received 7 and 3 pellets on the preceding runs (S^7 and S^3), respectively. Thus, the memories S^{14}, S^7, and S^3 become positive discriminative stimuli (S+s) for the instrumental response. In contrast to the first four runs (when subjects are reinforced), they are not reinforced on the fifth run, after receiving a 1-pellet reward on the fourth run. Therefore, the memory of having received 1 pellet on the preceding trial (S^1) becomes a negative discriminative stimulus (S−) for the instrumental response. According to this analysis, animals are slow to respond on the fifth run because the memory of 1 pellet on the preceding trial acts as an S−.

Consistent with the sequential-association theory, rats have been shown to have remarkable ability to remember the reward (or nonreward) outcomes of prior runs. They can remember, for example, as many as eight prior discrete hedonic events (one reward, followed by seven nonreward) (Capaldi & Verry, 1981). The sequential-association theory has also been surprisingly successful in explaining some results that at first glance seemed to be uniquely predicted by the pattern-learning hypothesis. Consider, for example, the effects of phrasing on pattern learning. As we described above, when the subsequence of food quantities 14-7-3-1-0 is repeated five times each day without interruption, tracking of the pattern is much better if each completion of the subsequence is marked by a phrasing cue. This outcome is clearly predicted by the pattern-learning hypothesis because phrasing cues that mark subsequences make the structure of a long pattern much more easily discerned. Capaldi, Verry, Nawrocki, and Miller (1984) have suggested an alternative interpretation. If the sequence 14-7-3-1-0 is repeated over and over without phrasing cues, the 0-pellet run is followed by the 14-pellet run. Therefore, the memory of no reward (S^0) is present when the subject receives 14 pellets, making S^0 a discriminative stimulus for running. The memory of 0 pellets is similar to the memory of 1 pellet (S^1). Therefore, the discriminative properties of S^0 are assumed to generalize to S^1. This encourages the subject to respond rapidly on the run that follows the 1-pellet reward. The result is that the subject does not slow down on the 0-pellet run in the 14-7-3-1-0 sequence, and tracking is not observed.

How might phrasing cues reduce the discriminative properties of S^1 and slow down responding on a 0-pellet run in the 14-7-3-1-0 sequence? Capaldi, Verry, Nawrocki, and Miller (1984) suggest that this occurs because phrasing cues become associated with the reward outcome that follows them. Consider introducing phrasing cues "X" between repetitions of a subsequence as follows: X-14-7-3-1-0-X-14-7-3-1-0 and so on. Now the 14-pellet reward is no longer given after the 0-pellet reward but after the phrasing cues symbolized by "X." Therefore, the memory of "X" rather than the memory of the 0-pellet reward will become associated with the 14-pellet reward. "X" will also block the association of S^0 with the 14-pellet reward because "X" is a better predictor of the 14 pellets. Since S^0 does not become a discriminative stimulus for running in this case, generalization of discriminative control from S^0 to S^1 does not occur. The result is that the subject is not encouraged to respond on 0-pellet runs in response to the memory of a 1-pellet reward, and the slowdown effect on 0-pellet runs is allowed to emerge. According to this analysis, phrasing cues act not by clarifying the structural organization of the food quantity sequence but by preventing the acquisition of discriminative control by stimuli that would otherwise lead to responding on 0-pellet runs.

The ingenious theoretical and experimental analysis of the phrasing effect provided by Capaldi, Verry, Nawrocki, and Miller (1984) makes clear that sequential-association theory has to be considered a serious alternative to the serial-pattern-learning hypothesis. However, the theory is not likely to provide an explanation of all serial pattern results. For example, as Capaldi and his associates have noted (see Capaldi & Molina, 1979), the sequential-association theory cannot explain the difference, described earlier, between a strong monotonic sequence (14-7-3-1-0) and a weak one (14-5-5-1-0). Significantly better tracking occurs in the strong than in the weak monotonic sequence. In both these sequences the memory of a 1-pellet reward (S^1) is assumed to become a negative discriminative stimulus because the run after the 1-pellet reward ends in 0 pellets. In

the strong sequence (14-7-3-1-0), the most similar positive discriminative stimulus is the memory of 3 pellets (S^3). In contrast, in the weak monotonic sequence (14-5-5-1-0), the most similar positive discriminative stimulus is the memory of 5 pellets (S^5). More stimulus generalization should occur from S^3 to S^1 than from S^5 to S^1. Therefore, S^1 should be less effective in inhibiting running in the strong monotonic sequence (14-7-3-1-0) than in the weak monotonic sequence (14-5-5-1-0). The fact that the opposite outcome was observed is contrary to this prediction.

Although the sequential-association theory has difficulty explaining certain patterning results, it is very successful in explaining other results. Capaldi and Molina (1979), for example, have shown that, with some reward sequences, discriminability of the memories of prior response outcomes is more important in predicting behavior than is the structural pattern of the sequences. The pattern-learning hypothesis and the sequential-association theory are both supported by evidence. Although the pattern-learning hypothesis has not withstood all challenges, it has been very successful in stimulating research that probably would not have been performed otherwise (such as that on the effects of phrasing cues). The task for future investigators is to delineate more clearly the circumstances in which sequential associations or pattern structure predominates in controlling behavior (Roitblat, Pologe, & Scopatz, 1983).

Concept Formation in Animals

Organisms experience a great variety of stimuli during their lifetime. However, as we have seen, they often do not respond to these stimuli as independent and isolated events. We discussed one type of perceptual organization in the preceding section, responding to a series of stimuli on the basis of the structural pattern of the series. Reactions to stimuli can also be organized by classes, or categories, that an individual stimulus may represent. Consider, for example, seeing a chair. You may note some of its specific features, such as its color, shape, height, firmness, and materials. However, you will also note that it is an instance of the category "chair." We can all agree on what things are chairs and what things are not. Specifying the critical features that constitute the concept "chair" is much more difficult. Many chairs are brown, have four legs, have a seat at about knee level, are hard, and are made of wood. However, something can be a chair without having any of these characteristics. Although it is not well understood how human beings form concepts, there is no doubt that concepts are very important in human behavior. We have concepts of physical entities, such as chairs, houses, trees, water, cats, and dogs. We also have concepts of events, such as a thunderstorm or a fight, and abstract concepts, such as loyalty, fairness, and intelligence. One reason concepts are very important in human behavior is that they form the building blocks of language. Words, in large measure, are labels for concepts.

Because complex concepts are critical to language, the study of concept formation in animals has been an integral part of efforts to teach linguistic skills to animals (for example, D. Premack, 1976). Much of this research has been conducted with chimpanzees. There is no doubt that chimpanzees are capable of learning complex concepts. However, chimpanzees have a much more developed nervous system than most animals. Therefore, one may well wonder whether an organism such as the pigeon, which has a much more rudimentary brain, is also capable of responding on the basis of a concept. In Chapter 11 we briefly discussed learning of the concept "same as" in connection with interpretations of matching-to-sample behavior (see "General versus Specific Rule Learning"). In the present section we will concentrate on how pigeons learn **perceptual concepts**— concepts involved in recognizing objects like a tree, a body of water, or a person (see Cerella, 1982; Herrnstein, 1984; Lea, 1984 for recent reviews of research and theory in this area).

One of the most thorough analyses of concept formation in the pigeon was carried out by Herrnstein, Loveland, and Cable (1976). They investigated pigeons' ability to respond to instances of three concepts—tree, water, and a particular person—on the basis of two-dimensional pictures illustrating these concepts. Their method basically involved discrimination training. In the "tree" experiment, for example, color slides of various scenes were projected on the wall of the experimental chamber near a response key. If the scene contained a tree or some part of a tree, the pigeons were reinforced with food for pecking the response key. If the picture did not contain a tree or any part of one, pecking was not reinforced. Each experimental session consisted of 80 slide presentations, about 40 of which included a tree. During training the stimuli for any given day were randomly selected from 500–700 pictures depicting various scenes from all four seasons of the year in New England. The reinforced stimuli included trees (or parts of trees) of all descriptions. However, the trees were not necessarily the main point of interest in the pictures. Some slides showed a tree far away, others showed trees that were partly obstructed so that only some of the branches were visible, for example.

During training the same photographs were occasionally used more than once. Subjects soon learned the requirements of the task and pecked the response key at a much higher rate in the presence of pictures containing a tree than in the presence of pictures without trees. What might have been responsible for the accuracy of their performance? One possibility is that the pigeons memorized what the reinforced and nonreinforced pictures looked like without paying particular attention to the presence or absence of trees. This is a distinct possibility when small numbers of pictures are used, because pigeons have remarkably good memory for visual scenes. They can memorize at least 80 different pictures. In a recent study, for example, Greene (1983) trained a discrimination between the presence and absence of a person by repeatedly presenting 80 pictures of various scenes (40 with the person and 40 without). With the use of special tests, she was able to show that the pigeons had learned to respond correctly when a picture with the person was presented not by responding to the person but by memorizing the background of each reinforced picture.

Memorization of individual reinforced and nonreinforced pictures probably was not responsible for the pigeons' successful performance in the study by Herrnstein et al. (1976), however, because 500–700 pictures were used, and only occasionally were pictures repeated. Herrnstein et al. also tried to rule out picture memorization by testing subjects with a completely new set of pictures at the end of training. The pigeons performed nearly as accurately on the new pictures as on the pictures used during initial training. Much higher rates of pecking occurred in the presence of new slides that contained a tree (or part of one) than in the presence of new slides that did not contain trees. Similar results were obtained in experiments involving the presence or absence of water (lakes, ocean, puddles, and so on) or the presence or absence of a particular person (in various types of clothing, in various situations, doing various things).

If pigeons in studies like those of Herrnstein et al. (1976) do not memorize individual reinforced and nonreinforced pictures, how do they learn to respond correctly? Consider what adult human beings might do if faced with a similar task. Keep in mind that the pigeons were not given verbal instructions (nor could they be) to the effect that responding in the presence of trees would be reinforced. Without such instructions, people would no doubt make errors until they learned that the problem required responding when a tree or part of a tree was being shown. They would not have to learn the concept of a tree during the experiment. They would just have to learn what to do whenever they saw a picture with some part of a tree. Perhaps pigeons approach the problem the same way. Perhaps they too already "know" what trees are and simply have to learn what to do whenever they see an instance of a tree. They may have learned the concept of a tree through their previous experience or may "know" about trees innately. Innate predispositions for concepts of important naturally occurring things like trees, water, and people may be adaptive for birds. Attractive as this hypothesis may be, however, it cannot explain other examples of concept formation in pigeons. For example, studies have shown that pigeons can learn to respond on the basis of the presence or absence of fish in underwater photographs (Herrnstein & deVilliers, 1980). Pigeons never have the opportunity to see underwater scenes during their life, nor is the ability to form a concept of fish likely to be adaptive for pigeons. Other experiments have shown that pigeons can learn entirely artificial concepts, such as the letter "A" appearing in diverse type styles (Morgan, Fitch, Holman, & Lea, 1976).

If concept-formation studies do not involve memorization of specific instances or use of already existing concepts, what do they involve? Another possibility is *feature analysis*. Perhaps the reinforced pictures all had a particular stimulus feature in common, and the instrumental response became conditioned to this stimulus feature. According to this account, subjects responded appropriately to new pictures because the new pictures contained the critical stimulus feature. Investigators of perceptual concept formation have argued against a simple feature-analysis explanation because a feature common to all positive instances of a concept is often impossible to identify. In the tree-concept experiment, for example, many of the trees shown had green coloration and were leafy, vertical, woody, and branching. However, the pigeons also responded to pictures of trees that did not have these characteristics. In addition, they failed to respond to pictures that did not have a tree but had some green, leafy, vertical, woody, and branching components. The problem of identifying a tree by critical stimulus features is similar to the problem of specifying the concept "chair" in this way. It is difficult to abstract a critical stimulus feature or critical combination of features.

Because of difficulties in identifying critical stimulus features in perceptual concept experiments, investigators have come to view perceptual concepts as involving the application of a **polymorphic rule** in the construction of a category (for example, Herrnstein, 1984; Lea & Harrison, 1978). Applying a polymorphic rule requires identification of stimulus features. However, a polymorphic rule does not treat any particular stimulus feature as either necessary or sufficient for inclusion in a category. A variety of features are considered to be important, but no feature by itself or in combination with other features is critical for identifying an instance as belonging to a category. Thus, being woody, leafy, and vertical may all be important features of trees, but none of these features is necessary or sufficient for identifying something as a tree.

Explanation of perceptual concepts as resulting

from the application of polymorphic rules has retained feature analysis as an important aspect of concept learning and has stimulated investigators to identify relevant features in concept discrimination procedures (Lea & Ryan, 1983). A related issue is thus raised: What makes something a feature of an object or an event? Are features inherent elemental properties of objects or are they "creations" of the perceiving organism? These questions are similar to the central issue of stimulus control we addressed in Chapter 8: What makes certain aspects of the environment gain control over instrumental behavior? Features arise from the way an animal sees an object or event. They are determined in part by perceptual predispositions and by contingencies of reinforcement. In a sense, a concept discrimination procedure shapes the formation of a perceptual concept by reinforcing some stimuli and not others. If responding to all four-legged creatures is reinforced and responding to all other creatures is not reinforced, a very broad concept is acquired. In contrast, reinforcement of responding to examples of collies but not examples of German shepherds would lead to the acquisition of a more restricted concept. Finally, such concept learning shaped by contingencies of reinforcement is likely to be circumscribed by innate predispositions to categorize stimuli in particular ways (Herrnstein, 1984; Marler, 1982).

Inferential and Analogical Reasoning

The present section on inferential and analogical reasoning and the section on language learning that follows discuss aspects of behavior that until recently have been considered to reflect uniquely human intellectual abilities. Both these aspects of intellectual functioning have been studied in chimpanzees. Research on language learning in chimpanzees has met much more controversy than research on inferential and analogical reasoning. However, both areas of research are fascinating and provide empirical evidence relevant to age-old beliefs about the special role of human beings in the animal kingdom.

Transitive inferential reasoning

Earlier in this chapter, we discussed how rats learn about a sequence of food quantities, such as different numbers of food pellets arranged in a monotonic order (14-7-3-1-0). In those experiments, the subjects were repeatedly exposed to the full series of stimuli. Can animals infer the order of a monotonic series of stimuli from experience only with segments of the series? Douglas Gillan (1981, 1983) recently addressed this question with chimpanzees.

The ability to infer the order of a monotonic series from experience with just segments of the series can be an adaptive skill. Consider, for example, a social group of three monkeys, A, B, and C. Assume that monkeys A and B got into a fight, and A defeated B. Monkeys B and C also got into a fight, and B defeated C. Should C, knowing the outcomes of these two fights, pick a fight with A? Since C has never fought A, on the basis of its direct experiences C would have no way of knowing the outcome. However, the knowledge that A can defeat B and that B can defeat C suggests that A would defeat C. Such reasoning involves making a transitive inference.

A **transitive inference** is a decision based on reconstruction of a monotonic series after experience with just segments of the series. Evidence for such inferential reasoning can be obtained by asking subjects to judge the order of a novel pair of stimuli after training with other stimulus pairs. As we shall see, however, the training stimulus pairs have to be chosen carefully so that they permit reconstruction of the monotonic series.

Gillan (1981, 1983) tested transitive inferential reasoning in three 5–6-year-old female chimpanzees, Jessie, Luvie, and Sadie. Although the subjects had been previously used in other tests of animal cognition, they had not been taught a language system. Five food containers with different-colored lids (red, blue, orange, black, or white) were used in the experiment. The experimenter arranged the five containers, designated by letters A through E, in a serial order, A < B < C < D < E. However, on a given trial, only two adjacent pairs of containers were presented at a time: A < B, B < C, C < D, or D < E. Each time, the chimpanzees had to choose the container that was "greater than" its comparison in the monotonic series. Thus, B was correct in the choice A versus B, but B was incorrect in the choice between B and C. The correct choice was reinforced by a favored piece of food (candy, crackers, or pretzels) that had been placed in the correct container for that trial.

Training continued for about 2 months with 12–24 trials per session. Sadie performed most accurately at the end of training, responding correctly on 89% of the adjacent choices. Luvie's and Jessie's accuracy scores were only 72% and 69%, respectively. The critical test phase of the experiment involved presenting the chimpanzees with a choice between two stimuli they had not encountered together during training, B versus D. If training with adjacent pairs of stimuli enabled the chimpanzees to infer the entire monotonic series, then they would choose D as being "greater than" B. Because this inferential reasoning requires knowledge of the order of adjacent pairs of stimuli, performance on the choice of B versus D should be related to accuracy in responding to adjacent choices. The results generally supported these predictions. Sadie, who had been most accurate in choices between adjacent stimuli, correctly chose D over B on 12 out of 12 test trials. Luvie and Jessie performed less well, selecting D on only 5 and 7 out of 12 test trials, respectively.

After the first test session, Luvie was given additional training with adjacent stimulus pairs and then again tested on B versus D. This time her accuracy on the adjacent stimulus pairs improved to 88%, and she correctly chose D over B on 10 out of 12 test trials. Thus, she also showed generalization of correct choice behavior to a nonadjacent stimulus pair.

The choice of stimulus D over B by Sadie and Luvie during the test sessions is difficult to explain without postulating inferential reasoning. They had not encountered this particular choice during training and therefore had not been conditioned to make a particular response in the presence of this combination of stimuli. In addition, stimuli B and D were equally often paired with reinforcement during training because each stimulus appeared both as the correct choice on some training trials (A versus B; C versus D) and as the incorrect choice on other trials (B versus C; D versus E). Therefore, the frequency of

reinforcement (or nonreinforcement) of choices of B and D cannot explain the choice between them during testing.

In the study, choice between nonadjacent stimuli during testing (B versus D) was assumed to reflect the fact that the training stimuli constituted a monotonic series. Sadie and Luvie presumably inferred this sequence. If this is true, then the choice between nonadjacent stimuli during testing should be disrupted by disrupting the monotonic order of the training stimuli. Gillan tested this prediction with additional training of Sadie. During the additional training, Sadie continued to receive trials of A < B, B < C, C < D, and D < E. Another element, F, was added to these comparisons, and subjects received trials in which F was reinforced in a choice with E (E < F). Thus, stimuli A through F were arranged in a monotonic order, A < B < C < D < E < F, and Sadie was reinforced for always choosing the "greater" stimulus in each pair of training stimuli. Sadie also received training with the pair of stimuli A versus F. To maintain the monotonic order of stimuli A through F, F should have been reinforced in the choice with A. Instead, Gillan provided reinforcement for A, thus destroying the monotonic order set up by the other training trials. Given stimulus pairs A < B, B < C, C < D, D < E, E < F, and F < A, stimuli A through F cannot be arranged in a monotonic order.

Sadie took a long time to learn to make the correct choice with the new pairs of stimuli. In particular, she made a lot of mistakes on A versus F, selecting F instead of A. But finally she did reach 90% accuracy and was tested with novel nonadjacent stimulus pairs B versus D, B versus E, and C versus E. It is important to note that, during training, these stimuli (B through E) had occurred in pairs that could be arranged in a monotonic order (B < C < D < E). Only stimuli A and F were involved in a training pair that destroyed the monotonic sequence. Nevertheless, choices on nonadjacent stimuli B through E were severely disrupted. Disruption of the monotonic order by manipulating stimuli A and F reduced Sadie's performance on choices among stimuli B through E to chance. These results provide strong evidence that Sadie's choice behavior reflected an inference about the structure of the entire series of stimuli based on training experiences with adjacent stimulus pairs.

Analogical reasoning

In the above studies, chimpanzees were required to make an inference about the order of a series of stimuli. In **analogical reasoning** the task is to infer a relation between a sample pair of stimuli and apply this relation to a new pair of test stimuli. Assessments of human intellectual ability often include tests of analogical reasoning. For example, a test item may be "*Train* is to *track* as *car* is to _____." To answer the item correctly, one first has to infer the relation "rides on" from the sample stimuli *train* and *track*. Applying this relation to the test stimulus *car* provides the answer *road*. Gillan, Premack, and Woodruff (1981; see also Gillan, 1983) demonstrated analogical reasoning in a 16-year-old chimpanzee, Sarah, who had previously received extensive training on various cognitive tasks. Sarah had also been taught a symbolic

language, which we will describe in the next section (see Figure 12.9).

In one set of experiments, Sarah was tested with a series of perceptual analogies. The stimuli were a series of geometric shapes cut from colored construction paper and glued onto cardboard. They varied in shape, color, size, and the presence or absence of an easily noticed black dot. Figure 12.7 shows two examples of test problems. The stimuli were presented to Sarah on a stimulus tray, as they appear in Figure 12.7. The sample stimuli for a given trial were presented on the left side. In problem A of Figure 12.7 these were a large and a small sawtooth. A symbol that Sarah had previously learned stood for "equal to" was placed next to the sample stimuli, and this was followed by one of the test stimuli. The bottom of the stimulus tray contained two choice stimuli, one of which correctly completed the analogy. In problem A, the relation between the bottom and top sample stimuli was "smaller than." Because the test stimulus on the right was a large triangle with a dot, the

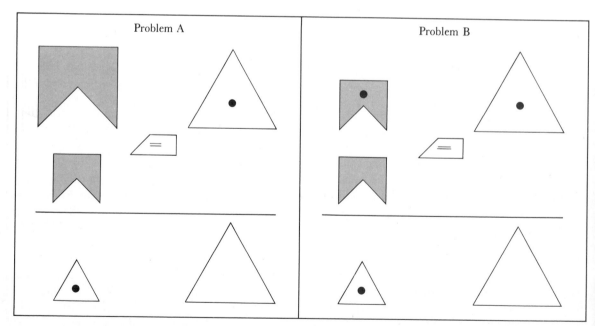

FIGURE 12.7.   Geometric stimuli and structure of problems used by Gillan, Premack, and Woodruff (1981) in a test of analogical reasoning in the chimpanzee. Problems are presented above the horizontal line, and possible answers are presented below the line.   *(After Gillan, Premack, & Woodruff, 1981.)*

correct stimulus for completing the analogy was a small triangle with a dot.

Problem B in Figure 12.7 used the same choice stimuli on the bottom of the stimulus tray as problem A. However, this time the top and bottom sample stimuli differed in that the bottom one lacked a dot. Therefore, the correct choice was the large triangle without the dot. Gillan et al. (1981) used 26 pairs of problems like the pair shown in Figure 12.7. (The two problems of a pair were mixed in with all the other problems so that they did not appear in consecutive order.) The use of pairs of problems that had the same choice stimuli but different correct responses prevented Sarah from solving the analogies by always picking certain favored stimuli.

Sarah was remarkably adept at solving the perceptual analogies. On the first 52 different problems she was presented, she made the correct response 85% of the time. Sarah's performance was uniformly good in every session. During the first session with 12 problems, she was correct on 83% of them. Thus, her per-

formance probably reflected past learning rather than learning during the course of the experiment.

The experiment described above required abstracting and applying perceptual relations ("smaller than," "lacking a dot," and the like). In a later study, Gillan et al. (1981) tested Sarah on conceptual analogies. Here the physical appearance of the stimuli provided no clue to the relevant relation. Rather, the relevant relation was based on the functions of the objects presented. Figure 12.8 shows a pair of problems of this type. The samples were again presented on the left of the stimulus tray, the test stimuli on the right, and the choice alternatives on the bottom. In problem A of Figure 12.8, the samples are a lock and a key. The functional relation between them is that the key opens the lock. The test stimulus is a can, and the choices are a can opener and a paintbrush. The correct choice is the can opener because it has the same functional relation to the can as the key has to the lock. In problem B the same choices are again used, but this time the relation being tested is "to

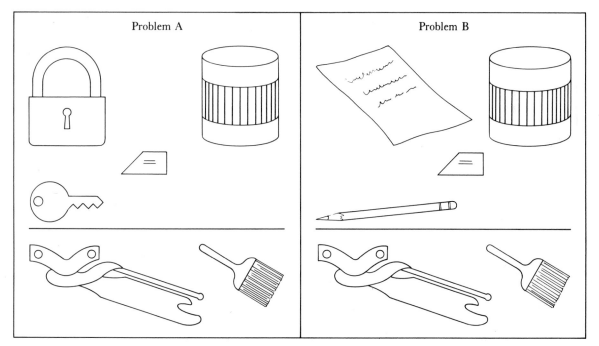

FIGURE 12.8.   Objects used by Gillan, Premack, and Woodruff (1981) in a test of analogical reasoning in the chimpanzee. Problems are presented above the horizontal line, and possible answers are presented below.   *(From Gillan, Premack, & Woodruff, 1981.)*

mark or color," making the brush the correct choice.

Sarah was tested with 9 pairs of problems like those shown in Figure 12.8. All the problems used objects familiar to Sarah. Again her performance was remarkably accurate. She made the correct choice on 83% of the 18 different problems.

The above demonstrations of inferential and analogical reasoning are important because they show that these intellectual skills are not uniquely human. The studies of inferential reasoning were conducted with chimpanzees that did not have prior language training. Therefore, we can conclude that inferential reasoning in chimpanzees is possible without language skills. Since Sarah did have extensive language training, further research is required to determine whether analogical reasoning is also possible without language. Now that we know that chimpanzees are capable of inferential and analogical reasoning, investigators may be encouraged to study these intellectual abilities in other species as well.

Teaching Language to Chimpanzees

Perhaps the most complex cognitive skill is the use of language. In fact, many have assumed that language use is so complex and specialized that it exists only in human beings. According to this view, the ability to use language depends on certain innate processes that have evolved only in our own species (for example, Chomsky, 1972; Lennenberg, 1967). In contrast, others have proposed that human beings use language because they are especially intelligent and because they have had the necessary training—not because they are the only organisms with the required genetic background. This second view suggests that nonhuman animals may also acquire language, provided that they are sufficiently intelligent and receive the proper training. Encouraged by this possibility, a number of people have tried to teach language skills to animals. If this effort were successful, it would end, once and for all, debates about the uniqueness of human beings in the acquisition of language. If we could teach language to animals, we might also be able to communicate with them and thereby gain

unique insights into their lives. Talking to an animal would be something like talking to someone from outer space. We might see for the first time how the world looks through the experiences of nonhuman individuals. We might also gain unique insights into ourselves. We would see for the first time how our own actions are viewed by an organism not biased by human experiences and ethnocentricity.

Most efforts to teach animals language have involved the chimpanzee because of all the primates, the chimpanzee is the most similar to human beings. Despite many similarities, however, chimpanzees do not learn to speak when they are given the same types of experiences that children have as they learn to speak. This became clear through observations of chimpanzees reared as children in people's homes. Nadezhda Kohts, of the Darwinian museum in Moscow, raised a chimpanzee in her home from 1913 to 1916 without once having it imitate the human voice or utter a word of Russian (see A. J. Premack, 1976). More detailed accounts of life with a chimpanzee are available from the experiences of Winthrop and Louise Kellogg, who raised a baby chimpanzee along with their baby boy in the 1930s (Kellogg, 1933). Their adopted charge also did not learn to speak in the normal manner. Undaunted by this evidence, Cathy and Keith Hayes raised a chimpanzee named Viki with the explicit intent of teaching her to talk (Hayes & Hayes, 1951). Despite several years of effort, Viki learned to say only three words: *mama, papa,* and *cup.*

For nearly 20 years the thorough efforts and failure of the Hayeses to teach language to Viki discouraged others from trying to teach chimpanzees to talk. However, there has been a considerable resurgence of interest in teaching language to chimpanzees in recent years, stimulated in part by the innovative approach of Allen and Beatrice Gardner (Gardner & Gardner, 1969, 1975, 1978). Instead of trying to teach their chimpanzee Washoe to talk using vocal speech, they tried to teach her to communicate using American Sign Language. American Sign Language consists of manual gestures in place of words and is used by deaf people in North America. Chimpanzees are much more adept at making hand movements and gestures than at making the mouth, tongue, and lip movements required for the production of speech sounds. Washoe was a good learner. She learned to sign 132 words. Washoe's success suggests that earlier efforts to teach speech to chimpanzees may have failed not because of the inability of the chimpanzee to engage in language communication but because an inappropriate medium (vocalization) was used. Washoe held out the promise that, given the appropriate medium for language, meaningful communication might still be established between chimpanzees and human beings.

Contemporary research on language in nonhuman primates is being conducted in two ways. Some investigators have continued to use the approach adopted by the Gardners in teaching American Sign Language to chimpanzees (for example, Fouts, 1972; Terrace, 1979; Terrace, Petitto, Sanders, & Bever, 1979) and gorillas (Patterson, 1978). Another approach has also stayed away from trying to teach chimpanzees vocalization. However, instead of adopting a human language that is in active use, such as sign language, the second approach has involved artificial language. One artificial language was developed and used by David Premack and his associates and consists of plastic forms of various shapes in place of words (Premack, 1971b, 1976). Figure 12.9 shows examples of the plastic symbols, which have a metal backing and are placed on a magnetized board in a vertical order, as in Chinese, to create sentences. Another artificial language, developed by Duane Rumbaugh and his colleagues at the Yerkes Primate Research Center, uses geometric shapes of various colors to represent words (Rumbaugh, 1977).

In investigations based on artificial languages, the context of the language training is often different than in attempts to teach sign language to chimpanzees. Sign-language training is usually conducted within the context of an established social relationship between the trainer and the chimpanzee. The chimpanzee may not be raised as a child in someone's family. However, it lives in a rich nonlaboratory environment and is cared for by a small number of people throughout the day, each of whom is adept at sign language. Every effort is made to engage the chimpanzee in active conversation (through signing) during its waking hours. Thus, the language training

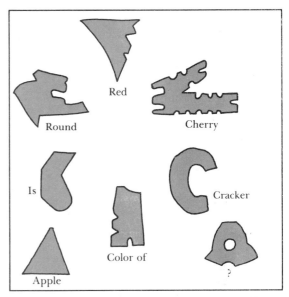

FIGURE 12.9. Examples of symbols in the artificial language developed by David Premack and his associates. *(From D. Premack, 1976.)*

is a part of the subject's "natural" experiences. New signs are learned during games, in the course of getting dressed or undressed, or when going from place to place. Organized training sessions are also held. However, the social relationship between the trainer and the subject is used to encourage the signing behavior, rather than explicit reinforcers such as candy, cookies, or drinks. The intent is to teach language to the chimpanzee in the way that children presumably learn to talk during the normal course of interacting with parents and siblings.

In contrast to the efforts to create a naturalistic context for the training of sign language, investigators using artificial languages usually conduct language training in a more confined laboratory situation with the use of explicit reinforcers. In the Yerkes project, for example, the word symbols appear on keys of a keyboard (like a typewriter), which is hooked up to a computer. The chimpanzee can "talk" to the computer and make various requests. The computer in turn communicates with the chimpanzee with symbols presented on a display console. This arrangement is very different from the type of social interaction in which children typically learn language. However, the computer communication method makes it much easier to obtain a permanent record of all the language responses of the subject. These responses can be automatically recorded for later analysis.

The considerable effort that has been devoted to teaching language to nonhuman primates has yielded at least one undisputed result. It is clear that chimpanzees and gorillas can learn to use arbitrary stimuli (manual gestures, plastic objects, or colored geometric shapes) as symbols for things and relations in their environment. Nonhuman primates are capable of learning a vocabulary well in excess of 100 words. Washoe's vocabulary after 51 months of training, in the order in which she first signed each word (Gardner & Gardner, 1975), is presented by way of example.

Come-gimme	Open
More	Tickle (touch)
Up	Go
Sweet	Out
Hurry	Dr. G.
Listen (hear)	Naomi
Toothbrush	Fruit (apple)
Drink	Comb
Hurt	Dirty
Sorry	String
Funny	Tree
Please	Light
Food-eat	Red
Flower	Hammer
Blanket (cover)	White
Dog	We
You	Meat
Wiper (napkin)	Smoke
In	Chair
Brush (rub)	Leaf
Hat	Enough
Me	Bug
Shoes	Ride
Roger	Cow
Smell	No
Good	Green
Washoe	Cheese
Pants	Black

Clothes	Berry (strawberry)
Cat	Spoon
Key	Window
Baby	Grass
Clean	Climb
Catch	Car
Down	Spin
Look	Yours
Susan	Kiss
Book	Can't
Oil	Hand
Mine	Tomato
Bed	Cucumber (green slices)
Banana	Dennis
Hug	Ron
Bird	Bite
Pencil (write)	Pipe
Mrs. G.	Cry
Quiet	Time
Greg	Pin
Help	Purse
Wende	Knife
Lollipop	Mirror
Water	Cereal
Woman	Swallow
Different	Hole
Same	Butterfly
Larry	Lock
Man	Linn
House	Ice (cold)
Run	Floor
Smile	Good-by
Hose	Nut
Stamp (letter)	Want (hunger)
Airplane	There
Telephone	Don
Hot (warm)	Bath
Fork	Who

Although it is agreed that nonhuman primates can learn a vocabulary, language is more than just a collection of words. In addition to a vocabulary, language involves arrangement of words in sequence according to certain rules set forth by the grammar of the language. Hence, a critical issue in teaching language to nonhuman primates is whether they can learn to construct word sequences on the basis of grammatical rules. There is considerable dispute about this. The smallest sequence of words possible is two words. However, the utterance of a pair of words does not prove that the subject is using grammar to create the sequence. One incident that has been the subject of controversy occurred when the chimp Washoe saw a swan in the water. She had never been exposed to a swan before. When asked "What is that?" she replied "Water bird." In this sequence was Washoe using "water" as an adjective to specify the kind of bird she saw? Perhaps she was. However, on the basis of just this much information, an equally plausible interpretation is that she signed "water" because she saw the water and "bird" because she saw a bird. That is, she may have signed "water bird" as two independent words rather than as an utterance of two words related to each other as adjective and noun (Terrace et al., 1979).

Difficulties of interpretation may also arise with words arranged in a sentence. Consider the following sentence that could have been made by a chimpanzee in the Yerkes project: "Please machine make music." If the subject pressed the appropriate symbols in the appropriate order on the computer keyboard, the machine complied and made music for the chimpanzee. However, pressing those keys in that order does not prove that the subject could construct a sentence. The chimpanzee may have just memorized a sequence of symbols to get reinforced. If the chimpanzee is using grammatical rules, then on other occasions it should be able to use a variety of other words in place of each of the words in the original sentence. Furthermore, these substitutions should be appropriate to the context in which they are made. The chimpanzee should be able to use the grammatical structure of "Please machine make music" to make up sentences such as "Please Peter make music" when Peter is there, "Please machine stop music" if the music has been playing for a while, or "Please machine make cookie" when it is hungry.

An analysis of the verbal behavior of Lana, the most famous of the chimpanzees in the Yerkes project, early in her training indicated that she did not learn such a flexible use of grammar to create new sentences. Rather, Lana appeared to have learned a set of stock sentences (such as "Please machine make music"), which she used repeatedly, changing only one or two of the words to suit the occasion (Thompson & Church, 1980). Thus, in the sentence "Please machine make music," she rarely changed any words except the last. By changing the last word, she could use the same stock sentence to ask the machine to show a movie, show slides, turn on the television, open the door, or open the window. This kind of behavior does not reflect true language skill.

Since then, the computer that controls Lana's language experiences has been reprogrammed to permit greater variation in sentence structure, and Lana has shown a corresponding increase in the range of sentences she produces (Pate & Rumbaugh, 1983). Instead of relying on 6 stock sentences, she has been observed to use 67 different sentence forms, some with as many as 135 possible alternatives for the various words. Other evidence of increase in the sophistication of her language skills is that she frequently expresses the same information using different sentence structures.

Questions have also been raised about the sentence-forming abilities of chimpanzees taught sign language. Terrace and his associates have analyzed instances in which their chimpanzee Nim spontaneously made more than one sign in a row to see whether these sign combinations provided evidence for grammatical structure (see Terrace, 1979; Terrace et al., 1979). Several aspects of this analysis indicated that the sign combinations were not governed by the kinds of grammatical rules that seem to govern early speech in children. First, a careful study of videotape recordings of Nim with his teachers showed that many sequences of signs were not spontaneous but were repetitions of signs the teacher had recently made. If in fact Nim was just imitating his teachers, his sign sequences cannot be interpreted as evidence of sentence construction. Another aspect of Nim's performance that suggests he was not learning language the way a child learns is that the average number of signs he made in a sequence never increased beyond two. In contrast, once children who are learning to speak (or to sign if they are deaf) begin to make utterances of more than one word, the average length of their utterances increases rapidly.

In addition, the maximum length of their utterances is close to the average length. Thus, a child who says two words at a time on the average will not make utterances that are more than 3–7 words long. Such results were not observed with Nim. Even when he signed two words in sequence on the average, occasionally he made utterances with as many as 16 signs. However, his longer utterances did not add meaningful information to his shorter sign sequences. Rather, they often included repetitions. For example, his most frequent four-sign combination was "eat drink eat drink." From such evidence Terrace and his associates concluded that their chimpanzee did not learn to use language despite the fact that he learned a vocabulary of well over 100 words.

The evidence obtained with the chimpanzee Nim indicates that he did not learn to construct sentences in about three and a half years of extensive training. What this implies for the issue of language in chimpanzees is a subject of heated debate. Terrace and his colleagues claim that the evidence that has been provided on the linguistic behavior of other nonhuman primates also does not demonstrate conclusively that these subjects were able to construct grammatical word combinations. However, other investigators contest this charge. Thus, the issue of language in nonhuman primates remains very much unresolved. We can expect that future discussions will help define what constitutes conclusive evidence of language in chimpanzees and that future investigations will involve more stringent documentation and analysis of results. It will be exciting to see how these developments ultimately resolve the issue of language in nonhuman animals.

Applying Language Training to Verbally Handicapped Children

The theoretical premise on which the language-training research with chimpanzees was initiated is that language use is an intellectual function separable from speech. This idea, together with the particular procedures used with chimpanzees, has been extended to some very exciting work with retarded and autistic children. Children with physical, emotional, or mental handicaps frequently do not communicate effectively through speech. Human speech is, after all, a complicated affair. It requires good auditory coding and memory, as well as the ability to prepare and deliver complicated vocal movements. The production of sound must, in addition, convey information. The children we will describe here may have problems in any one or all of these areas. Many retarded children make only a few utterances. Half of all autistic children never learn to speak, and the majority of those who do learn speak abnormally (Bartak, Rutter, & Cox, 1975; Rimland, 1964). Many exhibit echolalia, a parrotlike imitation of others' vocalizations. Other handicapped children—those with cerebral palsy, for example—often do not have sufficient motor control over their vocal apparatus to communicate by speaking. We will describe some of the training techniques that most closely correspond to the research with chimpanzees. In these techniques the language training initially bypasses speech mechanisms and uses nonverbal responses instead.

One approach to language training of nonverbal children is similar to the Gardners' work using sign language with chimpanzees. Several impressive projects based on this technique have been conducted (see Fay & Schuler, 1980, for a review). Schaeffer (1980) described work with three autistic boys. Two of the boys were initially mute and one was echolalic. Language training involved teaching sign language and vocal imitation in separate sessions. As a result of the procedure, the boys learned to sign spontaneously. That is, they were able to put signs together to communicate their own desires, produce new configurations, and generalize signed concepts beyond what was originally taught to them. After three or four months of training, they actually began to speak. This is a remarkable result because traditional speech therapy has been notoriously difficult and, by and large, unsuccessful with autistic children (for example, Hingtgen & Churchill, 1969). When speech emerged, the therapists used signed speech—speech used concomitantly with signing. The three boys became relatively proficient and spontaneous with signed speech. After about five months the boys began speaking without signing. Eventually they were able to communicate as creatively without signing as with the manual signs.

The facilitation of spoken language by sign-language training has also been observed in other studies. Creedon (1975, 1976) taught sign language to a number of autistic children. The children were taught to sign in groups that also included parents and peers. Each new sign was reinforced with social reinforcers—hugs, tickles, and the like. All the children learned to sign to communicate basic needs and desires. Some of them, as in Schaeffer's study, started speaking spontaneously along with the signing. Initially they produced only approximations to single words. Later intonation patterns and more accurate vocalizations appeared. In addition, Creedon reported that the children showed improvement on various scales of behavioral development and exhibited fewer behavior problems.

Why is sign-language training so effective with nonverbal children? Several ideas have been suggested. One possibility is that some of the hand movements involved in signing are already in the child's behavioral repertoire. Autistic children use their hands to reach for desired objects or to push away undesired ones in much the same way that normal children do. As Schaeffer states, they already know the relationship between what they do with their hands and getting their needs fulfilled. They are already capable of adjusting hand responses to fit various situations. Schaeffer's training program uses goal-directed hand movement as the foundation for teaching sign language. Creedon reports that sign language is very easy to prompt and is readily reinforceable. Most autistic children do not have motor impairments that would make signing difficult. This may allow the initiation of spontaneous and creative signing. Once manual language has been established, acquisition of spoken language involves only changing the medium of communication.

David and Ann Premack also worked with an autistic boy (Premack & Premack, 1974), along with chimpanzees, using their system of plastic symbols (see Figure 12.9). They found that the boy required far fewer trials than chimpanzees. Carrier and his associates have done more extensive work with mentally retarded children (see Hollis & Carrier, 1975). They tested a program called Non-Speech Language Initiation Program (Non-SLIP) with 180 retarded children. After 2 years, 125 subjects had completed the program and were ready to start speech training. As in the other studies, many children started to initiate speech while still working in the nonverbal language program.

The Premack-type language system is particularly useful for children who have limited motor abilities. Manipulating plastic symbols is much easier than forming manual signs. The Premack language system is also advantageous for children with memory deficits because the plastic symbols can be left in view as long as necessary. Spoken words and manual signs are brief and have to be remembered for satisfactory communication.

Research on language training offers great promise for people with verbal handicaps. Several possibilities are now available to free those who are locked in themselves, allowing them to communicate their needs and feelings to others. The joy of a child who can for the first time make his or her needs known is indeed a worthwhile result of our scientific pursuits.

References

Adams, G. P. (1903). On the negative and positive phototropism of the earthworm *Allolobophora foetida* as determined by light of different intensities. *American Journal of Physiology, 9,* 26-34.

Ader, R. (1985). Conditioned taste aversions and immunopharmacology. *Annals of the New York Academy of Sciences.*

Ader, R., & Cohen, N. (1982). Behaviorally conditioned immunosuppression and murine systemic lupus erythematosus. *Science, 215,* 1534-1536.

Ader, R., Cohen, N., & Bovbjerg, D. (1982). Conditioned suppression of humoral immunity in the rat. *Journal of Comparative and Physiological Psychology, 96,* 517-521.

Ainslie, G., & Herrnstein, R. J. (1981). Preference reversal and delayed reinforcement. *Animal Learning & Behavior, 9,* 476-482.

Albert, M. S., Butters, N., & Levin, J. (1979). Temporal gradients in the retrograde amnesia of patients with alcoholic Korsakoff's disease. *Archives of Neurology, 36,* 211-216.

Allison, J. (1983). *Behavioral economics.* New York: Praeger.

Alloy, L. B., & Seligman, M. E. P. (1979). On the cognitive component of learned helplessness and depression. In G. H. Bower (Ed.), *The psychology of learning and motivation* (Vol. 13). New York: Academic Press.

Amsel, A. (1958). The role of frustrative nonreward in noncontinuous reward situations. *Psychological Bulletin, 55,* 102-119.

Amsel, A. (1962). Frustrative nonreward in partial reinforcement and discrimination learning. *Psychological Review, 69,* 306-328.

Amsel, A. (1967). Partial reinforcement effects on vigor and persistence. In K. W. Spence & J. T. Spence (Eds.), *The psychology of learning and motivation* (Vol. 1). New York: Academic Press.

Amsel, A. (1972). Inhibition and mediation in classical, Pavlovian, and instrumental conditioning. In R. A. Boakes & M. S. Halliday (Eds.), *Inhibition and learning.* London: Academic Press.

Amsel, A. (1979). The ontogeny of appetitive learning and persistence in the rat. In N. E. Spear & B. A. Campbell (Eds.), *Ontogeny of learning and memory.* Hillsdale, N.J.: Erlbaum.

Amsel, A., & Rashotte, M. E. (1984). *Mechanisms of adaptive behavior: Clark L. Hull's theoretical papers, with commentary.* New York: Columbia University Press.

Anderson, D. C., Crowell, C. R., Cunningham, C. L., & Lupo, J. V. (1979). Behavior during shock exposure as a determinant of subsequent interference with shuttle box escape-avoidance learning in the rat. *Journal of Experimental Psychology: Animal Behavior Processes, 5,* 243-257.

Anderson, M. C., & Shettleworth, S. J. (1977). Behavioral adaptation to fixed-interval and fixed-time food delivery in golden hamsters. *Journal of the Experimental Analysis of Behavior, 25,* 33-49.

Anger, D. (1963). The role of temporal discrimination in the reinforcement of Sidman avoidance behavior. *Journal of the Experimental Analysis of Behavior, 6,* 477-506.

Anisman, H., de Catanzaro, D., & Remington, G. (1978). Escape performance following exposure to inescapable shock: Deficits in motor response maintenance. *Journal of Experimental Psychology: Animal Behavior Processes, 4,* 197-218.

Anisman, H., Hamilton, M., & Zacharko, R. M. (1984). Cue and response-choice acquisition and reversal after exposure to uncontrollable shock: Induction of response perseveration. *Journal of Experimental Psychology: Animal Behavior Processes, 10,* 229-243.

Annable, A., & Wearden, J. H. (1979). Grooming movements as operants in the rat. *Journal of the Experimental Analysis of Behavior, 32,* 297-304.

Archer, T., & Sjoden, P.-O. (1982). Higher-order conditioning and sensory preconditioning of a taste aversion with an exteroceptive CS_1. *Quarterly Journal of Experimental Psychology, 34B,* 1-17.

Ayllon, T., & Azrin, N. (1968). *The token-economy: A motivational system for therapy and rehabilitation.* New York: Appleton-Century-Crofts.

Azrin, N. H. (1956). Some effects of two intermittent schedules of immediate and non-immediate punishment. *Journal of Psychology, 42,* 3-21.

Azrin, N. H. (1958). Some effects of noise on human behavior. *Journal of the Experimental Analysis of Behavior, 1,* 183-200.

Azrin, N. H. (1959). Punishment and recovery during fixed ratio performance. *Journal of the Experimental Analysis of Behavior, 2,* 301-305.

Azrin, N. H. (1960). Effects of punishment intensity during variable-interval reinforcement. *Journal of the Experimental Analysis of Behavior, 3,* 123-142.

Azrin, N. H., & Hake, D. F. (1969). Positive conditioned suppression: Conditioned suppression using positive reinforcers as the unconditioned stimuli. *Journal of the Experimental Analysis of Behavior, 12,* 167-173.

Azrin, N. H., Hake, D. F., Holz, W. C., & Hutchinson, R. R. (1965). Motivational aspects of escape from punishment. *Journal of the Experimental Analysis of Behavior, 8,* 31-44.

Azrin, N. H., & Holz, W. C. (1961). Punishment during fixed-interval reinforcement. *Journal of the Experimental Analysis of Behavior, 4,* 343-347.

Azrin, N. H., & Holz, W. C. (1966). Punishment. In W. K.

Honig (Ed.), *Operant behavior: Areas of research and application*. New York: Appleton-Century-Crofts.

Azrin, N. H., Holz, W. C., & Hake, D. F. (1963). Fixed-ratio punishment. *Journal of the Experimental Analysis of Behavior, 6,* 141–148.

Azrin, N. H., Hutchinson, R. R., & Hake, D. F. (1966). Extinction-induced aggression. *Journal of the Experimental Analysis of Behavior, 9,* 191–204.

Baerends, G. P. (1957). The ethological analysis of fish behavior. In M. E. Brown (Ed.), *The physiology of fishes*. New York: Academic Press.

Baker, A. G., & Baker, P. A. (1985). Does inhibition differ from excitation? Proactive interference, contextual conditioning, and extinction. In R. R. Miller & N. E. Spear (Eds.), *Information processing in animals: Conditioned inhibition*. Hillsdale, N.J.: Erlbaum.

Baker, A. G., & Mackintosh, N. J. (1977). Excitatory and inhibitory conditioning following uncorrelated presentations of CS and UCS. *Animal Learning & Behavior, 5,* 315–319.

Baker, A. G., & Mercier, P. (1982). Extinction of the context and latent inhibition. *Learning and Motivation, 13,* 391–416.

Baker, A. G., Mercier, P., Gabel, J., & Baker, P. A. (1981). Contextual conditioning and the US preexposure effect in conditioned fear. *Journal of Experimental Psychology: Animal Behavior Processes, 7,* 109–128.

Baker, A. G., Singh, M., & Bindra, D. (1985). Some effects of contextual conditioning and US predictability on Pavlovian conditioning. In P. Balsam & A. Tomie (Eds.), *Context and learning*. Hillsdale, N.J.: Erlbaum.

Balaz, M. A., Kasprow, W. J., & Miller, R. R. (1982). Blocking with a single compound trial. *Animal Learning & Behavior, 10,* 271–276.

Balda, R. P., & Turek, R. J. (1984). The cache-recovery system as an example of memory capabilities in Clark's nutcracker. In H. L. Roitblat, T. G. Bever, & H. S. Terrace (Eds.), *Animal cognition*. Hillsdale, N.J.: Erlbaum.

Banks, R. K. (1976). Resistance to punishment as a function of intensity and frequency of prior punishment experience. *Learning and Motivation, 7,* 551–558.

Barker, L. M., Best, M. R., & Domjan, M. (Eds.). (1977). *Learning mechanisms in food selection*. Waco, Texas: Baylor University Press.

Barnett, S. A. (1981). *Modern ethology*. New York: Oxford University Press.

Baron, A. (1965). Delayed punishment of a runway response. *Journal of Comparative and Physiological Psychology, 60,* 131–134.

Barrera, F. J. (1974). Centrifugal election of signal directed pecking. *Journal of the Experimental Analysis of Behavior, 22,* 341–355.

Bartak, L., Rutter, M., & Cox, A. (1975). A comparative study of infantile autism and specific developmental receptive language disorder: I. The children. *British Journal of Psychiatry, 126,* 127–145.

Batson, J. D., & Best, M. R. (1981). Single-element assessment of conditioned inhibition. *Bulletin of the Psychonomic Society, 18,* 328–330.

Battalio, R. C., Kagel, J. H., & Winkler, R. C. (1975). Analysis of individual behavior in a controlled environment: An economist's perspective. In C. G. Miles (Ed.), *Experimentation in controlled environments: Its implications for economic behav-*

ior and social policy making. Toronto: Addiction Research Foundation.

Baum, M. (1969). Extinction of avoidance response following response prevention: Some parametric investigations. *Canadian Journal of Psychology, 23,* 1–10.

Baum, M. (1970). Extinction of avoidance responding through response prevention (flooding). *Psychological Bulletin, 74,* 276–284.

Baum, W. M. (1975). Time allocation in human vigilance. *Journal of the Experimental Analysis of Behavior, 23,* 45–53.

Baum, W. M. (1979). Matching, undermatching, and overmatching in studies of choice. *Journal of the Experimental Analysis of Behavior, 32,* 269–281.

Baum, W. M. (1981). Optimization and the matching law as accounts of instrumental behavior. *Journal of the Experimental Analysis of Behavior, 36,* 387–403.

Baxter, D. J., & Zamble, E. (1982). Reinforcer and response specificity in appetitive transfer of control. *Animal Learning & Behavior, 10,* 201–210.

Beatty, W. W., & Shavalia, D. A. (1980a). Rat spatial memory: Resistance to retroactive interference at long retention intervals. *Animal Learning & Behavior, 8,* 550–552.

Beatty, W. W., & Shavalia, D. A. (1980b). Spatial memory in rats: Time course of working memory and effects of anesthetics. *Behavioral and Neural Biology, 28,* 454–462.

Bechterev, V. M. (1913). *La psychologie objective*. Paris: Alcan.

Benedict, J. O., & Ayres, J. J. B. (1972). Factors affecting conditioning in the truly random control procedure in the rat. *Journal of Comparative and Physiological Psychology, 78,* 323–330.

Berlyne, D. E. (1969). The reward value of indifferent stimulation. In J. Tapp (Ed.), *Reinforcement and behavior*. New York: Academic Press.

Bernstein, D. A., & McAlister, A. (1976). The modification of smoking behavior: Progress and problems. *Addictive Behavior, 1,* 89–102.

Bernstein, D. J., & Ebbesen, E. B. (1978). Reinforcement and substitution in humans: A multiple-response analysis. *Journal of the Experimental Analysis of Behavior, 30,* 243–253.

Bernstein, I. L. (1978). Learned taste aversions in children receiving chemotherapy. *Science, 200,* 1302–1303.

Bernstein, I. L., & Webster, M. M. (1980). Learned taste aversions in humans. *Physiology and Behavior, 25,* 363–366.

Best, M. R. (1975). Conditioned and latent inhibition in taste-aversion learning: Clarifying the role of learned safety. *Journal of Experimental Psychology: Animal Behavior Processes, 1,* 97–113.

Best, M. R., & Gemberling, G. A. (1977). The role of short-term processes in the CS preexposure effect and the delay of reinforcement gradient in long-delay taste-aversion learning. *Journal of Experimental Psychology: Animal Behavior Processes, 3,* 253–263.

Best, P. J., Best, M. R., & Henggeler, S. (1977). The contribution of environmental noningestive cues in conditioning with aversive internal consequences. In L. M. Barker, M. R. Best, & M. Domjan (Eds.), *Learning mechanisms in food selection*. Waco, Texas: Baylor University Press.

Bindra, D. (1969). The interrelated mechanisms of reinforcement and motivation and the nature of their influence on response. In W. J. Arnold & D. Levine (Eds.), *Nebraska Sympo-*

sium on Motivation (Vol. 17). Lincoln: University of Nebraska Press.

Bitterman, M. E. (1964). Classical conditioning in the goldfish as a function of the CS-US interval. *Journal of Comparative and Physiological Psychology, 58,* 359–366.

Bitterman, M. E. (1975). The comparative analysis of learning. *Science, 188,* 699–709.

Bjork, R. A. (1972). The updating of human memory. In G. H. Bower (Ed.), *The psychology of learning and motivation* (Vol. 12). New York: Academic Press.

Black, A. H. (1971). Autonomic aversive conditioning in infrahuman subjects. In F. R. Brush (Ed.), *Aversive conditioning and learning.* New York: Academic Press.

Black, A. H. (1977). Comments on "Learned helplessness: Theory and evidence" by Maier and Seligman. *Journal of Experimental Psychology: General, 106,* 41–43.

Blackman, D. (1977). Conditioned suppression and the effects of classical conditioning on operant behavior. In W. K. Honig & J. E. R. Staddon (Eds.), *Handbook of operant behavior.* Englewood Cliffs, N.J.: Prentice-Hall.

Blakemore, C., & Cooper, G. F. (1970). Development of the brain depends on visual environment. *Science, 228,* 477–478.

Blough, D. S. (1959). Delayed matching in the pigeon. *Journal of the Experimental Analysis of Behavior, 2,* 151–160.

Boakes, R. A. (1979). Interactions between type I and type II processes involving positive reinforcement. In A. Dickinson & R. A. Boakes (Eds.), *Mechanisms of learning and motivation.* Hillsdale, N.J.: Erlbaum.

Boakes, R. A. (1984). *From Darwin to behaviourism.* Cambridge: Cambridge University Press.

Boakes, R. A., & Halliday, M. S. (Eds.). (1972). *Inhibition and learning.* London: Academic Press.

Boakes, R. A., Poli, M., Lockwood, M. J., & Goodall, G. (1978). A study of misbehavior: Token reinforcement in the rat. *Journal of the Experimental Analysis of Behavior, 29,* 115–134.

Boice, R. (1973). Domestication. *Psychological Bulletin, 80,* 215–230.

Boice, R. (1977). Burrows of wild and albino rats: Effects of domestication, outdoor raising, age, experience, and maternal state. *Journal of Comparative and Physiological Psychology, 91,* 649–661.

Boice, R. (1981). Behavioral comparability of wild and domesticated rats. *Behavior Genetics, 11,* 545–553.

Boland, F. J., Mellor, C. S., & Revusky, S. (1978). Chemical aversion treatment of alcoholism: Lithium as the aversive agent. *Behaviour Research and Therapy, 16,* 401–409.

Bolles, R. C. (1969). Avoidance and escape learning: Simultaneous acquisition of different responses. *Journal of Comparative and Physiological Psychology, 68,* 355–358.

Bolles, R. C. (1970). Species-specific defense reactions and avoidance learning. *Psychological Review, 71,* 32–48.

Bolles, R. C. (1971). Species-specific defense reaction. In F. R. Brush (Ed.), *Aversive conditioning and learning.* New York: Academic Press.

Bolles, R. C. (1972). The avoidance learning problem. In G. H. Bower (Ed.), *The psychology of learning and motivation* (Vol. 6). New York: Academic Press.

Bolles, R. C. (1975). *Theory of motivation* (2nd ed.). New York: Harper & Row.

Bolles, R. C., & Fanselow, M. S. (1980). A perceptual-defensive-recuperative model of fear and pain. *Behavioral and Brain Sciences, 3,* 291–323.

Bolles, R. C., & Grossen, N. E. (1969). Effects of an informational stimulus on the acquisition of avoidance behavior in rats. *Journal of Comparative and Physiological Psychology, 68,* 90–99.

Bolles, R. C., Holtz, R., Dunn, T., & Hill, W. (1980). Comparisons of stimulus learning and response learning in a punishment situation. *Learning and Motivation, 11,* 78–96.

Bolles, R. C., Stokes, L. W., & Younger, M. S. (1966). Does CS termination reinforce avoidance behavior? *Journal of Comparative and Physiological Psychology, 62,* 201–207.

Bond, A. B., Cook, R. G., & Lamb, M. R. (1981). Spatial memory and the performance of rats and pigeons in the radial-arm maze. *Animal Learning & Behavior, 9,* 575–580.

Bouton, M. E. (1984). Differential control by context in the inflation and reinstatement paradigms. *Journal of Experimental Psychology: Animal Behavior Processes, 10,* 56–74.

Bouton, M. E., & Bolles, R. C. (1980). Conditioned fear assessed by freezing and by the suppression of three different baselines. *Animal Learning & Behavior, 8,* 429–434.

Bouton, M. E., & Bolles, R. C. (1985). Contexts, event-memories, and extinction. In P. Balsam & A. Tomie (Eds.), *Context and learning.* Hillsdale, N.J.: Erlbaum.

Bovbjerg, D., Ader, R., & Cohen, N. (1984). Acquisition and extinction of conditioned suppression of a graft-vs-host response in the rat. *Journal of Immunology, 132,* 111–113.

Breland, K., & Breland, M. (1961). The misbehavior of organisms. *American Psychologist, 16,* 681–684.

Brogden, W. J., Lipman, E. A., & Culler, E. (1938). The role of incentive in conditioning and extinction. *American Journal of Psychology, 51,* 109–117.

Brown, J. S. (1969). Factors affecting self-punitive behavior. In B. Campbell & R. M. Church (Eds.), *Punishment and aversive behavior.* New York: Appleton-Century-Crofts.

Brown, J. S., & Cunningham, C. L. (1981). The paradox of persisting self-punitive behavior. *Neuroscience & Biobehavioral Reviews, 5,* 343–354.

Brown, J. S., & Jacobs, A. (1949). The role of fear in the motivation and acquisition of responses. *Journal of Experimental Psychology, 39,* 747–759.

Brown, P. L., & Jenkins, H. M. (1968). Auto-shaping the pigeon's key peck. *Journal of the Experimental Analysis of Behavior, 11,* 1–8.

Bull, J. A., III. (1970). An interaction between appetitive Pavlovian CS's and instrumental avoidance responding. *Learning and Motivation, 1,* 18–26.

Bull, J. A., III, & Overmier, J. B. (1968). Additive and subtractive properties of excitation and inhibition. *Journal of Comparative and Physiological Psychology, 66,* 511–514.

Burkhard, B. (1981). Preference and response substitutability with maximization of behavioral value. In M. Commons, R. J. Herrnstein, & H. Rachlin (Eds.), *Quantitative analysis of behavior* (Vol. 2). Cambridge, Mass.: Ballinger.

Burkhard, B., Rachlin, H., & Schrader, S. (1978). Reinforcement and punishment in a closed system. *Learning and Motivation, 9,* 392–410.

Burkhardt, P. E., & Ayres, J. J. B. (1978). CS and US duration effects in one-trial simultaneous conditioning as assessed by conditioned suppression of licking in rats. *Animal Learning and Behavior, 6,* 225–230.

Butters, N., & Cermak, L. S. (1980). *Alcoholic Korsakoff's syndrome: An information processing approach to amnesia.* New York: Academic Press.

Caggiula, A. R., & Hoebel, B. G. (1966). "Copulation-reward" site in the posterior hypothalamus. *Science, 153,* 1284–1285.

Camp, D. S., Raymond, G. A., & Church, R. M. (1967). Temporal relationship between response and punishment. *Journal of Experimental Psychology, 74,* 114–123.

Campagnoni, F. R., Cohen, P. S., & Yoburn, B. C. (1981). Organization of attack and other behaviors of White King pigeons exposed to intermittent water presentations. *Animal Learning & Behavior, 9,* 491–500.

Campbell, B. A., & Church, R. M. (Eds.). (1969). *Punishment and aversive behavior.* Englewood Cliffs, N.J.: Prentice-Hall.

Campbell, B. A., & Randall, P. K. (1976). The effect of reinstatement stimulus conditions on the maintenance of long-term memory. *Developmental Psychobiology, 9,* 325–333.

Campbell, H. J. (1971, October). Pleasure-seeking brains: Artificial tickles, natural joys of thought. *Smithsonian,* pp. 14–23.

Cannon, D. S., & Baker, T. B. (1981). Emetic and electric shock alcohol aversion therapy: Assessment of conditioning. *Journal of Consulting and Clinical Psychology, 49,* 20–33.

Cannon, D. S., Best, M. R., Batson, J. D., & Feldman, M. (1983). Taste familiarity and apomorphine-induced taste aversions in humans. *Behaviour Research and Therapy, 21,* 669–673.

Cantor, M. B. (1981). Bad habits: Models of induced ingestion in satiated rats and people. In S. Miller (Ed.), *Behavior and nutrition.* Philadelphia: Franklin Institute Press.

Cantor, M. B., Smith, S. E., & Bryan, B. R. (1982). Induced bad habits: Adjunctive ingestion and grooming in human subjects. *Appetite, 3,* 1–12.

Cantor, M. B., & Wilson, J. F. (1984). Feeding the face: New directions in adjunctive behavior research. In F. R. Brush & J. B. Overmier (Eds.), *Affect, conditioning, and cognition.* Hillsdale, N.J.: Erlbaum.

Capaldi, E. J. (1967). A sequential hypothesis of instrumental learning. In K. W. Spence & J. T. Spence (Eds.), *The psychology of learning and motivation* (Vol. 1). New York: Academic Press.

Capaldi, E. J. (1971). Memory and learning: A sequential viewpoint. In W. K. Honig & P. H. R. James (Eds.), *Animal memory.* New York: Academic Press.

Capaldi, E. J., & Molina, P. (1979). Element discriminability as a determinant of serial-pattern learning. *Animal Learning and Behavior, 7,* 318–322.

Capaldi, E. J., Nawrocki, T. M., & Verry, D. R. (1982). Difficult serial anticipation learning in rats: Rule-encoding vs. memory. *Animal Learning & Memory, 10,* 167–170.

Capaldi, E. J., Nawrocki, T. M., & Verry, D. R. (1984). Stimulus control in instrumental discrimination learning and reinforcement schedule situations. *Journal of Experimental Psychology: Animal Behavior Processes, 10,* 46–55.

Capaldi, E. J., & Verry, D. R. (1981). Serial order anticipation learning in rats: Memory for multiple hedonic events and their order. *Animal Learning & Behavior, 9,* 441–453.

Capaldi, E. J., Verry, D. R., & Davidson, T. L. (1980). Why rule encoding by animals in serial learning remains to be established. *Animal Learning & Memory, 8,* 691–692.

Capaldi, E. J., Verry, D. R., Nawrocki, T. M., & Miller, D. J. (1984). Serial learning, interim associations, phrasing cues, interference, overshadowing, chunking, memory, and extinction. *Animal Learning & Behavior, 12,* 7–20.

Carew, T. J., Hawkins, R. D., & Kandel, E. R. (1983). Differential classical conditioning of a defensive withdrawal reflex in *Aplysia californica. Science, 219,* 397–400.

Carr, E. G., & Lovaas, O. I. (1983). Contingent electric shock treatment for severe behavior problems. In S. Axelrod & J. Apsche (Eds.), *The effects of punishment on human behavior.* New York: Academic Press.

Caspy, T., & Lubow, R. E. (1981). Generality of US preexposure effects: Transfer from food to shock or shock to food with and without the same response requirements. *Animal Learning & Behavior, 9,* 524–532.

Catania, A. C. (1963). Concurrent performances: A baseline for the study of reinforcement magnitude. *Journal of the Experimental Analysis of Behavior, 6,* 299–300.

Cerella, J. (1982). Mechanisms of concept formation in the pigeon. In D. J. Ingle, M. A. Goodale, & R. J. W. Mansfield (Eds.), *Analysis of visual behavior.* Cambridge, Mass.: M.I.T. Press.

Cerletti, U., & Bini, L. (1938). Electric shock treatment. *Bollettino ed atti della Accademia medica di Roma, 64,* 36.

Chance, W. T. (1980). Autoanalgesia: Opiate and non-opiate mechanisms. *Neuroscience and Biobehavioral Reviews, 4,* 55–67.

Channell, S., & Hall, G. (1983). Contextual effects in latent inhibition with an appetitive conditioning procedure. *Animal Learning & Behavior, 11,* 67–74.

Charlton, S. G. (1983). Differential conditionability: Reinforcing grooming in golden hamsters. *Animal Learning & Behavior, 11,* 27–34.

Charlton, S. G., & Ferraro, D. P. (1982). Effects of deprivation on the differential conditionability of behavior in golden hamsters. *Experimental Animal Behaviour, 1,* 18–29.

Cheatle, M. D., & Rudy, J. W. (1978). Analysis of second-order odor-aversion conditioning in neonatal rats: Implications for Kamin's blocking effect. *Journal of Experimental Psychology: Animal Behavior Processes, 4,* 237–249.

Cherek, D. R. (1982). Schedule-induced cigarette self-administration. *Pharmacology Biochemistry & Behavior, 17,* 523–527.

Chomsky, N. (1972). *Language and mind.* New York: Harcourt Brace Jovanovich.

Chung, S.-H. (1965). Effects of delayed reinforcement in a concurrent situation. *Journal of the Experimental Analysis of Behavior, 8,* 439–444.

Chung, S.-H., & Herrnstein, R. J. (1967). Choice and delay of reinforcement. *Journal of the Experimental Analysis of Behavior, 10,* 67–74.

Church, R. M. (1963). The varied effects of punishment on behavior. *Psychological Review, 70,* 369–402.

Church, R. M. (1969). Response suppression. In B. A. Campbell & R. M. Church (Eds.), *Punishment and aversive behavior.* New York: Appleton-Century-Crofts.

Church, R. M. (1978). The internal clock. In S. H. Hulse, H. Fowler, & W. K. Honig (Eds.), *Cognitive processes in animal behavior.* Hillsdale, N.J.: Erlbaum.

Church, R. M., Getty, D. J., & Lerner, N. D. (1976). Duration discrimination by rats. *Journal of Experimental Psychology: Animal Behavior Processes, 2,* 303–312.

Church, R. M., & Raymond, G. A. (1967). Influence of the schedule of positive reinforcement on punished behavior. *Journal of Comparative and Physiological Psychology, 63,* 329–332.

Church, R. M., Wooten, C. L., & Matthews, T. J. (1970). Discriminative punishment and the conditioned emotional response. *Learning and Motivation, 1,* 1–17.

Cicala, G. A., & Owen, J. W. (1976). Warning signal termination and a feedback signal may not serve the same function. *Learning and Motivation, 7,* 356–367.

Cleland, G. G., & Davey, G. C. L. (1982). The effects of satiation and reinforcer devaluation on signal-centered behavior in the rat. *Learning and Motivation, 13,* 343–360.

Cohen, L. B. (1976). Habituation of infant visual attention. In T. J. Tighe & R. N. Leaton (Eds.), *Habituation: Perspectives from child development, animal behavior, and neurophysiology.* Hillsdale, N.J.: Erlbaum.

Cohen, P. S., & Looney, T. A. (1984). Induction by reinforcer schedules. *Journal of the Experimental Analysis of Behavior, 41,* 345–353.

Cole, S., Hainsworth, F. R., Kamil, A. C., Mercier, T., & Wolf, L. L. (1982). Spatial learning as an adaptation in hummingbirds. *Science, 217,* 655–657.

Coleman, S. R. (1975). Consequences of response-contingent change in unconditioned stimulus intensity upon the rabbit (*Oryctolagus cuniculus*) nictitating membrane response. *Journal of Comparative and Physiological Psychology, 88,* 591–595.

Coleman, S. R., & Gormezano, I. (1979). Classical conditioning and the "Law of Effect": Historical and empirical assessment. *Behaviorism, 7,* 1–33.

Collier, G. H. (1983). Life in a closed economy: The ecology of learning and motivation. In M. D. Zeiler & P. Harzem (Eds.), *Advances in analysis of behaviour.* Vol. 3: *Biological factors in learning.* Chichester, England: Wiley.

Commons, M. L., Herrnstein, R. J., & Rachlin, H. (Eds.). (1982). *Quantitative analyses of behavior.* Vol. 2: *Matching and maximizing accounts.* Cambridge, Mass.: Ballinger.

Cook, R. G. (1980). Retroactive interference in pigeon short-term memory by a reduction in ambient illumination. *Journal of Experimental Psychology: Animal Behavior Processes, 6,* 326–338.

Conger, R., & Killeen, P. (1974). Use of concurrent operants in small group research. *Pacific Sociological Review, 17,* 399–416.

Coons, E. E., & Miller, N. E. (1960). Conflict vs. consolidation of memory traces to explain "retrograde amnesia" produced by ECS. *Journal of Comparative and Physiological Psychology, 53,* 524–531.

Coulter, X., Riccio, D. C., & Page, H. A. (1969). Effects of blocking an instrumental avoidance response: Facilitated extinction but persistence of "fear." *Journal of Comparative and Physiological Psychology, 68,* 377–381.

Couvillon, P. A., & Bitterman, M. E. (1980). Some phenomena of associative learning in honeybees. *Journal of Comparative and Physiological Psychology, 94,* 878–885.

Couvillon, P. A., & Bitterman, M. E. (1982). Compound conditioning in honeybees. *Journal of Comparative and Physiological Psychology, 96,* 192–199.

Crawford, M., & Masterson, F. (1978). Components of the flight response can reinforce bar-press avoidance learning. *Journal of Experimental Psychology: Animal Behavior Processes, 4,* 144–151.

Creedon, M. P. (1975). *Appropriate behavior through communication.* Chicago: Dysfunctioning Child Center, Michael Reese Medical Center.

Creedon, M. P. (1976). *The David School: A simultaneous communication model.* Paper presented at meeting of the National Society for Autistic Children, Oak Brook, Ill.

Crespi, L. P. (1942). Quantitative variation in incentive and performance in the white rat. *American Journal of Psychology, 55,* 467–517.

Cronin, P. B. (1980). Reinstatement of postresponse stimuli prior to reward in delayed-reward discrimination learning by pigeons. *Animal Learning & Behavior, 8,* 352–358.

Crowell, C. R., Hinson, R. E., & Siegel, S. (1981). The role of conditional drug responses in tolerance to the hypothermic effects of ethanol. *Psychopharmacology, 73,* 51–54.

Crozier, W. J., & Navez, A. E. (1930). The geotropic orientation of gastropods. *Journal of General Physiology, 3,* 3–37.

Culler, E. A. (1938). Recent advances in some concepts of conditioning. *Psychological Review, 45,* 134–153.

Dafters, R., Hetherington, M., & McCartney, H. (1983). Blocking and sensory preconditioning effects in morphine analgesic tolerance: Support for a Pavlovian conditioning model of drug tolerance. *Quarterly Journal of Experimental Psychology, 35B,* 1–11.

D'Amato, M. R. (1973). Delayed matching and short-term memory in monkeys. In G. H. Bower (Ed.), *The psychology of learning and motivation* (Vol. 7). New York: Academic Press.

D'Amato, M. R., Fazzaro, J., & Etkin, M. (1968). Anticipatory responding and avoidance discrimination as factors in avoidance conditioning. *Journal of Comparative and Physiological Psychology, 77,* 41–47.

D'Amato, M. R., & Salmon, D. P. (1982). Tune discrimination in monkeys (*Cebus apella*) and in rats. *Animal Learning & Behavior, 10,* 126–134.

Dardano, J. F., & Sauerbrunn, D. (1964). An aversive stimulus as a correlated block counter in FR performance. *Journal of the Experimental Analysis of Behavior, 7,* 37–43.

Davey, G. C. L., & Cleland, G. G. (1982). Topography of signal-centered behavior in the rat: Effects of deprivation state and reinforcer type. *Journal of the Experimental Analysis of Behavior, 38,* 291–304.

Davey, G. C. L., Cleland, G. G., Oakley, D. A., & Jacobs, J. L. (1984). The effect of early feeding experience on signal-directed response topography in the rat. *Physiology & Behavior, 32,* 11–15.

Davis, E. R., & Platt, J. R. (1983). Contiguity and contingency in the acquisition and maintenance of an operant. *Learning and Motivation, 14,* 487–512.

Davis, H. (1968). Conditioned suppression: A survey of the literature. *Psychonomic Monograph Supplements, 2* (14, Whole No. 30), 283–291.

Davis, H., & Kreuter, C. (1972). Conditioned suppression of an avoidance response by a stimulus paired with food. *Journal of the Experimental Analysis of Behavior, 17,* 277–285.

Davis, H., & Memmott, J. (1982). Counting behavior in animals: A critical evaluation. *Psychological Bulletin, 92,* 547–571.

Davis, H., & Shattuck, D. (1980). Transfer of conditioned suppression and conditioned acceleration from instrumental to consummatory baselines. *Animal Learning & Behavior, 8,* 253–257.

Davis, M. (1970). Effects of interstimulus interval length and variability on startle-response habituation in the rat. *Journal of Comparative and Physiological Psychology, 72,* 177–192.

Davis, M. (1974). Sensitization of the rat startle response by noise. *Journal of Comparative and Physiological Psychology, 87,* 571–581.

Davis, M., & File, S. E. (1984). Intrinsic and extrinsic mechanisms of habituation and sensitization: Implications for the design and analysis of experiments. In H. V. S. Peeke & L. Petrinovich (Eds.), *Habituation, sensitization, and behavior.* New York: Academic Press.

Delprato, D. J. (1969). Extinction of one-way avoidance and delayed warning signal termination. *Journal of Experimental Psychology, 80,* 192–193.

Desiderato, O. (1969). Generalization of excitation and inhibition in control of avoidance responding by Pavlovian CS's in dogs. *Journal of Comparative and Physiological Psychology, 68,* 611–616.

Deutsch, J. A. (1960). *The structural basis of behavior.* Chicago: University of Chicago Press.

Deutsch, R. (1974). Conditioned hypoglycemia: A mechanism for saccharin-induced sensitivity to insulin in the rat. *Journal of Comparative and Physiological Psychology, 86,* 350–358.

deVilliers, P. A. (1974). The law of effect and avoidance: A quantitative relationship between response rate and shock-frequency reduction. *Journal of the Experimental Analysis of Behavior, 21,* 223–235.

Deweer, B., Sara, S. J., & Hars, B. (1980). Contextual cues and memory retrieval in rats: Alleviation of forgetting by a pretest exposure to background stimuli. *Animal Learning & Behavior, 8,* 265–272.

Dickinson, A., Nicholas, D. J., & Mackintosh, N. J. (1983). A re-examination of one-trial blocking in conditioned suppression. *Quarterly Journal of Experimental Psychology, 35,* 67–79.

Dickinson, A., & Pearce, J. M. (1977). Inhibitory interactions between appetitive and aversive stimuli. *Psychological Bulletin, 84,* 690–711.

Dinsmoor, J. A. (1952). A discrimination based on punishment. *Quarterly Journal of Experimental Psychology, 4,* 27–45.

Dinsmoor, J. A. (1954). Punishment: I. The avoidance hypothesis. *Psychological Review, 61,* 34–46.

Dinsmoor, J. A. (1962). Variable-interval escape from stimuli accompanied by shocks. *Journal of the Experimental Analysis of Behavior, 5,* 41–48.

Dinsmoor, J. A. (1977). Escape, avoidance, punishment: Where do we stand? *Journal of the Experimental Analysis of Behavior, 28,* 83–95.

Dinsmoor, J. A., & Sears, G. W. (1973). Control of avoidance by a response-produced stimulus. *Learning and Motivation, 4,* 284–293.

Dixon, L. (1981). A functional analysis of photo-object matching skills of severely retarded adolescents. *Journal of Applied Behavior Analysis, 14,* 465–478.

Dobrzecka, C., Szwejkowska, G., & Konorski, J. (1966). Qualitative versus directional cues in two forms of differentiation. *Science, 153,* 87–89.

Domjan, M. (1976). Determinants of the enhancement of flavored-water intake by prior exposure. *Journal of Experimental Psychology: Animal Behavior Processes, 2,* 17–27.

Domjan, M. (1980). Ingestional aversion learning: Unique and general processes. In J. S. Rosenblatt, R. A. Hinde, C. Beer, & M. Busnel (Eds.), *Advances in the study of behavior* (Vol 11). New York: Academic Press.

Domjan, M. (1983). Biological constraints on instrumental and classical conditioning: Implications for general process theory. In G. H. Bower (Ed.), *The psychology of learning and motivation* (Vol. 17). New York: Academic Press.

Domjan, M. (1985). Long-delay and selective association learning revisited. *Annals of the New York Academy of Sciences.*

Domjan, M., & Best, M. R. (1977). Paradoxical effects of proximal unconditioned stimulus preexposure: Interference with and conditioning of a taste aversion. *Journal of Experimental Psychology: Animal Behavior Processes, 3,* 310–321.

Domjan, M., & Wilson, N. E. (1972). Specificity of cue to consequence in aversion learning in the rat. *Psychonomic Science, 26,* 143–145.

Donegan, N. H., & Wagner, A. R. (1981). Conditioned diminution and facilitation of the UCR: A sometimes-opponent-process interpretation. In I. Gormezano, W. F. Prokasy, & R. F. Thompson (Eds.), *Classical conditioning III: Behavioral, neurophysiological, and neurochemical studies in the rabbit.* Hillsdale, N.J.: Erlbaum.

Dougan, J. D., McSweeney, F. K., O'Reilly, P. E., & Eacker, J. N. (1983). Negative automaintenance: Pavlovian conditioning or differential reinforcement? *Behaviour Analysis Letters, 3,* 201–212.

Duncan, C. P. (1949). The retroactive effect of electroshock on learning. *Journal of Comparative and Physiological Psychology, 42,* 32–44.

Dunham, P. J. (1971). Punishment: Method and theory. *Psychological Review, 78,* 58–70.

Dunham, P. J. (1972). Some effects of punishment on unpunished responding. *Journal of the Experimental Analysis of Behavior, 17,* 443–450.

Dunham, P. J. (1978). Changes in unpunished responding during response-contingent punishment. *Animal Learning & Behavior, 6,* 174–180.

Dunn, R., & Fantino, E. (1982). Choice and the relative immediacy of reinforcement. *Journal of the Experimental Analysis of Behavior, 38,* 321–326.

Durlach, P. J., & Rescorla, R. A. (1980). Potentiation rather than overshadowing in flavor-aversion learning: An analysis in terms of within-compound associations. *Journal of Experimental Psychology: Animal Behavior Processes, 6,* 175–187.

Dweck, C. S., & Wagner, A. R. (1970). Situational cues and correlation between conditioned stimulus and unconditioned stimulus as determinants of the conditioned emotional response. *Psychonomic Science, 18,* 145–147.

Eibl-Eibesfeldt, I. (1970). *Ethology: The biology of behavior.* New York: Holt, Rinehart and Winston.

Eikelboom, R., & Stewart, J. (1982). Conditioning of drug-induced physiological responses. *Psychological Review, 89,* 507–528.

Elkins, R. L. (1975). Aversion therapy for alcoholism: Chemical, electrical, or verbal imaginary? *International Journal of the Addictions, 10,* 157–209.

Ellins, S. R., Cramer, R. E., & Martin, G. C. (1982). Discrimination reversal learning in newts. *Animal Learning & Behavior, 10,* 301–304.

Ellis, A. (1962). *Reason and emotion in psychotherapy.* New York: Lyle Stuart.

Ellison, G. D. (1964). Differential salivary conditioning to traces. *Journal of Comparative and Physiological Psychology, 57,* 373–380.

Ellison, G. D., & Konorski, J. (1964). Separation of the salivary and motor responses in instrumental conditioning. *Science, 146,* 1071–1072.

Emmelkamp, P. M. G. (1982a). *Phobic and obsessive-compulsive disorders: Theory, research, and practice.* New York: Plenum.

Emmelkamp, P. M. G. (1982b). Recent developments in the behavioral treatment of obsessive-compulsive disorders. In J. Boulougouris (Ed.), *Learning theories approaches in psychiatry.* New York: Wiley.

Emmelkamp, P. M. G., & Wessels, H. (1975). Flooding in

imagination vs. flooding *in vivo*. *Behaviour Research and Therapy, 13,* 7–16.

Engberg, L. A., Hansen, G., Welker, R. L., & Thomas, D. R. (1972). Acquisition of key-pecking via autoshaping as a function of prior experience: "Learned laziness"? *Science, 178,* 1002–1004.

Epstein, S. M. (1967). Toward a unified theory of anxiety. In B. Maher (Ed.), *Progress in experimental personality research* (Vol. 4). New York: Academic Press.

Erickson, L. M., Tiffany, S. T., Martin, E. M., & Baker, T. B. (1983). Aversive smoking therapies: A conditioning analysis of therapeutic effectiveness. *Behaviour Research and Therapy, 21,* 595–611.

Eslinger, P. J., & Ludvigson, H. W. (1980). Are there constraints on learned responses to odors from rewarded and nonrewarded rats? *Animal Learning & Behavior, 8,* 452–456.

Esplin, D. W., & Woodbury, D. M. (1961). Spinal reflexes and seizure patterns in the two-toed sloth. *Science, 133,* 1426–1427.

Estes, W. K. (1943). Discriminative conditioning: I. A discriminative property of conditioned anticipation. *Journal of Experimental Psychology, 32,* 150–155.

Estes, W. K. (1944). An experimental study of punishment. *Psychological Monographs, 57* (3, Whole No. 263).

Estes, W. K. (1948). Discriminative conditioning: II. Effects of a Pavlovian conditioned stimulus upon a subsequently established operant response. *Journal of Experimental Psychology, 38,* 173–177.

Estes, W. K. (1969). Outline of a theory of punishment. In B. A. Campbell & R. M. Church (Eds.), *Punishment and aversive behavior.* New York: Appleton-Century-Crofts.

Estes, W. K., & Skinner, B. F. (1941). Some quantitative properties of anxiety. *Journal of Experimental Psychology, 29,* 390–400.

Fagen, J. W., & Rovee-Collier, C. (1983). Memory retrieval: A time-locked process in infancy. *Science, 222,* 1349–1351.

Falk, J. L. (1961). Production of polydipsia in normal rats by an intermittent food schedule. *Science, 133,* 195–196.

Falk, J. L. (1972). The nature and determinants of adjunctive behavior. In R. M. Gilbert & J. D. Keehn (Eds.), *Schedule effects: Drug, drinking, and aggression.* Toronto: Addiction Research Foundation and University of Toronto Press.

Fanselow, M. S., & Baackes, M. P. (1982). Conditioned fear-induced opiate analgesia on the formalin test: Evidence for two aversive motivational systems. *Learning and Motivation, 13,* 200–221.

Farley, J., & Alkon, D. L. (1980). Neural organization predicts stimulus specificity for a retained associative behavioral change. *Science, 210,* 1373–1375.

Farley, J., Richards, W. G., Ling, L. J., Liman, E., & Alkon, D. L. (1983). Membrane changes in a single photoreceptor cause associative learning in *Hermissenda. Science, 221,* 1201–1203.

Farthing, G. W., & Opuda, M. J. (1974). Transfer of matching-to-sample in pigeons. *Journal of the Experimental Analysis of Behavior, 21,* 199–213.

Fay, W. H., & Schuler, A. L. (1980). *Emerging language in autistic children. Language intervention series.* Baltimore, Md.: University Park Press.

Feldman, D. T., & Gordon, W. C. (1979). The alleviation of short-term retention decrements with reactivation. *Learning and Motivation, 10,* 198–210.

Feldman, M. P., & MacCulloch, M. J. (1971). *Homosexual behavior: Therapy and assessment.* Oxford: Pergamon Press.

Ferster, C. B., & Skinner, B. F. (1957). *Schedules of reinforcement.* New York: Appleton-Century-Crofts.

Flaherty, C. F. (1982). Incentive contrast: A review of behavioral changes following shifts in reward. *Animal Learning & Behavior, 10,* 409–440.

Flexner, J. B., Flexner, L. B., & Stellar, E. (1963). Memory in mice as affected by intracerebral puromycin. *Science, 141,* 57–59.

Flory, R. (1969). Attack behavior as a function of minimum interfood interval. *Journal of the Experimental Analysis of Behavior, 12,* 825–828.

Foree, D. D., & LoLordo, V. M. (1973). Attention in the pigeon: The differential effects of food-getting vs. shock avoidance procedures. *Journal of Comparative and Physiological Psychology, 85,* 551–558.

Foree, D. D., & LoLordo, V. M. (1975). Stimulus-reinforcer interactions in the pigeon: The role of electric shock and the avoidance contingency. *Journal of Experimental Psychology: Animal Behavior Processes, 1,* 39–46.

Fountain, S. B., Evensen, J. C., & Hulse, S. H. (1983). Formal structure and pattern length in serial pattern learning by rats. *Animal Learning & Behavior, 11,* 186–192.

Fountain, S. B., Henne, D. R., & Hulse, S. H. (1984). Phrasing cues and hierarchical organization in serial pattern learning by rats. *Journal of Experimental Psychology: Animal Behavior Processes, 10,* 30–45.

Fountain, S. B., & Hulse, S. H. (1981). Extrapolation of serial stimulus patterns by rats. *Animal Learning & Behavior, 9,* 381–384.

Fouts, R. (1972). Use of guidance in teaching sign language to a chimpanzee. *Journal of Comparative and Physiological Psychology, 80,* 515–522.

Fowler, H., Kleiman, M., & Lysle, D. (1985). Factors controlling the acquisition and extinction of conditioned inhibition suggest a "slave" process. In R. R. Miller & N. E. Spear (Eds.), *Information processing in animals: Conditioned inhibition.* Hillsdale, N.J.: Erlbaum.

Fox, L. (1966). Effecting the use of efficient study habits. In R. Ulrich, T. Stachnik, & J. Mabry (Eds.), *Control of human behavior.* Glenview, Ill.: Scott, Foresman.

Foxx, R. M., & Azrin, N. H. (1973). The elimination of autistic self-stimulatory behavior by overcorrection. *Journal of Applied Behavioral Analysis, 6,* 1–14.

Fraenkel, G. S., & Gunn, D. L. (1961). *The orientation of animals* (2nd ed.). New York: Dover.

Frankel, F. D. (1975). The role of response-punishment contingency in the suppression of a positively-reinforced operant. *Learning and Motivation, 6,* 385–403.

Gaffan, E. A., & Davies, J. (1981). The role of exploration in win-shift and win-stay performance on a radial maze. *Learning and Motivation, 12,* 282–299.

Galassi, J. P., Frierson, H. T., & Sharer, R. (1981). Behavior of high, moderate and low-test-anxious students during an actual test situation. *Journal of Consulting and Clinical Psychology, 49,* 51–62.

Galef, B. G., Jr., & Osborne, B. (1978). Novel taste facilitation of the association of visual cues with toxicosis in rats. *Journal of Comparative and Physiological Psychology, 92,* 907–916.

Gamzu, E. R. (1985). A pharmacological perspective on drugs used in establishing conditioned food aversions. *Annals of the New York Academy of Sciences.*

Gamzu, E. R., & Williams, D. R. (1971). Classical conditioning of a complex skeletal act. *Science, 171,* 923–925.

Gamzu, E. R., & Williams, D. R. (1973). Associative factors underlying the pigeon's key pecking in autoshaping procedures. *Journal of the Experimental Analysis of Behavior, 19,* 225–232.

Gantt, W. H. (1966). Conditional or conditioned, reflex or response? *Conditioned Reflex, 1,* 69–74.

Garb, J. J., & Stunkard, A. J. (1974). Taste aversions in man. *American Journal of Psychiatry, 131,* 1204–1207.

Garber, J., & Seligman, M. E. P. (Eds.). (1980). *Human helplessness: Theory and application.* New York: Academic Press.

Garcia, J., Ervin, F. R., & Koelling, R. A. (1966). Learning with prolonged delay of reinforcement. *Psychonomic Science, 5,* 121–122.

Garcia, J., Hankins, W. G., & Rusiniak, K. W. (1974). Behavioral regulation of the milieu interne in man and rat. *Science, 185,* 824–831.

Garcia, J., & Koelling, R. A. (1966). Relation of cue to consequence in avoidance learning. *Psychonomic Science, 4,* 123–124.

Gardner, E. T., & Lewis, P. (1976). Negative reinforcement with shock-frequency increase. *Journal of the Experimental Analysis of Behavior, 25,* 3–14.

Gardner, R. A., & Gardner, B. T. (1969). Teaching sign language to a chimpanzee. *Science, 165,* 664–672.

Gardner, R. A., & Gardner, B. T. (1975). Early signs of language in child and chimpanzee. *Science, 187,* 752–753.

Gardner, R. A., & Gardner, B. T. (1978). Comparative psychology and language acquisition. *Annals of the New York Academy of Science, 309,* 37–76.

Gemberling, G. A., & Domjan, M. (1982). Selective association in one-day-old rats: Taste-toxicosis and texture-shock aversion learning. *Journal of Comparative and Physiological Psychology, 96,* 105–113.

Gentry, G. D., & Marr, M. J. (1980). Choice and reinforcement delay. *Journal of the Experimental Analysis of Behavior, 33,* 27–37.

Gentry, W. D. (1968). Fixed-ratio schedule-induced aggression. *Journal of the Experimental Analysis of Behavior, 11,* 813–817.

Gibbon, J., & Church, R. M. (1984). Sources of variance in an information processing theory of timing. In H. L. Roitblat, T. G. Bever, & H. S. Terrace (Eds.), *Animal cognition.* Hillsdale, N.J.: Erlbaum.

Gibbon, J., Church, R. M., & Meck, W. H. (1984). Scalar timing in memory. *Annals of the New York Academy of Sciences, 423,* 52–77.

Gillan, D. J. (1981). Reasoning in the chimpanzee: II. Transitive inference. *Journal of Experimental Psychology: Animal Behavior Processes, 7,* 150–164.

Gillan, D. J. (1983). Inferences and the acquisition of knowledge by chimpanzees. In M. L. Commons, R. J. Herrnstein, & A. R. Wagner (Eds.), *Quantitative analyses of behavior.* Vol. 4: *Discrimination processes.* Cambridge, Mass.: Ballinger.

Gillan, D. J., Premack, D., & Woodruff, G. (1981). Reasoning in the chimpanzee: I. Analogical reasoning. *Journal of Experimental Psychology: Animal Behavior Processes, 7,* 1–17.

Gillette, K., Martin, G. M., & Bellingham, W. P. (1980). Differential use of food and water cues in the formation of conditioned aversions by domestic chicks (*Gallus gallus*). *Journal of Experimental Psychology: Animal Behavior Processes, 6,* 99–111.

Glickman, S. E., & Schiff, B. B. (1967). A biological theory of reinforcement. *Psychological Review, 74,* 81–109.

Gold, P. E., Haycock, J. W., Macri, J., & McGaugh, J. L. (1973). Retrograde amnesia and the "reminder effect": An alternative interpretation. *Science, 180,* 1199–1201.

Goldstein, A. J., & Chambless, D. L. (1978). A reanalysis of agoraphobia. *Behavior Therapy, 9,* 47–59.

Gonzalez, R. C., Gentry, G. V., & Bitterman, M. E. (1954). Relational discrimination of intermediate size in the chimpanzee. *Journal of Comparative and Physiological Psychology, 47,* 385–388.

Goodman, J. H., & Fowler, H. (1983). Blocking and enhancement of fear conditioning by appetitive CSs. *Animal Learning & Behavior, 11,* 75–82.

Gordon, W. C. (1981). Mechanisms for cue-induced retention enhancement. In N. E. Spear & R. R. Miller (Eds.), *Information processing in animals: Memory mechanisms.* Hillsdale, N.J.: Erlbaum.

Gordon, W. C., Brennan, M. J., & Schlesinger, J. L. (1976). The interaction of memories in the rat: Effects on short-term retention performance. *Learning and Motivation, 7,* 406–417.

Gordon, W. C., & Feldman, D. T. (1978). Reactivation-induced interference in a short-term retention paradigm. *Learning and Motivation, 9,* 164–178.

Gordon, W. C., McCracken, K. M., Dess-Beech, N., & Mowrer, R. R. (1981). Mechanisms for the cueing phenomenon: The addition of the cueing context to the training memory. *Learning and Motivation, 12,* 196–211.

Gordon, W. C., & Mowrer, R. R. (1980). An extinction trial as a reminder treatment following electroconvulsive shock. *Animal Learning & Behavior, 8,* 363–367.

Gormezano, I. (1966). Classical conditioning. In J. B. Sidowski (Ed.), *Experimental methods and instrumentation in psychology.* New York: McGraw-Hill.

Gormezano, I., & Coleman, S. R. (1973). The law of effect and CR contingent modification of the UCS. *Conditioned Reflex, 8,* 41–56.

Gormezano, I., & Hiller, G. W. (1972). Omission training of the jaw-movement response of the rabbit to a water US. *Psychonomic Science, 29,* 276–278.

Gormezano, I., & Kehoe, E. J. (1981). Classical conditioning and the law of contiguity. In P. Harzem & M. D. Zeiler (Eds.), *Predictability, correlation, and contiguity.* Chichester, England: Wiley.

Gormezano, I., Kehoe, E. J., & Marshall, B. S. (1983). Twenty years of classical conditioning research with the rabbit. In J. M. Prague & A. N. Epstein (Eds.), *Progress in psychobiology and physiological psychology* (Vol. 10). New York: Academic Press.

Graham, J. M., & Desjardins, C. (1980). Classical conditioning: Induction of luteinizing hormone and testosterone secretion in anticipation of sexual activity. *Science, 210,* 1039–1041.

Grant, D. S. (1975). Proactive interference in pigeon short-term memory. *Journal of Experimental Psychology: Animal Behavior Processes, 1,* 207–220.

Grant, D. S. (1976). Effect of sample presentation time on long-delay matching in the pigeon. *Learning and Motivation, 7,* 580–590.

Grant, D. S. (1982a). Intratrial proactive interference in pigeon short-term memory: Manipulation of stimulus dimension and dimensional similarity. *Learning and Motivation, 13,* 417–433.

Grant, D. S. (1982b). Stimulus control of information processing in rat short-term memory. *Journal of Experimental Psychology: Animal Behavior Processes, 8,* 154–164.

Grant, D. S., & Roberts, W. A. (1973). Trace interaction in

pigeon short-term memory. *Journal of Experimental Psychology, 101,* 21–29.

Grant, D. S., & Roberts, W. A. (1976). Sources of retroactive inhibition in pigeon short-term memory. *Journal of Experimental Psychology: Animal Behavior Processes, 2,* 1–16.

Greene, S. L. (1983). Feature memorization in pigeon concept formation. In M. L. Commons, R. J. Herrnstein, & A. R. Wagner (Eds.), *Quantitative analyses of behavior.* Vol. 4: *Discrimination processes.* Cambridge, Mass.: Ballinger.

Grice, G. R. (1948). The relation of secondary reinforcement to delayed reward in visual discrimination learning. *Journal of Experimental Psychology, 38,* 1–16.

Griffin, D. R. (1976). *The question of animal awareness.* New York: Rockefeller University Press.

Griffin, D. R. (Ed.). (1982). *Animal mind—human mind.* Berlin: Springer-Verlag.

Grossen, N. E., & Kelley, M. J. (1972). Species-specific behavior and acquisition of avoidance behavior in rats. *Journal of Comparative and Physiological Psychology, 81,* 307–310.

Grossen, N. E., Kostansek, D. J., & Bolles, R. C. (1969). Effects of appetitive discriminative stimuli on avoidance behavior. *Journal of Experimental Psychology, 81,* 340–343.

Groves, P. M., Lee, D., & Thompson, R. F. (1969). Effects of stimulus frequency and intensity on habituation and sensitization in acute spinal cat. *Physiology and Behavior, 4,* 383–388.

Groves, P. M., & Thompson, R. F. (1970). Habituation: A dual-process theory. *Psychological Review, 77,* 419–450.

Guha, D., Dutta, S. N., & Pradhan, S. N. (1974). Conditioning of gastric secretion by epinephrine in rats. *Proceedings of the Society for Experimental Biology and Medicine, 147,* 817–819.

Gunther, M. (1961). Infant behavior at the breast. In B. Foss (Ed.), *Determinants of infant behavior.* London: Wiley.

Gutman, A., & Maier, S. F. (1978). Operant and Pavlovian factors in cross-response transfer of inhibitory stimulus control. *Learning and Motivation, 9,* 231–254.

Guttman, N., & Kalish, H. I. (1956). Discriminability and stimulus generalization. *Journal of Experimental Psychology, 51,* 79–88.

Haig, K. A., Rawlins, J. N. P., Olton, D. S., Mead, A., & Taylor, B. (1983). Food searching strategies of rats: Variables affecting the relative strength of stay and shift strategies. *Journal of Experimental Psychology: Animal Behavior Processes, 9,* 337–348.

Hake, D. F., & Azrin, N. H. (1965). Conditioned punishment. *Journal of the Experimental Analysis of Behavior, 8,* 279–293.

Hale, E. B., & Almquist, J. O. (1960). Relation of sexual behavior to germ cell output in farm animals. *Journal of Dairy Science,* Supplement, *43,* 145–149.

Hall, G., Kaye, H., & Pearce, J. M. (1985). Attention and conditioned inhibition. In R. R. Miller & N. E. Spear (Eds.), *Information processing in animals: Conditioned inhibition.* Hillsdale, N.J.: Erlbaum.

Hall, G., & Pearce, J. M. (1979). Latent inhibition of a CS during CS-US pairings. *Journal of Experimental Psychology: Animal Behavior Processes, 5,* 31–42.

Hammond, L. J. (1966). Increased responding to CS— in differential CER. *Psychonomic Science, 5,* 337–338.

Hammond, L. J. (1968). Retardation of fear acquisition by a previously inhibitory CS. *Journal of Comparative and Physiological Psychology, 66,* 756–759.

Hankins, W. G., Rusiniak, K. W., & Garcia, J. (1976). Dissoci-

ation of odor and taste in shock-avoidance learning. *Behavioral Biology, 18,* 345–358.

Hanson, H. M. (1959). Effects of discrimination training on stimulus generalization. *Journal of Experimental Psychology, 58,* 321–333.

Hanson, S. J., & Timberlake, W. (1983). Regulation during challenge: A general model of learned performance under schedule constraint. *Psychological Review, 90,* 261–282.

Harlow, H. F. (1969). Age-mate or peer affectional system. In D. S. Lehrman, R. H. Hinde, & E. Shaw (Eds.), *Advances in the study of behavior* (Vol. 2). New York: Academic Press.

Haroutunian, V., & Riccio, D. C. (1979). Drug-induced "arousal" and the effectiveness of CS exposure in the reinstatement of memory. *Behavioral and Neural Biology, 26,* 115–120.

Hart, B. L. (1973). Reflexive behavior. In G. Bermant (Ed.), *Perspectives in animal behavior.* Glenview, Ill.: Scott, Foresman.

Hart, B. L. (1983). Role of testosterone secretion and penile reflexes in sexual behavior and sperm competition in male rats: A theoretical contribution. *Physiology and Behavior, 31,* 823–827.

Hawkins, R. D., Abrams, T. W., Carew, T. J., & Kandel, E. R. (1983). A cellular mechanism of classical conditioning in *Aplysia:* Activity-dependent amplification of presynaptic facilitation. *Science, 219,* 400–405.

Hawkins, R. D., & Kandel, E. R. (1984). Is there a cell-biological alphabet for simple forms of learning? *Psychological Review, 91,* 375–391.

Hayes, K. J., & Hayes, C. (1951). The intellectual development of a home-raised chimpanzee. *Proceedings of the American Philosophical Society, 95,* 105–109.

Hearst, E. (1968). Discrimination learning as the summation of excitation and inhibition. *Science, 162,* 1303–1306.

Hearst, E. (1969). Excitation, inhibition, and discrimination learning. In N. J. Mackintosh & W. K. Honig (Eds.), *Fundamental issues in associative learning.* Halifax: Dalhousie University Press.

Hearst, E. (1975). Pavlovian conditioning and directed movements. In G. Bower (Ed.), *The psychology of learning and motivation* (Vol. 9). New York: Academic Press.

Hearst, E., & Franklin, S. R. (1977). Positive and negative relations between a signal and food: Approach-withdrawal behavior to the signal. *Journal of Experimental Psychology: Animal Behavior Processes, 3,* 37–52.

Hearst, E., & Jenkins, H. M. (1974). *Sign-tracking: The stimulus-reinforcer relation and directed action.* Austin, Texas: Psychonomic Society.

Hearst, E., & Peterson, G. B. (1973). Transfer of conditioned excitation and inhibition from one operant response to another. *Journal of Experimental Psychology, 99,* 360–368.

Hearst, E., & Sidman, M. (1961). Some behavioral effects of a concurrently positive and negative stimulus. *Journal of the Experimental Analysis of Behavior, 4,* 251–256.

Hebb, D. O. (1956). The distinction between "classical" and "instrumental." *Canadian Journal of Psychology, 10,* 165–166.

Heingartner, A., & Hall, J. V. (1974). Affective consequences in adults and children of repeated exposure to auditory stimuli. *Journal of Personality and Social Psychology, 29.* 719–723.

Hendersen, R. W., Patterson, J. M., & Jackson, R. L. (1980). Acquisition and retention of control of instrumental behavior by a cue signaling airblast: How specific are conditioned anticipations? *Learning and Motivation, 11,* 407–426.

Herberg, L. J. (1963). Seminal ejaculation following positively reinforcing electrical stimulation of the rat hypothalamus. *Journal of Comparative and Physiological Psychology, 56,* 679–685.

Herman, L. M., & Thompson, R. K. R. (1982). Symbolic, identity, and probe delayed matching to sounds by the bottle-nosed dolphin. *Animal Learning & Behavior, 10,* 22–34.

Herman, R. L., & Azrin, N. H. (1964). Punishment by noise in an alternative response situation. *Journal of the Experimental Analysis of Behavior, 7,* 185–188.

Herrnstein, R. J. (1961). Relative and absolute strength of response as a function of frequency of reinforcement. *Journal of the Experimental Analysis of Behavior, 4,* 267–272.

Herrnstein, R. J. (1969). Method and theory in the study of avoidance. *Psychological Review, 76,* 49–69.

Herrnstein, R. J. (1970). On the law of effect. *Journal of the Experimental Analysis of Behavior, 13,* 243–266.

Herrnstein, R. J. (1984). Objects, categories, and discriminative stimuli. In H. L. Roitblat, T. G. Bever, & H. S. Terrace (Eds.), *Animal cognition.* Hillsdale, N.J.: Erlbaum.

Herrnstein, R. J., & deVilliers, P. A. (1980). Fish as a natural category for people and pigeons. In G. H. Bower (Ed.), *The psychology of learning and motivation* (Vol. 14). New York: Academic Press.

Herrnstein, R. J., & Heyman, G. M. (1979). Is matching compatible with reinforcement maximization on concurrent variable interval, variable ratio? *Journal of the Experimental Analysis of Behavior, 31,* 209–223.

Herrnstein, R. J., & Hineline, P. N. (1966). Negative reinforcement as shock-frequency reduction. *Journal of the Experimental Analysis of Behavior, 9,* 421–430.

Herrnstein, R. J., Loveland, D. H., & Cable, C. (1976). Natural concepts in pigeons. *Journal of Experimental Psychology: Animal Behavior Processes, 2,* 285–301.

Herrnstein, R. J., & Vaughan, W., Jr. (1980). Melioration and behavioral allocation. In J. E. R. Staddon (Ed.), *Limits to action.* New York: Academic Press.

Heth, C. D. (1976). Simultaneous and backward fear conditioning as a function of number of CS-UCS pairings. *Journal of Experimental Psychology: Animal Behavior Processes, 2,* 117–129.

Heth, C. D., & Rescorla, R. A. (1973). Simultaneous and backward fear conditioning in the rat. *Journal of Comparative and Physiological Psychology, 82,* 434–443.

Heyman, G. M. (1983). Optimization theory: Close but no cigar. *Behaviour Analysis Letters, 3,* 17–26.

Hilgard, E. R. (1936). The nature of the conditioned response: I. The case for and against stimulus substitution. *Psychological Review, 43,* 366–385.

Hilgard, E. R., & Marquis, D. G. (1935). Acquisition, extinction, and retention of conditioned lid responses to light in dogs. *Journal of Comparative Psychology, 19,* 29–58.

Hinde, R. A. (1954). Factors governing the changes in strength of a partially inborn response, as shown by the mobbing behavior of the chaffinch (*Fringilla coelebs*): I. The nature of the response, and an examination of its course. *Proceedings of the Royal Society,* Series B, *142,* 306–331.

Hineline, P. N. (1970). Negative reinforcement without shock reduction. *Journal of the Experimental Analysis of Behavior, 14,* 259–268.

Hineline, P. N. (1977). Negative reinforcement and avoidance. In W. K. Honig & J. E. R. Staddon (Eds.), *Handbook of operant behavior.* Englewood Cliffs, N.J.: Prentice-Hall.

Hineline, P. N. (1981). The several roles of stimuli in negative reinforcement. In P. Harzem & M. D. Zeiler (Eds.), *Predictability, correlation, and contiguity.* Chichester, England: Wiley.

Hingtgen, J. N., & Churchill, D. W. (1969). Identification of perceptual limitations in mute autistic children: Identification by the use of behavior modification. *Archives of General Psychiatry, 21,* 68–71.

Hinson, J. M., & Staddon, J. E. R. (1983a). Hill-climbing by pigeons. *Journal of the Experimental Analysis of Behavior, 39,* 25–47.

Hinson, J. M., & Staddon, J. E. R. (1983b). Matching, maximizing, and hill-climbing. *Journal of the Experimental Analysis of Behavior, 40,* 321–331.

Hinson, R. E. (1982). Effects of UCS preexposure on excitatory and inhibitory rabbit eyelid conditioning: An associative effect of conditioned contextual stimuli. *Journal of Experimental Psychology: Animal Behavior Processes, 8,* 49–61.

Hinson, R. E., & Siegel, S. (1980). Trace conditioning as an inhibitory procedure. *Animal Learning & Behavior, 8,* 60–66.

Hittesdorf, M., & Richards, R. W. (1982). Aversive second-order conditioning in the pigeon: Elimination of conditioning to CS1 and effects on established second-order conditioning. *Canadian Journal of Psychology, 36,* 462–477.

Hodgson, R. J., & Rachman, S. J. (1972). The effects of contamination and washing in obsessional patients. *Behaviour Research and Therapy, 10,* 111–117.

Hoebel, B. G., & Teitelbaum, P. (1962). Hypothalamic control of feeding and self-stimulation. *Science, 135,* 375–377.

Hoffman, H. S. (1966). The analysis of discriminated avoidance. In W. K. Honig (Ed.), *Operant behavior: Areas of research and application.* New York: Appleton-Century-Crofts.

Hoffman, H. S., & Fleshler, M. (1964). An apparatus for the measurement of the startle-response in the rat. *American Journal of Psychology, 77,* 307–308.

Hoffman, H. S., & Solomon, R. L. (1974). An opponent-process theory of motivation: III. Some affective dynamics in imprinting. *Learning and Motivation, 5,* 149–164.

Hogan, J. A. (1974). Responses in Pavlovian conditioning studies. *Science, 186,* 156–157.

Holland, P. C. (1977). Conditioned stimulus as a determinant of the form of the Pavlovian conditioned response. *Journal of Experimental Psychology: Animal Behavior Processes, 3,* 77–104.

Holland, P. C. (1980). Influence of visual conditioned stimulus characteristics on the form of Pavlovian appetitive conditioned responding in rats. *Journal of Experimental Psychology: Animal Behavior Processes, 6,* 81–97.

Holland, P. C. (1985). The nature of conditioned inhibition in serial and simultaneous feature negative discriminations. In R. R. Miller & N. E. Spear (Eds.), *Information processing in animals: Conditioned inhibition.* Hillsdale, N.J.: Erlbaum.

Holland, P. C., & Rescorla, R. A. (1975a). The effect of two ways of devaluing the unconditioned stimulus after first- and second-order appetitive conditioning. *Journal of Experimental Psychology: Animal Behavior Processes, 1,* 355–363.

Holland, P. C., & Rescorla, R. A. (1975b). Second-order conditioning with food unconditioned stimulus. *Journal of Comparative and Physiological Psychology, 88,* 459–467.

Holland, P. C., & Straub, J. J. (1979). Differential effect of two ways of devaluing the unconditioned stimulus after Pavlovian appetitive conditioning. *Journal of Experimental Psychology: Animal Behavior Processes, 5,* 65–78.

Hollis, J. H., & Carrier, J. K. (1975). Research implications for communicative deficiencies. *Exceptional children, 41,* 405–412.

Hollis, K. L. (1982). Pavlovian conditioning of signal-centered action patterns and autonomic behavior: A biological analysis of function. *Advances in the Study of Behavior, 12,* 1–64.

Hollis, K. L. (1984a). The biological function of Pavlovian conditioning: The best defense is a good offense. *Journal of Experimental Psychology: Animal Learning and Behavior, 10,* 413–425.

Hollis, K. L. (1984b). Cause and function of animal learning processes. In P. Marler & H. S. Terrace (Eds.), *The biology of learning.* New York: Springer-Verlag.

Holman, J. G., & Mackintosh, N. J. (1981). The control of appetitive instrumental responding does not depend on classical conditioning to the discriminative stimulus. *Quarterly Journal of Experimental Psychology, 33B,* 21–31.

Holz, W. C., & Azrin, N. H. (1961). Discriminative properties of punishment. *Journal of the Experimental Analysis of Behavior, 4,* 225–232.

Honig, W. K. (1978). Studies of working memory in the pigeon. In S. H. Hulse, H. Fowler, & W. K. Honig (Eds.), *Cognitive processes in animal behavior.* Hillsdale, N.J.: Erlbaum.

Honig, W. K., Boneau, C. A., Burstein, K. R., & Pennypacker, H. S. (1963). Positive and negative generalization gradients obtained under equivalent training conditions. *Journal of Comparative and Physiological Psychology, 56,* 111–116.

Honig, W. K., & James, P. H. R. (Eds.). (1971). *Animal memory.* New York: Academic Press.

Honig, W. K., & Urcuoli, P. J. (1981). The legacy of Guttman and Kalish (1956): 25 years of research on stimulus generalization. *Journal of the Experimental Analysis of Behavior, 36,* 405–445.

Hugdahl, K., Fredrickson, M., & Ohman, A. (1977). "Preparedness" and "arousability" as determinants of electrodermal conditioning. *Behaviour Research and Therapy, 15,* 345–353.

Hull, C. L. (1930). Knowledge and purpose as habit mechanisms. *Psychological Review, 30,* 511–525.

Hull, C. L. (1931). Goal attraction and directing ideas conceived as habit phenomena. *Psychological Review, 38,* 487–506.

Hulse, S. H. (1978). Cognitive structure and serial pattern learning by animals. In S. H. Hulse, H. Fowler, & W. K. Honig (Eds.), *Cognitive processes in animal behavior.* Hillsdale, N.J.: Erlbaum.

Hulse, S. H., Cynx, J., & Humpal, J. (1984). Cognitive processing of pitch and rhythm structures by birds. In H. L. Roitblat, T. G. Bever, & H. S. Terrace (Eds.), *Animal cognition.* Hillsdale, N.J.: Erlbaum.

Hulse, S. H., & Dorsky, N. P. (1977). Structural complexity as a determinant of serial pattern learning. *Learning and Motivation, 8,* 488–506.

Hulse, S. H., & Dorsky, N. P. (1979). Serial pattern learning by rats: Transfer of a formally defined stimulus relationship and the significance of nonreinforcement. *Animal Learning & Behavior, 7,* 211–220.

Hulse, S. H., Fowler, H., & Honig, W. K. (Eds.). (1978). *Cognitive processes in animal behavior.* Hillsdale, N.J.: Erlbaum.

Hunter, W. S. (1913). The delayed reaction in animals and children. *Behavior Monographs, 2,* serial #6.

Hursh, S. R., Navarick, D. J., & Fantino, E. (1974). "Automaintenance": The role of reinforcement. *Journal of the Experimental Analysis of Behavior, 21,* 117–124.

Hutchinson, R. R. (1977). By-products of aversive control. In W. K. Honig & J. E. R. Staddon (Eds.), *Handbook of operant behavior.* Englewood Cliffs, N.J.: Prentice-Hall.

Hutchinson, R. R., Azrin, N. H., & Hake, D. F. (1966). An automatic method for the study of aggression in squirrel monkeys. *Journal of the Experimental Analysis of Behavior, 9,* 233–237.

Hutchinson, R. R., Azrin, N. H., & Hunt, G. M. (1968). Attack produced by intermittent reinforcement of a concurrent operant response. *Journal of the Experimental Analysis of Behavior, 11,* 489–495.

Hutt, P. J. (1954). Rate of bar pressing as a function of quality and quantity of food reward. *Journal of Comparative and Physiological Psychology, 47,* 235–239.

Hymowitz, N. (1979). Suppression of responding during signaled and unsignaled shock. *Psychological Bulletin, 86,* 175–190.

Imada, H., & Imada, S. (1983). Thorndike's (1898) puzzle-box experiments revisited. *Kwansei Gakuin University Annual Studies, 32,* 167–184.

Innis, N. K., Reberg, D., Mann, B., Jacobson, J., & Turton, D. (1983). Schedule-induced behavior for food and water: Effects of interval duration. *Behaviour Analysis Letters, 3,* 191–200.

Innis, N. K., Simmelhag-Grant, V. L., & Staddon, J. E. R. (1983). Behavior induced by periodic food delivery: The effects of interfood interval. *Journal of the Experimental Analysis of Behavior, 39,* 309–322.

Irwin, J., Suissa, A., & Anisman, H. (1980). Differential effects of inescapable shock on escape performance and discrimination learning in a water escape task. *Journal of Experimental Psychology: Animal Behavior Processes, 6,* 21–40.

Israel, A. C., Devine, V. T., O'Dea, M. A., & Hamdi, M. E. (1974). Effect of delayed conditioned stimulus termination on extinction of an avoidance response following differential termination conditions during acquisition. *Journal of Experimental Psychology, 103,* 360–362.

Iversen, I. H., Ragnarsdottir, G. A., & Randrup, K. I. (1984). Operant conditioning of autogrooming in vervet monkeys (*Cercopithecus aethiops*). *Journal of the Experimental Analysis of Behavior, 42,* 171–189.

Jackson, R. L., Alexander, J. H., & Maier, S. F. (1980). Learned helplessness, inactivity, and associative deficits: Effects of inescapable shock on response choice escape learning. *Journal of Experimental Psychology: Animal Behavior Processes, 6,* 1–20.

Jackson, R. L., Maier, S. F., & Coon, D. J. (1979). Long-term analgesic effects of inescapable shock and learned helplessness. *Science, 206,* 91–93.

Jacobs, W. J., & LoLordo, V. M. (1980). Constraints on Pavlovian aversive conditioning: Implications for avoidance learning in the rat. *Learning and Motivation, 11,* 427–455.

Jarrard, L. E., & Moise, S. L. (1971). Short-term memory in the monkey. In L. E. Jarrard (Ed.), *Cognitive processes of non-human primates.* New York: Academic Press.

Jarvik, M. E., Goldfarb, T. L., & Carley, J. L. (1969). Influence of interference on delayed matching in monkeys. *Journal of Experimental Psychology, 81,* 1–6.

Jenkins, H. M. (1962). Resistance to extinction when partial reinforcement is followed by regular reinforcement. *Journal of Experimental Psychology, 64,* 441–450.

Jenkins, H. M. (1977). Sensitivity of different response systems to stimulus-reinforcer and response-reinforcer relations. In H. Davis & H. M. B. Hurwitz (Eds.), *Operant-Pavlovian interactions.* Hillsdale, N.J.: Erlbaum.

Jenkins, H. M., Barrera, F. J., Ireland, C., & Woodside, B. (1978). Signal-centered action patterns of dogs in appetitive classical conditioning. *Learning and Motivation, 9,* 272–296.

Jenkins, H. M., & Harrison, R. H. (1960). Effects of discrimination training on auditory generalization. *Journal of Experimental Psychology, 59,* 246–253.

Jenkins, H. M., & Harrison, R. H. (1962). Generalization gradients of inhibition following auditory discrimination learning. *Journal of the Experimental Analysis of Behavior, 5,* 435–441.

Jenkins, H. M., & Moore, B. R. (1973). The form of the auto-shaped response with food or water reinforcers. *Journal of the Experimental Analysis of Behavior, 20,* 163–181.

Jenkins, P. E. (1981). The determiners of key peck duration. *Animal Learning & Behavior, 9,* 501–507.

Jones, F. R. H. (1955). Photo-kinesis in the ammocoete larva of the brook lamprey. *Journal of Experimental Biology, 32,* 492–503.

Jones, M. R. (1974). Cognitive representations of serial patterns. In B. Kantowitz (Ed.), *Human information processing: Tutorials in performance and cognition.* Hillsdale, N.J.: Erlbaum.

Kachanoff, R., Leveille, R., McClelland, J. P., & Wayner, M. J. (1973). Schedule-induced behavior in humans. *Physiology and Behavior, 11,* 395–398.

Kagan, J. (1979). Growing by leaps: The form of early development. *The Sciences, 19,* 8–12, 32.

Kagel, J. H., Battalio, R. C., Green, L., & Rachlin, H. (1980). Consumer demand theory applied to choice behavior of rats. In J. E. R. Staddon (Ed.), *Limits to action.* New York: Academic Press.

Kagel, J. H., Rachlin, H., Green, L., Battalio, R. C., Basmann, R. L., & Klemm, W. R. (1975). Experimental studies of consumer demand behavior using laboratory animals. *Economic Inquiry, 13,* 22–38.

Kalat, J. W. (1974). Taste salience depends on novelty, not concentration, in taste-aversion learning in the rat. *Journal of Comparative and Physiological Psychology, 86,* 47–50.

Kamil, A. C. (1978). Systematic foraging by a nectar-feeding bird, the amakihi (*Loxops virens*). *Journal of Comparative and Physiological Psychology, 92,* 388–396.

Kamil, A. C., & Sargent, T. D. (Eds.). (1981). *Foraging behavior.* New York: Garland STPM.

Kamil, A. C., & Yoerg, S. I. (1982). Learning and foraging behavior. In P. P. G. Bateson & P. H. Klopfer (Eds.), *Perspectives in ethology* (Vol. 5). New York: Plenum.

Kamin, L. J. (1956). The effects of termination of the CS and avoidance of the US on avoidance learning. *Journal of Comparative and Physiological Psychology, 49,* 420–424.

Kamin, L. J. (1965). Temporal and intensity characteristics of the conditioned stimulus. In W. F. Prokasy (Ed.), *Classical conditioning.* New York: Appleton-Century-Crofts.

Kamin, L. J. (1968). "Attention-like" processes in classical conditioning. In M. R. Jones (Ed.), *Miami Symposium on the Prediction of Behavior: Aversive stimulation.* Miami: University of Miami Press.

Kamin, L. J. (1969). Predictability, surprise, attention, and conditioning. In B. A. Campbell & R. M. Church (Eds.), *Punishment and aversive behavior.* New York: Appleton-Century-Crofts.

Kamin, L. J., & Brimer, C. J. (1963). The effects of intensity of conditioned and unconditioned stimuli on a conditioned emotional response. *Canadian Journal of Psychology, 17,* 194–198.

Kamin, L. J., Brimer, C. J., & Black, A. H. (1963). Conditioned suppression as a monitor of fear of the CS in the course of avoidance training. *Journal of Comparative and Physiological Psychology, 56,* 497–501.

Kamin, L. J., & Schaub, R. E. (1963). Effects of conditioned stimulus intensity on the conditioned emotional response. *Journal of Comparative and Physiological Psychology, 56,* 502–507.

Kandel, E. R. (1976). *Cellular basis of behavior: An introduction to behavioral neurobiology.* San Francisco: W. H. Freeman.

Kandel, E. R., & Schwartz, J. H. (1982). Molecular biology of learning: Modulation of transmitter release. *Science, 218,* 433–443.

Kaplan, P. S. (1984). The importance of relative temporal parameters in trace autoshaping: From excitation to inhibition. *Journal of Experimental Psychology: Animal Behavior Processes, 10,* 113–126.

Karpicke, J. (1978). Directed approach responses and positive conditioned suppression in the rat. *Animal Learning & Behavior, 6,* 216–224.

Karpicke, J., Christoph, G., Peterson, G., & Hearst, E. (1977). Signal location and positive versus negative conditioned suppression in the rat. *Journal of Experimental Psychology: Animal Behavior Processes, 3,* 105–118.

Kasprow, W. J., Cacheiro, H., Balaz, M. A., & Miller, R. R. (1982). Reminder-induced recovery of associations to an overshadowed stimulus. *Learning and Motivation, 13,* 155–166.

Katzev, R. D. (1967). Extinguishing avoidance responses as a function of delayed warning signal termination. *Journal of Experimental Psychology, 75,* 339–344.

Katzev, R. D. (1972). What is both necessary and sufficient to maintain avoidance responding in the shuttle box? *Quarterly Journal of Experimental Psychology, 24,* 310–317.

Katzev, R. D., & Berman, J. S. (1974). Effect of exposure to conditioned stimulus and control of its termination in the extinction of avoidance behavior. *Journal of Comparative and Physiological Psychology, 87,* 347–353.

Kaufman, L. W., & Collier, G. (1983). Cost and meal pattern in wild-caught rats. *Physiology and Behavior, 30,* 445–449.

Kazdin, A. E. (1977). *The token economy.* New York: Plenum Press.

Keehn, J. D., & Nakkash, S. (1959). Effect of a signal contingent upon an avoidance response. *Nature, 184,* 566–568.

Kellogg, W. N. (1933). *The ape and the child.* New York: McGraw-Hill.

Kelsey, J. E., & Allison, J. (1976). Fixed-ratio lever pressing by VMH rats: Work vs. accessibility of sucrose reward. *Physiology & Behavior, 17,* 749–754.

Kempe, R. S., & Kempe, C. H. (1978). *Child abuse: The developing child.* Cambridge, Mass.: Harvard University Press.

Kendler, T. S. (1950). An experimental investigation of transposition as a function of the difference between training and test stimuli. *Journal of Experimental Psychology, 40,* 552–562.

Kidd, R. F., & Chayet, E. F. (1984). Why do victims fail to report? The psychology of criminal victimization. *Journal of Social Issues, 40,* 39–50.

Killeen, P. R. (1968). On the measurement of reinforcement frequency in the study of preference. *Journal of the Experimental Analysis of Behavior, 11,* 263–269.

Killeen, P. R. (1972). The matching law. *Journal of the Experimental Analysis of Behavior, 17,* 489–495.

Killeen, P. R. (1981). Learning as causal inference. In M. L. Commons & J. A. Nevin (Eds.), *Quantitative analyses of behavior.* Vol. 1: *Discriminative properties of reinforcement schedules.* Cambridge, Mass.: Ballinger.

Killeen, P. R. (1982). Incentive theory: II. Models for choice. *Journal of the Experimental Analysis of Behavior, 38,* 217–232.

Killeen, P. R., & Smith, J. P. (1984). Perception of contingency in conditioning: Scalar timing, response, bias, and erasure of memory by reinforcement. *Journal of Experimental Psychology: Animal Behavior Processes, 10,* 333–345.

Kintsch, W., & Witte, R. S. (1962). Concurrent conditioning of bar press and salivation responses. *Journal of Comparative and Physiological Psychology, 52,* 963–968.

Klein, M., & Rilling, M. (1974). Generalization of free-operant avoidance behavior in pigeons. *Journal of the Experimental Analysis of Behavior, 21,* 75–88.

Köhler, W. (1939). Simple structural functions in the chimpanzee and in the chicken. In W. D. Ellis (Ed.), *A source book of Gestalt psychology.* New York: Harcourt Brace Jovanovich.

Konorski, J. (1948). *Conditioned reflexes and neuron organization.* Cambridge: Cambridge University Press.

Konorski, J., & Miller, S. (1930). Méthode d'examen de l'analysateur moteur par les réactions salivomatrices. *Compte et Mémoires de la Société de Biologie, 104,* 907–910.

Konorski, J., & Szwejkowska, G. (1950). Chronic extinction and restoration of conditioned reflexes: I. Extinction against the excitatory background. *Acta Biologiae Experimentalis, 15,* 155–170.

Konorski, J., & Szwejkowska, G. (1952). Chronic extinction and restoration of conditioned reflexes: IV. The dependence of the course of extinction and restoration of conditioned reflexes on the "history" of the conditioned stimulus (The principle of the primacy of first training). *Acta Biologiae Experimentalis, 16,* 95–113.

Korol, B., Sletten, I. W., & Brown, M. I. (1966). Conditioned physiological adaptation to anticholinergic drugs. *American Journal of Physiology, 211,* 911–914.

Krane, R. V., & Wagner, A. R. (1975). Taste aversion learning with a delayed shock US: Implications for the "generality of the laws of learning." *Journal of Comparative and Physiological Psychology, 88,* 882–889.

Krebs, J. R., Erichsen, J. T., Webber, M. I., & Charnov, E. L. (1977). Optimal prey selection in the great tit (*Parus major*). *Animal Behaviour, 25,* 30–38.

Krebs, J. R., Houston, A. I., & Charnov, E. L. (1981). Some recent developments in optimal foraging. In A. C. Kamil & T. D. Sargent (Eds.), *Foraging behavior.* New York: Garland STPM.

Krebs, J. R., Kacelnik, A., & Taylor, P. (1978). Test of optimal sampling by foraging great tits. *Nature, 275,* 27–31.

Krebs, J. R., & McCleery, R. H. (1984). Optimization in behavioural ecology. In J. R. Krebs & N. B. Davies (Eds.), *Behavioural ecology* (2nd ed.). Sunderland, Mass.: Sinauer Associates.

Krebs, J. R., Ryan, J. C., & Charnov, E. L. (1974). Hunting by expectation or optimal foraging? A study of patch use by chickadees. *Animal Behaviour, 22,* 953–964.

Kremer, E. F. (1978). The Rescorla-Wagner model: Losses in associative strength in compound conditioned stimuli. *Journal of Experimental Psychology: Animal Behavior Processes, 4,* 22–36.

Kremer, E. F., & Kamin, L. J. (1971). The truly random control procedure: Associative or nonassociative effects in rats. *Journal of Comparative and Physiological Psychology, 74,* 203–210.

Kruse, J. M., Overmier, J. B., Konz, W. A., & Rokke, E. (1983). Pavlovian conditioned stimulus effects upon instrumental choice behavior are reinforcer specific. *Learning and Motivation, 14,* 165–181.

Kucharski, D., & Spear, N. E. (1984). Potentiation of a conditioned taste aversion in preweanling and adult rats. *Behavioral and Neural Biology, 40,* 44–57.

Lang, W. J., Brown, M. L., Gershon, S., & Korol, B. (1966). Classical and physiologic adaptive conditioned responses to anticholinergic drugs in conscious dogs. *International Journal of Neuropharmacology, 5,* 311–315.

Lashley, K. S., & Wade, M. (1946). The Pavlovian theory of generalization. *Psychological Review, 53,* 72–87.

La Vigna, G. W. (1977). Communication training in mute autistic adolescents using the written word. *Journal of Autism and Childhood Schizophrenia, 7,* 135–149.

Lea, S. E. G. (1978). The psychology and economics of demand. *Psychological Bulletin, 85,* 441–466.

Lea, S. E. G. (1984). In what sense do pigeons learn concepts? In H. L. Roitblat, T. G. Bever, & H. S. Terrace (Eds.), *Animal cognition.* Hillsdale, N.J.: Erlbaum.

Lea, S. E. G., & Harrison, S. N. (1978). Discrimination of polymorphous stimulus sets by pigeons. *Quarterly Journal of Experimental Psychology, 30,* 521–537.

Lea, S. E. G., & Roper, T. J. (1977). Demand for food on fixed-ratio schedules as a function of the quality of concurrently available reinforcement. *Journal of the Experimental Analysis of Behavior, 27,* 371–380.

Lea, S. E. G., & Ryan, C. M. E. (1983). Feature analysis of pigeon's acquisition of concept discrimination. In M. L. Commons, R. J. Herrnstein, & A. R. Wagner (Eds.), *Quantitative analyses of behavior.* Vol. 4: *Discrimination processes.* Cambridge, Mass.: Ballinger.

Leaton, R. N. (1976). Long-term retention of the habituation of lick suppression and startle response produced by a single auditory stimulus. *Journal of Experimental Psychology: Animal Behavior Processes, 2,* 248–259.

Leclerc, R., & Reberg, D. (1980). Sign-tracking in aversive conditioning. *Learning and Motivation, 11,* 302–317.

Leitenberg, H., Gross, J., Peterson, J., & Rosen, J. (1984). Analysis of an anxiety model and the process of change during exposure plus response prevention treatment of bulimia nervosa. *Behavior Therapy, 15,* 3–20.

Lemere, F., & Voegtlin, W. L. (1950). An evaluation of the aversion treatment of alcoholism. *Quarterly Journal of Studies on Alcohol, 11,* 199–204.

Lennenberg, E. H. (1967). *Biological foundations of language.* New York: Wiley.

Leon, G. R. (1974). *Case histories of deviant behavior: A social learning analysis.* Boston: Holbrook Press.

Lett, B.T. (1980). Taste potentiates color-sickness associations in pigeons and quail. *Animal Learning & Behavior, 8,* 193–198.

Lett, B. T. (1982). Taste potentiation in poison avoidance learning. In M. L. Commons, R. J. Herrnstein, & A. R. Wagner (Eds.), *Quantitative analyses of behavior*. Vol. 3: *Acquisition*. Cambridge, Mass.: Ballinger.

Levine, F. M., & Sandeen, E. (1985). *Conceptualization in psychotherapy: The models approach*. Hillsdale, N.J.: Erlbaum.

Levis, D. J. (1976). Learned helplessness: A reply and alternative S-R interpretation. *Journal of Experimental Psychology: General, 105,* 47–65.

Levis, D. J. (1981). Extrapolation of two-factor learning theory of infrahuman avoidance behavior to psychopathology, *Neuroscience & Biobehavioral Reviews, 5,* 355–370.

Levitsky, D., & Collier, G. (1968). Schedule-induced wheel running. *Physiology and Behavior, 3,* 571–573.

Lewis, A. (1942). Incidence of neurosis in England under war conditions. *Lancet, 2,* 175–183.

Lewis, D. J. (1979). Psychobiology of active and inactive memory. *Psychological Bulletin, 86,* 1054–1083.

Leyland, C. M. (1977). Higher order autoshaping. *Quarterly Journal of Experimental Psychology, 29,* 607–619.

Lichtenstein, E., & Danaher, B. G. (1976). Modification of smoking behavior: A critical analysis of theory, research, and practice. In M. Hersen, R. M. Eisler, & P. M. Miller (Eds.), *Progress in behavior modification* (Vol. 3). New York: Academic Press.

Lieberman, D. A., McIntosh, D. C., & Thomas, G. V. (1979). Learning when reward is delayed: A marking hypothesis. *Journal of Experimental Psychology: Animal Behavior Processes, 5,* 224–242.

Linden, D. R. (1969). Attenuation and reestablishment of the CER by discriminated avoidance conditioning in rats. *Journal of Comparative and Physiological Psychology, 69,* 573–578.

Lipsitt, L. P., & Kaye, H. (1965). Changes in neonatal response to optimizing and non-optimizing suckling stimulation. *Psychonomic Science, 2,* 221–222.

Lockard, R. B. (1968). The albino rat: A defensible choice or a bad habit? *American Psychologist, 23,* 734–742.

Locurto, C. M. (1981). Contributions of autoshaping to the partitioning of conditioned behavior. In C. M. Locurto, H. S. Terrace, & J. Gibbon (Eds.), *Autoshaping and conditioning theory*. New York: Academic Press.

Locurto, C. M., Terrace, H. S., & Gibbon, J. (1981). *Autoshaping and conditioning theory*. New York: Academic Press.

Logan, F. A. (1959). The Hull-Spence approach. In S. Koch (Ed.), *Psychology: A study of science* (Vol. 2). New York: McGraw-Hill.

Logue, A. W. (1982). Expecting shock. *Behavioral and Brain Sciences, 5,* 680–681.

Logue, A. W. (1985). Conditioned food aversion learning in humans. *Annals of the New York Academy of Sciences.*

Logue, A. W., Ophir, I., & Strauss, K. E. (1981). The acquisition of taste aversions in humans. *Behaviour Research and Therapy, 19,* 319–333.

Logue, A. W., Rodriguez, M. L., Peña-Correal, T. E., & Mauro, B. C. (in press). Choice in a self-control paradigm: Quantification of experience-based differences. *Journal of the Experimental Analysis of Behavior, 41,* 53–67.

LoLordo, V. M. (1971). Facilitation of food-reinforced responding by a signal for response-independent food. *Journal of the Experimental Analysis of Behavior, 15,* 49–55.

LoLordo, V. M. (1979). Selective associations. In A. Dickinson

& R. A. Boakes (Eds.), *Mechanisms of learning and motivation*. Hillsdale, N.J.: Erlbaum.

LoLordo, V. M., & Fairless, J. L. (1985). Pavlovian conditioned inhibition: The literature since 1969. In R. R. Miller & N. E. Spear (Eds.), *Information processing in animals: Conditioned inhibition*. Hillsdale, N.J.: Erlbaum.

LoLordo, V. M., & Furrow, D. R. (1976). Control by the auditory or the visual element of a compound discriminative stimulus: Effects of feedback. *Journal of the Experimental Analysis of Behavior, 25,* 251–256.

LoLordo, V. M., & Jacobs, W. J. (1983). Constraints on aversive conditioning in the rat: Some theoretical accounts. In M. D. Zeiler & P. Harzem (Eds.), *Advances in analysis of behaviour* (Vol. 3). Chichester, England: Wiley.

LoLordo, V. M., Jacobs, W. J., & Foree, D. D. (1982). Failure to block control by a relevant stimulus. *Animal Learning & Behavior, 10,* 183–193.

LoLordo, V. M., McMillan, J. C., & Riley, A. L. (1974). The effects upon food-reinforced pecking and treadle-pressing of auditory and visual signals for response-independent food. *Learning and Motivation, 5,* 24–41.

Looney, T. A., & Cohen, P. S. (1982). Aggression induced by intermittent positive reinforcement. *Neuroscience and Biobehavioral Reviews, 6,* 15–37.

Lorenz, K., & Tinbergen, N. (1939). Taxis und Instinkthandlung in der Eirollbewegung der Graugans: I. *Zeitschrift für Tierpsychologie, 3,* 1–29.

Lovaas, O. I., & Newsom, C. D. (1976). Behavior modification with psychotic children. In H. Leitenberg (Ed.), *Handbook of behavior modification and behavior therapy*. Englewood Cliffs, N.J.: Prentice-Hall.

Lovibond, P. F. (1983). Facilitation of instrumental behavior by a Pavlovian appetitive conditioned stimulus. *Journal of Experimental Psychology: Animal Behavior Processes, 9,* 225–247.

Lubow, R. E. (1973). Latent inhibition. *Psychological Bulletin, 79,* 398–407.

Lubow, R. E., & Moore, A. U. (1959). Latent inhibition: The effect of nonreinforced preexposure to the conditioned stimulus. *Journal of Comparative and Physiological Psychology, 52,* 415–419.

Lyon, D. O. (1968). Conditioned suppression: Operant variables and aversive control. *Psychological Record, 18,* 317–338.

MacCorquodale, K., & Meehl, P. E. (1948). On the distinction between hypothetical constructs and intervening variables. *Psychological Review, 55,* 97–105.

Mackintosh, J. J. (1977). Stimulus control: Attentional factors. In W. K. Honig & J. E. R. Staddon (Eds.), *Handbook of operant behavior*. Englewood Cliffs, N.J.: Prentice-Hall.

Mackintosh, N. J., Bygrave, D. J., & Picton, B. M. B. (1977). Locus of the effect of a surprising reinforcer in the attenuation of blocking. *Quarterly Journal of Experimental Psychology, 29,* 327–336.

MacLennan, A. J., Jackson, R. L., & Maier, S. F. (1980). Conditioned analgesia in the rat. *Bulletin of the Psychonomic Society, 15,* 387–390.

Mactutus, C. F., Ferek, J. M., George, C. A., & Riccio, D. C. (1982). Hypothermia-induced amnesia for newly acquired and old reactivated memories: Commonalities and distinctions. *Physiological Psychology, 10,* 79–95.

Mactutus, C. F., Riccio, D. C., & Ferek, J. M. (1979). Retrograde amnesia for old (reactivated) memory: Some anomalous characteristics. *Science, 204,* 1319–1320.

Mahoney, W. J., & Ayres, J. J. B. (1976). One-trial simultaneous and backward conditioning as reflected in conditioned suppression of licking in rats. *Animal Learning and Behavior, 4,* 357–362.

Maier, S. F., Davies, S., Grau, J. W., Jackson, R. L., Morrison, D. H., Moye, T., Madden, J., & Barchas, J. D. (1980). Opiate antagonists and long-term analgesic reaction induced by inescapable shock in rats. *Journal of Comparative and Physiological Psychology, 94,* 1172–1183.

Maier, S. F., Drugan, R., Grau, J. W., Hyson, R., MacLennan, A. J., Moye, T., Madden, J., IV, & Barchas, J. D. (1983). Learned helplessness, pain inhibition, and the endogenous opiates. In M. D. Zeiler & P. Harzem (Eds.), *Biological factors in learning.* Chichester, England: Wiley.

Maier, S. F., & Jackson, R. L. (1979). Learned helplessness: All of us were right (and wrong): Inescapable shock has multiple effects. In G. H. Bower (Ed.), *The psychology of learning and motivation* (Vol. 13). New York: Academic Press.

Maier, S. F., Rapaport, P., & Wheatley, K. L. (1976). Conditioned inhibition and the UCS-CS interval. *Animal Learning and Behavior, 4,* 217–220.

Maier, S. F., & Seligman, M. E. P. (1976). Learned helplessness: Theory and evidence. *Journal of Experimental Psychology: General, 105,* 3–46.

Maier, S. F., Sherman, J. E., Lewis, J. W., Terman, G. W., & Liebeskind, J. C. (1983). The opioid/nonopioid nature of stress-induced analgesia and learned helplessness. *Journal of Experimental Psychology: Animal Behavior Processes, 9,* 80–90.

Maki, W. S. (1979). Pigeon's short-term memories for surprising vs. expected reinforcement and nonreinforcement. *Animal Learning & Behavior, 7,* 31–37.

Maki, W. S., Brokofsky, S., & Berg, B. (1979). Spatial memory in rats: Resistance to retroactive interference. *Animal Learning & Behavior, 7,* 25–30.

Maki, W. S., & Hegvik, D. K. (1980). Directed forgetting in pigeons. *Animal Learning & Behavior, 8,* 567–574.

Maki, W. S., Moe, J. C., & Bierley, C. M. (1977). Short-term memory for stimuli, responses, and reinforcers. *Journal of Experimental Psychology: Animal Behavior Processes, 3,* 156–177.

Maki, W. S., Olson, D., & Rego, S. (1981). Directed forgetting in pigeons: Analysis of cue functions. *Animal Learning & Behavior, 9,* 189–195.

Marchant, H. G., III, Mis, F. W., & Moore, J. W. (1972). Conditioned inhibition of the rabbit's nictitating membrane response. *Journal of Experimental Psychology, 95,* 408–411.

Margules, D. L., & Olds, J. (1962). Identical "feeding" and "rewarding" systems in the lateral hypothalamus of rats. *Science, 135,* 374–375.

Maricq, A. V., Roberts, S., & Church, R. M. (1981). Methamphetamine and time estimation. *Journal of Experimental Psychology: Animal Behavior Processes, 7,* 18–30.

Marler, P. R. (1982). Avian and primate communication: The problem of natural categories. *Neuroscience & Biobehavioral Reviews, 6,* 87–94.

Marsh, G. (1972). Prediction of the peak shift in pigeons from gradients of excitation and inhibition. *Journal of Comparative and Physiological Psychology, 81,* 262–266.

Martinez, J. J., Jensen, R. A., & McGaugh, J. L. (1981). Attenuation of experimentally-induced amnesia. *Progress in Neurobiology, 16,* 155–186.

Masserman, J. H. (1946). *Principles of dynamic psychiatry.* Philadelphia: Saunders.

Mast, M., Blanchard, R. J., & Blanchard, D. C. (1982). The relationship of freezing and response suppression in a CER situation. *Psychological Record, 32,* 151–167.

Masterson, F. A., & Crawford, M. (1982). The defense motivation system: A theory of avoidance behavior. *Behavioral and Brain Sciences, 5,* 661–696.

Masterson, F. A., Crawford, M., & Bartter, W. D. (1978). Brief escape from a dangerous place: The role of reinforcement in the rat's one-way avoidance acquisition. *Learning and Motivation, 9,* 141–163.

Matysiak, J., & Green, L. (1984). On the directionality of classically-conditioned glycemic responses. *Physiology and Behavior, 32,* 5–9.

Mayer-Gross, W. (1943). Retrograde amnesia. *Lancet, 2,* 603–605.

Mazmanian, D. S., & Roberts, W. A. (1983). Spatial memory in rats under restricted viewing conditions. *Learning and Motivation, 14,* 123–139.

Mazur, J. E. (1981). Optimization theory fails to predict performance of pigeons in a two-response situation. *Science, 214,* 823–825.

Mazur, J. E., & Wagner, A. R. (1982). An episodic model of associative learning. In M. L. Commons, R. J. Herrnstein, & A. R. Wagner (Eds.), *Quantitative analyses of behavior. Vol. 3: Acquisition.* Cambridge, Mass.: Ballinger.

McAllister, W. R., & McAllister, D. E. (1971). Behavioral measurement of fear. In F. R. Brush (Ed.), *Aversive conditioning and learning.* New York: Academic Press.

McAllister, W. R., McAllister, D. E., & Benton, M. M. (1983). Measurement of fear of the conditioned stimulus and of situational cues at several stages of two-way avoidance learning. *Learning and Motivation, 14,* 92–106.

McDowell, J. J. (1981). On the validity and utility of Herrnstein's hyperbola in applied behavioral analysis. In C. M. Bradshaw, E. Szabadi, & C. F. Lowe (Eds.), *Quantification of steady-state operant behaviour.* Amsterdam: Elsevier/North-Holland.

McDowell, J. J. (1982). The importance of Herrnstein's mathematical statement of the law of effect for behavior therapy. *American Psychologist, 37,* 771–779.

McGaugh, J. L., & Herz, M. J. (1972). *Memory consolidation.* San Francisco: Albion.

McGaugh, J. L., & Petrinovich, L. F. (1965). Effects of drugs on learning and memory. *International Review of Neurobiology, 8,* 139–196.

McSweeney, F. K., Melville, C. L., Buck, M. A., & Whipple, J. E. (1983). Local rates of responding and reinforcement during concurrent schedules. *Journal of the Experimental Analysis of Behavior, 40,* 79–98.

Meck, W. H. (1983). Selective adjustment of the speed of internal clock and memory processes. *Journal of Experimental Psychology: Animal Behavior Processes, 9,* 171–201.

Meck, W. H., & Church, R. M. (1982). Abstraction of temporal attributes. *Journal of Experimental Psychology: Animal Behavior Processes, 8,* 226–243.

Meck, W. H., & Church, R. M. (1983). A mode control model of counting and timing processes. *Journal of Experimental Psychology: Animal Behavior Processes, 9,* 320–334.

Meck, W. H., Church, R. M., & Olton, D. S. (in press).

Hippocampus, time, and memory. *Behavioral Neuroscience.*

Medin, D. L. (1980). Proactive interference in monkeys: Delay and intersample interval effects are noncomparable. *Animal Learning & Behavior, 8,* 553–560.

Medin, D. L., Roberts, W. A., & Davis, R. T. (1976). *Processes of animal memory.* Hillsdale, N.J.: Erlbaum.

Meehl, P. E. (1950). On the circularity of the law of effect. *Psychological Bulletin, 47,* 52–75.

Mehrabian, A. (1970). A semantic space for nonverbal behavior. *Journal of Consulting and Clinical Psychology, 35,* 248–257.

Mehrabian, A., & Weiner, M. (1966). Decoding of inconsistent communications. *Journal of Personality and Social Psychology, 6,* 109–114.

Mellgren, R. L. (1972). Positive and negative contrast effects using delayed reinforcement. *Learning and Motivation, 3,* 185–193.

Mellgren, R. L. (1982). Foraging in a simulated natural environment: There's a rat loose in the lab. *Journal of the Experimental Analysis of Behavior, 38,* 93–100.

Mellgren, R. L., Mays, M. Z., & Haddad, N. F. (1983). Discrimination and generalization by rats of temporal stimuli lasting for minutes. *Learning and Motivation, 14,* 75–91.

Meltzer, D., & Brahlek, J. A. (1970). Conditioned suppression and conditioned enhancement with the same positive UCS: An effect of CS duration. *Journal of the Experimental Analysis of Behavior, 13,* 67–73.

Melvin, K. B. (1971). Vicious circle behavior. In H. D. Kimmel (Ed.), *Experimental psychopathology.* New York: Academic Press.

Melvin, K. B., & Ervey, D. H. (1973). Facilitative and suppressive effects of punishment of species-typical aggressive display in *Betta splendens. Journal of Comparative and Physiological Psychology, 83,* 451–457.

Mendelson, J. (1967). Lateral hypothalamic stimulation in satiated rats: The rewarding effects of self-induced drinking. *Science, 157,* 1077–1079.

Mendelson, J., & Chillag, D. (1970). Schedule-induced air licking in rats. *Physiology and Behavior, 5,* 535–537.

Menzel, R. (1983). Neurobiology of learning and memory: The honeybee as a model system. *Naturwissenschaften, 70,* 504–511.

Miczek, K. A., & Grossman, S. (1971). Positive conditioned suppression: Effects of CS duration. *Journal of the Experimental Analysis of Behavior, 15,* 243–247.

Milgram, N. W., Krames, L., & Alloway, T. M. (Eds.). (1977). *Food aversion learning.* New York: Plenum.

Millar, A., & Navarick, D. J. (1984). Self-control and choice in humans: Effects of video game playing as a positive reinforcer. *Learning and Motivation, 15,* 203–218.

Miller, N. E. (1948). Studies of fear as an acquirable drive: I. Fear as motivation and fear-reduction as reinforcement in the learning of new responses. *Journal of Experimental Psychology, 38,* 89–101.

Miller, N. E. (1951). Learnable drives and rewards. In S. S. Stevens (Ed.), *Handbook of experimental psychology.* New York: Wiley.

Miller, N. E. (1960). Learning resistance to pain and fear: Effects of overlearning, exposure, and rewarded exposure in context. *Journal of Experimental Psychology, 60,* 137–145.

Miller, N. E., & DeBold, R. C. (1965). Classically conditioned tongue-licking and operant bar-pressing recorded simulta-neously in the rat. *Journal of Comparative and Physiological Psychology, 59,* 109–111.

Miller, N. E., & Kessen, M. L. (1952). Reward effect of food via stomach fistula compared with those of food via mouth. *Journal of Comparative and Physiological Psychology, 45,* 555–564.

Miller, R. R. (1982). Effects of intertrial reinstatement of training stimuli on complex maze learning rats: Evidence that "acquisition" curves reflect more than acquisition. *Journal of Experimental Psychology: Animal Behavior Processes, 8,* 86–109.

Miller, R. R., & Spear, N. E. (Eds.). (1985). *Information processing in animals: Conditioned inhibition.* Hillsdale, N.J.: Erlbaum.

Miller, R. R., & Springer, A. D. (1973). Amnesia, consolidation, and retrieval. *Psychological Review, 80,* 69–79.

Miller, V., & Domjan, M. (1981). Selective sensitization induced by lithium malaise and footshock in rats. *Behavioral and Neural Biology, 31,* 42–55.

Milner, P. M. (1970). *Physiological psychology.* New York: Holt, Rinehart and Winston.

Milner, P. M. (1976). Theories of reinforcement, drive, and motivation. In L. L. Iverson, S. D. Iverson, & S. H. Snyder (Eds.), *Handbook of psychopharmacology* (Vol. 7). New York: Plenum.

Mineka, S. (1979). The role of fear in theories of avoidance learning, flooding, and extinction. *Psychological Bulletin, 86,* 985–1010.

Mineka, S. (in press). The frightful complexity of the origins of fears. In J. B. Overmier & F. R. Brush (Eds.), *Affect, conditioning, and cognition: Essays on the determinants of behavior.* Hillsdale, N.J.: Erlbaum.

Mineka, S., & Gino, A. (1979). Dissociative effects of different types and amounts of nonreinforced CS exposure on avoidance extinction and the CER. *Learning and Motivation, 10,* 141–160.

Mineka, S., & Gino, A. (1980). Dissociation between conditioned emotional response and extended avoidance performance. *Learning and Motivation, 11,* 476–502.

Mineka, S., Miller, S., Gino, A., & Giencke, L. (1981). Dissociative effects of flooding on a multivariate assessment of fear reduction and on jump-up avoidance extinction. *Learning and Motivation, 12,* 435–461.

Mineka, S., Suomi, S. J., & DeLizio, R. (1981). Multiple separations in adolescent monkeys: An opponent-process interpretation. *Journal of Experimental Psychology: General, 110,* 56–85.

Misanin, J. R., Miller, R. R., & Lewis, D. J. (1968). Retrograde amnesia produced by electroconvulsive shock after reactivation of a consolidated memory trace. *Science, 160,* 554–555.

Mogenson, G. J., & Cioe, J. (1977). Central reinforcement: A bridge between brain function and behavior. In W. K. Honig & J. E. R. Staddon (Eds.), *Handbook of operant behavior.* Englewood Cliffs, N.J.: Prentice-Hall.

Mogenson, G. J., & Huang, Y. H. (1973). The neurobiology of motivated behavior. In G. A. Kerkut & J. W. Phillis (Eds.), *Progress in neurobiology* (Vol. 1). Oxford: Pergamon Press.

Mogenson, G. J., & Kaplinsky, M. (1970). Brain self-stimulation and mechanisms of reinforcement. *Learning and Motivation, 1,* 186–198.

Mogenson, G. J., & Morgan, C. W. (1967). Effects of induced drinking on self-stimulation of the lateral hypothalamus. *Experimental Brain Research, 3,* 111–116.

Mogenson, G. J., & Stevenson, J. A. F. (1966). Drinking and self-stimulation with electrical stimulation of the lateral hypothalamus. *Physiology and Behavior, 1,* 251–254.

Morgan, M. J., Fitch, M. D., Holman, J. G., & Lea, S. E. G. (1976). Pigeons learn the concept of an "A." *Perception, 5,* 57–66.

Morris, R. G. M. (1974). Pavlovian conditioned inhibition of fear during shuttlebox avoidance behavior. *Learning and Motivation, 5,* 424–447.

Morris, R. G. M. (1975). Preconditioning of reinforcing properties to an exteroceptive feedback stimulus. *Learning and Motivation, 6,* 289–298.

Morris, R. G. M. (1981). Spatial localization does not require the presence of local cues. *Learning and Motivation, 12,* 239–260.

Moscovitch, A., & LoLordo, V. M. (1968). Role of safety in the Pavlovian backward fear conditioning procedure. *Journal of Comparative and Physiological Psychology, 66,* 673–678.

Mowrer, O. H. (1947). On the dual nature of learning: A reinterpretation of "conditioning" and "problem-solving." *Harvard Educational Review, 17,* 102–150.

Mowrer, O. H. (1960). *Learning theory and behavior.* New York: Wiley.

Mowrer, O. H., & Lamoreaux, R. R. (1942). Avoidance conditioning and signal duration: A study of secondary motivation and reward. *Psychological Monographs, 54* (Whole No. 247).

Mowrer, R. R., & Gordon, W. C. (1983). Effects of cuing in an "irrelevant" context. *Animal Learning & Behavior, 11,* 401–406.

Moye, T. B., Coon, D. J., Grau, J. W., & Maier, S. F. (1981). Therapy and immunization of long-term analgesia in rats. *Learning and Motivation, 12,* 133–148.

Moye, T. B., Hyson, R. L., Grau, J. W., & Maier, S. F. (1983). Immunization of opioid analgesia: Effects of prior escapable shock on subsequent shock-induced and morphine-induced antinociception. *Learning and Motivation, 14,* 238–251.

Moye, T. B., & Thomas, D. R. (1982). Effects of memory reactivation treatments on postdiscrimination generalization performance in pigeons. *Animal Learning & Behavior, 10,* 159–166.

Murphy, B. T., & Levine, F. M. (1982). *Nonverbal behavior in peer-victimized children.* Paper presented at meeting of the Association for the Advancement of Behavior Therapy.

Nairne, J. S., & Rescorla, R. A. (1981). Second-order conditioning with diffuse auditory reinforcers in the pigeon. *Learning and Motivation, 12,* 65–91.

Nation, J. R., & Cooney, J. B. (1982). The time course of extinction-induced aggressive behavior in humans: Evidence for a stage model of extinction. *Learning and Motivation, 13,* 95–112.

Nevin, J. A. (1969). Interval reinforcement of choice behavior in discrete trials. *Journal of the Experimental Analysis of Behavior, 12,* 875–885.

Nevin, J. A. (1979). Overall matching versus momentary maximizing: Nevin (1969) revisited. *Journal of Experimental Psychology: Animal Behavior Processes, 5,* 300–306.

Obál, F. (1966). The fundamentals of the central nervous system of vegetative homeostasis. *Acta Physiologica Academiae Scientiarum Hungaricae, 30,* 15–29.

Olds, J. (1956). Runway and maze behavior controlled by basomedial forebrain stimulation in the rat. *Journal of Comparative and Physiological Psychology, 49,* 507–512.

Olds, J. (1958). Effects of hunger and male sex hormone on self-stimulation of the brain. *Journal of Comparative and Physiological Psychology, 51,* 320–324.

Olds, J., & Milner, P. (1954). Positive reinforcement produced by electrical stimulation of septal area and other regions of the rat brain. *Journal of Comparative and Physiological Psychology, 47,* 419–427.

O'Leary, K. D., & Wilson, G. T. (1975). *Behavior therapy: Applications and outcome.* Englewood Cliffs, N.J.: Prentice-Hall.

Oliverio, A., & Castellano, C. (1982). Classical conditioning of stress-induced analgesia. *Physiology and Behavior, 25,* 171–172.

Olson, D. J., & Maki, W. S. (1983). Characteristics of spatial memory in pigeons. *Journal of Experimental Psychology: Animal Behavior Processes, 9,* 266–280.

Olton, D. S. (1978). Characteristics of spatial memory. In S. H. Hulse, H. Fowler, & W. K. Honig (Eds.), *Cognitive processes in animal behavior.* Hillsdale, N.J.: Erlbaum.

Olton, D. S. (1979). Mazes, maps, and memory. *American Psychologist, 34,* 583–596.

Olton, D. S., Collison, C., & Werz, M. A. (1977). Spatial memory and radial arm maze performance of rats. *Learning and Motivation, 8,* 289–314.

Olton, D. S., & Samuelson, R. J. (1976). Remembrance of places passed: Spatial memory in rats. *Journal of Experimental Psychology: Animal Behavior Processes, 2,* 97–116.

Oscar-Berman, M. (1980). Neuropsychological consequences of long-term chronic alcoholism. *American Scientist, 68,* 410–419.

Ost, J. W. P., & Lauer, D. W. (1965). Some investigations of salivary conditioning in the dog. In W. F. Prokasy (Ed.), *Classical conditioning.* New York: Appleton-Century-Crofts.

Overman, W. H., McLain, C., Ormsby, G. E., & Brooks, V. (1983). Visual recognition memory in squirrel monkeys. *Animal Learning & Behavior, 11,* 483–488.

Overmier, J. B., Bull, J. A., & Pack, K. (1971). On instrumental response interaction as explaining the influences of Pavlovian CSs upon avoidance behavior. *Learning and Motivation, 2,* 103–112.

Overmier, J. B., & Lawry, J. A. (1979). Pavlovian conditioning and the mediation of behavior. In G. H. Bower (Ed.), *The psychology of learning and motivation* (Vol. 13). New York: Academic Press.

Overmier, J. B., & Seligman, M. E. P. (1967). Effects of inescapable shock upon subsequent escape and avoidance learning. *Journal of Comparative and Physiological Psychology, 63,* 23–33.

Owen, J. W., Cicala, G. A., & Herdegen, R. T. (1978). Fear inhibition and species specific defense reaction termination may contribute independently to avoidance learning. *Learning and Motivation, 9,* 297–313.

Palmerino, C. C., Rusiniak, K. W., & Garcia, J. (1980). Flavor-illness aversions: The peculiar roles of odor and taste in memory for poison. *Science, 208,* 753–755.

Parker, G. (1977). Cyclone Tracy and Darwin evacuees: On the restoration of the species. *British Journal of Psychiatry, 130,* 548–555.

Pate, J. L., & Rumbaugh, D. M. (1983). The language-like

behavior of Lana chimpanzee: Is it merely discrimination and paired-associate learning? *Animal Learning & Behavior, 11,* 134–138.

Patten, R. L., & Rudy, J. W. (1967). The Sheffield omission of training procedure applied to the conditioning of the licking response in rats. *Psychonomic Science, 8,* 463–464.

Patterson, F. G. (1978). The gestures of a gorilla: Language acquisition in another pongid. *Brain and Language, 5,* 56–71.

Pavlov, I. P. (1927). *Conditioned reflexes* (G. V. Anrep, trans.). London: Oxford University Press.

Pearce, J. M., Colwill, R. M., & Hall, G. (1978). Instrumental conditioning of scratching in the laboratory rat. *Learning and Motivation, 9,* 255–271.

Pearce, J. M., & Hall, G. (1980). A model for Pavlovian learning: Variations in the effectiveness of conditioned but not of unconditioned stimuli. *Psychological Review, 87,* 532–552.

Peden, B. F., Browne, M. P., & Hearst, E. (1977). Persistent approaches to a signal for food despite food omission for approaching. *Journal of Experimental Psychology: Animal Behavior Processes, 3,* 377–399.

Peeke, H. V. S., & Petrinovich, L. (Eds.). (1984). *Habituation, sensitization, and behavior.* New York: Academic Press.

Peele, D. B., Casey, J., & Silberberg, A. (1984). Primacy of interresponse-time reinforcement in accounting for rate differences under variable-ratio and variable-interval schedules. *Journal of Experimental Psychology: Animal Behavior Processes, 10,* 149–167.

Pelchat, M. L., Grill, H. J., Rozin, P., & Jacobs, J. (1983). Quality of acquired responses to tastes by *Rattus norvegicus* depends on type of associated discomfort. *Journal of Comparative Psychology, 97,* 140–153.

Perkins, C. C., Jr. (1955). The stimulus conditions which follow learned responses. *Psychological Review, 62,* 341–348.

Perkins, C. C., Jr. (1968). An analysis of the concept of reinforcement. *Psychological Review, 75,* 155–172.

Perry, D. G., & Parke, R. D. (1975). Punishment and alternative response training as determinants of response inhibition in children. *Genetic Psychology Monographs, 91,* 257–279.

Peterson, C., & Seligman, M. E. P. (1984). Causal explanations as a risk factor for depression: Theory and evidence. *Psychological Review, 91,* 347–374.

Peterson, G. B., Ackil, J. E., Frommer, G. P., & Hearst, E. S. (1972). Conditioned approach and contact behavior toward signals for food and brain-stimulation reinforcement. *Science, 177,* 1009–1011.

Peterson, G. B., & Trapold, M. A. (1980). Effects of altering outcome expectancies on pigeons' delayed conditional discrimination performance. *Learning and Motivation, 11,* 267–288.

Peterson, N. (1962). Effect of monochromatic rearing on the control of responding by wavelength. *Science, 136,* 774–775.

Pfaffman, C. (1960). The pleasures of sensation. *Psychological Review, 67,* 253–268.

Phillips, A. G., & Mogenson, G. J. (1968). Effects of taste on self-stimulation and induced drinking. *Journal of Comparative and Physiological Psychology, 66,* 654–660.

Pickens, R., & Dougherty, J. (1971). Conditioning the activity effects of drugs. In T. Thompson & C. Schuster (Eds.), *Stimulus properties of drugs.* New York: Appleton-Century-Crofts.

Platt, S. A., Holliday, M., & Drudge, O. W. (1980). Discrimination learning of an instrumental response in individual *Dro-sophila melanogaster. Journal of Experimental Psychology: Animal Behavior Processes, 6,* 301–311.

Plotkin, H. C., & Odling-Smee, F. J. (1979). Learning, change, and evolution: An enquiry into the teleonomy of learning. In J. S. Rosenblatt, R. A. Hinde, C. Beer, & M.-C. Busnel (Eds.), *Advances in the study of behavior* (Vol. 10). New York: Academic Press.

Porter, D., & Neuringer, A. (1984). Music discrimination by pigeons. *Journal of Experimental Psychology: Animal Behavior Processes, 10,* 138–148.

Postman, L. (1971). Transfer, interference, and forgetting. In J. W. Kling & L. A. Riggs (Eds.), *Woodworth and Schlosberg's experimental psychology* (3rd ed.). New York: Holt, Rinehart and Winston.

Poulos, C. X., & Hinson, R. E. (1982). Pavlovian conditioned tolerance to haloperidol catalepsy: Evidence of dynamic adaptation in the dopaminergic system. *Science, 218,* 491–492.

Poulos, C. X., Hinson, R. E., & Siegel, S. (1981). The role of Pavlovian processes in drug tolerance and dependence: Implications for treatment. *Addictive Behaviors, 6,* 205–211.

Prelec, D. (1982). Matching, maximizing, and the hyperbolic reinforcement feedback function. *Psychological Review, 89,* 189–230.

Premack, A. J. (1976). *Why chimps can read.* New York: Harper & Row.

Premack, D. (1961). Predicting instrumental performance from the independent rate of the contingent response. *Journal of Experimental Psychology, 61,* 163–171.

Premack, D. (1962). Reversibility of the reinforcement relation. *Science, 136,* 255–257.

Premack, D. (1963). Prediction of the comparative reinforcement values of running and drinking. *Science, 139,* 1062–1063.

Premack, D. (1965). Reinforcement theory. In D. Levine (Ed.), *Nebraska Symposium on Motivation* (Vol. 13). Lincoln: University of Nebraska Press.

Premack, D. (1971a). Catching up with common sense, or two sides of a generalization: Reinforcement and punishment. In R. Glaser (Ed.), *The nature of reinforcement.* New York: Academic Press.

Premack, D. (1971b). Language in chimpanzee? *Science, 172,* 808–822.

Premack, D. (1976). *Intelligence in ape and man.* Hillsdale, N.J.: Erlbaum.

Premack, D., & Premack, A. J. (1974). Teaching visual languages to apes and language-deficient persons. In R. L. Schiefelbusch & L. L. Loyd (Eds.), *Language perspectives: Acquisition, retardation, and intervention.* Baltimore, Md.: University Park Press.

Pribram, K. H. (1984). Brain systems and cognitive learning processes. In H. L. Roitblat, T. G. Bever, & H. S. Terrace (Eds.), *Animal cognition.* Hillsdale, N.J.: Erlbaum.

Quartermain, D., McEwen, B. S., & Azmitia, E. C., Jr. (1970). Amnesia produced by electroconvulsive shock or cycloheximide: Conditions for recovery. *Science, 169,* 683–686.

Quinsey, V. L. (1971). Conditioned suppression with no CS-US contingency in the rat. *Canadian Journal of Psychology, 25,* 69–82.

Rachlin, H. C. (1971). On the tautology of the matching law. *Journal of the Experimental Analysis of Behavior, 15,* 249–251.

Rachlin, H. C. (1978). A molar theory of reinforcement schedules. *Journal of the Experimental Analysis of Behavior, 30,* 345–360.

Rachlin, H. C., Battalio, R., Kagel, J., & Green, L. (1981). Maximization theory in behavioral psychology. *Behavioral and Brain Sciences, 4,* 371–417.

Rachlin, H. C., & Burkhard, B. (1978). The temporal triangle: Response substitution in instrumental conditioning. *Psychological Review, 85,* 22–47.

Rachlin, H. C., & Green, L. (1972). Commitment, choice, and self-control. *Journal of the Experimental Analysis of Behavior, 17,* 15–22.

Rachlin, H. C., Green, L., Kagel, J. H., & Battalio, R. C. (1976). Economic demand theory and studies of choice. In G. H. Bower (Ed.), *The psychology of learning and motivation* (Vol. 10). New York: Academic Press.

Rachlin, H. C., & Herrnstein, R. L. (1969). Hedonism revisited: On the negative law of effect. In B. A. Campbell & R. M. Church (Eds.), *Punishment and aversive behavior.* New York: Appleton-Century-Crofts.

Rachman, S. J. (1978). An anatomy of obsessions. *Behavior Analysis and Modification, 2,* 253–278.

Rachman, S. J., & Teasdale, J. (1969). *Aversion therapy and behavior disorders: An analysis.* Coral Gables, Fla.: University of Miami Press.

Rachman, S. J., & Wilson, G. T. (1980). *The effects of psychological therapy.* Oxford: Pergamon Press.

Randich, A. (1981). The US preexposure phenomenon in the conditioned suppression paradigm: A role for conditioned situational stimuli. *Learning and Motivation, 12,* 321–341.

Randich, A., & LoLordo, V. M. (1979). Associative and nonassociative theories of the UCS preexposure phenomenon: Implications for Pavlovian conditioning. *Psychological Bulletin, 86,* 523–548.

Randich, A., & Ross, R. T. (1985). The role of contextual stimuli in mediating the effects of pre- and postexposure to the unconditioned stimulus alone on acquisition and retention of conditioned suppression. In P. Balsam & A. Tomie (Eds.), *Context and learning.* Hillsdale, N.J.: Erlbaum.

Rashotte, M. E., Griffin, R. W., & Sisk, C. L. (1977). Second-order conditioning of the pigeon's keypeck. *Animal Learning & Behavior, 5,* 25–38.

Reberg, D. (1972). Compound tests for excitation in early acquisition and after prolonged extinction of conditioned suppression. *Learning and Motivation, 3,* 246–258.

Reberg, D., & Black, A. H. (1969). Compound testing of individually conditioned stimuli as an index of excitatory and inhibitory properties. *Psychonomic Science, 17,* 30–31.

Reberg, D., Innis, N. K., Mann, B., & Eizenga, C. (1978). "Superstitious" behavior resulting from periodic response-independent presentations of food or water. *Animal Behaviour, 26,* 506–519.

Reberg, D., Mann, B., & Innis, N. K. (1977). Superstitious behavior for food and water in the rat. *Physiology and Behavior, 19,* 803–806.

Rescorla, R. A. (1967a). Inhibition of delay in Pavlovian fear conditioning. *Journal of Comparative and Physiological Psychology, 64,* 114–120.

Rescorla, R. A. (1967b). Pavlovian conditioning and its proper control procedures. *Psychological Review, 74,* 71–80.

Rescorla, R. A. (1968). Pavlovian conditioned fear in Sidman avoidance learning. *Journal of Comparative and Physiological Psychology, 65,* 55–60.

Rescorla, R. A. (1969a). Conditioned inhibition of fear resulting from negative CS-US contingencies. *Journal of Comparative and Physiological Psychology, 67,* 504–509.

Rescorla, R. A. (1969b). Pavlovian conditioned inhibition. *Psychological Bulletin, 72,* 77–94.

Rescorla, R. A. (1973). Effect of US habituation following conditioning. *Journal of Comparative and Physiological Psychology, 82,* 137–143.

Rescorla, R. A. (1974). Effect of inflation on the unconditioned stimulus value following conditioning. *Journal of Comparative and Physiological Psychology, 86,* 101–106.

Rescorla, R. A. (1979). Aspects of the reinforcer learned in second-order Pavlovian conditioning. *Journal of Experimental Psychology: Animal Behavior Processes, 5,* 79–95.

Rescorla, R. A. (1980a). *Pavlovian second-order conditioning.* Hillsdale, N.J.: Erlbaum.

Rescorla, R. A. (1980b). Simultaneous and successive associations in sensory preconditioning. *Journal of Experimental Psychology: Animal Behavior Processes, 6,* 207–216.

Rescorla, R. A. (1982). Simultaneous second-order conditioning produces S-S learning in conditioned suppression. *Journal of Experimental Psychology: Animal Behavior Processes, 8,* 23–32.

Rescorla, R. A. (1985). Conditioned inhibition and facilitation. In R. R. Miller & N. E. Spear (Eds.), *Information processing in animals: Conditioned inhibition.* Hillsdale, N.J.: Erlbaum.

Rescorla, R. A., & Cunningham, C. L. (1977). The erasure of reinstatement. *Animal Learning & Behavior, 5,* 386–394.

Rescorla, R. A., & Cunningham, C. L. (1979). Spatial contiguity facilitates Pavlovian second-order conditioning. *Journal of Experimental Psychology: Animal Behavior Processes, 5,* 152–161.

Rescorla, R. A., & Durlach, P. J. (1981). Within-event learning in Pavlovian conditioning. In N. E. Spear & R. R. Miller (Eds.), *Information processing in animals: Memory mechanisms.* Hillsdale, N.J.: Erlbaum.

Rescorla, R. A., Durlach, P. J., & Grau, J. W. (1985). Contextual learning in Pavlovian conditioning. In P. Balsam & A. Tomie (Eds.), *Context and learning.* Hillsdale, N.J.: Erlbaum.

Rescorla, R. A., & Furrow, D. R. (1977). Stimulus similarity as a determinant of Pavlovian conditioning. *Journal of Experimental Psychology: Animal Behavior Processes, 3,* 203–215.

Rescorla, R. A., & Gillan, D. J. (1980). An analysis of the facilitative effect of similarity on second-order conditioning. *Journal of Experimental Psychology: Animal Behavior Processes, 6,* 339–351.

Rescorla, R. A., & Heth, D. C. (1975). Reinstatement of fear to an extinguished conditioned stimulus. *Journal of Experimental Psychology: Animal Behavior Processes, 1,* 88–96.

Rescorla, R. A., & LoLordo, V. M. (1965). Inhibition of avoidance behavior. *Journal of Comparative and Physiological Psychology, 59,* 406–412.

Rescorla, R. A., & Solomon, R. L. (1967). Two-process learning theory: Relationships between Pavlovian conditioning and instrumental learning. *Psychological Review, 74,* 151–182.

Rescorla, R. A., & Wagner, A. R. (1972). A theory of Pavlovian conditioning: Variations in the effectiveness of reinforcement and nonreinforcement. In A. H. Black & W. F. Prokasy (Eds.),

Classical conditioning II: Current research and theory. New York: Appleton-Century-Crofts.

Resick, P. A. (1983).   The rape reaction: Research findings and implications for intervention. *Behavior Therapist, 6,* 126–132.

Restle, F., & Brown, E. (1970).   Organization of serial pattern learning. In G. H. Bower & J. T. Spence (Eds.), *The psychology of learning and motivation* (Vol. 4). New York: Academic Press.

Revusky, S. H., & Garcia, J. (1970).   Learned associations over long delays. In G. H. Bower & J. T. Spence (Eds.), *The psychology of learning and motivation* (Vol. 4). New York: Academic Press.

Reynolds, G. S. (1961a).   Attention in the pigeon. *Journal of the Experimental Analysis of Behavior, 4,* 203–208.

Reynolds, G. S. (1961b).   Behavioral contrast. *Journal of the Experimental Analysis of Behavior, 4,* 57–71.

Reynolds, G. S. (1968).   *A primer of operant conditioning.* Glenview, Ill.: Scott, Foresman.

Reynolds, T. J., & Medin, D. L. (1981).   Stimulus interaction and between-trials proactive interference in monkeys. *Journal of Experimental Psychology: Animal Behavior Processes, 7,* 334–347.

Riccio, D. C., Hodges, L. A., & Randall, P. R. (1968).   Retrograde amnesia produced by hypothermia in rats. *Journal of Comparative and Physiological Psychology, 3,* 618–622.

Riccio, D. C., & Richardson, R. (in press).   The status of memory following experimentally-induced amnesias: Gone, but not forgotten. *Physiological Psychology.*

Riccio, D. C., Urda, M., & Thomas, D. R. (1966).   Stimulus control in pigeons based on proprioceptive stimuli from floor inclination. *Science, 153,* 434–436.

Richardson, R., Riccio, D. C., & Jonke, T. (1983).   Alleviation of infantile amnesia in rats by means of a pharmacological contextual state. *Developmental Psychobiology, 16,* 511–518.

Richelle, M., & Lejeune, H. (1980).   *Time in animal behavior.* New York: Pergamon Press.

Richter, C. P. (1953).   Experimentally produced behavior reactions to food poisoning in wild and domesticated rats. *Annals of the New York Academy of Sciences, 56,* 225–239.

Riegert, P. W. (1959).   Humidity reactions of *Melanoplus birittatus* (Say) and *Camnula pellucida* (Scudd.) (Orthoptera, Acrididae): Reactions of normal grasshoppers. *Canadian Entomologist, 91,* 35–40.

Riley, A. L., & Tuck, D. L. (1985).   Conditioned food aversions: A bibliography. *Annals of the New York Academy of Sciences.*

Rilling, M. (1977).   Stimulus control and inhibitory processes. In W. K. Honig, & J. E. R. Staddon (Eds.), *Handbook of operant behavior.* Englewood Cliffs, N.J.: Prentice-Hall.

Rilling, M., Kendrick, D. F., & Stonebraker, T. B. (1984).   Directed forgetting in context. In G. H. Bower (Ed.), *The psychology of learning and motivation* (Vol. 18). New York: Academic Press.

Rimland, B. (1964).   *Infantile autism: The syndrome and its implications for a neural theory of behavior.* Englewood Cliffs, N.J.: Prentice-Hall.

Rizley, R. C., & Rescorla, R. A. (1972).   Associations in second-order conditioning and sensory preconditioning. *Journal of Comparative and Physiological Psychology, 81,* 1–11.

Roberts, S. (1981).   Isolation of an internal clock. *Journal of Experimental Psychology: Animal Behavior Processes, 7,* 242–268.

Roberts, S. (1982).   Cross-modal use of an internal clock. *Journal of Experimental Psychology: Animal Behavior Processes, 8,* 2–22.

Roberts, S., & Church, R. M. (1978).   Control of an internal clock. *Journal of Experimental Psychology: Animal Behavior Processes, 4,* 318–337.

Roberts, W. A. (1979).   Spatial memory in the rat on a hierarchical maze. *Learning and Motivation, 10,* 117–140.

Roberts, W. A. (1984).   Some issues in animal spatial memory. In H. L. Roitblat, T. G. Bever, & H. S. Terrace (Eds.), *Animal cognition.* Hillsdale, N.J.: Erlbaum.

Roberts, W. A., & Grant, D. S. (1976).   Studies of short-term memory in the pigeon using the delayed matching to sample procedure. In D. L. Medin, W. A. Roberts, & R. T. Davis (Eds.), *Processes of animal memory.* Hillsdale, N.J.: Erlbaum.

Roberts, W. A., & Grant, D. S. (1978).   An analysis of light-induced retroactive inhibition in pigeon short-term memory. *Journal of Experimental Psychology: Animal Behavior Processes, 4,* 219–236.

Roberts, W. A., Mazmanian, D. S., & Kraemer, P. J. (1984).   Directed forgetting in monkeys. *Animal Learning & Behavior, 12,* 29–40.

Roitblat, H. L. (1982).   The meaning of representation in animal memory. *Behavioral and Brain Sciences, 5,* 353–406.

Roitblat, H. L. (1984).   Representations in pigeon working memory. In H. L. Roitblat, T. G. Bever, & H. S. Terrace (Eds.), *Animal cognition.* Hillsdale, N.J.: Erlbaum.

Roitblat, H. L., Bever, T. G., & Terrace, H. S. (Eds.). (1984).   *Animal cognition.* Hillsdale, N.J.: Erlbaum.

Roitblat, H. L., Pologe, B., & Scopatz, R. A. (1983).   The representation of items in serial position. *Animal Learning & Behavior, 11,* 489–498.

Roitblat, H. L., Tham, W., & Golub, L. (1982).   Performance of *Betta splendens* in a radial arm maze. *Animal Learning & Behavior, 10,* 108–114.

Roper, G., Rachman, S., & Hodgson, R. (1973).   An experiment on obsessional checking. *Behaviour Research and Therapy, 11,* 271–277.

Roper, T. J. (1981).   What is meant by the term "schedule-induced," and how general is schedule induction? *Animal Learning & Behavior, 9,* 433–440.

Roper, T. J., Edwards, L., & Crossland, G. (1983).   Factors affecting schedule-induced wood-chewing in rats: Percentage and rate of reinforcement, and operant requirement. *Animal Learning & Behavior, 11,* 35–43.

Rosellini, R. A., & DeCola, J. P. (1981).   Inescapable shock interferes with the acquisition of a low-activity response in an appetitive context. *Animal Learning & Behavior, 9,* 487–490.

Rosellini, R. A., DeCola, J. P., Plonsky, M., Warren, D. A., & Stilman, A. J. (1984).   Uncontrollable shock proactively increases sensitivity to response-reinforcer independence in rats. *Journal of Experimental Psychology: Animal Behavior Processes, 10,* 346–359.

Rosellini, R. A., DeCola, J. P., & Shapiro, N. R. (1982).   Cross-motivational effects of inescapable shock are associative in nature. *Journal of Experimental Psychology: Animal Behavior Processes, 8,* 376–388.

Rosen, J. C., & Leitenberg, H. L. (1982).   Bulimia nervosa: Treatment with exposure and response prevention. *Behavior Therapy, 13,* 117–124.

Ross, R. T. (1983). Relationships between the determinants of performance in serial feature-positive discriminations. *Journal of Experimental Psychology: Animal Behavior Processes, 9,* 349–373.

Ross, R. T., & Holland, P. C. (1981). Conditioning of simultaneous and serial feature-positive discriminations. *Animal Learning & Behavior, 9,* 293–303.

Ross, R. T., & Randich, A. (1984). Unconditioned stress-induced analgesia following exposure to brief footshock. *Journal of Experimental Psychology: Animal Behavior Processes, 10,* 127–137.

Rovee, C. K., & Rovee, D. T. (1969). Conjugate reinforcement of infant exploratory behavior. *Journal of Experimental Child Psychology, 8,* 33–39.

Rovee-Collier, C. K. (1983). Infants as problem-solvers: A psychobiological perspective. In M. D. Zeiler & P. Harzem (Eds.), *Advances in analysis of behaviour.* Vol. 3: *Biological factors in learning.* Chichester, England: Wiley.

Rovee-Collier, C. K., Sullivan, M. W., Enright, M., Lucas, D., & Fagen, J. W. (1980). Reactivation of infant memory. *Science, 208,* 1159–1161.

Rozin, P., & Kalat, J. W. (1971). Specific hungers and poison avoidance as adaptive specializations of learning. *Psychological Review, 78,* 459–486.

Rudolph, R. L., & Van Houten, R. (1977). Auditory stimulus control in pigeons: Jenkins and Harrison (1960) revisited. *Journal of the Experimental Analysis of Behavior, 27,* 327–330.

Rumbaugh, D. M. (Ed.). (1977). *Language learning by a chimpanzee: The Lana project.* New York: Academic Press.

Rusiniak, K. W., Hankins, W. G., Garcia, J., & Brett, L. P. (1979). Flavor-illness aversions: Potentiation of odor by taste in rats. *Behavioral and Neural Biology, 25,* 1–17.

Rusiniak, K. W., Palmerino, C. C., & Garcia, J. (1982). Potentiation of odor by taste in rats: Tests of some nonassociative factors. *Journal of Comparative and Physiological Psychology, 96,* 775–780.

Rusiniak, K. W., Palmerino, C. C., Rice, A. G., Forthman, D. L., & Garcia, J. (1982). Flavor-illness aversions: Potentiation of odor by taste with toxin but not shock in rats. *Journal of Comparative and Physiological Psychology, 96,* 527–539.

Russell, W. R., & Nathan, P. W. (1946). Traumatic amnesia. *Brain, 69,* 280–300.

Rzoska, J. (1953). Bait shyness, a study in rat behaviour. *British Journal of Animal Behaviour, 1,* 128–135.

Sahley, C., Rudy, J. W., & Gelperin, A. (1981). An analysis of associative learning in a terrestrial mollusc: I. Higher-order conditioning, blocking, and a transient US-pre-exposure effect. *Journal of Comparative Physiology-A, 144,* 1–8.

Schachter, S. (1971a). *Emotion, obesity, and crime.* New York: Academic Press.

Schachter, S. (1971b). Some extraordinary facts about obese humans and rats. *American Psychologist, 26,* 129–144.

Schachtman, T. R., Gee, J.-L., Kasprow, W. J., & Miller, R. R. (1983). Reminder-induced recovery from blocking as a function of the number of compound trials. *Learning and Motivation, 14,* 154–164.

Schaeffer, B. (1980). Spontaneous language through signed speech. In R. L. Schiefelbusch (Ed.), *Nonspeech language and communication: Analysis and intervention.* Baltimore, Md.: University Park Press.

Schiff, R., Smith, N., & Prochaska, J. (1972). Extinction of avoidance in rats as a function of duration and number of blocked trials. *Journal of Comparative and Physiological Psychology, 81,* 356–359.

Schindler, C. W., & Weiss, S. J. (1982). The influence of positive and negative reinforcement on selective attention in the rat. *Learning and Motivation, 13,* 304–323.

Schlosberg, H. (1934). Conditioned responses in the white rat. *Journal of Genetic Psychology, 45,* 303–335.

Schlosberg, H. (1936). Conditioned responses in the white rat: II. Conditioned responses based upon shock to the foreleg. *Journal of Genetic Psychology, 49,* 107–138.

Schlosberg, H. (1937). The relationship between success and the laws of conditioning. *Psychological Review, 44,* 379–394.

Schmahl, D., Lichtenstein, E., & Harris, D. (1972). Successful treatment of habitual smokers with warm, smoky air and rapid smoking. *Journal of Consulting and Clinical Psychology, 38,* 105–111.

Schneider, A. M., Tyler, J., & Jinich, D. (1974). Recovery from retrograde amnesia: A learning process. *Science, 184,* 87–88.

Schneiderman, N., Fuentes, I., & Gormezano, I. (1962). Acquisition and extinction of the classically conditioned eyelid response in the albino rabbit. *Science, 136,* 650–652.

Schneiderman, N., & Gormezano, I. (1964). Conditioning of the nictitating membrane of the rabbit as a function of CS-US interval. *Journal of Comparative and Physiological Psychology, 57,* 188–195.

Schull, J. (1979). A conditioned opponent theory of Pavlovian conditioning and habituation. In G. H. Bower (Ed.), *The psychology of learning and motivation* (Vol. 13). New York: Academic Press.

Schuster, R. H., & Rachlin, H. (1968). Indifference between punishment and free shock: Evidence for the negative law of effect. *Journal of the Experimental Analysis of Behavior, 11,* 777–786.

Schwartz, B. (1976). Positive and negative conditioned suppression in the pigeon: Effects of the locus and modality of the CS. *Learning and Motivation, 7,* 86–100.

Schwartz, B. (1981). Reinforcement creates behavioral units. *Behavioural Analysis Letters, 1,* 33–41.

Schwartz, B., & Williams, D. R. (1972). The role of the response-reinforcer contingency in negative automaintenance. *Journal of the Experimental Analysis of Behavior, 17,* 351–357.

Scobie, S. R. (1972). Interaction of an aversive Pavlovian conditioned stimulus with aversively and appetitively motivated operants in rats. *Journal of Comparative and Physiological Psychology, 79,* 171–188.

Seligman, M. E. P. (1968). Chronic fear produced by unpredictable electric shock. *Journal of Comparative and Physiological Psychology, 66,* 402–411.

Seligman, M. E. P., & Binik, Y. M. (1977). The safety signal hypothesis. In H. Davis & H. M. B. Hurwitz (Eds.), *Operant-Pavlovian interactions.* Hillsdale, N.J.: Erlbaum.

Seligman, M. E. P., & Maier, S. F. (1967). Failure to escape traumatic shock. *Journal of Experimental Psychology, 74,* 1–9.

Seligman, M. E. P., & Meyer, B. (1970). Chronic fear and ulcers in rats as a function of the unpredictability of safety. *Journal of Comparative and Physiological Psychology, 73,* 202–207.

Seligman, M. E. P., & Weiss, J. (1980). Coping behavior: Learned helplessness, physiological activity, and learned inactivity. *Behaviour Research and Therapy, 18,* 459–512.

Sevenster, P. (1973). Incompatibility of response and reward. In R. A. Hinde & J. Stevenson-Hinde (Eds.), *Constraints on learning*. London: Academic Press.

Shapiro, K. L., Jacobs, W. J., & LoLordo, V. M. (1980). Stimulus-reinforcer interactions in Pavlovian conditioning of pigeons: Implications for selective associations. *Animal Learning & Behavior, 8*, 586–594.

Shapiro, K. L., & LoLordo, V. M. (1982). Constraints on Pavlovian conditioning of the pigeon: Relative conditioned reinforcing effects of red-light and tone CSs paired with food. *Learning and Motivation, 13*, 68–80.

Shapiro, M. M. (1960). Respondent salivary conditioning during operant lever pressing in dogs. *Science, 132*, 619–620.

Shapiro, M. M. (1961). Salivary conditioning in dogs during fixed-interval reinforcement contingent upon lever pressing. *Journal of the Experimental Analysis of Behavior, 4*, 361–364.

Shapiro, M. M. (1962). Temporal relationship between salivation and lever pressing with differential reinforcement of low rates. *Journal of Comparative and Physiological Psychology, 55*, 567–571.

Shapiro, N. R., Dudek, B. C., & Rosellini, R. A. (1983). The role of associative factors in tolerance to the hypothermic effects of morphine in mice. *Pharmacology Biochemistry & Behavior, 19*, 327–333.

Sheffield, F. D. (1948). Avoidance training and the contiguity principle. *Journal of Comparative and Physiological Psychology, 41*, 165–177.

Sheffield, F. D. (1965). Relation between classical conditioning and instrumental learning. In W. F. Prokasy (Ed.), *Classical conditioning*. New York: Appleton-Century-Crofts.

Sheffield, F. D., Roby, T. B., & Campbell, B. A. (1954). Drive reduction versus consummatory behavior as determinants of reinforcement. *Journal of Comparative and Physiological Psychology, 47*, 349–354.

Sheffield, F. D., Wulff, J. J., & Backer, R. (1951). Reward value of copulation without sex drive reduction. *Journal of Comparative and Physiological Psychology, 44*, 3–8.

Sherman, A. R. (1972). Real-life exposure as a primary therapeutic factor in the desensitization treatment of fear. *Journal of Abnormal Psychology, 79*, 19–28.

Shettleworth, S. J. (1972). Constraints on learning. In D. S. Lehrman, R. A. Hinde, & E. Shaw (Eds.), *Advances in the study of behavior* (Vol. 4). New York: Academic Press.

Shettleworth, S. J. (1975). Reinforcement and the organization of behavior in golden hamsters: Hunger, environment, and food reinforcement. *Journal of Experimental Psychology: Animal Behavior Processes, 1*, 56–87.

Shettleworth, S. J. (1978a). Reinforcement and the organization of behavior in golden hamsters: Punishment of three action patterns. *Learning and Motivation, 9*, 99–123.

Shettleworth, S. J. (1978b). Reinforcement and the organization of behavior in golden hamsters: Sunflower seed and nest paper reinforcers. *Animal Learning & Behavior, 6*, 352–362.

Shettleworth, S. J. (1981). Reinforcement and the organization of behavior in golden hamsters: Differential overshadowing of a CS by different responses. *Quarterly Journal of Experimental Psychology, 33B*, 241–255.

Shettleworth, S. J. (1983a). Function and mechanism in learning. In M. D. Zeiler & P. Harzem (Eds.), *Advances in analysis of behaviour* (Vol. 3). Chichester, England: Wiley.

Shettleworth, S. J. (1983b). Memory in food-hoarding birds. *Scientific American, 248*, 102–110.

Shettleworth, S. J. (1984). Learning and behavioural ecology. In J. R. Krebs & N. B. Davies (Eds.), *Behavioural ecology* (2nd ed.). Sunderland, Mass.: Sinauer Associates.

Shettleworth, S. J., & Krebs, J. R. (1982). How marsh tits find their hoards: The roles of site preference and spatial memory. *Journal of Experimental Psychology: Animal Behavior Processes, 8*, 354–375.

Shimp, C. P. (1966). Probabilistically reinforced choice behavior in pigeons. *Journal of the Experimental Analysis of Behavior, 9*, 443–455.

Shimp, C. P. (1969). Optimum behavior in free-operant experiments. *Psychological Review, 76*, 97–112.

Shurtleff, D., & Ayres, J. J. B. (1981). One-trial backward excitatory fear conditioning in rats: Acquisition, retention, extinction, and spontaneous recovery. *Animal Learning & Behavior, 9*, 65–74.

Sidman, M. (1953a). Avoidance conditioning with brief shock and no exteroceptive warning signal. *Science, 118*, 157–158.

Sidman, M. (1953b). Two temporal parameters of the maintenance of avoidance behavior by the white rat. *Journal of Comparative and Physiological Psychology, 46*, 253–261.

Sidman, M. (1960). *Tactics of scientific research*. New York: Basic Books.

Sidman, M. (1962). Reduction of shock frequency as reinforcement for avoidance behavior. *Journal of the Experimental Analysis of Behavior, 5*, 247–257.

Sidman, M. (1966). Avoidance behavior. In W. K. Honig (Ed.), *Operant behavior*. New York: Appleton-Century-Crofts.

Siegel, S. (1975a). Conditioning insulin effects. *Journal of Comparative and Physiological Psychology, 89*, 189–199.

Siegel, S. (1975b). Evidence from rats that morphine tolerance is a learned response. *Journal of Comparative and Physiological Psychology, 89*, 498–506.

Siegel, S. (1976). Morphine analgesic tolerance: Its situation specificity supports a Pavlovian conditioning model. *Science, 193*, 323–325.

Siegel, S. (1977a). Morphine tolerance acquisition as an associative process. *Journal of Experimental Psychology: Animal Behavior Processes, 3*, 1–13.

Siegel, S. (1977b). A Pavlovian conditioning analysis of morphine tolerance (and opiate dependence). In N. A. Krasnegor (Ed.), *Behavioral tolerance: Research and treatment implications*. National Institute for Drug Abuse, Monograph No. 18. Government Printing Office Stock No. 017-024-00699-8. Washington, D.C.: Government Printing Office.

Siegel, S. (1978). Tolerance to the hyperthermic effect of morphine in the rat is a learned response. *Journal of Comparative and Physiological Psychology, 92*, 1137–1149.

Siegel, S. (1983). Classical conditioning, drug tolerance, and drug dependence. In Y. Israel, F. B. Glaser, H. Kalant, R. E. Popham, W. Schmidt, & R. G. Smart (Eds.), *Research advances in alcohol and drug problems* (Vol. 7). New York: Plenum.

Siegel, S., & Domjan, M. (1971). Backward conditioning as an inhibitory procedure. *Learning and Motivation, 2*, 1–11.

Siegel, S., Hinson, R. E., & Krank, M. D. (1978). The role of predrug signals in morphine analgesic tolerance: Support for a Pavlovian conditioning model of tolerance. *Journal of Experimental Psychology: Animal Behavior Processes, 4*, 188–196.

Siegel, S., Hinson, R. E., Krank, M. D., & McCully, J. (1982).

Heroin "overdose" death: Contribution of drug-associated environmental cues. *Science, 216,* 436–437.

Sigmundi, R. A., & Bolles, R. C. (1983). CS modality, context conditioning, and conditioned freezing. *Animal Learning & Behavior, 11,* 205–212.

Simon, H. A., & Kotovsky, K. (1963). Human acquisition of concepts for sequential patterns. *Psychological Review, 70,* 534–546.

Skinner, B. F. (1938). *The behavior of organisms.* New York: Appleton-Century-Crofts.

Skinner, B. F. (1948). "Superstition" in the pigeon. *Journal of Experimental Psychology, 38,* 168–172.

Skinner, B. F. (1953). *Science and human behavior.* New York: Macmillan.

Slamecka, N. J., & Ceraso, J. (1960). Retroactive and proactive inhibition of verbal learning. *Psychological Bulletin, 57,* 449–475.

Small, W. S. (1899). An experimental study of the mental processes of the rat: I. *American Journal of Psychology, 11,* 133–164.

Small, W. S. (1900). An experimental study of the mental processes of the rat: II. *American Journal of Psychology, 12,* 206–239.

Smith, J. C., & Roll, D. L. (1967). Trace conditioning with X-rays as an aversive stimulus. *Psychonomic Science, 9,* 11–12.

Smith, M. C., Coleman, S. R., & Gormezano, I. (1969). Classical conditioning of the rabbit's nictitating membrane response at backward, simultaneous, and forward CS-US intervals. *Journal of Comparative and Physiological Psychology, 69,* 226–231.

Snyderman, M. (1983). Delay and amount of reward in a concurrent chain. *Journal of the Experimental Analysis of Behavior, 39,* 437–447.

Solnick, J. V., Kannenberg, C. H., Eckerman, D. A., & Waller, M. B. (1980). An experimental analysis of impulsivity and impulse control in humans. *Learning and Motivation, 11,* 61–77.

Solomon, R. L. (1964). Punishment. *American Psychologist, 19,* 239–253.

Solomon, R. L. (1977). An opponent-process theory of acquired motivation: The affective dynamics of addiction. In J. D. Maser & M. E. P. Seligman (Eds.), *Psychopathology: Experimental models.* San Francisco: W. H. Freeman.

Solomon, R. L. (1980). The opponent-process theory of acquired motivation: The costs of pleasure and the benefits of pain. *American Psychologist, 35,* 691–712.

Solomon, R. L., & Corbit, J. D. (1973). An opponent-process theory of motivation: II. Cigarette addiction. *Journal of Abnormal Psychology, 81,* 158–171.

Solomon, R. L., & Corbit, J. D. (1974). An opponent-process theory of motivation: I. The temporal dynamics of affect. *Psychological Review, 81,* 119–145.

Solomon, R. L., Kamin, L. J., & Wynne, L. C. (1953). Traumatic avoidance learning: The outcomes of several extinction procedures with dogs. *Journal of Abnormal and Social Psychology, 48,* 291–302.

Solomon, R. L., & Wynne, L. C. (1953). Traumatic avoidance learning: Acquisition in normal dogs. *Psychological Monographs, 67* (Whole No. 354).

Soltysik, S. S., Wolfe, G. E., Nicholas, T., Wilson, W. J., & Garcia-Sanchez, L. (1983). Blocking of inhibitory conditioning within a serial conditioned stimulus-conditioned inhibitor

compound: Maintenance of acquired behavior without an unconditioned stimulus. *Learning and Motivation, 14,* 1–29.

Spear, N. E. (1973). Retrieval of memory in animals. *Psychological Review, 80,* 163–194.

Spear, N. E. (1976). Retrieval of memories: A psychobiological approach. In W. K. Estes (Ed.), *Handbook of learning and cognitive processes* (Vol. 4). Hillsdale, N.J.: Erlbaum.

Spear, N. E. (1978). *The processing of memories: Forgetting and retention.* Hillsdale, N.J.: Erlbaum.

Spear, N. E. (1981). Extending the domain of memory retrieval. In N. E. Spear & R. R. Miller (Eds.), *Information processing in animals: Memory mechanisms.* Hillsdale, N.J.: Erlbaum.

Spear, N. E., Hamberg, J. M., & Bryan, R. (1980). Forgetting of recently acquired or recently reactivated memories. *Learning and Motivation, 11,* 456–475.

Spear, N. E., & Miller, R. R. (Eds.). (1981). *Informaton processing in animals: Memory mechanisms.* Hillsdale, N.J.: Erlbaum.

Spear, N. E., Smith, G. J., Bryan, R. G., Gordon, W. C., Timmons, R., & Chiszar, D. A. (1980). Contextual influences on the interaction between conflicting memories in the rat. *Animal Learning & Behavior, 8,* 273–281.

Spence, K. W. (1936). The nature of discrimination learning in animals. *Psychological Review, 43,* 427–449.

Spence, K. W. (1937). The differential response in animals to stimuli varying within a single dimension. *Psychological Review, 44,* 430–444.

Spence, K. W. (1956). *Behavior theory and conditioning.* New Haven, Conn.: Yale University Press.

Spetch, M. L., & Wilkie, D. M. (1981). Duration discrimination is better with food access as the signal than with light as the signal. *Learning and Motivation, 12,* 40–64.

Spetch, M. L., Wilkie, D. M., & Pinel, J. P. J. (1981). Backward conditioning: A reevaluation of the empirical evidence. *Psychological Bulletin, 89,* 163–175.

Staddon, J. E. R. (1979). Operant behavior as adaptation to constraint. *Journal of Experimental Psychology: General, 108,* 48–67.

Staddon, J. E. R. (1980). Optimality analyses of operant behavior and their relation to optimal foraging. In J. E. R. Staddon (Ed.), *Limits to action.* New York: Academic Press.

Staddon, J. E. R. (1983). *Adaptive behavior and learning.* Cambridge: Cambridge University Press.

Staddon, J. E. R., & Hinson, J. M. (1983). Optimization: A result or a mechanism? *Science, 221,* 976–977.

Staddon, J. E. R., & Simmelhag, V. L. (1971). The "superstition" experiment: A reexamination of its implications for the principles of adaptive behavior. *Psychological Review, 78,* 3–43.

Starr, M. D. (1978). An opponent-process theory of motivation: VI. Time and intensity variables in the development of separation-induced distress calling in ducklings. *Journal of Experimental Psychology: Animal Behavior Processes, 4,* 338–355.

Starr, M. D., & Mineka, S. (1977). Determinants of fear over the course of avoidance learning. *Learning and Motivation, 8,* 332–350.

Steinert, P., Fallon, D., & Wallace, J. (1976). Matching to sample in goldfish (*Carassuis auratus*). *Bulletin of the Psychonomic Society, 8,* 265.

Stephenson, D., & Siddle, D. (1983). Theories of habituation. In D. Siddle (Ed.), *Orienting and habituation: Perspectives in human research.* Chichester, England: Wiley.

Stiers, M., & Silberberg, A. (1974). Lever-contact responses in rats: Automaintenance with and without a negative response-reinforcer dependency. *Journal of the Experimental Analysis of Behavior, 22,* 497–506.

Stonebraker, T. B., & Rilling, M. (1981). Control of delayed matching-to-sample performance using directed forgetting techniques. *Animal Learning & Behavior, 9,* 196–201.

Straub, R. O., & Terrace, H. S. (1981). Generalization of serial learning in the pigeon. *Animal Learning & Memory, 9,* 454–468.

Stuart, R. B., & Davis, B. (1972). *Slim chance in a fat world: Behavioral control of obesity.* Champaign, Ill.: Research Press.

Stunkard, A. J., & Mahoney, M. J. (1976). Behavioral treatment of eating disorders. In H. Leitenberg (Ed.), *Handbook of behavior modification and behavior therapy.* Englewood Cliffs, N.J.: Prentice-Hall.

Suomi, S. J., Mineka, S., & Harlow, H. F. (1983). Social separation in monkeys as viewed from several motivational perspectives. In E. Satinoff & P. Teitelbaum (Eds.), *Handbook of neurobiology.* Vol. 6: *Motivation.* New York: Plenum.

Susswein, A. J., & Schwarz, M. (1983). A learned change of response to inedible food in *Aplysia. Behavioral and Neural Biology, 39,* 1–6.

Sutherland, N. S., & Mackintosh, M. J. (1971). *Mechanisms of animal discrimination learning.* New York: Academic Press.

Suzuki, S., Augerinos, G., & Black, A. H. (1980). Stimulus control of spatial behavior on the eight-arm maze in rats. *Learning and Motivation, 11,* 1–18.

Terrace, H. S. (1964). Wavelength generalization after discrimination learning with and without errors. *Science, 144,* 78–80.

Terrace, H. S. (1966a). Discrimination learning and inhibition. *Science, 154,* 1677–1680.

Terrace, H. S. (1966b). Stimulus control. In W. K. Honig (Ed.), *Operant behavior: Areas of research and application.* New York: Appleton-Century-Crofts.

Terrace, H. S. (1972). By-products of discrimination learning. In G. H. Bower (Ed.), *The psychology of learning and motivation* (Vol. 5). New York: Academic Press.

Terrace, H. S. (1979). *Nim.* New York: Knopf.

Terrace, H. S. (1984). Animal cognition. In H. L. Roitblat, T. G. Bever, & H. S. Terrace (Eds.), *Animal cognition.* Hillsdale, N.J.: Erlbaum.

Terrace, H. S., Petitto, L. A., Sanders, R. J., & Bever, T. G. (1979). Can an ape create a sentence? *Science, 206,* 891–1201.

Terry, W. S. (1976). Effects of priming unconditioned stimulus representation in short-term memory on Pavlovian conditioning. *Journal of Experimental Psychology: Animal Behavior Processes, 2,* 354–369.

Terry, W. S., & Wagner, A. R. (1975). Short-term memory for "surprising" versus "expected" unconditioned stimuli in Pavlovian conditioning. *Journal of Experimental Psychology: Animal Behavior Processes, 1,* 122–133.

Testa, T. J. (1974). Causal relationships and the acquisition of avoidance responses. *Psychological Review, 81,* 491–505.

Theios, J. (1962). The partial reinforcement effect sustained through blocks of continuous reinforcement. *Journal of Experimental Psychology, 64,* 1–6.

Thomas, D. R., Mariner, R. W., & Sherry, G. (1969). Role of preexperimental experience in the development of stimulus control. *Journal of Experimental Psychology, 79,* 375–376.

Thomas, D. R., McKelvie, A. R., Ranney, M., & Moye, T. B. (1981). Interference in pigeons' long-term memory viewed as a retrieval problem. *Animal Learning & Behavior, 9,* 581–586.

Thomas, G. V. (1981). Contiguity, reinforcement rate and the law of effect. *Quarterly Journal of Experimental Psychology, 33B,* 33–43.

Thomas, G. V., Lieberman, D. A., McIntosh, D. C., & Ronaldson, P. (1983). The role of marking when reward is delayed. *Journal of Experimental Psychology: Animal Behavior Processes, 9,* 401–411.

Thomas, J. R. (1968). Fixed ratio punishment by timeout of concurrent variable-interval behavior. *Journal of the Experimental Analysis of Behavior, 11,* 609–616.

Thompson, C. R., & Church, R. M. (1980). An explanation of the language of a chimpanzee. *Science, 208,* 313–314.

Thompson, R. F., Groves, P. M., Teyler, T. J., & Roemer, R. A. (1973). A dual-process theory of habituation: Theory and behavior. In H. V. S. Peeke & M. J. Herz (Eds.), *Habituation.* New York: Academic Press.

Thompson, R. F., & Spencer, W. A. (1966). Habituation: A model phenomenon for the study of neuronal substrates of behavior. *Psychological Review, 73,* 16–43.

Thompson, R. K. R., Van Hemel, P. E., Winston, K. M., & Pappas, N. (1983). Modality-specific interference with overt mediation by pigeons in a delayed discrimination task. *Learning and Motivation, 14,* 271–303.

Thorndike, E. L. (1898). Animal intelligence: An experimental study of the association processes in animals. *Psychological Review Monograph, 2* (Whole No. 8).

Thorndike, E. L. (1911). *Animal intelligence: Experimental studies.* New York: Macmillan.

Thorndike, E. L. (1932). *The fundamentals of learning.* New York: Teachers College, Columbia University.

Tiffany, S. T., & Baker, T. B. (1981). Morphine tolerance in rats: Congruence with a Pavlovian paradigm. *Journal of Comparative and Physiological Psychology, 95,* 747–762.

Timberlake, W. (1980). A molar equilibrium theory of learned performance. In G. H. Bower (Ed.), *The psychology of learning and motivation* (Vol. 14). New York: Academic Press.

Timberlake, W. (1983a). The functional organization of appetitive behavior: Behavior systems and learning. In M. D. Zeiler & P. Harzem (Eds.), *Advances in analysis of behavior.* Vol. 3: *Biological factors in learning.* Chicester, England: Wiley.

Timberlake, W. (1983b). Rats' responses to a moving object related to food or water: A behavior-systems analysis. *Animal Learning & Behavior, 11,* 309–320.

Timberlake, W. (1984). Behavior regulation and learned performance: Some misapprehensions and disagreements. *Journal of the Experimental Analysis of Behavior, 41,* 355–375.

Timberlake, W., & Allison, J. (1974). Response deprivation: An empirical approach to instrumental performance. *Psychological Review, 81,* 146–164.

Timberlake, W., & Grant, D. S. (1975). Auto-shaping in rats to the presentation of another rat predicting food. *Science, 190,* 690–692.

Timberlake, W., Wahl, G., & King, D. (1982). Stimulus and response contingencies in the misbehavior of rats. *Journal of Experimental Psychology: Animal Behavior Processes, 8,* 62–85.

Tinbergen, N. (1951). *The study of instinct.* Oxford: Clarendon Press.

Tinbergen, N., & Perdeck, A. C. (1950). On the stimulus situation releasing the begging response in the newly hatched herring gull chick (*Larus argentatus argentatus Pont.*). *Behaviour, 3,* 1–39.

Tolman, E. C. (1932). *Purposive behavior in animals and men.* New York: Appleton-Century-Crofts.

Tolman, E. C. (1938). The determiners of behavior at a choice point. *Psychological Review, 45,* 1–41.

Trapold, M. A., & Winokur, S. (1967). Transfer from classical conditioning to acquisition, extinction, and stimulus generalization of a positively reinforced instrumental response. *Journal of Experimental Psychology, 73,* 517–525.

Trenholme, I. A., & Baron, A. (1975). Immediate and delayed punishment of human behavior by loss of reinforcement. *Learning and Motivation, 6,* 62–79.

Twitmyer, E. B. (1974). A study of the knee jerk. *Journal of Experimental Psychology, 103,* 1047–1066.

Ulrich, R. E., Hutchinson, R. R., & Azrin, N. H. (1965). Pain-elicited aggression. *Psychological Record, 15,* 111–126.

Underwood, B. J. (1957). Interference and forgetting. *Psychological Review, 64,* 49–60.

Vaughan, W., Jr. (1981). Melioration, matching, and maximizing. *Journal of the Experimental Analysis of Behavior, 36,* 141–149.

Villareal, J. (1967). *Schedule-induced pica.* Paper presented at the meeting of the Eastern Psychological Association, Boston.

Wagner, A. R. (1976). Priming in STM: An information processing mechanism for self-generated or retrieval-generated depression in performance. In T. J. Tighe & R. N. Leaton (Eds.), *Habituation: Perspectives from child development, animal behavior, and neurophysiology.* Hillsdale, N.J.: Erlbaum.

Wagner, A. R. (1978). Expectancies and the priming of STM. In S. H. Hulse, H. Fowler, & W. K. Honig (Eds.), *Cognitive processes in animal behavior.* Hillsdale, N.J.: Erlbaum.

Wagner, A. R. (1979). Habituation and memory. In A. Dickinson & R. A. Boakes (Eds.), *Mechanisms of learning and motivation: A memorial to Jerzy Konorski.* Hillsdale, N.J.: Erlbaum.

Wagner, A. R. (1981). SOP: A model of automatic memory processing in animal behavior. In N. E. Spear & R. R. Miller (Eds.), *Information processing in animals: Memory mechanisms.* Hillsdale, N.J.: Erlbaum.

Wagner, A. R., & Larew, M. B. (1985). Opponent processes and Pavlovian inhibition. In R. R. Miller & N. E. Spear (Eds.), *Information processing in animals: Conditioned inhibition.* Hillsdale, N.J.: Erlbaum.

Wagner, A. R., Logan, F. A., Haberlandt, K., & Price, T. (1968). Stimulus selection in animal discrimination learning. *Journal of Experimental Psychology, 76,* 171–180.

Wagner, A. R., & Rescorla, R. A. (1972). Inhibition in Pavlovian conditioning: Application of a theory. In R. A. Boakes & M. S. Halliday (Eds.), *Inhibition and learning.* London: Academic Press.

Wallace, J., Steinert, P. A., Scobie, S. R., & Spear, N. E. (1980). Stimulus modality and short-term memory in rats. *Animal Learning & Behavior, 8,* 10–16.

Wallace, M., Singer, G., Wayner, M. J., & Cook, P. (1975). Adjunctive behavior in humans during game playing. *Physiology and Behavior, 14,* 651–654.

Walter, H. E. (1907). The reaction of planarians to light. *Journal of Experimental Zoology, 5,* 35–162.

Walters, G. C., & Glazer, R. D. (1971). Punishment of instinctive behavior in the Mongolian gerbil. *Journal of Comparative and Physiological Psychology, 75,* 331–340.

Walters, G. C., & Grusec, J. F. (1977). *Punishment.* San Francisco: W. H. Freeman.

Wasserman, E. A. (1973). Pavlovian conditioning with heat reinforcement produces stimulus-directed pecking in chicks. *Science, 181,* 875–877.

Wasserman, E. A. (1974). Responses in Pavlovian conditioning studies (reply to Hogan). *Science, 186,* 157.

Wasserman, E. A. (1981a). Comparative psychology returns: A review of Hulse, Fowler, and Honig's *Cognitive processes in animal behavior. Journal of the Experimental Analysis of Behavior, 35,* 243–257.

Wasserman, E. A. (1981b). Response evocation in autoshaping: Contributions of cognitive and comparative-evolutionary analyses to an understanding of directed action. In C. M. Locurto, H. S. Terrace, & J. Gibbon (Eds.), *Autoshaping and conditioning theory.* New York: Academic Press.

Wasserman, E. A., DeLong, R. E., & Larew, M. B. (1984). Temporal order and duration: Their discrimination and retention by pigeons. *Annals of the New York Academy of Sciences, 423,* 103–115.

Wasserman, E. A., Franklin, S. R., & Hearst, E. (1974). Pavlovian appetitive contingencies and approach versus withdrawal to conditioned stimuli in pigeons. *Journal of Comparative and Physiological Psychology, 86,* 616–627.

Watson, J. B. (1913). Psychology as the behaviorist views it. *Psychological Review, 20,* 158–177.

Watson, J. B. (1924). *Behaviorism.* New York: Norton.

Watson, J. B., & Raynor, R. (1920). Conditioned emotional reactions. *Journal of Experimental Psychology, 3,* 1–14.

Wearden, J. H., & Burgess, I. S. (1982). Matching since Baum (1979). *Journal of the Experimental Analysis of Behavior, 38,* 339–348.

Weinberger, N. (1965). Effect of detainment on extinction of avoidance responses. *Journal of Comparative and Physiological Psychology, 60,* 135–138.

Weisman, R. G., & Litner, J. S. (1969). The course of Pavlovian excitation and inhibition of fear in rats. *Journal of Comparative and Physiological Psychology, 69,* 667–672.

Weisman, R. G., & Litner, J. S. (1972). The role of Pavlovian events in avoidance training. In R. A. Boakes & M. S. Halliday (Eds.), *Inhibition and learning.* London: Academic Press.

Weisman, R. G., & Premack, D. (1966). *Reinforcement and punishment produced by the same response depending upon the probability relation between the instrumental and contingent responses.* Paper presented at the meeting of the Psychonomic Society, St. Louis.

Weiss, J. M. (1970). Somatic effects of predictable and unpredictable shock. *Psychosomatic Medicine, 32,* 397–409.

Weiss, J. M. (1971). Effects of coping behavior in different warning signal conditions on stress pathology in rats. *Journal of Comparative and Physiological Psychology, 77,* 1–13.

Weiss, S. J., & Schindler, C. W. (1981). Generalization peak shift in rats under conditions of positive reinforcement and avoidance. *Journal of the Experimental Analysis of Behavior, 35,* 175–185.

Weiss-Fogh, T. (1949). An aerodynamic sense organ stimulating and regulating flight in locusts. *Nature, 164,* 873–874.

Welsh, J. H. (1933). Light intensity and the extent of activity of locomotor muscles as opposed to cilia. *Biological Bulletin, 65,* 168–174.

Wesierska, M., & Zielinski, K. (1980). Enhancement of bar-pressing rate in rats by the conditioned inhibitor of the CER. *Acta Neurobiologica Experimentalis, 40,* 945–963.

Westbrook, R. F., Smith, F. J., & Charnock, D. J. (in press). The long-term extinction of an aversion: Role of the interval between non-reinforced presentations of the averted stimulus. *Quarterly Journal of Experimental Psychology.*

Wetherington, C. L. (1982). Is adjunctive behavior a third class of behavior? *Neuroscience and Biobehavioral Reviews, 6,* 329–350.

Whitlow, J. W., Jr. (1975). Short-term memory in habituation and dishabituation. *Journal of Experimental Psychology: Animal Behavior Processes, 1,* 189–206.

Whitlow, J. W., Jr., & Wagner, A. R. (1984). Memory and habituation. In H. V. S. Peeke & L. Petrinovich (Eds.), *Habituation, sensitization, and behavior.* New York: Academic Press.

Wiens, A. N., & Menustik, C. E. (1983). Treatment outcome and patient characteristics in an aversion therapy program for alcoholism. *American Psychologist, 38,* 1089–1096.

Wigglesworth, V. B., & Gillett, J. D. (1934). The function of the antennae of *Rhodnius prolixus* (Hemiptera) and the mechanisms of orientation to the host. *Journal of Experimental Biology, 11,* 120–139.

Wilkie, D. M. (1983). Pigeons' spatial memory: II. Acquisition of delayed matching of key location and transfer to new locations. *Journal of the Experimental Analysis of Behavior, 39,* 69–76.

Wilkie, D. M., & Slobin, P. (1983). Gerbils in space: Performance on the 17-arm radial maze. *Journal of the Experimental Analysis of Behavior, 40,* 301–312.

Wilkie, D. M., & Summers, R. J. (1982). Pigeons' spatial memory: Factors affecting delayed matching of key location. *Journal of the Experimental Analysis of Behavior, 37,* 45–56.

Willer, J. C., Dehen, H., & Cambier, J. (1981). Stress-induced analgesia in humans: Endogenous opioids and naloxone-reversible depression of pain reflexes. *Science, 212,* 689–691.

Williams, B. A. (1983). Another look at contrast in multiple schedules. *Journal of the Experimental Analysis of Behavior, 39,* 345–384.

Williams, B. A. (in press). Reinforcement, choice, and response strength. In R. C. Atkinson, R. J. Herrnstein, G. Lindzey, & R. D. Luce (Eds.), *Steven's handbook of experimental psychology* (2nd ed.). New York: Wiley.

Williams, D. R. (1965). Classical conditioning and incentive motivation. In W. F. Prokasy (Ed.), *Classical conditioning.* New York: Appleton-Century-Crofts.

Williams, D. R., & Williams, H. (1969). Automaintenance in the pigeon: Sustained pecking despite contingent non-reinforcement. *Journal of the Experimental Analysis of Behavior, 12,* 511–520.

Winter, J., & Perkins, C. C. (1982). Immediate reinforcement in delayed reward learning in pigeons. *Journal of the Experimental Analysis of Behavior, 38,* 169–179.

Winkler, R. C. (1980). Behavioral economics, token economies, and applied behavior analysis. In J. E. R. Staddon (Ed.), *Limits to action: The allocation of individual behavior.* New York: Academic Press.

Wolfe, J. B. (1934). The effect of delayed reward upon learning in the white rat. *Journal of Comparative and Physiological Psychology, 17,* 1–21.

Woodworth, R. S., & Schlosberg, H. (1954). *Experimental psychology.* New York: Holt, Rinehart and Winston.

Worsham, R. W., & D'Amato, M. R. (1973). Ambient light, white noise, and monkey vocalization as sources of interference in visual short-term memory of monkeys. *Journal of Experimental Psychology, 99,* 99–105.

Wright, A. A., & Sands, S. F. (1981). A model of detection and decision processes during matching to sample by pigeons: Performance with 88 different wavelengths in delayed and simultaneous matching tasks. *Journal of Experimental Psychology: Animal Behavior Processes, 7,* 191–216.

Wright, A. A., Urcuioli, P. J., Sands, S. F., & Santiago, H. C. (1981). Interference of delayed matching to sample in pigeons: Effects of interpolation at different periods within a trial and stimulus similarity. *Animal Learning & Behavior, 9,* 595–603.

Yerkes, R. M., & Morgulis, S. (1909). The method of Pavlov in animal psychology. *Psychological Bulletin, 6,* 257–273.

Yoerg, S. I., & Kamil, A. C. (1982). Response strategies in the radial arm maze: Running around in circles. *Animal Learning & Behavior, 10,* 530–534.

Zener, K. (1937). The significance of behavior accompanying conditioned salivary secretion for theories of the conditioned response. *American Journal of Psychology, 50,* 384–403.

Zentall, T. R., Edwards, C. A., Moore, B. S., & Hogan, D. E. (1981). Identity: The basis for both matching and oddity learning in pigeons. *Journal of Experimental Psychology: Animal Behavior Processes, 7,* 70–86.

Zentall, T. R., Hogan, D. E., & Edwards, C. A. (1984). Cognitive factors in conditional learning by pigeons. In H. L. Roitblat, T. G. Bever, & H. S. Terrace (Eds.), *Animal cognition.* Hillsdale, N.J.: Erlbaum.

Zimmer-Hart, C. L., & Rescorla, R. A. (1974). Extinction of Pavlovian conditioned inhibition. *Journal of Comparative and Physiological Psychology, 86,* 837–845.

Zoladek, L., & Roberts, W. A. (1978). The sensory basis of spatial memory in the rat. *Animal Learning & Behavior, 6,* 77–81.

Name Index

Subject Index

Credits

This page constitutes an extension of the copyright page.